THE
WORLD
TREASURY OF
GRAND OPERA

THE
WORLD
TREASURY OF

edited by

GEORGE R. MAREK

GRAND OPERA

ITS TRIUMPHS, TRIALS AND GREAT PERSONALITIES

Essay Index Reprint Series

BOOKS FOR LIBRARIES PRESS
FREEPORT, NEW YORK

Copyright © 1957 by
George Richard Marek.

Reprinted 1971 by arrangement with
Harper & Row, Publishers, Inc.

Library of Congress Cataloging in Publication Data

Marek, George Richard, 1902-   ed.
    The world treasury of grand opera.
    (Essay index reprint series)
    Reprint of the 1957 ed.
    1. Opera--Addresses, essays, lectures.
I. Title.
ML1700.1.M33 1972   782.1'08   74-167383
ISBN 0-8369-2463-0

PRINTED IN THE UNITED STATES OF AMERICA
BY
NEW WORLD BOOK MANUFACTURING CO., INC.
HALLANDALE, FLORIDA 33009

CONTENTS

FRENCH OPERA

GERMAN OPERA

THE CRISIS OF OPERA

INTRODUCTION

It is very pleasant to ride one's hobbyhorse into the byways. To an opera lover, the next best thing to hearing an opera is to talk about it. Such a conversation, to be held with kindred souls, ranges, as this book does, from the operas themselves, their composers, the dramatic material they used, the social background of their work, to the merits, or, even more interesting, the demerits, of certain singers. The next best thing to personal discussion is reading about opera. It is to be hoped that the contents of this anthology may, in turn, stimulate new discussion and eventually lead to deeper understanding of the operatic art. The remarks introducing the sections on Italian, French, and German opera are designed to bind the material together and to provide a summary view.

I have been going to the opera for thirty years, man and standee, and I have been reading about opera for almost that length of time. I have made my selections by the *da capo* test: those pieces which I found worth rereading. Music is notoriously a difficult art about which to write in words. Considering how much has been written about opera, it is astonishing that not more has been well written. It is as difficult to find another Ernest Newman in musical writing as it is another Bernard Berenson in the visual arts or another J. Dover Wilson in Shakespearean analysis. I have searched for good presentation as well as for the merely instructive, and I have included some material just because I found it amusing. All of it is, I trust, good reading, and a number of the selections may have the merit of unfamiliarity. I apologize for many omissions, particularly that of Russian opera. I have had no access to the best Russian sources.

I wish to thank Miss Ann M. Lingg, who aided me in the research, and Mr. John Appleton of Harper & Brothers for his many suggestions.

I shall be very pleased if this book helps to while away the reader's time between performances.

GEORGE R. MAREK

New York
February, 1957

ITALIAN OPERA

THE NATURE OF THE LADY

George R. Marek

She is fascinating. She is beautiful. Yet many consider her features too regular for complete beauty, her mien too soft for enduring loveliness. She is eager as a child to give pleasure. Yet there are some who find that she is overeager and that she dispenses her favors a little too readily. She is capable of noble and composed emotion, of aristocratic behavior in the presence of sadness. Yet at other times and for not completely convincing reasons she becomes overwrought. Then she dashes with quick steps into all four corners of the room, she pulls her hair, she sobs and sheds thick, glossy tears, tears more sweet than salty. Her actions do not always make sense; at times they seem unreasonable. Yet her behavior follows a logic of its own. She will renounce a good man who has committed only the slightest of discourtesies toward her and yet will be faithful to a lover who persists in offending her, who commits the most boorish infidelities, and who is unattractive to boot. She is likely to swoon at a slight brawl, but she is also likely to look with equanimity on the sight of a gory battlefield. She is passionately fond of masquerades and adores dressing up in various costumes, being sure each time that she is not going to be recognized. She shares with other females a love for beautiful clothes, for stylish pageantry and for jewels. She is not infallible in distinguishing diamonds from paste. She is almost always interested in love, but she is by no means capable of sexual love only. She believes that all mothers are good, all white-haired people worthy of respect. She meditates on disease and is especially sympathetic to tubercular patients. But she can at once drive away her morbid thoughts and can smile and be gay. Her voice is her best feature. She has it under control at all times, she uses it with complete skill. She whispers adorably, she pleads irresistibly, she commands majestically, and she tells a story well. When she is in a tight situation, she uses that voice; it touches our hearts and we come to her aid. But once in a while that voice, so seraphic, so supple, and so warm, rises to a shrillness and breaks out in accents of vulgarity which make us suspect that she has spent a considerable part of her life in the marketplace. She is loved by many people; indeed, people of the most diverse tastes, education, temperament, nationality, and degree of worldliness are united in pronouncing her charms. A man can be a simpleton and love her; a man can be a scholar and love her still. Yet there are some reasonable and knowledgeable people who despise her and, worse still, find her boring.

This is Italian opera.

Let us see how the art got to be where it is. Let us see how the lady's character was formed. Italian opera did not follow as firm a course as the course of the symphony from Stamitz to Shostakovitch. It has meant different things to different audiences at different periods. We can almost say that it has *been* a different thing at different periods.

The play was at one time the reason for going to the opera, the scenery at another time, the singer (and the singer alone) at still another. Only one characteristic has the lady possessed since birth: Italian opera was always a public art, designed for popularity, intended to entertain people who step up to the box office and pay for their admission. In this respect Italian opera is more closely related to the spoken theater than it is to other forms of music, including other forms of opera. We have only to bear in mind that French opera began as a court entertainment, a private amateur theatrical, or that Wagner envisaged a theater for which people would *not* have to pay admission and to which they would come for moral betterment as much as for entertainment, to see the validity of this definition.

It all started with a song. A madrigal. During the last part of the sixteenth century, the singing of madrigals was a diversion much favored by the young gentlemen about town, the young men who carried on their elegantly draped shoulders the high tradition of the Renaissance. Look at the Bronzino portrait in the Frick Museum: the cavalier looks as if he might burst into song any moment. Madrigals—unaccompanied compositions to be sung by two or three voices —were beautiful and intricate. If madrigals were such a success when they were sung on the sun-baked streets of Naples or on the shadow-lapped bridges of Venice, or in the jewel-candied palaces of Florence, why would it not be a good idea to put them on the stage? A group of experimental-minded Florentines devised a series of entertainments in which actors spoke the lines of a play while a group of singers, unseen behind the stage, sang madrigals in subdued voices. This presentation was not entirely satisfactory. It was soon elaborated. Music played by stringed instruments was added. This combination of speech and music was the beginning of opera, though the word was still more important than the singing, the play overshadowing the music. It is interesting to note that the avowed goal of these performances was the restoration of the Greek drama. Wagner sought the same goal a century and a half later. The subjects chosen were mythological and heroic. The play was to be heightened and underscored by the use of music and chanting as the Greeks had done it and as we do it (though a little differently) in our films.

Such was the plan of Giulio Caccini, who in 1601 published a manifesto, calling it proudly *Le Nuove Musiche* (*The New Music*). The new music was given impetus by a wedding ceremony of no small importance. In 1600 Henry IV of France married Marie de Medici. For the wedding, which took place in Florence, the bride, a lady fond of music and the arts, commissioned two composers to collaborate on an opera on the subject of Eurydice. The two composers were Jacopo Peri and Caccini. The opera was performed at the Pitti Palace in Florence on the sixth of October. Incidentally, this being a wedding and a festive occasion, the sad tale of Eurydice was given a happy ending.

Most historians consider *Eurydice* to be the first opera. From Florence the novelty spread to the other Italian cities. It spread rapidly, as desirable novelties do. Monteverdi, a remarkable genius, wrote twenty-one of these new-fashioned works. Venice, a city friendly to all entertainments for the stage, had several good theaters in which operas could be given. Padua, the university city, played opera for its students. Rome, the world city, used the entertainment for its own magnificent purposes.

It did not take very long before Italian opera changed its nature. The art, which had been conceived as an auxiliary to a play, yielded to the demand of its spectators to hear a good tune. The music became more important, the play less so. Monteverdi wrote good tunes. The audiences liked the tunes, even if the singing slowed up the progress of the play.

The Italians did not only want to hear good tunes, they wanted to have something worth while to look at. The "scenic phase" of opera began. We are speaking of a time when enormous wealth was concentrated in few pockets, when Rome was rich and threw its might about. The age was propitious to architecture. The cardinals and princes of the period expended their wealth on stone. They thought that be it ever so flaunting there was no place like home. Huge edifices, bold palaces, were being erected in the city. The delight in architecture was accompanied by a love of gadgets. The middle of the seventeenth century was an era of hydraulic and torsional inventions. It was to be expected that the audiences of the time would not be satisfied with puny scenery and simple backdrops. Elaborate stage marvels were produced. Fire, water, platforms, pulleys, wheels, springs —and hordes of people—collaborated to give the public something to gape at. Cardinal Barberini built a magnificent new theater near his Palace of the Four Fountains. He opened the theater with a perform- ance of *Sant' Alessio* by Stefano Landi. It was a good opera, but the chief curiosity of the spectators centered on the new stage equipment. Cardinal Barberini was himself an inventor and a passionate devotee of mechanics. (When he was closeted with his favorite architect, all matters of state or religion had to be held in abeyance. He once kept the French ambassador waiting several hours because he was poring over a new blueprint.) The new theater was capable of holding four thousand spectators. And these spectators saw at the première and at subsequent performances effects such as these: The stage is flooded with water and on it is fought a sea battle. Real ships are used, large enough to hold men and to be maneuvered around the stage. . . . The heavens open (the heavens were always opening and things were always descending from them; the platform used for this effect was "capable of lifting more than a hundred persons at a time") and reveal Jupiter flanked by the gods. He hurls a bolt of lightning and destroys the castle of Mars. This castle is built of wood and burns on the stage with real fire. . . . Pegasus, played by a trained horse, floats down from heaven standing on top of a fountain, the fountain gushing water during its descent, while the nine Muses picturesquely drape themselves around the fountain.

Battles were fought by armies which overflowed from the stage to the auditorium, where they executed, in time to the music, elabo- rate maneuvers. For the victory processions, trained elephants, camels, stags drawing chariots, and dancing horses were used. The opera often ended with indoor fireworks. We do not understand how they managed it all. No wonder the architect's name was given equal prominence on the playbill with the name of the composer!

The mechanical age was succeeded by an age more sophisticated and less vigorous. Soft-spoken manners, precious wit, love of small perfection became the fashion. Exquisite was the motto, and ex- quisite became the voice of opera. The late seventeenth and the eighteenth century delighted in a form of singing which was made possible by a creature neither man nor woman. In the conservatories of Italy young *castrati* were being trained through years of rigorous study to sing in voices made sexless but given matchless flexibility. These epicene voices had a very wide range and were as malleable as rich clay. Other singers—normal men and women (or as normal as any singer can be)—vied with the skill of the *castrato*. The singer became the reason why anybody went to the opera. Music, orchestra, and scenery played subsidiary roles. Operas were written for individual singers, parts tailor-made to fit the singer's preferences and to take advantage of his strong points. Operas began to be mere improvisations. The composer set down the main outlines, indicated the melodies, and constructed the ensembles (as few as possible, so as not to detract attention from solo arias), and the singer did the rest. He added coloratura, cadenzas, and other embroideries. But at his best he was not merely a vocal athlete. He was almost a composer in his own right. His vocal traceries, his intricate elaborations, had originality, grace, and beauty. Fleeting though the art was and insubstantial, it was an art. To hear this superhuman chant, nobody cared what happened to the play. The young people who flocked to the opera houses acclaimed the singers and shouted their names. After a particularly well-executed aria, a few enthusiastic spectators climbed to the stage to embrace the singers. It was the singer first and last, though a few of the spectators remained curious about the dramatic content of the opera. To these studious spectators a libretto was offered for sale at the entrance of the theater. Since the theater was sparsely illuminated, you received with your libretto a little stub of a candle which, once inside, you could light and by which you could read. Performances lasted from four to six hours. You grew hungry during the performance. If you did, you had only to beckon to one of the several hawkers who wended their way through the audience and who sold candied chestnuts, oranges, apples, and pear compote. If a singer sang badly, these fruits could be hurled at him.

The audience listened with passion to the notes that were held for unbelievable lengths, to the trills that were trilled so that each note was as exactly equivalent to the next as the ticking of a watch, to the runs of notes, now legato, now of pinpoint staccato, which played hide-and-seek with the melody. When the singing stopped, they discussed the merits of favorite singers, their probable earnings, their voyages to the leading opera houses of the Continent and of England,

and their marital and extramarital affairs. The feuds between singers were fought not only by those directly involved but also by their public. The men who stood during the performance used their fists, the gentlemen who sat during the performance used the rapier.

One does not have to be a historian of the theater to be able to predict what happens when the actor or the singer becomes all-powerful. Sooner or later such a theater goes to pieces. What happened in Italy happened to the English stage at about this time. As Margaret Barton has pointed out in her biography of Garrick, the actors tampered with Shakespeare's plays. They thought nothing of giving *King Lear* a happy ending. *Macbeth*'s witches became comic characters. During performances actors conversed with friends in the audience, and if in ill humor they ostentatiously spat on the stage. Audiences shouted and made comments. Every so often a young drunk climbed onto the stage to kiss the leading lady.

In Italy the operatic theater sank to a vaudeville of improvisation —and the operatic composer became a discouraged servant. What was the use of creating anything careful, of taking trouble with an opera, when the singers paid little heed to your work and when the public cared less? It is a sentimental notion that an artist can create his work independent of his time, that he can rise completely above contemporary conditions, heedless of the consumers of his wares. The artist needs his public. To a certain extent even the great artist gives the public what the public wants. Rather, he gives the public more than it wants. He builds on the known, adding the unknown, the new, the daring, the experimental to his structure. But he must have some basis to build on. His work cannot float in an ideal, separate ether. The art that we call timeless was anchored in its time. It bore some relation to the everyday world, the comfortable or disconsolate world in which lived those people who cooked the artist's dinner, who cleaned his room, and who paid him his money. When you find a period where people don't care what goes into a book, you will find few good authors. When you find a period where paintings are out of fashion, you will find few first-rate painters. And if this is true of all art, it is especially true of the art of the theater. Less than books or paintings or sculpture can a play or an opera live the sheltered life. It must be exposed to the public, it must live with its audience.

Italian opera left to the ministrations of the singers not only became questionable music but lost the sense of the theater. As early as 1720 a satiric writer, Marcello by name, published a report on operatic conditions in which he made fun of these conditions by pretending to offer good advice to all those who took part in an opera performance. The opera composer, he writes, "will hurry or slow down the pace of an aria, according to the caprice of the singers, and will conceal the displeasure which their insolence causes him by the reflection that his reputation, his solvency, and all his interest are in their hands. . . . The director will see that all the best songs go to the prima donna, and if it becomes necessary to shorten the opera he will never allow her arias to be cut, but rather other entire scenes." If a singer

has a scene with another actor, whom he is supposed to address when singing an air, he will take care to pay no attention to him, but will bow to the spectators in the loges, smile at the orchestra and the other players, in order that the audience may clearly understand that he is the *Signor Alipi Forconi, Musico,* and not the Prince Zoroaster, whom he is representing. . . .

All the while the ritornello of his air is being played the singer should walk about the stage, take snuff, complain to his friends that he is in bad voice, that he has a cold, etc., and while singing his aria he shall take care to remember that at the cadence he may pause as long as he pleases, and make runs, decorations, and ornaments according to his fancy; during which time the leader of the orchestra shall leave his place at the harpsichord, take a pinch of snuff, and wait until it shall please the singer to finish.

Nevertheless, the opera house lost none of its popularity as a place of entertainment. It was, aside from the church, the most pleasant place in which to see your friends, meet your mistress, show the Milanese silk of your new dress, and receive the gossip of the day. The opera house was the best-heated, the best-lighted public building. The boxes were handsomely decorated and were illuminated with lanterns to make sure that the entire audience could see the occupants. The leading families of the town owned the boxes outright. This custom persisted almost to our own day. In the early days of the Metropolitan Opera House the boxes were owned by the stockholders, and the rich families of Milan each owned a box at La Scala. They vied with one another in decorating the boxes to their own taste, using their own silks and velvets. The more "social" operagoing became, the less attention was paid to what went on, on the stage. Hogarth painted an audience of the time. He called the picture "A Good Audience." You see, in one of the boxes, a cavalier conversing with an orange girl, the subject of the conversation being plainly expressed in his smirk. Another young man is making good progress with *his* girl who, at the moment, is unbuttoning his coat. The audience in the pit is laughing. Only the musicians are glum and serious.

No wonder that to such an audience stereotyped entertainments were offered. In serious opera the subjects were still classical-allegorical-mythological. Comic operas were a little more inventive, a little less stilted. Essentially both kinds of opera were parades of arias. Between the arias people played chess; a visitor to Rome reported that "chess serves to fill out the boredom of the recitatives and the music serves to check too great a passion for chess." [1] I do not know what ambidextrous mind first reasoned that if people liked opera and liked gambling, then why not give them both at the same time and make doubly sure of their patronage. It is a fact that in the late eighteenth century most of Italy's opera houses were run in connection with a gambling casino. If the performance did not please you, you could get to the gaming tables without having to step out in the rain.

These coarse conditions lasted until the first part of the nineteenth century, when three men came along to pull opera out of its doldrums. The first of these was the brilliant and intellectual Rossini, the second, the careful and gentle Bellini, the third, the prolific Donizetti. Rossini was not a reformer in the pedagogic sense of the word. He did not set out to prove theories or uplift the stage. He wanted to do merely what others had done before him, that is, to entertain audiences and thereby earn fame and money. But he saw that things in the opera house were at sixes and sevens. He rebelled against the power of the performers. When he found that a certain singer so titivated one of his melodies that Rossini himself was not sure of recognizing his own brain child, he cried with Hamlet, "O, reform it altogether!"

Here it is again a question of the relationship between a man's talent and the time he lives in. A man comes upon the scene and writes something that is beautiful and new. He refreshes and reforms his art. But in order for him to do so, the art must be ready to be reformed. When Rossini came upon the scene, the art no longer served as it was. People were beginning to tire of the overelaborate style. And there may have been many who were beginning to demand from opera a deeper satisfaction than butterfly entertainment. Moreover,

[1] Quoted by D. Grout, *A Short History of Opera,* and by Alberto Ghislanzoni, *Il Problema dell'Opera.*

a practical consideration was involved: the supply of *castrati* was becoming sparse. They were no longer so good as they used to be. Rossini argued, not unreasonably, that he could write better music than the music singers could invent. He demanded that the singers sing what he had composed. He gave a more important role to the orchestra. He enriched and varied the ensembles. In short, he put new life into the art. And a very sparkling life it was, though he made the mistake of setting any play to music without bothering to inquire whether it *was* a play. Rossini, born in 1792, is the bridge between the eighteenth and the nineteenth centuries. He started his career in an age when the composer was still the servant of the singer,[2] and lived to see the time (though he had given up writing operas long before) when Wagner was postulating his exacting theories of music drama. The residue of this long lifetime is unfortunately small, stray jewels from a capacious casket, consisting of the glittering overtures in the concert hall and of *The Barber of Seville* in the opera house. It was his own fault: a double fault, compounded not only of slipshod librettos basted together for a season's use, but also of music which, though highly original compared with the work of any other contemporary Italian composer, constantly cribbed from itself. One Rossini opera sounds like another Rossini opera; devices such as the famous Rossini crescendo are ubiquitous, the formula all too apparent. But alike or not, transparent or not, the wonder is that every time one hears a Rossini opera it proves to be an exhilarating experience. *La Cenerentola* (*Cinderella*) has recently captivated new audiences; *Otello*, particularly its beautiful last act, makes a deep impression; *L'Italiana in Algerì* contains wit which almost matches the *Barber*'s; and *William Tell* contains moments of power seemingly surpassing the composer's capacity. For *William Tell* is a work on which Rossini expended a doughty effort, so that he gave too much and produced an opera that needs tightening and adaptation should it ever be revived again. Someday there is going to take place a Rossini revival, and not of *William Tell* alone. His music is too good to be lost forever.

Now a generation of new singers was growing up. Men like the tenor Rubini, the bass Lablache, women like Pasta and Grisi, if they were no longer improvisers, had other virtues. They knew how to

[2] "The Maestro Rossini obliges himself to make, if necessary, all the changes . . . to suit the capabilities or exigencies of the singers," read his contract for *The Barber of Seville*.

produce a voice warm and rich, such a voice, such a tone as a cellist who is in love might summon. They breathed with the poise of a diplomat. Long, long was the sound and even the tone. They melted one tone into the next and the sweet liquid flowed straight to the heart of the hearer. The age of beautiful singing, of *bel canto*, was in the ascendancy. Bellini and Donizetti were there to serve it.

These were men conscious of their importance. No longer meek, they and others of their time regained the upper hand as composers. They still cared little about the play or fitting the music to the dramatic situation, or of expressing music in other terms than beautiful singing. Their arias were accompanied for the most part merely by a rocking motion in the orchestra. (Except in Donizetti's comic operas, *Don Pasquale* and *L'Elisir d'Amore*, which are Rossini's cousins both in orchestral expressiveness and in vocal charm.) They concocted much that was hasty pudding. Donizetti composed his operas even faster than Rossini did. *Don Pasquale* was composed in eleven days, *Lucia di Lammermoor* in six weeks. What of it? *Don Pasquale* is, as I just said, replete with vocal charm which would not have been improved by eleven weeks of polishing. *Lucia* is an uneven opera. It sinks in the Mad Scene to tricky banality and rises in its final scene to a noble beauty which foreshadows the best Verdi. The Sextet is deservedly famous, and as Cecil Gray has pointed out, it is "one of the very finest examples of concerted vocal writing in the whole range of opera." Altogether, the public's verdict on *Lucia* is a just one, as public verdicts have a habit of being: an old-fashioned opera but a masterpiece.

Bellini's working methods were different from Donizetti's. Not only was he the more careful craftsman but he claimed to have derived his melodies from the tone fall of the spoken line. He tells us that before he set words to music, he declaimed the parts spoken by the different characters and observed the inflections of his own voice and "the degree of haste or languor in the delivery." Little of this is to be heard in *I Puritani, La Sonnambula,* or *Norma.* What is to be heard is not a lyric line tied to speech but lyricism independent, soaring, free floating, a song molded with the kind of self-assurance which takes its time. His masterpiece is *Norma,* a work of highest value. It influenced not only Italian opera but all romantic music; its elegiac melodies echo through the scores of Chopin, Liszt, Debussy, and Puccini.

In 1813 northern Italy was still a possession of Napoleon. In that year, an innkeeper in the small town of Roncole registered with the French authorities the birth of a male child, the given names being Joseph Fortunin François. Had Verdi been born a year later, his first name might well have been registered as Josef, for by that time the Austrians were in charge. But he grew up as Giuseppe in a country of strife, in a period when Italians bent their effort to the task of becoming Italians instead of remaining provincials. In that period Italian men and women were proud and ambitious, even if for all too brief a time, a people who could pull at the bellrope of liberty together. When Verdi was born he was born in a country that was no country. But Mazzini, Garibaldi, Cavour led Italians and the people fought for liberty. Verdi lived to see a nation.

In Verdi's early operas were to be heard patriotic and revolutionary appeals. His first big success was *Nabucco*. It contains a famous chorus of slaves [3] which became a rallying song for the Italians. *Nabucco* was such a success that La Scala, where the work was first performed, handed him a contract with a blank space for the fee. Giuseppina Strepponi, the young singer with whom he fell in love, advised him to ask the fee received by Bellini for *Norma*. That was the highest compliment one could pay a composer. His next work, *I Lombardi*, provoked a patriotic demonstration against the Austrian oppressors. Even his name became a political anagram: Viva Emmanuele, Re d'Italia. Though these early operas showed flashes of genius, they were as yet too slam-bang in style, too melodramatic in character, too "Italianate" to capture the sedate international audience. They are worth noting here because they show us that opera had become an art which roused Italians to truculent fervor; it was propaganda, it was a Patrick Henry manifesto set to music,[4] and as such was to be watched with a suspicious and a drooping eye by the gentlemen at the censorship office. Even later Verdi had his troubles with the censor. *Rigoletto*, said the government official, was a subject so disrespectful to royalty that he was surprised that the "illustrious Maestro" would waste his talent on it. Verdi's *Un Ballo in Maschera* was to be produced at the San Carlo in Naples. The censor of Naples disapproved of the subject and required fundamental alterations in the libretto. Verdi refused to comply. The San Carlo Theater threatened him with a breach-of-contract suit. But the people of Naples

[3] "*Va pensiero sull' ali dorate!*" ("Fly, thought, on golden wings!")
[4] The patriotic use of Italian opera forms the basis of the plot in George Meredith's novel, *Sandra Belloni*.

so ardently took Verdi's part that the management of the theater had no choice but to absolve Verdi of his obligation, fearing that if they did not a real revolution would break out. That is how seriously operatic matters were now considered.

And no wonder! For no matter in what fabled and removed countries and times their subjects were set, these new operas by the new genius, so modest and yet so exacting, were no longer removed, calm, classical, no longer mythological charades, no longer "polite," if we may so express ourselves. The music was full of wine of current vintage. Verdi gave a new contemporaneousness to the old art. It was no longer merely beautiful behind the footlights; it was heady and haunting in your daily life. And indeed many of the tunes became the popular songs of the day.

But Verdi's genius, even in its early stage, transcended considerations of patriotism and transcended also the humming appeal of good melodies. He knew how to write superb melodies. He also knew how to give his audience a good show. But over and above that he knew how to fuse music and drama, making the alloy far stronger than it had been. He wrought a miracle of ligation.

What is an opera, a *good* opera? (Let's not ask, "What is a music drama?" The distinction between opera and music drama is largely snobbery.) Opera is defined as a play set to music. But that elementary definition does not tell the story. It is possible to take a good play, to bestrew it with arias, duets, and ensembles at given points, and yet *not* achieve an opera. Why does the result not measure up? What essential ingredient is missing? The essential ingredient in opera is this: the play must be expressed *through* the music; it cannot merely be illustrated or underscored or overlaid by music. The music itself must contain the drama that the spoken play expresses in words. The drama cannot be confined to the libretto; there must take place a true amalgamation between plot and song, between action as it is expressed in the book and action as it is expressed in the music.

Verdi achieved this. He achieved it in an original fashion. He made opera more human. Himself a normal man, he is the great composer of the normal situation. A girl parting from her beloved—has that situation ever been more heartbreakingly expressed than in *Traviata*'s simple, "*Amami, Alfredo!*"? A father's struggle against the man who is going to hurt his child—we experience it in *Rigoletto*, enveloped in darkness. A woman's longing for peace—Verdi sets it down with complete conviction in *"Pace, pace, mio dio"* in *The Force of Destiny*, an aria which remembers Bellini's melody but is less remote, is nearer to our heart.

We are not belittling Verdi when we call him normal. He was of course normal in the way of a genius, which means that he combined great sensitivity with great intellect. It was perhaps from Shakespeare, whom he worshiped, that he absorbed some of the lifelike directness which he put into his music. That is not to say that Verdi was free of faults. His plots occasionally strut with melodrama, his music is sometimes overly theatrical, he whips up excitement by a stretto device. No matter! Enough strength and beauty are left to satisfy us— seemingly forever.

Thanks to Verdi, Italian opera became more than ever a truly popular art. The triple constellation which emerged in his middle period, *Rigoletto, Il Trovatore,* and *La Traviata,* along with the later *Aïda,* a work of consummate dramatic and musical skill, are as beloved today as they were half a century ago.

Verdi was to go on after *Aïda* to compose two nonpopular operas. He produced *Otello* and *Falstaff,* two lonely masterpieces. *Otello,* of which I would not hesitate to say that it is one of the three greatest works written for the lyric stage, is only now achieving some degree of popular understanding. *Falstaff* has never been a popular opera; it is too fine-spun, too subtle for the wide-open spaces of the opera house. And it is only in a recording such as Toscanini gave us that we can savor its grace and rejoice over its wit.

Unique as these two works are, they are still Italian operas, they are still operas by Verdi. And they share with other Italian operas the characteristic of combining stirring and poignant music with the entertainment offered by good theater. They work with a double thrust. They connect tangible characters, people of flesh and blood (though sometimes of too much flesh and too little blood), to the incorporeal world of sound. This twin interest—linking the "real" and the "unreal," combining the easily imagined with the highly fanciful—this is what gives opera much of its fascination. Here we must also find the explanation for the enduring success of the two works of the Veristic school, Mascagni's *Cavalleria Rusticana,* an opera of fairly gross taste, and of Leoncavallo's *I Pagliacci,* which is better music, though the clown with the broken heart drops tears of grease paint.

In the textbooks Puccini is counted as a pupil of the Veristic school.

He is not, really. He is much better than that. As a musician he is
the successor of Verdi—though he himself did not enjoy being called
that—who at the same time had carefully cocked his ear in the direction of Wagner and Debussy and, after absorbing a variety of styles,
created a very personal musical speech, a speech so personal that it
can be recognized after three bars. Like Verdi and Bellini, he was a
natural-born melodist. He said, "The simple passages are the most
difficult for me—I can always think of a melody." But the simple
passages that he did write are often beautiful. He knew how to set to
music everyday speech, love's give and take, the small ecstasy, the
jealousy of a winter's tale. He was not interested in heroes and
heroines. It was ordinary people who interested him in *La Bohème*
and in *Butterfly* and even in *Tosca*. His female characters he took to
his heart. They resemble one another: Mimi and Cio-Cio-San and Liù
are cousins in calamity. Puccini's instinct for the theater is almost
always sure, and his orchestra serves that instinct. In passages such
as the introduction of the third act of *Bohème* or the love duet in the
first act of *Butterfly* his orchestral writing is superb. That he was a
craftsman of almost fanatical punctiliousness is proved by his struggle
with the texts and by a study of his manuscripts. His reward is the
fact that *Bohème, Butterfly*, and *Tosca* are the only three operas
which rival Verdi's operas in popularity. He is not only Verdi's successor—inferior but nonetheless a master—but up to the present the
last of a long line of composers who succeeded in making Italian
opera a truly popular art.

We may end our informal history by reasserting that this art is an
international commodity. Italian opera is a language understood by
people who do not understand a word of Italian. Antonio Ghislanzoni, the librettist of *Aïda*, once remarked on this quality in a bit of
humorous verse:

> La nostra musica
> nell' universo
> regnò sovrana
> finchè fu musica
> italiana.
> Volle esser musica
> cosmopolita
> allor d'Italia
> non è più uscita.

(Our music reigned supreme in the universe as long
as it was Italian music. The moment it became
cosmopolitan music, it never got out of Italy.)

Italy has always been a country where the musical exports far out-
balanced the imports. Italian opera is an export article, which by and
large does not deteriorate in transit. Even translation into German—
than which there is nothing more incongruous—does not entirely spoil
the products of Verdi and Puccini. They have always been almost as
much at home in Paris or Vienna or New York as in Milan.

A lady who is that much at home everywhere may occasionally o'er-
step the modesty of nature and tear a passion to tatters, but if she
does we forgive her.

ROSSINI AS A COMPOSER

Francis Toye

This is the summarizing chapter of the biography written by the English critic.

"A tragedy of bad librettos."

The precise balance to be struck between the merits and defects of Rossini as a composer must always remain perforce a matter of opinion. His music will never appeal greatly to those who attach supreme value to profundity of feeling or intellect. The latter, at any rate, could scarcely be expected of him. Rossini was clearheaded, shrewd, urbane, but in no way intellectual. The extraordinary thing is rather, with an education so neglected, with a career during the first thirty years of his life so feverish and so vagabond, that he should have risen to the heights he did. Partly, no doubt, his lack of profound feeling can be ascribed to the same cause. Fétis observed with considerable perspicacity that, till he left Italy after *Semiramide*, Rossini never could have had the time even to cultivate a genuine friendship. Thrown constantly into contact with thousands of people in one town after another, his life must have been passed in a kind of delirium of sensations; and I think that this is reflected in his music. Doubtless, there was a great change in later life, when he made many real friends, but early habits leave an ineradicable mark, and, in any case, it must be remembered that he wrote very little music after the age of thirty-six.

Every student of Rossini has noticed, moreover, his comparative inability to portray the emotion of love in its more tender aspect. For my part, I doubt if he ever felt it. The countless amorous intrigues of his youth seem to have been nothing but the usual fleeting affairs of theatrical life. He must at one time have felt a certain amount of passion for Isabella Colbran, and she, poor woman, certainly grew to

Reprinted from *Rossini* by Francis Toye, by permission of Alfred A. Knopf, Inc.

love him, but one has an uneasy suspicion that in that alliance material considerations counted at least as much as affection. In all probability he cared more deeply for Olympe Pélissier. By then, however, he had practically given up composition, and was, moreover, a sick man, full of self-pity, who needed protection and care, not stimulus to artistic creation. The most poignant emotion he ever knew was undoubtedly adoration of his mother, which some biographers have found reflected in certain pages of *William Tell*. It may be so. In any case, such filial devotion, however passionate, has nothing to do with the point.

To his faulty education, too, must be ascribed that indifference to the literary value of words and situations so noticeable in many of the operas. Any music would serve to express them provided it sounded agreeable in itself. His sluggishness and extraordinary facility combined further to induce in him a regrettable lack of self-criticism. Much of his subject matter suffers from excessive similarity; he was far too easily satisfied with ideas as they first presented themselves, far too tolerant of repetitions and the continuous employment of stereotyped devices such as the famous crescendo. His excessive borrowings have been commented on already; they were in reality part and parcel of the same attitude of mind.

Rossini's operatic career might be summarized as a tragedy of bad librettos, for only once, in fact, was he really well served. But he must bear some of the responsibility. Had he, like Verdi, possessed the character and the determination to insist on his own way and reject even one-third of the fifteen librettos that he set to music in the space of four years; had he, like Beethoven, written three overtures for one opera instead of fitting one overture to three operas, there would have been a very different tale to tell. At the same time it must be remembered that the conditions of the Italian theater made any such proceeding exceedingly difficult. We should not so much blame Rossini as commiserate him on having been unable to rise above the handicaps of his life and circumstances. All things said and done, what he did in fact accomplish remains little less than a miracle.

Besides, as regards some of his defects there is, to say the least, another side to the medal. His carelessness in the setting of words, for instance, proceeded to some extent from the remarkably pure musicality of his inspiration. Music as pure sound, rhythm as pure rhythm, meant everything to him; words very little. "Give me a laundry list," he is reported once to have said, "and I will set it to music." He could, and did, compose music under any kind of conditions, amidst the chatter of friends, the clamor of copyists, out fishing and in bed. Now this musicality is, perhaps, his principal attraction, to it must be ascribed the spontaneity, the vivacity, the charm which are characteristic of his work. He did not always make the best of his extraordinary natural gift in this respect, but he rarely allows us to forget that he possessed it. His music is never anything but indisputably musical, the precise reverse of Meyerbeer's; indeed, that is why most musicians have kept somewhere in their hearts a warm spot for Rossini, be his faults what they may. The "storms" in some half-dozen of his operas provide a good instance of this musicality. They are never just imitative, but always translated into purely musical terms, often subtly attuned, as, for instance, in *La Cenerentola*, to the psychology of that particular score. In fact, one of the very few abstract principles which he laid down as a dogma was that music should be "ideal and expressive," not imitative.

Generally speaking, however, Rossini never dogmatized; his approach to music was instinctive rather than intellectual. This is shown in his famous saying that there are only two kinds of music, the good and the bad; or that other, less known, where he states that every kind of music is good except the boring kind. These are scarcely the utterances of a man who attached any value to aesthetic theories as such. The fact of the matter is that Rossini regarded himself as an artist-craftsman producing music when and where required, entirely devoid of the pretensions invented subsequently by the Romantic movement, which at no time affected Italy as it affected Germany, France or England, and, before he went to Paris, had made no impression whatever south of the Alps. Besides, there is always a tendency to forget that for all practical purposes Rossini's musical career ended in 1829. To some extent, therefore, he remains in essence more akin to an eighteenth-century, than to a nineteenth-century, composer.

As regards Rossini's technical ability there can scarcely be two opinions. No man not a consummate technician could have written *William Tell*, while the wonderful ensembles in the earlier operas suffice by themselves to attest his mastery. These ensembles lack as a rule the power of characterization later attained by Verdi, but as examples of skill and effectiveness in vocal part writing they are supreme. Yet Rossini always professed indifference to scholastic ingenuity as such. "*Voilà du temps perdu*," he added in pencil after writing some eight-part contrapuntal essay or other. He disliked the pedants as much as they disliked him, and I have a shrewd suspicion that many of the "irregularities" in his music were due as much to a wanton pleasure in annoying them as to carelessness and indifference.

His excellence in orchestration, too, has not, I think, been sufficiently emphasized. None of his Italian contemporaries, not even Verdi till the *Ballo in Maschera* period, scored as well as he did. It has been said, indeed, that, with his retirement in 1829, Italian writing for the orchestra took a definite step backward. All through the Rossini operas we find instruments treated with great skill, with an unerring instinct for their potentialities of expression. The overtures, in particular, deserve the highest praise in this respect. Take, for instance, the writing for the cellos in the *William Tell* Overture. It is so masterly that the famous cellist Servais told Rossini that he had no need to be informed that the composer had himself studied the cello in his youth. And for sheer brilliance and effectiveness the rest of the orchestration is equally remarkable. Nor should the comparative simplicity of the effects in the earlier overtures such as *L'Italiana*, *The Barber*, *La Gazza Ladra* and *Semiramide* blind us to the surety of touch, the felicity of inspiration, that were necessary to invent them at that time. Everything "comes off" as well today as ever it did. Nobody who has heard them played by a Toscanini or a Beecham is likely to stand in need of conversion on that score. As a matter of fact, these overtures are little masterpieces from every point of view. In them we find displayed to the best advantage that rhythm in which Rossini so excelled and to which he attached so much importance, saying that in it resided all the power and expressiveness of music. The subject material itself is nearly always excellent and highly individual; the form is as clear as the treatment. Possibly the very attractiveness of these overtures has led some of our musicians unduly to underrate them.

Finally, Rossini's exceptional knowledge and love of the human voice cannot be too strongly insisted upon. Himself a singer from childhood, he understood it as scarcely any other composer has understood it, and his writing for it sets a standard. There is no question here of demanding effects, as Verdi too often does, mainly from notes at the extremity of the singer's compass; the whole range of the voice is expected to pay its due contribution, while it is scarcely possible in all the operas and songs to find a vocal phrase which, granted the technique prevalent at the time, is not delightfully singable. It is not surprising that he should have excelled in this respect, for, of all forms of musical expression, Rossini loved singing the best. Inevitably, such enthusiasm on the part of so famous a composer produced its effect, particularly in France, where Rossini's influence is said to have altered for the better the whole style of French singing. The gradual decline in the art during the last thirty years of his life (a decline that has been progressing with increasing rapidity ever since) filled him with dismay. He told Michotte, indeed, that his main ambition in the *Petite Messe* was to leave a final legacy which might serve as an example of how to write for the voice. Yet he never willingly suffered the tyranny of singers, and he refused to allow that they had any share in the work of artistic creation. "A good singer," he wrote in 1851, "should only be the conscientious interpreter of the composer's ideas, endeavoring to express them as effectively as possible and to present them as clearly as they can be presented. . . . In short the composer and the poet alone have any serious claim to be regarded as creators."

In view of all the reproaches that have been leveled at Rossini for writing solely to show off the virtuosity of his singers, this insistence is decidedly interesting. There is no reason to think that he did not in the main succeed in putting it into practice, though there were occasions, in particular where Isabella Colbran was concerned, when he certainly did not. In fact Isabella, quite unintentionally, did him definite harm, in that in all probability a desire to minister to her particular talents led him to write *opera seria* when, as Beethoven suggested and he himself admitted, he would have been better employed in writing *opera buffa*. A man of stronger character would have noted the pitfall, to bridge or avoid it, but once again it must be insisted that there was nothing grand or heroic about Rossini; for him the easiest path was the obvious, the only path. Can one imagine Verdi advising a young friend, as Rossini did, to get out of a difficulty by a lie, if necessary? His general attitude toward music has not unfairly been described as indicative of a pronounced taste rather than passion or semireligious veneration. His real justification is that he possessed in an exceptional degree the most essential attributes of a composer, melodic and rhythmical inventiveness, and that he brought into music a great healthy laugh which will always endear him to the artist if not to the educationalist. Wagner, who . . . described him as the first man he had met in the world of art who was truly great and

worthy of reverence, wrote after his death an epitaph that was alike
kind, wise and just:

Rossini can scarcely be handed to posterity in a more false guise than by
stamping him as a hero of Art on the one hand or degrading him to a
flippant wag on the other. . . . No; Rossini will never be judged aright
until someone attempts an intelligent history of the culture of our current
century. . . . Were this character of our age correctly drawn, it would then
be possible to allot to Rossini also his true and fitting station in it. And
that station would be no lowly one, for, with the same title as Palestrina,
Bach and Mozart belonged to their age, Rossini belongs to his. . . . Then,
and not till then, will it be possible to estimate Rossini at his true and
quite peculiar worth; for what fell short of full dignity would have to be
accounted to neither his natural gifts nor his artistic conscience, but
simply to his public and environment, which made it difficult for a man
of his nature to raise himself above his age and thereby share the grandeur
of the veritable art-heroes.

SOME PERSONAL RECOLLECTIONS OF ROSSINI

Camille Saint-Saëns

> Almost all who came in contact with Rossini remem-
> bered him with the special affection one reserves for a
> fat man. Brilliant, sociable, and genuinely interested in
> all that was going on in music during the fruitful dec-
> ades of the middle nineteenth century, Rossini held open
> house Saturday nights to which came the best of Pari-
> sian intellectual society. . . . The composer of *Sam-*
> *son et Delila* describes a benevolent hoax.

"The duo is not mine."

I was twenty years old when M. and Mme. Viardot presented
me to Rossini. He invited me to his little evening receptions, where
he welcomed me with the bland amiability of which he was past master. About a month later, when he found I did not want him to give
me a private hearing either as a composer or as a pianist, he changed
his attitude toward me.

"Come and see me in the morning," he said, "and we'll have a
little chat."

I hastened to accept this flattering invitation, and found a Rossini
totally different from that of the evening before, interesting to the
highest degree, open-minded, with ideas which, if not advanced, were
at least large and lofty in spirit. He gave evidence of this in his
defense of the famous *Mass* of Liszt in face of almost unanimous hostility, when it was performed for the first time at the church of Saint
Eustache.

"You have written," he said one day, "a duo for flute and clarinet
for Messieurs Dorus and Leroy. Won't you ask these musicians if
they will consent to play it at one of my *soirées*?"

The two great artists hardly needed to be asked, and an unfor-

From *Musica*, Paris.

gettable incident followed. As Rossini never had printed programs for these occasions, he arranged to have it understood that the work was composed by himself. One can imagine how successful it was under those circumstances. The piece over and done with, Rossini took me into the dining room and made me sit near him, holding me by the hand in a way that made it impossible for me to escape. Then came the procession of admirers and flatterers. "Ah, *maître*! what a masterpiece! what a marvel! . . ."

And as soon as the victim had unwoven this garland of praise, Rossini would reply, tranquilly: "I entirely agree with your opinion; but the duo is not mine, it is by this gentleman. . . ." Such acts of kindness, mingled with pleasantry, speak more for this great man than a wealth of commentary. For Rossini was a great man. The young gentlemen of our age are badly situated to judge his works, written, as he himself said, for singers and a public which no longer exist. "People have reproached me," he said to me one day, "for the big crescendo in my overtures. But if they didn't have the crescendo they would never have the operas performed."

In our day the public is enslaved. Have I not seen on the programs of a certain concert hall, "All signs of disapproval will be severely repressed"? Formerly, especially in Italy, the public was the master and its approval was law. It came before the candles were lighted, and insisted on the big overture with the big crescendo; it demanded cavatinas, duos, ensembles; it came to hear the singers and not to assist at a lyric drama. Rossini, in several of his works, and above all in *Otello*, made great strides in dramatic truthfulness in his operas. In *Moses* and in *The Siege of Corinth* (without mentioning *William Tell*), he opened up new avenues which even yet have not been fully explored, in spite of the meagerness of the means at his disposal. But—as Victor Hugo has gloriously demonstrated—poverty of means is no obstacle to genius any more than a wealth of means is an advantage to mediocrity.

With Stanzieri, a charming young man of whom Rossini was very fond, but who was somewhat lacking in "polish," and Diémer, still young but a great virtuoso, I became "pianist in ordinary" to the household. We frequently had the pleasure of hearing the little piano pieces which the master amused himself by scribbling in his idle moments. I willingly accompanied the singers when Rossini did not wish to do so himself, though he accompanied admirably, for he played the piano to perfection. But, unfortunately, I did not participate in the *soirée* at which Patti was heard at Rossini's house for the first time. After the performance of the aria from his *Barber*, everyone will recall how Rossini, with the most complimentary air imaginable, said to her: "Who was the composer of the aria you have just sung to us?"

I saw him the next day, and he was not yet calmed down.

"I know well enough," he said, "that my arias ought to be embroidered somewhat; they were designed for that. But in the recitatives, to leave not a note as I wrote it—that is too much! . . ."

And in his irritation he inveighed against sopranos who insist on singing arias written for contraltos, leaving unsung the arias written for sopranos.

The diva herself was highly indignant. But she reflected that it would be a serious matter to have Rossini for an enemy. . . . A few days after, she came, repentant, to ask his advice. She did well in so doing, for at that time her brilliant, fascinating talent was not fully developed.

THE BARBER OF SEVILLE

Ernest Newman

> Virtually all of Ernest Newman's essays on operas could
> be reprinted in an anthology. He looks behind the
> music and here helps us to understand not only *The
> Barber* but also Mozart's opera.

"The absurd comedy of the world."

The Caron de Beaumarchais, to whom we owe *The Barber
of Seville* and *The Marriage of Figaro*, began life in a humble way in
January, 1732, as Pierre Augustin Caron, the son of a Paris clockmaker. The boy was trained in his father's profession, and at twenty
invented a new watch escapement. His idea was stolen by a rival:
a lawsuit followed: the young Caron saw to it that the affair received
plenty of publicity, and it all ended very much in his favor. The incident was symbolic and prophetic: all his long life he was at variance
with someone or other, and practically always victor by virtue of his
superior adroitness and his satiric tongue and pen.

By now he had attracted the attention of the Court. He was appointed clockmaker to Louis XV, and before long we find him, rather
surprisingly, teaching the guitar and harp to His Majesty's daughters
and organizing the Court musical entertainments and ballets. In
1755 he married a rich widow, eleven years his senior, who died after
some eighteen months of wedlock. Much of the money he inherited
from her was lost in lawsuits with her relations. There remained in
his hands, however, a small landed property of hers that carried with
it the title of De Beaumarchais, by which he chose to be known for
the rest of his life. In 1768 he married another widow, who also died
within a couple of years.

A born adventurer, cool, audacious, infinitely resourceful and none
too scrupulous, for the next thirty years or so he was ready to try his

Reprinted from *Seventeen Famous Operas* by Ernest Newman, by permission of
Alfred A. Knopf, Inc. Copyright 1954 by Ernest Newman.

hand at anything that looked like turning out profitably and at the same time attracted him by a spice of difficulty and danger in it. He was equally happy gunrunning for the American insurgents (or, during the Terror, for the Dutch), acting as a royalist spy and purloiner of secret documents in London, or insinuating his plays into the Paris theaters and fighting the actors for his author's fees. (Literary men should remember him with gratitude as the founder of the Société des Auteurs Dramatiques, the prime object of which was to see that the actors at the Comédie Française did not bamboozle play-wrights out of their royalties.) He was a man who would have come to the front in any age and any milieu: today he would no doubt be equally notorious, equally successful, as a dealer in armaments, a secret service agent, a Hollywood magnate, a playwright and a smuggler of Swiss watches, nylons or foreign currency.

His excursions into serious drama were not a success; sentimentality did not sit well on him. His literary fame rests today almost entirely on three works—the two immortal Figaro comedies and the *Mémoires*;[1] and the last is as great in its way as the two stage works by which he is mostly known now. In his late thirties he had become closely associated with one of the big financiers of the day, a certain Pâris-Duverney, who had no doubt found him very useful in some of his business transactions and was appropriately grateful. Beaumarchais soon found himself sufficiently in funds to buy for fifty thousand livres an appointment as royal secretary that carried with it a title to nobility: when detractors ventured to throw doubts on his claim to be one of the aristocracy he would reply, with a frankness rare among recipients of titles, "If you don't believe me I'll show you the receipt." On the first of April, 1770, he and Pâris-Duverney had a final settlement of accounts, the financier acknowledging in writing that he owed Beaumarchais fifteen thousand livres. Four months later Pâris-Duverney died. His nephew and general heir, Count de la Blache, reluctant to let this ripe plum slip out of his hands, accused Beaumarchais of having falsified the books, and alleged him to be indebted to the estate to the tune of 139,000 livres. The case was decided legally first against Beaumarchais, then in his favor; but he had been imprudent enough just then to incur the hostility of the powerful Duke de Chaulnes by filching the latter's mistress from him, and

---

[1] Not "*mémoires*" in the autobiographical sense of the term, but "documents relating to . . ."; the full description of the work in question is *Mémoires dans l'affaire Goezman*.

there was a quarrel that ended in both the Duke and Beaumarchais being placed under arrest.

This gave La Blache an opportunity to reopen his case. When, in the second act of *The Barber*, Bartolo hints at getting Count Almaviva out of the way by attacking him in a night ambuscade, the wily Basilio cries "Fie!" on him for the crudity of his technique. Basilio knows a better way of ruining the Count's chances with Rosina—by means of calumny, a subject on which he grows eloquent. "Calumny, Monsieur! You do wrong to despise it. I have seen the most respectable men pretty well annihilated by it. Take my word for it, there is no stupid vileness, no horror, no absurdity that you can't get the loungers of a big town to believe—and here in Madrid we have some real experts in that line!" La Blache, with his adversary temporarily out of the way, renewed the battle for the precious livres, and found calumny his best weapon. Forged letters from and to Beaumarchais were put into circulation, and he was accused of having got rid of both his wives by poison. The upshot of it all was that La Blache won his case on a retrial, and Beaumarchais, at the age of forty-one, was well-nigh ruined.

But, as usual, disaster and conflict brought out all that was best in him; his genius needed rough friction to develop all its latent light and heat. The climax in the Pâris-Duverney dispute had come in April, 1773. A legal councilor named Goezman had been entrusted with the preparation of a report on the case, which was to come before the tribunal on the fifth of that month. On the first, Beaumarchais, who was, of course, seriously hampered in both defense and attack by the circumstances of his imprisonment, obtained permission to leave the jail on each of the next few mornings on the conditions that he would be accompanied everywhere by a certain M. Santerre, that he would not occupy himself in his free time with anything but the coming lawsuit, and that he would return to the prison each day at nightfall. The person who mattered most to him was of course Goezman, who, he feared, was not as well acquainted with the financial details of the Pâris-Duverney matter as he would have liked him to be; so Beaumarchais's first, indeed only, care was to have a little confidential talk with this influential gentleman.

Friends had told him that his judge Goezman's young wife took an interest of her own occasionally in the cases that came before her husband: as Beaumarchais puts it ironically in his first *Mémoire*, she had assured his chief informant that if a litigant's nature was generous and his cause just, and he asked of her nothing that was inconsistent with her honesty, she would not resent the offer of a little private gift as an outrage on her delicacy. The friend who was acting for Beaumarchais learned that Mme. Goezman was so anxious to do all a poor weak woman could do to further the interests of justice that for a trifle of a hundred louis d'or she would arrange for her husband to grant Beaumarchais an audience before the case came on. On the third of April the latter did indeed manage to see the judge, but only for a few minutes before the great man's supper. A promise of a longer talk the next day was made, but not kept. Thereupon Mme. Goezman guaranteed him an interview on the following morning—the fifth of April—in return for a further disinterested transfer of a hundred louis; but as Beaumarchais did not possess that sum she was content with a watch set with diamonds—plus fifteen louis, intended, so she said, for her husband's secretary. But again Beaumarchais was refused the door, making the ninth time in all the case was heard on that fateful fifth, and, after an all-day sitting of the court, judgment was given against him.

His adversaries were sure he was forever down and out: but little did they know their man. It had been one of the conditions of the understanding with Mme. Goezman that if the promised interview with her husband did not materialize and Beaumarchais lost his case she would return the gifts. This she did, so far as the hundred louis and the watch were concerned, but not as regards the fifteen louis for the secretary—which the latter denied ever having been offered him. Thereupon Beaumarchais began to make trouble. The details of the affair having become public property—Beaumarchais had seen to that —Goezman was forced to come into the open with a charge that the litigant, having tried to suborn one of his judges and failed, was now calumniating the latter's innocent wife. The old intrigues, machinations and chicaneries began all over again, but now on a much larger scale, more and more people being dragged into the affair. Beaumarchais took bold aggressive action: since the courts would not give him justice as he conceived it he would appeal to the public. This he did in four *Mémoires*, masterpieces of wit, humor, gay argument and urbane malice that were the delight of a town always appreciative of good rapier play. The full story of his own conduct in the affair was told with irresistible vivacity. Mme. Goezman cut a sorry figure in court under his relentless examination. He had turned her inside out, made her contradict herself—in a moment of flurry she was indiscreet enough to deny that she had ever received the fifteen louis—showed her up in all her feminine silliness, disarmed her at times with flattery—gallantly declining to believe that a woman who looked, as he assured her, no more than eighteen could possibly be thirty, as she said—goaded her into threatening him with personal violence, worked her up at one moment into a wildcat fury and the next baffled her by his imperturbable politeness, so that on one occasion, after a particularly devastating handling of her, she smilingly accepted his arm as they left the court. Beaumarchais had everyone on his side: Voltaire, no mean controversialist himself, was enchanted with the *Mémoires*: "Don't tell me," he chuckled, "that this man poisoned his wives; he's much too gay and amusing for that."

Everyone on his side—except his judges, who had lost their heads completely. Their verdict, delivered on February 26, 1774, after an all-day sitting, was worthy of one of his own comedies. The *Mémoires* were condemned to be burned by the public executioner as defamatory, scandalous, and heaven knows what else; Mme. Goezman was censured and ordered to refund the fifteen louis; Goezman, an awkward episode in whose private life Beaumarchais had unkindly dragged into the open, was so discredited that he had to give up his post; and both Beaumarchais and Mme. Goezman were ordered to appear before the tribunal and beg its pardon on their knees.[2] Beaumarchais must have enjoyed the whole thing immensely; he had become overnight the most popular man in Paris, for every one of his opponents and judges was hated for some reason or other by some one or other from the King down to the man in the street,[3] so that the butchery gave general satisfaction. But the King, who thought the scandal had gone far enough for public safety, had a hint conveyed to Beaumarchais that he did not wish him to develop it any further: meanwhile, till a new trial of the case could be ordered, he was entrusted with a confidential mission in London.[4] *L'Affaire Goezman* is of particular importance to us today because so much of the actual Beaumarchais went straight into the making of the immortal Figaro, and

[2] Beaumarchais was spared this ignominy, however.

[3] The King's favorite, Mme. Dubarry, had the episode of Beaumarchais's public tussle with Mme. Goezman dramatized and staged at the Court.

[4] We cannot follow the remainder of his busy and varied life in detail here. He got into trouble with the French revolutionaries in 1792, but somehow survived the Terror. After three years in Holland, still active in the business of gun supplies, he returned in 1796 to Paris, really ruined at last, and died on the eighteenth of May, 1799.

something of the acid fun he had poked at French administrators of justice finds its echo in the scene in the third act of *The Marriage of Figaro*, in which the breach of promise case of Marcellina v. Figaro, Bartolo intervening, is solemnly tried by that moral pillar of society, Count Almaviva.

Le Barbier de Séville had been written in 1772: it was then an *opéra comique*, that is to say a mixture of spoken play and music, which accounts for the relatively large proportion of the latter still surviving in the present form of the work. The play was intended for the Comédie Italienne, but was refused there because the actor who was to play the barber Figaro jibbed at the part, he having been at one time a barber's apprentice. Recast as an ordinary play, *Le Barbier* was accepted by the Comédie Française and actually put into rehearsal; but the theater closed down on it when Beaumarchais was committed to prison at the same time as the Duc de Chaulnes. In 1774, when the Comédie Française was willing to take it up again, the police forbade a production, for the Goezman affair was then in full swing and it was rumored that the comedy contained attacks on the magistrature. It was not until February, 1775, that *Le Barbier de Séville, ou la Précaution Inutile*, in five acts, appeared on the stage. It failed decisively on the first night. Beaumarchais, always the realist, saw where he had gone wrong and at once proceeded to put things right. He cut a large quantity of dead wood out of the overgrown tree, suppressed a whole act that had been added to the original *opéra comique*, and shortened the action and the speeches at several points. The second performance was a complete success; and when he printed the play he added a long and brilliant "Letter" to his critics in which he anticipated the publicity technique of Bernard Shaw.

Figaro, as the author introduces him to us in the opening act of the play, was essentially Beaumarchais himself. Like the latter, he had tried his hand at everything. In Madrid he had been in the service of the rich young grandee Count Almaviva, who, while admiring his remarkable talents, obviously would not trust him any further than he could see him: the Count's first words on recognizing him at dead of night outside Rosina's house in Seville are "Why, it's that rogue Figaro!" The latter gives him an account of his vicissitudes since the pair had last met. Almaviva had recommended him for government employment: he had been given a medical job, not, however, in the hospitals, as he had expected, but in the Andalusian stables, where, he now claims, by dosing human beings with the medicines intended for the horses he had not only put money in his pocket but effected some remarkable cures: if occasionally his human patients had died, well, as he philosophically remarks, "There's no universal remedy." He had been dismissed, according to his own account, from sheer jealousy and stupidity on the part of the Minister concerned, who held that literary ambitions were incompatible with a talent for business—for Figaro, it appears, had been writing madrigals and contributing to the papers. But he had taken his dismissal philosophically, maintaining—and here it is the actual Beaumarchais who is speaking from experience—that an exalted personage is doing a poor man like him all the good he can when he refrains from doing him any harm. When the Count smilingly remarks that he remembers quite well what Figaro was when in his service—a bit of a rascal, a good-for-nothing, lazy, disorderly—he gets the biting riposte, "Ah, Monseigneur, with your high ideal of the virtues necessary to a servant, how many masters, would you say, are fit to be valets?" a fencing pass that wins the admiration of the broad-minded young grandee.

Figaro, on the occasion of that meeting, resumes the story of his life. He had gone back to Madrid, where he had attempted dramatic authorship. In this he had failed, though he could not understand why, for, as he admits, he had done everything possible to ensure success, employing all the arts of the paid claque and getting himself and his piece talked about in advance in the cafés. But the cabals had beaten him; his play had been hissed, and if ever he sees a chance to get his own back—! The Count interrupts him: "Don't you know that in the law courts one has only twenty-four hours in which to call down curses on his judges?" to which Figaro replies grimly, "In the theater one has twenty-four years."

Having found it impossible to make any headway in Madrid against the butting animals and stinging insects that everywhere made the literary man's life a burden to him, and being out of funds and very much in debt, he had decided that the honorable emoluments of the razor were preferable to the empty honors of the pen; so he had traveled across Spain, practicing his new profession of barber, "made much of in one town, jailed in another, but always superior to events . . . laughing at the fools, defying the rascals, taking my property lightheartedly and shaving all and sundry." At last he had come to Seville, where he still is, ready to do anything that Count Almaviva may demand of him. His gay philosophy of life, he assures the Count, is the product of his misfortunes: he forces himself to laugh at everything to keep himself from weeping. He is at every point Beaumarchais himself to the life.

There let us leave him and Beaumarchais for a moment and turn to Rossini.

He was in his twenty-fourth year when he wrote *Il Barbiere di Siviglia*. Young as he was he already had several operas to his credit. To some of these, in whole or in part, the Rossini lover still turns with delight, particularly *La Cambiale di Matrimonio* (*Marriage by Bill of Exchange*, 1810), *La Pietra del Paragone* (*The Touchstone*, 1812), *Il Signor Bruschino* (1812), *Tancredi* (1813) and *L'Italiana in Algeri* (*The Italian Girl in Algiers*, 1813); while the sparkling overture to *La Scala di Seta* (*The Silk Ladder*, 1812) has won for itself a secure place in our concert rooms. With the *Barber of Seville* subject he had had more than one predecessor: in addition to the well-known work of Paisiello (1782) there had been at least four French or German treatments of the theme. Morlacchi, the Italian director of the Dresden Opera from 1810 to 1841, had produced a *Barbiere di Siviglia* there in 1814.

Rossini had been commissioned in December, 1815, by Duke Francesco Sforza-Cesarini, the director of the Argentina Theatre in Rome, to provide an *opera buffa* in which a notable Spanish tenor, Garcia, was to "star." The libretto having been found unsatisfactory, Rossini himself, it is conjectured, suggested the Beaumarchais comedy to his librettist Sterbini, who made a very good job of it. (It is astonishing how naturally and easily both *The Barber* and *The Marriage of Figaro* adapt themselves to the purposes of the musical stage.) As Paisiello still had his fanatical admirers, Sterbini and Rossini thought it diplomatic to call their own work, in the first place, not *The Barber of Seville* but *Almaviva, or the Vain Precaution*, and to make it known that they did so out of deference to the older composer. But their own precaution proved to be in vain; the partisans of Paisiello, joining forces with the personal enemies of the impresario, saw to it that the first performance, on the twentieth of February, 1816, failed miserably. Presumably these gentry, satisfied with their victory, did not turn up on the second night, when the general Roman public, left to itself, welcomed the new work warmly. The Figaro was Zamboni, the Almaviva Manuel del Popolo Garcia,[5] who, on the opening night (though not afterward) was allowed to substitute for Rossini's music for the serenade to Rosina some arrangements of his own of Spanish folk melodies, which, he had no doubt thought, supplied a local color that was lacking in the score.

According to the legends, Rossini dashed off the music of the opera in anything from eight days to a fortnight; his own account of the affair in later years varied from twelve days to thirteen. The score was certainly completed within about three weeks at the most. Verdi's summing up of the matter in one of his letters says the sensible thing —Rossini had certainly lived with the characters for some time previously, and they must have taken musical shape in his mind before ever he put pen to paper. Donizetti's dry comment when he was told that the score had been completed in thirteen days was "Yes, but then Rossini always was a lazy fellow."

The nineteenth-century German and English writers on music managed to persuade themselves, and did their best to persuade the world, that Mozart, in his *Marriage of Figaro*, had raised what had been in Beaumarchais a mere "sordid comedy of intrigue" to a loftier ethical sphere—a signal example of the moral sense, as Oscar Wilde put it, intruding where it is not wanted. But whatever we may think of the Beaumarchais-Mozart case there can be no doubt that the one and only *Barber of Seville* in music is and always will be Rossini's. The subject had gone, so far as the music was concerned, to the right man at the right time; Rossini alone had the sprightliness of spirit, the combination of lightness and certainty of touch, and the southern vivacity appropriate to the mercurial Figaro; and the *Barber*, as Verdi said, with its copiousness of genuine musical ideas, its comic verve and its veracity of declamation, remains to this day the best of all Italian *opere buffe*. It was a young man's work, something that even its creator could achieve to the same degree only once in his life. Weber rightly pointed out that in *The Seraglio* was incarnated "what every man's joyous youthful years are to him, the bloom of which he will never recapture": as Mozart grew in experience of life he was bound to write a *Figaro* and a *Don Giovanni*, "but with the best will

[5] He had been born, appropriately enough, in Seville. His daughter Maria was the famous Malibran; another, Pauline, was the still more famous Mme. Viardot. His son Manuel Patricio Garcia began as a bass singer but ultimately settled down to teaching. He died in London in July, 1906, at the age of 101. He was the inventor of the laryngoscope.

in the world he could never have written another *Seraglio*." Rossini still had a rich comic vein to explore, but a *Barber* he would never accomplish again; there is in it an enjoyment of the absurd comedy of the world, a delight in a coltish kicking up of the heels, that comes to an artist only once in life, and that when he is young and the sap of life in him rich and abundant.

HOW TO WRITE AN OVERTURE

Gioacchino Rossini

A letter to an unknown young composer.

"Wait until the eve of the performance."

Wait until the eve of the performance. Nothing stimulates the inspiration more than sheer necessity, the presence of a copyist who is waiting for your work, and the insistence of a frantic impresario who is tearing out his hair by the handful. At my time all the impresarios in Italy were bald at the age of thirty.

I wrote the Overture to *Otello* in a small room in the Barbaja Palace, where the baldest and fiercest of all impresarios forcefully locked me into my room, alone with a plate of spaghetti, and under the threat not to let me out until I had finished my last note.

I wrote the Overture to *The Thieving Magpie* on the day of the première, under the roof of La Scala, where the director had imprisoned me. I was guarded by four stagehands, who had instructions to throw my manuscript out of the window—page by page—down to the copyists who were waiting below to transcribe it.

With the *Barber*, I had a much easier time; I did not compose an overture at all, but took the one intended for the opera *Elizabetta*. The public was quite satisfied.

I composed the Overture to *Count Ory* while fishing, my feet in the water, in the company of Mr. Agnado, who was giving me a lecture on Spanish financial conditions.

The Overture to *William Tell* was written under almost similar circumstances.

As far as *Moses* is concerned, I did not write anything.

BELLINI DESCRIBED BY HEINE

Heinrich Heine, poet of tear-drenched verse, was also a keen and occasionally a cynical observer of contemporary celebrities. Heine met the composer of *Norma* in Paris.

"A sigh in pumps and silk stockings."

Bellini was a tall, up-shooting, slender figure, which always moved gracefully; coquettish, looking as if just emerged from a bandbox; a regular, but large, delicately rose-tinted face; light, almost golden hair, worn in wavy curls; a high, very high, marble forehead, straight nose, light blue eyes, well-sized mouth, and rounded chin. His features had something vague in them, a want of character, something milklike, and in his milklike face flitted sometimes a painful-pleasing expression of sorrow. It was this shallow sorrow that the young maestro seemed most willing to represent in his whole appearance. His hair was dressed so fancifully sad; his clothes fitted so languishingly around his delicate body; he carried his cane so idyl-like, that he reminded me of the young shepherds we find in our pastorals, with their crooks decorated with ribbons. His whole walk was so innocent, so airy, so sentimental. The man looked like a sigh in pumps and silk stockings. . . .

It is a prejudice to suppose that genius must die early. I believe from thirty to thirty-four has been called the dangerous time for geniuses. How often I have tormented poor Bellini with this, and jestingly prophesied to him that he in his quality of genius must soon die. Strange! In spite of the jesting tone he was yet uneasy about this prophecy. He called me his *jettatore*,[1] and made always the *jettatore* sign. . . . He wished so much to remain alive. He found much favor with women, but I doubt if he ever awakened a strong passion. Although Bellini had already lived several years in France, he nevertheless spoke French as badly as can perhaps be spoken in England. Yes, when one was with him in society, and he murdered the poor

[1] Possessor of the evil eye.—Editor.

French words, one sometimes thought the world could not but perish amid peals of thunder. A deathlike silence then reigned in the whole room; deadly terror was painted on all faces, with chalk or with vermilion; the women did not know whether to faint or flee; the men looked in dismay at their trousers to convince themselves that they really wore such things; and, what was the most frightful thing of all, this terror excited at the same time a convulsive desire to laugh, which scarcely allowed itself to be suppressed. Therefore when one was in society with Bellini his vicinity could not but always inspire a certain anxiety which through a horrible charm was at once repellent and attractive. Sometimes his involuntary puns were merely of an amusing kind, and in their droll absurdity they reminded one of the castle of his compatriot, the Prince of Pallagonia, which Goethe depicts in his *Italienische Reise* as a museum of strange distortions and an incongruous combination of deformities. As Bellini on such occasions always believed that he had said something quite innocent and quite serious, his countenance formed just the maddest contrast with his words. Not till later till I had already known Bellini for a long time, did I feel for him some affection. This arose especially when I observed that his character was thoroughly noble and good. I remember one moment when Bellini appeared to me in so lovable a light that I looked at him with pleasure, and made up my mind to get to know him better. But, unfortunately, it was the last moment I was to see him in this life. This was one evening after we had dined together at the house of a great lady who had the smallest feet in Paris, and had become very genial, and the sweetest melodies sounded at the pianoforte. I see him still, the good Bellini, as he at last, exhausted by the many mad Bellinisms he had chattered, sat down upon a chair. This chair was very low, almost like a footstool, so that Bellini therefore came to sit as it were at the feet of a beautiful lady, who had stretched herself opposite him on a sofa and looked down on Bellini with sweet mischievousness, whilst he tried hard to entertain her with some small talk. I believe the beautiful lady did not listen at all to Bellini's small talk. She had taken out of his hands his little Spanish cane and quite calmly made use of it to destroy the elegant, artificially arranged curls on the temples of the young maestro.

A PERFORMANCE OF *LUCIA*
from *Where Angels Fear to Tread*

E. M. Forster

Like Flaubert, E. M. Forster is a craftsman of almost
fanatic patience. Nineteen years before publishing his
best-known novel, *A Passage to India,* he wrote the
novel, *Where Angels Fear to Tread.* This scene from
the earlier work may be considered a companion to the
similar scene in Flaubert.

He had been to this theater many years before, on the occasion of a performance of *La Zia di Carlo.* Since then it had been
thoroughly done up, in the tints of the beet root and the tomato, and
was in many other ways a credit to the little town. The orchestra had
been enlarged, some of the boxes had terra-cotta draperies, and over
each box was now suspended an enormous tablet, neatly framed,
bearing upon it the number of that box. There was also a drop scene,
representing a pink and purple landscape, wherein sported many a
lady lightly clad, and two more ladies lay along the top of the
proscenium to steady a large and pallid clock. So rich and so appalling
was the effect, that Philip could scarcely suppress a cry. There is
something majestic in the bad taste of Italy; it is not the bad taste of
a country which knows no better; it has not the nervous vulgarity of
England, or the blinded vulgarity of Germany. It observes beauty,
and chooses to pass it by. But it attains to beauty's confidence. This
tiny theater of Monteriano spraddled and swaggered with the best of
them, and these ladies with their clock would have nodded to the
young men on the ceiling of the Sistine.

Philip had tried for a box, but all the best were taken: it was rather
a grand performance, and he had to be content with stalls. Harriet
was fretful and insular. Miss Abbott was pleasant, and insisted on

praising everything: her only regret was that she had no pretty clothes with her.

"We do all right," said Philip, amused at her unwonted vanity.

"Yes, I know; but pretty things pack as easily as ugly ones. We had no need to come to Italy like guys."

This time he did not reply, "But we're here to rescue a baby." For he saw a charming picture, as charming a picture as he had seen for years—the hot red theater; outside the theater, towers and dark gates and medieval walls; beyond the walls olive trees in the starlight and white winding roads and fireflies and untroubled dust; and here in the middle of it all, Miss Abbott, wishing she had not come looking like a guy. She had made the right remark. Most undoubtedly she had made the right remark. This stiff suburban woman was unbending before the shrine.

"Don't you like it at all?" he asked her.

"Most awfully." And by this bald interchange they convinced each other that Romance was here.

Harriet, meanwhile, had been coughing ominously at the drop scene, which presently rose on the grounds of Ravenswood, and the chorus of Scotch retainers burst into cry. The audience accompanied with tappings and drummings, swaying in the melody like corn in the wind. Harriet, though she did not care for music, knew how to listen to it. She uttered an acid "Shish!"

"Shut it," whispered her brother.

"We must make a stand from the beginning. They're talking."

"It is tiresome," murmured Miss Abbott; "but perhaps it isn't for us to interfere."

Harriet shook her head and shished again. The people were quiet, not because it is wrong to talk during a chorus, but because it is natural to be civil to a visitor. For a little time she kept the whole house in order, and could smile at her brother complacently.

Her success annoyed him. He had grasped the principle of opera in Italy—it aims not at illusion but at entertainment—and he did not want this great evening party to turn into a prayer meeting. But soon the boxes began to fill, and Harriet's power was over. Families greeted each other across the auditorium. People in the pit hailed their brothers and sons in the chorus, and told them how well they were singing. When Lucia appeared by the fountain there was loud applause, and cries of "Welcome to Monteriano!"

"Ridiculous babies!" said Harriet, settling down in her stall.

"Why, it is the famous hot lady of the Apennines," cried Philip; "the one who had never, never before—"

"Ugh! Don't. She will be very vulgar. And I'm sure it's even worse here than in the tunnel. I wish we'd never—"

Lucia began to sing, and there was a moment's silence. She was stout and ugly; but her voice was still beautiful, and as she sang the theater murmured like a hive of happy bees. All through the coloratura she was accompanied by sighs, and its top note was drowned in a shout of universal joy.

So the opera proceeded. The singers drew inspiration from the audience, and the two great sextets were rendered not unworthily. Miss Abbott fell into the spirit of the thing. She, too, chatted and laughed and applauded and encored, and rejoiced in the existence of beauty. As for Philip, he forgot himself as well as his mission. He was not even an enthusiastic visitor. For he had been in this place always. It was his home.

Harriet, like M. Bovary on a more famous occasion, was trying to follow the plot. Occasionally she nudged her companions, and asked them what had become of Walter Scott. She looked round grimly. The audience sounded drunk, and even Caroline, who never took a drop, was swaying oddly. Violent waves of excitement, all arising from very little, went sweeping round the theater. The climax was reached in the Mad Scene. Lucia, clad in white, as befitting her malady, suddenly gathered up her streaming hair and bowed her acknowledgment to the audience. Then from the back of the stage —she feigned not to see it—there advanced a kind of bamboo clotheshorse, stuck all over with bouquets. It was very ugly, and most of the flowers in it were false. Lucia knew this, and so did the audience; and they all knew that the clotheshorse was a piece of stage property, brought in to make the performance go year after year. None the less did it unloose the great deeps. With a scream of amazement and joy she embraced the animal, pulled out one or two practicable blossoms, pressed them to her lips, and flung them into her admirers. They flung them back, with loud melodious cries, and a little boy in one of the stage boxes snatched up his sister's carnations and offered them. "*Che carino!*" exclaimed the singer. She darted at the little boy and kissed him. Now the noise became tremendous. "Silence! silence!" shouted many old gentlemen behind. "Let the divine creature continue!" But the young men in the adjacent box were imploring Lucia to extend her civility to them. She refused, with a humorous, expressive gesture. One of them hurled a bouquet at her. She spurned it with her foot. Then, encouraged by the roars of the audience, she picked it up and tossed it to them. Harriet was always unfortunate. The bouquet struck her full in the chest, and a little billet-doux fell out of it into her lap.

"Call this classical!" she cried, rising from her seat. "It's not even respectable! Philip! take me out at once."

MADAME BOVARY GOES TO HEAR LUCIA

Gustave Flaubert

In the opera house, Emma meets once again her Monsieur Léon and once again indulges in her romantic speculations.

The crowd was waiting against the wall, symmetrically enclosed between the balustrades. At the corner of the neighboring streets huge bills repeated in quaint letters "Lucie de Lammermoor— Lagardy—Opera—" etc. The weather was fine, the people were hot, perspiration trickled amid the curls, and handkerchiefs taken from pockets were mopping red foreheads; and now and then a warm wind that blew from the river gently stirred the border of the awnings over the doors of the public houses. A little lower down, however, one was refreshed by a current of icy air that smelt of tallow, leather, and oil. This was an exhalation from the Rue des Charrettes, full of large black warehouses where they made casks.

For fear of seeming ridiculous, Emma before going in wished to have a little stroll in the harbor, and Bovary prudently kept his tickets in his hand, in the pocket of his trousers, which he pressed against his stomach.

Her heart began to beat as soon as she reached the vestibule. She involuntarily smiled with vanity on seeing the crowd rushing to the right by the other corridor while she went up the staircase to the reserved seats. She was as pleased as a child to push with her finger the large tapestried door. She breathed in with all her might the dusty smell of the lobbies, and when she was seated in her box she bent forward with the air of a duchess.

The theater was beginning to fill; opera glasses were taken from their cases, and the subscribers, catching sight of one another, were bowing. They came to seek relaxation in the fine arts after the anx-

From *Madame Bovary* by Gustave Flaubert, translated by Eleanor Marx Aveling, by permission of Rinehart & Company, Inc.

ieties of business; but "business" was not forgotten; they still talked cottons, spirits of wine, or indigo. The heads of old men were to be seen, inexpressive and peaceful, with their hair and complexions looking like silver medals tarnished by steam of lead. The young beaux were strutting around below, showing in the opening of their waistcoats their pink or apple-green cravats, and Madame Bovary from above admired them leaning on their canes with golden knobs in the open palm of their yellow gloves.

Now the lights of the orchestra were lit, the chandelier, let down from the ceiling, threw by the glimmering of its facets a sudden gaiety over the theater; then the musicians came in one after the other; and first there was the protracted hubbub of the basses grumbling, violins squeaking, cornets trumpeting, flutes and flageolets fifing. But three knocks were heard on the stage, a rolling of drums began, the brass instruments played some chords, and the curtain rising, discovered a country scene.

It was the crossroads of a wood, with a fountain shaded by an oak to the left. Peasants and lords with plaids on their shoulders were singing a hunting song together; then a captain suddenly came on, who evoked the spirit of evil by lifting both his arms to heaven. Another appeared; they went away, and the hunters started afresh.

She felt herself transported to the reading of her youth, into the midst of Walter Scott. She seemed to hear through the mist the sound of the Scotch bagpipes re-echoing over the heather. Then her remembrance of the novel helping her to understand the libretto, she followed the story phrase by phrase, while vague thoughts that came back to her dispersed at once with the bursts of music. She gave herself up to the lullaby of the melodies, and felt all her being vibrate as if the violin bows were drawn over her nerves. She had not eyes enough to look at the costumes, the scenery, the actors, the painted trees that shook when anyone walked, and the velvet caps, cloaks, swords—all those imaginary things that floated amid the harmony as in the atmosphere of another world. But a young woman stepped forward, throwing a purse to a squire in green. She was left alone, and the flute was heard like the murmur of a fountain or the warbling of birds. Lucie attacked her cavatina in G major bravely. She plained of love; she longed for wings. Emma, too, fleeing from life, would have liked to fly away in an embrace. Suddenly Edgar Lagardy appeared.

He had that splendid pallor that gives something of the majesty of marble to the ardent races of the South. His vigorous form was tightly clad in a brown doublet; a small chiseled poniard hung against his left thigh, and he cast round languorous looks showing his white teeth. They said that a Polish princess having heard him sing one night on the beach at Biarritz, where he mended boats, had fallen in love with him. She had ruined herself for him. He had deserted her for other women, and this sentimental celebrity did not fail to enhance his artistic reputation. The crafty actor took care always to slip into his advertisements some poetic phrase on the fascination of his person and the susceptibility of his soul. A fine organ, imperturbable coolness, more temperament than intelligence, more power of emphasis than real singing, made up the charm of this admirable charlatan nature, in which there was something of the hairdresser and the toreador.

From the first scene he evoked enthusiasm. He pressed Lucie in his arms, he left her, he came back, he seemed desperate; he had outbursts of rage, then elegiac gurglings of infinite sweetness, and the notes escaped from his bare neck full of sobs and kisses. Emma leaned forward to see him, clutching the velvet of the box with her nails. She was filling her heart with these melodious lamentations that were drawn out to the accompaniment of the double basses, like the cries of the drowning in the tumult of a tempest. She recognized all the intoxication and the anguish that had almost killed her. The voice of the prima donna seemed to her to be but echoes of her conscience, and this illusion that charmed her, some very thing of her own life. But no one on earth had loved her with such love. He had not wept like Edgar that last moonlit night when they said, "To-morrow! tomorrow!" The theater rang with cheers; they recommenced the entire movement; the lovers spoke of the flowers on their tomb, of vows, exile, fate, hopes; and when they uttered the final adieu, Emma gave a sharp cry that mingled with the vibrations of the last chords.

"But why," asked Bovary, "does that gentleman persecute her?"

"No, no!" she answered; "he is her lover!"

"But he vows vengeance on her family, while the other one who came on before said, 'I love Lucie and she loves me!' Besides, he went off with her father arm in arm. For he certainly is her father, isn't he—the ugly little man with a cock's feather in his hat?"

Despite Emma's explanations, as soon as the recitative duet began in which Gilbert lays bare his abominable machinations to his master

Ashton, Charles, seeing the false troth ring that is to deceive Lucie, thought it was a love gift sent by Edgar. He confessed, moreover, that he did not understand the story because of the music which interfered very much with the words.

"What does it matter?" said Emma. "Do be quiet!"

"Yes, but you know," he went on, leaning against her shoulder, "I like to understand things."

"Be quiet! be quiet!" she cried impatiently.

Lucie advanced, half supported by her women, a wreath of orange blossoms in her hair, and paler than the white satin of her gown. Emma dreamed of her marriage day; she saw herself at home again amid the wheat in the little path as they walked to the church. Oh, why had not she, like this woman, resisted, implored? She, on the contrary, had been joyous, without seeing the abyss into which she was throwing herself. Ah! if in the freshness of her beauty, before the soiling of marriage and the disillusions of adultery, she could have anchored her life upon some great, strong heart, then virtue, tenderness, voluptuousness, and duty blending, she would never have fallen from so high a happiness. But that happiness, no doubt, was a lie invented for the despair of all desire. She now knew the smallness of the passions that art exaggerated. So, striving to divert her thoughts, Emma determined now to see in this reproduction of her sorrows only a plastic fantasy, well enough to please the eye, and she even smiled internally with disdainful pity when at the back of the stage under the velvet hangings a man appeared in a black cloak.

His large Spanish hat fell at a gesture he made, and immediately the instruments and the singers began the Sextet. Edgar, flashing with fury, dominated all the others with his clearer voice; Ashton hurled homicidal provocations at him in deep notes; Lucie uttered her shrill plaint, Arthur at one side, his modulated tones in the middle register, and the bass of the minister pealed forth like an organ, while the voices of the women repeating his words took them up in chorus delightfully. They were all in a row gesticulating, and anger, vengeance, jealousy, terror, and stupefaction breathed forth at once from their half-opened mouths. The outraged lover brandished his naked sword; his guipure ruffle rose with jerks to the movements of his chest, and he walked from right to left with long strides, clanking against the boards the silver-gilt spurs of his soft boots, widening out at the ankles. He, she thought, must have an inexhaustible love to lavish it upon the crowd with such effusion. All her small fault-findings faded before the poetry of the part that absorbed her; and, drawn toward this man by the illusion of the character, she tried to imagine to herself his life —that life resonant, extraordinary, splendid, and that might have been hers if fate had willed it. They would have known one another, loved one another. With him, through all the kingdoms of Europe she would have traveled from capital to capital, sharing his fatigues and his pride, picking up the flowers thrown to him, herself embroidering his costumes. Then each evening, at the back of a box, behind the golden trelliswork, she would have drunk in eagerly the expansions of this soul that would have sung for her alone; from the stage, even as he acted, he would have looked at her. But the mad idea seized her that he was looking at her; it was certain. She longed to run to his arms, to take refuge in his strength, as in the incarnation of love itself, and to say to him, to cry out, "Take me away! carry me with you! let us go! Thine, thine! all my ardor and all my dreams!"

The curtain fell.

The smell of the gas mingled with that of the breaths; the waving of the fans made the air more suffocating. Emma wanted to go out; the crowd filled the corridors, and she fell back in her armchair with palpitations that choked her. Charles, fearing that she would faint, ran to the refreshment room to get a glass of barley water.

He had great difficulty in getting back to his seat, for his elbows were jerked at every step because of the glass he held in his hands, and he even spilt three-fourths on the shoulders of a Rouen lady in short sleeves, who feeling the cold liquid running down her loins, uttered cries like a peacock, as if she were being assassinated. Her husband, who was a mill owner, railed at the clumsy fellow, and while she was with her handkerchief wiping the stains from her handsome cherry-colored taffeta gown, he angrily muttered about indemnity, costs, reimbursement. At last Charles reached his wife, saying to her, quite out of breath—

"*Ma foi!* I thought I should have had to stay there. There is such a crowd—*such* a crowd!"

He added—

"Just guess whom I met up there! Monsieur Léon!"

"Léon?"

"Himself! He's coming along to pay his respects." And as he finished these words the ex-clerk of Yonville entered the box.

He held out his hand with the ease of a gentleman; and Madame

Bovary extended hers, without doubt obeying the attraction of a stronger will. She had not felt it since that spring evening when the rain fell upon the green leaves, and they had said good-by standing at the window. But soon recalling herself to the necessities of the situation, with an effort she shook off the torpor of her memories, and began stammering a few hurried words.

"Ah, good day! What! you here?"

"Silence!" cried a voice from the orchestra, for the third act was beginning.

"So you are at Rouen?"

"Yes."

"And since when?"

"Put them out! put them out!" People were looking at them. They were silent.

But from that moment she listened no more; and the chorus of the guests, the scene between Ashton and his servant, the grand duet in D major, all were for her as far off as if the instruments had grown less sonorous and the characters more remote. She remembered the games of cards at the druggist's, and the walk to the nurse's, the reading in the arbor, the *tête-à-tête* by the fireside—all that poor love, so calm and so protracted, so discreet, so tender, and that she had nevertheless forgotten. And why had he come back? What combination of circumstances had brought him back into her life? He was standing behind her, leaning with his shoulder against the wall of the box; now and again she felt herself shuddering beneath the hot breath from his nostrils falling upon her hair.

"Does this amuse you?" he said, bending over her so closely that the end of his mustache brushed her cheek. She replied carelessly—

"Oh, dear me, no, not much."

Then he proposed that they should leave the theater and go and take an ice somewhere.

"Oh, not yet; let us stay," said Bovary. "Her hair's undone; this is going to be tragic."

But the Mad Scene did not at all interest Emma, and the acting of the singer seemed to her exaggerated.

"She screams too loud," said she, turning to Charles, who was listening.

"Yes—perhaps—a little," he replied, undecided between the frankness of his pleasure and his respect for his wife's opinion.

Then with a sigh Léon said—
"The heat is—"
"Unbearable! Yes!"
"Do you feel unwell?" asked Bovary.
"Yes, I am stifling; let us go."

A PORTRAIT OF VERDI

Franz Werfel

Of all that has been written about Verdi, the best has been written by non-Italian writers. (See Toye, Hussey, Pougin, etc.) Franz Werfel not only made a German adaptation of *La Forza del Destino* but also edited Verdi's letters in an edition which he preceded by a lengthy preface. The present excerpt, presenting a view of the composer as a man, is taken from this preface. If that view be tinged with sentimentality, we may accept it as a poet's sentimentality. The translation is by Barrows Mussey.

"A very star in the murk."

Giuseppe Verdi was born in 1813, the same year that brought into the world his great rival, the enemy and dragon-slayer of Italian opera, Richard Wagner. The little house where Verdi was born stands in a small village in the former Duchy of Parma, bearing the name of Roncole. Not far away the Po sends its muddy torrent across the vast plain that stretches down from the curve of the Alps to the Adriatic. This plain was Verdi's homeland, which he loved and served throughout a long life.

Above the narrow front door of the crumbling little house in Roncole, which is preserved by the State as a national shrine, was a sign: *"Sale e Tabacchi,"* and perhaps also, *"Vini nostrani."* Carlo Verdi, the tavernkeeper and grocer of the hamlet, sold to the starved peasants of the Napoleonic and post-Napoleonic era the few poor luxuries they enjoyed. His son Giuseppe grew up in the most abject poverty. A smoke-blackened taproom, an open fireplace, a shop counter, and two tiny bedrooms adjoining, were enough for the family. On Sunday a few peasants brooded over their wine in the tiny taproom.

From *Verdi, the Man in His Letters* by Franz Werfel, by permission of Mrs. Alma Werfel.

The mythology of Verdi's childhood is very scanty. One pretty story tells of the terrified tumult that filled the towns and villages of Parma when the marauding troops of Eugène Beauharnais left the country, and the soldiers of the Holy Alliance occupied it instead. Among the latter, the Cossacks in particular enjoyed a reputation as bad as it was undeserved for butchering or at least abducting children. And the women of Roncole, the story says, roamed the neighborhood, seeking a safe hiding place for their littlest ones. Young Luisa Verdi (her maiden name was Utini) took her baby, Beppino, wrapped him in her apron, and, with the newborn infant, climbed to the top of the campanile, the belfry of the village church. There she knew she was safe from the bearskin-capped kidnapers, although the icy December winds blew with Cossack fierceness about her and the baby. This legend is not a bad symbol of a man who was to tower above the country all his life, as lonely, high, and resounding as a campanile.

Of all human capacities, music is the earliest to be in evidence. Most great musicians were probably child prodigies. Whether they were so in the eyes of the world depended on the surroundings they grew up in. Not all six-year-old geniuses have had for fathers a Leopold Mozart, that excellent music master, model pedagogue, and tireless impresario all in one. Still it must be accounted greatly to the credit of the poor tavernkeeper, Carlo Verdi, that one day he took his rude staff in hand, and tramped the dusty highway to the county seat, Busseto, to ask the advice of an important personage about his little son.

It is not known who first drew his attention to Beppino's musical nature. Carlo Verdi and his wife were completely untutored souls who knew nothing of music. (Yet the parents were very early at considerable expense to put a rickety spinet under Beppino's tiny hands.) It may have been Bagasset to whom Giuseppe Verdi owed his discovery. Bagasset stands with one foot in mythology, the other in biographical reality. Bagasset was a wandering musician who strolled about the neighboring villages, playing at church festivals, weddings, and other gala occasions. Judging by the sound of his name, Bagasset should have tooted the bassoon or the clarinet. Actually, however, he sawed out the popular tunes of the day on a whining fiddle. It is said that little Verdi dogged his footsteps, and sat beside him by the hour when he was performing somewhere. Bagasset was warmly remembered by the Maestro, who was not a sentimental man. Visitors at the country seat of Sant' Agata are said to have met the old strolling musician there as late as the end of the fifties.

If Bagasset was not the discoverer of Verdi, probably the pastor of Roncole was. There had been difficulties with the pastor during Mass on Sunday. Beppino usually assisted at the altar. But this particular Sunday the organ was playing. The organ very seldom played in the church at Roncole—almost never except when an organist from the neighborhood came to the village on a visit. Beppino, absorbed in the swelling tones, completely forgot his surroundings, and failed in his duties during the Holy Office. He did not make the responses. He did not kneel. He forgot to swing the censer. The pastor had already growled softly at him twice. When this proved unavailing, he gave him a nudge, whereupon the little lad fell in a faint on the altar steps. This scene indicates an extremely delicate nervous system. Village lads do not usually fall in a faint when awakened from musical dreams by a gentle poke in the ribs. At the same time the scene shows the close connection between native genius and the capacity for intense concentration.

But no matter who was the first to think there was a musician in Beppino, only one man far and wide could help—Antonio Barezzi. The village innkeeper of Roncole had modest business relations with him. Prosperous Antonio Barezzi was the largest merchant in the city of Busseto. Today we would say he was the owner of the most splendid department store in town or county, where every kind of wares could be had, from foodstuffs to farm tools, from textiles to saddlery and hunting guns. Barezzi's house on the main marketplace was one of the most stately in all Busseto. Above the vaulted storerooms of the ground floor were the living quarters of the family, including a large hall where the members of the Società Filarmonica met for rehearsals two or three times a week. For Signor Barezzi— to whom Carlo Verdi presented his request touching on Giuseppe— was not only a good man of business, but far more, a rabid music lover, for which his memory will bloom eternal. Antonio Barezzi called himself president of the above-mentioned Società Filarmonica —a pompous title that must not, incidentally, be taken to indicate a philharmonic orchestra in the modern sense, but a primitive brass band, a "Banda Municipale," such as is fortunately maintained to this day in the tiniest villages of Italy. The president was also a member of the orchestra. He doughtily tooted the clarinet. On Sunday after High Mass there was usually a concert in the town square.

Otherwise they participated in solemn church functions, and carried deserving fellow citizens to the grave with a solemn, querulous accompaniment.

Whether in those days an opera season occasionally strayed to Busseto, and the Società Filarmonica was privileged to function as a theater orchestra, scholarship can no longer determine. But from the bottom of our hearts we hope so. For in the first place an Italian town is almost unthinkable without a traveling opera troupe, and in the second place President Barezzi's musical ambition was high. Not contenting himself with arranging Rossini overtures and popular opera potpourris for his venturesome philharmonists, he independently commissioned local composers to write marches, church music, and even cantatas. Signor Antonio was also constantly on the lookout for new talent. To this local pride and ambition of his we owe the fact that he did not simply eject Verdi the tavernkeeper, but sent for Beppino, then ten years old, to come to the house and be looked over.

Honest Signor Antonio proved that he had a keen eye. After the first visit of the shy, awkward, taciturn village lad he decided to pay out of his own pocket for Giuseppe Verdi's musical education and regular schooling. From that moment Antonio Barezzi was the guardian angel of Verdi's youth, a portly, easygoing, perpetually curious, rather commonplace guardian angel with a heart as warm as a child's.

Beppino was now sent to board with a maker of wooden shoes named Pugnatta. Life here was perhaps even more poverty-stricken than at home. But what did that count for now that the great dream seemed to be reaching fulfillment?

The musical luminary of Busseto at the time was a certain Maestro Provesi. In the early nineteenth century even the smallest Italian town had a local musical figure. In many cases these men were priests. Priests had played an honorable part in the musical history of Italy, especially as teachers. The celebrated Padre Martini of Bologna was still universally remembered—a wizard of counterpoint who survived from the classical age into the new century. Rossini, and for a while young Donizetti, too, had studied under him. True enough, honest Provesi was no Padre Martini. His skill was modest. He taught his pupils the first elements of harmony and musical composition. No less important, however, was the humanistic training that the boy owed to the priest who taught him at the secondary school, Don Seletti—a good command of Latin, a profound knowledge of the

Bible, and a highly polished feeling for language, versification, and meter, which was to be astonishingly revealed in his many letters to librettists.

But even in the first few years of his training the boy had to perform practical services of every sort. He was sent as an organist to villages all over the province. In winter this was no small matter. He had to go out in the black of night, and trudge by the hour along the frost-bitten highway to be in time at the church in some remote village. One Sunday morning in January there was almost a mishap. The climate of the region is very harsh; that morning there was a blustering storm; the boy went astray in the darkness, and fell exhausted in the snow somewhere off the road. Finally a peasant came along in a cart, and heard his cries for help.

Another share of his musical services fell to the Società Filarmonica. Signor Antonio very soon began to trust his protégé. Only a few years had passed before Giuseppe was the factotum of the orchestra. He learned quickly how a piece of music is arranged and orchestrated for that kind of musical organization. Along with these arrangements he began to write various marches, serenades, and overtures for the Società himself. The most important thing, however, was that he gained an exact knowledge and command of the special nature of the instruments, particularly the winds. Decades later, when he used the bass clarinet and double bassoon, instruments of modern romantic orchestral coloration not very common at that time, thus embarrassing the smaller theaters, he said with a laugh, "Even as a young lad between 1820 and 1830 I composed solos for bass clarinet and double bassoon."

But once again it was Antonio Barezzi who realized that his Busseto Società Filarmonica and honest Maestro Provesi were not the school for a composer with a great future. And that such a future awaited Giuseppe, Signor Antonio no longer questioned. He had grown very fond of the lean village boy with the fine, clear brow and the strangely deep-seated blue eyes. He received him into his own family, where he grew up among the Barezzi children. Giuseppe had now finished the Latin school. He ought to go to Milan, thought the merchant of Busseto. There, at the celebrated Conservatory, he should receive his musical ordination. Those who had gone through the Conservatory classes had a head start in their careers. Besides, Milan was at that time the musical capital of Italy, as Naples had been a generation or two earlier. It was the great mart for singers, maestros, and impresarios, and, above all, the mart for all opera scores. In Milan was the world famous Teatro della Scala, with its tremendous stage and auditorium. The Scala was the dream of all musicians. To an Italian, of course, music and opera are one and the same. It would cost a pretty penny, Signor Antonio reflected.

Before the examination commission of the Imperiale e Reale Conservatorio di Milano the eighteen-year-old Giuseppe Verdi suffered one of the severest defeats of his life. Here, under the presidency of the redoubtable Basily, were assembled the musical pedants and pigtails of the Lombard capital. Only one of the professors, old Rolla, a friend of Abbé Provesi's who had received a letter of recommendation from him, was not quite so icy to the ill-dressed and unimpressive village youth. Verdi submitted some of his compositions, presumably written for the "Banda" of Busseto. The eyes of the examination commission rested unkindly upon them. Then he was instructed to play something on the piano. The bashful Verdi, although an accomplished pianist, was never fond of showing off, least of all before commissioners. To please the bewigged pedants and prove his own good taste he should have chosen some sonata by Galuppi, Scarlatti, or something by Mozart. Instead he played a dry-as-dust virtuoso piece by Kalkbrenner.

A few days later old Rolla informed him that he must put the Conservatory out of his mind. Let him look around for a teacher in the city.

A better businessman and worse music lover than Antonio Barezzi would probably have said after this that that fellow Verdi had turned out to be a fraud.

Signor Antonio said nothing of the sort, but told Giuseppe to stay on in Milan at his expense, and pick out a teacher. Giuseppe found one. His name was Lavigna, and he was the conductor at the Scala. Judging by his success, Maestro Lavigna was not a bad master. His hobby, Verdi himself tells us, was the analysis of the score of Mozart's *Don Giovanni*. Every morning he used to say: "Well, Giuseppe, to-day we'll have another look at the introduction and the grand finale." This choice of subjects seems to point to Lavigna as the man who awakened in his pupil the fondness for dramatic contrapuntal contrasts that astonishes the student even in Verdi's early operas, and reaches its highest perfection in *Rigoletto*.

The young man from Roncole stayed in the capital for several years. He tried every way of earning his living as a musician. He failed.

Disappointment followed upon disappointment. On the advice of a well-wisher he began to compose an opera to an old libretto of the celebrated Felice Romani. (Afterward he wrote out with his own hand the whole material of the opera, solos, choruses, and orchestral parts.) But who had any use for the tragic opera of a young man from Roncole?

It was no use. Time passed. The disaster grew more and more acute. One could not dawdle about the great city forever, making constant demands upon Papa Barezzi to keep from starving. One day Verdi had a letter from Busseto. It reported that the position of organist there had fallen vacant, and been thrown open to competition. Why should he not compete for it?

Hard as it must have been for Giuseppe Verdi to come home defeated, having drawn a blank, home he went. He sought and secured the organist's position, though even this modest good fortune was spoiled for him by all sorts of intrigues and rivalries. Antonio Barezzi received him with open arms. The failure at Milan had not shaken his firm belief in Verdi.

During the three years that he served as organist at Busseto, the young Maestro finished his opera, *Oberto, Conte di San Bonifacio.* In later times Verdi needed three or four months at most to have a work finished and on paper. By disposition he believed in rapid, nay, frenzied work. Only in his eighties, finishing his last and next-to-last operas, did he take as long as he had for his first product.

We possess an album of romanzas that may date from the days of *Oberto.* They are of great biographical interest because they show a sadness of soul, a melancholy that has none of the rhythmic elasticity of the later Verdi. These romanzas sing in resigned tones of death and exile. Memorably enough, Gretchen's two songs from Goethe's *Faust* are in the album.

The sadness of his first creative period is surprising because it was during those very three years that Verdi laid the foundations for his life's happiness, or at least believed he was doing so. Margherita Barezzi, one of Signor Antonio's daughters, fell in love with him, and he with her. Margherita was a pretty creature, and highly musical. The pair had met over the piano. The girl was a true daughter of her father. She shared his faith in and admiration for Verdi; she was fired with ambition for him and his career.

It was a simple love story, quite without complications, the kindliest that could be imagined—two fine, healthy young people, well suited to each other, who had known each other from childhood. There was not even an angry rich-merchant papa to rage at his daughter's taking a poor devil instead of a rich suitor. On the contrary, he was delighted with his daughter's choice, for after all he was getting for a son-in-law a genius whose intellectual father he himself was. The wedding soon took place. Encouraging reports came from Milan, making it seem not impossible that a theater manager might put on *Oberto*. Verdi would try his luck in the capital once again. Now he was not alone. He had a wife who loved him; and there was a child on the way. This time he would, he must, succeed!

With warm blessings and a monthly allowance from kindly old Signor Antonio, the young couple took the mail coach to Milan. It would be a very modest, limited life that lay before them, but the proud Margherita knew what it meant to be the wife of a young artist who, though he might be struggling now for recognition, was assured beyond doubt of great fame. In a damp inhospitable house in one of the inhospitable alleyways near the Porta Ticinese they found very small, cheap quarters. But gray-shrouded Destiny waited, immobile in the corner of that dark dwelling, upon the new tenant, Verdi—an implacable tragedy such as few men and artists have had to endure.

Giuseppe Verdi tells of this tragedy in his own words. . . . Simple and utterly unadorned, this one literary document that we possess from his hand has an incomparable purity and dignity. It is very characteristic, too, that the real tragedy, the death of his two children and his young wife, which came blow upon blow, is reported here in a few lines. He speaks at greater length of the agonies caused by unpaid rent. Again and again it is the same bashfulness, the same pride. Verdi is muffling his heart.

The autobiographical sketch ends with a description of the opening night of the biblical opera *Nabucodonosor*, or *Nabucco*, as it was popularly abbreviated.

Nabucco was Verdi's third opera and first success after the crushing reverses of his youth. This work, which celebrated its hundredth birthday in 1942, abounds in beautiful music, true Verdi music. It is full of long melodies, sustained, syncopated, rhythmic, but full above all of sweeping choral passages depicting the yearning, the sadness and wildness of the biblical exiles. In the most splendid of these choruses, "*Va, pensiero sull' ali dorate,*" Verdi reached the highest summit that any musician can attain. That tune made him, then and for all time, the singer of his people's liberty. The very day after *Nabucco* opened, people were singing the song in the streets. It became the anthem of revolt against foreign rule and oppression. For the past hundred years every Italian child has known and sung it. . . .

The psalm from *Nabucco* runs through Verdi's life like a sort of reminiscence. One of his biographers tells the following moving story: When Signor Antonio, very old, was on his deathbed, Giuseppe Verdi hurried to his bedside from Turin, or perhaps it was from Paris. He sat quietly beside the dying man, who was breathing heavily. Barezzi could barely speak. Or possibly he lacked the courage to confess his wish. His eyes uneasily indicated the open door to the next room. Verdi understood his benefactor. Slowly getting up, he went softly in to the piano, and played the chords of yearning from *Nabucco:* "*Va, pensiero*—Fly, thought, on golden wings."

This story was published during the master's lifetime, and we can accept it; for, great disavower of all untruths and exaggerations that he was, he made no denial. The last word of the good merchant of Busseto was very rightly: "Verdi . . ."

With the triumph of *Nabucco* the story of Giuseppe Verdi's youth comes to an end; indeed we might almost say his biography ended then, insofar as action, grave misfortune, and outward struggle are concerned. What follows is one great upward climb, interrupted of course by reverses and bypaths, but all moving unmistakably in one direction. The outward struggles become inner struggles, hidden from the world, but none the less intense for that. From here on the biography of Verdi is the biography of his operas. It becomes a biography of nineteenth-century Italian opera and its life-and-death struggle. . . .

To do justice to Verdi's accomplishment between 1842 and 1851, between *Nabucco* and *Rigoletto*, we must cast a glance at the musical theater of the leading countries at the time. A French or German composer worked under quite different conditions from those of an Italian. France was Paris, and therefore there was in France only one opera stage, the Grand Opera—"La Grande Boutique," as it was derisively called. The road to this pretentious palace was as good as barred to a young musician. The doors of the great opera opened not to talent but to connections, guile, intrigues, and universally recognized mediocrity. This was the experience of young Richard Wagner, who had to starve in Paris. And the young French musicians shared his experience. The art of the nineteenth century in France had to make its way against the "Salon" in every field.

In small-town Germany with its decorous "Court and City Theaters" there was not even the impulse of protest and desperate ambition that the metropolis gives to all those who are striving. The enemy Wagner had to defeat at home was none other than the provincial likeness of everything that was applauded as success in the great world. In untouched solitude he built up his sound-swept cloud theater out of nothing.

How different was Italy! That country was still inexhaustible soil for the most intoxicating of all the arts. As wine was the Italian sun turned fluid, so opera put it into sound. The opera troupes were still traveling from town to town. There were an imposing number of magnificent singers, who had in their throats not only the national gift of voice and the certain something of *bel canto*, but overwhelming expressiveness and the tradition bred by two hundred years of an opera civilization. And the strand was not severed. As one vanished, another appeared. After a Malibran, a Rubini, and a Lablache came a Coletti and a Tadolini; after these shining stars the sun of Adelina Patti rose, and then came a Tamagno, a Maurel, and finally in our own century Caruso and Battistini.

In Italy opera is life, and by no means an unimportant part of it. Basevi gives statistics to show that within the first decade of the Verdi era in Italy more than five hundred new operas were written and performed. (To appreciate the full weight of this figure, we must keep in mind that nowadays there are frequent years when no new work is performed at all in the largest opera houses.) Whereas everywhere else the supply of dramatic music far exceeded the demand, in Italy the reverse was true. Furthermore, until late in the second half of the nineteenth century the opera houses of the world lived almost entirely on the Italian output. The maestros were swept helplessly into the swift torrent of activity, and were no longer free to take refuge on the shore. Thus the magnificent talents of Bellini and Donizetti came to an early end. The latter went mad at forty-five, and it is still uncertain how much of his malady was due to the exhaustion of a brain and a nervous system that sometimes produced as many as six operas a year. The opera is a dangerous goddess. It is intoxication and release. Like ancient tragedy, it is truly descended from Dionysus. Often indeed it strikes its priests dead with the fatal thyrsus, the ivy-twined staff.

Even Rossini, a true genius, suddenly fell silent at thirty-seven after *Guglielmo Tell,* and although he lived to be seventy he never wrote another opera. If this was what happened to the great, what must have been the lot of the comet swarm of lesser lights, the Mercadantes and Pacinis, every one of whom after all had it in him to sing a true melody? Only Giuseppe Verdi alone, the strongest of them all, remained victorious, with, against, and above the current.

We must remember: in the time during which young Wagner could concentrate his efforts on four works, from *Rienzi* to *Lohengrin,* young Verdi was compelled to write *seventeen* operas. Compelled? Yes, compelled. It may be true that the spirit of a young man who had struggled through a hard childhood, hunger, failure, a dreadful blow of fate, would succumb more easily than others would to the temptations of money and success. But this was not what forced upon Verdi the killing output of his first working decade. It was the audience, the people themselves. It was the active, overpowering *need* for his music all over the country. His employers, the impresarios and publishers, merely exploited this national need.

In *Nabucco* the twenty-eight-year-old Maestro spoke the decisive words: "*Va, pensiero.*" The majestic new anthem sounded. The tingling agility of Rossini, the divinely gentle melancholy of Bellini, the sensually ecstatic melodiousness of Donizetti gradually faded into the shadows of the past. Quite beyond the purely musical values, suddenly something new struck a surprising chord: energy and angry passion. Roughness, "*ruvidezza,*" the Italians call it. Hidden under this *ruvidezza* is a pounding, a grinding, an underground rumbling, which produced the amazing effect known to Italy under the apt name of *furore.* . . .

The Scala at Milan performed a few of the young composer's scores. Soon Naples, Rome, Venice, Florence, Genoa, Trieste, had their turn. Each city wanted a new opera for its carnival. What a heady potion it must have been for the peasant lad from Roncole to find the world thirsting for his music, which but yesterday no one would touch! He made contracts. But they weighed him down grievously once the first intoxication was over. For instance, a contract said: "The composer shall receive the libretto four months before the first orchestra rehearsal." The Maestro had, in other words, only a few weeks to familiarize himself with the libretto, make changes, sketch out the music, elaborate it, and finally finish the score. Thus *Rigoletto* was set to music and orchestrated within forty days—a stupendous accomplishment even mechanically, and artistically quite beyond belief. Giuseppe Verdi never put down musical ideas in note-books for later use. All his music sprang to life straight out of the libretto. Thus we have to admire not only the imagination but the capacity for work that could get the immortal profusion of tunes in *Rigoletto* down on paper in a single month. The Maestro wrote: "In my younger days I often sat at my desk without interruption from early morning until late at night, with nothing inside me but a cup of black coffee." Again he sighs: "I must go back to my music, though it is real agony."

While most of the maestros around him composed in order to supply the demand, our young artist, who might have taken an easier road, made life difficult for himself and others. He did something quite unheard-of in refusing to allow the singers supplementary arias and rondos; he would not tolerate the slightest alteration in his music, and people had to grit their teeth and hold the final rehearsal in cos-tume and mask. So, when his artistic conscience was in question, he tyrannized over the tyrants. And the ones over whom he tyrannized most implacably were the fiercest tyrants of all, the theater managers and publishers. . . . It would be a mistake to read any kind of greed or avarice into his letters to middlemen. Verdi was not con-cerned with money. The deepest sense of justice alone fixed his rela-tionship to the men of business. At the very time when other young composers were wearing out shoe leather trying to procure a perform-ance somewhere, Giuseppe Verdi was fiercely ready to withdraw any of his operas, no matter how great the financial loss, if a single one of his artistic stipulations was not met. Even in his early days he be-gan including in his contracts a clause by which any change or omis-sion in a score, even the mere transposition of a part, carried a penalty of a thousand francs. The publisher was made liable for it. Money was mere empty air to Verdi the moment art was put in question. Never for a single instant of his life was his thinking commercial. When he was thirty-three he forbade Ricordi, the publisher, to let the Scala at Milan perform his new opera. Imagine: the Scala was the great shrine of the Italian melo-drama, and Verdi scarcely more than a be-ginner. A success at the Scala would bring in a fortune. But never mind! At this shrine they had treated his music lightly. Therefore he put a ban on the Scala, which was never really revoked until the creative period of his old age.

It would be a grave mistake to take the expression "tyrant" too literally, and suppose Verdi a dictatorial character who could not forget a bitter childhood, and was retaliating, once he had attained some small power, on all those who were subject to it. The Maestro never demanded anything for himself personally except that he should be left out of account. Whatever he required had to do with the objective cause represented by a work of art that is to be offered to the public.

He would repeat a hundred times over: "I wrote the opera this way and no other way; probably someone else would have done it much better. But as I couldn't make it any better myself, the opera has got to be played as I planned it, or else everyone will suffer a fiasco—the impresario, the singer, and I."

Seventeen works came into being in this fashion, among them such beautiful and daring ones as *Macbeth, Luisa Miller, La Battaglia di Legnano*. The greatness of Verdi by comparison with his predecessors and competitors can best be judged by the fact that under these back-breaking conditions his work was never irresponsible or superficial, understandable as that would have been. His purity of artistic purpose challenged the Italian show business, and imposed his own laws upon it, so far as his operas were concerned. The impresario, the singer, the conductor, the orchestra, and not least the librettist had found a terrible new taskmaster. Particularly in the matter of librettists . . . Verdi was always his own playwright, planning the scenario for himself, shaping the characters, writing the dialogue, and leaving the literary men with nothing to do but turn his swift prose into meters that he had carefully worked out beforehand. The librettist served him solely as a verse-maker. Even today there are critics who maintain that Giuseppe Verdi draped his music on lifeless librettos, like a dress on a window dummy. This, they say, is the failing that distinguishes Italian opera from high musical drama.

Actually, however, the Maestro not only illuminated every character and every situation to its depths with the incorruptible sensitivity of a great dramatist before starting to work on the composition, but did the same for each word down to its very syllables. His letters to his librettists are the living proof that never a word was too unimportant for him to weigh its suggestive effect. The analysis of the librettos of *Un Ballo in Maschera* and *Aïda* . . . ought to be part of the curriculum in every dramatic and musical school.

It was another important trait of his character that the Maestro, despite his superiority, never insisted on the poet's removing or adding anything; with all modesty he would simply clothe his wish in the form of a suggestion.

Nothing could better characterize the relationship of Verdi to the theater than the following excerpt from the yellowed memoirs of Nina Barbieri the singer, describing the rehearsals and performance of the opera *Macbeth*. This took place in 1847, in the days of the most extreme Italian melodrama, which was usually whipped to the footlights after two or three orchestra rehearsals. By way of comparison: the German musical drama was hardly born. Richard Wagner had just finished *Tannhäuser*. Of the three Shakespeare operas that Verdi composed—it is still uncertain whether part of the music was ever written for the fourth, *King Lear*—*Macbeth* is the earliest and in a sense the most interesting. Considering the age and society to which it was presented, the theme was impossibly daring. Scotch mist, witches, ghosts, murders, darkness, and not a trace of a love story to bring in a lilting tune. And the composer of this dreadful "thriller" was a child of the Italian sun! Today we know that the solution Verdi found for the subject was as bold as the subject itself. *Macbeth* is not a bit less new and revolutionary in the history of opera than *Tannhäuser*. Verdi at thirty-three, hand in hand with Shakespeare, took the leap from the old melodrama to the modern musical drama without being untrue for a single beat to his own style or convictions. But Italy was not yet ripe to understand him. Although the première of *Macbeth* was a success, still it was a success of misunderstanding. Verdi could feel that no one would follow him into the new country he had conquered.

The singer who played Lady Macbeth describes very vividly the struggle that the Maestro carried on against the conventional theater on behalf of his *Macbeth*.

More than a hundred piano and orchestral rehearsals of *Macbeth* were held, for Verdi never seemed satisfied, and kept demanding that the singers give a more and more concentrated rendering of their parts. With his excessive requirements and reserved, taciturn character they had very little liking for him. In the morning and evening, when the Maestro came to rehearsal, all eyes on the stage and in the rehearsal rooms would search his face to see whether he had some new torture for us. If he came in with a pleasant smile, it was as good as certain that he would demand endless hours of overtime rehearsal. As I remember it, the opera had two climaxes—the sleepwalking scene and my duet with Macbeth after the murder. No one will believe it, but it is a fact that the sleepwalking scene alone required more than three months of rehearsals. For three months I tried, morning and evening, to play the part of a person talking in his sleep, uttering words, as the Maestro insisted, without moving the lips. Eyes closed, the whole face as rigid as a mask—often it was enough to drive one crazy. . . .

Incredible though it sounds, the duet with the baritone, *Fatal, mia donna, un mormore,* was rehearsed a hundred and fifty times. Verdi was determined that in our mouths the music should seem rather spoken than sung. Well, even that was got through with. On the evening of the final rehearsal, Verdi absolutely insisted on everyone's singing in costume, something previously unheard of. And there was no such thing as defying his will. At last we were all dressed, and the orchestra was waiting with instruments ready tuned, when Verdi suddenly beckoned Varese, the baritone, and me to him in the wings, and asked us to do him the favor of running through that accursed duet once more with him in the rehearsal room.

He was a tyrant who had to be implicitly obeyed. I can still remember the black look Varese shot at Verdi as he came into the rehearsal room, his hand clutching the pommel of his sword as if to transfix the Maestro like King Duncan. But he too submitted, and the hundred-and-fiftieth trial took place with the impatient audience already making an uproar in the theater. But anyone who merely said that the duet was enthusiastically received would be saying nothing at all. For it was something unheard-of, something quite new, something unimagined. Wherever I sang Macbeth, every night of the Teatro Pergola season (where it was first performed), we had to repeat the duet two, three, four times, once even five times!

Nor shall I forget how Verdi, silent and uneasy, kept circling about me before the sleepwalking scene on the opening night. It was evident that for him the success of the opera, great as it already seemed to be, could only be decided by that scene. I will let the newspapers of the time be my judge whether I captured the musical and dramatic intent of the great master. All I know is this: the storm of applause had not yet died down, and I was standing in my dressing room, trembling in every limb, unable to utter a word, when the door flew open—I was already half undressed—, and Verdi stood before me. He gesticulated, and his lips moved as if he were trying to make a speech, but not a word came out. I could not speak either, only laugh and cry. But I saw that Verdi's eyes were red too. He squeezed my hand, and rushed out. It was a magnificent reward for those months of work and strain.

The cool objectivity of the thirty-year-old was admirable. He was no touchy author, skulking shyly around the theater, upsetting the cast by remarks now abject, now presumptuous. Young Verdi walked into the auditorium, and by virtue of an inflexible will and an inborn authority the master who would take absolute command was there. It was not important that a man by the name of Giuseppe Verdi had written the work to be performed. His work was now separate from himself. It no longer belonged to him. He had only to make sure that everything he had felt and thought through should be transposed into reality with the greatest possible perfection. The vainest of all human institutions, the theater, encountered the incredible phenomenon of an artist without vanity.

We have, then, seen how Giuseppe Verdi was guided by the requirements of the Italian opera, and how he soon began to determine those requirements for himself. With all his love of the new and daring, he could not, like Richard Wagner, shatter the sacred canons of the opera form, established through centuries and handed down by his predecessors. More than that, he actually hoped, by wise development and tireless innovation, to preserve, keep, and hand on to an unknown future the hallowed form of *bel canto*. This after all was the meaning of his mission and his struggle from the very beginning.

At thirty-four years of age Giuseppe Verdi first reached the outside world. He wrote *I Masnadieri* (Schiller's *The Robbers*) for Her Majesty's Theatre in London, and *Gerusalemme* for the Grand Opera in Paris. This was the first long journey he ever took, to rehearse the two works on the spot. England and English ways made a great impression on Verdi, the realist. Through all the fog and coal smoke of London industry he recognized the vigor of the Anglo-Saxon race. "Who can resist this nation?" he exclaimed. But he confessed also that the fog and smoke made him ill, that he was yearning for the sun of home, counting the days.

Verdi had far less admiration for Paris than for London. "I have no great longing to go to Paris. . . . The city is without special attractions for me, but I shall like it very well, because I can lead the kind of life I want to lead there. . . ." How prophetic was this "I shall like it very well"! He was to like Paris very well indeed. "It is a great pleasure to be able to do as one pleases here." A constant urge for independence was one of Verdi's strongest characteristics. From now on he spent several weeks, often even months, of every year in Paris, enjoying his stay most when it was not disturbed by performances of his operas. When he did work in Paris, he worked more leisurely than in the old days. He generally settled in the *faubourgs*.

He would stroll for hours on the boulevards, through the gardens and along the quays on the Seine.

But alas, Paris was not only the city of the boulevards, of Montmartre, of gardens and quays where one could take the fresh air, strolling free and unobserved through the silver-gray of early spring as if one had no duty to the jealous goddess, Opera. Paris was also the capital of the intellectual world, the center of the politics, literature, painting, and music of the whole age. Here the great artists of all countries first received the cachet that gave them world rank. And in Paris likewise the moths gathered around the flame. These were the literati, the journalists, the theatrical people, the critics, the dilettantes, the frequenters of cafés, the snobs. They cooked up public opinion on books, plays, operas, pictures. This was a realm of presumption united in the *esprit de corps* of negation. After all, anyone who is a cipher almost becomes a unit if he calls a unit a cipher.

The man from Roncole made his first acquaintance with this realm of presumption, headed by the higher criticism, when he came to Paris. It is indicative, and we are almost inclined to take it for a trait of character, that the first operas Verdi wrote for the "Grande Boutique"—*Gerusalemme* and *I Vespri Siciliani*—were almost more Italian than those he had written for Italy. And this at a time and in a city whose nerves were already beginning to be frayed by Italian music. Rossini, Donizetti, Bellini had been accepted and domesticated as typifying the gracious lightheartedness of a fading era. But enough of that, thought the literati and critics. Here was this man from Roncole daring to put his vulgar male choruses in polka time on the grand opera stage!

At all the rehearsals there was a whispering behind Verdi's back: "*Pas de bon goût.*" Again and again the awful words "bad taste"— and then the dagger thrusts: "Banality," "triviality." True, the audience applauded these banalities, they captured the people, and the hand organs played them in the courtyards of Paris. But to offset this, Verdi could read in the newspapers of Paris and all the other great cities what a pitiful street musician he was, and how his popular operatic music was worlds beneath that which could be taken seriously as true art.

Probably no master in history has ever been treated so ill by the "higher criticism" as Verdi. A good example is the reviews of the celebrated Viennese critic Hanslick. When this brilliant stylist attacked Wagner (to which attack he owed his fame), he did so with obvious misgivings of conscience, with reservations, respectfully, as it were in self-defense. Quite otherwise with Verdi. Here Hanslick rolled up his sleeves at leisure, for he had nothing to fear. With witty relish he exposed the ludicrousness of his victim. And the other luminaries of musical criticism in France, England, America, and Germany followed the same course.

Then when *Aïda,* the *Requiem, Otello,* and *Falstaff* made their appearance, these gentry were not in the least abashed. They pointed out with the benevolence to which, after all, old age has a right that the bad boy had improved; they even ventured the melancholy remark that there had been considerably more "red blood" in the naughty pranks of youth than in these masterpieces of maturity.

The way Giuseppe Verdi managed to deal with this ill usage at the hands of critics and intellectual snobs was a marvelous proof of spiritual fortitude. He was not exasperated; but neither was he self-satisfied with his popular success. He did not swerve an inch from his path; neither was he rigidly unyielding. He looked the forces of negation squarely in the eye. He tried to find the truth even in scorn and dispraise, and to see his own back, as it were, with the coldest objectivity.

He never for an instant questioned the laws of the Italian operatic form, forged in a hundred fires. Dramatic singing was and would remain king, divided between recitatives and arias. In the recitatives the action advanced, producing the necessary calm for the arias. A sustained melody required to be relieved by a quicker, electrifying rhythm. This is not only an operatic law, but a prime law of music in general, which a composer offends against to his own cost. And so, at a time when all the electrifying accelerations, known as *cabalette,* had long since been extirpated root and branch, Verdi asked the librettist of *Aïda* to furnish the necessary verses for such a cabaletta, expressly adding: "*Cabalette* are perfectly acceptable to me." The opposing tendency could not shake his conviction.

In Paris Verdi heard a great deal of music, and certainly not that of Auber and Meyerbeer alone. Presumably he met with an occasional piece by Berlioz in the concert halls. An alien world, an antagonistic world. He recognized progress; he meant to progress himself. But the musical progress that found expression in broken color tones and romantic torment of the nerves was not his kind. Giuseppe Verdi had other talents to contribute to the battle going on for a new art: an uncompromising sense of proportion, polished acuteness, inexhaustible feeling and invention, justness to the point of mania, and an enlightened realism that was scarcely understood until recently, but has come to mean eternal youth for his music.

The realist reached out for new subjects, subjects inconceivable in the lyric theater as it had previously existed. He put a hunchbacked cripple on the stage (*Rigoletto*) and a tubercular cocotte (*La Traviata*). For perhaps the first time the traditional opera stage was trodden not by costumed singers, but by suffering human beings. Now that three generations have been familiar with these most popular of all operas, we can no longer realize the revolutionary courage required to approach such provocative themes in defiance of censorship and the reigning aesthetic code. And the Maestro—as he says himself—would not have been afraid to turn the most treacherous of all situations into a true Verdi love duet: the seducer and the seduced in the bedroom. "That would be a duet, a magnificent duet . . . but we should be whipped out of town."

So that we may have a proper understanding of his life and works, let us sum up once again: an Italian of vigorous peasant stock, whose apprentice years came during the time when Rossini, Bellini, and Donizetti dominated the opera houses of the world with a yearly triumph, and it was the dream of all dramatic composers to emulate these three bright stars. An Italian from a wretched village, from the deepest poverty, who was not accepted for the Conservatory at Milan, and had to learn his trade from a theater conductor who went through a few opera scores with him for no reward in order to teach his pupil the skills essential for success. An Italian who presumably heard very few classical or preclassical pieces of music in his youth. An Italian who soon became the father of a family under harassing circumstances, who had to struggle desperately, and for whom art could not be a dream, but had to mean bread. An Italian who, through a dreadful occurrence, lost everything, wife and children; whose opera was hissed off the stage during those days of horror; but who pulled himself together on the threshold of nothingness, and within a few years turned out three times six melodic dramas, some to become immortal, while his music as a whole blossomed into the marching song of national rebirth.

One may well ask whether after such a career this Italian would not have had every right to be weary. Might he not have been satisfied with what he had attained? What was the world to him; what were Paris, the critics, the snobs; what was German music? "After *La Traviata*," Verdi once wrote, "I could have taken things easy, and written an opera every year on the tried-and-true model. . . ."

He did not take things easy. He did not sidestep the crisis that threatened Italian opera. He met the challenge of that crisis. His clear mind remained free. Abuse of the opera, as old as opera itself, began to pile up from all sides, not least in Italy. Verdi turned an attentive ear. He did not fly into a rage when he saw the enemy conquering position after position in his own country. In later times he merely shook his head when invited to join a "chamber music society" or the "committee of a symphony orchestra." Why, could not these fools see that they were serving a strange god ill-disposed toward singing—that they were giving aid and comfort to the enemy? The enemy of pure song, the enemy of Italian opera was the symphonic tendency, or in other words German music, along with its priests, worshipers, and imitators the world over.

Giuseppe Verdi knew his own goal. He recognized that at this turning-point any artist who stood still and dwelt in the past was lost. With cool, keen eyes he watched the enemy. He was always ready to accept even from the foe anything that squared with his own natural conviction. And so Giuseppe Verdi moved forward bravely and circumspectly, like a good soldier.

The road from *Nabucco, Ernani, Macbeth*, to *Rigoletto, Il Trovatore, Un Ballo in Maschera* and then to *La Forza del Destino* and *Don Carlos*, is a straight climb. But the advance is the smaller marvel, as against the man's fidelity to himself during this progress. There is no essential difference between the scores of *Nabucco* and *Otello*. It is not the form that changes significantly, but the spiritual expression, which is ennobled beyond all imagining.

At one particular time, it is true, the hazards around Giuseppe Verdi multiplied. This was between 1865 and 1870, when the Maestro wrote *Don Carlos* for Paris, a work that betrays an almost frantic straining of every nerve, even a certain overloading. Acute ears immediately caught the danger. It was no less a figure than the composer of *Carmen* who expressed his anxiety for Verdi in a letter written after *Don Carlos*. What, was even this old, strong Italian to succumb to the new god? The danger that Bizet saw threatening Verdi had a name: Richard Wagner.

This is not the place to draw comparisons in musical history. And anyway, comparison of great opposites is a simple and therefore very precarious matter. These two men often lived near each other in space, and they never met. That is symbol enough.

The question whether Giuseppe Verdi matched the greatness of Richard Wagner or not is unimportant. All that matters is the fact that he was the only one to hold out against that greatness. Wagner was more than a brilliant playwright and dramatic composer, he was the creator of a new musical language. No matter whether one loves or hates that language, all his contemporaries succumbed to it, and so have all his successors down to the present day. All composers after 1870 spoke and still speak the language of Wagner, with variants that will be blurred a hundred years hence. Even the cacophonies and rhythmic spasms of ultramodern music spring from an effort to burn Wagner's language out of the blood stream by an artificial fever.

The vigor of Verdi's personality saved him from two evils—being seduced by Wagner, and becoming antiquated through Wagner. He once said to the Marchese Monaldi: *"Vi pare, che sotto questo sole e questo cielo io avrei potuto scrivere il Tristano o la Tetralogia? Siamo Italiani, per Dio! In tutto! Anche nella musica!"* [1] But it was not sun and sky alone that saved him from losing himself; the opera of Italy, for which he had had to work so hard in his younger days, saved him to become its savior. Not for a moment did he waver in his principles. The drama is man. Therefore the opera too is man— that is, the human voice; that is, singing. The melodies of the instrument called man obey different laws from the themes of the orchestral instruments. Anyone who does not realize this mistakes the meaning of opera and the conditions necessary for its existence. If the human being and his melodies are pushed into the background in favor of any orchestral fabric, no matter how compelling, the idea of opera is destroyed. Verdi once called it "the invasion of the baroque." And he was right when he said that this invasion of the baroque was by no means new in the history of opera, but had occurred once or twice already in the course of the centuries. To him wrong did not become right simply because a great man did it with every resource of his genius. Verdi shrugged his shoulders. How uncomfortable the Germans made him, with their perpetual rebellion against the fundamental facts of humanity, their fanatical craving to conquer and devour everything that might oppose them! . . .

The Wagner peril may often have shaken Verdi's self-assurance,

---

[1] "Do you think that under this sun and this sky I could have written *Tristan* or the *Ring*? We are Italians, by God! In everything! Including music!"

but never his artistic conscience. He looked around him. All the composers, Italian and non-Italian, were wavering, more or less submitting to the new principle. The Italian opera was like a beleaguered fortress; and within this beleaguered fortress the traitors of the "Fifth Column," as we would call it today, were at work. A friend of Verdi's, the conductor Angelo Mariani, one of the most influential musicians in Italy, had gone over to the Wagnerians, and he put on *Lohengrin* at Bologna, with tremendous thumping of the publicity tub. Once again Giuseppe Verdi muffled his heart. He even sat with a copy of the piano score at the dress rehearsal, and looked his adversary in the eye.

About this time Verdi, still under sixty, summoned all his forces, and made a triumphant sortie from the beleaguered fortress. This sortie bears the name of *Aïda*. Although it was written to order for the gala opening of the Suez Canal, this strange occasional piece has historical significance of a high order. *Aïda* stands for the self-defense, salvation and renewal of Italian opera as against the assault of the symphonic drama. It is the final relieving of the beleaguered fortress. In this music Verdi struggled to give to excited song, *canto concitato*, a fanatic force of expression previously unknown even in his own works. One dramatic melody rushed headlong upon the heels of the next, and each one depicted with the sharpest perfection the passion of the characters involved. The instrumental accompaniment was accompaniment still, even with all the sunset gold that had come into the colors, and the quivering variation of the rhythms. Today we have discovered at last that *Aïda* is not merely a popular opera written for an occasion, but a victorious battle in a long war.

The European critics of the time, faced with these new facts, hastily improved the opportunity to distinguish themselves in regard to their old friend by misunderstanding his epoch-making work from beginning to end. Whereas to them Verdi had once been the tasteless theater composer with a few pretty tunes, after *Aïda* he quickly advanced to the post of imitator and puny offshoot of Wagner. This horrid stigma he was never again to escape.

Let it be said again and again, with every emphasis: Giuseppe Verdi adopted *nothing* from Richard Wagner. Though jealous Wagnerians may lay claim here to an unusual harmony, an orchestral coloration, there to a series of tones, a reminiscence, it is all empty labor; such things are in the air of the times, in the common development. They mean nothing at all. It would be equally futile to maintain that Wagner had been influenced by Verdi because, for instance, the "Pact Motif" in the *Ring of the Nibelungs* resembled the descending series of notes characterizing the agreement between Rigoletto and the bandit Sparafucile at the end of the scene. From *Nabucco* to *Falstaff* the language of Verdi is always the same, a curt, hard, aphoristic language, and nothing is more alien to it than the long-drawn expression of Wagner, meant to persuade and overwhelm the listener. The last two works, *Otello* and *Falstaff*, still criticized by the obtuse as being like Wagner, are precisely the best proof of this statement. Not a single symphonic measure is to be found in them that would subordinate the song to the thematic fabric; but we do find the entire older opera brilliantly abbreviated with new inspiration. What had been an aria was now compressed into the small space of a "phrase," drenched in melody and harmony; man singing was triumphant as always, and the orchestra never took the lead, but obediently lived and trembled with man and his fate. In *Otello* and *Falstaff* the aesthetic contradictions that have always been inherent in the "reborn tragedy" are almost resolved.

It is plain that Verdi suffered through and from Wagner. This suffering was a secret motif of his letters and utterances from the time of *Don Carlos*. It broke through whenever he wrote about "music of the future" or "high art," about the founding of symphony orchestras in Italy, about the decline in singing, and similar subjects. Once he complained with unaccustomed frankness: "A pretty fate, to wind up after more than thirty-five years' work as an imitator of Wagner!" And again: "If only I had never written *Aïda,* or at least never published it!" and went on: "Not a word did I hear that was worthy of art!"

He was right. Despite the world success of *Aïda* no one understood the battle that was fought out in that work.

It is hardly too fantastic a supposition to connect the long hiatus in production between Verdi's sixtieth and seventy-third year with the depressions here hinted at. "Why should I write?" he keeps asking.

Yet still Giuseppe Verdi never hated Richard Wagner, although there must have been talebearers in abundance. The great Italian probably knew that the great German despised him, for that is the kind of contempt one can feel, and it is the severest test of a man's sense of justice. (Wagner was in the habit of citing the aria of Germont, the father in *La Traviata,* on the piano as proof of the decline of Italian opera.) Yet Verdi never made the slightest remark pointing to any hatred of Wagner. All hatred is plebeian, for it presumes that a spirit can be degraded. Verdi's spirit could not be degraded.

The Verdis—several years after the death of Margherita Barezzi the Maestro had married Giuseppina Strepponi, the diva of his *Nabucco*, and a popular idol—the Verdis usually spent the winter months in the mild climate of Genoa, in a big apartment on the second floor of the Palazzo Doria. It was in one of the high-windowed rooms of that palace, on the evening of February 13, 1883, that seventy-three-year-old Giuseppe Verdi opened his newspaper, and read the dispatch announcing to the world that Richard Wagner had died suddenly a few hours before in the Palazzo Vendramin at Venice. What was in the Maestro's heart as he slowly put the paper containing this report back on his desk? The most conscientious biographer, scrupulously refraining from all fictional adornment, could hardly keep from dreaming in retrospect of that great moment. . . .

Wagner was dead. The fire whose smoke and flames had choked Italian opera and its master for decades was extinct. Wagner was dead. But Verdi was alive, and the living man is always right. The living man is victorious over the dead, invariably. And the victor was not only alive at seventy, but sound, healthier than in his youth, and he could feel the strength for new deeds, whereas the dead man must now remain mutely idle forever. Would it not have been only human if the black lightning of unutterable triumph had quivered through Verdi's heart at that moment?

Fortunately we have a document to show. It is a letter to Giulio Ricordi, the son of the publisher, his young friend and confidant.

Here is the letter, faithfully reproduced:

Sad sad sad!
Wagner is dead!
When I read this news yesterday, I may truthfully say that I was completely crushed.
Let us say no more! It is a great personality that has disappeared. A name which leaves a mighty imprint upon the history of art. . . .

It is impossible to study the facsimile of this letter long enough. First, the *"Triste triste triste,"* with no commas, the words breathed on paper in almost tremulous script. It is unquestionably a magnanimous expression of true regret, behind which no secret satisfaction can hide. The word "Wagner" is written with "V" instead of

"W." It seems as if in his emotion Verdi were unable for a moment to recall his rival's painfully familiar name. And then, most striking of all, Verdi has crossed out the adjective "mighty" (*potente*), replacing it with the superlative "most mighty" (*potentissima*). The justice of the Maestro, no lover of superlatives, would not permit the weaker term he had first chosen.

Thus a warrior dips his sword to the fallen foe. With a pure heart.

At the same time of life when Giuseppe Verdi first came in contact with foreign countries, with the great world, with Paris, he bought a house, home, and fields on his native soil, not far from Roncole. This considerable country estate is named after the hamlet of Sant' Agata. Like the giant in the Greek myth, the Maestro now could touch the earth from which he sprang, renewing his strength from it. Though art and its own work might require long stays in Milan, Genoa, Rome, Naples, Paris, yes, even St. Petersburg and Madrid, though he had to violate his principles by making a European tour as conductor of his *Requiem* in 1875, he was everywhere an impatient guest; at Sant' Agata alone he was at home and under his own roof.

When Giuseppe Verdi bought the estate of Sant' Agata, it was a run-down establishment off the main road, a flat, dreary piece of land with a tumble-down house, in the middle of the most desolate neighborhood imaginable. The Maestro had spent many long weeks in Florence, Naples, Rome; had not those landscapes and their beauty lured him to settle under the cypresses, laurels and mimosas? Had he so little "artistic" feeling that he must needs choose the most monotonous and melancholy spot in Italy for his permanent abode? The peasant lad of Roncole was not tempted by the hills of Tuscany and the magic gardens of Sorrento, but by the prosaic yet fertile soil of his fathers. There he built his house.

He built a manor house. It is a bright, fairly extensive building, a ground floor and second story, completely unadorned. Around this house, as grave and clear as its master, stretches a great park. Close at hand are trimmed hedges, flowerbeds and circles. But the further the park reaches from the house, the more it is left to itself. Verdi's pride was the beautiful trees. Oh, it was not easy to bring the shoots here, to plant and raise them.

Years passed. The crowns grew thicker and closer, and then long, dark avenues ran through the park, which had once been a stretch of desert. The Maestro had a happy touch with growing things. Nevertheless the old dissembler wrote in late 1865 about the "wonders of Sant' Agata":

Four walls protect me against the sun and against the inclemency of the weather; a few dozen trees, largely planted by my own hand, and a puddle that I would dignify with the name of "lake" if I had water to fill it. . . .

The interior of those four walls, which did far more than protect him from sun and weather, gives the same impression as Verdi the man. The study was large, not remarkably light. One might call it sunny darkness. A massive desk stood in the room, a second, smaller desk to the left of it. Next to that a heavy bookcase. Among Verdi's books were not only several editions of Shakespeare, but the theoretical writings of Richard Wagner. The latter in turn were a proof of the long, concerted struggle that the Maestro carried on for the existence or nonexistence of Italian opera. Pushed over against the side wall stood a big piano, a gift from the firm of Erard. Over it hung a portrait of none other than good Signor Antonio, the excellent merchant of Busseto.

All this was very simple, with but little of the overcrowding characterizing the period between 1870 and 1900, which could never get enough of heavy curtains and furniture like fortresses or mountains that scarcely left room to force one's way among them.

Now let us hear a visitor describing Sant' Agata. It is Antonio Ghislanzoni, the librettist of *Aïda*:

"Nature has bestowed no charms on this landscape. The plain rolls monotonously on. Rich for the countryman, poor for the poet. In the middle of a long avenue of poplars the eye, surprised and touched with melancholy, rests upon two weeping willows that flank a garden gate. The two giant trees, which would scarcely attract attention elsewhere, tease the mind here like some strange and unfamiliar spectacle. He who planted those trees at this spot can be no ordinary man. . . . He may even be a misanthrope, for a drawbridge furnishes the only communication between his property and the world."

As Ghislanzoni goes on with his description, although he praises the beauty of the park, he cannot escape a certain melancholy. He comes to the conclusion:

"If a genius inhabits this house, it must be a genius of pain and passion."

Having cast a glance at the strange lake in the middle of the park, the visitor ends his observations.

"The broad lands of the master spread out beyond the lake. Their cultivation bears testimony to the scientific principles that he has introduced here from less naturally fortunate foreign countries. Verdi's gift of keen observation has turned every advance in English and French agriculture to the profit of his own country. While the weeping willows, the dark thickets of trees, the melancholy lake, all reflect the dreamy passion of the artist, the fields outside reveal the orderly energy and acute understanding of the man."

The last sentence raises a great contradiction. Dreamy passion and a sense of reality! Can this conflict be resolved within a single soul? The nineteenth-century conception of artists denied the possibility. To that age the romantic was the archetype of the artist. The romantic blithely ignored reality. He did not feel himself bound by "bourgeois" morality. He was proud of not understanding about money, business, the requirements of the human life that went on far below at his feet. If he had to go hungry, he regarded it as sacrilege against genius on the part of bourgeois society. Since religion was fading away, and people no longer believed in God, the romantic artist in his overweening pride set himself up as a sort of substitute. Do not the features of Richard Wagner shine through this hasty sketch?

In the outer conduct of his life, too, Giuseppe Verdi remained the great contrast to his rival. The author of almost thirty opera scores, the composer of the *Messa di Requiem* and *Quatro Pezzi Sacri*, was anything but the mere proprietor of a splendid estate and a handsome country retreat. He was a conscientious farmer, a large-scale agriculturist through and through, and this not in the ordinary but in the creative sense. He had his fair share of all the work, plans, schemes, alarms, troubles, cares, joys and pains of the real, serious landowner. The model estate of Sant' Agata brought about reforms in the agriculture of the whole district. Constant new innovations and improvements surprised the conservative, skeptical peasants of the province. Verdi dug canals, introduced the threshing machine and the steam plow, started dairy farms round about, built roads.

He kept increasing his holdings. The soil of Sant' Agata swallowed a considerable part of the sums his operas earned. Music made Verdi a rich man. He was proud of the fortune that he owed to his pen. No wonder that envy circulated every imaginable slander upon his person. Verdi, they said, was greedy and miserly. But this greedy miser never worshiped money for a single hour of his life. He never put his money to work on the stock exchanges, in the world of shares and complicated interest. What he did not spend on living and farming, he invested in the more patriotic than profitable Italian funds. Verdi was never avaricious; he was the very opposite—he was thrifty. And he could think and act selflessly, like a patriarch, in a thrifty and constructive fashion, as the following episode shows.

About 1880 Italy went through a grave economic depression. Unemployment waxed from month to month. People in town and country, and particularly in the country, could no longer earn their bread. Emigration to America assumed alarming proportions. While the romantic artists of the time simply took no notice of such things, the Italian operatic composer Verdi immediately turned to in his own locality with a vigorous hand. In the middle of winter he left the comfortable Palazzo Doria, and went to Sant' Agata. There he not only started a long-planned remodeling of the house, but had three large dairy farms and agricultural establishments set up on his own land, so that he could give work and bread to two hundred unemployed peasants and their numerous families. Soon he could exclaim with satisfaction: "Nobody is emigrating from my village now!"

Giuseppe Verdi, whose prophetic eye foresaw the world wars of our day during the Franco-Prussian conflict of 1870, predicted no less prophetically: "For you must know, you city dwellers, that the misery among the poor is great, very great, immensely great. . . . And if nothing is done to meet it, whether from below or from above, we shall live to see a great catastrophe. . . ."

Verdi was no friend of the Socialists, as indeed he was no friend of any one political party. But his was a resolutely responsible social spirit like that of no other musician in his day. And he saw not the slightest contradiction between speech and action.

He showed the same integrity and purity of character in all questions of public welfare. He hated it when it was only the alms to ease the consciences of the well-to-do. He refused to participate in anything that smelled of "benevolence," of "charity." He would take any burden upon himself, even that of doing good. For instance, he not only built the hospital in the neighboring town of Villanova out of his own pocket, but supervised the administration of the place, looked after the wine, milk, and meat, and made sure that the patients were not stinted in any way. But if the papers printed a story that Giuseppe Verdi had made a donation for the renovation of the little church in his native village, or that Busseto was to have a theater, he would fly into a rage; and this newspaper scribbling was not too trifling for him to correct it with brusque denials.

His servants and employees, too, the master of Sant' Agata treated like a patriarch. They feared him, for he was a real master, caring for his property even when he was away in Paris or Genoa. "Is the coachman exercising the horses every day?" (Verdi loved his horses as Leo Tolstoy did.) Who had dared to turn over the key of the machine shed to unauthorized persons against his orders? What? The cholera was raging in northern Italy, and the overseer did not even think it worth while to write him a line as to whether all was well at home? But it was not his property alone that the master cared for with all his heart, it was his people even more. There is testimony to this in his will, where even the least and youngest of his servants was not forgotten, and in a multitude of other cases. For instance to save some poor wretch, the son of a coachman, from military service he moved heaven and earth, wrote begging letters (what an agony!) to influential acquaintances, and was finally forced to realize that even the great Verdi was a little man in the eyes of bureaucracy.

The Maestro suffered a great deal of annoyance in his days at Sant' Agata from the affair of the theater at Busseto. This went far back, into the lifetime of Barezzi. Old Signor Antonio, a celebrity himself through the glory of the man he had discovered and helped—oh, fame is a drink that does not quench the thirst it feeds—had probably originated the idea that the city of Busseto should build a Teatro Verdi in honor of its great son. A few Bussetans approached the Maestro with the idea, and immediately sustained a sharp rebuff. The years hurried on. Meanwhile the plan of a Festspielhaus at Bayreuth came into being, dedicated to the works of one man. "Bayreuth" became a regular headline in the European press. Who knows, perhaps the Bayreuth festivals made the honest Bussetans even more eager for their Teatro Verdi. They went after Signor Carrara, the Maestro's attorney. The refusal was even sharper than before: "I tell you, I have never seen the use of a theater in Busseto."

Several times more the game was repeated, always with the same result. Verdi did not want a Teatro Verdi.

Often as he had thrown himself body and soul into giving his music a perfect performance, he never thought for a moment of establishing a fixed tradition, let alone of making Busseto into a Bayreuth. His labor of love in his old age was not to be devoted to his own operas, but to the human beings who had been the voice of those operas, the veterans of song and orchestra pit. On the Piazzale Michelangelo in Milan the Maestro bought a piece of ground. On this plot—on the outskirts of the city, from which one saw the blue range of the Alps on the horizon—he put up an imposing new building. It was a home for aged musicians, bearing the more tactful name of *Casa di Riposo*. In this house of rest a group of old musicians, a hundred at a time, were and still are housed and fed for the remainder of their lives. Along with the endowment given by the Maestro, the royalties on Verdi's operas form the permanent income of the home. As long as those operas live and bring returns, a hundred retired artists will have food and shelter, generation after generation.

Here is the everyday routine of Sant' Agata. Giuseppe Verdi rises early. Like most Italians, he takes nothing but a cup of unsweetened black coffee. Then he goes out on horseback—in later years he has the carriage hitched up—to inspect the work in fields, barnyards, and at the dairy farms, or to call on some of his tenants. He is the squire, not the Maestro. Between nine and ten he comes home. Meanwhile the mail has arrived. The mail is of course the great daily event at any country house. Signora Giuseppina has sorted the letters, separating the nuisances attendant on a celebrity from the important correspondence. Some time is spent every day in dealing with this. If guests come, they generally arrive about noon. Verdi's equipage usually fetches them from the nearest railway station, Firenzuola-Arda. His circle of friends is small, and grows no larger despite the vast number of connections formed in the course of a long, brilliant life. Only seldom does an outsider come in, like Monsieur du Locle, the director of the Paris Grand Opera, who asks Verdi in vain for a new work for his institution. After 1870 the group of friends consists chiefly of the singer Teresina Stolz, a Czech with a superb voice who created *Aïda* at the Scala, Giulio Ricordi and Arrigo Boito, the poet-composer of *Mefistofele*, a vigorous talent and more vigorous intellect who writes the masterly librettos of *Otello* and *Falstaff* for Verdi.

The main meal comes at about six in the evening. Verdi has the reputation of a lover and connoisseur of good cooking; though he does not compare with Rossini in that respect, he sets a splendid table. He loves the light wine of Italy and heavy Havana cigars, nor does he disdain a game of cards after the evening meal.

Music seems to cut no great figure in the house. Verdi is not fond of musical discussions. He warns some of his visitors that they will find no scores at his house, and a piano with broken strings.

Yet sometimes, later in the evening or at night, after the guests are all gone, Signora Giuseppina will be sitting alone in her room. Perhaps she is thinking how it all came about. Once, long ago, she was the young, radiant diva, and the Maestro a modest, rather somber man to whom her patronage helped bring victory and great glory. And now? Muffled tones come from Verdi's room. Peppina drops her sewing, and lifts her head. What is this? Why, that's new! What the woman does now requires some courage. But she cannot help herself. Slowly, on tiptoe she creeps nearer, listens at the door, and finally opens it. One of those melodies has just been born that seem as old as the world the very first time they are heard: *"Addio di bei giorni"* from *La Traviata*. *"Ai nostri monti ritorneremo"* from *Il Trovatore*. *"Rivedrai le foreste imbalsamate"* from *Aïda*. Giuseppe Verdi's face is hot, his eyes are moist; the tremendous emotional power of his soul, which he hides so manfully from the world, is revealed now to his wife, his old companion in music. . . .

The signature Giuseppe Verdi put at the end of his letters changed somewhat as decades passed. One need not be a graphologist to understand the spiritual meaning of the twined circle that the Maestro drew more and more closely about his name. The signed name itself represents the ego, exposed to the shameless presumptions of a perpetually exigent world. No matter how strongly this ego believes itself armored with hardness and equanimity, it is and remains a touch-me-not, achingly excitable, mortally wounded by every unkind breath. To protect this ego, which is embodied in the name, the writing hand puts a sort of hedge around it, a sheltering fence or wall, at once cautious and vigorous. This is the meaning of the loop that encircles the name, leaving a smaller and smaller opening for the admittance of the world as time goes on:

Excitability and sensitivity of the ego are the natural and necessary concomitants of every artist personality. In most cases they lead to a morbid access of self-conceit, to an egocentric intoxication that would deny the autonomy of the outer world, and subjugate that world to the desires and purposes of the perpetually suffering ego. Quite otherwise with Verdi. Through all his letters from young manhood on runs the pedagogical determination to push the ego into the background. Fie upon this ego writ large, with its vain self-mirroring! We meet with a chained and sifted ego that has been many times subdued, and seldom permits itself an unchecked outburst. On the other hand all the cool, critical forces hostile to self-conceit come to the fore.

If a playwright or actor has a failure he will generally put the blame, once he recovers from the first stupefaction, not on himself but on his associates, on an unhappy combination of circumstances, or even on the audience. The vain egocentric is quite incapable of thinking himself wrong. Verdi, on the contrary, records failures suffered by himself with a coolness bordering on a kind of strange malicious satisfaction.

He is still young, and has the success of *Nabucco* just behind him; a new opera, *I Lombardi*, is performed at Venice. So much depends on his not suffering a reverse now! Fifteen minutes after the curtain falls upon the last act, the thirty-year-old writes to a woman friend:

I Lombardi has fizzled completely. It was one of the truly classical fizzles. Everything was disliked or just barely tolerated. . . . This is the simple but true history, and I tell it without pleasure, but without pain either. . . .

Some ten years later *La Traviata* suffered a failure of such proportions, on its first performance (also in Venice), that the final curtain went down to the pitiless laughter of the audience. Imagine this happening to *La Traviata* on the first evening of what was to be its perennial stage life! And Verdi wrote one of his rare autograph letters that have become famous:

La Traviata was a fiasco yesterday. Was it my fault, or the singers'? Time will tell.

This letter of three sentences is like a crystal. A gem of human veracity.

The man who cultivated this chaste truthfulness was an operatic composer, and lived in the world of the theater, a world of constant overweening pretension and self-adoration. No wonder that his aversion to what he called "advertising" started early, and sprouted later into the most acute disgust! Other artists are delighted to see their names often in print, even if only in connection with gossip or vapid anecdotes. Even as a young man Verdi was made violently uncomfortable by such occurrences. And in his old age he suffered from a strange onomatophobia: "I am horrified," he said, "when I read my own name; it smells dusty. . . ."

At the time of *Aïda* the name of Giuseppe Verdi became one of the show pieces of world publicity. The Khedive of Egypt commissioned an opera for the opening of the Suez Canal. The choice, according to the rapturous tales of publicity, wavered between Richard Wagner and Giuseppe Verdi. And the publicity went rapturously on: the Khedive was paying two hundred thousand louis d'or upon delivery of the score. (Actually it was a hundred and fifty thousand francs.) The material for the opera came from the great Egyptologist, Mariette Bey. Emperors and kings announced their attendance. The entire press of the world was sending special correspondents to Cairo. Day after day the chant of publicity went on, compounded of truth and exaggeration. Would not any author have rubbed his hands? The name of the work was echoing in everyone's ears long before it was written.

But the Maestro's stomach was turned by the constant tub-thumping. When Filippo Filippi, the critic (incidentally one of the deserters to Wagner), proudly informed him that he too was going to Cairo for his newspaper, Verdi burst out into a song of fury, a veritable diatribe against advertising:

I have a feeling that if this sort of thing goes on, art will no longer be art, but an empty trade, a pleasure journey, a hunt, a mere something that people run after, to which they would like to give, if not success, at least publicity at any price. What it makes me feel is disgust and humiliation! I always think with pleasure of my early days, when I came before the public with my works almost without a friend, without a soul to talk about me, without preparation, without the well-known influence; I was ready to take any bullets that came, and more than happy if I succeeded in creating a musical impression. And now, what machinery for one opera! Journalists, soloists, chorus men, directors, professors, etc. Each one must contribute his mite to the structure of advertising. . . .

Even the sedate, easygoing publicity of that day was enough to send the blood to his head. What did all these people mean by their "German bustle," stewing a work of art for months in the "witches' caldron of public opinion"? When he quoted this, Verdi was thinking of Meyerbeer and the Wagner of the Paris *Tannhäuser*. Can any cause in this world be sustained by persuasion? What have connec-

tions, dinners, diplomats, ministers, patronage, bribery, newspaper
stories to do with a work of art? Is a work of art any the better because a mandarin of criticism nods at it, or a clique of half-baked
minds is artificially worked up about it? There is an incorruptible
relationship between tune and listener: either the tune sticks to the
listener's consciousness, or it evaporates forever. Any attempt at pro-
moting or mediating is contrary to nature, nay, impossible. Not only
his innate repugnance but his clear thinking made it impossible for
Verdi to understand how creative human beings could so completely
mistake the laws of life. Thus even theoretic work on behalf of his
own cause was unknown to him. This was where he differed most
sharply from Wagner. He was not a Messiah, but *simply* a master of
Italian operatic music. And how could a master overrate or underrate
himself and his work? How could a master venture to thrust upon
the world anything that it did not take of its own accord? Mastery is
sure repose within the natural organization of things.

And so it was an actual fact that during his long stays in Paris
throughout forty years Giuseppe Verdi never gave any interviews, was
scarcely ever visible at great receptions, avoided the salons as sedulously as he did the coteries of the artists, and jealously preserved his
untouchable solitude. He knew neither Meyerbeer nor Berlioz nor
Gounod personally, and in fact he seems never to have met Rossini,
of whom he thought very highly.

This same Rossini once discovered that his countryman from
Roncole—he called him "the musician with the helmet on his head"
—who after all was hoping for success as an operatic composer in
Paris, could not even be persuaded to pay the necessary and usual
calls.

The hedging line around Giuseppe Verdi's signature drew closer
and closer. Then came the years of silence, the years of the strange
hiatus in his output. His successful operas dominated the repertory
of the world without diminution. But there was quiet around him
now. He no longer had to curse publicity. Divine honors were paid to
the name of Richard Wagner. Verdi was merely considered a popular
operatic composer. No progressive music lover of the time would have
dared to give him the same rank as his rival.

The connoisseurs nodded mournfully: *Aïda* was the swan song of
Italian opera, which had been annihilated once and for all by the
musical drama of Wagner. The world was convinced that the old
Maestro himself had spoken his last word with *Aïda*, and would

write no more. Verdi was seventy. The papers began to bestow on him, free of charge, the honorary title of "the venerable ancient of Sant' Agata." He was seventy-two; seventy-three.

And then one evening at the Scala in Milan the tremendous, dissonant opening chord of *Otello* came crashing out, that blow of a giant's fist, smashing the stone of the tomb. "I am here still!" Italian opera cried, and this in an orchestral medium that no one would have thought it capable of.

And the venerable ancient of Sant' Agata was eighty when the Scala echoed with the first chord of *Falstaff*, a fierce new proof of strength, this time on the weak beat of common time. Tempestuously bidding defiance to the accustomed measures, *Falstaff* burst upon an astonished world. By these two works Verdi hurled the Italian opera, which without him would have succumbed to the crisis, like a golden discus into a remote future. The dream of the learned gentlemen of Florence was fulfilled, if in an unexpected way. Here were none of the good old vices that had become attached to opera in the course of the ages. But neither was there the bloated excess, the garrulous monotony and superabundance of the symphonic drama. And everything, everything was song. *Otello* is the suffering mortal who is musically revealed down to the faintest tremor of his nervous system. Never before had music succeeded in reproducing so sharply the physiological process of spiritual anguish.

And *Falstaff* is the comedy of overcoming the world, just as *Parsifal* is the mystery play of overcoming the world. But what a contrast! In *Falstaff* the innate irony of Italian opera takes wings again; there is a sort of underlying terpsichorean feeling that the things of this world are not quite real, but the sport of the gods. The work ends with a tremendous choral fugue, expressing in this most earnest of all musical forms the conviction that everything on earth is a jest:

"*Tutto nel mondo è burla.*"

Yes, everything on earth is a jest. And within this jest man is "*il nato burlone*," the born fool, the unconscious jester of fate. Pleasure passes away, even pain, more real than pleasure, passes away. All that remains is the strange fame, the jest in the cosmic form of a fugue. But in *Falstaff* too everything, everything is pure song. There is even a loving couple that sing the sweetest melodies. It is true that these tunes breathe a touching coolness which by no means belongs to the love songs of *La Traviata* and *Aïda*. It cannot be denied that a man of eighty wrote those songs. They are like the enchanting frost flowers on a window, through which the deep blue eyes of old age smile out upon a sunny winter landscape.

But now the time to cease work was irrevocably at hand. Verdi had covered a long, long road, a road of labor, a road of the soul. He had fought his battle through to the end. His uncompromising nature, a "thou must" as hard as diamond, had never allowed him to weary, never to temporize, and had kept him young, a man of the future, up to the very arctic zone of life. Fame had been no temptation to him, and even true inspiration no excuse. His constant intellectual labor produced not nervous exhaustion but another kind of hard work, farming. Progressively, year after year, there developed within this man of the theater a divine striving for anonymity, or, to put it more clearly, a striving for an existence without outward seeming.

There he went, the old man, through the streets of Milan, Genoa, Rome; everyone turned to look, but it no longer troubled him. The hedge of anonymity had grown together around him. It was seldom that now he had an outburst of anger or disgust. Like a bluish shadow the chivalrous humor of *Falstaff* lay upon its old creator, rendering him gentle.

Sometimes still a cloud would gather over Verdi's head. The King of Italy and his ministers were planning to make the Maestro "Marchese of Busseto." Unpleasantly surprised, he humbly requested to be spared this elevation to the nobility: he would feel ridiculous. This was neither pride nor democratic principles, but a delicate sense of dignity.

During those years Verdi often stayed at the spa of Montecatini. Montecatini was alive with organ grinders. The Maestro had to run the gauntlet of his own tunes, for the hand organs relentlessly ground out the *"Miserere"* from *Il Trovatore* and the Quartet from *Rigoletto*. One day Verdi assembled these honest men of music, and paid them a stiff ransom to desist from further propagation of his songs. He may have succeeded in the little watering place of Montecatini, but he did not succeed anywhere else in the world.

But another time, in Rome, Verdi happened by chance to hear a distant orchestra playing the introduction to the last act of *La Traviata*. Unable to control himself, he began to weep, melting over his own coals, as Goethe has it.

"Old as I am, there's still a little heart left in me," he once confessed, "and I can still weep. . . ."

After Giuseppina died, the peaceful companion of half a century's

life and music, he could no longer endure the loneliness of Sant'
Agata. He moved to the Grand Hôtel Milan in Milan. There anyone
might see him, in the lobby, in the writing room, in the lift, even in
the restaurant. He put no outer barrier between himself and the
crowd, as if he no longer bore the burden of his own name. He did
not turn away callers. He received not only his friends Ricordi and
Boito, but such young musicians as Mascagni and Giordano. He
watched the world and the new century that had dawned. But
already he seemed to be on the far shore.

The end came suddenly. A stroke. The cause was a shirt stud. A
niece who was taking care of the Maestro had gone out of the room
for a moment. He was just dressing. The stud slipped from his fingers,
and rolled under the bed. But old Verdi was the old Verdi still. He
did not believe he needed help or attendance any more than he ever
had. He knelt down quickly, and stuck his head under the bed to
look for the little button. And then death came to him.

But death had no easy time with him. For seven days the struggle
went on between death and Giuseppe Verdi. That iron body, that
magnificent generator of all earthly harmonies and rhythms, defended
itself valiantly. Outside, in front of the Grand Hôtel Milan, a dark
silent crowd stood gathered for seven days. The traffic was diverted
from the Via Manzoni. Nobody in the city seemed to speak above a
whisper.

D'Annunzio, the poet, wrote a great ode about the death of Verdi.
He saw the figures of Dante, Michelangelo, and Leonardo in the
Milan hotel room, bending over the unconscious form. The finest
stanza of the poem tells with ecstatic rapture what Verdi meant to
the people of Italy and to the world:

> He nurtured us, as Nature's hand,
> The free, circumambient universe
> Of air, sustains mankind.
> His life of beauty and manly strength,
>   Alone,
> Swept high above us like the singing seas of heaven.
>   He found his song
> In the very breath of the suffering throng.
>   Let mourning and hope echo forth:
>   He loved and wept for all men.

On January 27, 1901, the heartbeat of Italy stopped for an instant.
Italy knew that the music of Verdi was like the air, without which

there could be no life. But now he was gone, he who had found his song in the very breath of the suffering throng, who lived for all and wept for all in his melodies. Italy would give her great son such a funeral as had never been seen before.

With accustomed foresight, none other than the Maestro in person upset the plans. When the will was read, people were dismayed to find the following provision:

"I wish my funeral to be very simple, and to take place at daybreak or at the time of the angelus in the evening, without singing or music."

This was what had to be done, and done it was. But fortunately there was another clause in the will. Verdi wished to be buried in the chapel of his Casa di Riposo. This required some time and preparation, and made a second funeral necessary, about which the will was silent.

The second interment, a few months later—the coffin was taken from the Milan Monumental Cemetery to the Casa di Riposo—was a great national ceremony. Hundreds of thousands swarmed around the cortège. The royal family took part, the government, the army on parade. And then came one of the great and rare moments when people and music become one. Without any preconcerted plan, by some inexplicable inspiration, there suddenly rose out of the monstrous soul of the multitude the chorus from *Nabucco* with which Giuseppe Verdi had become the voice of consolation and hope for his people, sixty years before.

"*Va, pensiero sull' ali dorate!*" The song of the enslaved by the waters of Babylon, after the words of the Psalm. . . .

Opinion about Verdi's music fluctuates with the times, yet it is hard to imagine that human hearts and ears will ever be closed to the slender beam of his dramatic melody. His life is a parable, an example pointing toward the future. In this time of change and upheaval we have buried so many gods! . . .

At such a moment as this, a life full of truth and without illusions, like that of the poet and farmer Giuseppe Verdi, seems a very star in the murk.

VERDI THE MUSICIAN

Francis Toye

From the biography which, though first published in 1931, still stands as the most authoritative work on the composer.

"Art devoid of spontaneity, naturalness, and simplicity ceases to be Art."

Perhaps the basis of Verdi's aesthetic creed is best shown in his views on musical education. They were eminently practical. First and foremost, he believed in rigid discipline and hard work. He did not believe in theories or systems. He thought a general literary and, especially, a historical culture more important than concern with abstract questions of aesthetics; the acquisition of fluency by means of assiduous practice in strict counterpoint and the writing of fugues more desirable than conscious stimulation of the imaginative faculties. "The student with genius," he once wrote, "who has been well initiated into the mysteries of the art will end by accomplishing that which no master could ever have taught him."

He did not consider it advisable that a student should be largely preoccupied with contemporary music, because of the danger of such preoccupation developing an idolatrous enthusiasm for some composer or other liable to stifle individuality. In the ultimate resort he certainly regarded the fearless expression of personality as the cardinal virtue in a composer and the lack of it as the outstanding defect in the music of his younger contemporaries. A letter to Arrivabene written in 1875 gives his point of view in a nutshell:

I am unable to say what will emerge from the present musical ferment. Some want to specialize in melody like Bellini, others in harmony like Meyerbeer. I am not in favor of either. I should like a young man, when he begins to write, never to think about being a melodist or a futurist or

Reprinted from *Giuseppe Verdi: His Life and Works* by Francis Toye, by permission of Alfred A. Knopf, Inc. Copyright 1946 by Alfred A. Knopf, Inc.

any other of the devils created by this kind of pedantry. Melody and harmony should only be means to make music in the hands of the artist. If the day ever comes when we cease to talk of melody or harmony; of Italian or German schools; of past or future, etc., etc.—then perhaps the kingdom of art will be established.

Another calamity of the present time is that all the works of these young men are the products of *fear*. Everybody is excessively self-conscious in his writing and when these young men sit down to compose, their predominant idea is to avoid antagonizing the public and to enter into the good graces of the critics.

You tell me that my success is due to a fusion of the two schools. *I never gave either of them a thought. . . .*

Verdi was undoubtedly justified in claiming that he had never given a thought to the theoretical advantage of this or that school. In some respects it might have been better if he had, but in others he was the gainer. The essential practicality of his mind was to a large extent responsible for the individuality and the sincerity of his music. His creed coincided with the injunction of the Preacher to do with his might whatever his hand found to do. That is not to say that he was unconscious of the shortcomings of his own cultural limitations. On the contrary, he often deplored the circumstances of his upbringing and asked with true, not affected, modesty what the judgment of a peasant like himself could be worth. Nevertheless, in his heart he did not believe in judgments at all, either his own or those of other composers, however eminent. He believed in personal taste. Toward the end of his life, in 1893, when a fellow composer submitted a sonata for his opinion, he answered as follows:

Everybody has and should have his own way of feeling; wherefore judgments are always diverse and useless, sometimes false. Boito (who was there) joined with me in admiring your composition, especially the very beautiful and expressive phrase at the beginning. If I told you that the composition in general seemed to me too much based on dissonance, you could answer: "Why not? Dissonance as well as consonance is an element of music; I prefer the former, etc." And you would be right. On the other hand, why should I necessarily be wrong?

Two years later, writing to the same musician, he insisted that "judgments have no value even when they are sincere. Everybody judges according to his personal feelings, and the public interprets the judgment of others in exactly the same way." Other instances of his emphatic views in this sense have already been given elsewhere. In short, though Verdi doubtless believed as firmly as Rossini that music could be divided only into two categories, the good and the bad, he did not pretend to know any infallible method of distinguishing the two, except perhaps a definite insistence that music of one kind should never pretend to be of another. For himself, he recognized as valid the claims of every school and of every period. "I admit the past and the present," he wrote to Arrivabene in 1882, "and I would admit the future, too, if I knew it and found it good."

Verdi never pretended to an intellectual outlook in which he did not, in fact, believe. He scarcely ever consulted the scores of other men and he was not ashamed to admit that music on a merely visual acquaintance meant nothing to him. As late as 1880 he avowed that in his opinion a good cabaletta was preferable to all the harmonic and orchestral ingenuities at present in vogue. Indeed, anticipating the extreme moderns of our own day, he thought that much of the vaunted progress in music was in reality a step backward, not forward, because "Art devoid of spontaneity, naturalness, and simplicity ceases to be Art." "In the Arts," he wrote in 1884, "excessive (I say, excessive) reflection stifles inspiration." To sincerity he was prepared to sacrifice everything, even those attributes of contemporary music which, as he wrote to Bellaigue in 1893, he recognized as genuine improvements and admirable in themselves. It must not be imagined from this that Verdi was ever a mere *laudator temporis acti*. On the contrary, he once summed up his views with typical simplicity and conciseness thus: "One must belong to one's own epoch." Though enthusiastic for celebrations in honor of Palestrina and Cimarosa, he poked fun at those who made an excessive cult of the past, suggesting on one occasion, when some commemoration or other was mooted, that it might be a good idea to start a movement for an erection of a statue to Pythagoras and, if that were a success, to Jubal as well. He frequently commented adversely on the tendency of the public never to honor the living equally with the dead, on their readiness to turn against a composer who had achieved success while still young.

Indeed, the ignorance, the stupidity and, above all, the fickleness of the public were constant themes with him and he preached rigid indifference to them as necessary to the true artist. The finest day in an artist's life, he thought, was when he could turn round and say: "Fools, you were wrong!" Yet his letters show him as fully recognizing the truth of the apparent paradox that in the ultimate result the judgment of the public is the sole true criterion of values. At the very end of his life he did not even hesitate to say, with an admission of his prosaic outlook in certain respects, that the takings of the box office provided the "only infallible thermometer" of success or failure, though he did not think that such a test was necessarily applicable immediately.

To the opinions of professional criticism, on the other hand, he paid little attention, despite personal respect for individual critics such as Filippi and, even more, Bellaigue. Somewhere or other he makes the odd statement that, whereas the artist should look into the future, it is not only the right but the duty of the critic to judge according to established standards; which seems to imply that he did not even expect exceptional insight or flair in that quarter. The truth of the matter is that Verdi could never forget that critics were also journalists—that is to say, members of a tribe especially obnoxious to him as being connected with what he probably hated more than anything else in the world: publicity.

Though Verdi was conscious of musical claims superior to considerations of nationality and environment, he was throughout his life an ardent apostle of what we now should call musical nationalism. During the seventies and the eighties he was exceedingly distressed, as we have seen, by what he considered the excessive Germanization of Italian music. He wished the Germans to remain German and the Italians Italian, emphasizing the fact that the music of the former was primarily instrumental, that of the latter, vocal. He never ceased to urge on his countrymen the importance of regarding Palestrina as the basis of their national music. It would be interesting to know precisely the time when Verdi developed this enthusiasm for Palestrina. Did it date from his student days or did it come later? The sole certainty is that it existed at the time of the composition of *Aïda*; in fact, one of the choruses in that opera was originally planned as an essay in the manner of Palestrina.

When Boito, in 1887, asked Verdi's opinion as to the best six composers to study for the purposes of choral singing, he answered in a letter so interesting that it deserves quotation:

I send you some names, the first that come into my mind. They are more than six, but there were so many excellent men in the period you mention that it is difficult to know whom to choose.

1500
- *Palestrina (*in primis et ante omnia*)
- Victoria
- Luca Marenzio (a very pure writer)
- Allegri (he who wrote the *Miserere*)

And the many other excellent composers in that century, except Monteverdi, whose part-writing was poor.

1600
Beginning
- *Carissimi
- Cavalli

Later
- Lotti
- *Scarlatti, A. (who is full of harmonic treasures also)
- *Marcello
- Leo

1800
Beginning
- *Pergolesi
- Jomelli

Later   * Piccini (the first, I believe, to write quintets, sextets etc. Composer of the first genuine *opera buffa, Cecchina*).

If you are really limited to six, those marked * seem to me entitled to preference.

The list is interesting for many reasons, not least because there figures in it Piccini, often summarily dismissed by people totally ignorant of his music as a mere worthless antagonist of Gluck; for whom, incidentally, Verdi entertained by no means the conventional reverence, describing him as "not much superior to the best men of his time despite his powerful dramatic sense, and definitely inferior to Handel as a musician."

Verdi also wished to see vocal rather than string quartets popular in Italy, reiterating, even at the time when he himself had written a string quartet, his belief in their greater conformity with Italian musical traditions. In 1879, when the Scala orchestra began giving concerts in Milan under Mancinelli, he was pleased at their success but skeptical as to their utility. "I do not know," he wrote to the Countess Maffei, "how it can help *our* art. Let us be frank; *our* art is not instrumental." A year before he had not been at all enthusiastic about the visit of the same orchestra to Paris under Faccio, though on this occasion the remarkable triumph of the enterprise led him to say that his advice was probably bad, as usual.

His whole attitude with regard to nationalism in general and Germany and Italy in particular is well illustrated by his correspondence

with Hans von Bülow. Von Bülow had in the heyday of his Wagnerian enthusiasm written a scathing criticism of the *Requiem Mass*
after one of the original performances at La Scala. Prompted, it is
said, by Brahms, he subsequently recanted and with typical impetuosity wrote, in 1892, a letter to Verdi so apposite that a portion of it
must be quoted:

I began with the study of your last works, *Aïda, Otello,* and the
Requiem, of which a recent performance, though quite mediocre, moved
me to tears. I have studied them not only according to the letter that
killeth but the spirit that giveth life. Let me say, illustrious Master, that
now I admire, I love you! . . . And, faithful to the Prussian motto: *Suum
Cuique,* I exclaim with enthusiasm: Long live Verdi, the Wagner of our
Allies!

It may be doubted whether Verdi, who had little love for the Triple
Alliance, altogether relished this peroration, but the letter caused him
real joy. Perhaps he found in it some compensation for the defection
of Mariani twenty years before. He answered with charm and dignity,
writing among other things:

If the artists of north and south have different tendencies, it is well that
these should be different. Everybody should preserve the characteristics of
his own nation, as Wagner so rightly observed. You are fortunate in that
you are still the sons of Bach. And we? We too, sons of Palestrina, once
had a great school of our own, but it has become bastard and looks like
perishing utterly.

Much emphasis has been laid on Verdi's independent evolution
. . . in the analyses of the various works. Such emphasis is not meant
to imply that Verdi differed in this respect from other composers—
for instance, the genesis of Wagner's mature works is often discernible
in his earlier operas—but an uncompromising assertion of the fact
was necessary, since, up to recent times at any rate, it has been customary to admit Verdi as a great composer only after he came within
the orbit of Teutonic influence. The fallacy is complete, because there
was always a quality of greatness in Verdi's music and he never in any
real sense came within the orbit of Teutonic influence.

Nevertheless, like every composer, Verdi was influenced by the
work of other men. At the outset of his career the contours of his
melody owed much to Bellini, for whom three years before his death
he had not lost his admiration. He found Bellini's orchestration and
harmony poor, but the sentiment and the melancholy of his music

as a whole entirely individual. Above all, he admired the length of his melodies, describing the *lento a piacere* phrase in the introduction to *Norma* as one of the most beautiful things ever written. To Rossini his debt was greater or at any rate more definite. For instance, the theme of the "*Sì, Vendetta*" duet in *Rigoletto* is strikingly akin to a passage in Rossini's *Otello*, while the accompaniment of the "*Miserere*" in *Il Trovatore* is almost identical with that of "*Qual mesto gemito*" in *Semiramide*. There never was a composer so utterly devoid of snobbery as Verdi, who, despite his profound reverence for Beethoven in general and the Ninth Symphony in particular, did not hesitate to say that the workmanship of the last movement of that symphony was very bad and was not ashamed to own that he found some of Bach's *B Minor Mass* arid, and classical music occasionally dull. Wherefore he did not judge it necessary to claim perfection for everything Rossini had written though he admired him wholeheartedly not only for his music but for his mental capacity. He thought that *The Barber of Seville* was the best comic opera ever written, that *William Tell* was a great masterpiece, and that other operas contained passages of sublime beauty. Rossini, it may be remarked, returned a portion at least of the admiration, for he once described Verdi as the most original and robust of contemporary composers and paid tribute to his character as a rare example of private and public virtue.

In later life Verdi was influenced, like every other opera composer of the generation, by Meyerbeer. . . . Except, possibly, in the case of *I Vespri Siciliani*, Verdi never capitulated to it, but traces of Meyerbeerian procedure may be found in most of his operas, even, according to Stanford, in *Falstaff*, though completely assimilated and individualized. Pizzi tells us that Verdi entertained a genuine admiration for Meyerbeer's intellectual qualities despite the fact that he was repelled by "the banker's" intrigues and journalistic maneuvers in pursuit of success. He praised warmly the blend of fantasy and realism in *Robert le Diable*, the dramatic power of *Le Prophète*, and, like everybody else, Wagner included, he raved over the fourth act of *Les Huguenots* though he found the opera as a whole heavy and long.

Verdi's relations with Berlioz were more cordial—on both sides. Berlioz describes Verdi in his *Mémoires* as a "noble and honorable artist." Verdi, writing to Escudier, bids him salute Berlioz, "whom I love as a man and respect as an artist." Again, in a letter to Arrivabene written in 1882, Verdi summed up Berlioz as follows:

Berlioz was a poor sick fellow, full of fury against the world at large, bitter and spiteful. His intellect was vast and keen. He had a natural flair for scoring and anticipated Wagner in many orchestral effects. (The Wagnerians will not admit this, but it is so.) He did not know the meaning of moderation and was deficient in that calm, that balance, let us say, which produces complete works of art. Even when he did praiseworthy things he exaggerated. . . .

One would gladly know more of the relations between these two remarkable men, so utterly different yet obviously sympathetic one to the other. Verdi must have learnt much from Berlioz as regards scoring, a notable instance being the use of the echoing trumpets in the *Dies Irae* section of the *Mass*, whereof the *Kyrie*, it should be noted in passing, also shows unmistakable traces of the influence of Cherubini's fine Masses.

A certain amount has already been written about the relations of Verdi and Wagner, but something must be added. First of all, with reference to Wagner's attitude to Verdi—a slight task, for it can scarcely be said to have existed. Wagner just ignored his greatest operatic contemporary. So far as I am aware, Verdi is not once mentioned by name in the whole course of Wagner's letters and writings. There is a contemptuous reference to "the new *furia* of modern operas as exemplified in *I Vespri Siciliani* and other nights of carnage." There is an equally contemptuous expression of sympathy for a favorite singer who had to abandon *The Flying Dutchman* for *Il Trovatore*. Otherwise, Verdi is casually included in such a label as "Donizetti and Co."; nothing more. The omission is perhaps more striking than surprising. Wagner, who, according to J. W. Klein, would not even read Berlioz's operas though urged to do so by no less a person than Liszt, was notoriously indifferent to the music of his contemporaries. In view of his own wonderful achievements his indifference and egotism were justified, for, all things said and done, the music written by a composer is the only thing that ultimately matters. This is Wagner's real justification. The justification sometimes put forward, to the effect that Verdi had written nothing worthy of his attention before his death in 1883, will not hold water. Even granted— and few people nowadays would grant it—that there was nothing in the earlier operas up to and including *Don Carlos* to awaken interest and admiration, both *Aïda* and the Requiem Mass were composed and performed everywhere before Wagner wrote the last of his innumerable pages of prose. His neglect is all the more remarkable because (again according to Klein) Wagner's devoted disciple Cornelius greatly admired *Aïda,* while the *Requiem* had been the subject of much comment in the musical world. The presumable explanation of the matter is that Wagner had early in life made up his mind about Verdi and never troubled to examine the facts anew. To him, Verdi was only one of the Italian composers who wrote for the opera public as distinct from that nebulous abstraction which he christened "the Folk." As if in Italy, at any rate, they were not one and the same thing!

Verdi, however, unlike Wagner, was curious about his rival's music. He deplored the celebrated fiasco of *Tannhäuser* in Paris, because it deprived him of the opportunity of hearing the opera. Radiciotti says that he first heard the overture at a concert at the Paris Opéra in 1865 and, like Berlioz on a first hearing of the first act of *Tristan,* found it "mad." If, as seems likely, this was the first occasion on which Verdi heard Wagner's music, the case for any conscious imitation in *Don Carlos* becomes very slender. It is certain that he heard one of the Bologna performances of *Lohengrin* in November, 1871.

There exists at Busseto a vocal score of *Lohengrin,* with pencil annotations made by Verdi during some actual performance. Many of these notes are criticism, mainly unfavorable, of the performance; which creates a difficulty in reconciling it with the Bologna production, usually considered by everybody, including Wagner himself, to have been of the first class. Verdi also attended a performance of *Lohengrin* in Vienna some time or other, for he mentioned the fact to Pizzi, and it is conceivable, therefore, that this was the performance in question, though Lualdi, who has carefully examined and described the notes on the score, does not even suggest such a possibility.

I was fortunate enough myself to look at these notes, which are often scarcely legible. Some are profoundly interesting. For instance, Verdi found all the swan music ugly; he did not like, or at any rate did not understand, the first scene of the second act, but praised the end of the third; while his previous study of the score is attested by the remark that the wedding march did not sound so effective as he thought it would. His general impression, noted at the end, was that the reflective music was better than the music of action, that there were too many words moving too slowly, that there was abuse of organ-like effects in the writing for the woodwind. Except for some criticism of the string writing he generally admired the orchestration and found the music as a whole beautiful when the underlying thought was clear.

It should be noticed how scrupulously fair Verdi was in all this to the music of a man who was being used as a kind of cudgel to beat him to the ground, in the midst, possibly, of all the bitterness caused by the defection of a valued friend. He never made any secret of his admiration for Wagner's genius. Writing late in life, he summed up his music as "music where there is life, blood, and nerves; music, therefore, that is entitled to survive. Wagner shows artistic patriotism to an exceptional degree. He pushed his passion so far in this respect as to write in accordance with a preconceived artistic idea. This preconceived idea did him harm; but most of the harm came not so much from himself as from his imitators." Nevertheless, admiration for Wagner as a composer was a very different matter from acceptance of the dogmatic tenets of Wagnerism, which he found ridiculous and pretentious. Indeed, it is not too much to say that Verdi hated Wagnerism and all that it stood for, while he was always ready to poke fun at the "Music of the Future," expressly stating on one occasion that he saw no reason to fear it.

Both as men and as artists Wagner and Verdi stood at opposite poles. Verdi always remained conscious and proud of his Latin birth and characteristics. He held in abomination the uncouth heroes of the Nibelung saga, Siegfried in particular. He disliked the great length of Wagner's operas almost as much as the total darkness accompanying their performance, which, he said, induced a torpor in everybody, the Germans included; though his prophecy that they would on that account never become popular in Italy has been falsified by events. As Monaldi truly wrote, Verdi was always primarily an instinctive artist, bent only on improving his artistry; he was never a philosopher or an aesthetic speculator like Wagner. Moreover, unlike Wagner, whose object was the concentration of all the arts in the theater, Verdi sought first and foremost the greatest possible musical perfection. Even in the realm of music pure and simple their ideals were fundamentally different, for Wagner had symphonic aspirations, while Verdi believed (to quote his own words) that opera was opera and a symphony a symphony. Verdi stated in so many words his conviction that a theatrical composer must be prepared on occasions to sacrifice portions of his music, however admirable, in the interests of succinctness; Wagner's prolixity, though perhaps inseparable from his resourcefulness and inventive fertility, has been singled out as his most obvious weakness. As regards intellectual speculation Wagner was of course Verdi's superior; as regards inflexibility of determination there was nothing to choose between them. Perhaps Wagner's most remarkable achievement was that he invented an idiom that became for more than fifty years the musical language of the world. One of Verdi's greatest feats was that, almost alone among Wagner's contemporaries and immediate successors in Western Europe, he successfully avoided speaking that language.

In a sense the influence of Boito on Verdi was the most fruitful of all, but only in a strictly limited sense. The once prevalent idea to the effect that Verdi absorbed Wagnerian ideas and aspirations through the medium of Boito is not true. To begin with, Boito was in no sense a Wagnerite though he passionately admired Wagner's music. His judgment on Wagner, contained in a letter to Bellaigue, deserves to be better known: "Hybrid and monstrous, half-man and half-brute, fawn, satyr, centaur, or triton; or, better perhaps, half-god and half-ass, Dionysus in the divine frenzy of his inspiration, Bottom in his stupid obstinacy—how can we ever love him unreservedly?" Boito was far more a Verdian than a Wagnerian, for he preferred Verdi's outlook in every respect, aesthetic as well as social, even though he might have admitted the superiority of Wagner's intellectual equipment in most, and his musical equipment in some, respects. Second, Boito, whether a Wagnerite or not, seems to have had no direct musical influence on Verdi at all. What he did influence was his cultural outlook. Verdi always possessed an instinctive, uncultivated flair for what was great—for Shakespeare, Michelangelo, and Beethoven. Boito made it more conscious. He instilled into him a new respect for the literary value of a praise as distinct from its dramatic value; he made him see more clearly, perhaps, that it was not enough for a situation as a whole to be effective, but that the details of it as expressed in words must be of themselves worthy of their context. This is the most that can be claimed for him, and even here, remembering the libretto of *Aïda* or even of *King Lear*, it behooves us to walk warily. Boito's great and undeniable merit was to have made himself so beloved by Verdi that the composer accepted with enthusiasm from his hands incomparably the two best librettos in the history of Italian opera. His inquiring, restless mind may have stimulated Verdi's imagination, just as his wonderful, loyal devotion, amounting to real self-abnegation, may have been more responsible than we know or guess for encouraging the old man not to cease from his labors. But nothing can alter the fact that in the Verdi-Boito partnership Verdi remained always the dominant partner, the masculine element. May one venture to sum up the situation by suggesting that Boito became to Verdi in the aesthetic sense very much what Giuseppina Strepponi was in the life of every day?

In any attempt to sum up Verdi's characteristics as a musician due regard must be paid to the circumstances and the environment in which the major part of his working life was spent. Franz Werfel, in the introduction to his collection of Verdi's letters, has very justly emphasized the extraordinary pressure exercised on an Italian composer by the demands of the public in the first half of the nineteenth century. This pressure not only determined the enormous size of the output expected from a composer but rigorously dictated what he might and might not do. There is no parallel in modern music to such a state of things; perhaps the nearest analogy to it in England was the musical comedy stage in the days of George Edwardes. New operas were expected at regular and frequent intervals, written in conformity with conventions that could not be defied with impunity. Verdi, though first subordinating himself to these conventions, eventually, thanks to his iron will, did not so much defy as change them. But the process was arduous. He succeeded at the outset in adapting the prescribed mold to the expression of his new personal vigor. Thus, he curtailed the length of the operatic form—Mercadante, for instance, when he first heard *Nabucco* is said to have remarked that it was all over by the time he himself would have got to the end of the first act —and restricted the license of vocal embellishments which, despite the greater discipline already imposed by Rossini, still stood in the way of the unfettered presentation of the composer's intentions. In the main, however, he conformed to the conventional patterns strictly and, up to the time of *Rigoletto* at any rate, readily enough.

Inevitably such conditions affected the quality of Verdi's early output. Between March, 1842, and March, 1851, he wrote fourteen operas, one of them twice over! How could it be expected that he should always give of his best? The amazing thing is that these operas include not only *Nabucco* and *Ernani* and such "progressive" works as *Macbeth* and *Luisa Miller*, but *Rigoletto* itself. There was, however, a good as well as a bad side to this operatic tyranny. It developed a standard of craftsmanship scarcely realized in the world of music today. The treadmill was undoubtedly responsible for much worthless music, but it left Verdi with an unrivaled capacity "to bend the notes" (his favorite phrase) to the service of his meaning. Moreover, the very exclusivism of the system worked in the end to his advantage. Italy neither knew nor cared anything about the music of other countries. The harmonic language of her composers might be a quarter of a century behind that of the rest of Europe; the standard of her orchestral performances infinitely lower. Provided her singers maintained their world-wide supremacy, she remained indifferent. This state of things undoubtedly explains the backwardness of Verdi's harmony in comparison with that of several of his contemporaries in other countries. It probably explains also his very tentative experiments in orchestral effects; for what was the use of making experiments if there were no orchestras capable of carrying them out? But mark the result! He never was lured into that overindulgence in harmonic or orchestral ingenuity which has proved a refuge to so many second-rate composers in distress. He was forced to concentrate on the intrinsic value of the bare musical idea ungarnished by any more or less adventitious trappings. The way in which he laughed at himself and all his colleagues for overworking the chord of the diminished seventh is very revelatory in this respect. When, however, the musical ideas he had to express demanded greater harmonic freedom, he did not, like so many composers, take other people's ideas ready-made, but gradually and laboriously evolved a genuine idiom of his own. His attitude to orchestration followed a precisely similar orbit, with the result that alike in middle life, when they were comparatively backward, and in late life, when they were comparatively advanced, both his harmony and his orchestration remained entirely individual, indissolubly part and parcel of what he had to say. It was largely, then, this habit of self-reliance and self-containedness that enabled him to achieve the almost unique distinction, already noted, of withstanding the potent magic of the Wizard of Bayreuth, because, with insignificant exceptions, he never borrowed anything from anybody that could not be assimilated and individualized.

Doubtless, he was further assisted by another aspect of his musical psychology: lack of a sense of shame. Attaching little value to cleverness for its own sake, Verdi never hesitated to write down his musical ideas as he really felt them without a thought, so it seems, as to whether they were original, refined, calculated to elicit admiration or the reverse. Beyond question this was responsible for occasional vulgarities, but they were always the vulgarities produced by exuberance of vitality or sentiment. Many lesser composers have been possessed of better taste, for a certain kind of good taste has always been the hereditary enemy of genius. Verdi's unswerving search for truth, alike in music and life, was not a cold but a passionate quest, forming the nucleus of that compelling sincerity which has often been stressed as the outstanding feature of his art, and which, by a curious paradox, is perhaps more, not less, indispensable to a writer for the artificial medium of the theater than to any other.

But, in a sense, the whole character of this apparently so simple man was a paradox. With an unsurpassed instinct for the theater he hated everything the theater stood for, just as he despised the race of singers while rating the human voice as the most potent means of musical expression. His haughty contempt of the public was only equaled by the humility with which he bowed to the ultimate validity of their judgment. A believer in tradition, he persistently protested against belittlement of the present; an exponent of nationalism in practice, he preached the importance in theory of considerations superior to nationalism. He was a skeptic and an enthusiast, a pessimist who never capitulated to pessimism. The most proud and secretive of men, he remained the most modest and expansive of musicians. No one ever lived a more practical or a better-balanced life, yet the soul of his music was romance, expressed in violent contrasts and quivering emotion. Most paradoxical of all, as has been truly observed, this man to whom the world owes some of its most passionate love songs has not, to my knowledge, left behind him a single love letter.

Verdi's unbounded vitality, his fundamental simplicity and integrity, fused these incompatibilities, more apparent of course than real, into a personality of such force that still today the music in which it was expressed can thrill and stimulate us in a manner peculiar to great art and, in some measure, to itself. Boito defined Verdi's predominant quality alike in his music and his life as that of putting "the right note in the right place." No praise could be higher, for, in art as in letters, that quality is the monopoly of the true poet, the supreme master. . . .

VERDI REFUNDS

One Prospero Bertani owes a measure of immortality
to the fact that he did *not* enjoy *Aïda*.

"He promises never to hear another one of my new operas."

REGGIO, May 7, 1872

To GIUSEPPE VERDI

On the second of this month, attracted by the sensation which your
opera, "Aïda," was making I went to Parma. Half an hour before
the performance began I was already in my seat, No. 120. I admired
the scenery, listened with great pleasure to the excellent singers, and
took pains to let nothing escape me. After the performance was over,
I asked myself whether I was satisfied. The answer was in the negative. I returned to Reggio and on the way back in the railroad carriage, I listened to the verdicts of my fellow travelers. Nearly all of
them agreed that "Aïda" was a work of the highest rank.

Thereupon I conceived a desire to hear it again, and so on the
fourth I returned to Parma. I made the most desperate efforts to obtain a reserved seat, and there was such a crowd that I had to spend
five lire to see the performance in comfort.

I came to the following conclusion: the opera contains absolutely
nothing thrilling or electrifying, and if it were not for the magnificent
scenery, the audience would not sit through it to the end. It will fill
the theater a few more times and then gather dust in the archives.
Now, my dear Signor Verdi, you can imagine my regret at having
spent 32 lire for these two performances. Add to this the aggravating
circumstance that I am dependent on my family, and you will understand that this money preys on my mind like a terrible spectre. Therefore I address myself frankly and openly to you, so that you may
send me this sum. Here is the account:

From *Verdi, the Man in His Letters* by Franz Werfel.

Railroad: one way	2.60	lire
Railroad: return trip	3.30	"
Theater	8.00	"
Disgustingly bad dinner at the station	2.00	"
	15.90	lire
Multiplied by 2	x 2	"
	31.80	lire

In the hope that you will extricate me from this dilemma, I am yours sincerely,

BERTANI

My address: Bertani, Prospero; Via San Domenico, No. 5

VERDI'S REPLY (ADDRESSED TO RICORDI)   May, 1872

. . . As you may readily imagine, in order to save this scion of his family from the specters that pursue him, I shall gladly pay the little bill he sends me. Be so kind, therefore, as to have one of your agents send the sum of 27 lire, 80 centesimi to this Signor Prospero Bertani, Via San Domenico, No. 5. True, that isn't the whole sum he demands, but for me to pay for his dinner too would be wearing the joke a bit thin. He could perfectly well have eaten at home. Naturally, he must send you a receipt, as well as a written declaration that he promises never to hear another one of my new operas, so that he won't expose himself again to the danger of being pursued by specters, and that he may spare me further travel expenses!

May 15, 1872

I, the undersigned, certify herewith that I have received the sum of 27.80 lire from Maestro Giuseppe Verdi, as reimbursement of my expenses for a trip to Parma to hear the opera, "Aïda." The Maestro felt it was fair that this sum should be restored to me, since I did not find his opera to my taste. At the same time, it is agreed that I shall undertake no trip to hear any of the Maestro's new operas in the future, unless he takes all the expenses upon himself, whatever my opinion of his work may be.

In confirmation whereof I have affixed my signature,

BERTANI PROSPERO

THREE LETTERS BY VERDI TO
HIS PUBLISHERS

> Never the most patient of men, Verdi, as he grew older, became less tolerant of capricious performances or fulsome discussions of his art. He once said that if he returned to a performance three weeks after the première, he could hardly recognize his own opera. What would he think of our current workaday performances? These letters were written shortly after the Italian première of Aïda at La Scala.

"Is that art?"

[Probably 1872]

To Giulio Ricordi

Nicolini always cuts his part!!! . . . Aldighieri several times in the duet in the third act!! Even the second finale was cut down one evening!!! Aside from the fact that the romanza was transposed downward, some measures in it were changed.

A mediocre Aïda! A soprano singing Amneris! And on top of all that, a conductor who dares to change the tempi!!! . . . . I hardly think we need to have conductors and singers discover new effects; and for my part I vow that no one has ever, ever, ever even succeeded in bringing out all the effects that I intended. . . . No one!! Never, never. . . . Neither singers nor conductors!!

. . . But now it is the style to applaud conductors too, and I deplore it not only in the interest of the few whom I admire, but still more because I see that the bad habits of one theater spread to others, without ever stopping. Once we had to bear the tyranny of the prima donnas; now comes that of the conductors as well!

Well? And you talk to me about composing, about art and so on!!! . . . . Is that art?

I close with the request that you tell the house of Ricordi that I

From *Verdi, the Man in His Letters* by Franz Werfel.

cannot tolerate the above-mentioned state of affairs, that the house of Ricordi may, if it pleases, withdraw my three last scores from circulation (and I should be very glad of it) but that I will not tolerate any changes being made. Whatever may happen, I repeat: I cannot tolerate it. . . .

To Giulio Ricordi   [A few days later]

After an interval of twenty-five years at La Scala I have been whistled off after the first act of "La Forza del Destino." After "Aïda," endless chatter about how I am no longer the Verdi of "Un Ballo in Maschera" (the very "Masked Ball" that was first whistled off at La Scala); how the only compensation (according to Arcais) is the fourth act; how I don't know how to write for singers; how the few bearable things are all in the second and fourth act (nothing in the third); and how on top of all that I am an imitator of Wagner!!! A fine outcome after thirty-five years to wind up as an imitator!!!

This much is sure, that such chatter will not sway me a hair's breadth from my goal, any more than it ever has done; I have always known what I wanted. Now that I am where I stand, whether high or low, I can say: If this is so, do what you please. If I want to make music, I can do it in my own room, without having to listen to the opinion of scholars and blockheads.

I cannot take your statement that "the complete salvation of the theater and of art is in your hands," for anything but a joke. No, no. Make no doubt of it, there will always be composers; and I too would repeat the toast proposed by Boito to Faccio at the performance of his first work: ". . . And perhaps the man is already born who will smash the altar." Amen!

To Giulio Ricordi   Genoa, March 31, 1872

Dear Giulio:
So this evening will be the last for "Aïda." I can breathe: It won't be talked about any more, or at least nothing but a few, final words. Maybe some new insults accusing me of Wagnerism, and then *Requiescat in pace!*

And now will you be good enough to tell me what sacrifices this opera of mine has cost the management? Don't be surprised at the question; I am bound to suppose there must have been sacrifices, seeing that none of the gentlemen, after all my work and thousands of lire in expenses, have given me so much as a "Thank you, Dog."

Or should I by chance be thanking them for having accepted and performed poor old "Aïda," which brought in 165,000 lire of profit in twenty performances, not counting the season tickets and the galleries? Ah, Shakespeare, Shakespeare! The great searcher of the human heart! But I shall never learn.

VERDI COMPOSES *OTELLO*

Francis Toye

It was the breaking of a silence which had lasted fifteen
years. In 1871 Verdi finished *Aïda*. Aside from a revision of the earlier *Simone Boccanegra* and two minor
liturgical compositions, no new work had come from
his pen. Then, at the age of seventy-three, in 1886, the
world learned that Verdi, the retired farmer, had composed another opera. They could hardly divine its
stature!

"For a long time he intended to call the opera 'Iago.' "

Despite revisions, despite depression, the idea of *Otello* lurked
always at the back of Verdi's mind. During the year 1881 and spo-
radically during the ensuing years he was in correspondence with his
friend the painter Morelli about the characters and costumes of the
play. Apparently Morelli would have liked Othello himself to be
dressed as an ordinary Venetian, but Verdi replied that, as Shakespeare had chosen to make a Moor out of Giacomo Moro (a Venetian general in the original Italian story on which the play is based), a
Moor he would have to remain. His chief preoccupation was with
Iago. Morelli's idea of Iago was a small man of cunning aspect,
dressed in black. Verdi approved the black, but confessed that his
own idea of Iago was quite different. "If I were an actor," he wrote,

and had to act Iago, I should like to portray rather a spare, tall man with
thin lips, small eyes set close together like a monkey's, a high, receding
forehead, and head well developed at the back. His manner should be
vague, nonchalant, indifferent to everything, skeptical, pungent. He should
throw off good and evil sentiments lightly, as if he were thinking of something quite different from his actual utterances. Thus, if somebody reproached him, saying: "What you propose is infamous," he would reply:

Reprinted from *Giuseppe Verdi: His Life and Works* by Francis Toye, by permission
of Alfred A. Knopf, Inc. Copyright 1946 by Alfred A. Knopf, Inc.

"Really? . . . I did not think it was . . . don't let us talk about it any more!" A man like this might deceive anybody, even his own wife to a certain extent. A small malevolent-looking man arouses suspicion in everybody and deceives no one.

Morelli was told that he ought to paint a picture of Othello prostrate on the ground after the terrible insinuations of Iago, and he in fact made a sketch for such a picture, which Boito vainly tried to describe to Verdi in March, 1884; but the picture itself had not even then materialized. There is no doubt that the figure of Iago, in whom he saw an embodiment of the kind of priest he so much disliked, especially fascinated Verdi. It was no mere coincidence that for a long time he intended to call the opera "Iago."

The whole project nearly came to grief in 1884. After the production of *Mefistofele* at Naples, a banquet was given to Boito, at which he was reported by a newspaper to have said that he was sorry not to be setting "Iago" himself. Verdi, in his touchy mood, thought that Boito implied that his music would not be satisfactory and offered to restore the manuscript as a free gift, "without the slightest resentment." Boito, whose relations with Verdi had been growing steadily more intimate, had no difficulty in proving that he had been misreported. He refused point-blank to accept Verdi's offer, and the storm blew over. Verdi, however, refused to guarantee to complete the opera, writing to Boito on the twenty-sixth of April, 1884, that there had been too much talk about it, that he had worked and lived too long, that the years not only of his life but of his labor were excessive: "Heaven forbid that the public should have to say to me too openly: 'Enough.' " Ten days later he wrote to Franco Faccio in much the same strain: "So, in your opinion, I ought really to finish this *Otello*? But why? And for whom? It is a matter of indifference to me and still more to the public."

Verdi speaks of "finishing" the opera, but it is, to say the least, doubtful whether he had as yet composed much of the music. He certainly told both Arrivabene and Giulio Ricordi in March, 1883 that he had not written a note at that time. Checchi makes the definite statement that he did not begin writing the score until November, 1885 (and, incidentally, that he scored the whole of the first act during the fortnight that he passed at Montecatini during the summer of 1886, working not more than two or three hours a day); but this seems scarcely possible in view of the fact that Verdi wrote to Maurel on the thirtieth of December, 1885 to the effect that *Otello* "is not completely finished, as has been stated, but is well advanced toward completion. I am in no hurry to finish it, because up to now I have not made up my mind to produce it"—his hesitation being due, apparently, to the impossible economic conditions prevailing in the theater.

Besides, he informed the publisher Leduc in January, 1886, "My *Otello* (no longer 'Iago') is not finished. True, I did a lot of work on it toward the end of last winter and at the beginning of the autumn, but many things still have to be done to complete the score." Knowing Verdi's habitual procedure, we may surmise that he had most of the music in his mind before he started to write it down. He may even have made definite sketches; in any case it would be perhaps unwise to take his denials to Ricordi and Arrivabene too literally. Where his compositions were concerned, Verdi always showed himself extraordinarily secretive even with his most intimate friends.

Rumor became busy with his intentions. As early as March, 1883, Verdi was surprised to read in a paper that "Maurel has again told us that Verdi is preparing a huge surprise for the musical world and in his 'Iago' will give the young 'musicians of the future' a very stiff lesson." He was not at all pleased. "Heaven forbid!" he wrote to Ricordi; "it never has been and never will be my intention to give lessons to anybody. I admire everything I like without prejudice for or against any particular school. I am guided by my own tastes and I let everybody else do as he pleases."

As the facts with regard to the progress of the opera became known, interest not only in Milan but in Paris increased. Maurel wrote, reminding Verdi of a promise to entrust to him the part of Iago. Verdi, though protesting that he never could have made a promise that he was not absolutely sure of being able to fulfill, replied that he could imagine no better interpreter possible, and for the time being closed the subject. A year later, in January, 1886, Maurel again returned to the charge, this time trying to persuade Verdi to allow *Otello* to be produced at the Paris Opéra Comique under the direction of Carvalho, who was prepared to do everything conceivable to satisfy the composer's requirements. Verdi, though much pleased, politely refused.

You who know Boito will not need to be told that in *Otello* he has fashioned a libretto wherein situations and verses alike are extraordinarily powerful. I have tried to give to these verses the most true and significant accents in my power. This quality (it may turn out to be a defect) would be largely lost in translation. It is imperative, then, that *Otello* should be given for the first time in Italian. . . . But, I repeat, any such considera- tion is premature.

Several celebrated singers wrote in the hope of procuring parts in the new opera, but on some excuse or other all were discouraged except Tamagno, who was told to come quietly to Genoa on his way back from Madrid to talk things over. The journalists began to take a hand in the game, tackling the notoriously reserved Boito with no success at all and eliciting from Guilio Ricordi, afraid perhaps of his own expansiveness, only the deliberate misstatement that it was a thousand pities that Verdi would or could write no more music. Needless to say, the inscrutable composer himself vouchsafed no in- formation. Outwardly his attention seemed occupied with quite other matters. For instance, he was considering the presentation to the village of Villanova of a tiny hospital with twelve beds, in order to save the poorer inhabitants the tiresome and often fatal journey to Piacenza; while the newspapers credited him with the further intention of restoring the church of the hamlet of Sant' Agata. Since Verdi, who regarded the report as tendentious, never had any such intention, this led to correspondence in which he complained that the newspapers seemed determined to make him out much richer than he was. "You must know better than anybody else," he wrote to Ricordi, "that when I composed a great deal, the price paid for operas was low; now that it is high I hardly compose at all." Even as late as March, 1886, he found time to go to Paris for a week or two, "a little to hear Maurel, a little to see if they are madder than they used to be, a little just to have a change." In July he journeyed post-haste to Milan to be present at the deathbed of the Countess Maffei, his friend for forty-four years and the recipient of his most intimate con- fidences.

Nevertheless, on the first of November, 1886, *Otello* was finished, the fact being announced to Boito in the following laconic note:

> DEAR BOITO,—
>   It is finished.
>   Here's a health to us . . . (and also to Him . . .).
>   Good-by.
>   G. VERDI

On the eighteenth of December the last pages were sent from Genoa to the copyist. Verdi hated to see them go. He felt as if he had lost a friend. "Poor Otello!" he wrote to Boito, "he will come back here no more."

The production was announced for the fifth of February, 1887, at La Scala, but Verdi had reserved the right, though the public was unaware of the fact, to withdraw the opera at any time during rehearsal or even after the dress rehearsal.[1] Curiosity and excitement were rife in the city. The choice of subject, inseparably associated in the mind of the older generation with Rossini, provoked comment, not all of it favorable. With an insignificant exception, no new work by Verdi had been heard for nearly thirteen years. Some remembered his own declaration that he was too old to write any more, that "music needs youthfulness of the senses, impetuousness of the blood, fullness of life"; that the children of old men "are rickety, anemic and worse." Others, pointing to Verdi's well-known vitality in comparison with his years, recalled the fact that Professor Fedeli, who looked after him during his annual cure at Montecatini, had declared that he was still perfectly capable of work. Nobody had the slightest idea what the new opera would be like as regards either nature or style, especially as the La Scala rule of exclusion from rehearsals had been enforced even more rigidly than usual.

Though the speculators took advantage of the situation to push up the price of seats to fantastic heights, the theater, with the exception of the royal box, was completely filled a quarter of an hour before the performance; the rush for the cheaper seats nearly ended in a free fight, and the approaches to La Scala were thronged throughout the evening by crowds of people unable to gain admission but determined to play some part, however vicarious, in such a historic event.

Monaldi, who was present, gives an extremely vivid account of the scene in the theater, with its atmosphere of tense expectancy. The orchestra, under Faccio, numbered a hundred; so did the chorus. Managers and critics from all Europe were present in force, including Reyer from Paris, Bennett and Hueffer from London. What would their verdict be? As to the reception of the opera by the public there was soon no doubt. Twice in the first act, after the fire chorus and

---

[1] This little-known fact is established by a letter to Giulio Ricordi that appeared in the *Berliner Tageblatt* and is included by Werfel in his collection of Verdi's letters. It is of importance as illustrating the sense of experiment felt by Verdi in his new venture.

Iago's drinking song, they tried, though vainly, to call Verdi onto the stage. When, at the end of the act, Verdi took his call, "one immense simultaneous shout makes the theater rock. Verdi slightly bends his head and smiles, the frantic enthusiasm of the huge assembly bringing tears to his eyes. He seems to feel the necessity to retire, which the public, with a tardy respect for his age, finally permits him to do."

At the end of the opera renewed and even greater enthusiasm! When the composer left the theater, a crowd of admirers, who throughout the day had lined the streets to applaud his every appearance, unharnessed the horses from his carriage and drew it to the Hotel de Milano, where he always stayed. Bellaigue relates that here, in the midst of those he loved most, Peppina, Teresina Stolz, Faccio, Boito, and Ricordi, listening to the acclamations of the crowds outside, he was assailed by melancholy. "I feel," he said, "as if I had fired off my last cartridge. Oh, the solitude of Sant' Agata, hitherto peopled by all the creatures of my imagination whom, well or ill, I translated into terms of music! Tonight the public has torn away the veil that concealed my last mysteries. I have nothing left."

And as they spoke of his glory, he continued: "Oh, glory, glory! I so loved my solitude in the company of Othello and Desdemona! Now the crowd, always greedy for something new, has taken them away from me, leaving me nothing but the remembrance of our secret conversation, our dear, past intimacy." But the mood, which will readily be understood by anyone who has experienced the vicissitudes of artistic creation, soon passed, and with a smile on his austere face the old man said: "My friends, if I were thirty years younger I should like to begin a new opera tomorrow, on the condition that Boito provided the libretto."

When the press notices appeared, the judgment of the critics was as favorable as that of the public. In the *Corriere della Sera*, then beginning to occupy the predominant position in Italian journalism that it still holds, there were criticisms of the first three performances, on the whole exceptionally intelligent. "In no other opera," writes the critic, "has Verdi devoted so much care to detail as in this *Otello*. The recitatives, which are of unique beauty, will, I am sure, after two or three hearings prove to be not one of its least attractions for the public. A most marked feature of this opera is the manner in which Verdi has underlined, as it were, the words that are most important for dramatic expression; while the scoring, even on a first hearing, appeared to be of rare beauty and perfectly balanced." The critic then proceeds to detailed praise, especially of the final duet of the first act, "which alone would suffice to make the fortune of any opera"; of the great ensemble at the end of the third, and of the whole of the last act. He also makes the interesting remark that the measure of the success of the second as compared with the first performance was more like a hundred to one than two to one. Perhaps in part this may have been due to the greater restraint of the audience— an innovation particularly welcome to Verdi. "Do you know the greatest pleasure I had in Milan?" he said to Ricordi; "it was the discovery that the public was intelligent and perceptive enough to guess my wish that the acts should not be interrupted by calls or encores."

The *Nuova Antologia* considered as the greatest merit of Verdi in *Otello* the fact that he had not allowed himself, as regards form, to be bound by any rigid system, especially the Wagnerian system of the leitmotiv. "In his desire for the music to illustrate and comment on the drama he has reserved for himself full liberty of form, abolishing the old divisions and conventions of separate numbers. All the scenes in an act are closely linked together, but it is not true, as has been erroneously asserted, that every act makes an indivisible whole." The critic of the *Secolo* summed up the leading characteristic of the opera with acumen when he wrote: "This is dramatic declamation in strict time substituted for classical recitative on the one hand and Wagnerian polyphony on the other."

The French and the Germans were in agreement with their Italian colleagues. Reyer in the *Journal des Débats* waxed positively lyrical. He particularly emphasized the absence of motifs in *Otello* and the fact that the orchestra, for all the care bestowed upon it, was never allowed preponderance over the singers. "This is sufficient proof, I think, that the score of *Otello*, despite its evident tendencies and the determination to sacrifice every conventional effect to dramatic truth, cannot be compared or likened in any way to works entirely different in type and character. There is no excuse for anybody to believe that the composer in modifying his style has for one moment lost sight of the claims of his own personality." The reference is clearly to Wagner, a similar conclusion being reached by the *Wiener Zeitung*, which affirmed that the obvious change in Verdi's style was due to evolution, not imitation, and that for this reason Verdi's *Otello* was in some respects more remarkable than Wagner's *Parsifal*.

The English critics, Bennett in the *Daily Telegraph* and Hueffer in *The Times*, concurred in the general verdict, the former praising unreservedly Verdi's declamation and power of musical accent, the latter describing his success with the dialogues as astonishing. "The doctrine of Wagner," wrote *The Times*, "is carried out with a rigour that would have astonished Wagner himself . . . but every bar teems with individual and national impulse. In no other opera has Verdi been more himself than in 'Otello.' . . . This is the most remarkable first performance of modern times."

The two English critics agreed, moreover, in rating the last act as the most beautiful in the entire opera and, what is especially interesting, in stating that the performance left something to be desired. This is important, because we are often asked to believe that one of the reasons why *Otello* made its way comparatively slowly in the Italian theaters was the fact that the superlative excellence of the first performance discouraged emulation. As regards detail, the critics differed. Both agreed that the double bass recitative before the entrance of Othello in the last act (strangely enough, encored) was exceedingly badly played. Both agreed that Signora Pantaleoni left a great deal to be desired as Desdemona, that Maurel's performance of Iago was superb. But whereas *The Times* described the famous Tamagno as "almost as good . . . with a voice which though without much charm in the middle register goes up to B flat with perfect ease," the *Daily Telegraph* dismissed him somewhat cavalierly as being "not quite equal to the part." Again the *Daily Telegraph* characterized the chorus as "moderately good," and wrote that "even Signor Faccio's orchestra, usually so capable, fell short of perfection at important moments." *The Times*, on the other hand, considered the performances of the chorus and orchestra "the most satisfactory features throughout, though the brass was too strong and the woodwind was not strong enough." Moreover, the critics differed amusingly with regard to certain points about the opera itself, Hueffer singling out the ensemble at the end of the third act for especial praise but thinking that Verdi would have been well advised to make use of motifs in the opera generally, Bennett commending Verdi for the absence of motifs but finding fault with the ensemble in question as "excessively elaborate." Finally, it is interesting to note that nearly all the critics of every nationality concurred in considering the third act as the most difficult of digestion for the public.

On the whole, then, contemporary criticism assigned to *Otello* precisely the merits now universally recognized. It may be doubted whether any other opera has achieved a more satisfactory fusion between music and words, a relationship between voice and orchestra more perfect. We know little or nothing of the details of the collaboration between Boito and Verdi, what changes, if any, Verdi made in Boito's original libretto, what share, if any, Boito had in suggesting a particular line of musical treatment. It is said that Boito advised against the great ensemble at the end of the third act, but that Verdi insisted, probably because it provided a characteristic example of Italian operatic construction. It is said that Verdi had qualms about Iago's Credo, which Boito, drawing on isolated passages in various Shakespearean plays, had inserted in the libretto. Whatever the contributory means, however, the final result was a remarkable, probably unparalleled, example of felicitous collaboration.

A considerable portion of the credit must be assigned to Boito, for his adaptation of Shakespeare's play to operatic purposes is beyond praise. A lesser man could hardly have escaped the lure of the first act. Boito, to avoid excessive length, discarded it altogether, making use only of some relevant allusions and a few lines of exceptional beauty inserted into the love duet. Certain important points, of course, such as Iago's vague suspicions of Othello and Emilia and the warning by Desdemona's father to Othello that a girl who can deceive her father may also deceive her husband, are inevitably jettisoned; but it is difficult to see how the material as a whole could have been better dealt with. Boito's treatment of the climax of the tragedy is, if anything, an improvement on Shakespeare's, while all through the opera he showed the greatest ingenuity in providing Verdi with every possible opportunity for lyrical expression without sacrificing the truth or the rapidity of the dramatic action. His verses, his general handling, reflect throughout the essential spirit of Shakespeare, though it is said that he was only able to read the play in a French translation.

Verdi's music is something of a miracle; in my opinion, more of a miracle than the music of *Falstaff*, usually considered the most extraordinary phenomenon of the century. But is it, in reality, so remarkable that a man of eighty should have written the masterpiece of sparkling wit and mellow wisdom that is *Falstaff* as that a man of seventy-four should have written the masterpiece of intensity and passion that is *Otello*? Doubtless the technical handling of *Falstaff* is, if possible, even more masterly than the technical handling of *Otello*;

but the vitality of *Otello* from the first bar to the last, no whit inferior to the vitality of *Aïda* or *Il Trovatore*, would, if it did not exist, be considered incredible in the work of so old a man. The amazing skill with which Verdi follows every shade of meaning, every change of mood throughout the drama; the flexibility of the dialogue, with the points continuously emphasized in an orchestration that is never superfluous, always true to the psychology of the situation; the harmonic invention, as, for instance, in Iago's famous drinking song, where the chromatics suggest in the most subtle manner the Satanic design underlying what appears to be mere boisterous revelry; the ability with which the various personalities are differentiated in the concerted numbers; the lyrical perfection of the opening of the last act, in which, as Mr. Anthony Asquith once beautifully said, "one seems to hear the overtones of Shakespeare"—all these are remarkable enough. But the miracle lies elsewhere. It is to be sought in the intense malignity of Iago, in the passionate, animal jealousy of Othello, in the yearning ache perceptible under the tenderness of that duet between Othello and Desdemona which remains, perhaps, the most satisfactory interpretation of true love, as distinct from passion or lust, in all the annals of opera. How could a man of over seventy feel these things so acutely as to translate them with such poignancy into music? We are fortunately not called upon to solve the riddle, only to be grateful for the fact. There is no question that *Otello* is the greatest tragic opera of Italy; it should rank with *Tristan and Isolde* as one of the two greatest tragic operas of the world.

Despite his triumph, Verdi may well have been glad to leave Milan. To begin with, even his exceptional vitality must have felt the strain of the three months of hard work preparatory to the production of his opera. But this, though exhausting, was not distasteful. What, in view of his temperament, he probably disliked most was the necessity to live so much in public. In addition to the crowds and the journalists, there had been the formal acceptance of tributes from admirers—monstrous things, most of them, such as the cup shaped like a winged dragon carrying a shell with a pearl in the middle, the gift of Signora Pantaleoni—of which the only one that he can have valued at all was the bronze-gilt wreath given him by Faccio on behalf of the orchestra after the dress rehearsal. There had been formal interviews with the authorities of the theater and of the municipality, at which everyone said polite things about everyone else. The sole function of importance that he seems to have avoided was a lunch given by the Mayor of Milan to distinguished foreign visitors, whereat, as a matter of fact, that functionary made an exceptionally illuminating speech descriptive of the bond between Verdi and Shakespeare: "In both," he said, "we find the same richness of color, the same capacity to create characters. In the works of the English poet and the Italian composer we feel the same sense of tragedy, making us shudder or weep." Verdi, in spite of his regrets, must have heaved a sigh of relief as his train steamed out of Milan and he became once more "the placid farmer of Sant' Agata."

OTELLO'S PREMIÈRE

Blanche Roosevelt

> Victorian authoress and biographer of Longfellow, Blanche Roosevelt journeyed to Milan to be present at *the* event. She gathered her impressions into an effusive book, cast as a series of letters to her friend Wilkie Collins, author of *The Moonstone*.

"At last, at last, the great day has come."

OTELLOPOLIS, February 5th, 1887

At last, at last the great day has come and gone, and Verdi has added the crown jewel to his diadem of triumphs. I cannot tell you the anxiety felt in the city before nightfall. As early as five A.M. everyone was astir, and when Gianetta brought my tea she informed me that she had already been to La Scala: the posters were unchanged, the opera would surely come off, unless—you may imagine I sent her about her business with her "unlesses"—unless the tenor, or the soprano, or the wig-maker, or the some particular hinge of the cast, she explained, "did not 'run ill' before seven P.M." Speaking of wig-makers, she also reminds me that any number of ladies in the hotel were having their hair dressed even at that unearthly hour—not me— eight "an may it please you," making preparations exactly as if the occasion were a State ball or a Royal wedding. These ladies will sit all day with bejeweled and elaborately dressed pates, and not dare to lie down, or sit back, or lean over, for fear of ruining their puffs, etc.

You may imagine the excitement was not lost on me. I hastily dressed, and before noon was in the streets. Streets? There were no streets—at least, no crossings—visible, and had the blocks of houses not divided the town architecturally, everything would have been run together, like honey, with human beings, human beings, human beings! I never knew how the day passed. Vergil ran up against the

From *Verdi, Milan and Othello* by Blanche Roosevelt.

La Scala doctor, and actually turned pale as the M.D. went to speak to him. "Don't tell me!" Vergil cried. "All right," laughed Doctor L.; "he is not quite well, but will sing, of course." The "he" meant, naturally, the tenor. I met Madame M. leaning over the piazza. "And to think of it!" she cried; "it is four o'clock. Iago's wig was brought home, and fits so badly that not even *glue* will stick it on to his head. He simply won't sing if—" "Don't," I cried; "I will give him my hair, every inch of it, and sew it on to a pate myself, rather than that." Just then the wig-maker came round a corner. Madame M. gave him one look; I slipped into the Galleria, and was busy staring at photographs. Poor wretch! that look reminded me of legends of Sioux scalping their victims, and the fitful dripping tress that decorates the successful warrior's belt, flashed before my eyes. "The end of this day will be human gore," I muttered; then turned to look again into the square. It was alive. An hour passed; men, women, children, beggars and ballias, hand-organs pealing forth Verdi tunes, Ernani, "Fly with me," and Manrico, "Do not leave me"; pardon the vernacular. Leonardo da Vinci's statue gleamed out of the sea of faces like a white eaglet's plume drifting toward a storm-swept sea. The windows of the tall houses looking out on the quadrangle were a mass of shifting heads: balconies were freighted with excited humanity, and the Italian-terraced roofs, where people were eating and drinking and shouting, were literally black with moving forms. But the exteriors of these old stone palaces was the most curious sight. The panels were a perfect kaleidoscope of light and color. You know the Italian women are fond of bright raiment. When they have not covered their heads with their pretty black veils, they wear veils in cream color studded with artificial flowers; they wear hats which would shame a hothouse for brilliancy, and their necks are hung with gewgaws; their bodices glow like an Oriental chasuble; then, too, these creatures looked so happy, laughing eyes, glittering teeth, bodies swaying to the pantomime of anticipated pleasure: all this made an impression on me I shall not soon forget; and as to the others, their spirits were so contagious that the crowd seemed charged with electricity.

The Piazza della Scala was a sight to see, and the cries of "Viva Verdi! viva Verdi!" were so deafening that I longed for cotton in my ears. Poor Verdi! had he been there, he would certainly have been torn to pieces, as a crowd in its enthusiasm rarely distinguishes between glory and assassination. You will ask what I was doing in the streets at such a time; and I will answer: I don't know; I merely obeyed the common impulse—went where the others did: the truth is, I also wanted to watch the Scala billboard, to see that no change would be made in the announcements. We all stood staring at the old theater, just as those idiots on the Paris boulevards on a summer night watch the magic lantern, to read the different advertisements for enterprising firms: and this, you say, in dead of winter? O, an Italian does not feel the cold on an occasion like this.

But to return. In case there had been any change of program I need not say there would not have been found a person in all Milan courageous enough to have put up the notice. There was death in the eyes of some of those men, waiting like hungry wolves since the night before to be first to crowd into the pit and galleries. Well, at last— after dinner—I didn't dine, I swallowed food—we started to the theater. The carriage had to be sent off long before we reached the door, the horses could not make their way through the crowd. At best, human beings one by one between a line of police could struggle toward the entrance. I expected my dress would be in rags; however, I managed to get in whole, and once there the sight was indescribable. La Scala has never before held such an audience, and although it was fully an hour before the time to commence, every seat was occupied.

The light murmur of expectant voices issuing from three thousand throats, audible, but discreetly indistinct, reminded me of the sounds in an enchanted forest on a summer night. No one was too exalted or too proud on this greatest of all solemnities to jostle the *contadina* on the doorstep, or the fruit vendor humming a Verdinian measure under the portico of La Scala; all were frantic to be seated before the curtain rose. Only in Italy could such a scene take place; for here pride of birth, or rank, or position gives way before the homage which a land of song sows in perennial laurel at the feet of her great composers.

From pit to dome, the immense auditorium was one mass of eager faces, sparkling eyes, brilliant toilettes, and splendid jewels. The Italian Court was a rainbow of colors, and Queen Margherita's ladies of honor like a hothouse bouquet of rarest exotics. The first and second tiers of boxes were so packed with the Milanese high-bred women, so covered with dazzling jewels and filmy laces, that the house seemed spanned with a river of light, up, up, up to where the last gallery was lost in a dainty cornice of gold. The gleam of diamond tiara and corsage bouquet shot oblong rays on the black-coated background; while the new electric lights, imprisoned in their dead-white globes, shed so

unearthly a radiance over the auditorium that we all looked like specters uprising from some fantastic dead-and-gone rout. As to the platea
or "stalls," it was simply marvelous. I know of no city in the world
which could present a spectacle of similar brilliancy. In the first place,
it was packed with officers—certainly the handsomest men in the
world—gorgeous in the varied and brilliant Italian uniform: staff
officers in full dress, and scarred veterans with their whole record in
speaking breast decorations; and the women—such pretty women as
one could see only in Italy; for the Italians are a decorative race when
seen in Italy, and picturesque, my dear friend, is the only word possible to describe them. The men look well anywhere; the women may
not shine on the Corso, but at the play they will put women of every
other nation in the shade. They are a special embellishment, a part
of the gorgeousness, the glitter, the performance. They know just how
to dress, and just what jewels to wear; how to sit, how to stand, how
to listen at the right moment, and to look bored at the right moment;
in short, their princely boxes are packed with such a baggage of per-
fections that the universal playgoing world most unanimously acknowledge their rightful supremacy.

"And the other portions of the house?" you say. That is a just question; for La Scala is not alone in its nobility, its platea and boxes. Besides the celebrities here and there, the romancer who has left his pen,
the painter his brush, or the sculptor his chisel, La Scala's real public
is in the upper tiers, in pit, or *lobbione*. Besides the throng of strangers,
there were present all the old theatergoers who never miss a first night,
and those who go but on such occasions were there in full force, conspicuous in their habitual places. They never need programs, they
know the names of every living and working artist; they have heard
all the great singers since Catalani and Pasta; have seen all the dancers
since Taglioni, father and daughter. They have supped with Bellini
after success and failure; and they have seen Verdi on the one occasion when he was at his conductor's place in the orchestra. They know
La Scala and everything pertaining to it by heart; nine cases out of
ten, they are better musicians than those in the band, better artists
than those on the stage. They come to sit in judgment: to applaud
or hiss, as they honestly feel; to lend their presence to the event of
what is to them the entire world: the annual opening of a new opera,
or a first night at their renowned opera house; in short, they are a
part of it. They have not dined, perhaps not even breakfasted, and
their pockets are filled with chestnuts: grave, anxious, preoccupied,

they are at the theater doors hours before the opening of the doors, waiting their chance to rush pell-mell into the roof gallery, called the *lobbione*. There are many amongst them who have not tasted food for a week: the body may be starved, but never the soul. They consider no sacrifice too great to enable them to figure at a first night at La Scala: no king is prouder than this old and faithful person. Can you not recognize him? No detail of toilette is neglected: hair is pomaded; mustache waxed; linen spotless; cravat tied in perfect knot; habit guiltless of dust; a flower in the buttonhole, a rose or *garofano*; gloves of a sickly white, from having seen the cleaner's too often. Can you not remember him as, opera glass in hand, his eye roams over the sea of faces, calculating which tier is to have the honor of his first glance? Last night this ancient man stood in his place until he had seen each member of the orchestra come in; then he sat down, unfolded a silk handkerchief, spread it on his knees, and with a friendly wave of his hand saluted his brother fossils right and left, as much as to say:

"You see me; here I am. Do you think *Othello* could go on were I not present?"

When I saw him I knew that the opera was about to begin. The habitué wore the same eager look he has assumed twice or thrice a year for half a century of Carnivals; he has forgotten the hours of waiting at the street door, the scrimpy dinner, the meager lunch of polenta, and the long, uneventful year. He is a part of the whole, and believes he is responsible for this night's failure or success.

I saw the ancient man stir, saw the glass move and the handkerchief flutter; saw him reseat and settle himself more comfortably; then I said to myself, "Ah, the opera is about to begin: now for *Othello*."

It is generally supposed that on a first night Verdi conducts his operas, but the idea is an erroneous one. With very few exceptions, for forty years or more he has not taken his place in the orchestra leader's chair. On this occasion he would have been too nervous to have attempted such a thing. The present incumbent of the leader's place at La Scala is Franco Faccio, an admirable musician and composer, one who knows his band as a flautist knows his stops, and who for years has directed Verdi's operas under the Maestro's own eye and dictation. Faccio's appearance in the conductor's chair, which he has filled so long and so well, was a signal for thunders of applause. . . .

The scenery, costumes, choruses, and orchestra were nearly perfect; the cast was certainly weak. Victor Maurel is the only real artist in the opera, and he is a Frenchman. In voice, acting, appearance, and dress he is the ideal of what an operatic artist should be, and the ideal of what any operatic Iago could be. He sang as even his best friends never dreamed he could sing, and his acting was the consummate work which we always have at his artistic hands. He entered at once into the fullest sympathies of the audience, and I could not help then and there contrasting the Iagos we have seen in other countries with the Iagos we always see in Italy. Iago even seems a *persona grata* to the public; the qualities which raise a thrill of horror in the righteous Anglo-Saxon are received by this susceptible nation with placid contentment and relief. His vileness, ruses, and perfidy are accepted for their art, not their nature; his ingenious devices arouse heartfelt plaudits, and let me add that never will you hear a gallery god in Italy express any disapprobation with a successful knave. Had Iago not succeeded there is every reason to believe that *Othello* would be left out of the Italian Shakespearean repertory. On noting his more than prominence in this opera, rendered doubly so by Maurel's sublime creation, I could well understand Boito's and Verdi's inclination to call their work *Iago*, and not *Othello*. Iago is essentially Italian, not in the sense of vice, but of artistic villainy: he reasons from the personal standpoint, and his reasons find a universal echo in the land which gave birth to such a student of human nature as Machiavelli. Othello, you will see, is an inferior creature, and plays an inferior part. . . .

Tamagno, the tenor, looked and acted Othello, but he did not sing—he bleated. Desdemona has never been a favorite of mine in history, and the present exponent of the role suggested to me all my thousand unavenged wrongs laid at the door of Brabantio's daughter. Madame Pantaleone is an excellent person, but as Desdemona she ought to have been suppressed the night before at her dress rehearsal. Her voice is naturally fine and dramatic, but she has no more knowledge of the pure art of singing than I have of the real science of astronomy. She has a vile emission of tone in the medium open notes; the upper notes are clear, but rarely in tune. The lovely music assigned to Othello's wife must have splendid resisting powers not to have fallen flat in her hands or throat. In appearance Madame Pantaleone is likewise unfortunate: she is short, slightly cross-eyed, and of a physical plainness, which dwarfed the already insignificant Desdemona. She acted very well in the first and third acts, but not so well in the last. Of the other singers, I will add that Petrovitch as Emilia was deservedly hooted; V. Fornari as Roderigo was not important to help or hinder the work; and M. Paroli as Cassio was a really fair second tenor; he, at least, knows how to sing, but Nature evidently never intended him to sing at La Scala.

The ovations to Verdi and Boito reached the climax of enthusiasm. Verdi was presented with a silver album filled with the autographs and cards of every citizen in Milan. He was called out twenty times, and at the last recalls hats and handkerchiefs were waved, and the house rose in a body. The emotion was something indescribable, and many wept. Verdi's carriage was dragged by citizens to the hotel. He was toasted and serenaded; and at five in the morning I had not closed my eyes in sleep for the crowds still singing and shrieking *"Viva Verdi! viva Verdi!"* Who shall say that this cry will not re-echo all over the world?

FALSTAFF

Francis Toye

Written for a recent recording of the opera.

"Falstaff has never quite won the place in the affection of the public to which it is so obviously entitled by its merits."

Everybody knows that *Falstaff* was the last opera written by Verdi, but perhaps comparatively few people realize how different was his attitude to it and its immediate predecessor, *Otello*, from that adopted toward all his other operas up to and including *Aïda*. Throughout his working life Verdi had regarded himself first and foremost as a craftsman, commissioned and paid to do a certain job; when once he had undertaken to deliver the goods he felt conscientiously bound to do so to the very best of his ability.

Nothing of the kind applied to the composition of *Otello* or *Falstaff*. By the time he began writing the former he himself, not to say the public at large, regarded his professional career as finished; he was more than seventy years old, he had saved enough money to satisfy all his needs, and he made no secret of the fact that his dearest wish was to be left alone. Had he not met and made friends with Boito; had not his wife, Giuseppina, been the very clever and intelligent woman she was; had his publisher, Ricordi, not been exceptionally astute we can hardly doubt that Verdi's two great masterpieces would never have come to life at all.

Perhaps the psychological difference may be conveniently summed up by saying that Verdi regarded them both as his private possessions. He refused to guarantee that he would ever finish them; he reserved the right to withdraw them from performance even after the dress rehearsal; he viewed both as experiments undertaken to pass the time away; he grew to love both dearly. Inevitably this is even more true of *Falstaff* than of *Otello* because he was eighty years old when *Falstaff* was produced, difficult though it may be for us to realize the fact, and

By permission of Angel Records.

the giving of *Falstaff* to the public was as if the last and best loved of his children were leaving the old man's home. This sadness is attested by the curious little *envoi* discovered in the score wherein Verdi bids farewell to Falstaff and wishes him Godspeed in his career throughout the world. There is no need, however, to shed too many tears. Verdi insisted over and over again that he had found great enjoyment in writing this, his last opera. To how many creative artists of any kind has such pleasure been vouchsafed between the ages, say, of seventy-eight and eighty?

So far as *Falstaff* is concerned almost all the credit not only of leading the old horse to the water but of making him drink must unquestionably be assigned to Boito. Verdi had always wished to write a comic opera, not a little perhaps because Rossini had once expressed doubts of his ability to do so, but the ambition remained vague. He seems to have toyed with several possible subjects including, it is said, *Don Quixote*. It was Boito who definitely anchored his choice to *The Merry Wives of Windsor*, going so far, we are told, as to sketch a scenario in forty-eight hours so as not to allow his collaborator's enthusiasm time to cool. It is significant that after this first sketch at any rate Verdi at no time even suggested any change in the libretto—a rare phenomenon indeed!—which shows to what extent his imagination had been captured and his trust in Boito fortified.

It will be noted that the subject is defined as *The Merry Wives of Windsor*. As will presently appear *Falstaff* is by no means identical with *The Merry Wives*, but on the whole too much has been made of Boito's assimilation of material from *Henry IV*. Some material from this source was, it is true, introduced: the famous Monologue on Honor, for instance, and the allusion to Bardolph's red nose, but these amount to very little. More important in all probability is the treatment of the character of Falstaff himself. Boito's Falstaff is not quite the gross buffoon of *The Merry Wives*; he has something of the more subtle Falstaff of the historical play. Many readers will remember how at the end as a kind of self-justification after his indignities and discomfitures Falstaff proclaims himself the origin of all the fun without whom none of these diverting episodes could have taken place. Surely this is pure *Henry IV*? There is no trace or hint of anything of the kind in *The Merry Wives*. It has been said that Boito somewhat Latinized the fat knight; it is probably true; I see no objection.

Boito's great achievement, however, lay rather in his treatment of the original Shakespearean farce. Mostly this consists of changes in the matter of omission, but partly of invention also. For instance, the number of characters as of incidents is considerably reduced. Thus, Page goes altogether, as do Evans and Shallow; Dr. Caius in the opera is a kind of amalgam of Dr. Caius and Slender in the play; Falstaff pays one visit instead of two to Alice's house, the searching of the basket being an addition from the omitted episode; Ford, masquerading as Brook, only comes once to see Falstaff; and so on. The most important inventions are to be found in the delicious comedy of Falstaff and Ford at the end of their interview; in the charming love passages of Nannetta and Fenton, which scarcely exist in Shakespeare; in all the business with the screen in the second act; in many details of the final scene, especially in my view the actual end which, by bringing the characters to the front of the stage, not as characters but as themselves, to sing the well-known final fugue links the opera to the oldest traditions of Italian *opera buffa*.

From sheer sentiment no Englishman can ever help regretting "Sweet Anne Page," not so much because she has here become Anne Ford as because of the long association of the phrase with the ridiculous Slender. Nevertheless I would venture to assert that on the whole Boito's *Falstaff* is a better comedy than *The Merry Wives of Windsor*; the action is less diffuse; the intrigue more tidy and concentrated. True, no Anglo-Saxon will ever understand why Boito chose to accent the name of the Duke of Norfolk on the last syllable, thus making it well-nigh impossible to translate the incomparable *"Quand' ero Paggio"* into English, but on the whole his rendering of Shakespeare remains beyond praise, on the same level as his rendering of Shakespeare's *Othello*. The literary quality of his dialogue as such has also at all times been greatly admired, though few are likely to deny that in his partiality for certain recondite words he sounds excessively pedantic. This, however, presupposes an exceptional familiarity with Italian.

In any case nobody to the best of my belief has ever questioned the pre-eminence of Boito's *Falstaff* among operatic librettos of this kind, its supreme merit being that just at the right time it provided Verdi with exactly what he needed to enable him to give full rein to all the fantasy and robust humor latent in his genius. Rarely if ever has there been a more happy fusion of words and music.

Attention has already been called to Verdi's possessive attitude toward *Falstaff*, and to the pleasure he so frequently expressed in working on the score and in the experiments he was making. He seems quite deliberately to have tackled the job in a more leisurely fashion than had been his wont hitherto—only two hours' work a day, it is said. Yet I hardly think it is true to say that the listener is ever conscious of any sense of experiment for the good reason that all the experiments were completely successful. Indeed the technical brilliance and mastery shown in *Falstaff* still continue to astonish the world. Detailed and complete analysis of the score would be impossible even if desirable; to provide anything adequate a whole pamphlet would be necessary. All that can be done here is to indicate what seem to me the salient features.

First and foremost emphasis must be laid on the distinctly Beethovenish quality of the music. Stanford pointed this out in the admirable article he wrote on the occasion of the first performance to which I shall refer again later. He was quite right; the flavor of Beethoven is unmistakable especially, perhaps, at the very beginning of the opera. Nor is this at all surprising. Boito, a considerable composer himself be it remembered, was a fervent admirer of Beethoven and despite gratuitous assertions to the contrary it was toward Beethoven rather than Wagner that he led Verdi. Not that Verdi needed much leading; several earlier operas already show the influence of Beethoven. There is little, if any, trace of Wagner's influence in *Falstaff* as many critics, foreign as well as Italian, were at pains to point out at the time of its production. For my part I can see no relationship between *Falstaff* and, say, *Die Meistersinger* except the importance and the mastery of the orchestra common to both. People have talked of the motifs that play an important part in Verdi's last opera. Strictly speaking, however, they are not motifs so much as labels associated with emotions and incidents as well as with characters. There was nothing new about this so far as Verdi was concerned. The reader has only to think of the lovely melody expressive of Alfredo's love for Violetta in *La Traviata* as recalled in the last act, of the motto-theme in *La Forza del Destino*, even the miserable tune associated with the sworn friendship of Carlo and Rodrigo in *Don Carlos*. True, the musical labels in *Falstaff* are both more varied and more numerous. They are also extraordinarily felicitous. You cannot hear the phrase attached to Mistress Quickly's curtsey or the assignation made with Mistress Alice between two and three o'clock without knowing at once and exactly where you are. Best of all, perhaps, is the delicious musical expression of the love of Fenton and Nannetta. The old man seems to have been able to give to this an almost uncanny quality of tenderness; there is nothing of adult passion about it; it is essentially the love music of a boy and girl; it is exactly right; so far as I know its particular quality is unique in operatic literature.

Returning to the first act attention must of course be called to the Monologue on Honor, where the trills and the grunts on the wood-wind so well illustrate Falstaff's contempt of the practical advantages of being an honorable man. Not inaptly has this monologue been called the humorous counterpart of Iago's Credo in *Otello*. When we come to the second scene the woodwind is gay instead of cynical, a perfect accompaniment to the mischievous laughter of the Merry Wives. Perhaps the gem of the scene is the unaccompanied quartet, but the whole ensemble is a masterpiece; on paper it looks so complicated, but in performance it becomes as clear as crystal.

There can be no doubt that the scene between Falstaff and Ford posing as Master Brook contains the outstanding music of the first scene of the second act, though I myself have a predilection for the almost physical self-satisfaction of the soliloquy *"Va vecchio John"* with its staccato brass accompaniment and flaring orchestral conclusion. Nevertheless to Ford's famous Monologue on Jealousy must go pride of place. This magnificent music rings so fierce, so genuine, that many modern listeners have found difficulty in not taking it seriously. An Elizabethan would have found no such difficulty. Does it not deal with cuckoldry, always in itself funny? It is significant, too, that at the first performance at least one Italian critic singled it out as the funniest passage in the whole opera! So much does what seems or does not seem funny remain conditioned by time and place. The classical instance of course is Malvolio whose plight has provoked sympathy and pity in many a modern. Any such feeling would have been inconceivable to an Elizabethan contemporary; Malvolio deserved his misfortunes and was thus perforce an object of ridicule. The music when Falstaff returns dressed up in his best clothes after Ford's outburst provides just the right foil to end the scene. It is enchanting, while the simultaneous exit of the two men through the door has become a veritable byword.

There is less to be said about the music of the second scene of the act, though it would be difficult to overpraise the hurly-burly and the rapid movement of the ensemble which culminates in the throwing of Falstaff, concealed in the clothes hamper, into the Thames. In the earlier part of the scene, however, occurs the *"Quand' ero Paggio,"* probably the best-known number of the entire opera. It lasts scarcely a minute; it is like the sparkle of a gem that vanishes almost before one becomes aware of it; there is nothing else in operatic literature quite like it. Incidentally, one of the two major alterations made by Verdi after the completion of the score occurs toward the end of this scene, the second being in the first scene of the third act.

Perhaps the most remarkable thing about this first scene is that it does not strike one as an anticlimax as it so easily might have done. To me the plot hatched by the women always conveys the impression of a lighthearted parody of all the somber conspiracies of the earlier Verdian operas such as *Rigoletto* and *Un Ballo in Maschera*. Besides, at the beginning of the scene occurs what is one of the most interesting things in the entire opera: the brilliance of the orchestral writing when the gradually expanding effect of wine on Falstaff is illustrated by a trill progressively taken up by the whole orchestra including trombones and trumpets with the big drum tremolando. An astonishing piece of virtuosity!

Everybody, including Stanford, has commented on the originality of the Fairy Music in the concluding scene, so entirely different from the Fairy Music of Weber or of Mendelssohn. In fact, of course, it is not Fairy Music at all; it is music of pure fantasy; it might just as appropriately have been framed in the garden of Busseto as in the glades of Windsor Forest. It does, however, possess an ethereal quality all of its own which, combined with the exquisite duet between Nannetta and Fenton, produces an atmosphere that could scarcely be more individual. Rightly or wrongly, I always feel conscious that here is the music of an old man and for this reason there is an effect of pathos—quite unconscious, of course, and serene, but still pathos—which almost brings tears to the eyes. If only on this account I regard the final fugue as just right. As a fugue it has been criticized, but that is of no importance one way or the other. What is of importance is that after the fantasy of the sham spirits, the very real sentiment of the two lovers, the comic tortures of Falstaff, it comes to remind us that none of this is to be taken seriously, that the world is a madhouse anyway and that men and women, whether wise or foolish, whether virtuous or gross, are mere puppets more than a little ridiculous. I would not have a note or a word of it changed.

Not the least interesting thing about *Falstaff* is that critical opinion and appraisement of its merits have not notably changed in the sixty odd years that have elapsed since it was first produced. Naturally no collection of people has been or ever will be in complete agreement as to the various influences traceable in the score; some mention Rossini and Mozart; others Beethoven and Wagner. For my part I am conscious of little of any of these apart from Beethoven's. It is all Verdi's very own—and in any case the matter is of little moment. But except that nowadays he would scarcely be bowled over by the sheer virtuosity of the orchestral score as were his predecessors (in particular his Italian predecessors), a modern critic would find and does in fact find almost exactly the same things to note and praise. This is not so common a phenomenon in operatic history as might be supposed. How many operas have been acclaimed as masterpieces only to be relegated sooner rather than later to a lower category or even to complete oblivion! How many operas that first failed to please either public or critics have come to rank among the established treasures of the world! *Falstaff* first took its place as a masterpiece on the ninth of February, 1893, and has retained it ever since.

Nevertheless *Falstaff* has never quite won the place in the affection of the public to which it is so obviously entitled by its merits. Everybody acknowledges its originality, its brilliance and its charm, but somehow the passionate love bestowed on other, usually less worthy, operas is withheld. I think the reason for this lamentable fact is fairly clear. As Stanford truly pointed out in the article already referred to, incidentally by far the best of the original contemporary press notices, there is a lack of any central melody for the average, even the average cultivated, listener to take hold of. For instance, the music of the two young lovers, so exquisite in itself, is almost too frail to provide the necessary repose in such a whirl of brilliance; "*Quand' ero Paggio*," as already noted, is a mere flash, gone in a moment. Perhaps the whole matter may be summed up by saying that for almost any dilettante *Falstaff* moves too fast; just as he begins to apprehend one beauty he is hurried on to another. It is not till the score is known in every detail that all its subtleties of manner and matter can be appreciated. The ordinary member of the operatic public can scarcely be expected to possess such knowledge. Yet to acquire it would be well worth his while—and, incidentally, I can think of no better method than listening repeatedly to a recording on the gramophone—because *Falstaff* remains one of the great masterpieces of the world, a well-nigh inexhaustible source of surprise and delight. Stanford summed up the opera beautifully: "It is as sunny as the composer's garden at Busseto, clear as crystal in construction, tender and explosive by turns, humorous and witty without a touch of extravagance or a note of vulgarity. Each act goes as quickly as lightning, without halt, almost without slow tempi."

Precisely.

BEFORE *FALSTAFF* WAS PERFORMED

Anonymous

> *Falstaff*'s première took place on February 9, 1893. On April 23, 1892, there appeared in the *Saturday Review* (London) this article, the author of which I have been unable to identify. The assertion that the part of Falstaff was especially written for Maurel contradicts one of Verdi's own letters to Ricordi. Victor Maurel, the famous French baritone, felt that he had first call on the part. Verdi wished to accept no such restriction and threatened to put *Falstaff* "on the funeral pyre . . . together with his great belly."

"A Verdi that nobody suspects will be revealed here."

Verdi's characteristic answer to a timid question addressed to him at the railway station, as the Maestro was leaving Milan a few days ago, gave the first authentic piece of news about the termination of a work which the whole artistic world awaits with impatience, and which but a short time ago ran the risk of not being completed. The influenza demon had singled out the lord and lady of Sant' Agata for an attack and left evil traces of his visit. There was a well-established project of giving *Falstaff* this May at the Dal Verme, and that had to be abandoned on account of the Maestro's illness. As late as January last Verdi was raging like a caged lion at his inability to work eight hours at a stretch as he used to do. "At the rate I am working now I shall never finish *Falstaff*," would he roar; "I have been hardly an hour at my desk, and I am already tired." The work done was lying on the table; several sheets of music paper covered with small but distinct writing, without a single erasure or correction, the succession of notes and musical signs formed evidently as rapidly as if it were a matter of mere copy—and copy it was, only the original was in these marvelous brains; for Verdi copies only from the dictates of his fancy,

From *Saturday Review*, London, April 23, 1892.

and his MS. sheets go straight from his hands to the publishers as soon as they are finished. The whole of the orchestral score is already in the possession of Messrs. Ricordi, and it is decided that *Falstaff* will be given in the next Carnival season. Of course, the Scala is the only theater in Italy where the event ought to take place; but Verdi is full of artistic scruples, and cannot make up his mind as to that. "*Falstaff* is a musical comedy," he says, "full of such details that I must have my artists and the public near one another; the dimensions of a big house may smother these details, and then *Falstaff* will be like a picture with a frame too large for it." In other words, Verdi wants to put into practice the precept of Berlioz—"*Faire vibrer le public avec les artistes*"—and he feels that the *ambiente* of the Scala is against this vibration. However, the predilection for the house and for Milan may go a long way toward obviating that difficulty; and, as a matter of fact, during his visit here for the Rossinian Commemoration, Verdi amused himself on the stage of the Scala by having a "vanishing trick" performed before him—we refer here to the chest in which Falstaff hides, and which is thrown instantly through the window into the Thames, the "defenestration" taking place before the public. Verdi observes, "I do not want Maurel to break his arms and legs at every performance." The Maestro was very pleased with the working of the trick, and laughed heartily at the sound of genuine splash of water accompanying it. But when the difficulty of the choice of the *locale* is overcome, there remains another, much more important, that of interpreters. The character of the music of *Falstaff* in general and of the recitatives in particular is such that, according to Verdi, only native singers, well accustomed to the "*parlare sciolto*," are likely to give him satisfaction. He is especially anxious about the female parts, of which there are four (light soprano, dramatic soprano, mezzo-soprano, and contralto), and he knows, alas! that "*parlare sciolto*" is in inverse proportion to "*cantare bene*" amongst the fair representatives of the lyric art in Italy. One fact is positive, that M. Maurel is to create the part of the protagonist; for the opera has been written especially for him.

It may not be without interest to know how Verdi came to choose such a libretto for what he intends to be his last work.

The Master's original idea, after the first performance of *Otello*, was to write *Romeo and Juliet*, "*per il suo caro Maurel*," as he calls him. But Gounod's *Romeò*, with the accent on the last syllable, was revived just then in Paris, and we shall never cease to regret that an excessive feeling of delicacy should have actuated Verdi to abandon that project. After that he toyed for a time with *The Taming of the Shrew*, and finally, having called Boito to the rescue, took a fancy to Sir John. *Et voilà.*

The opera, though containing several thousand notes more than *Otello*, will not take more than two and a half hours to perform. Boito's book is taken from the two *Henrys* and *The Merry Wives of Windsor*, and the *clou* of the work is said to be Falstaff's monologue about honor.

As for the music in general, we may say that no description can give an adequate idea of the humor, the youthfulness, and the piquancy of the vocal or orchestral part, and of the rhythms—and that a Verdi that nobody suspects will be revealed here.

A PERFORMANCE OF *TRAVIATA*
from *On the Eve*

Ivan Turgeniev

> Turgeniev's *On the Eve* is a story of the love of two
> young people, Elena and Insarov, in which the fate of
> Violetta is paralleled by the fate of Insarov. In search of
> the benefits of the sun, the young couple go to Italy,
> where they witness a provincial performance of *La
> Traviata*. Turgeniev expressed in this scene the magic
> of a stage performance, even a bad performance—that
> magic which crosses the frontier "beyond which beauty
> dwells."

After dinner they went to the theater. They were giving a
Verdi opera—a rather commonplace one, to tell the truth, but one
that had already made the round of all the opera houses in Europe and
was well known in Russia too—*La Traviata*. The season in Venice was
over and the singers did not rise above the level of mediocrity. They
all shouted as loud as their lungs could manage. Violetta's part was
sung by a little-known artiste who, to judge by the coldness of her reception, was not a popular favorite, though she was not without
talent. She was a dark-eyed girl, young and not particularly beautiful,
with an uneven and already tired voice. She was dressed in ridicu-
lously gaudy, ugly clothes with a red net over her hair. Her dress,
which was made of faded blue satin, was too tight over her bosom,
and her thick suede gloves came up to her bony elbows. Yes, how was
she, the daughter of some obscure shepherd from Bergamo, to know
how the *"Dames aux Camélias"* of Paris dressed? Nor did she know
how to move about the stage, though there was a good deal of sincerity and guileless simplicity in her acting and she sang with the
peculiar passion of expression and rhythm which only Italians can
achieve.

From *On the Eve* by Ivan Turgeniev, translated by Moura Budberg, by permission
of The Cresset Press.

Elena and Insarov sat alone in the dark box, very close to the stage. They were still in the frivolous mood that had overcome them in the Accademia di Belle Arti. When the father of the unfortunate youth, who falls into the toils of the seductress, appeared on the stage in a pea-colored frockcoat and disheveled white wig, opened his mouth crookedly and, obviously uncertain of the effect, emitted a dismal bass tremolo, they both almost burst out laughing. Violetta's acting, however, impressed them.

"That poor girl gets so little applause," said Elena, "yet I prefer her a thousand times to some self-confident, second-rate celebrity, who would be affected, pretentious and give herself airs. This one seems to take it very seriously—you can see she's not even aware of the audience."

Insarov leant on the edge of the box and looked intently at Violetta.

"Yes," he murmured, "it's no joke in her case—there's a kind of odor of death about her."

Elena was silent.

The third act began. The curtain went up. Elena felt herself shudder at the sight of the bed, the drawn curtains, the medicine bottles, the shaded light. She recalled the not so distant past. "And the future? The present?" flashed through her brain. As though on purpose, the actress' feigned cough was answered from the box by Insarov's hoarse and genuine one. Elena glanced at him out of the corner of her eye, and her face immediately assumed a calm and unconcerned expression. Insarov, who understood what she meant, smiled and began softly to join in the singing. Very soon, however, he was silent again. Violetta's acting improved all the time, became more uninhibited. She discarded everything unessential and superfluous, and found herself—a rare, a sublime happiness for an artist. She had suddenly crossed the frontier line which it is impossible to define, but beyond which beauty dwells. The audience held its breath in surprise. The ungainly girl with the tired voice had begun to control it, to dominate it. But her voice did not sound tired any more; it had warmed up, had gained strength. When Alfredo appeared, Violetta's cry of joy almost provoked the storm, which the Italians call *fanatismo*, and compared with which our restrained applause is nothing at all. . . . Another moment and the audience became spellbound again. It was the duet, the best moment of the opera, in which the composer succeeded in expressing all the regrets of misspent and foolish youth, the dying struggle of desperate and hopeless love. Carried away, transported by the wave of general sympathy, with tears of joy and real suffering in her eyes, the singer surrendered to the wave that was lifting her, her face became transformed and as the grim phantom of rapidly approaching death confronted her, the words—"*Lasciami vivere . . . morir si giovane . . .*"—were torn from her in a prayer of such passionate appeal to divine mercy that the whole theater shook with frenzied applause and rapturous cries.

Elena felt quite numb. She began searching gently for Insarov's hand and squeezed it tightly. He responded with the same pressure, but she did not look at him, nor he at her. This pressure of their hands now meant something different from what it had a few hours earlier in the gondola.

They glided back again to their hotel on the Grand Canal. Night had fallen, a bright and balmy one. The same palaces stretched out in front of them, but they seemed different. Those of them that were lit by the moon had a pale golden sheen in which the details of ornamentation and the outlines of windows and balconies seemed to vanish; they stood out more distinctly on those buildings which were lightly wrapped in shadow. The gondolas with their little red lights seemed to glide more swiftly and noiselessly than ever, their steel prows glittered mysteriously, the oars rose and fell mysteriously among the silver scales of the ruffled water; apart from the sporadic muffled cries of the gondoliers, who never sing nowadays, there was scarcely a sound to be heard.

The hotel where Insarov and Elena were staying was on the Riva degli Schiavoni. They got out of the gondola before reaching it and walked several times round the Piazza di San Marco. Under the colonnades crowds of idle people had collected in front of the small cafés. There is a peculiar fascination in walking about among strangers in a strange town with somebody one loves—everything seems beautiful and significant and one cannot help wanting everyone else to share one's own peace, serenity and happiness. But Elena was no longer able to surrender lightheartedly to her own happiness; her heart, shaken by recent impressions, could not recover its calm and as they passed the Palace of the Doges, Insarov pointed, without comment, to the Austrian guns poking out of the basement, and pulled his hat down lower over his forehead. Besides, he felt tired; and, with a last glance at St. Mark's and its domes, the bluish lead of which gleamed in the moonlight with a phosphorescent glow, they slowly wandered back to their hotel.

Their little room looked out over the wide lagoon that spreads from the Riva degli Schiavoni to the Giudecca. Almost directly opposite the hotel rose the spear-headed tower of San Giorgio Maggiore; to the right, high up in the air, glittered the golden dome of the Dogana; and, arrayed like a bride—most beautiful of churches—Palladio's Redentore. On the left were silhouetted the dark outlines of ships' masts and yardarms, the funnels of steamers, and an occasional half-folded sail hanging like a large wing among the almost motionless rigging.

Insarov sat down by the window, but Elena would not let him admire the view for long. He suddenly felt feverish and overcome by weakness. She put him to bed and, after waiting for him to go to sleep, returned silently to the window. What a mild and gentle night it was—blue as lapis lazuli and as soft as a dove. Surely, it seemed to her, all pain and sorrow must be stilled and assuaged beneath this limpid sky, and under the moon's benign and purifying influence.

"Oh God," thought Elena, "why should there be such things as death and parting and illness and tears—why, on the other hand, this loveliness, this blissful feeling of hope, the reassuring sense of a secure shelter, of unfailing protection, of eternal guardianship? What does it all mean—this smiling, friendly sky, this calm and happy earth? Is it possible that it's only inside ourselves after all and that outside there is nothing but eternal cold and silence? Is it possible that here we are alone—alone—and that up there, in the unfathomable depths and abysses of space, everything is hostile to us? If so, why is it that we long for prayer and for the relief it brings? ("*Morir si giovane*" echoed in her heart.) Was it impossible to ward off danger, to have one's prayers answered? Oh God, was it after all then impossible to believe in miracles?"

She rested her head on her folded hands. "Enough?" she whispered, "have I really had enough? I've been happy, not only for minutes, for hours, for days, but for weeks on end I've been happy. And by what right?" She felt frightened by her happiness. "What if it can't go on?" she thought; "if it can only be had at a price? We've been in heaven, after all, and we're only human beings, poor, sinful human beings. '*Morir si giovane*. . . .' Haunt me no more, dark phantom! It's not only for my sake that he must live. But what if this is our punishment?" she thought again; "what if we now have to settle in full for the wrong we have done? My conscience was silent, is silent even now, but is this a proof of innocence? Oh God, are we in truth such sinners! Thou who hast created this sky, this night, is it Thy will to punish us for having loved? And if it is, if he is guilty, if I am guilty . . ." she added with a sudden outburst, "—Oh, then, Oh God, grant that we should both die at least an honorable and glorious death, over there, on his native soil, not here in this obscure room. . . .

"And what of the grief of my poor lonely mother?" she asked herself, and became confused and found no answer to her question. Elena did not realize that the happiness of one involves the misery of another, that even one person's prosperity and comfort require—as a statue requires a pedestal—the disadvantage and discomfort of others.

"Rendich!" Insarov murmured in his sleep.

Elena approached him on tiptoe, bent over him and wiped the perspiration from his forehead. He tossed a little on his pillow and was quiet again. She returned to the window and her thoughts again assailed her. She began to persuade herself, to reassure herself that there was no ground for alarm. She was even ashamed of her apprehensiveness.

"Is he really in danger? Isn't he much better?" she whispered. "If we hadn't been to the theater this evening, none of this would have occurred to me."

At this moment, she saw a white sea gull flying high over the water. It had probably been startled by a fisherman and flew noiselessly, with an uneven flight, as though looking for a place to settle. "If it flies this way," thought Elena, "it will be a good omen." The sea gull circled over one spot, folded its wings and, as though hit by a bullet, dropped out of sight with a plaintive wail, somewhere behind a dark ship. Elena shuddered and was ashamed of having done so, and without undressing she lay down on the bed by Insarov's side. He was breathing heavily and quickly.

VERISMO OPERA

W. H. Auden

A contemporary poet and essayist, himself the coauthor
of an operatic libretto (Stravinsky's *The Rake's Progress*), discusses the style of *Cavalleria* and *Pagliacci*.
The essay was written as a preface to a recording.

"With a strong dose of salt."

While we all know that every moment of life is a living moment, it is impossible for us not to feel that some moments are more
lively than others, that certain experiences are clues to the meaning
and essential structure of the whole flux of experience in a way that
others are not. This selection is, in part, imposed by experience itself—
certain events overwhelm us with their importance without our knowing why—and in part the result of a predisposition on our side, by
personal temperament and by social tradition, to be open to some
kinds of events and closed to others. Dante's encounter with Beatrice,
for example, was *given* him, but he would probably not have received
or interpreted the revelation exactly the way that he did if the love
poetry of Provence had never been written. On the other hand, many
people before Wordsworth must have experienced feelings about
Nature similar to his, but they had dismissed them as not very
relevant.

Every artist holds, usually in common with his contemporaries, certain presuppositions about the real *Nature*, concealed behind or
within the stream of phenomena, to which it is his artistic duty to be
true, and it is these which condition the kind of art he produces as
distinct from its quality.

Suppose that a dramatist believes that the most interesting and
significant characteristic of man is his power to choose between right
and wrong, his responsibility for his actions; then, out of the infinite

By permission of W. H. Auden and Radio Corporation of America.

number of characters and situations that life offers him, he will select situations in which the temptation to choose wrong is at its greatest and the actual consequences incurred by the choice are most serious, and he will select characters who are really free to choose, who are least in the position to blame their choice afterward on circumstances or others.

At most periods in history he could find both of these most easily among the lives of the rich and powerful, and least among the lives of the poor. A king can commit a murder without fear of punishment by human law; a poor man cannot, so that, if he commits one, we feel he must be mad and therefore not responsible, and if he refrains we feel that the law, not he, is largely responsible. A king who steals a country is more interesting dramatically than a starving peasant who steals a loaf, firstly because the country is so much bigger, and secondly because the king is not driven, like the peasant, by an impersonal natural need outside his control, but by a personal ambition which he could restrain.

For many centuries the dramatic role of the poor was to provide comic relief, to be shown, that is, in situations and with emotions similar to those of their betters but with this difference that, in their case, the outcome was not tragic suffering. Needless to say, no dramatist ever believed that in real life the poor did not suffer but, if the dramatic function of suffering is to indicate moral guilt, then the relatively innocent cannot be shown on the stage as suffering. The comic similarity of their passions is a criticism of the great, a reminder that the king, too, is but a man, and the difference in destiny a reminder that the poor who, within their narrower captivity, commit the same crimes are, by comparison, innocent.

Such a view might be termed the traditional view of Western culture against which naturalism was one form of revolt. As a literary movement, nineteenth-century naturalism was a corollary of nineteenth-century science, in particular of its biology. The evidences of Evolution, the discovery of some of the laws of genetics, for example, had shown that man was much more deeply embedded in the necessities of the natural order than he had imagined, and many began to believe that it was only a matter of time before the whole of man's existence, including his historical personality, would be found to be phenomena explicable in terms of the laws of science.

If the most significant characteristic of man is the complex of biological needs he shares with all members of his species, then the best lives for the writer to observe are those in which the role of natural necessity is clearest, namely, the lives of the very poor.

The difficulty for the naturalistic writer is that he cannot hold consistently to his principles without ceasing to be an artist and becoming a statistician, for an artist is by definition interested in uniqueness. There can no more be an art about the common man than there can be a medicine about the uncommon man. To think of another as common is to be indifferent to his personal fate; to the degree that one loves or hates another, one is conscious of his or her uniqueness. All the characters in literature with universal appeal, those that seem to reveal every man to himself, are in character and situation very uncommon indeed. A writer who is committed to a naturalist doctrine is driven by his need as an artist to be interesting to find a substitute for the tragic situation in the pathetic, situations of fantastic undeserved misfortune, and a substitute for the morally responsible hero in the pathological case.

The role of impersonal necessity, the necessities of nature or the necessities of the social order in its totality, upon the human person can be presented in fiction, in epic poetry and, better still, in the movies, because these media can verbally describe or visually picture that nature and that order; but in drama, where they are forced to remain offstage—there can be no dramatic equivalent to Hardy's description of Egdon Heath in *The Return of the Native*—this is very difficult. And in opera it is impossible, firstly, because music is, in its essence dynamic, an expression of will and self-affirmation and, secondly, because opera, like ballet, is a virtuoso art; whatever his role, an actor who sings is more an uncommon man, more a master of his fate, even as a self-destroyer, than an actor who speaks. Passivity or collapse of the will cannot be expressed in song; if, for example, a tenor really sings the word *"Piango"* ("I'm crying"), he does not cry, a fact of which some tenors, alas, are only too aware. It is significant as a warning sign that the concluding line of *Cavalleria Rusticana,* *"Hanno ammazzato compare Turiddu"* ("They've killed our friend Turiddu"), and the concluding line of Pagliacci, *"La commedia è finita"* ("The comedy is over"), are spoken, not sung.

In practice, the theory of *verismo,* as applied to opera, meant substituting, in place of the heroic artistocratic setting of the traditional *opera seria,* various exotic settings; social and geographic instead of gods and princes. It gave us courtesans (*La Traviata, Manon*), gypsies and bullfighters (*Carmen*), a diva (*Tosca*), bohemian artists (*La Bohème*), the Far East (*Madama Butterfly*), etc., social types and situations every bit as unfamiliar to the average operagoer as those of Olympus or Versailles.

Giovanni Verga was no doctrinaire naturalist. He wrote about the Sicilian peasants because he had grown up among them, knew them intimately, loved them and therefore could see them as unique beings. The original short story *"Cavalleria Rusticana"* which appeared in *Vita dei Campi* (1880) differs in several important respects from the dramatized version which Verga wrote four years later, and upon which the libretto is based. In the short story the hero Turiddu is the relatively innocent victim of his poverty and his good looks. Santuzza is not the abused defenseless creature we know from the opera but a rich man's daughter who knows very well how to look after herself. Turiddu serenades her but he has no chance of marrying her since he has no money and though she likes him, she does not lose her head. Her betrayal to Alfio of Turiddu's affair with Lola is therefore much more malicious and unsympathetic than it is in the opera. Finally, the reason that Turiddu gives Alfio for insisting upon a fight to the death is not Santuzza's future—he has completely forgotten her —but the future of his penniless old mother.

Santuzza's seduction and pregnancy, Turiddu's brutal rejection of her, her curse upon him, his final remorse were all added by Verga when he had to build up Santuzza into a big and sympathetic role for Duse. As a subject for a short libretto, it is excellent. The situation is strong, self-contained and immediately clear; it provides roles for a convenient number and range of voices; and the emotions involved are both singable emotions and easy to contrast musically. The psychology is straightforward enough for song but not silly: how right it is, for instance, that Turiddu should reproach Santuzza for having let him seduce her—*"Pentirsi è vano dopo l'offesa"* ("Repentance after the offense is futile"). Thanks to the swiftness with which music can express a change in feeling, even Turiddu's sudden switch of attitude from contempt to remorse becomes much more plausible in the opera than it seems in the spoken drama. Targioni-Tozzetti and Menasci quite rightly stuck pretty closely to Verga's story, their chief addition being the lines in which Turiddu begs Lucia to accept Santuzza as a daughter. But, having at their disposal as librettists what a dramatist no longer has, a chorus, they took full advantage of it. The choral episodes, the chorus of spring, the mule-driving song, the Easter hymn, the drinking song take up more than a quarter of the score. It might have been expected that, particularly in so short a work, to keep postponing and interrupting the action so much would be fatal; but, in fact, if one asks what was the chief contribution of the librettists toward giving the work the peculiar impact and popularity it has, I think one must say it was precisely these episodes. Thanks to them, the action of the protagonists, their personal tragedy, is seen against an immense background, the recurrent death and rebirth of nature, the liturgical celebration of the once-and-for-all death and resurrection of the redeemer of man, the age-old social rites of the poor, so that their local history takes on a rhythmical significance; Turiddu's death is, as it were, a ritual sacrifice in atonement for the sins of the whole community. One of the most moving moments in the opera, for example—and nothing could be less *verismo*—occurs when Santuzza, the excommunicated girl who believes that she is damned, is translated out of her situation and starts singing out over the chorus, like Deborah the Prophetess, "*Inneggiamo il Signor non è morto!*" ("Let us sing! Christ is not dead!").

If the interplay of rite and personal action which is the secret of *Cavalleria Rusticana* is not a typical concern of the *verismo* school, the libretto interest of *Pagliacci* is even less naturalistic, for the subject is the psychological conundrum—"Who is the real me? Who is the real you?" This is presented through three contradictions. Firstly, the contradiction between the artist who creates his work out of real joys and sufferings and his audience whom it amuses, who enjoy through it imaginary joys and sufferings which are probably quite different from those of its creator. Secondly, the contradiction between the actors who do not feel the emotions they are portraying and the audience who do, at least, imaginatively. And lastly the contradiction between the actors as professionals who have to portray imaginary feelings and the actors as men and women who have real feelings of their own. We are all actors; we frequently have with others to hide our real feelings and, alone with ourselves, we are constantly the victims of self-deception. We can never be certain that we know what is going on in the hearts of others, though we usually overestimate our knowledge—both the shock of discovering an infidelity and the tortures of jealousy are due to this. On the other hand, we are too certain that nobody else sees the real us.

In the Prologue Tonio, speaking on behalf of Leoncavallo and then of the cast, reminds the audience that the artist and the actor are men. When we reach the play within the play all the contradictions are going simultaneously. Nedda is half-actress, half-woman, for she is expressing her real feelings in an imaginary situation; she is in love but not with Beppe who is playing Harlequin. Beppe is pure actor; as a man he is not in love with anybody. Tonio and Canio are themselves, for their real feelings and the situation correspond, to the greater amusement of the audience for it makes them *act* so convincingly. Finally there is Nedda's lover Silvio, the member of the audience who has got into the act, though as yet invisibly. When Nedda as Columbine recites to Harlequin the line written for her "*A stanotte e per sempre sarò tua!*" ("Till tonight, then! And forever I'll be yours!"), Canio as Pagliaccio is tortured because he has heard her use as herself these identical words to the lover he has not seen. One has only to imagine what the opera would be like if, with the same situation between the characters, the *Commedia* were omitted, to see how much the interest of the opera depends on the question of Illusion and Reality, a problem which is supposed only to concern *idealists*.

About the music of these two operas, I can, of course, only speak as a layman. The first thing that strikes me on hearing them is the extraordinary strength and vitality of the Italian operatic tradition. Since 1800 Italian opera had already produced four fertile geniuses, Bellini, Rossini, Donizetti and Verdi, yet there was still enough left to allow, not only the lesser but still formidable figure of Puccini, but also the talents of Ponchielli, Giordano, Mascagni and Leoncavallo to create original and successful works. Today, indeed—it may have seemed different in the nineties—we are more conscious in the works of these later composers of the continuity of the tradition than of any revolutionary novelty. We do not emerge from the house, after hearing *Cavalleria* or *Pagliacci* for the first time, saying to ourselves, "What a strange new kind of opera! How shall I classify it? I've got it. *Verismo*." No, before the first ten bars are over, we are thinking: "Ah, another Italian opera. How jolly!"

Comparing one with the other (a rather silly but inevitable habit), Leoncavallo strikes me as much more technically adroit. One of the strange things about Mascagni is the almost old-fashioned simplicity of his musical means; he writes as if he were scarcely aware of even the middle Verdi. There are dull passages in *Cavalleria Rusticana*; the music of the mule-driving song and the drinking song seems to me pretty *imaginary*. Yet, in the dramatic passages, the very primitive awkwardness of the music seems to *go with* the characters and give them a conviction which Leoncavallo fails to give to his down-at-heel actors. For instance, when I listen to Turiddu rejecting Santuzza in the duet, "*No, no! Turiddu, rimani*" ("No, no! Turiddu! Remain"), I can believe that I am listening to a village Don Giovanni, but when I listen to Silvio making love to Nedda in the duet, "*Decidi, il mio destin*" ("Tell me my fate, I pray"), I know that I am listening to a baritone. As a listener, then, I prefer Mascagni; if I were a singer, I dare say my preference would be reversed.

In making their way round the world, *Cav & Pag* have had two great advantages: they are relatively cheap to produce and the vocal writing is effective but does not make excessive demands so that they are enjoyable even when performed by provincial touring companies, whereas works like *La Gioconda* or *Fedora* are intolerable without great stars. Take, for example, the famous aria "*Vesti la giubba*": if the singer is in good voice, he has a fine opportunity to put it through its paces; if his voice is going, he can always throw away the notes and just bellow, a procedure which some audiences seem to prefer.

The idea of *verismo* may have meant a lot to Mascagni and Leoncavallo; I don't know. All the various artistic battle cries, Classicism, Romanticism, Naturalism, Surrealism, The-language-really-used-by-men, The-music-of-the-future, etc., are of interest to art historians because of the practical help which, however absurd they may seem as theories, they have been to artists in discovering how to create the kind of works which were proper to their powers. As listeners, readers and spectators, we should take them all with a strong dose of salt, remembering that a work of art is not *about* this or that kind of life; it *has* life, drawn, certainly, from human experience but transmuted, as a tree transmutes water and sunlight into treehood, into its own unique being. Every encounter with a work of art is a personal encounter; what it *says* is not information but a revelation of itself which is simultaneously a revelation of ourselves. We may dislike any particular work we encounter or prefer another to it but, to the degree that our dislike or our preference is genuine, we admit its genuineness as a work of art. The only real negative judgment—it may be we, not the work, that are at fault—is indifference. As Rossini put it: "All kinds of music are good except the boring kind."

HOW I WROTE *PAGLIACCI*

Ruggiero Leoncavallo

Leoncavallo was *very* fond of being interviewed. The sketch was written in 1902 for the *North American Review*.

"I had taken my plot from an event that really took place."

I was born at Naples in March, 1858, my parents being the late Cavaliere Vincenzo Leoncavallo, President of the High Court of Justice, and Virginie d'Aurion, daughter of a celebrated Neapolitan painter, many of whose works are now in the Royal Palace at Naples. I studied first at Naples, where I entered the Conservatoire as a day scholar at the age of eight, and received my diploma when sixteen; my professors of composition were Serrao and de Piamcesi: a cantata was the work I wrote on leaving the Conservatoire. Afterward, I went to Bologna to complete my literary studies at the University, under the direction of the great Italian poet, Carducci; and I received my diploma as doctor of letters at the age of twenty. I was not obliged to do any military service, as, at the time of conscription, my brother was in the army. So I began my peregrinations as a concert pianist in Egypt, where at that time I had an uncle, Leoncavallo Bey, who was Director of the Press at the Foreign Office.

There I played at Court, and Mahmoud Hamdy, the brother of the Viceroy Tewfik, appointed me as his private musician. I was driven out of Egypt by the war with the English, Mahmoud having sided with Arabi Pasha, who had promised officially to give me the appointment of head of the Egyptian military bands, with a liberal salary. Instead of this fine promise being fulfilled, I was fortunate in saving my life after Tel-el-Kebir, by means of a twenty-four hours' ride in Arab costume to Ismaïlia. There I resumed European dress, but being penniless, I was obliged to give a concert at Port Said in the house of M. Desavary, representative of M. de Lesseps. The proceeds

From the *North American Review*, 1908.

of this concert amounted to five or six hundred francs, with which I was enabled to take an English boat, the *Propitious*. I recalled this episode to Her Most Gracious Majesty, Queen Victoria, when I had the honor and happiness of seeing her, a few years ago, at Nice. Arrived at Marseilles, I immediately took a train (not *de luxe!* nor, alas, express!) which brought me to Paris, where, in the depths of want, I was forced to begin my career as an accompanist in café concerts. I shall always remember one evening when I was engaged by a large wine merchant at Creil for eight francs, plus the amount of the fare there and back, and supper. When I was introduced into the concert room (!), to my surprise I found no piano, but a small harmonium, and the *artistes* who sang had no music, but only those small leaflets that are sold for a sou in the streets, giving the melody only without accompaniment; this did not prevent the *artistes*, however, from asking, before they began: "A *tone and a half lower, please, Maître!*" It seems that I did marvels in the way of accompaniment, for the next day all the small agencies of the suburban café concerts were asking for *the little Italian who was so clever*, according to the recommendation of the *artistes* whom I had accompanied. Little by little, my reputation reached the *Eldorado*, when the then director, M. Renard, asked me to write some songs for his "stars." These songs were successful, and were paid for by Père Bathlot at the princely rate of twenty or thirty francs apiece, without counting my royalties, which used to rise to the giddy height of seventy to eighty centimes an evening.

Later on I quitted the sphere of café concerts, and got singing pupils among the *artistes*, whose repertoire I used to work up for them. It was at this period that I had the pleasure of making the acquaintance of M. Maurel and the Maestro Massenet, who from the first treated me with great kindness.

Having met with many kind people at Paris who did their best to help me and assist me toward the attainment of a higher position, I succeeded at last in making a good living. About that time I wrote a symphonic poem on de Musset's "*Nuit de Mai,*" which is still unknown, although it was on the point of being performed by Colonne, who had promised to introduce it. When one day in conversation with M. Maurel on the subject of my hopes for the future, I read him the poem of the "*Medicis*," which I had just completed; this great artist was so struck by the magnitude of my self-imposed task and the quality of the poem, that he advised me, as an Italian, to go to Milan, where he was to take part in the first rehearsal of *Otello*, promising me an introduction and recommendation to M. Ricordi.

Relying on this promise, I pawned the furniture of my little flat and went to Milan, where M. Maurel kept his word, and presented me and recommended me to M. Ricordi, who finally gave me a commission to write the music for the libretto of the "*Medicis*," which I had read to him, for the sum of 2,400 francs, payable in sums of 200 francs a month, thus obliging me to finish my opera in the course of a year. But, alas, although the opera was ready at the end of the year, M. Ricordi was by no means ready to produce it! And I waited thus in vain for three years, during which I recommenced at Milan the melancholy task of teaching, which I had hoped I might never have to resume!

After the success of *Cavalleria*, by Mascagni, I lost all patience, and I shut myself up in sheer desperation, resolved to make a last struggle. In five months I wrote the words and the music of *Pagliacci*, which was acquired by M. Sonzogno, after he had only read the libretto, and which Maurel admired so much that he insisted on producing it at Milan on May 17, 1892. The success of this piece, as is known, was as striking as that of *Cavalleria*, and its fame spread like wildfire. When this work was translated, M. Mendès, seeing that it bore some resemblance to his *Femme de Tabarins*, honestly believed that I had borrowed the subject of my work from him, and he even took steps toward bringing an action, which he frankly withdrew, with a letter published in the *Figaro*, after having found that there were other *Tabarins* written before his own. The truth is that I was then completely ignorant of the work of this writer, whom I admire so much, and I had taken my plot from an event that really took place in Calabria and was brought before my father when he was holding the Court of Justice at Cosenza. And what is stranger still, as I have since learned, the protagonist of my work is still living, and having been released from prison, is now in the service of Baroness Sprovieri in Calabria. If the action had come to trial, he would have been willing to come and give evidence in my favor. I regret that this did not happen, as we should have had a very dramatic scene during the evidence of poor Alessandro (the real name of my Canio) when he was relating his crime, his jealous fury and his sufferings!

DEATH OF A LIBRETTO

Henry W. Simon

Concerning the demotion of a plot and the transplantation of its characters.

"The censors were able to make hash of the details of the story."

It is customary—and superficially reasonable—when explaining some of the palpable absurdities of the libretto of *Un Ballo in Maschera* to blame the Italian censors who demanded changes. They read an adaptation of a competent, hitherto successful and unexceptionable historical melodrama by Scribe; they became frightened; they demanded extensive changes; they compromised; and the result was the patchwork that we have today. Instead of a Swedish monarch who really was murdered at a masked ball, we have a fictitious and impossible British aristocrat, usually costumed as a Puritan, acting as the colonial governor of a Boston that never was on sea or land. Lord Riccardo Warwick is surrounded by a European court with all its trappings. In addition, he has a mulatto secretary who lives in a handsome house complete with beautiful, aristocratic wife, servants, and painted portrait of his friend; he plays good-natured kingly practical jokes in the company of his adoring subjects, who hail him as a sort of benevolent despot whenever they have the chance; and he is murdered at a masked ball by a couple of aristocratic guests known only by the simple but unaristocratic names of Sam and Tom.

The changes are, of course, deplorable. But that some changes should have been demanded may not appear to be so completely unreasonable as one is led to believe through reading only biographies of Verdi and commentaries on his operas. Censors have always been sensitive to the political dynamite inherent in popular art—particularly if it happens to be good art as well as popular. At the time of the Essex rebellion, in the reign of the first Elizabeth, Shakespeare's company of players got into trouble for a performance of

By permission of Radio Corporation of America.

Richard II, wherein the monarch is murdered. One can come closer with the story of the difficulties encountered by Da Ponte, Mozart's librettist, in securing permission for the production of *Le Nozze di Figaro*. One can come still closer to Verdi's own day with the now almost forgotten but then still familiar story of the political violence inspired by a performance of Auber's *Masaniello* in Brussels on August 25, 1830. The Dutch were driven out of Belgium on that occasion.

It was in 1859 that *Un Ballo in Maschera* was scheduled to be produced at Naples; and in 1859 thrones, national boundaries, and political ideas were extremely insecure. A serious attempt at assassinating Napoleon III had recently been made, and a movement was afoot to create a united Italy. Naples was still an independent principality; and if the movement were to succeed, King Ferdinand II of Naples (and presumably his censors) would lose their jobs if not their heads. Not too many months had gone by since an infuriated soldier had attempted to take the life of the unpopular Ferdinand himself—or "King Bomba," as he was contemptuously called. In fact, at the very time when Verdi was waging his presumably private war with the Neapolitan censors about his libretto, crowds gathered outside his hotel to raise, for the first time, a political cry that later became familiar throughout Italy. Verdi was known to be heart and soul in favor of the nationalist movement, and the cry was *"Viva Verdi!"*—V-E-R-D-I being, in wall inscriptions, written as an acrostic for *Vittoria Emmanuele, Re d'Italia*. Add to this the fact that Napoleon III was an opponent of Italian nationalism, and Felice Orsini, his would-be assassin, was an Italian, and it is not hard to see why the censors might have some fears. True, the prolific and now all but forgotten Mercadante had already set Scribe's original text without inciting riots, and so had Auber, whose capacity for igniting political violence through operatics had already been demonstrated. But these productions dated back to the thirties of the century, when Italy was not seated on a powder keg, and Auber's very successful work never was produced south of the Alps.

Even Verdi, a notoriously fair-minded and decent man, was ready to see that some change might be reasonable. He was irked, but he thought it would be a fairly uncomplicated matter. He changed Scribe's title from *Gustave III* to *Una Vendetta in Domino* and reduced the rank of his hero from King of Sweden to Duke of Pomerania.

But it wasn't so simple as all that. When the censors finally saw the completed libretto (only a prose summary had been submitted in the first place), they "suggested" the following:

1. Change the scene from eighteenth-century Sweden or Pomerania to fourteenth-century Florence.
2. Make it a story of the fight between the Guelphs and the Ghibellenes.
3. Change the name to *Adelia degli Adimari.* (Verdi was especially outraged by this: he thought the title meaningless.)
4. Make the soprano the baritone's sister instead of his wife.
5. Omit the dance.
6. Have the murder take place off stage.
7. Omit the gallows.
8. Omit the drawing of the lots.
9. Change practically every name. (One of the suggested changes here was especially odd: the pageboy Oscar was to be called by the name of Napoleon III's would-be assassin, Orsini.)

In addition, by Verdi's own count, 207 of his librettist Antonio Somma's 884 verses were to be stricken out or altered.

With the best intentions in the world, it is impossible to imagine today just what prompted some of these suggestions. Nevertheless, Verdi did his best—within his demanding artistic conscience—to comply. He compromised by calling the opera by its present title, which was Scribe's original subtitle. He sent letters to Somma, discussing details; and in one of these letters he even said that the libretto "in my opinion, has lost but little; as a matter of fact, I think it has gained at some point." The letters—like all of those from Verdi to his librettists—are masterpieces of tact and replete with practical, constructive criticism. One sample here will have to suffice us:

You have let some words slip in which the public may find in bad taste and disapprove . . . *Un pugnale t'aspetta* [A dagger awaits you] is worse than *l'assassinio* [the assassination]. The Censor will not allow it. So find a phrase, a circumlocution, which means the same thing, such as—*da mano amico uciso sarai* [You will be slain by the hand of a friend].[1] . . . Further on, the stanza *Dunque l'onta* [Then the shame] etc., seems to me weak for the situation. The rhyme *lui . . . nui* is too hard for music. . . . From now on, I think everything will go smoothly.

[1] As Verdi must have known, his suggested line did not fit the music he had already composed. Somma took his suggestion, nevertheless, and made it fit the notes precisely, thus: *"per man d'un amico"* ("by the hand of a friend").

There is no use in following all the details of the quarrel with the censors. Their ideas were so far apart from Verdi's that no solution seemed possible to the composer. He decided to withdraw the work entirely—a serious matter for the management, for Verdi's popularity was enormous and the première of a new opera by him was a great event. Every pressure was brought on him to make him change his mind. On the one hand, the Count of Syracuse suggested a meeting with King Ferdinand with a view to getting some royal pressure put on the censors. On the other hand, Verdi was seriously threatened with prison and a huge fine. The latter course would never have done: to punish an opera composer so well beloved as Verdi might itself have brought on trouble from the people. He was therefore finally allowed to depart in peace with the proviso that he should return to Naples and supervise a production of *Simone Boccanegra*. He did this soon after.

Meantime, La Scala, at Milan, made moves to get the première of the new opera. Verdi, however, preferred to have the first performance in Rome, which had already seen Scribe's original play without exciting either the populace or the censors. But Rome also felt jittery. It was by compromise with the Eternal City's minions that Boston, Massachusetts, was finally decided on for the locale. Verdi did not argue much this time. He was tired. He had, at this point, composed and supervised the productions of nineteen operas in sixteen years. As he put it, "Since *Nabucco* I have had not one hour of repose. Sixteen years' hard labor!"

At Verdi's request, Somma went to Rome to help make the changes demanded by this second set of censors. Apparently his heart was not in it; for, despite the composer's evident dismay, Somma did not let his own name appear on the printed libretto or score: it was only after his death that he received the doubtful honor. This refusal of Somma's can only be attributed to his judgment of the caliber of the work as it finally appeared. Certainly it was not the result of any displeasure over his relationship with Verdi; for he continued to work on a libretto of *King Lear* (which the composer called "magnificent," which he did a certain amount of work on, and which he finally laid aside with great regret), and he continued to suggest other subjects for collaboration, such as *Ivan the Terrible*. But *Un Ballo in Maschera* remains the only published work of Verdi's which today bears the name of Antonio Somma as librettist.

Verdi himself arrived in Rome only one month before the première, which occurred on February 17, 1859, at the Teatro Apollo. He was not pleased with either the libretto or the cast; and the critics and public were not pleased with the work as a whole. Failing to make the expected profits, Vincenzo Jacovacci, the Apollo's penny-pinching impresario, wrote to Verdi suggesting that the publisher, Ricordi, might agree to reduce the rental fees for the score. Verdi, who had mistrusted Jacovacci from the beginning, flatly refused to have anything to do with the suggestion. His letter, however, was far from flat. He called the cast "that awful company of singers you palmed off on me." "Cross your heart," he went on, "and admit that I was a model of self-abnegation for not taking the score and just clearing out in search of dogs who wouldn't have bellowed so much as those singers." And then the letter continues, sarcastically, to suggest that if Jacovacci wants to produce operas without paying publishers or composers, he should mount Paisiello's *Nina Pazza*, Gluck's *Armide* and Lully's *Alceste*—all in the public domain and royalty-free. Furthermore, they are beautiful music and will get nothing but praise "if only because people cannot say nasty things about those who have not yet done them the little favor of dying."

Despite its initial failure, **Un Ballo** has been performed—and continues to be performed—all over Italy; and it has made its way into every opera house of any importance on both sides of the Atlantic, as well as in Australia. It has been produced in Rumanian, Bulgarian, Lithuanian, Estonian, Lettish, Slovenian, and Croatian besides the more conventional tongues. It reached New York (in German) two years after its première, and a few months later two London theaters (Her Majesty's and Covent Garden) raced to see who could produce it first. Her Majesty's won by seven days. At the Metropolitan Opera House, where it was first given, in German, in 1889, it has been revived a number of times—in 1903 (for one performance only), in 1905 (for two performances), in 1913, in 1940, and in 1954–55.

Yet, in the eighty years of Metropolitan history, **Un Ballo** has achieved barely two dozen performances. Great singers have been given it—quite different from Verdi's original "dogs." Caruso, Scotti, Plançon, E. de Reszke, Eames, Destinn, Hempel, Matzenauer, Homer, Peerce, Milanov, Warren—almost every great singer of the Italian wing has sung one role or another but never with enough acclaim to keep audiences coming for more than a season or two. Compared with Verdi's great hits—*La Traviata, Rigoletto, Aïda*—the numbers are pitiful. And a similar account might be given with all the Western world's great opera houses. The opera is slightly more popular than *Simone Boccanegra*, slightly less than *La Forza del Destino*, its proximate neighbors in the Verdi canon. But compared with some of their earlier and later neighbors, they are all three rarities—and one may guess that the trouble is the classical one of which all composers who did not write their own books have at one time or another complained—libretto trouble.

One may guess, further, that *Un Ballo*'s libretto trouble stems from the work of the censors. Auber's setting, first performed in 1833, was highly successful. Indeed, when Verdi's was first put on in London, over a quarter of a century later, odious comparisons were made. That knowledgeable, workmanlike, but often mistaken anti-Verdian, Henry Chorley, wrote later in his *Reminiscences*: "I was never fully aware of the value of Auber's music till I heard the assault made by Signor Verdi on the same subject."

That the setting is the principal weakness of the libretto has been guessed by various impresarios, and they have done something about it. As early as 1861, the Paris production at the Théâtre Italien placed the story, ironically perhaps, in the Kingdom of Naples. (In this version, which is still used sometimes on the Continent, Riccardo becomes the Duke of Olivaies, Governor of Naples. And—so that everyone may be properly confused—the Italians call Oscar *Oscar* when they use the Neapolitan setting but *Edgar* when they use the Boston. And Amelia becomes *Adelia* in Boston but remains *Amelia* in Naples.) The great Mario had the leading role. No success; and when the Lyrique got around to mounting it, eight years later, the plot was shipped back again to Boston. Not till 1935, in Copenhagen, did anyone show enough imagination to try to lay the scene where it was originally intended to be—in Sweden. The Metropolitan borrowed the idea from the Danes and tried the same thing in New York in 1940. It made visually a most handsome opening-night opera, with gorgeous blue Swedish court costumes and a magnificently spacious witch's hovel. The cast, too, which included Jussi Bjoerling, Zinka Milanov, and Alexander Sved (in his debut), was highly and deservedly praised by the newspapers. But a change of air and costumes turned out to be not enough. When we recall that almost all the names of the characters had been changed as well as nearly a quarter of the original verses, it is not hard to see why. The original villains of the piece, for example, were Count Horn and Count Wart-ung. By the time the Roman censors had got through with them, they were Samuele and Tommaso, two very low-grade characters. In the original they made an attempt on King Gustave's life in the second scene; in the Roman version, they are present in the witch's den for no conceivable reason. Samuele and Tommaso they remained at the Metropolitan and they showed up at the witch's den only because their voices are needed in the ensemble numbers. Giving them pretty clothes to wear, then, made matters perhaps worse than better. Ulrica, "an Indian of low pedigree" in the Italian libretto, had a slightly darkened make-up; King Gustave remained Riccardo of Warwick. In other respects, there might have been some improvement. For instance, the delightful foppish pageboy Oscar (the only name, incidentally, retained from Scribe's original) did appear to be more appropriately deposited in the middle of an eighteenth-century European court than in a colonial governor's mansion. But at best, in many ways, the change was still a painful compromise. The censors had done their work too thoroughly.

For such reasons, a radio or phonograph performance of *Un Ballo in Maschera* suffers less and gains more than most operas when sub-stituted for a stage performance. The musical projection of the general dramatic themes—love vs. duty, loss of friendship, secret ambition, thwarted ardor, etc.—gains from being disembodied and divorced from the ludicrously compromised visualization. Take merely one ex-ample—the most famous aria in the opera, *"Eri tu."* Whether the baritone is dressed as an eighteenth-century English Puritan or as an eighteenth-century Swedish aristocrat, his name—Renato—is equally preposterous. (Scribe—and Somma originally—had called him Ankar-ström.) But everyone knows that as Verdi projected him, he is just one thing—an Italian baritone pouring out his heart. He believes that his wife has been faithless to him with his leader and closest friend. He has told her she must die, and has consented to give her time only for a last brief interview with their little son. All this we learn equally well from a disembodied version. And when she has gone, he addresses the portrait of his friend, swearing vengeance. The bold, marked rhythm of the orchestra as it repeats the tonic chord of D minor, prepares with the brasses the entry of the assertive bari-tone on the dominant note. Then, later, the woodwinds sing in thirds, as the baritone reflects on all he is losing. It is better not to watch our staunch Puritan standing around miserably awaiting his cue. It is far better to hear him join mellifluously with the woodwinds in one of the finest melodies ever written for an opera singer.

The student of the development of Verdi as a composer has also a great deal to learn from careful listening to the opera. The very first pages—the *Preludio*—strike a new note. For the first time, Verdi takes a theme from his opera (the theme always associated with the conspirators) and develops it contrapuntally, in a sort of fugato. He also takes (as he had done in the Prelude to *La Traviata*) a love theme; but this time he contrasts the two in striking juxtaposition. In a later opera, *Aïda*, he was to do even better, developing the tender Aïda theme in a really magnificent fashion juxtaposed to the ominous theme of the high priests. But nothing like what he accomplished in the Prelude to *Un Ballo* had he ever done before.

He also develops, in this opera, a new side of his musico-dramatic emotional armory. In *Rigoletto* and *La Traviata* there had been scenes of some gaiety; in the early *Un Giorno di Regno* he had even tried—with marked lack of success—to compose a two-act comedy. But in *Un Ballo* we get, for the first time, the portrait of a gay and charming character in gay and charming music—Oscar, whom some critics, in what appears to me to be exaggerated enthusiasm, have put into the rarefied company of Cherubino. Good as the latter or not, it is still a highly successful picture; and even those silly conspirators, Sam and Tom, afford, in Verdi's musical portraiture of them, a kind of light, evil ironic vein. Verdi developed this side of his art even more in his next opera, *La Forza del Destino*; and in *Falstaff*, of course, it found its full flowering.

But the finest touch of this new light artillery lies in the second-scene quintet, where Riccardo tries to laugh off Ulrica's dire prediction. In the throat of a fine tenor the principal melody becomes the nearest thing to a really melodic chuckle any composer ever wrote. Nevertheless, the serious overtones of the dramatic situation are equally well brought out in the ensemble. It is, in fact, just as much the great ensemble numbers that distinguish *Un Ballo* as anything else; and the different emotions that Verdi was always able to project simultaneously in such writing are overwhelmingly eloquent here.

The censors were able to make hash of the details of the story. They could not (and let's give them credit: they could scarcely have wished to) dim any of the luster of Verdi's music.

IN DEFENSE OF PUCCINI

Mosco Carner

In spite of Puccini's great popularity, a defense still seems possible and, indeed, advisable. Only recently a serious and thoughtful writer called *Tosca* a "cheap piece."

"An individual musical personality."

There was a time, not so very long ago, when the subject of Puccini was taboo among the so-called serious musicians: to confess to a sneaking liking for his music was tantamount to cultivating a taste for the low and meretricious in art. Slush and sentimentality, librettos that conformed to the standards of the penny-dreadful and the cheap erotic novel, a shameless exploitation of hoary stage tricks: such and more was said in condemnation of Puccini's operas by the musical mandarins of a generation or so ago. Oddly enough, the strongest anti-Puccinian phalanx was to be found in the composer's own country where it was headed by the powerful Torrefranca, a critic who thought it worth while devoting a whole book to the subject, a book in which the unhappy composer was pilloried and pulled to bits in the most scientific fashion. What is the position today? The hostile pamphlets have wandered into limbo and the unfriendly cliques have disappeared. What has remained is Puccini's music, most of it as fresh and spontaneous today as it was when it first conquered the world.

Some of us may for temperamental reasons still dislike it. For there is no denying its predominantly sentimental character. It is certainly no food for the purist. And those brought up in the tradition of the "*Musikdrama*" and all it implies cannot help picking holes—and quite large ones at that—in the fabric of the Puccinian opera. But there is one great thing that cannot be overlooked: Puccini's operas are theater *par excellence*. An inborn dramatic instinct, a keen sense for the imponderables of the stage, an almost unfailing power to write music that fits the action as a glove fits the hand, and last, but by no means least, a rich vein of warm lyrical invention: this is, in a nutshell, the secret of Puccini's operatic art. Add to it big rewarding parts which for their perfect rendering call for that rare bird the singer-cum-actor, swift-moving scenes full of action, dramatic tension and suspense, and brilliant orchestral writing, and you have the explanation of the fact that out of the twelve operas Puccini wrote, at least half a dozen are among the mainstays of every big opera house. Of how many modern operas can the same be said? Strauss was the only one among Puccini's contemporaries who rivaled him in that respect. Of the works of his Italian contemporaries, the Catalinis, Cileas, Franchettis, Mascagnis, Leoncavallos, and Giordanos, none was able to hold our attention for very long, with the sole exception of the Veristic twins *Cavalleria* and *I Pagliacci* which, for all their merits, reach neither the craftsmanship nor the musical quality of *Tosca* and *Il Tabarro*.

Thus Puccini remains the only successor of any caliber of his great compatriot Verdi. Verdi was his starting-point and forever his operatic idol. True, Puccini neither had his great commanding personality nor was the "radius of dramatic action" of Puccini's operas as wide and full as that of Verdi's; but within his limitations, his power to move and to carry the spectator with him was equal to that of the composer of *La Traviata* and *Otello*. What earned him his "bad" reputation was his strong bent for the markedly erotic type of opera: the chief protagonist of ten of his operas is the woman. His was a special type of woman, the little creature of frail femininity whose whole *raison d'être*, as Puccini saw it, was love, without which she must perish. It is true that in this Puccini continued a line that had started in French opera with Gounod, Thomas, and Massenet. Yet it was the Italian who developed that operatic type to perfection by adding an at once realistic and more individual note. Even in his *Turandot*, in which Puccini succeeded in getting away from the little woman idea, a last vestige of his natural bent remained with the figure of Liù to whom, significantly enough, he gave the best and most moving music of the whole opera. (An even greater significance attaches to the fact that this character was the composer's, not Gozzi's, creation.) To have blamed him for this peculiar predilection was as stupid as it was beside the point. The theater is not a moral institution, and no matter what kind of subject is brought onto the stage, its sole criterion is its dramatic propriety and its artistic handling. In Puccini's case it was the subject, with a special type of woman as heroine and charged with a tense erotic atmosphere, that provided the spark for his musico-dramatic inspiration and that resulted in most successful works for the stage.

Yet there was more in Puccini than the successful musical raconteur of the amorous lives and love tragedies of Manon, Mimi, Cio-Cio-San, Tosca, Angelica, and Giorgetta. With two masterpieces, *Gianni Schicchi* and *Turandot*, he revealed new facets of his operatic genius. His excursion into Florentine comedy came as unexpectedly as that into Chinese fairy tales. (The parallel with the "new" Verdi of *Otello* and *Falstaff* is worth noting.) *Gianni Schicchi* was perhaps the more startling of the two as its light-handed and witty treatment and the champagne-like sparkle of its music seemed so far removed from the usual Puccinian domain of sentimental love stories with their full-blooded and passionate music. In *Turandot* he returned again to a partly tragic love story, but it moves no longer on the more or less commonplace erotic plane of his sentimental operas. What Puccini had in mind when he cast about for a new subject and lighted upon Gozzi's play was, in his own words, "to try new paths." These new paths led to a work in which the composer not only reached the consummation of his technical mastery but achieved something that had seemed to lie beyond his powers: a style of expression that was at once virile, heroic, and grandiose. With *Turandot* Puccini wrote a work that can be mentioned in a breath with Verdi's *Aïda* and *Otello*. True, it shows signs that the composer's melodic inspiration was no longer as fresh and spontaneous as it used to be; there are enough traces of laborious work. Yet in its rare combination of sustained passionate passages (Turandot and Calaf), of most moving lyricism (Liù) and of delightful comic relief (Ping, Pang, Pong), all tinged with beautiful exotic colors, it shows the hand of a master.

But Puccini was not only a master of his craft. He was more than that: he was an individual musical personality. And this despite the more or less eclectic nature of his technique. In his musico-dramatic treatment he takes a leaf or two out of both Wagner's and Verdi's scores. He adopts a pseudo-symphonic method by occasionally using leitmotivs and working them into a simple homophonic texture. His chief method of building up a musical scene is to construct a mosaic of small melodic units, a device which he uses so skillfully that it produces the effect of a constant and spontaneous flow, as in Liù's first aria and the concluding chorus of the first act of *Turandot*. In his harmony he keeps abreast of his time. He is as much at home in

Wagnerian chromaticism as he is in the color harmonies of the French Impressionists and the feasts of dissonance and polytonality of the last postwar period.[1] (See the opening of the first and second acts of *Turandot.*) Above all, he has a rare gift of absorbing all these heterogeneous elements and fusing them into a language entirely his own.

This applies particularly to his lyrical phrase. There is no mistaking its individuality. Passionate, ardent, spontaneous, and full of *morbidezza*, it is specially in the expression of mental pain, suffering, and emotional fatigue that Puccini's lyricism reaches its highest degree of poignancy and beauty. Here Puccini created a new type of operatic melody, the melody that in a forcible screwing-up of its line reaches the climax only with an effort, and then gradually drops down in exhaustion, as is most beautifully shown in the duet between Mimi and Rudolfo in the last act of *La Bohème,* in Cavaradossi's passionate outburst shortly before his execution and Liù's moving appeal to Turandot. Here Puccini is at his best, his purest, and his most individual.

[1] World War I.

BUTTERFLY'S FAILURE

George R. Marek

The editor of an anthology ought not to choose material from his own writings. My excuse for overstepping the bounds of modesty is merely that I know of no other detailed account of an event which remains a tantalizing operatic mystery.

"Grunts, growls, groans, laughter."

Butterfly was offered to La Scala—and promptly accepted. It was understood that La Scala, under the management of Giulio Gatti-Casazza, would give the opera the finest possible production. The scenery was designed in Paris by the famous stage designer Jusseaume. Giovanni Zenatello was Pinkerton, Giuseppe de Luca Sharpless, the conductor Campanini. And Cio-Cio-San was Rosina Storchio, a superb singer and a beautiful woman, small, delicate, intelligent, sensitive to direction, young, and suffused with artistic sincerity. All who worked with her remember her affectionately and speak of her with smiling admiration. She was one of Toscanini's favorite singers. In short, the cast, as Gatti-Casazza says in his *Memories of Opera*, was "ideal."

Puccini was confident. He had completed the music at a time when he had been an invalid and suffering pain. But of invalidism, he knew, there was no trace in the score. He had given his best. Confined to the wheelchair, he had refined the music in the crucible of concentration. He had worked over every passage, correcting and improving countless times, as the manuscript shows. He loved Cio-Cio-San, this child of a strange country, more than he had loved any of his previous heroines. "There is no comparison," he said, "between my love for Mimi, Musetta, Manon, and Tosca and that love which I have in my heart for her for whom I wrote music in the night. . . ." During the rehearsals at La Scala, over which Tito Ricordi presided, the

From *Puccini* by George R. Marek, by permission of Simon and Schuster, Inc.

stagehands, men not easily impressed, walked on tiptoe, often stopped their work altogether, and listened with tears in their eyes. After the dress rehearsal, the orchestra rose to its feet and congratulated the composer with the greatest sincerity. Yes, for once there was no doubt about it: this was going to be a success. Puccini always begged his family to stay away from his premières. This was the one and only time that he not only permitted them to come but actually invited his sisters to Milan. At the beginning of the performance, three of them, decorously clad in black, were to be seen ensconced in a box.

Expectation was enormous. Admission prices were raised. Twenty-five thousand lire were taken in at the box office, a record. On the day of the performance, Puccini sent Rosina Storchio a note:

February 17, 1904

DEAREST ROSINA:

My good wishes are not necessary. So true, so fine, so moving is your wonderful art that the public must succumb to it! I hope that through you I will gain my victory. Until tonight, then—with confidence and much affection.

The night came. The audience assembled. The curtain rose. The beginning of the opera, up to the entrance of Butterfly, was heard in silence. An ominous sign, for Italian audiences do not listen in silence when they like what they are hearing. Just before the entrance of Butterfly—Storchio was standing in the wings with Puccini, her hands cold as ice—a super came by mumbling, "What is the matter with the public?" Storchio broke out into a cold sweat. The assistant conductor pointed: it was her cue. She sang backstage the first phrase of Cio-Cio-San's, that enchanting phrase, "One more step and we have arrived." She was on the stage. Silence. No applause. She continued to sing. And suddenly there was a shout from the balcony, "That is *Bohème*." Immediately the cry was echoed by other voices: "*Bohème! Bohème!* We've heard that already. Give us something new!" Then all was quiet again. Quiet during the wedding ceremony. Quiet during the long love duet. At the climax of the duet a few handclaps; so sparse were they that in the darkness of the theater they sounded like an emphasis on silence. The curtain fell. Again a little applause—very little—mixed with hisses. There were three curtain calls, in two of which the reluctant Puccini, leaning on his cane, participated.

During the first intermission, no one came backstage, not a friend, not a journalist. An actor once told me that failure could always be recognized after the first act. If no one appeared to make a fuss over you, you were ready to look for another job. There were two hectic spots on Puccini's face as he walked up and down, smoking one cigarette after another, unmindful of the two firemen stationed backstage. Tito Ricordi was cold and composed. He went over to Storchio and said, "At the second act the reaction will set in. I swear to you that it will be a success."

The second act began. At one moment Storchio turned around quickly. A draft caught her kimono and it ballooned up. At that a hoarse voice in the audience shouted, "Butterfly is pregnant." Storchio began to weep. She finished "Un bel dì" in a voice thickened by tears. There was again scattered applause. But when she introduced the child to Sharpless, pandemonium broke loose. Grunts, growls, groans, laughter, ironic cries of "Bis!," obscene remarks, hisses hailed down on the performers. From then on hardly a note was heard in silence. The derogatory noises reached their climax during the Intermezzo. (We must remember that Butterfly in the original version was given in two acts, the Intermezzo connecting Scenes 1 and 2 of Act II.) Tito had had the unfortunate idea of reinforcing the effect of the music by producing from hidden parts of the auditorium itself the gentle chirping of birds. As the sky darkened and night fell, as Butterfly, Suzuki, and the child stood looking out over the landscape, these aviary twitterings were to be heard. A tasteless bit of realism, which gave a cue to the audience. They answered: they barked like dogs, burst into cock-a-doodle-doos of roosters, brayed like asses, and mooed like cows as if—Storchio said—dawn in Japan were taking place in Noah's Ark. Nothing after that failed to strike the audience as funny. The final scene, the preparation for the suicide and the suicide itself, was heard in comparative quiet, but when the curtain fell, Butterfly ended amidst laughter and derogatory shouts. There were no curtain calls, not a single one.

Long before the opera ended, the composer's son Tonio had come backstage. The boy hurled himself into the arms of Puccini, crying, "Oh, Father! Father!" Puccini hid in one of the dressing rooms, but the furor and the noise reached him there also. He heard "those whistles, those terrible whistles, which humiliate you, which slap you down, which tear your heart into pieces. . . . How is it possible that the public, even if the work be a mistake, can be so ferocious; how is it possible that it cannot pity, that it cannot consider that behind the scenery on that stage there stands an artist who has attempted to create something, a father who loves his work and who suffers to see it tortured, offended, abused? Good people, one by one, the spectators. But together, once out for evil, they are rabble."

Puccini slunk home. He had not far to go: his apartment in the Via Verdi was across the street from the Scala. Even these few steps were painful: he hid himself against the walls as if—he said—he had been a man who had committed a dirty crime. He could not understand. As he sat with Elvira, Tito, and Giulio through a sleepless night, he demanded to know how it could have happened that he, who thought himself loved, if not by all, certainly by many, could now be "one against the crowd, defenseless, at the mercy of a furious audience who turned into ridicule the opera born in the deepest recesses of my heart. . . . My whole life passed before me. There were some things beyond the ken of the public's judgment of one night. . . . And I determined that *Madama Butterfly*, however miserably it might have fallen when it took the first step, should not stop here at the Scala of Milan, but would continue its way in the world. . . . I thought of Bellini, remembering the enormous fiasco at the Scala [of *Norma*]; I thought of the cries which met Rossini at the first performance of *The Barber*; I thought of Wagner and the sounds of the hunting horns blown by the Parisian aristocrats who drowned his *Tannhäuser* in ridicule. . . ."

Then other friends came in and Puccini turned to them in a burst of unjust anger: "Have you too whistled at my opera? Did you too shout? Do as you like. I know what I have accomplished, even if the others do not. *Butterfly* is my best opera." After this he became calmer.

His humiliation was not over. Morning came and with it the cries of the newsboys. In his apartment he could not shut out the sounds of those headlines. Of all of them—"BUTTERFLY A FAILURE," "PUCCINI HISSED," "FIASCO AT THE SCALA," etc.—the one which hurt him most was "BUTTERFLY DIABETIC OPERA, RESULT OF AUTOMOBILE ACCIDENT."

There is no question but that the disgraceful scene in the theater had been organized. This was not spontaneous disapproval. It was a deliberate affront, engineered and staged. Ricordi's statements, made after the première, and other evidence leave no doubt on the matter. Ricordi said:

After this pandemonium, throughout which practically nothing could be heard, the public left the theater as pleased as Punch. And one had never before seen so many happy, or such joyously satisfied, faces—satisfied as if by a triumph in which all had shared. In the atrium of the theater the joy was at its height, and there were those who rubbed their hands, underlining the gesture with the solemn words, *Consummatum est, parce sepulto!* The performance given in the pit seems to have been as well organized as that on the stage, since it too began punctually with the beginning of the opera. This is a true account of the evening.[1]

Colombo, Sr., who was at the time working for Ricordi and later became the manager of the firm, told me that he had worked for weeks to make sure that the piano scores of *Butterfly* were available in the music stores of Milan on the day of the performance. They were displayed in all the shop windows. The day after, every one of these scores disappeared. This could not have been done, he said, except through concerted action on the part of a clique working together.

Who was this clique? Who were the people who set into motion one of the most spectacular scandals in operatic history? We shall never know precisely. We shall not be able to name the instigators, unless documents come to the surface. This is most unlikely, as intrigues of this kind are not documented. Knowing Italian operatic life, we can guess that the group consisted of rival composers and their adherents, the same group, probably, who had planned to threaten the first performance of *Tosca*. Not much love was lost between Puccini and his colleagues. He held himself apart. He did not fraternize with the crowd that visited the Galleria in Milan and frequented the salons. He was too outspoken in his opinion of contemporary Italian music. More important, he was now so ubiquitously popular that a check to his career seemed a necessary measure. Puccini himself said that "there were people there who for years had waited for the joy of laying me low—at whatever cost."

But even a well-organized faction could hardly have produced the result they did, if the nonprofessional audience at the Scala had genuinely enjoyed the opera. The audience did *not* enjoy it. Even spectators of good will could hardly have done so. After the first outcries of the troublemakers, the opera's spell was broken. Puccini said that *Butterfly* was "a work of suggestion. Once the suggestion was breached, the magic faded." But there was another reason. *But-*

[1] From *Letters of Giacomo Puccini.*

terfly was, in its original version, not nearly so stageworthy a work as it is now. Mosco Carner has made a special study of the original and the revised scores. The revisions, he says in *Of Men and Music*, at first glance do not seem to amount to much; "but on closer examination, most of them are found to be important and necessary." There were only two acts, making each act of a greater length than the Italian public was used to. "For once, Puccini's unfailing sense for the balance of acts failed completely; for not only was there a striking disproportion between the lengths of the first and second acts— the former lasting about fifty-five minutes, the latter about ninety minutes—but the second in itself was too long."

There is very little action of any kind in the first act of the opera except the wedding ceremony. And that wedding ceremony was presented in tiresome detail. Butterfly's relatives were introduced, Japanese refreshments were served, and Pinkerton commented on them. This was followed by an episode in which Butterfly's uncle, Yakusidé, got drunk. Puccini shortened the scene in the revision.

In the second act, the scene of Butterfly's make-up was too dragged out. Moreover, in the original version it was Kate Pinkerton who asked Butterfly for the child, at the very moment when Cio-Cio-San realizes that Pinkerton has betrayed her. This, says Carner, "was a piece of most sadistic cruelty and utter tastelessness withall." He concludes: "In comparing the two versions on paper, the difference may not seem very striking. But on the stage, with its subtle laws of weight, balance, timing, and 'spacing' of scenes, Puccini's revisions went a long way. They most probably saved the work from remaining a 'near miss.' " Giuseppe de Luca confirmed this opinion. He told me that in performance the difference between the two versions was considerable.

On the morning of the eighteenth, Puccini held a meeting at his apartment at which were present Tito and Giulio Ricordi, Illica and Giacosa—and Rosina Storchio. The following decisions were taken: (1) The opera was to be withdrawn immediately. The second performance, already announced, was to be canceled. (2) The composer's, the librettists', and Ricordi's share in the proceeds of the performance were to be restituted to the management of La Scala. This was a heroic gesture: the sum involved was twenty thousand lire. (3) Puccini was to withdraw the score from general circulation, canceling also a projected performance in Rome, and he was to revise it, dividing the opera into three acts. (4) The revisions completed, the opera was to be given in its new version not in Milan but in a smaller theater, as a tryout.

Under the circumstances, a calm, critical appraisal of the opera was impossible. Giovanni Pozza, of the *Corriere della Sera*, was the most sympathetic of the critics. He found much fault with the work, calling attention to "details which were too minute," and with the action, which was "uselessly repeated and prolix." But he also found much beauty in the music, and ended his article with, "The opera did not pass the test. All the same, I persist in believing that this work, abbreviated and lightened, will rise again. Scattered through it are too many beautiful pages, it is stamped with too much elegance and grace. Better to await, before pronouncing the final word, a judgment more calm and considered."

But Puccini's humiliation was even yet not complete. The fiasco was too good a subject for the newspapers to let go.

On the twentieth of February, *Il Secolo* carried an announcement concerning the withdrawal of the opera, "in spite of insistent protests by the management of the theater." (This was true: Gatti-Casazza liked the work and did not wish to withdraw it.) *Faust* was going to be substituted for the next performance. The article continued:

It is easily understood that *Butterfly* could not be given again after the crushing result which *La Perseveranza* has frankly called a fiasco. A second performance would have provoked a scandal which would have called for decided action on the part of the Milanese public, who do not relish being mocked. This opera is not one of those, like *The Barber of Seville*, which carry in them the seeds of resurrection. It reveals that Maestro Puccini was in a hurry. Importuned as he was to bring out the work this season, sick as he was, he did not find original inspiration and took recourse to melodies from his previous operas, and even helped himself to melodies of other composers. In his defense we must say that the libretto was artistically unfortunate. . . . The opera is dead.

But perhaps because meanness was applied with so heavy a hand, a sense of justice and fairness began to spring up among the public. Voices were raised to defend the work. As early as the nineteenth of February, an anonymous letter appeared in the *Corriere della Sera*. It read in part:

I am neither a critic nor a musician, but music may be enjoyed by anyone who possesses good, sensitive ears, and as to the theater, I understand it as anybody would who goes there frequently. This does not give me the right to voice my modest judgment about *Butterfly* publicly. But there is one matter on which I do consider myself competent, and that is manners. Permit me to say, therefore, that while last night a performance of an opera took place which may or may not have been worthy of applause, in the audience something took place which lacked all courtesy. This Giacomo Puccini was, a few hours before the curtain went up, the idol of the public. His melodies sound in all ears and are on all lips. . . . It sufficed that a new opera was given which did not please, to turn this favorite into more or less of a delinquent. A hunt of wild ferocity went on last night. Why? Did none of those people in the audience ever make a mistake? Are there no businessmen who mismanage an affair? Lawyers who lose a case? Engineers who miscalculate? And does a similar vindictive ire surge up at every error? A business deal, a lawsuit, a mathematical calculation are minor episodes. An opera is quite another matter, especially an opera by Puccini. . . . I witnessed disgusting scenes. There were people there who, at every attempt to applaud, wore an expression of atrocious suffering. So much so, that at a certain point I turned to a man who whimpered, roared, and sweated hatred from all pores, and said to him, "Puccini must have accomplished something if he made you that ferocious."

There are plenty of signs around prohibiting spitting on the floor. This is good for physical hygiene. Is nothing to be done for moral hygiene?

ONE OF THE PUBLIC

Puccini never forgot the seventeenth of February, 1904. For a long time it made him unsure of his own judgment. He no longer understood *Il Signor Pubblico*, he said. Particularly did he fear and distrust from now on the public of the Scala. Eventually the howl of the fiasco became dim, yet it never entirely ceased to sound in the dark background of his mind.

At the time, he was particularly friendly with two brothers, Ippolito and Camillo Bondi, music lovers both, who had been kind to him in his youth. The heirs of the Bondi family gave me the letters of Puccini written immediately after *Butterfly*:

[To Camillo]   MILAN, February 18, 1904

With a sad but strong heart I tell you that it was a lynching! Those cannibals didn't listen to one single note—what a terrible orgy of madmen drunk with hate! But my *Butterfly* remains as it is: the most felt and most expressive opera that I have conceived! I shall win in the end, you'll see— if it is given in a smaller theater, less permeated by hatred and passion. Here I have withdrawn the opera and refunded the money, in agreement with my collaborators; and I shall not give it in Rome if I can free myself of that contract, because I am sure that even there I would have trouble, as the atmosphere is not serene—and besides, I don't want to give it there! I shall give it in a smaller theater, in another city, where there is tranquillity. Enough—You'll see if I am right.

[To Camillo]   MILAN, February 22, 1904
I am still shocked by all that happened—not so much for what they did to my poor *Butterfly*, but for the poison that they spat at me as an artist and as a man! And I can't explain why all this was done to me, who live far away from all human contacts. They have printed all kinds of things! Now they say that I am going to rewrite the opera and that it will take me six months! Nothing of the kind! I am not rewriting anything, or, at least, very few details—I shall make a few cuts and divide the second act in two—something which I had already thought of doing during the rehearsals, but it was then too near the first performance. . . . That first performance was a Dantean Inferno, prepared in advance. . . .

[To Ippolito]   MILAN, February 22, 1904
The reaction of the public has begun here, and the fact that the opera was withdrawn after the first performance has made quite an impression. . . . I thank you from the bottom of my heart for your kind interest in me and my opera. Isn't it true that it is not the awful thing that every one (*I say every one*) of those cannibals said it was?

Puccini returned to Torre del Lago to make his corrections. Tito Ricordi, who had not lost faith in *Butterfly*, chose Brescia for the première of the revised version. This performance took place on the twenty-eighth of May, 1904, with Salomea Krucenisca as Butterfly (Storchio had gone to South America).

Brescia is near Milan. At any rate, the representatives of the Milan press could hardly have been prevented from coming to Brescia to find out what new excitement was in store. The performance, says Fraccaroli, seemed more like a first night at the Scala than a provincial opening. The curious and the sensation seekers were everywhere. Tension was high.

And yet how different were the results! At the very opening of the curtain, the scenery was applauded. The first small tenor aria was greeted with shouts of approval. The public insisted that it be repeated. Repeated it was, and Puccini had to bow on the stage. Thunders of applause at Butterfly's entrance. Once more Puccini had to show himself. During the love duet, the audience sat quiet. Here and there applause broke out but this was indignantly hushed—the spectators, provincial and cosmopolitan, wished to savor the music to the full. But at the climax, when Butterfly sang, "Sweet night, how many stars!" there came a clapping of hands so overwhelming that it covered voices and orchestra. The curtain fell, and then the audience really broke loose. Nothing would do but that the curtain had again to be raised and the entire love duet repeated! Friends, critics, composers—including Arrigo Boito—rushed backstage among a general hubbub of jubilation.

The excitement continued in the second act. Four numbers were encored: "*Un bel di,*" the reading of the letter, the flower duet, and the Intermezzo. Puccini had to appear ten times. Brescia did its best to compensate him for what had been done to him in Milan.

Not a soul went home at the end. They stood, they screamed, they waved, while over and over again Puccini bowed.

In the spring of that year, Toscanini took *Butterfly* to Buenos Aires. There, with Rosina Storchio in the part, it was as great a triumph as it had been in Brescia.

Never again did *Butterfly* fail. No other first performance proved short of a triumph. Within a few years it rivaled *Bohème* in popularity. Like *Bohème, Butterfly* evoked in operagoers a feeling of special tenderness, a smiling personal affection. Everybody wanted to pet and be good to the little geisha girl—everybody, that is, who liked Puccini's music.

But like a father who cannot forget that his child has been a sickly infant, however sturdy he proves to be when he grows up, Puccini continued to regard the opera with sentimental anxiety. Rosina Storchio gave Puccini a painting of herself in the role. He hung this above his desk in the Via Verdi apartment. He looked at it often, and quoted the line from the opera, "*Rinnegata e felice*"—"Renounced but happy."

FRENCH OPERA

FOR THE FAMILY TRADE

George R. Marek

The nation which contributed Voltaire to satire, Descartes to cool reason, Cézanne to painting, Racine to measured verse, and practically all there is to know to the knowledge of good food, has contributed relatively little to opera. Opera does not spring naturally from the Gallic soul, nor does it rest securely in the French heart. Why is it that so great a difference exists in the operatic climate in two neighboring countries, France and Italy, countries which in other arts and habits and ways of looking at life show many similarities? No completely satisfactory explanation can be brought forth—for mysteries and contradictions reside in nations as well as in individuals —but perhaps we can come near the mark by remembering the essential nature of the French mind—rational, logical, realistic, humorous, and quick to observe absurdities. In France to wear one's heart on one's sleeve is the habit of a simpleton. The obvious is suspect. In music, as well as in literature, the French ideal lies in subtlety, in the blended nuance, in twice-distilled refinement. At its worst this tendency produces salon pieces and Colette's novelettes, at its best Proust and Debussy. Such an environment is not the right one for the big climax and the strong situation which opera demands. Nor has the favorite French verse form, the Alexandrine, and the tradition of speaking and singing verse in a special way, with the final *e* pronounced, been helpful to dramatic singing. More important, the French are purists and like their arts unmixed. Early France achieved eminence in classical tragedy through Corneille and Racine. Early also the French ballet was developed, formal, frail, and elegant. People had little mind to mix tragedy and ballet into an art form which its detractors call "hybrid."

Whatever the reasons, French opera did not begin as an art of the people. French opera was not born as popular entertainment in the popular theaters of small and large towns. No traveling opera groups existed in France such as those which in Italy brought the works of

Rossini to any town of any size. French opera was conceived as court entertainment and was performed in charming theaters to which only the well-born were admitted, theaters as ornate as a pastry cook's creation. Later, much later, the court theater was companioned by the theater for the upper middle class, for the good bourgeois family trade, and in these theaters French opera did reach plain popularity, but all the same, the French attitude toward opera has never lost a certain "precious" quality.

Once we have conjectured, however, the historical reasons why France did not produce a Verdi or a Wagner, we must make room for the exceptions, important and valuable exceptions though few in number, and we must note the paradox that one opera, as stageworthy as any work of Puccini and as strong as all but the greatest works of Verdi, was a French work. That opera was, of course, *Carmen.*

Opera got started in France almost a century later than in Italy. Its first important composer was Jean Baptiste Lully, who, as a matter of fact, was an Italian born in Florence. He went to Paris at the age of fourteen and, after having protested that opera in French was impossible, changed his opinion or thought it profitable to change it, and produced a score of works which were performed successfully at the court of Louis XIV. To the modern ear Lully's music sounds less attractive than the music of Monteverdi, whose contemporary he was. Listen to *Armide* and you will hear music which is stately, formal, and often quite monotonous. Lully reflected the splendor of the age of the Sun King; his operas are replete with scenes which have little to do with the dramatic business at hand but are mere representational episodes intended to ravish the eye (and only incidentally the ear) of an exigent aristocracy. As in Italian opera of the seventeenth century, the preferred French subjects were classical and mythological. As much stage apparatus as possible was used. Gods and Furies, shepherds and shepherdesses, half the protagonists of the *Aeneid* appeared on the scene. Emphasis was placed on ballet, an emphasis which French opera was never to lose. Lully did make important contributions to the art. He strove to compose recitatives congenial to the fall and flow of the French language, and he gave importance to instrumental music as well as to chorus and ballet, accomplishments which contrasted with Italian opera, with its concentration on the individual singer.

After the death of Lully, a half-century elapsed before another genius came upon the scene. This was Rameau. By that time the severe formality of Louis XIV had given way to the arabesque grace of Louis XV, and consequently Rameau's operas introduced a lighter note, a new gaiety and charm. There are fewer battles and more shepherds. Rameau did not have his first serious opera produced until he was fifty-one. His style, formed on organ music, was a good deal more contrapuntal than that of his predecessor. The best music in his operas is to be found in the instrumental interludes, the overtures, the descriptive music which occurs during sunrises, thunderstorms, earthquakes (for example, the earthquake in *Les Indes Galantes*), and of course in dances.

Both Rameau and Lully possess merely historic interest today, though the Paris Opéra did recently revive *Les Indes Galantes*. They presented the opera with all the trappings of ballet and stage mechanism which were originally intended for it. The effects were elaborate and the performance was a great success in Paris. It is unlikely that this success could be repeated in any other opera house.

The greatest master of eighteenth-century French opera, the one whose music we hear with pleasure today, was not French at all, or rather he was French only in expediency. Christoph Willibald Gluck was born in Bohemia and found his early employment in Vienna. He produced a quantity of the kind of Italian operas then fashionable in Vienna. At Vienna also he met Metastasio, the obliging poet who furnished operatic librettos for half the composers of the time, including Gluck. Nothing in Gluck's early career presaged the power and originality which the composer was to summon later. But then he came under the spell of the new ideals which were flowing through the world, ideals which swept away the interlocking order of the baroque, the style which had for years sported in exuberant strength but had by now weakened into merely ornamental fussiness, a manner of which people had become tired and which skeptics such as Voltaire had ridiculed. Now, in a new renaissance, smaller and less vigorous but important nonetheless, artists sought for naturalness and simplicity. The foremost propounder of this demand was Jean-Jacques Rousseau. It was at this fortunate time that Gluck met a fine poet, Rangiero Calzabigi, who admired Shakespeare and wished to offer poetic dramas different in style from those of Metastasio. Gluck was inspired by the poet, as he himself has graciously acknowledged, and the first product of this new collaboration was the masterpiece *Orfeo ed Euridice*. Here indeed was something new, though by coincidence the subject was not only old but the very same subject which had served the first Italian opera. The libretto was new in that it stripped away all that was superfluous or merely showy. The austere story is now austerely told. Euridice has already died before the curtain rises, and the first scene consists of a lament by Orfeo, joined by the chorus. What is true of the libretto is true of the music. Here we find no unnecessary ornamentation, no coloratura arias, no stagey tricks. All is seemingly simple. But how beautiful it all is! How noble! And how fresh it must have seemed to contemporary audiences! The scene of the Furies, whose repeated cries soften before Orfeo's song and, being unable to resist the power of music, ebb away in a long sigh, that scene retains more dramatic power than the whole frantic song contest in *Tannhäuser* which is also meant to prove that music hath charms. Finally, the scene in the Elysian Fields, with its famous ballet and its exquisite air, *"Che puro ciel"* ("How pure the sky"), is the very distillation of serenity.

Orfeo was a success in Vienna, where it was first performed in 1762, as well as in Paris twelve years later, where it was given with a French libretto and the added ballet music without which no Parisian production was possible. His next important work, *Alceste*, was welcomed with equal fervor. When the score was published, it was furnished with a preface in which Gluck put into words his thoughts for the reform of opera. This has become a famous document, even though, or perhaps because, it contained few thoughts which had not been expressed by the operatic composer before this and no principle which was not generally recognized as valid. Gluck and his poet inveighed against the tyranny and caprices of the opera singers. They pointed out how weak were musical formulas applied to the text without regard to the meaning of the words. And they avowed that they had striven to restrict music to its true task of serving poetry, by expressing the situations of the story without interrupting the action or smothering it under superfluous ornaments. As has been pointed out many times, Gluck's manifesto foreshadowed the more elaborate theories of Wagner. In neither case did practice follow theory. Of neither composer's music could it be said that it merely served the poetry. Gluck is alive because of his music and not because of Calzabigi's words; Wagner is alive because of his music and often in spite of his poetry. At any rate, Gluck's declared loyalty to dramatic situation and textual meaning did serve to free opera from a style heavily artificial and excessively pretty. Gluck's ideas stood him in good stead when he had begun to feel that Vienna did not sufficiently appreciate his genius and that he needed a new field to conquer. He had suffered financial reverses and so he cast a glance toward the richest and most brilliant European capital, Paris. Marie Antoinette had formerly been a pupil of his and was still interested in him. Gluck's ideas blended with the stream of the new French thought and its demand for simplicity, clarity, and naturalness. So to Paris he went and began the composition of *Iphigénie en Aulide*. This work triumphed. It marked an advance even over Gluck's own *Orfeo* in the coherency and large line of the music.

With this work and the French version of *Orfeo* Gluck became a French composer, lionized by most of Paris, attacked on the other hand by a group led by the composer Piccini, who believed the Italian school to be superior. The quarrel between the Gluckists and the Piccinists became one of those *causes célèbres* in which the French delight. It helped Gluck's reputation.

Gluck's last important work, and one which has unaccountably been neglected, was *Iphigénie en Tauride*. An excellent text spurred Gluck on to his best effort, one from which later composers, including Berlioz and Wagner, drew inspiration. His music here has further grown in stature and intensity and his melodies, while still simple, have become richer, thus somewhat negating his own theory, a regular occurrence among theorists who happen at the same time to be geniuses.

French opera had to wait a long time before it profited by Gluck's greatness. Other countries, notably Austria and Germany, were quicker to take up his innovations. But Paris remained the capital of opera even after the Revolution. Classical subjects remained in vogue, and so it happened that another non-French composer, an Italian, Luigi Cherubini, became the most important voice of post-Revolutionary France. His *Médée* and *Les Deux Journées* were greatly admired by Beethoven, although Cherubini on his part did not in the least understand Beethoven. Cherubini's music resembles the huge canvases of David and Géricault. Like those paintings they take pleasure in sheer size, strive for a classicism which imagines itself noble when it is merely broadly posed, and are for the most part as cold as a government edifice. Cherubini means little to us today: he owes his present fame not to his music but to the remarkable portrait which Ingres painted of him (*Médée*, however, was given recently in Italy and in New York, with some success.)

He bequeathed the doctrine of grandness to Gasparo Spontini, who at the turn of the century came forward with his *La Vestale,* composed to an exciting libretto which combines a passionate love story with many spectacular crowd scenes and stage effects. *La Vestale* had its première in 1807, and a whole generation elapsed before French opera once more produced an important composer. Once more this man was not born a Frenchman; he was German by birth. Giacomo Meyerbeer—his hybrid name itself gives a clue to his style—began as a pupil of Weber to write German operas, soon achieved success in Italy with works in the Italian style, and, when he arrived in Paris in 1826, perceiving the opportunity which existed there, set himself to master the French style as it had been developed by Cherubini and Spontini, the one important French opera by Rossini, *Guillaume Tell,* and the one beautiful and thoroughly French opera—still occasionally performed—Halévy's *La Juive.*

Meyerbeer is a curious phenomenon. His almost total eclipse today marks an unjust reaction against his one-time towering popularity. This eclipse reflects not only certain grave defects in his music, the chief being an amount of bombast which we are no longer willing to condone, and the cold-blooded calculation of some of his effects, but also his denigration by Wagner, who began by attempting to out-Meyerbeer Meyerbeer in *Rienzi* but later used him as a theoretician's whipping boy, as the bad-boy example of everything which music drama ought not to allow, although the echoes of Meyerbeer's style can be clearly traced in *Lohengrin* and to a lesser degree in *Tannhäuser.*

It is possible that Meyerbeer could today enjoy a revival, were it not for two difficulties: First, the necessity of finding singers to do justice to his elaborate and surcharged music, music which takes over from the Italian *bel canto* the long line and ornate melody but adds to it an amount of dramatic propulsion and movement which Bellini would have found excessive. Singers singing Meyerbeer must be masters not only of lyric but of dramatic singing. Meyerbeer therefore served well the talents of Caruso, Plançon, Battistini, or Ponselle. But who can interpret him today? The second reason which militates against a Meyerbeer revival is the sheer expense of mounting his operas. His crowds are huge and his spectacular scenes require much apparatus and many stagehands. Moreover, his scores are overlong. And if we are to summarize all his faults, we may as well admit that a good deal of his music is vulgar. But now let us turn to his virtues. For there is no question that he had virtues, that he contributed

values to operatic music, helped to make grand opera grander, and influenced not only Wagner but Verdi. He lacked the heart of the
greatest of the Italians. Yet the *auto-da-fé* scene in Verdi's *Don
Carlos*, and better still the Triumphal Scene of *Aïda*, owe much to
Meyerbeer's grandiose conceptions.

But we do scant justice to Meyerbeer's importance if we only speak
of him in connection with others. Taking him for himself, and listening to the operas in an unhistorical mood, one hears much that is
thrilling and much that is fine. His three most famous works, *Les
Huguenots*, *Le Prophète*, and *L'Africaine*, contain passages of such
excellence that one regrets their disappearance. The last act of the
Huguenots, several parts of *Le Prophète*, including again the final act,
and the finale of Act II of *L'Africaine*—in all these Meyerbeer reached
the heights. That he occasionally could summon a lyrical and quiet
beauty is attested by the famous aria, "O Paradiso!" [1] from *L'Africaine*.

It is possible, as I have suggested, that Meyerbeer is due for a revival, particularly if somebody takes the trouble to cut the operas
reasonably and to stage them with *élan*. More probably a revival of
Meyerbeer may come through recordings if it is to come at all.
Through recordings it may be possible to present with present-day
singers a reasonable facsimile of the Meyerbeer color. He is, one must
repeat, not a French composer, though for good and bad he dominated
the French stage for decades. He is an international composer, producing opera without national characteristics. It is quite possible to
sing Meyerbeer in Italian; one cannot sing *Carmen* or *Louise* in Italian
without harming the music.

Along with this internationally minded grand opera, there grew up
in France a form of opera peculiarly French, French in charm and
softness, French in the refinement of the mixture of virtue and fault,
sadness and merriment, sweetness and scorn, superficiality and insight.
That is the *opéra comique*. The *opéra comique* is a lyric opera of
smaller proportions, not necessarily and indeed not primarily a comic
opera, but one which at first combined music with spoken dialogue.
It developed as a kind of antidote against the pomposities of the
grand form, and it stood between the grand opera and the operetta,
of which lighthearted and fluttering form the chief practitioners
were Daniel Auber, Ferdinand Herold, Adolphe Adams, and—most
successful, most melodious, and cleverest of all—Jacques Offenbach
who, after entertaining the Paris of the Second Empire with such

[1] I have used the Italian title, the aria being better known in that language.

ebullient works as *La Belle Hélène* and *La Grande Duchesse de Gérol-stein* and *Orphée aux Enfers* and *La Périchole*, rose to one grand opera, or almost grand, one combining elements of the tragic, the fantastic, and of the operetta, *Les Contes d'Hoffmann*. Here again we must observe that Offenbach, the most French of the French light composers, was born at Cologne, the son of a Jewish cantor. Paris was (and still is) a magnet for talent. So powerful is it as a mentor that the immigrant soon speaks idiomatic French.

It is then in the *opéra comique* that we find the truest expression of the French genius, its ability to delight us in a theater which makes no exorbitant claims on our mental capacities.

The two composers who achieved the greatest success before the Franco-Prussian War were Ambrose Thomas and Charles Gounod. Thomas's *Hamlet* we can dismiss, the subject being far above his ability as a composer. But his *Mignon* retains a certain amount of in-genuous effectiveness: for *"Connais tu le pays?"* and the Gavotte we are willing to condone the silliness of Philine and her *"Je suis Titania."*

What shall we say of *Faust*, which at one time was the most popu-lar opera in America as well as in France? As a treatment of the drama, it is not to be taken seriously. Nothing is left of Goethe's poem except a naïve love story. There lie more fantasy and power in ten pages of Berlioz's flawed *Damnation of Faust* than in the whole huge box of Gounod's confections. But if you can accept the reduction of the theme to an *opéra comique*—and obviously thousands of people can—you find that the bonbons in the elaborate red-wrapped box *are* sweet. Gounod had the talent to write a pretty tune, to make love melodiously, to pen a stirring chorus, and to furnish a soprano with an effective coloratura aria. That has proved to be enough for close to a hundred years of fame. As a matter of fact, we may give Gounod a little more. In the Garden Scene of *Faust* we feel, for once, a mood and an atmosphere. It is a scene, not a parade of tunes. A twilight suffuses the quartet and the duet; we hear music which, though by this time it may sound fairly undevilish and decorous, yet does sug-gest the passion of the lovers and the shadow passing across the pas-sion. There are such moments of genuine dramatic persuasion even in his other operas, in *Roméo et Juliette* and in *Mireille*.

It is difficult for us now to realize how important was Gounod's in-fluence, how seriously his music was considered, in what esteem this white-bearded prophet was held for many years, an esteem which made life arduous for any French composer who happened to write not quite so prettily. Gounod, not Berlioz, was the apostle of the new music. *Faust*, not *Les Troyens*, was the "modern" work.

But "modern" or not, the form suited French society, diverse groups of it, the gentlemen who wore the ribbon of the *Légion* and the monocle, descendants of the once formal court circle for which Lully labored and who were still interested in the *corps de ballet*, as well as the ladies with a *"de"* before their names who, wrapped in layers of ruffles and beclouded by perfume, sighed over the easy melodies. It suited the demimonde and the young men dancing attendance on them as much as it did the solid frugal citizens who wanted good entertainment for their francs. After 1870 almost every important new French opera saw the light not at the stately Opéra but at the less ornate and more modest Opéra Comique. Here then are to be found the historic premières, here French opera continues its course: Bizet's *Carmen* (1875), Delibes's *Lakmé* (1883), Massenet's *Manon* (1884), Charpentier's *Louise* (1900), and Debussy's *Pelléas et Mélisande* (1902).

The most indispensable of these, the work of greatest power, the drama which many have called "the perfect opera," is *Carmen*. Here at last we have an opera that is both truly French and not in the least local. In *Carmen* is combined Gallic directness with genuine passion and uncompromising malevolence. Here we find the courage which throws out of the window the mincing prettiness which mars so many products of the *opéra comique* style. Only once does the music stray into the soft ground of excessive sweetness. That is in the character of Micaela. She is a cousin of Marguerite, and a bore. Aside from this flaw, *Carmen* is a straight, strong music drama, its characters comprehensible and coherent. What counts is that *Carmen* is coherent *musically* as well as dramatically. Story and character are shaped and expressed by music; this is music which is searching, subtle, and beautiful without being recondite.

In short, *Carmen* is more than an opera of inspired melodies strung together on a stylish ribbon. The melodies are there, to be sure, and it is they which give the opera its primary popularity. It is from its musical construction, however—orchestral writing (which is superb!) as well as vocal line—that we derive the deep satisfaction which vouchsafes the work continuing life. *Carmen* is not likely to go out of fashion, as *Faust* will. In almost every scene the music captures the right mood, be it the exuberance of the first act with the fine differentiation between the soldiers, the chorus of the youngsters, and the bustle of the factory girls—a panorama neither Spanish nor French but above time or place; be it the somber scene in the third act in which Carmen seeks her fortune in the cards, a scene to be regarded as one of the best on the lyric stage; or be it the ultimate duet of Don José and Carmen, with its tones of pride and hurt, with its conclusion of foreordained destiny that knows no compromise.

Carmen at its first performance was neither a success nor a failure. The story that Bizet died of a broken heart shortly after the première of *Carmen* is one of those musical legends which have been carefully contradicted only to be told again as fact. True, the opera did not immediately score a triumph, but this was due less to any difficulties which the music might have presented than to the shocking seriousness of the story. Nonetheless, the respectable families and their daughters, gathered in the opera house to meet eligible young men, very soon accepted the strong dose. At that, they probably preferred *Lakmé, Manon,* and *Werther.*

After Bizet there again occurred a descent into prettiness. Two years later, Saint-Saëns's famous work came along. (However, it was premièred in Weimar, not in Paris.) *Samson et Dalila* is not much of an opera. It is more of a worldly oratorio with a few good choruses and a good tenor aria to give some relief to Delilah's seduction scene, which is the reason for the opera and which, to be sure, is quite seductive.

Massenet's operas are a great deal better. He was a man of the theater who knew how to create effects. His method is highly individual: he works in pastel colors which somehow or other manage to be strong enough to shimmer in the opera house. He is erotic without being impolite, and he is always easy to listen to. *Manon* is his masterpiece, and in *Manon* Massenet has given us, along with some dull stretches, scenes which almost persuade us that they are powerful, such as the St. Sulpice scene. *Thaïs* is marred by cloying sentimentality, but *Werther* is a fragrant work, containing some of Massenet's best music.

The lovable but faulty heroine who had become since Marguerite the favorite figure in the Paris theater is to be found in a work of great merit which came along just as the nineteenth century turned into the twentieth. Gustave Charpentier, pupil of Massenet, created in *Louise* his one and only important work. Now the heroine is simply and straightforwardly a Parisian working girl, and the story, written by Charpentier himself, introduces such everyday touches as the family supper of a Parisian working-class family, the reading of a news-paper, and the gossip in a dressmaker's shop. These are contrasted with and made larger by the symbol of the city itself; it is Paris, not one of the city's daughters, who is the real protagonist of the opera. The mood of the great city is admirably captured in the music. Mont-martre, the little streets, the unbelievable and eccentric figures which in Paris happen to be true, the very air of Paris, gay and sordid, are expressed in music which owes a little to Wagner and a little to Massenet but is nonetheless original. Within this atmosphere the drama achieves a fluid expression: the scene between Louise and her father in the first act is tender and touching, and the love music of Act III, which culminates in the beautiful aria, *"Depuis le jour,"* much too frequently taken out of context, can stand comparison with the best love scenes of Puccini. *Louise* also is likely to prove an en-during work, or would be if it were possible for each generation to find a Mary Garden to interpret the part.

Two years after *Louise*, there was performed at the Opéra Comique a work of such newness, one composed in so fresh a musical language, as to seem to have no connection with all that had gone before. That work was Debussy's *Pelléas et Mélisande*. It, like *Carmen*, marks one of the high points of the French genius. Nothing of Gounod or Thomas is left in this score, and neither does it owe anything to Wagner,[2] although the life of the opera pulses in the orchestra and the symphonic web is as fine-spun as it is in *Die Meistersinger*. It is music of allusion and understatement, of hints and ripples below the surface, of lights unseen except in reflection, of words unheard except in echoes. But though this music never shouts and though, as a matter of fact, there are but four loud passages in the entire score, this is not a small-scale composition. Too much has been made of Debussy as a "miniaturist," when as a matter of fact his picture is not small but a deep canvas on which the design is accomplished by brush strokes that suggest rather than spell out. As before one of the Venetian pic-tures of Monet one has to stand some distance away before the design appears, the whispers become audible and the colors begin to glow. A full and rich life it is, with the instruments of the orchestra treated as if they were protagonists, given almost equal prominence with Méli-sande and with Golaud, with the strings divided and the woodwinds each adding a separate voice. No, this opera is not small. It is so large that it was able to create and populate its own world, one never

[2] Except, perhaps, through purposeful contradiction!

recaptured or even imitated since. Intense and fascinating is this music, with its marvelously evocative interludes, its strange setting of the dank woods, the castle in which the sun shines palely, the fountains which drip limpid water, and the souls which cannot rise above their own weariness. But though *Pelléas* is so individual that it lies outside the pale of all we ordinarily think of when we think of "opera," it is yet French as Proust is French; even in this world the characteristics, the good characteristics, of the French genius can be found. Indeed, *Pelléas* carries to a new height the art of treating the French language musically.

With *Pelléas* we have arrived at the end of the history, though there remain some delightful works of smaller consequence, works such as *Ariane et Barbe-Bleue* by Dukas; the one-act comic opera by Ravel, *L'Heure Espagnole*; Henri Rabaud's Oriental opera, *Marouf*, and Honneger's *Jeanne au Bucher*, which have won a place in the international repertoire.

In summary, we may attempt to assay the virtues of French opera: One of its great contributions is the belief already held by Lully that an opera is first a play on the stage, that the music must heighten the play, and that therefore the musical idiom must fit the words. In French opera the connection is closer between text and music than it is in Italian opera; that is why it is well-nigh impossible to translate French opera successfully. One of the difficulties in performing French opera lies in the fact that to give it well—musically— one has to find singers who speak perfect French. It is possible for a singer to get away with indifferent Italian: not with indifferent French. This is another way of saying that French music has served to express the beauty of the French language.

A second characteristic is the amount of attention paid to spectacle and ballet. French audiences never lost their interest in the ballet, and even Italian operas, including those of Verdi, had to have a ballet when they were given in Paris, with the result that Verdi wrote some of his poorest music to satisfy Parisian performances. The center of interest in French opera lies often not in characters, not even in individual arias, but in the total effect of the spectacle, of which the ballet is an integral part. In short, French opera is an opera of ensemble.

The natural result of these two tendencies is the fact that by and large French librettos are good, and the French lyric stage avoids such gore-and-slaughter absurdities as beset *Il Trovatore*. On the other hand, the preoccupation of Gallic art with the pleasing, the urbane, the sweet, one might almost say the polite, has prevented French opera from rising to the heights. The elemental force which we find in Wagner, the setting to great melody of ubiquitous emotions which we find in Verdi, are absent in music which makes its appeal first by sensuousness. French opera is refined even when it is vulgar. In the valley it charms us; the mountaintop is not its natural dwelling.

GLUCK DECLARES HIS PRINCIPLES

These principles, so important to the development of French opera and later influential in shaping Wagner's theories, were stated in the dedication to Gluck's *Alceste* (1769).

"I do not wish to arrest an actor in the greatest heat of dialogue"

YOUR ROYAL HIGHNESS:

When I undertook to write the music for *Alceste*, I resolved to divest it entirely of all those abuses, introduced into it either by the mistaken vanity of singers or by the too great complaisance of composers, which have so long disfigured Italian opera and made of the most splendid and most beautiful of spectacles the most ridiculous and wearisome. I have striven to restrict music to its true office of serving poetry by means of expression and by following the situations of the story, without interrupting the action or stifling it with a useless superfluity of ornaments; and I believed that it should do this in the same way as telling colors affect a correct and well-ordered drawing, by a well-assorted contrast of light and shade, which serves to animate the figures without altering their contours. Thus I did not wish to arrest an actor in the greatest heat of dialogue in order to wait for a tiresome ritornello, nor to hold him up in the middle of a word on a vowel favorable to his voice, nor to make display of the agility of his fine voice in some long-drawn passage, nor to wait while the orchestra gives him time to recover his breath for a cadenza. I did not think it my duty to pass quickly over the second section of an aria of which the words are perhaps the most impassioned and important, in order to repeat regularly four times over those of the first part, and to finish the aria where its sense may perhaps not end for the convenience of the singer who wishes to show that he can capriciously vary a passage in a number of guises; in short, I have sought to abolish all the abuses against which good sense and reason have long cried out in vain.

I have felt that the overture ought to apprise the spectators of the nature of the action that is to be represented and to form, so to speak, its argument; that the concerted instruments should be introduced in proportion to the interest and the intensity of the words, and not leave that sharp contrast between the aria and the recitative in the dialogue, so as not to break a period unreasonably or wantonly disturb the force and heat of the action.

Furthermore, I believed that my greatest labor should be devoted to seeking a beautiful simplicity, and I have avoided making displays of difficulty at the expense of clearness; nor did I judge it desirable to discover novelties if it was not naturally suggested by the situation and the expression; and there is no rule which I have not thought it right to set aside willingly for the sake of an intended effect.

Such are my principles. By good fortune my designs were wonderfully furthered by the libretto, in which the celebrated author, devising a new dramatic scheme, for florid descriptions, unnatural paragons, and sententious, cold morality, had substituted heartfelt language, strong passions, interesting situations and an endlessly varied spectacle. The success of the work justified my maxims, and the universal approbation of so enlightened a city has made it clearly evident that simplicity, truth and naturalness are the great principles of beauty in all artistic manifestations. For all that, in spite of repeated urgings on the part of some most eminent persons to decide upon the publication of this opera of mine in print, I was well aware of all the risk run in combating such firmly and profoundly rooted prejudices, and I thus felt the necessity of fortifying myself with the most powerful patronage of YOUR ROYAL HIGHNESS, whose August Name I beg you may have the grace to prefix to this my opera, a name which with so much justice enjoys the suffrages of an enlightened Europe. The great protector of the fine arts, who reigns over a nation that had the glory of making them arise again from universal oppression and which itself has produced the greatest models, in a city that was always the first to shake off the yoke of vulgar prejudices in order to clear a path for perfection, may alone undertake the reform of that noble spectacle in which all the fine arts take so great a share. If this should succeed, the glory of having moved the first stone will remain for me, and in this public testimonial of Your Highness's furtherance of the same, I have the honor to subscribe myself, with the most humble respect,

Your Royal Highness's

Most humble, most devoted, and most obliged servant,

CHRISTOFORO GLUCK

NAPOLEON AS AN OPERATIC DICTATOR

Martial Teneo

> M. Teneo was librarian to the Paris Opéra. His re-
> searches indicate what happens to an artistic institu-
> tion when a dictator takes hold of it. M. Teneo admires
> Napoleon; one may, however, draw one's own conclu-
> sions.

"And flattery also played its part."

At the beginning of 1803 Bonaparte expressed to Morel, the
new director, his displeasure at several abuses and cases of negligence:
"The leading artists play far too seldom, and the repertory is often
changed owing to their fault. The execution of the songs by the
chorus is very careless, especially in the case of the women; they often
sing out of tune and hardly ever keep together. If this continues he
will be forced to have recourse to severe measures. Wishing that the
obsequies of General Leclerc at Soissons should leave nothing to be
desired, he requests the director of the Opéra to place at the disposal
of the organizer, M. Frémont, all decorations, hangings and other
things which it is possible for him to use without injury to the service
of the theater."

Kept constantly informed by the reports drawn up for him by Vély,
secretary to the Opéra, he forbade the performance of the ballet *Lucas
et Laurette* as "unworthy of the Théâtre des Arts, its triviality forming
a contrast with the magnificence of the first theater of the capital."

In January, 1804, the efforts made by foreigners to engage the artists
of the Opéra became so alarming that Morel felt bound to request
the Prefect of the Palace "to take measures for the preservation of a
theater which France, the capital and the arts regard as a national
property which it is useful and necessary to preserve." Soon, on March
29, the director alleges that it is urgent that Bonaparte should decree:

From *Fortnightly Review*, June 1921.

"1. That the Théâtre des Arts forms part of the Household of the First Consul; 2. that the artists are engaged for a fixed term of years; 3. that none of them can leave France or obtain a passport without a special permit; 4. that those who leave the country shall be treated as *émigrés*; 5. that anyone trying to engage them shall be dealt with according to the law on causing desertion." Later on Bonaparte ratified these provisions, but at the moment he did not pay much attention to them, since he was still feeling the effects of the asassination of the Duc d'Enghien, and was preparing the way for the Empire.

After the visit of the Senate to St. Cloud on May 18 to salute Napoleon I, Emperor of the French, in the person of General Bonaparte, the sovereign, in spite of the heavy work imposed upon him by his new dignity, took a more active interest than ever in the Opéra. By orders and decrees, as well as by personal influence, he set out to restore to the great lyric stage its former brilliance. And flattery also played its part. Bonet, recently appointed director, becomes almost servile. On May 28 he writes to De Luçay: "It is customary for the orchestra of the theater to announce to the public by a roll of drums the arrival of His Majesty the Emperor. Do you not think it would be fitting to show the same mark of respect to Her Majesty the Empress? This arrangement would offer the management and the public a new opportunity for expressing to Their Imperial Majesties the sentiments of respect and love which are in every heart. I have the honor to request you, M. le Préfet, kindly to consider in the light of your wise judgment this proposition, which is inspired by my own private feelings, and to make known to me your decision on the subject." I feel sure that this letter, perhaps inspired by Josephine, remained unanswered.

The Emperor had now turned the Théâtre des Arts into his Imperial Academy of Music. Orders were given by him to remove from the front of the theater "one of those inscriptions which recall the time when France, deprived of a lasting form of government, was a prey to the evils of anarchy."

July 13, 1804, is a date of importance in musical history. Napoleon and the Empress were present at the second performance of Le Sueur's *Ossian, ou Les Bardes.* The composer, who had been unpopular at court up till then owing to his disputes with Sarrette, the director of the Conservatoire, had just achieved a master stroke by dedicating his work to the Emperor in the following terms:

Sire, your glorious name at the head of the opera of *Ossian* recommends it to posterity. The glory of this hero of the third century filled a part of our continent: if my voice has sometimes been raised in the attempt to sing his praise, it is because my heart had before it constantly as a model the living picture of a hero, the pride of our age, whose name and glory fill the globe upon which we live—I might almost say, the universe; is this presuming too far? He fulfills the designs of the Author of all things; he occupies the thoughts of the Mover of the world; his destiny is as conspicuous as the stars which shine upon us. But how could I rise to the level of this model, the object of my songs? He is bound to be that of centuries to come. I see in him the heroes of future races, inflamed by the thought that they may deserve comparison with him. Tears rise to their eyes as they follow his history. One day they in their turn will receive the tribute of these tears of sublime emulation; they will receive it from the traveler who reads upon their tombs: "They had something of Napoleon in them." Yours respectfully, Le Sueur.

In spite of its inflated style, which is almost worthy of a madman, this dedication flattered Napoleon. And so for the whole evening he insisted on keeping the musician at his side in his box.

On October 28 Napoleon, accompanied by the Empress, was present at the thirteenth performance of *Les Bardes*, for which he had a particular affection, not only because the poems of Ossian formed one of his bedside books, but because this work was the most noble homage offered to his fame. "The performance started at half-past seven," says Police Inspector Rebory; "there was never such a crowded audience as at the thirteenth performance of *Les Bardes*. Even by doubling the guard it was hard to control the crowds which streamed into all the streets adjacent to the Academy. The receipts amounted to 8,947 francs." At the end of November the Emperor, with the idea of maintaining his popularity in the Army, had three hundred tickets at half price for the pit and an equal number for the fourth tier sent by the Opéra to General César Berthier for every performance during the Coronation festivities—that is to say, up to December 18.

On December 16 the Municipal Council gave a *fête* in honor of the Emperor at the Hôtel de Ville, his presence at which from three o'clock, the hour of the banquet, to nine o'clock, after the concert and fireworks, gave extraordinary animation to the proceedings. Some verses by M. de Propiac, entitled *"Le Vœu de Paris,"* were sung to the music of Plantade, a fact of which the historians all seem to be ignorant!

In February, 1805, Napoleon conceived the idea of trying to reduce the expenses of the Opéra, and had a new budget drawn up by the Arch-Chancellor, entailing a reduction of the staff of the orchestra, the singers, the dancers, the choruses, and the attendants. M. de Luçay at once tried to prove to him that such a measure would involve the ruin of the Academy of Music. If the orchestra was to have only sixty-two players instead of eighty, it would lose its great reputation; the singing could not recover from the dismissal of fourteen artists, etc. On the contrary, the estimates ought to be increased to a million and a half francs: "His Majesty would then preserve the magnificence and reputation of this theater, the first in Europe; in that case, too, He would increase its resources and achieve those economies which He proposes." This motion is supported by the written opinion of the heads of the singing, dancing and orchestral staffs and the chief machinist, all of whom agree in rejecting the proposed measures.

The Emperor, who knew when to yield to argument, now left things as they were and departed to be crowned King of Italy. After his return on July 11 he went to the Opéra with the Empress on the nineteenth to get into touch with the public again and excite their applause. Two days later he flew into a violent rage because Fanny de Beauharnais, an aunt of Josephine's, had personally recommended the musician Porta and his opera, *Le Vieux de la Montagne*, to M. de Luçay. This work had been refused by the jury; now Fanny said that she knew it had been rehearsed, that the Empress had heard it and had promised her patronage to the author, and, finally, that it depended on the Prefect of the Palace to see that Porta should "triumph over Envy, which is always the enemy of superior merit." But Napoleon had recently declared definitely that no work was to be given without his orders. This was quite enough to ensure that *Le Vieux de la Montagne* was never heard of again. . . .

By the beginning of 1810 Napoleon was divorced and entirely taken up with his marriage to Marie Louise, which was to take place on April 1. He was soon anxious to show her off at the theater, and especially at the Opéra. On June 10 Rémusat writes to Picard: "I send you official notice, my dear Director, that Their Majesties will go to the Opéra on Tuesday and that His Majesty desires that after *Le Devin du Village* the ballet of *Persée et Andromède* should be played. Make it known to everybody; you are even at liberty to announce it in the papers; do not fail to do the latter, for the Emperor is reckoning on it to attract a large audience."

This was an unforgettable evening for Marie Louise. The public applause was so great that it drowned the fanfares of the orchestra. The receipts, which totaled 8,885 francs, bear witness to the general enthusiasm.

On the twenty-fourth Their Majesties were again at the Opéra to hear *Colinette à la Cour* and the ballet of *Télémaque* (a fact hitherto unrecorded); on the thirty-first they arrived at the beginning of the third act of *Le Triomphe de Trajan*. "They then repeated the Nuptial March, and each of the allusions with which the work is filled aroused applause, which led the Emperor, who shared the general emotion, to make an imposing bow." Finally, on September 23, Napoleon and Marie Louise heard Catel's *Les Bayadères*. On Wednesday, November 28, Rémusat sent word to Picard: "Announce everywhere and put it in the papers that the Emperor is going to the Opéra on Friday; insist that all the leading artists shall appear, and as *Alceste* might perhaps appear a little *triste* and consequently too long, have a few cuts made, especially in Lainez's *rôle*." And on November 30 the Imperial pair did indeed hear *Alceste*, and a cantata by D'Esménard and Méhul containing allusions to the Empress's pregnancy, a fact which had made Napoleon hesitate as to whether he should allow this work of topical interest. There was a brilliant assembly, applause, and thousands of bunches of laurel were presented to Their Majesties (receipts, 7,329 francs).

It was at this time that the Emperor announced his intention of going to the Opéra every Friday. He did go on December 7, with the Empress, to see the ballet of *Psyché* (receipts 6,636 francs), but he was not there again till the twenty-eighth for *Le Jugement de Paris* and *Aristipe*. On that very morning Rémusat had written to Picard: "Make the report of the Emperor's visit as widely known as possible; that will make people come. And do not forget to let the police know." But the announcement was too late, they took only 3,867 francs.

GOUNOD'S *FAUST*

Herbert F. Peyser

> A sympathetic appraisal, written originally for *Opera News*, the publication of the Metropolitan Opera Guild.

"An iron constitution."

A few years before his death Goethe lamented to his friend Eckermann that it was impossible to find anybody who could write the proper music for *Faust*. "Such music ought to be in the character of *Don Juan*," he ventured; "Mozart should have composed *Faust*."

Mozart, alas, had at that time been dead nearly forty years. Eckermann suggested—of all people—Rossini. Goethe retorted with another impossible name—Meyerbeer. In later days the French librettist, Jules Barbier, approached Meyerbeer with the idea of a *Faust* opera. The composer of *The Huguenots*, whatever else his artistic sins, is reported to have answered in a manner that does him credit: "*Faust* is the ark of the covenant, a sanctuary not to be approached with profane music."

Goethe, who was notoriously unmusical, never seems to have thought of the one man of his time sent by heaven to interpret *Faust* in tone—his devoted admirer, Beethoven. Beethoven, indeed, had been pondering *Faust* music as far back as 1808. Fourteen years later Rochlitz, at the instigation of the publisher Haertel, laid the idea before him. Beethoven exclaimed: "That would be a work! Something might come of it!" But he had other creative projects on his mind and nothing did come of it.

Nevertheless *Faust* composers, large and small, were presently crowding the scene. Some wrote incidental music—the sort of thing Goethe had in mind and Beethoven might have provided. Others turned the huge tragedy into operas of one kind or another. The vast majority of these composers do not matter. Their labors are

By permission of the Metropolitan Opera Guild.

long forgotten except to antiquarians. Only two men have distilled for us in music the essence of certain fundamental aspects of Goethe's mighty poem—Liszt in his *Faust* Symphony, Wagner in his overture portraying Faust in bitter meditation and solitude. Berlioz in a work which is neither fish nor flesh—neither outright opera nor downright cantata—did, however, show here and there a singularly penetrating vision.

Yet to the man in the street—or in the grand tier box, the parquet, the dress circle or the top gallery—*Faust* in tone means the opera of Gounod. So far as he is concerned, Boito's *Mefistofele* is a side issue or less and diversified *Fausts* of Spohr, of Donizetti, of Schumann nothing at all. The writer of these lines recalls an episode of his student days when a noted professor of literature in Columbia University holding forth on Goethe's masterpiece declared that the chief thing most people remembered of the tragedy was Gounod's opera and the principal thing in that, the Soldiers' Chorus. This, of course, is going a bit far but in its fashion it is indicative.

If there really is such a thing as the most popular opera in the world *Faust* comes about as close to it as anything else in lyric drama. It has no problems today, however it may once have suffered. It seems incredible to us that once upon a time George Eliot should have put herself on record as believing that the love scene, with all its charms, could never brook comparison with the one in *The Huguenots*. In common with works like *Trovatore, Rigoletto*, Rossini's *Barber* and a few others of their stripe *Faust* has an iron constitution. Even the poorest of performances cannot kill it. And if the description is at all permissible *Faust* might be characterized as the most operatic of operas. It contains about every feature, every specialty the average taste looks for in the entertainment furnished by the lyric theater. From the first it has been assailed because it was not the *Faust* of Goethe. Of course it is not the *Faust* of Goethe—neither is any other of the myriad *Faust* operas. If it were it would—depend on it!—be vastly less popular.

Exactly because the work is so little problematic, so full of operatic effects and stunts and features, so copiously supplied with dramatic, romantic and melodic attractions of one sort or another we may pass directly to a survey of the musical rewards which in such plethoric measure it offers us. This is not to say that all of its music is equally good. Far from it! A good deal is merely sweetly sentimental, some pages are affected with a kind of sugared religiosity; others, again, are an offense to cultured taste. Yet as so often happens in music some of the commonest things in it maintain an astonishing vitality.

It is really a pity that listeners ordinarily pay so little attention to the first two pages of the orchestral introduction, for these somber, brooding measures are worthy of the best man who ever ventured to approach Goethe's poem with musical intentions. Actually, they capture something essential of it. Unfortunately, after a dark, creeping, sinuous fugato of great promise, a platitudinous modulation and a few thin measures of harp scales introduce the melody of one of the numberless song hits of the opera, the tune sung afterward by Valentine to the words "*Avant de quitter ces lieux,*" ending in a typical Gounod cadence. Faust's gloomy monologue at the curtain rise is, like the first part of the overture, another inspiration that deserves a more careful hearing than it usually gets—particularly the phrase "*J'ai langui, triste et solitaire.*" Then, the pretty six-eight melody of the solo oboe which breaks in upon Faust's meditations is almost certain to linger in the ear, the more so as it is shortly repeated by a soprano chorus outside ("*Paresseuse fille*"). And the listener is almost certain to be challenged by Faust's resolute "*Salut! ô mon dernier matin,*" which, along with his utterances that immediately follow, are melodically very typical of what one might call Gounod's *Faust* style.

The appearance of Mephisto is musically none too striking for the composer has not at this point endeavored to portray the devil in very striking tones. He sets him before us chiefly as a gallant swaggerer in a red (or black) cloak with a sweeping feather in his cap—in brief, as he himself says, "a real gentleman." Then, after the devil has interrogated Faust as to his wishes and received the reply that more than all else the philosopher desires youth, the latter breaks into the fine, swinging tune "*A moi les plaisirs,*" which afterward becomes the basis of a duet. But before the act ends we have a lovely episode, the vision of Marguerite at the spinning wheel, the horns singing beneath a murmuring spinning figure of violins and harp a melody which we will hear more fully developed in the nocturnal duet between the lovers in Marguerite's garden.

The scene of the Kermesse is heaped with gaudy and richly varied melodic merchandise. There are, first of all, the lively and popular choruses—or rather one big chorus made up of half a dozen successive ones of burghers, students, soldiers, young girls, old men, matrons; all of them with jaunty melodies of their own, the rousing ensemble ending as it began. Then, to solemn, religious harmonies, appears Valentine, who presently delivers his song of farewell remembered from the overture. This air, incidentally, was added to the opera after its first hearing and to an Italian text (*"Dio possente"*). It appears here in three-part form, with a rather martial middle section not heard in the overture. The next considerable signpost is Mephisto's vigorous Song of the Golden Calf—a number with a dash that carries all before it.

A subsequent detail which ought not be overlooked is that downward chromatic rush of strings as Mephisto calls upon Bacchus to fill the cups of the crowd with fresh wine—a capital bit of musical description. It is scarcely necessary to direct the hearer's attention to the chorale of the swords—a number in Gounod's unmistakable churchly vein—in which the men, suddenly conscious of the evil identity of their strange visitor, exorcise him with the crosses on their swords. But this cloud is quickly dissipated by a wholly irresistible waltz. It is in reality not one waltz but four, the chorus singing a sort of counter melody against the main one and the melodies following. It might be argued that this waltz is too elegant for these burghers and peasants, yet who can resist the spirit and sweep of it? Suddenly a change comes over the music and, as Marguerite appears and, after a few words, quickly vanishes, we hear the graceful, adorable melody of the lovers' first meeting. Thereafter the waltz measures return, bringing the act to its close in a whirlwind of animation.

Deeper tones underlie the introduction to the second act. A rhythmic motive is followed by a meditative, weaving figure of violins, which spins its course in sixteenth notes. After a short, sweet clarinet phrase the orchestra announces Siebel's gracious flower song, almost too familiar a melody to require comment. The appearance of Faust and Mephisto brings us in short order to the tenor cavatina, *"Salut! demeure,"* a song of tenderest sentiment, and a delicacy of instrumental color (notice particularly the lovely orchestral prelude and postlude), which suggests Gounod's preoccupation with Mozart. The air is fashioned in ternary form, with a contrasting middle section, *"O nature, c'est là que tu la fis si belle."*

The chain of gems sparkles steadily with other bright inspirations— Marguerite's song of the King of Thulé, with its touch of northern mystery and the brief interrupting phrases as the maiden pauses in her spinning to meditate on the handsome cavalier who seems to love her; her startled surprise at discovering the casket of jewels; finally the Jewel Song itself—a *valse brillante*, seemingly a trifle incongruous for a girl of such simplicity as Marguerite, until we recall that the Marguerite which the librettists Barbier and Carré invented for Gounod is not the Gretchen of Goethe.

The fine quartet which grows out of the presence of Faust, Marguerite, Martha and Mephisto, is one of the high spots of the opera and a notable piece of collective characterization as well. But finer still is the love scene, exquisite in its melodic fragrance of the phrase, *"Laisse-moi contempler ton visage,"* and the manner in which another ravishing inspiration, *"O nuit d'amour,"* becomes by the simple process of inversion that wondrous phrase, *"Je veux t'aimer,"* which we heard in the momentary vision of Marguerite in the first act.

It is not possible, unfortunately, to signalize the various other beauties of the Garden Scene, though one cannot avoid mentioning Mephisto's broad invocation and the melting passage which Berlioz, at the first performance of the work, cited as the finest thing in the entire opera, *"Il m'aime, quel trouble en mon coeur."* And, as the curtain descends, this passage swells to a passionate and grandiose outburst.

The ensuing Cathedral Scene of the third act is one of the finest in the work. Contrasting with the devout chantings of priests and choir boys we catch the satanic utterances of Mephisto which are as the afflicting voices of conscience in Marguerite's ears. Amid the scourging dotted rhythm of the orchestra with the snarls of stopped horns the unhappy woman hears the accusing words of the fiend till, with a prodigious effort, she wrests her spirit from the diabolical torments in a paroxysm of supplication. The song in which she finds release, *"Seigneur, accueillez la prière,"* is perhaps not the loftiest type of musical inspiration, but rather a tune related to such religious outpourings as "The Palms" or as Adam's "Holy Night." Yet for all its sweet obviousness it is the right thing in this place and has a surging uplift which carries away the least susceptible.

The following scene opens with the universally familiar Soldiers' Chorus, a thoroughly blatant, rowdy and vulgar tune, which one excuses for better or worse as a piece of musical rubbish. But in a short time, as a French critic wrote, "the music fades into the distance, for the relief of our ears," and better things assert themselves—particularly Mephisto's sardonic Serenade, with its cynical accompaniment and the devilish laugh at the close with the malicious "Ha! Ha! Ha!" through two falling octaves. The big ensemble of the curse and death of Valentine, as the flame of insanity begins to burn athwart Marguerite's distraught features—this ensemble ending with the whispered choral prayer, "*Que le Seigneur aît son âme,*" achieves something of the pity and terror of the scene conceived by Goethe.

Of the Prison Scene, which closes the opera, not much need be said. Marguerite's momentary recall of the melodies associated with her happier days—the waltz, the love music—is touchingly reminiscent. But the climax of this act is the trio, with its interesting orchestra details (like the beating of horses' hoofs as Mephisto mentions his impatient steeds) and Marguerite's soaring, ecstatic melody, "*Anges purs, anges radieux,*" thrice repeated, each time a tone higher, and gleaming with a kind of supernal light. Marguerite's pardon and her redemption are proclaimed in a somewhat theatrical apotheosis to the Easter hymn, "Christ Is Risen," while angels bear her spirit heavenward.

FAUST IN MUSIC

Ernest Newman

> The fortunes and misfortunes of the great theme which
> has challenged many composers and has never been sat-
> isfactorily expressed in music. Compare with the pre-
> ceding article!

"A problem of discouraging difficulty."

The musical settings of *Faust*, in one form or another, now
number, I believe, something like thirty or thirty-five. It is perhaps the
most popular of all subjects with musicians, far outdistancing in favor
the Hamlets and Othellos and Romeo-and-Juliets and all the other
lay figures which composers are fond of using to show off their own
garments. It cannot be said that they have added very much, on the
whole, to our comprehension of the drama; indeed, with half a dozen
exceptions the Faust symphonies and Faust operas and Faust scenes
have quite failed to justify their existence. One of the main difficulties
in the way of the musician—even supposing him to have the brain
capacity to rise to the height of the psychology of the thing—is the
enormous range and wealth of material of the drama itself. The First
Part of Goethe's work alone, or the Second Part, is quite sufficient to
tax the constructive powers of any composer to the uttermost; but to
reshape the whole of *Faust* in music is a desperate undertaking. Since
Goethe's day we are bound to see the Faust picture through *his* eyes;
any harking back to earlier forms of it is quite out of the question.
And Goethe, while he has enormously extended and deepened the
spiritual elements of the story, has by this very means set the musician
a problem of discouraging difficulty. No musical version of the play,
in the first place, can be adequate unless it embraces Goethe's Second
Part as well as the First. Due opportunity, again, must be given for
the exposition of all the essential, the seminal "motives" of the drama,
and they are many indeed. The composer is thus on the horns of a
dilemma. If he wants his work to stand in the same gallery with

Courtesy Ernest Newman.

Goethe's, he has to run a line through Faust's soul long enough and sinuous enough to touch upon all its secret places; but anyone who tries to do this soon perceives how hard it is to focus so vast a scene and to keep the picture within one frame of reasonable size. An opera or a symphony that should attempt to cover all the psychological ground of the drama would take at least ten or twelve hours in performance. Apparently the only rational course for the future composer who may think of setting the Faust subject is to take two or three evenings over it, after the manner of Wagner's *Ring of the Nibelungs*; and until this is done we shall have to rest satisfied with the more or less inadequate versions we have at present.

The cosmic quality of the subject, one would think, should have attracted more of the first-rank men, considering how many of the second and third rank it has tempted to self-destruction. One wonders, for example, why it should have fallen to the lot of Gounod to give so many honest but uninstructed people their first, perhaps their only, idea of *Faust*—an experience something like getting one's first notions of *Hamlet* from the country booth. We can understand their taking the thing seriously, for I fancy we all took it seriously at one time—in the callow stage of our musical culture—and many quite respectable musicians do so still. Yet we have only to come back to it one day, after dropping acquaintance with it for many years, to see what a laughter-moving monstrosity the thing is. The book gets as near the inane at times as anything founded on Goethe could do, though the music has its good points, of course. In the overture and opening scene there really is some suggestion of the gravity and the spirituality of the problems of Faust's soul; but from the time Marguerite and Mephistopheles appear upon the scene the thing becomes for the most part mere opera, and Faust just the ordinary amorist— *l'homme moyen sensuel*. The melodrama, *qua* melodrama, is sometimes good of its kind; the Valentine scenes generally ring true, and now and then they become really impressive. There is plenty of lovely music, too, in the opera, which may suffice you if you are not very critical as to the poetic basis—if you do not attempt, that is, to get below the ear-tickling sounds and to see the characters as Goethe has drawn them. But once you begin to think of these matters you can only smile at Gounod and his fellow criminals who concocted the libretto.

Look at the Gounod overture, for example. For a couple of minutes it is worthy of almost the loftiest subject or of the best man who has taken up the *Faust* theme; and then how woefully it fizzles out, drifting back into its native habitat of banality, where the air is more congenial to it—for all the world like a man who goes to an Ibsen play, sternly resolved to be a serious moralist for one evening at least, but at the end of the first act makes for the nearest music hall or *café chantant*. One can see where it is all tending; Faust the philosopher has already, at this early stage of his career, become Faust the *boulevardier*. So with the opening scene, wherein we just catch the accent of Goethe for a breath or two, but never longer. And then that absurd devil Mephistopheles, with his stage strut, his stage idiom, his stage brain! "Are you afraid?" he asks Faust at his first red-fire appearance, when "Are you amused?" would be more appropriate. There is a touch of the genuine sardonic quality in his serenade; but on the whole he suggests not so much the spirit of denial as the spirit of the pantomime rally. Nor, till you quietly think about the structure of the libretto, do you realize how exceedingly funny it all is. In the drinking scene it is Wagner who gets up to sing the song of the rat; Wagner! who by no process of shuffling of names can be got out of our heads as the pupil and companion of Faust. It is true he does not go very far with the ballad, Mephistopheles interrupting him after the first line or two—for which Gounod, remembering that Berlioz had set the same song once for all, was no doubt duly grateful to the devil. Then Mephistopheles sings his fatuous air about the Calf of Gold, and quarrels with Valentine—who, oddly enough, is also of the party—about his sister. So the opera goes on—very charming where it has least to do with the subject, but merely feeble or ludicrous when it comes near enough to Goethe to suggest a comparison. For Gounod, whose own religion was merely Catholicism *sucré*, not only lacked the brain to grasp the austere philosophy of a subject of this kind; his musical faculty was not deep enough nor strong enough to save him from aiming perpetually at drama and achieving only melodrama. Watch him, for example, in the scenes where he is trying to carry on a dramatic dialogue, and see to what straits he is put in the effort to make the orchestra do something expressive in between the actors' speeches. See the catchpenny trade he drives in those stale operatic formulas for whose poetic equivalent we have to go to the country booth; see him capering about with his fussy little runs and twiddles, and striking all kinds of pompous musical poses, that really signify nothing at all, and only remind us of the conventional up-down-right-left-cut-thrust of stage fencing. And this banal thing, this cheap

vulgarization of Goethe, this blend of the pantomime, the novelette
and the Christmas card, still represents *Faust* in the minds of nine
musical amateurs out of ten! It is no more the real Faust than Sardou's *Robespierre*, for example, is the real Robespierre; in each case
a portentous name has simply been tacked on to a piece of very ordinary melodrama. The most pleasing elements in Gounod's work—the
really lovely, if not always profound, love music—are precisely those
that withdraw it furthest from Goethe; for here it is clearly not Faust
speaking to Marguerite, but any man to any woman, any Edwin to
any Angelina. Gounod's Marguerite alone suggests dimly the drama
of Goethe; but that is because she is the easiest of all the characters
to represent in music. In most of the settings of *Faust*, indeed, the
portrait of Marguerite carries a kind of conviction even when the
other two characters have nothing more in common with Faust and
Mephistopheles than the names. He must be a very inferior musician
who could fail here. The essence of Marguerite's character is simplicity, innocence, the absence of all complicating elements; and accordingly we find that all the settings of her have a strong family
resemblance to each other. Schumann's Marguerite is very German,
Liszt's very German but at the same time quite cosmopolitan, Berlioz's curiously *moyen-âge*, Gounod's decidedly modern and town-bred,
but all have the same fundamental qualities; none does violence to
our conception of the real Marguerite. Faust, however, has to be
something more than the seducer of Marguerite; we want to see some
traces in his music of the weariness of life, the disgust with knowledge, that distinguish him at the beginning of the drama; we want to
see him growing at once stronger and weaker as he develops, his
character being purged of its dross, his soul's insight into the world
of real things becoming prophetically clear just as he is bidden to leave
it. Unless some elements at least of this picture are given us, the
composer has no right to attach to his painting the title of *Faust*.

One wonders, again, why a musician like Boito should ever have
thought himself fit company for Marlowe and Goethe. Here is a poet
—one can cheerfully pay a tribute to his general culture if not to his
musicianship—with a semimusical gift that rarely rises above the
mediocre and generally dips a point or two below it, who not only
fancies he can throw new light on Faust's soul through his music, but
serenely undertakes a reconstruction of the drama that Goethe gave
him. Boito made such a really good libretto for Verdi out of *Othello*
that it is rather surprising what an abject mess he has made of *Faust*.

His hash of the great drama is really deplorable. His superior culture and his finer literary palate put him above the commonplace Gounod conception of the play as a melodramatic story of a man, a maid, and a devil. He knows there is a "problem," a "world-view," in it that really makes it what it is. But as soon as he begins to set the play to music he seems to forget what the problem is, where it begins and where it ends. The result is that he is not content to write a piece of plain, straightforward music of the ordinary operatic type, but must needs drag in just enough of Goethe's great plan to make the whole thing preposterous. I say nothing of his musical deficiencies—of his incurable old-Italian-opera tricks of style, his lame, blind, and halt melody, the monotonous tenuity of his harmony, the odd jumble of Wagner and Rossini in his idiom, his notion that the terrible is adequately expressed in five-finger exercises, and the horrible by a reproduction of the noises made when the bow is drawn across all four strings of the violin at once. These are mere details, as is also the fact that his powers of dramatic characterization are very limited, or that his choruses of angels would be more suitable to *contadini,* or that his Mephistopheles is transported bodily and mentally from the *buffo* stage. What is most awesome in Boito's opera is the pseudo-philosophical scheme of the libretto. He begins with a Prologue in Heaven that is almost entirely superfluous, not one-fifth of it being concerned with Faust. The first half of the first act might also be dispensed with entirely, for all it has to do with the problem of Faust's soul. The second half of this act, and the first half of the next, are, in the main, essential to the drama, though there is no need for musical composers to retain, in the garden scene, the episodes between Mephistopheles and Martha, that are right enough in the play, but mar the more ideal atmosphere of music. The descent into the *buffo* is perilously easy here; and it is much better to omit all this, as Schumann does, and concentrate the whole of the light on Faust and Marguerite.

Boito's next scene, however—the Walpurgis Night—is pure waste of time and space; there is a great deal too much of Mephistopheles and the chorus, and not half enough of Faust to let us grasp the bearing of the scene upon the evolution of his soul. The whole of the third act helps to carry on the story; but the fourth act—the classical Walpurgis Night—becomes pure nonsense in Boito's handling of it. Whatever meaning there may be in the Helen episode in Goethe's long allegory, there can be no sense at all in simply pushing her on the operatic stage in order to sing a duet with Faust, the pair having incontinently fallen in love at first sight—presumably behind the scenes. Finally, the Epilogue—the Death of Faust—ends the work only in an operatic, not a spiritual, sense; there being no spiritual connection between the earlier and the later Faust, no reason why he should die just then, no hint of the bearing of his death upon his life. And why in the name of common sense should Boito have permitted himself to rewrite the final act, the crowning pinnacle of the whole mighty structure that Goethe has so slowly, so painfully reared? In place of the great motives and profoundly moving scenes of the poetic drama—Faust's schemes for human happiness, the poor old couple and their little house on the shore, the conversation with the four gray women, the blinding and death of Faust, the coming of Mephistopheles with the Lemures to dig the grave, the pathetic death scene, the transportation of the purified Faust into that diviner air where he meets the purified Marguerite—instead of all this we have Faust back again in the old laboratory of the first act, Mephistopheles holding out banal operatic temptations to him, after the manner of Gounod, and Faust clinging for salvation to the Bible and going straight off to heaven on his knees, all in the most approved fashion of the Stratford-on-Avon novelette.[1] Yet, bad as it is, Boito's *Mefistofele* is not the worst that might be done with the drama. His musical faculties may be of the kind that move us to more laughter than is good for us; but he certainly had some understanding of the inner spirit as well as of the external action of Goethe's poem; and the very extent of his failure serves to show how difficult it is to mold the play to musical requirements. The difficulty lies not so much in finding appropriate musical episodes as in dealing with such a multiplicity of them as

[1] The reader may need to be reminded that the published score of *Mefistofele* is an abbreviation of the opera as it was originally given. The opening scene of the first act and the Walpurgis Night scene in the second have been cut down (see Mazzucato's article on Boito in *Grove's Dictionary*). "The grand scene at the Emperor's Palace," says Signor Mazzucato, is "entirely abandoned." "A strikingly original *intermezzo sinfonico* . . . stood between the fourth and fifth Acts; it was meant to illustrate the battle of the Emperor against the pseudo-Emperor, supported by the infernal legions led by Faust and Mephistopheles—the incident which in Goethe's poem leads to the last period of Faust's life. The three themes—that is, the *Fanfare* of the Emperor, the *Fanfare* of the pseudo-Emperor, and the *Fanfare infernale*—were beautiful in conception and interwoven in a masterly manner, and the scene was brought to a close by Mephistopheles leading off with 'Te Deum laudamus' after the victory." As to the beautiful conception and the masterly interweaving I am inclined to be skeptical; but in any case the inclusion of this scene simply puts Boito in a worse light than ever. The whole episode is practically without significance as far as regards Faust's spiritual evolution. So far as music is concerned, it merely gives the opportunity for a claptrap battle piece.

there is. The drama, indeed, is amazingly rich in musical "stuff"—as Wagner would have put it—of the first order; as Berlioz expressed it in connection with Gounod's *Faust*, "The librettists have passed over some admirably musical situations that it would have been necessary to invent if Goethe had not already done so."

There is a vast quantity of the poem, of course, that is as alien to the spirit of music as it is to that of literature. But there is a certain irreducible minimum that *must* be dealt with, if the musical setting is to aim at reproducing the spiritual problem of Goethe with anything like completeness. The Prelude and the Prologue in Heaven may, in case of need, be dispensed with; but almost all the First Part ought to be utilized, not following Goethe word for word, of course, but taking the pith of each scene. Here and there we come across sections that either defy musical treatment or are comparatively unimportant episodes in the poem. But the main psychological moments must all be dealt with; and the omission of any one of these cuts a piece out of the intellectual interest, breaks the subtle line of development, and makes all that comes after it seem insufficiently led up to. The First Part of Goethe's *Faust*, in fact, is in itself a masterpiece of construction, holding the balance most carefully and skillfully between dramatic action and philosophical reflection. Omit any of the steps by which the characters have been brought to the dramatic completeness in which we see them at the end of the First Part, and you break the spell that makes them real to us.

There is, then, in the First Part alone, more than enough to constitute the poetical material of at least two operas. Many composers have chosen to end their labors here, with the death of Marguerite and the flight of Mephistopheles with Faust; and from the purely operatic point of view there is much to be said for such a course. The First Part does at least run on the lines that are common to a philosophical drama and an opera; whereas the Second Part deliberately flouts the musical sense at point after point. In the First Part the poetry marches hand-in-hand with the ethical conception; in the Second Part the poetry has often to be dug out of the jungle of prosaic diffuseness in which Goethe has hidden it. Nevertheless one great purpose runs like a fine, continuous thread through all the seemingly unrelated incidents of the drama; and this line at least must be followed by the musician, though he may disregard the excursions from its direct course which Goethe so often permits himself. The poet's purpose, of course, was not complete, could not possibly be complete, without the Second Part. From the very beginning we feel that the vast issues must end, full-orbed, in something like the remote, non-earthly atmosphere of the opening; and we keep in our memory the words of the Prologue in Heaven—

> A good man, through obscurest aspiration,
> Has still an instinct of the one true way—

waiting for the ultimate gleam that shall make the darkness of Faust's first perplexed flight quite clear to us. Plainly one-half only of the problem had been stated in the First Part; and though comparatively few people read the Second Part and few of those who have read once read it twice, it is really the rounding-off of the philosophical conception here that gives the First Part its proper meaning. The human striving of the earlier poem demanded the later episodes, both as poetical completion and ethical solution. Without the Second Part, the First Part is a broken cadence, a discord only half resolved. Goethe himself, we are told, "compared the Prologue in Heaven to the Overture to Mozart's *Don Giovanni,* in which a certain musical phrase occurs which is not repeated until the finale." A musical setting can be adequate only if it really deals with the central spiritual forces of *Faust,* not only as they affect the protagonist up to the death of Marguerite, but in the crowded afteryears. Life was wider than art to Goethe; and the vastness and unwieldiness of the scheme of the play are mostly due to his attempt to embrace so much of life in it. The trouble with the average musical setting is that it fails to rise to the level of Goethe's own lofty humanism. The theatrical is there in plenty; but there is little that brings home to us the grave philosophy of the drama, little that speaks of that great, moving, human figure of the Second Part, beating his way painfully through the darkness to the light. Above all, one cannot spare the ethical elevation of that final scene, with its supremely pathetic picture of the man's defeat in the very moment of victory, and its mystical suggestion of this material defeat being in reality a spiritual triumph. Goethe, in fact, made the subject an essentially modern one—put into it the fever and the fret, the finer joys and finer despairs, the deepened philosophy and the more impassioned spiritual aspirations, of the generations that succeeded the great upheaval of the eighteenth century. In Marlowe's *Faustus* we feel that, powerful as the wings of the poet are, there still clings to them something of the grossness of the Middle Ages, and the grossness, only more superficially refined, of the Renaissance. The thick breath of materiality hangs like a cloud over Marlowe's drama. Faustus himself has in him much of the coarseness of tissue of the Elizabethan age. On the purely human side, especially in the later scenes, he does indeed touch and move us; but in the mainsprings of his being, in the limitations of his desire—

> Sweet Mephistopheles, thou pleasest me;
> Whilst I am here on earth, let me be cloyed
> With all things that delight the heart of man.
> My four-and-twenty years of liberty
> I'll spend in pleasure and in dalliance,
> That Faustus' name, whilst this bright frame doth stand,
> May be admired through the furthest land—

how immeasurably does he fall short of the philosophic Faust of Goethe—

> Two souls, alas! reside within my breast,
> And each withdraws from, and repels, its brother.
> One with tenacious organs holds in love
> And clinging lust the world in its embraces;
> The other strongly sweeps, this dust above,
> Into the high ancestral spaces.

The mere magic-working Mephistopheles of Marlowe, again, takes on, in the modern poet, something of the terrifying grandeur of one of the essential forces of the universe. How subtle is Goethe's insight into him, and how one longs to get something of that subtlety in his music—

> Part of that Power, not always understood,
> Which always wills the Bad, and always works the Good. . . .

> Part of the Part am I, once all, in primal Night—
> Part of the Darkness which brought forth the Light,
> The haughty Light, which now disputes the space,
> And claims of Mother Night her ancient place.

He is the element of destruction that is the other half of being; not a mere tempting devil, the crude beguiler of the theological fancy, but simply the evil side of Faust becoming self-conscious. See, for example, in the eleventh scene of the First Part, and again in the fourteenth scene, how he probes to the very depth of Faust's soul, dragging into the light the true motives that sway him, which Faust himself is incompetent to analyze. His taunt in the seventeenth scene, again, "Thou, full of sensual, supersensual desire," is a stroke of which Marlowe was incapable.

There are one or two scenes in the Second Part which lend themselves to music, but have been curiously neglected—it being strange, for example, that no musician of the first rank has set the scene of Faust's discovery of ideal beauty (Act I, Scene 7). But on the whole the Second Part is uncongenial to music, until we come to the gravely passionate human element at the end. Even to poetry Goethe's plan is somewhat unpropitious, as Schiller pointed out to him. "A source of anxiety to me," he wrote in 1797, "is that *Faust*, according to your design, seems to require such a great amount of material, if the idea is finally to appear complete; and I find no poetical hoop which can encircle such a cumulative mass. . . . For example, Faust must necessarily, to my thinking, be conducted into the active life of the world, and whatever part of it you may choose out of the great whole, the very nature of it seems to require too much particularity and diffuseness." If the "poetical hoop" was so hard to find, a musical hoop to contain such wildly mixed material is beyond the power of man to cast. All the musician can do is to make sure of the final scenes (from Act VII, Scene 4 onward); though even then—and this is the perpetual dilemma—one feels the need of some connecting link between the Faust whose life is drawing so near to the end, and the Faust whom we saw being torn away by Mephistopheles from Marguerite and the prison. As Schiller said, Faust must go "into the active life of the world" before that stupendous cadence can have its true significance; yet most of the intermediate scenes into which Goethe has put him can never be caught up into the being of music. As one looks at the poem itself, one admits despairingly that it would be impossible to build the first four acts into any operatic structure. But one broad purpose of spiritual development runs through even this desert of apparently endless aridity; and surely this might be treated by the musician, if not in operatic, at least in symphonic form. That is, between the stage of Faust's life that ends with the death of Marguerite and the awakening of Faust to a new joy in earth and a resolution to seek the highest good, and the stage where his own death puts the seal on the drama, we might have a symphonic interlude that would make the transition less abrupt for us. The comparative vagueness of the music in this form would match the increased indefiniteness of the poetical handling; while the more positive operatic form could be resumed in the fifth act, where the closeness of the association with actual life demands the continuous use of words. It is not an ideal device, perhaps, but it is the only adequate one. Only in some such manner as this can we hope to get the real *Faust* translated into music. As it is, the composers who have grasped the philosophy of the work have been restricted to a canvas far too small for the whole subject, while those who have not laid stress on the philosophy have simply not dealt with the Faust drama at all.

Men like Wagner and Rubinstein, again, who have really had the thinker's appreciation of the deeper currents of the theme, and have tried to express these in the single-movement form, have been woefully hampered by the limited space in which they have been compelled to work. Wagner, of course, never meant his Faust Overture to be a complete treatment of the subject; it was intended merely as one section of a large Faust Symphony. The general excellence and the one defect of the work inspire us with regret that the scheme as a whole was never carried out. Its one shortcoming is that it deals only with the melancholy, brooding, world-weary Faust of the opening of Goethe's poem, the egoistic Faust on whom the larger world issues have not yet dawned. We should like to have had Wagner's treatment of the final and complete Faust, taken out of himself, touched with sublimer sorrows and compassions, pouring out his soul upon the greater interests of humanity. As it is, however, we have in the Faust Overture the veritable Faust of the opening of Goethe's poem. No attempt is made at the portraiture of Marguerite—the beautiful theme in the middle section simply representing the "ever-womanly" floating before Faust's eye in vague suggestion—nor is there any Mephistopheles in the work. But in regard to the special task Wagner seems to have set himself, the translation into music of the first scene of Goethe's First Part, nothing more perfect could well be imagined. There are few more convincing pieces of musical portraiture than this great gray head, with the look of the weary Titan in the eyes, that looms out in heroic proportions from Wagner's score.

One of the least known of the settings of *Faust*—or at any rate of the fine settings of it—is that of Henri Hugo Pierson.[2] Though he was an Englishman, his music is practically unknown in England, for

[2] Henry Hugh Pearson was born at Oxford in 1815. He settled in Germany, where he found a more congenial musical atmosphere than was to be had at that time in England. After writing for a little while under the pseudonym of "Edgar Mansfeldt," he reverted to his own name, but metamorphosed it into Henri Hugo Pierson. His "Music to the Second Part of Goethe's *Faust*" was brought out at Hamburg in 1854. Pierson died in 1873.

which his residence in Germany is no doubt mainly responsible. It is
a pity such a man could not have found in his own country the conditions under which his talents could thrive and expand; for when one
realizes how much strength and originality there are in his music, one
feels that had he worked in England he might have helped to found
a native school, and so brought our musical renaissance to birth at
any rate a generation earlier than it has come. His music is always
that of a musician who is at the same time poet and thinker. The very
plan of his *Faust* is original. As its title indicates, it deals only with
the Second Part of Goethe's play. This in itself is a slight fault, for
it brings before us that tremendous drama of regeneration without
having prepared us for it by the previous drama of struggle and error.
Starting with Ariel and the Chorus of Fairies singing round the sleeping Faust, Pierson takes us through the scene in the Emperor's Castle,
the calling up of the apparitions of Paris and Helen, and the attempt
of Faust to seize the Grecian beauty—all from Act I. From the second
act we have Wagner and the birth of the Homunculus, and the journey of Faust, Mephistopheles, and the Homunculus through the air.
From the third act we have the scene before the Palace of Menelaus
(Helen and the Chorus of captive Trojan women), the coming of
Faust as a knight of the Middle Ages, his dialogue with Helen, the
appearance and death of Euphorion; from the fourth act, the battle
between the Emperor and his enemies; from the fifth act, the song
of Lynceus the warder, the entry of the four Gray Women—Want,
Guilt, Care, and Need—and the blinding of Faust; the digging of the
grave by the Lemures, the death of Faust, the choruses of the spirits
and the anchorites, the chorus of the younger seraphs and angels
ascending with the spirit of Faust, the scene in the empyrean, and
the final "Chorus Mysticus"—"*Alles Vergängliche ist nur ein Gleichniss.*"

The scheme, it will be seen at once, is not an ideal one. It achieves
comprehensiveness at the expense of organic unity. It keeps too strictly
to the letter and the order of Goethe's scenes; episodes like the battle, that are of the very slightest significance, are needlessly included;
other and more essential episodes are so lightly dwelt upon that their
full value can hardly be brought out; and others are omitted altogether. As a mere piece of architecture the thing is extremely im-
perfect. Too much use, again, is made of the melodrama—*i.e.* the
union of the reciting voice with the orchestra—one of the least justifiable and most trying forms of art ever invented. But with all its

faults of structure it is a notable work; the music redeems all its errors. The opening scene, with Ariel and the spirits, is exquisitely fresh and sunny; the death of Euphorion and the death of Faust are both very moving, and there are some fine choruses in the work, notably the "*Heilige Poesie.*" Pierson re-creates for us the philosophic atmosphere of the Second Part of *Faust*, and gives us the same impression of the largeness of the issues at work; which is no small achievement. It is a pity one of our Festival Committees could not be prevailed upon to let us hear the score, or at any rate a portion of it.

Unduly neglected, again, is Henry Litolff's setting of certain scenes from Goethe (Op. 103). Like Pierson, he adopts occasionally the unpleasant form of declamation with orchestral accompaniment. This spoils an otherwise fine treatment of the first scene (in Faust's study). It is really a symphonic poem with a vocal element here and there; and paradoxically enough, though Faust is restricted to declamation, the Earth Spirit sings his part to a melodic and very expressive *quasi recitativo*. The movement has the prevailing fault of all Litolff's writing—a certain slackness and want of resource in the development; but the ideas themselves are often most striking. The first scene concludes with a fine setting of the Easter Hymn. The second scene, before the City Gate, is exceedingly fresh and charming; while the seventh, the scene in the Cathedral (No. 20 of Goethe's First Part), is a masterly piece of work—finer even, perhaps, than Schumann's version of the same scene. If Goethe's drama has moved many of the second-rate musicians only to show how very second-rate they are, it has at all events stimulated others to efforts that at times put them very nearly in the ranks of the first-rate.

Rubinstein's orchestral poem *Faust*—which the composer styles simply "*Ein musikalisches Charakterbild*"—is not altogether easy to understand, in its literary intentions, in the absence of a guide. It is in one movement only, and contains apparently no allusion to Mephistopheles, nor, as far as can be gathered beyond doubt from the music itself, to Marguerite—for the suave melodies that are interposed as a contrast to the more passionate and more reflective utterances of Faust are not distinctively feminine in nature. They may have nothing at all to do with Marguerite, or they may represent Faust's attempt to resolve his philosophic doubts by a contemplation of the simpler and more constant elements of human nature—just as Wagner, in his Faust Overture, does not so much limn an actual Marguerite as suggest the consolation which the thought of womanly love can bring to the soul of Faust. Rubinstein's work, though not quite on the same plane as Wagner's, is yet exceedingly sincere. What it lacks is sufficient definiteness to make us refer it to Faust and to Faust only. It is clearly a strenuous picture of a lofty and noble soul, striving in its own way to read "the riddle of the painful earth," and mournfully acknowledging, at the last, that its only portion is defeat and disillusion. But this is a psychological frame that might be made to fit a score of pictures; and one misses, in Rubinstein's piece, the conclusive sense of congruence with Faust as we know him in Goethe's poem. There is nothing in it to clash with the poet's conception; the emotional atmosphere is the same in both; but in spite of the title the musician has put upon his work, it is less a study of individual character than a description of a type. Rubinstein's Faust is the least definite and the most symbolical of them all.

Rubinstein's tone poem and every other purely orchestral setting of the subject, however, pale before the magnificence of Liszt's Faust Symphony. Liszt writes three movements—entitled respectively "Faust," "Marguerite," "Mephistopheles"—and then sums up the whole work in a choral setting of Goethe's final lines, "*Alles Vergängliche ist nur ein Gleichniss*," etc. Here the larger scale on which the picture is painted permits Liszt both a breadth and an intimacy of psychology which are impossible in the one-movement overtures. In the long first movement (taking about twenty-five minutes in performance), we really do feel that Faust is being analyzed with something of the same elaboration and the same insight as in Goethe's poem. The handling is a trifle loose here and there, owing to Liszt repeating his material from time to time in obedience to literary rather than to musical necessities; but apart from this the "Faust" movement is extraordinarily fine character-drawing, and certainly the only instrumental Faust study that strikes one as being complete. In the "Marguerite" movement he incorporates very suggestively a reference here and there to the phrases of the "Faust," thus not only sketching Marguerite herself but giving the love scenes in a form of the highest concentration. This section is surpassingly beautiful throughout . . . almost the whole Marguerite is there, with her curious blend of sweetness, timidity, and passion; while Faust's interpositions are exceedingly noble. All that one misses in Liszt, I think, is the tragic Marguerite of the scene in the Cathedral and the prayer to the Mater Dolorosa. The "Mephistopheles" section is particularly ingenious. It consists, for the most part, of a kind of burlesque upon the subjects of the "Faust," which are here passed, as it were, through a continuous fire of irony and ridicule. This is a far more effective way of depicting "the spirit of denial" than making him mouth a farrago of pantomime bombast, in the manner of Boito. The being who exists, for the purposes of the drama, only in antagonism to Faust, whose main activity consists only in endeavoring to frustrate every good impulse of Faust's soul, is really best dealt with, in music, not as a positive individuality, but as the embodiment of negation—a malicious, saturnine parody of all the good that has gone to the making of Faust. The "Mephistopheles" is not only a piece of diabolically clever music, but the best picture we have of a character that in the hands of the average musician becomes either stupid, or vulgar, or both. As we listen to Liszt's music, we feel that we really have the Mephistopheles of Goethe's drama.

The Mephistopheles of Berlioz's *Faust* is interesting in another way. Berlioz, of course, played fast and loose in the most serene way with the drama as a whole, accepting, rejecting, or altering it just as it suited his musical scheme. He blandly avows, for example, that he takes Faust, in one scene, into Hungary, simply because he wants to insert in the score his arrangement of a celebrated Hungarian March! Moral criticism would be wasted on one so naked and unashamed as this—though perhaps after all it is only pedantry that would regard most of Berlioz's alterations of Goethe's drama as very serious perversions of the main Faust legend. So long as the central problems of the character are seen and stated, it matters very little through what incidents the composer chooses to bring them home to us. And Berlioz really has a very strong grip upon the inner meaning of the legend. His success, indeed, is somewhat surprising when we consider how he approached the work. He had been greatly impressed, in his youth, by Gérard de Nerval's translation of Goethe's poem; but instead of attempting a continuous setting of the work at this time (1829), he aimed only at setting eight disconnected scenes. These were (1) "The Easter Scene"; (2) "The Peasants' Dance"; (3) "The Chorus of Sylphs"; (4) "The Song of the Rat"; (5) "The Song of the Flea"; (6) "The Ballad of the King of Thulé"; (7) "Marguerite's Romance and the Soldiers' Chorus"; (8) "Mephistopheles' Serenade." Faust, therefore, had practically no part in this selection; and it was not till seventeen years later that Berlioz brought out his complete "dramatic legend." It looks as if his early interest in the work were more pictorial than philosophical, for the two songs of

Marguerite alone suggest the deeper emotional currents of the drama. Mephistopheles, however, seems to have captivated his young Romantic imagination from the first, and, in the ironic serenade to Marguerite, the character as he conceived it is already fully sketched. Berlioz's devil is, perhaps, the only operatic Mephistopheles that carries anything like conviction; he never, even for a moment, suggests the inanely grotesque figure of the pantomime. Of malicious, saturnine devilry there is plenty in him; no one, except Liszt, could compete with Berlioz on this ground. But there is more than this in the character. In such scenes as that on the banks of the Elbe, where he lulls Faust to sleep, there is a real suggestion of power, of dominion over ordinary things, that takes Mephistopheles out of the category of the merely theatrical and puts him in that of the philosophical.

Nor, in sheer character-drawing, can any other operatic Faust and Marguerite compare with the figures of Berlioz; and when we consider the piecemeal manner in which the work was built up, it is astonishing how just, how sure, how incisive this portraiture is. It may not be precisely Goethe; but it is a magnificent translation of Goethe into French. Faust, of course, is the Romantic Faust, with his passionate intimacy with nature. We miss in Berlioz what we get in Schumann, for example—the close following of Goethe's philosophical plan. Berlioz is not greatly interested in Faust's schemes for the regeneration of mankind; his own culture had not brought him into contact with Louis Blanc and Proudhon and Saint-Simon. But of its kind it is all amazingly fine. No other Marguerite except Liszt's and perhaps Schumann's, can compare with Berlioz's for pure pathos —the sensuous simplicity of soul that wrings the heart with compassion. Altogether, though the opera of Berlioz deals only with the more primordial passions of the drama, and ends in a manner rather too suggestive of a Christmas card conceived in a nightmare, it is more subtle, more profound, than almost any other work of the same order.

Only one setting surpasses it—that of Schumann; not because it achieves a finer individual portraiture than Berlioz's work, but because, on the whole, it stirs us more deeply in precisely the way we are stirred by Goethe's poem. Schumann's plan is peculiar and original. Whereas most other composers who have employed the operatic or cantata form have drawn largely on Goethe's First Part and almost ignored the Second, it is from the Second Part that two-thirds of Schumann's work are taken. Out of the First Part we have only the garden scene, Marguerite before the image of the Mater Dolorosa, and the scene in the cathedral. Faust, therefore, does not so far appear at all, except in the tiny garden scene; and the sole structural fault of the work is that something of the earlier Faust should have been shown to us, before he appears, in the next section, as the refined and vigorous humanist of Goethe's Second Part. Setting this defect aside, however, the remainder of the work gives us the quintessence of Goethe's drama. We have first the scene, at the opening of Goethe's Second Part, where Ariel and his fellow spirits sing round the sleeping Faust; then Faust's return to mental health and energy, and his resolve to devote himself henceforth to the highest activities of human life. Upon this scene there follows the visit of the four gray-haired women—Want, Guilt, Need, and Care—the blinding of Faust by the breath of Care, the last outburst of his passionate zeal for life and freedom, and his death. The remainder of the work is devoted to a textual setting, line for line, of the final scene of Goethe's poem—the hermits, the choruses of angels, the three women, the penitent (formerly Marguerite), the Mater Gloriosa, and the "Chorus Mysticus."

Schumann's scheme is thus in the highest degree philosophical. It austerely disregards the conventional elements that enter into the usual operatic *Faust*, and concentrates itself on the essential spiritual factors of the poem. Mephistopheles appears only for a moment in the garden duet, and again in Faust's death scene, so that there is no attempt at full portraiture of him. Schumann's Marguerite really suggests the Marguerite of Goethe. The same medieval atmosphere seems to environ her, both in the garden and in the cathedral. She is naïve in the scene with Faust as Goethe's Marguerite is naïve; and in the scene where she bends before the Mater Dolorosa, and again when the evil spirit, in the cathedral, harries her with his taunts, everything is set in the right key and the right color. In the portrait of Faust it is the thinker, the philosopher, that is uppermost throughout. All through Schumann's Second Part, indeed, we feel this constant preoccupation of the musician with the great human elements of the drama; while in the exquisite, subtilized mysticism of the Third Part these elements glow with a purer and rarer light. The work is uneven in its musical inspiration; but on the whole we can say that Schumann's is the real *German Faust*, the *Faust* of Goethe. Writing in his eightieth year, the old poet pointed out one of the main reasons for the enduring interest in his work:

The commendation which the work has received, far and near, may perhaps be owing to this quality—that it permanently preserves the period of a development of a human soul, which is tormented by all that afflicts mankind, shaken also by all that disturbs it, repelled by all that it finds repellent, and made happy by all that which it desires. The author is at present far removed from such conditions: the world, likewise, has to some extent other struggles to undergo: nevertheless, the state of men, in joy and sorrow, remains very much the same; and the latest born will still find cause to acquaint himself with what has been enjoyed and suffered before him, in order to adapt himself to that which awaits him.

It is this grave note, this width of outlook upon man and the world, that we have in Schumann's work in fuller quantity and richer quality than in any other setting of *Faust*. His is really the spirit of the *Faust* conceived by the great poet—full of a passionate reflection upon life, an uplifted, philosophical sense of tragedy, a mellow sympathy with and pity for the troubled heart of man. From first to last he has made his emotions out of the deeper, not out of the more superficial, passions of the play.

THE VOICE OF CARMEN

Paul Bekker

> "The one great masterpiece of French lyric opera" has always been particularly attractive to the Germans. The enthusiasm shown by Paul Bekker, one of Beethoven's renowned biographers and a musical philosopher who championed the cause of Schönberg, follows the tradition.

"Mirroring the man she is addressing."

And now appeared the one great masterpiece of French lyric opera, surpassing every example that had preceded it: *Carmen.*

That it was not immediately recognized, and that it later—fortunately for its effectiveness—received, instead of dialogue, recitatives from a hand other than that of the composer—these facts do not detract from the importance of the first appearance of *Carmen.* For it is already the work in which all the basic characteristics of the lyric opera are brought to their highest development—free, unforced, produced solely by the kindling power of the subject. Once more this subject exhibits the characteristic idea of the lyric opera: love and jealousy in a triangle of one woman and two men, in simple and moving form, free of all sentimentality. This is love as a primitive force, possessed almost of the power of destiny in classic drama. A connected feature is the spell of a special environment, important for the dramatic purpose of the lyric opera. Through the combination of Spanish and gypsy coloring, *Carmen* has an almost exotic charm, while the objectiveness of the action and its everyday nature create, through their apparent restraint and simple clarity, a counterspell that enhances the tension.

The conventional elements, on the other hand, are slight, notably in that part of the first act where the action is set in motion. The four-act form made necessary a certain tension. The sentimental figure of Micaela, and the picturesque choruses, dances, and portrayal of milieu, create a fullness of episodic detail that carries the action forward through the first three acts to a point from which such a landslide as occurs in the last act is possible. This last act is in every respect—as an artistic conception, as a dramatic contrasting of the voices, and as a revelation of their animal nature—the distilled content of the work. It is characteristic again that the climactic line leading to this fourth act was at first not recognized as such. The conventional first act was well received, but a flagging of enthusiasm led to the fiasco of the last act—confirmation of the fact that *Carmen* marks the turning point in the conception of the nature of the lyric opera.

Carmen is the basic type of the trio opera—not in its use of ensemble, but in the working-out of the acting characters. They are here conceived absolutely primitively—especially the woman. She has the Mignon mezzo tone quality, associated in German ideas with the somewhat unctuous alto, but really to be taken only as the voluptuous low tone of the French female voice. The physical demands made upon the voice are comparatively slight. The relation with language is basic. Every curve of the vocal line meets a requirement of the declamation. The latter is, so far as possible, related to dance and song form. The color of the voice is stressed, rather than its singing quality: in the Card Song, for example, the dark shades, in a heavy, dragging line; and, as a contrast, the dance rhythms, only sketchily clothed in tone, of the Seguidilla.

Similarly, every passage Carmen sings is a new mask, mirroring the man she is addressing. The receptive nature of woman is portrayed with uncanny realism in her change of tone as she addresses the passers-by, José, Zuniga, the smugglers, Escamillo. To each she is a different woman, changing the sound of her voice, the character of her melody, her mood, her tempo, and all within modest vocal limits. She is wholly herself only in the weary, scale-wise rise and fall of the melody of the Card Song, and in the dramatic arioso dialogue in the last act. The mimic significance of the voice, its true dramatic function and power of characterization, were never so strikingly displayed, and never with such subordination of all its singing qualities, in the ordinary sense; indeed the conception of woman as a primitive creature was never developed to such an extent out of the qualities of the voice itself. One recognizes the difference if one compares Carmen with the other female singing roles of the work: Frasquita, Mercédès, Micaela. All these are singers, standing in clearly defined relations to the conventional vocal types. Carmen remains outside their circle. For that very reason, she is the completed realization of an elemental nature evolved out of the possibilities for dramatic characterization that belong to the voice.

The two men are determined by the nature of this central female figure. José, the French tenor who depends on the lightness of his high register and the appealing softness of his voice, is here whipped out of a state of passive endurance into live, human, passionate action by the inciting temperament of the woman. His vocal line ends in the cry of the animal, and the last big duet scene of the couple ends in spoken words—tones that have lost definite pitch.

The baritone is a less active figure. He is not an active force, but a simple fact. His song, based on an elementary march type of melody, is solely a sort of refrain that marks every turn in the action. He simply embodies the natural masculinity of the baritone as opposed to the exceptional sensitivity indicated by the tenor. The background characters are only sketched: the mocked lover, the bass Zuniga; the two smugglers, descended from the buffo type and intensified to the point of crafty seriousness; Mercédès and Frasquita. But the manner in which they are used to paint the environment lifts them out of the class of mere dramatic properties and makes them organic and living types.

Then there is a new type of ensemble. It is recruited no longer from among the principals, but from the ranks of the minor players. In the Quintet, the chief ensemble of the whole work, only one of the principals takes part—Carmen. And even she is used at first only as a filling-in voice. The piece has no direct relation to the dramatic content of the work, nor is it, like similar pieces in Gounod or Verdi, a bringing together of the basic forces. From an external dramatic view it would seem to be only an effective interpolation. Its one important episode—Carmen's refusal to take part in the smuggling—could take place just as well outside this particular frame. This enclosing of a portion of the action corresponds to that of Carmen's Card Song in the women's trio of the third act. But the significance of the Quintet in relation to the atmosphere and the psychological preparation for the events that follow, is so important that its absence is not conceivable without injury to the effect of the whole. It is precisely here that the special treatment of the voices, their hurried whispering, brings about the intensification of the sense of a ruling destiny that determines events. The chorus also serves this same purpose of making clear the environment in which the action takes place. This is extensively the case in the first act, where it is minutely subdivided so that children's, men's, and women's choruses form numerous individual groups: strollers, soldiers, girls from the cigarette factory. And these groups are never brought together into a combined chorus. Not until the conventional climax in the finale of the second act is there a combined chorus tone that really sounds like an operatic ensemble. The smugglers' choruses of the third act preserve this character in their underlying coloring; and then the march in the fourth act is reduced again to the introduction of singing supernumeraries. At this point the chorus has fulfilled its purpose as an instrument of tonal illumination. Now it is only a matter of individuals, and the mass disappears.

The orchestral treatment is especially subtle, and particularly the treatment of the woodwinds. Every form of mass treatment vanishes; or, when it does occasionally appear, as in Escamillo's scenes, it is immediately recognizable as an effect for the sake of contrast. This orchestra is not the active bearer of the harmony, nor is it subordinated to the singing voice. It is the light and air in which the characters of the action live and breathe. It is not intellectually reflective, but it is full of intuitions and sudden realizations. It is silent in the moments of greatest dramatic tension, limited to a few chords of recitative accompaniment, only to break out anew in support and intensification of the singing voice. The elements of harmony, of chamber music, and of color are equally represented, but limited and defined by the laws of the most intensely concentrated expression. It is just in this almost aphoristic concentration, in the avoidance of everything in the nature of flourishes or fine phrases, that the sturdy vigor and force of Bizet's orchestra consists. The effect of something not fully expressed, something only indicated in the flash of a sharp light, characterizes the entire impression. The single flute or trumpet is not a solo in the old sense. It is an abbreviation for a sound conceived as fuller than this, here represented only by its most characteristic color. Only within an orchestral tone so purified, so full and yet so transparent, could the French singing voice move freely and independently.

It seems exaggerated, of course, to claim that all this, and with it the entire conception of everything that the *Carmen* style means to opera, was the result of taking a woman's voice as model, and of the urge to give it such expression, in speech and song, character and action, as would offer the most productive employment of its possibilities. But in view of the conditions that govern the creative process —conditions which have really nothing to do with purely rational considerations—the claim is justified. Only around such a concept as a center was it possible to construct a work that must, in its simple reality, display its national character in every fiber, to an extent never before reached by any French work. Carmen's voice is, with all its advantages and all its limitations, the musically sensitive basic type of a nation. In its entirely individual tonal nature it is suited as no other to the expression of a mixture of melancholy and frivolity, sensuality and contempt for death. It is a sort of translation of Don Giovanni into feminine terms, filled with the same uncontrollable temperament as its prototype. Only recognition of this deepest impulse makes clear the nature of the whole opera.

THE TWO MANONS

Edward Sackville-West

A comparison of Massenet's and Puccini's treatment of
Abbé Prévost's novel.

"Both works are indispensable."

The story of Manon Lescaut occupies a high place in a not
altogether reputable category: the unconscious work of art. Whatever we may think of the Abbé Prévost, we can hardly accuse him of
taking himself seriously: it is unlikely that he regarded the *Mémoires
d'un Homme de Qualité* (the hotchpotch of autobiography and fiction in which *Manon Lescaut* forms an enclave) as anything but an
easy way of making money, of which he was chronically short; nor
does he seem to have been at all aware that, in drawing so firmly the
full-length portrait of Manon herself, he was creating something new
in fiction. True, she had been preceded by Moll Flanders; but Defoe's
shrewd virago is quite without the pathos which is the underlying
note of Manon's nature. Moll's progeny, whether romanticized or not,
are the *femmes fatales* of nineteenth-century literature: Carmen,
Nana, and Wedekind's Lulu, with the Philine of *Wilhelm Meister*
as an earlier and perhaps borderline case. The offspring of Manon are
very different, as can be seen by simply naming the most famous of
them: *La Dame aux Camélias*, Sonia in Dostoevsky's *Crime and Punishment*, the Thaïs of Anatole France. The difference lies between
conscience and the lack of it: Carmen is out for what she can get,
and devil-take-the-hindmost, while Manon's devotion to self-interest
is not so wholehearted.

Prévost's novel, despite its atmosphere of brimming emotion, is
highly realistic. If Manon herself is not idealized, still fewer bones are
made about the "types" who prowl round her. Her brother Lescaut
is, quite simply, a pimp who sees no reason why he should not make
a good thing out of his pretty sister and her young lover. The aura

of squalid criminality which surrounds this "Mayfair man" is an impressive witness to Prévost's powers of observation, and affords an interesting glimpse (not the only one in the novel) of the Paris underworld during the *Ancien Régime*. Indeed, apart from Des Grieux *père* (well-meaning, worried, choleric, and misguided), the high-minded colony at New Orleans, Des Grieux's confidant, Tiberge, and the Father Superior of St. Sulpice, the milieu of the book is the lecherous and self-seeking world of *The Rake's Progress*. Des Grieux, on the other hand, is not a rake: he is a warmhearted ninny, dignified only by his blind passion for Manon—a passion which is ripened by adversity into self-sacrificing devotion. Even so, Prévost, who was here drawing freely on his own character, does not share the librettists' illusions about Des Grieux, admitting him to be fool enough to start a gambling hell in concert with the cynically untrustworthy Lescaut, and knave enough to try cheating at cards as a last resort, when he and Manon run out of money. But a knave and a fool are preferable to a prig, and as an offset to the reckless lovers and spirited gangsters Tiberge really will not do. The intolerable smugness exhaled by the well-known portrait of the Abbé Prévost finds all too ample scope in the sermonettes with which Tiberge thinks fit to regale Des Grieux —at moments, too, when only sympathy and practical help are of any use to him.

At this point we are faced by the one aspect of the novel which non-Catholic readers find so hard to accept--I mean the apparent levity with which Des Grieux allows himself to be persuaded by his father into taking Holy Orders, only to pop out of his cassock the moment Manon reappears. All this seems absurd, if not downright repulsive; and the author's specious moralizing, which in the operas we are spared, in the novel only makes matters worse. It should, however, be remembered that in Latin countries the distinction between sacred and profane love is largely a matter of feeling—the feeling of the moment. Des Grieux's behavior may well offend Anglican taste, but his own words—and the manner of his end—make it quite clear that he was at no time a hypocrite. *Autre temps, autres moeurs.* By a French believer of this period the mysteries of the Catholic faith were taken for granted and remained inextricably bound up with all ways of life, however vile. The love of God was always available, when Des Grieux chose to be aware of it; His mercy too, though it assumed unexpected forms. It may be added that presumably Des

Grieux took only Minor Orders, which can easily be quitted and which in the next century enabled the aging Liszt to make the best of both worlds.

The episode in the seminary of St. Sulpice, which looms so large in Massenet's opera, is only an interlude (though an important one) in a story which is crowded with incident from beginning to end. All the toing and froing, the arrests and escapes, the robberies, ambushes, plots and disguises, are partly due to the picaresque fashion of the period, to deviate from which would not have occurred to so helpless a writer as Prévost. The result is somewhat too complicated, but has the merit of throwing into high relief the pathetic plight of the lovers, as truants from society for whom there can be no respite for long. This aspect, which is responsible for some of the novel's appeal, is hard to convey within the very different time scheme of an opera; both Massenet and Puccini rely on their final scenes to make the point once and for all.

Among the many episodes with which the operas do not attempt to deal—at all events directly—at least five are of palmary importance to the psychological effect of the novel: Des Grieux's imprisonment at St. Lazare, his escape and rescue of Manon from the Hôpital; the murder of Lescaut; the young G.M., and his farcical abduction; Manon's attempt to recompense Des Grieux for her infidelity by sending him a letter of farewell in the hands of a pretty young prostitute; and finally the New Orleans episode, the lovers' attempt to enlist the Governor's favor, and Des Grieux's duel with Synnelet. The passage where Manon and Des Grieux are robbed by their servants is also of some importance, because it is this disaster which gives Lescaut the opportunity of tempting Des Grieux to repair his fortunes by setting up a gaming house. Equally, Manon's second escapade with old Monsieur de G.M., her affairs with the latter's son and with the Italian prince (inserted in the 1753 edition of the novel) help to emphasize the fact, which is vital to Prévost's conception of her nature, that, despite her profound and somehow childlike love for Des Grieux, Manon could never resist (*a*) luxury, (*b*) a man. (As we shall see, neither Massenet's nor Puccini's librettists allow her more than one lover, apart from Des Grieux.)

Of all these omissions perhaps the most unfortunate is the episode of the letter. To my mind this is the most powerful scene in the book, for it brings together, as in a counterpoint, the strength of Des Grieux's helpless love, Manon's thoughtless irresponsibility, and the pathos of the young girl who wishes to do a kindness to both of them, yet knows she is being made the instrument of a monstrous betrayal. Until this point the reader may not find it easy to share all Prévost's sympathy for his hero; but in this scene Des Grieux's despair is expressed with a violence and bitterness to which the reader cannot but respond. For the first time in the novel we are brought face to face with the uncomprehending cruelty of which natures like Manon's are capable, and from his own words we realize that at this moment—and *because of* what she has done—Des Grieux loves her more than ever before. It is a superb stroke of imagination and we cannot help regretting that neither of the operas takes advantage of its expressive possibilities. There is, perhaps, a reflection of it in Massenet's second act, where Manon allows Des Grieux to be arrested, in order to improve her own position; but the music here does not convey much more than a hint of the conflict which, in the letter scene of the novel, is so beautifully displayed.

It is one of the great merits of the novel that its final section is not a mere denouement in which the sense of character becomes lost under the pressure of action and circumstance. On the contrary, it reveals something we should not have expected—that Manon and Des Grieux are, after all, characters capable of learning by experience. But I prefer to leave consideration of the point till the end of this essay. Meanwhile, it is time to examine in further detail the manner in which the librettists concerned have set about reducing all the crowded incidents of the story to operatic proportions.

Up to the present time Prévost's novel has given rise to five operas and one ballet. These, in order of date, are as follows:

1. *Manon Lescaut* (1830), a ballet by Jacques Halévy. A successful early work by the composer of *La Juive*, the ballet has long since disappeared from any repertory.

2. An opera by Balfe to a text by Alfred Bunn, euphemistically entitled *The Maid of Artois* (1836). This opera was composed specially for the great soprano, Maria Malibran, who sang the role in England and the United States.

3. *Manon Lescaut* (1856), opera by Auber. The text, by Scribe, makes more of the American episode than any of the other versions. Though not much more than an interesting curiosity, this opera might be worth an occasional "festival" performance.

4. *Manon* (1884), opera by Massenet, text by Henri Meilhac and Philippe Gille. Meilhac was by this time a famous librettist. On most

occasions he collaborated with Ludovic Halévy—notably on the text of Bizet's *Carmen*. Gille also has a good many librettos to his credit. He was responsible for the final (two-act) version of Delibes's *Lakmé*.

5. *Manon Lescaut* (1893), opera by Puccini, text by Marco Praga, Domenico Oliva, and Luigi Illica. Illica had a hand in the texts of an enormous number of operas, including *La Bohème, Tosca,* and *Madama Butterfly*.

6. *Le Portrait de Manon* (1894), opera by Massenet, text by Georges Boyer. This one-acter, described as a "sequel" to *Manon,* imagines Des Grieux in old age, undertaking the painful task of preventing his nephew from marrying a girl whom he has discovered to be Manon's daughter. The music is a skillful and charming pastiche of eighteenth-century style. The *Portrait* did not have much success, and although it has occasionally been revived its existence remains largely unknown, even to admirers of *Manon*.

Of these six works, then, only two can be said to hold the stage today: Massenet's *Manon* and Puccini's *Manon Lescaut;* to which operas I shall therefore confine my attention. The divergency of treatment is considerable, and extends beyond the selection of episodes to the light in which the characters themselves are displayed.

It must be said at once that, until the end, Massenet's opera sticks much more closely to the *form* of the novel than does Puccini's. Meilhac and Gille divide the action into five acts (originally four: the second scene of Act IV later became Act V), each corresponding to a climactic phase of the story.

After a short Prelude, which sets the general tone of gaiety mingled with tender sentiment, the curtain rises on Act I: *The courtyard of the inn at Amiens.* The librettists have transferred to this act the material of Prévost's first Paris scenes. The chorus of burgesses, guards, and grisettes, who have come to meet the stagecoach, is joined by Lescaut and two Parisian figures, a tax farmer, Brétigny (the M. de B. of the novel), and the Minister of Finance, Guillot Morfontaine, in whom we discern the features of the elder G.M. When Manon arrives Lescaut greets her as his cousin (not his sister, as in the novel). He loses no time in establishing himself as her protector and the guardian of the family honor. (It may be observed here that the librettists' attempt to mitigate Lescaut's character and position has the unfortunate effect, throughout the opera, of diminishing his impact on the story.) Brétigny and Guillot both try to make love to Manon. Lescaut sees his chance, but when he follows the two men, in order to bargain with them, Des Grieux makes his entry. He is on his way to join his father, but stops on seeing Manon. The love duet which follows is the only passage of lyrical expansion in an act which is chiefly composed of choral sections interspersed with recitative. Their duet ended, Manon and Des Grieux make their escape in the carriage which Guillot had ordered for a similar purpose; and the act ends with the angry Finance Minister vowing vengeance, while Lescaut, by this time the worse for drink, curses everyone concerned in the name of "family honor."

Act II: *An apartment in the Rue Vivienne*. Manon and Des Grieux have set up house together, secretly, in Paris. Des Grieux is writing to apprise his father of his love. He and Manon read over the letter together: "She is called Manon. She is just sixteen." This charmingly contrived scene is interrupted by Lescaut and Brétigny. Lescaut pretends to be furious with the lovers, but Brétigny tries to mollify him. While Des Grieux takes Lescaut aside in order to show him the letter to his father, as proof of his honorable intentions, Brétigny reveals to Manon that the old Count Des Grieux has already secured an order for his son's arrest, and that the order will be executed that evening. If only Manon will accept his, Brétigny's, protection, she may be rich and secure. . . . When Lescaut and Brétigny have left, the lovers settle down, in chastened mood, to supper. The tone of this scene, with Manon's misgivings ("*Je suis que faiblesse et que fragilité*") and her farewell to "our pretty little table," were evidently suggested by the Rue Vivienne passage in the novel, but Des Grieux's famous "Dream" ("*En fermant les yeux*") borrows its Rousseauesque fancy from a later book—Bernardin de Saint-Pierre's *Paul et Virginie*. This touchingly beautiful air, with its simple accompaniment of two violins, captures to perfection the essentially French quality of the novel. The final scene, in which Des Grieux is arrested and taken away, is polished off in three pages of agitated music. There is, however, one delightful (and again characteristically French) moment of irony, when Des Grieux, before going to answer the knock on the door, exclaims: "I will dismiss him politely, then return and we will laugh together at your foolish fears."

The whole of this brief act is musically much richer than the first, and the passages of action and recitative are more firmly integrated in the melodic texture. The device of spoken dialogue over a musical background, which Massenet uses (but never abuses) throughout the opera, is introduced most effectively at the point where the lovers' duet is broken into, first by Des Grieux's suspicions of Manon's fidelity, secondly by the irruption of Lescaut and Brétigny. From the musical point of view the device is a great improvement on the earlier *opéra comique* method of interrupting the musical flow with spoken dialogue. It is also more dramatic than *secco* recitative, because the orchestral background is free to reutter themes which take on an expressive value from their former associations.

Act III, Scene 1: *Promenade de la Cour la Reine.* The Prelude to this scene reintroduces the gay music of the Prelude to Act I, and the scene itself gives Massenet an opportunity to insert the ballet considered indispensable to French operas of this period. The company is much the same as that of Act I, with the addition (for the first time in the opera) of Des Grieux's father, the Count. Manon appears, on the arm of Brétigny; the cynosure of all eyes, she rises to the occasion in two florid arias, the second of which—the gavotte (*"Obéissons, quand leur voix appelle"*)—is sometimes exchanged for the vocally more elaborate *fabliau* which Massenet composed especially for a celebrated Manon, Mme. Bréjean-Silver. In the scene which follows Manon overhears the Count telling Brétigny that his son has taken Orders. Questioned directly by her, he does not deny that Des Grieux still hankers after Manon. Taking a decision on the instant, and despite Lescaut's remonstrances, Manon leaves for St. Sulpice.

Act III, Scene 2: *The parlor of the seminary.* After a short scene in which the Count congratulates his son on a sermon he has just delivered ("Our family should be proud of having produced a new Bossuet"), Des Grieux, left alone, gives vent to his longing for Manon in the well-known aria *"Ah! fuyez, douce image."* At this moment Manon herself supervenes. As Prévost expressly states, she "had always been a believer"; for this reason, no doubt, Meilhac and Gille give her a speech (before Des Grieux perceives her presence) in which she naïvely asks God's pardon for abstracting her former lover from His service. And, in fact, in the scene which follows Manon takes the initiative for the first time in the opera. This kind of behavior on her part is not vouched for in the novel, where she remains purely passive throughout all her adventures. After a few perfunctory reproaches, Des Grieux gives way.

Act IV: *A gambling house.* During most of its course this act is one more interlude of gaiety between the passionate seriousness of Act III, Scene 2, and the final tragedy. Some of the musical material of the Cour la Reine scene is drawn upon, and again the company is the same. Two points must be noticed. (*a*) The fear of poverty, which in the novel is one of Manon's two chief springs of action, is here expressed unequivocally for the first time. (*b*) Des Grieux, fresh (in the opera, though not in the novel) from the seminary, seems not to care for his new surroundings. Prévost asserts that his hero did cheat at cards, whereas in the opera he is wrongfully accused of doing so by Guillot, who in revenge fetches the old Count. As an immediate result, the lovers are haled off in different directions by the police.

Act V: *On the road to Havre*. From the end of Act IV, Meilhac and Gille abandon any attempt to follow Prévost's scenario. Act V is extremely short: apart from a preliminary passage, in which Lescaut (in the novel he is by this time dead) performs the necessary service of buying off the guards for long enough to permit Manon to die in Des Grieux's arms, the scene consists of a duet. The passionate nostalgia for the early days of their love is admirably conveyed in Manon's simple phrases, spoken against a pianissimo background of the love motive which recurs in almost every scene of the opera.

It may be added here that Massenet's librettists do not specify the cause of Manon's death. In the novel, as in Puccini's opera, the lovers' flight into the desert, with all that this implies in the way of privation, may be accepted as sufficient. But the fatigue of a journey from Paris to Havre—even when aggravated by despair—seems a thin excuse. We should, perhaps, assume that, contrary to appearances, Manon had never (as the saying goes) been very strong.

The text of Puccini's *Manon Lescaut* is more tightly woven than that of *Manon*, and the numerous episodes of the novel are still further reduced. The subtitle, "Lyric Drama," is a significant contrast to Massenet's *"Opéra Comique,"* and in fact Puccini concentrates his interest on the two lovers to the exclusion of the Parisian atmosphere which plays so important—and so delightful—a part in Massenet's score. Puccini's Des Grieux is a far more single-minded character than Prévost's weak hero; at his first entry he strikes a "fated," Byronic attitude which he maintains to the end. Manon, too, is here neither sparkling nor frivolous; her pathos, which Massenet reserves till Act V, is established at the outset, in conformity with Puccini's overriding pity for the female sex. Lescaut is restored, both to his rightful position as Manon's brother, and to the formidable character he assumes in the novel. Like Massenet, Puccini omits Tiberge altogether; but I cannot help thinking that the student,

Edmondo, who opens Act I, and the relenting Lescaut of Act III, are to some extent conflations in which Tiberge is an element.

Act I: *Courtyard at Amiens.* The course of events resembles very closely that of Massenet's Act I. Guillot Morfontaine appears as Géronte de Ravoir, but holds the same official position and behaves in the same manner. On the other hand, we hear nothing about "family honor" from Lescaut, who proclaims himself a cynical villain in the style of Verdi's Iago. Manon's fear of poverty is not kept for a later scene (as in *Manon*), but is revealed to Géronte by Lescaut at the end of the act.

Act II: *Géronte's house in Paris.* The action here telescopes into a single scene the whole of Acts II and III of Massenet's opera. The lovers' first sojourn together is nostalgically described in Manon's aria, *"In quelle trine morbide"*; it is left to Lescaut to inform Manon that Des Grieux has taken to gambling (and cheating) in order to regain her love; and the fashionable gaiety of the Cour la Reine is squeezed into the scene in which Manon is serenaded with a madrigal and then given a lesson in dancing the minuet. When Des Grieux eventually appears, there is no mention of Holy Orders, or of Papa (both omitted altogether from this version of the story). Géronte surprises the lovers in each other's arms and goes out to fetch the police, who force the door and despite an attempt at rescue by Lescaut, succeed in arresting Manon and Des Grieux.

Although full of charming music, this act suffers from the librettists' attempt to cram so much into it. The changes of mood are too many and distractingly close together. The madrigal and the minuet are not integral to the whole conception (as is the Cour la Reine in Massenet's opera); though pretty enough in themselves, they have no dramatic justification. Only in the love duet does the composer find room to exploit his gift for lyrical eloquence. These pages are superbly convincing: the lovers' ecstasy is conveyed with a Wagnerian chromaticism which disappears in Puccini's later operas, but which is used here to excellent effect.

Between Acts II and III occurs the orchestral intermezzo ("The Prison and the Journey to Havre") which cause the aged Verdi to observe grumpily that no good would come of neglecting the distinction between opera and symphony. In the circumstances, however, there seems every justification for the interlude, since, after the crowded agitation of the preceding act, some point of rest—of meditation—is needed, in order to establish more firmly our sympathy with the lovers in their plight. The passage is furnished with an elucidatory quotation from the novel at the point where Des Grieux declares the lengths to which his love has led him. The first page of this beautiful interlude is in a recitative style, plainly influenced by Wagner; the rest is a reminiscent expansion of the love music, describing a dynamic curve, then dying away in a pianissimo version of the descending theme which forms the climax of the duet in Act II, at Des Grieux's words: *"Nell' occhio tuo profondo io leggo il mio destino."*

Act III: *The port of Havre.* In this scene Puccini keeps more closely than Massenet to the penultimate episode of the novel, except that here it is Lescaut—not Des Grieux himself—who persuades the Sergeant-at-arms to allow the Chevalier to board the ship with Manon. Musically, the act is remarkable for a fine ensemble (the four principals, supported by a chorus of townsfolk), marked *Largo sostenuto.* This starts with a new theme in E-flat, then takes up the chromatic sequence from the duet in Act II.

Act IV: *A desolate moorland near New Orleans.* This act dispenses with all Prévost's intrigues and consists simply of a *Liebestod* for Manon and Des Grieux. The text has been criticized for this, on the grounds that to take us all the way to America, merely for the sake of a duet, is pointlessly extravagant. This charge would be justified if the librettists had themselves invented the plot; but in the novel, as we know, Manon and Grieux did go to America and Manon died there: operagoers are expected, in cases like this, to know somewhat more about the story than can be conveyed in the text or a *compterendu,* and the circumstances of Manon's final tragedy have a bearing on her character. Puccini's instinct here was, I think, sounder than Massenet's; at all events, in the music with which the catastrophe inspired him he is at his very best. Indeed, it is doubtful whether he ever wrote anything more simply touching than Manon's outburst: *"Sola, perduta, abbandonata,"* in which the woodwind phrases suggest most vividly the boundless solitude in which she finds herself. This passage, the later section (*"Mio dolce amor, tu piangi"*), which resumes a strikingly tragic theme from Act III, and the broken phrases that illumine the ebbing consciousness of the dying woman—all these are truer to the spirit of Prévost's conclusion than the last act of Massenet's opera. For, when life has done its worst to them, Manon and Des Grieux lose their frivolity: they become aware of themselves at last as adult human beings, responsible for their own and each other's immortal souls. Des Grieux's outcry at the strangeness of God's justice ("He had patiently borne with me so long as I walked blindly along the paths of sin, and His hardest chastisements were held in store for when I began to return to virtue") indicate that his sojourn at St. Sulpice had after all not been an act of impertinence, and that at long last he has understood the meaning of his love.

If the two operas be compared solely on the ground of their fidelity, on the whole, to Prévost's novel, the palm must—and here I agree with the general verdict—be awarded to Massenet. Every inch a Parisian, and in sensibility strikingly feminine, Massenet combined a tenderness for women with an unillusioned perception of their weaknesses. Being a Frenchman he approached Prévost's novel, not simply as a love story, but as a love story conditioned, from beginning to end, by a sharply defined setting. The result is (if you like) sentimental, because the music, with its deliberate lightness of touch, avoids the tragic implications of the story, above all the increasing tenacity of Des Grieux's love—a feature of the novel which, perhaps more than any other, has captivated so many generations of readers. But if Manon is sentimental, it is never cheap—as Massenet's music sometimes is, in later operas such as Thaïs, which attempts more than lay within the scope of his imagination. In Manon, as in Werther, he found a subject that on the whole suited him perfectly; he clothed it in music like silk, thin but exquisitely woven, scored with a sparkle and a transparency that owe much to Bizet and provide an unerring support for the fluent rhetoric of his vocal line.

The virtues of Puccini's opera are, as I have tried to make clear, very different. Manon Lescaut was his first international success; in it his gift for big, soaring, full-bodied melody flowered with astonishing abundance. Puccini's interest in the story is indeed centered exclusively upon the lovers: this deprives his treatment of the localized interest which attaches to Massenet's version, but it strengthens the emotional and psychological appeal of the two central figures. If Puccini lacks the subtlety of Massenet, his portraits are more firmly drawn, by means of music that gains in sheer impact what it loses in refinement. The luscious harmony, the Wagnerian sequences, conceal with extraordinary skill Puccini's most fruitful discovery: the adaptation to operatic (and erotic) ends of those plainsong melodies with which in childhood and early youth (when he was organist and choirmaster at the church of San Martino, at Lucca) he had been saturated.

Massenet's opera stands on a level with Prévost's novel: if the latter be regarded as a "classic," the title can scarcely be denied to the opera too. Puccini's *Manon Lescaut* stands apart from both—inferior in some respects to *Manon,* but not intrinsically so. Both works are indispensable to lovers of opera, as we should perceive if we were called upon to make a permanent choice between them.

THE SPITE OF A POET

Victor Seroff

> That the greatly endowed are capable of being greatly silly is a fact which all too often peeps from the biographies. *Pelléas and Mélisande* was the cause of a bitter quarrel between Debussy and Maeterlinck.

"This performance will take place against my wishes."

"How will the world get along with these two poor creatures?" Debussy had written to Lerolle in 1894. ". . . They are so difficult to introduce into the world . . ." he had complained to Ysaye in 1896. For ten years these were Debussy's thoughts about *Pelléas et Mélisande* and there is no doubt, now that the opportunity had finally arrived, that his sole concern was with the best possible way of presenting his work. He certainly had not the slightest premonition of the "drama" his opera would cause even before the curtain rose for the dress rehearsal, a "drama" which involved two beautiful, ambitious and jealous prima donnas, their lovers, and Debussy, implicated only because of this concern with the forthcoming production.

The two prima donnas, Georgette Leblanc and Mary Garden, have both written their memoirs and have stated the case, each according, I presume, "to her best knowledge and belief," as contradictory as one would expect. Of these two accounts of the story, Georgette Leblanc's, written some twenty years after the events took place, is shorter and calmer, as befits the loser in a contest, while Mary Garden's, as told from a memory of fifty years, is so emotional—perhaps understandably—and so vague about dates, that it can serve only as an illustration of the characters entangled in an intrigue that gave Debussy an unnecessary headache.

Both women were singers well known to the audiences of the Opéra Comique, and both were closely connected with Albert Carré, the director, and André Messager, the conductor, who had the decisive

Victor Seroff, *Debussy: Musician of France*, copyright 1956, G. P. Putnam's Sons.

voices in choosing the cast. Mary Garden had had a two-year-long love affair with Messager and says in her memoirs that Carré had asked her to marry him. Georgette Leblanc had recently married Maeterlinck and in her story insinuates that Carré was not entirely indifferent to her. Such were the cast and the aphrodisiac atmosphere into which Debussy stepped with his score of *Pelléas et Mélisande.*

According to Leblanc—and it does not sound improbable—during or at the end of the summer of 1901, Debussy went to see Maeterlinck, who was then living in Paris on rue Raynouard in Passy. While Debussy played his score, Maeterlinck smoked his pipe and, having neither understanding nor interest in music, fell half asleep from boredom. Behind Debussy's back Georgette Leblanc made a desperate effort to keep her husband awake. Before Debussy left they spoke of possible choices for the roles and Leblanc expressed her ardent desire to sing Mélisande. Maeterlinck agreed and Debussy was "enchanted." They arranged immediately to study together, and they did—two or three times at the Maeterlincks' and twice at Debussy's apartment on rue Cardinet. Debussy seems to have been perfectly satisfied with Leblanc.

Meanwhile, an important conference was held at the Café Weber between Carré, Messager and Debussy. Many names were suggested and discarded in connection with the casting, and whether because they were reminded of a similar situation when Carré and Messager had spent months searching for the right person to play Louise before they discovered Mlle. Marthe Rioton, or for more personal reasons, Carré brought up the name of Garden and her sensational debut while substituting for Rioton, who fell ill during a performance of *Louise.* Debussy knew nothing about Mary Garden, but Carré insisted: "I think even her charming inexperience is an asset in this case."

Thereupon it was arranged for the cast to meet Debussy at Messager's apartment and to hear his work. "Debussy played his score and sang all the parts in that deep, sepulchral voice of his, but with an expression that grew more and more irresistible," Messager said. "The impression produced by his music that day was, I think, a unique experience. At first, there was an atmosphere of mistrust and antagonism; then gradually the attention of the hearers was caught and held; little by little emotion overcame them; and the last notes of Mélisande's death scene fell amidst silence and tears." Mary Garden says that she burst into "the most awful sobbing," and Madame

Messager began to sob along with her, and both of them fled into the next room.

On January 13 the rehearsals began and a few days later Maeterlinck read in the newspapers the name of Mary Garden as Mélisande and not that of his wife, Georgette Leblanc. Enraged—he was going to stop the production—Maeterlinck appealed to the Société des Auteurs, basing his complaint on the fact that the registration of *Pelléas* at the Society on December 30, 1901, was illegal, since it did not have his signature, and reserving all rights regarding the performance until he should be given the list of the cast for his approval. Called on for an explanation, Debussy quoted Maeterlinck's written authorization dated October 19, 1895, giving him the right to produce the opera "when, how and wherever" he liked. And as for Maeterlinck's assertion that only a few months previously Debussy had agreed to give Leblanc the role of Mélisande, Debussy denied it, saying that he had not committed himself any further than the casual "we will see."

On February 7, following Maeterlinck's formal complaint, Victorien Sardou, then presiding over La Commission des Auteurs, summoned both parties for the committee's next session, and on the fourteenth of the same month Debussy declared his firm stand in regard to Garden. The Commission proposed that both sides submit to arbitration. Debussy accepted. Maeterlinck promised to give his answer, and a week later announced that he had decided to appeal to the courts, bringing the case also against Carré, whom he considered equally responsible. On February 27 the court decided in Debussy's favor on a purely legalistic basis.

Brandishing his cane, Maeterlinck told Leblanc that he would use it on Debussy "to teach him how to live," and as their apartment was on the street level, walked out of the window with the air of a crusader on his way to revenge. Debussy took refuge in an armchair when the unexpected guest entered his apartment and Lily rushed to him with the smelling salts. She begged the poet to leave. What else could he do, Maeterlinck said later, "All crazy, all sick, these musicians!"

But Maeterlinck was not through. Leblanc was worried that Debussy would send his seconds to Maeterlinck, and Maeterlinck threatened to challenge Carré to a duel. Debussy had betrayed him, Maeterlinck raved. But the true villain was Carré who, he said, was taking vengeance on Leblanc because a few years previously, when Leblanc sang *Carmen* at the Opéra Comique, she had refused to become his mistress.

Debussy had no intention of fighting a duel, he had far more serious things on his mind. The rehearsals began in the middle of January and for three and a half months continued till the day of the performance—forty-one rehearsals with the cast, not counting those with the orchestra alone. Soon the initial enthusiasm began to sag. Debussy had left the copying of the orchestra parts to an inexperienced musician, a piano student, who though conscientiously counting all the "rests" would forget to mark the changes in meter and tonality and often simply mistook sharps for flats. This caused frequent interruptions during the rehearsals and the orchestra men rebelled. "A despicable pack of hounds," Debussy growled, and himself tried to help, explain and correct wherever he could.

Some members of the orchestra, particularly from the brass section, were so moved by Mélisande's death scene that they would come up to Messager and say: "We have very little to do in this part, and we don't know how it sounds to you here at your desk, but when Arkel says 'If I were God I would have pity on men' . . . that is truly beautiful." But there was a large section of the cast and musicians who were tired out from the unusually long rehearsing and were getting bored.

To Debussy all this was mere detail. For Carré had asked him to write some more music for the entr'actes in order to give him time to change the scenery. It had to fit what was already written and not disturb the composition as a whole. When not at the theater, Debussy worked at his desk, while Messager kept sending letters and telegrams asking for the music for the next scene and threatening to cancel rehearsals. These were piled together with notes from bailiffs and summonses to court for nonpayment of debts. Debussy spent the nights composing, rearranging and adding to his score to fit the needs of Carré's production and certainly did not think of Maeterlinck, who on March 19 came to the Opéra Comique, sat through two rehearsals, first of the orchestra and later of the whole company, and then without a word to anyone walked out. No one expected to hear from him again. But no one knew that Maeterlinck had changed his tactics.

He was not going to leave this "affair" in the hands of justice alone. He went to a fortuneteller, in good faith, as he said; that is, if he did not entirely believe in clairvoyant force, he was open-minded about

it and was ready to put it to a test. The whole business with *Pelléas*
seemed to him an excellent occasion for such an experiment, since,
he said, in this intrigue several powerful and hostile wills were engaged in a struggle against him. "The forces were well balanced and
according to human logic it was impossible to predict the outcome
and who was going to be the victor," Maeterlinck wrote later on,
describing in detail his visit to the fortuneteller.[1]

Maeterlinck chose the most famous clairvoyant in Paris. During
her trance the middle-aged woman claimed to have incarnated herself
into the spirit of a little girl named Julia. Sitting across the table from
Maeterlinck, she asked him to concentrate on the subject of his
trouble and to speak to her as he would to a girl of seven or eight.
Then her hands, her eyes and her whole body went through convulsions Maeterlinck found disagreeable to witness. With her hair dis-
arranged, the expression of her face completely changed to a naïve
and childish one, her voice a high descant, she began her discourse.

Maeterlinck was inclined to believe her as she slowly described
not only the places, but the faces and the characters of everyone involved in his "trouble."

"But how will it all end?" said Maeterlinck. "Will I be the one
who will win, or the enemy who resists me and wishes me ill?"

"Ah, this [that is, the future] is much harder to tell," the voice
said—and particularly because the enemy was not against Maeterlinck but "because of another person."—"I cannot see why he de-
tests her!" the voice continued. "Oh, how he hates her, how he hates
her! And it is because you love her that he does not want you to
do what you want to do for her."

"But," Maeterlinck anxiously asked, "will he go to the extreme,
isn't he going to compromise at all?"

"Oh, don't worry about him. I see he is sick and will not live long."

"Nonsense!" said Maeterlinck, "I saw him the day before yesterday.
He is perfectly well."

"No, no . . . this does not mean anything," the voice reassured,
"he is sick, it does not show, but he is very ill. He is going to die
soon."

"But when and how?"

"He is covered with blood. I see blood around him, everywhere."

"Blood? Does it mean a duel?" [Here Maeterlinck wrote in paren-

---

[1] In Maurice Maeterlinck's collection of six essays, *The Future* (not translated into
English).

thesis: "I was thinking for a while of finding a pretext to fight my adversary."] "Or an accident, murder, vengeance?" ["He was an unjust man without scruples who had hurt many people," Maeterlinck commented.]

"Oh, don't question me. I am very tired . . . let me go. . . . Be good, I will help you. . . ."

The same crisis of convulsions was repeated as at the beginning of the séance and the woman regained her own expression and her own voice as though she woke from a long sleep.

Apparently Maeterlinck followed her advice "to be good," for he did not challenge Carré. A short while later Carré actually fell ill, had to be operated on and almost fulfilled the prophecy.

Maeterlinck was not, however, at the end of his resources. When the rehearsals of *Pelléas* reached a peak of excitement and confusion because only two more weeks were left before the opening night, he sent a letter to *Le Figaro* which was published on April 14:

DEAR SIR:
The management of the Opéra Comique has announced a forthcoming production of *Pelléas et Mélisande*. This performance will take place against my wishes because MM. Carré and Debussy have disregarded my most legitimate rights. Actually M. Debussy, after having agreed with me on the choice of an artist, the only one in my opinion capable, following my intentions and my wishes, of creating the role of Mélisande, decided, supported by M. Carré's unjust opposition to my choice, to deny me the right to intervene by abusing a letter which I wrote him in all confidence some six years ago. This inelegant gesture was joined by strange practices, as is proved by the bill of acceptance of the piece, obviously antedated in order to establish that my protest came too late. Thus they succeeded in excluding me from my work and from then on it was treated like a conquered land. Arbitrary and absurd cuts have made the piece incomprehensible; they have preserved passages that I wished to suppress or improve as I did in the libretto which has just appeared and from which it will be seen how far the text adapted by the Opéra Comique differs from the authentic version. In short, the *Pelléas* in question has become strange and hostile to me, almost an enemy, and, stripped of all control over my work, I am reduced to wishing its immediate and decided failure.

This latest missive added fuel to the growing gossip, intrigue and criticism in connection with a work that had not yet been presented. "If Maeterlinck, the author himself, is against it, why argue about it?" was the common attitude. Debussy wrote and telegraphed Godet for his advice on what to do about Maeterlinck's letter. It was decided that Debussy should ignore it. But Carré wrote Octave Mirbeau, Maeterlinck's old friend, hoping through him to calm the furious poet. It was in vain. Mirbeau regretted the ridiculous attitude taken by Maeterlinck—"I have never seen a man so possessed by an evil spirit of a woman"—but he said there was nothing he could do against his blindness. "I cannot ask him to reason, for he does not reason any more."

Six months after the first performance of *Pelléas et Mélisande* Maeterlinck conceded his defeat. At the end of 1902 he wrote:

Julia's prophecy came to pass in part—that is, without my triumph in the major point, the "affair" turned out, nevertheless, satisfactory in other aspects. [Carré had engaged Leblanc for a title role in Dukas's *Ariane et Barbe-Bleue*, an opera written after Maeterlinck's play.] As for the death of my adversary, it has not happened yet and willingly I release the future from keeping the promise given me by an innocent child of the unknown world.

But Maeterlinck never forgave Debussy. In 1909 he attended a performance of *Pelléas et Mélisande* at the Manhattan Opera House in New York. He walked out after the first act.

GERMAN OPERA

AMBROSIA AND PRETZELS

George R. Marek

From the time in the seventeenth century when a certain Johann Wolfgang Franck (no ancestor of César Franck and no relation to Johann Wolfgang Goethe) began to compose fourteen operas, down to the latest product of Carl Orff, there have been presented in the German opera houses, large and small, provincial or attended by cosmopolitan guests, as many different operas as have come and gone across the boards of Italy. We are a little astonished by this productivity. We think of Italy as the field in which operas are harvested. We imagine that in whatever corner of Parnassus operatic composers congregate, the prevailing language would be Italian. It appears that on our visit there we will be asked, *"Sprechen Sie Deutsch?"*

Whom would we meet in this spectral company? Talents earnest but limited, musicians careful but uninspiring, composers punctilious but plodding, men whose operas are unseasoned with that dash of trivial spice which makes even a second-rate Italian opera palatable. We would hear them talk of lofty purposes, of presenting "Duty" (*"Pflicht,"* a favorite German word); but the music is likely to induce a yawn. German opera has used a quantity of green scenery representing forest and glade, but the green is a bit dusty and the foliage appears dry.

Except—! Except in the exceptions, the creations of a very few geniuses. All at once we leap to the heights, we hear the most inspired of music, we find ourselves—almost without knowing how we got there, almost without historic logic, taken as it were by surprise—in the presence of works which we can count among the richest legacies of the artistic spirit of *any* nation.

Hundreds of German operas, dozens of composers are drowned in oblivion. What remains? For all practical purposes, German opera, as it is still given in the world's opera houses, can be enumerated by counting composers on the fingers of one hand. Five suffice: Mozart,

Beethoven (he of course with only one opera), Weber, Wagner, and Richard Strauss. In English-speaking countries even this list would be pared to Mozart, Wagner, and Richard Strauss. Nor is the condition very different in the Fatherland. The current native repertoire of German opera houses is almost equally limited. Operatic taste in Germany is turning toward the Italians. The statistics of performances in West Germany of the 1954–55 season show that *Hänsel und Gretel* was the opera most frequently performed, with 251 performances. (*Hänsel und Gretel* is of course a special favorite of children, and as such to be considered outside the regular repertoire.) The next was *Butterfly* with 246 performances, the third *Bohème*, 225, the fourth *Aïda*, and the fifth *Figaro*. Lortzing's *Zar und Zimmermann* held the sixth position; it is a romantic, light opera popular in Germany though virtually unknown outside.

There you have it: Puccini and Verdi preceding Mozart, even as they do at the Metropolitan. Wagner appears in twenty-third place, with *Tannhäuser*. Travelers to the German summer festivals meet, in addition, performances of Nicolai's *Die lustigen Weiber von Windsor*, the opera which is a bumpkin cousin of *Falstaff*. These same festivals attempt to persuade the public that Pfitzner's *Palestrina* is important; the public fails to be persuaded. More international interest lingers in Alban Berg's galled and fascinating work, *Wozzeck*.

But never mind popularity and current tastes: it is still true that what remains after the inexorable melting down by history is the purest gold. Now we are permitted to mention Mozart's name; we can enjoy ourselves without reserve, without fatigue, without cessation. As long as the sense of beauty remains, so long will we continue to listen in wonder and in admiration to *Don Giovanni* and *Figaro*.

Now, too, appears Richard Wagner, the arrogant oracle who a generation ago stood on the high place, who now has come down a step or two, but who nonetheless, and with all the rebellion and irritation that his music may evoke, remains an overwhelming sorcerer.

Why is it that the peaks in the Teutonic range are so high amid so flat a terrain? One cause may lie in the German tendency to imitation, an adoption of and respect for foreign forms, against which tendency the Germans react from time to time with an exaggerated shudder—only to revert to it after the turmoil. For many years the opera houses of the small disjointed German states demanded works which were reworkings of the Italian *opera buffa* or of the French ballet opera. In Saxony as well as in the more cosmopolitan Vienna there were performed—to be sure with less expensive scenery, less elaborate costumes, and less graceful dancing—operas that came as near as possible to those to be heard in Paris or in Naples. In Mozart's time the successful opera composer was he who could concoct a dish with imported ingredients. The taste of the public and the court was hardly propitious to the development of a native art. Only the strongest could dare it. Even in Beethoven's time, when German symphonic music had already made its mark, Vienna wanted Rossini and nothing but Rossini.

Only gradually there sprang up a demand for truly home-cooked German opera. This demand was at first modest; it was satisfied in the late eighteenth century with the Singspiel. This "song-play" was a little play, comic in character, to which a little music was added. Sometimes it was caparisoned with a few magic tricks and was then called a *Zauberoper* (Magic Opera). To the first category belonged Mozart's *Abduction from the Seraglio*, out of the second grew *The Magic Flute*.

It has also been pointed out that the musical ability of Germany lies along symphonic rather than vocal lines. Such a statement must leave room for many exceptions. The German Lied is a vocal product, and where will you find the human voice more considerately treated than in the songs of Schubert, Schumann, and Brahms? Perhaps it is more accurate to say that the German genius is not altogether comfortable on the stage. Here again exceptions protrude, a long line of plays from Kleist and Lessing, Goethe and Schiller, to Sudermann and Hauptmann. The works of the German classics, fine as they may be in thought and poetry, do not as plays rival what the English or the Russian theater offers. And in opera, worthiness of sentiment, villains all black, knights all shining, and a traipsing forth of elves and gnomes substitute too often for dramatic vitality. It is significant that several of Germany's and Austria's greatest composers have failed in opera. The efforts of Mendelssohn (*Die Hochzeit des Camacho*) or Schumann (*Genoveva*), or the many operas by Schubert were all failures.

But Mozart did succeed. He who mastered almost every form gave his best music to opera. What Bernard Shaw said of one of the arias in *The Magic Flute*—"that is the only music which would sound well in the mouth of God"—could be said of most of the music of

Figaro or *Don Giovanni*. Aside from gracious loveliness and spry beauty, Mozart's contribution to opera is unique because he possessed to the highest degree two abilities, his ability at characterization and his skill at dramatic architecture. Mozart can be compared to Shakespeare; like him he seems to dip with both hands into the fullness of life and lift from it characters which have a way of staying with us as our best acquaintances. Like Shakespeare's, Mozart's power extends to minor characters. Shakespeare is able in *Macbeth* to put two murderers on the stage and give them separate individualities, though they appear and act as a "duet." Mozart is able to make personalities out of such episodic figures as Masetto or Barberina or Antonio. Nothing seems beyond his range: he is master of the pastel portrait of a young boy, Cherubino, awakening to the delights of love —and what a creation that is!—as well as of the heavy charcoal drawing of the coarse and sly servant, Leporello. But with all the clearness of characterization, with all the fullness of identifying music, there remains a mystery. We are permitted to fill up the mold with our own imagination, to complete the picture with our own minds. This is the secret of the greatest character creation: it makes room for a life beyond the frame, in the conjuring of which we ourselves may take a part. We may interpret Richard the Second or Cleopatra or Rosalind. And we may interpret the Countess or Don Giovanni or Donna Elvira or Donna Anna. This unhappy woman, Donna Anna, has given rise to many speculations and psychological interpretations, some of them so fanciful as, I'm sure, to astonish Mozart were he to hear them. That they are possible, that speculation can sport, is merely a testimony to his power.

As a dramatic-musical designer, Mozart's special contribution lies in the handling of the ensemble. Every opera composer writes ensembles. They are needed for weight, for the closing of acts, for the drumming up of excitement. Mozart's ensembles are never merely weighty, with the possible exception of the finale of the first act of *Don Giovanni*. They are the result of the protagonists rubbing against one another. Mozart makes his ensembles sound inevitable: they are the outgrowth of conflicts, whether in seriousness or fun. It is in the ensemble that opera has the advantage over the spoken play. Let several speak simultaneously and you have confusion. *Exeunt omnes.* Let them sing and you have heightening of tension. All remain to enjoy. Mozart's ensembles are enjoyed by all because they weave several strains, with each voice achieving freedom, into a clear and mobile unit. Of what marvels is he capable! One of Mozart's supreme achievements is the finale of the second act of *Figaro*, the most expansive and the most daring finale he attempted. Here each dramatic situation, beginning with the opening of the door from which Susanna steps, is expressed in music of incredible versatility and vivacity, without anyone's losing his individuality. And the orchestra plays as leading a role as the people involved. To name but one instance, its ticking provides commentary on Figaro's embarrassment when he does not know what paper dropped out of his pocket nor what is missing on the paper.

It is wrong to speak of Mozart as a German composer. Not only did he travel so extensively as a *Wunderkind* that he early acquired an international viewpoint, but it is obvious that three of his major operas, *Don Giovanni, Figaro,* and *Così fan Tutte,* are the results of his desire to give the public what it wanted in the Italian style. Still, he did write two important works in the German language: the one, *The Abduction from the Seraglio,* is in size and ambition nothing more than a Singspiel; the other, *The Magic Flute,* is a work of his last year, composed in the period of his last three symphonies, and is in some ways his most ambitious project. The libretto of *The Magic Flute,* concocted for him by an actor-impresario, exudes laudable sentiment, alludes to Freemasonry, and puts forth the proposition that Man ought to be kind. The opera is marred by contradiction, lack of clarity, and childishness. The Germans have taken it very seriously, because they stand in awe of moral sentiment on the stage, perhaps for the same reason that the English, with their bad cooking, have written so well about good food. (See Dickens and Gissing and Lamb.) All the philosophizing in the world and all the ethical loftiness cannot spirit away the awkwardness of the play, an awkwardness which proved too much even for Mozart. The serious characters of *The Magic Flute* are representatives and lack the individuality which endows Don Giovanni and Figaro with life. As to the comic parts, Papageno and Papagena are attractive enough in a naïve way, but they lack style and dash. Far more successful in the round is *Così fan Tutte,* an opera purposefully improbable and artificial. *Così* has puzzled the German pundits and is underestimated by the public, possibly because it contains no moral sentiment whatever. But once we acknowledge the defects of *The Magic Flute,* we must add with the utmost haste that it contains some of Mozart's most beautiful music; silly or not, the plot furnished him with the opportunity for sublime invention.

The Magic Flute served as inspiration to other German composers. They found there congenial motives, enough magic hocus-pocus to enliven stage proceedings, and, at the end, a moral drawn obediently and neatly. Beethoven searched for a libretto with "high moral sentiment"; he too admired The Magic Flute above all of Mozart's operas. He found such a libretto in the story of connubial fidelity. He felt that he needed to lighten this story by a subplot which would enable him to introduce two light characters, the jailer's daughter and her awkward suitor. It might have been better had he omitted Jaquino and Marzelline. Though there is humor in Beethoven's music, as in the "Pastoral" Symphony, and though lightness and grace were not beyond his power, as the Eighth Symphony proves, the mincing Singspiel style seems as incongruous to him as if the Moses of Michelangelo were to smile. This I think is what makes some spectators feel uncomfortable. For the objections often raised against the opera, that it is not vocal in style, or that its dramatic content is better expressed in the Leonore Overture than in the whole opera, seem to me hardly tenable. Perhaps I am prejudiced: I love the work. Surely the Quartet in the first act, the scene of the prisoners, Leonore's great aria, and the entire scene in the dungeon, with the possible exception of the initial tenor aria, and finally the superb choral conclusion, is music of true dramatic validity—and quite singable, too.

It was The Magic Flute, though, more than Fidelio, which influenced Karl Maria von Weber, whose Freischütz was the greatest success of Germany a generation after Fidelio. (Fidelio was premièred in 1805 and then was given in a revised version in 1814. Der Freischütz was given in 1822.) To a libretto which reads like one of the fairy tales collected by the brothers Grimm, Weber wrote music which was gentle and charming and redolent of the German forest. Once again we get our share of moralizing, here in the form of the deus ex machina hermit. We hark back to the old Singspiel in the figure of Ännchen. And we meet the triple-pure German maiden with the blond braids in Agathe. The lovers, Agathe and Max, are menaced by a fairy-tale devil, Caspar. All ends happily and magnanimously.

Spurred on by the success of Weber, German opera now delighted in the supernatural, set outdoors. Now the elves called through the woods; evil spirits were abroad; men transgressed but were forgiven; the girls prayed. The protagonist of Heinrich Marschner's *Hans Heiling*, composed to a libretto by Eduard Devrient originally written for Mendelssohn, was a half-mad half-sprite in love with a mortal woman.

Possibly as an antidote, the romantic comic opera became popular. The most successful of the comic composers was Lortzing, whose *Zar und Zimmermann* (*Czar and Carpenter*) abounds with pleasant melody; he also composed *Undine*, another serious romantic opera, the theme being again redemption through a woman's love. Other comic operas belonging to that period were *Die Lustigen Weiber von Windsor*, by Otto Nicolai, Lortzing's *Der Waffenschmied*, and *Der Barbier von Bagdad* by Peter Cornelius.

Though Wagner arrogated to himself the role of explorer and theatrical reformer, denying indebtedness to anyone of lesser stature than Shakespeare or Aeschylus, it is obvious that his dramatic motives were of the same web and woof as the material used in romantic opera, the German early nineteenth-century novel, and the German drama. Though written with epic pretension, refined psychologically, and sexually slanted, we recognize in *Der Fliegende Holländer, Tannhäuser*, and *Lohengrin* the familiar dramatic themes: the pure woman, the erring hero, the being half-human half-immortal, and of course redemption through love.

As a dramatist Wagner's vision was wide and bold, but the seer's sight was all too symbolic. All too often he ignores the individual characteristic, the telltale trait, the recognizably human feature which we demand even in super-life-size heroes and heroines, if we are to understand them. Though he is capable of creating characters, the *Ring* is a lot less personal than the *Iliad*. As to his plots, they move too slowly and, what is worse, they walk the same road twice.

Valhalla is cloud-capp'd, but the clouds can be moist and sticky. This puzzling genius used fairy tale and legend to twist them into psychological dramas in which protagonists often undefined, often unsympathetic, act out their turgid destiny. And Wagner believed he was creating an art of the people!

Yet with all that, what high dramatic moments are to be experienced in the *Ring*! Even if you care nothing for symbolism, you can respond to these moments as moving theater, as tragedy tense and taut. That is true even of *Tristan*, as a play the most obfuscated and philosophically burdened of Wagner's works. It is true even of *Parsifal*, though the verity of its religion must be deeply suspect and though its length is intolerable. As to *Die Meistersinger,* for once the philosopher doesn't get in the way of the playwright, and—wonder of wonders!—the portentous dramatist achieves a delightful comedy: it is the most successful of his plays and has been performed once or twice without the music.

However, we need not concern ourselves with it or the other dramatic poems as literature, except insofar as they serve as texts for music. Wagner would have wished otherwise. Today the philosopher, theorist, and poet must give way to the creator of works, call them operas or music dramas, which are performed in the opera house the night after *Il Trovatore.* We judge him as an operatic composer.

What, then, does Wagner mean to us today?

Judgment of Wagner has undergone some curious changes. It began with angry rejection of the "caterwauling dissonances," mixed with fascination, but quickly proceeded to acceptance and to popularity. His importance rose to all-embracing proportion until he came to be almost the be-all and end-all of music, whose influence none could unshackle. At that time his doctrines and philosophy were studied with utmost earnestness, and this continued among laymen for a period after musicians had begun to doubt. Reaction set in: it led to a gradual shedding of his theories, or rather, the balancing of them against other theories. New composers, first Debussy and later Stravinsky, turned away. But the public continued to love the music, without bothering much either with the theories or with the names of all the various leitmotivs. In the years between the two wars, Wagner rivaled Verdi in operatic popularity.

And today? His mighty dream is derogated, his music appears less often in concert halls, fewer are the performances in the opera house —though Bayreuth continues to draw eager tourists—and the demand for Wagner on records has decreased. Berenson has pointed out [1] that "Our reaction toward a creation of the past begins to be increasingly different from what it was in those who first enjoyed it. This feeling is continuously changing." Perhaps no other work of art has experienced such violent changes, such ups and downs. If at the moment Wagner is down, I venture to predict that he will rise again. Certain is that in the seventy-odd years since Wagner died in Venice, his work fulfilled, his mission accomplished (or so he thought), he has never once failed to evoke strong likes and dislikes, has never once wholly lost his grip on some part of the public. Perhaps the

[1] In *Aesthetics and History.*

present eclipse is due in part to nonmusical causes. Hitler cited him for his own purposes, and in the years through which we all lived, Wagner became a spokesman for hideousness. It is undeniable that he is not free of the special brand of Teutonic fanaticism which exacerbates anything that is not *echt Deutsch*. But this period has passed and is even now in the process of being forgotten, though something of the onus may cling to Wagner. On the other hand, his relative unpopularity today may be due to nothing more mysterious than the fact that great Wagnerian singers are unavailable, that we have no Flagstad or Leider or Lehmann or Schorr to interpret him.

We do listen to his work today from a different viewpoint. No longer is the canon of his musical text sacrosanct. We admit that Wotan talks too much and that King Mark's second-act speech is musically dreary. It is no longer a sin to make cuts in Wagner's music. As to his aesthetic theories, nobody pays any attention to them any longer. Time and again he has insisted on the equivalent role which poetry played in his work. We now know that there is nothing equivalent between Wagner the poet and Wagner the composer. Under what a gigantic illusion did he labor! For Wagner's poetry is mediocre—except, as I indicated, in *Die Meistersinger*—and often it is worse. Often his symbolism is fatuous, when it appears profound. It is not the talking bird or the golden apples or the *Tarnhelm* to which we object, but to the fact that these devices are weighed down with a bale of cosmic mysticism containing straw, not stardust.

But when we have said all that, there remains the music. And that music has the quality of renewing itself. Rest from it for a while, hear it again, and you feel astonished at its life, its copiousness, its freshness, its logic, its power, and its unique ability to set our nerves atingle. It may have certain faults, it may conquer you by weight— yet it is wonderful, "wonder full" in the true sense of the word. So it happens that young people of today, impatient with parable and symbolism, unwilling to take Schopenhauer seriously, yet respond unreservedly to *Tristan und Isolde*. That astonishing work still has something new, something not wholly fathomed, to say about longing and love. It is still an uncompanioned tone poem, exploring the stress of love in music that is as perturbing and as beautiful as love itself.

Love and the redemption through love—the theme that Wagner had inherited and made his own—finds expression not in *Tristan* alone, but in every one of these gigantic works. The theme rests at the base of the heroic proclamation; it pushes and swells through; it suffuses and floods the brassy utterances. The colloquy of Siegmund and Sieglinde, the parting of Wotan and Brünnhilde, the speculation of young Siegfried in the forest, the threnody of his death, the final cleansing apostrophe of Brünnhilde—in all these Wagner's music fulfills the demand of greatest art, the demand to discover and show us what lies in ourselves.

When Wagner gave us *Die Meistersinger*, the stars stood in happy conjunction. The native German bent toward lovely melody, a gift rooted in the German folk song and nourished by the Romantic composers, here seems to have met the German skill at musical polyphony, the ability to create a bold design and adumbrate it enchantingly. One has to go back to Schubert to find a like inventiveness of melody, a similar delight in song. One has to go back to Bach to find a like joyousness of design. This twice-endowed work has not aged. Eva is no older than she was in the last century, Hans Sachs remains as kindly, and the twilight of St. John's Eve glows on with unclouded beauty. "Glow" and "light" are the words we think of when we hear this music. As Donald Francis Tovey has remarked, *Die Meistersinger* is "bathed in sunshine, with no shadows deeper than moonshine."

One is tempted to say that *Die Meistersinger* embodies Wagner's greatness without perturbing us with Wagner's megalomania. Though the opera is long, and though we may feel that some of David's jokes are rather intramural, it does not weary us. There are not many passages through which we wish to coast, so exciting is the voice of the orchestra and so succulent are the melodies.

Now, as we turn away from the nineteenth century and its great genius who synthesized operatic and symphonic elements, we must turn to the final composer whose operas remain in the active repertoire, Richard Strauss, Wagner's successor and heir.

Tristan may excite our nerves to an unholy degree. Yet in *Tristan* we are still face to face, so to speak, with "normal" feelings. The sensitivity of *Tristan* has been twisted to the perverse in Richard Strauss's *Salome*, to the deranged in Richard Strauss's *Elektra*. That is not to say that these operas are not works of art, that they are pathological case histories set to music. They *are* works of art, the products of a master, subtle, intellectual, fascinating works which carry forward the Wagnerian eloquence of the orchestra. Still, they lack the repose, the breadth, and the universality which we find in Wagner. One may leave a performance of *Salome* or of *Elektra* shaken and feeling that one has undergone an uprooting experience. I doubt whether one leaves it feeling, "This applies to me." When one arrives at supreme art, when one hears the "Eroica" or looks at Botticelli's *Primavera* or pursues Hans Sachs's monologue or meets Prince Mishkin, one feels that in some measure or other, in some way or other, "This is I." The secret lies in kinship. Does one feel kin to *Salome* and *Elektra*, enormously clever and enormously effective as these works are?

Somewhat parallel to Wagner, it was in comedy that Richard Strauss achieved his best. Just as I believe *Till Eulenspiegel* to be his most successful tone poem, so is *Der Rosenkavalier* likely to be his most enduring work for the stage. The musician from Munich became Viennese and succumbed to three-quarter time. And the public responded, pleased and grateful. You find dull stretches in *Der Rosenkavalier*, such as the beginning of the third act or Baron Ochs's long *précis* of his amorous adventures, wittier in the words than in the music, but they are a small price to pay for the rich charm of the music, for the exquisite character creation of the Marschallin, for the gaiety of Octavian, for the champagne effulgence which we take home with us after hearing the final trio and the final duet. . . .

Perhaps it has been necessary for the Germans in their methodical way to produce a great many pretzels so that we might taste ambrosia. Such a statement supposes that musical history follows some sort of logic, a supposition which cannot be proved either right or wrong. Certain is only that when German opera is nourishing, it is ambrosial.

AN EARLY PORTRAIT OF MOZART

Adolph Heinrich von Schlichtegroll

> Schlichtegroll was the first serious biographer of Mozart. He owed many of his facts to personal interviews with Mozart's sister, Marianne. The book was translated into French by Stendhal under the pseudonym of Bombet.

"A being of superior order as soon as he sat down to a piano-forte."

As early as the year 1785, Haydn said to Mozart's father, who was then at Vienna: "I declare to you, before God, and on my honor, that I regard your son as the greatest composer I ever heard of."

Such was Mozart in music. To those acquainted with human nature, it will not appear surprising, that a man, whose talents in this department were the object of general admiration, should not appear to equal advantage in the other situations of life.

Mozart possessed no advantages of person, though his parents were noted for their beauty. Cabinis remarks, that "Sensibility may be compared to a fluid, the total quantity of which is determined; and which, whenever it flows more abundantly in any one channel, is proportionally diminished in the others."

Mozart never reached his natural growth. During his whole life his health was delicate. He was thin and pale; and though the form of his face was unusual, there was nothing striking in his physiognomy, but its extreme variableness. The expression of his countenance changed every moment, but indicated nothing more than the pleasure or pain which he experienced at the instant. He was remarkable for a habit, which is usually the attendant of stupidity. His body was perpetually in motion; he was either playing with his hands, or beating the ground with his foot. There was nothing extraordinary in his other habits, except his extreme fondness for the game of billiards. He had a table in his house, on which he played every day by himself, when he had not anyone to play with. His hands were so habituated to the piano, that he was rather clumsy in everything beside. At table, he never carved, or if he attempted to do so, it was with much awkwardness and difficulty. His wife usually undertook that office. The same man, who, from his earliest age, had shown the greatest expansion of mind in what related to his art, in other respects remained always a child. He never knew how properly to conduct himself. The management of domestic affairs, the proper use of money, the judicious selection of his pleasures, and temperance in the enjoyment of them, were never virtues to his taste. The gratification of the moment was always uppermost with him. His mind was so absorbed by a crowd of ideas, which rendered him incapable of all serious reflection, that, during his whole life, he stood in need of a guardian to take care of his temporal affairs. His father was well aware of his weakness in this respect, and it was on this account that he persuaded his wife to follow him to Paris, in 1777, his engagements not allowing him to leave Salzburg himself.

But this man, so absent, so devoted to trifling amusements, appeared a being of a superior order as soon as he sat down to a pianoforte. His mind then took wing, and his whole attention was directed to the sole object for which nature designed him, *the harmony of sounds*. The most numerous orchestra did not prevent him from observing the slightest false note, and he immediately pointed out, with surprising precision, by what instrument the fault had been committed, and the note which should have been made.

When Mozart went to Berlin, he arrived late in the evening. Scarcely had he alighted than he asked the waiter of the inn whether there was any opera that evening, "Yes, the *Entführung aus dem Serail*." "That is charming!" He immediately set out for the theater, and placed himself at the entrance of the pit, that he might listen without being observed. But, sometimes, he was so pleased with the execution of certain passages, and at others, so dissatisfied with the manner, or the time, in which they were performed, or with the embellishments added by the actors, that, continually expressing either his pleasure or disapprobation, he insensibly got up to the bar of the orchestra. The manager had taken the liberty of making some alterations in one of the airs. When they came to it, Mozart, unable to restrain himself any longer, called out, almost aloud, to the orchestra, in what way it ought to be played. Everybody turned to look at the man in a great coat, who was making all this noise. Some persons recognized Mozart, and in an instant, the musicians and actors were informed that he was in the theater. Some of them, and amongst the number a very good female singer, were so agitated at the intelligence, that they refused to come again upon the stage. The manager informed Mozart of the embarrassment he was in. He immediately went behind the scenes, and succeeded, by the compliments which he paid to the actors, in prevailing upon them to go on with the piece.

Music was his constant employment, and his most gratifying recreation. Never, even in his earliest childhood, was persuasion required to engage him to go to his piano. On the contrary, it was necessary to take care that he did not injure his health by his application. He was particularly fond of playing in the night. If he sat down to the instrument at nine o'clock in the evening, he never left it before midnight, and even then it was necessary to force him away from it, for he would have continued to modulate, and play voluntaries, the whole night. In his general habits he was the gentlest of men, but the least noise during the performance of music offended him violently. He was far above that affected or misplaced modesty, which prevents many performers from playing till they have been repeatedly entreated. The nobility of Vienna often reproached him with playing, with equal interest, before any persons that took pleasure in hearing him.

An amateur, in a town through which Mozart passed in one of his journeys, assembled a large party of his friends, to give them an opportunity of hearing this celebrated musician. Mozart came agreeably to his engagement, said very little, and sat down to the pianoforte. Thinking that none but connoisseurs were present, he began a slow movement, the harmony of which was sweet, but extremely simple, intending by it to prepare his auditors for the sentiment which he designed to introduce afterward. The company thought all this very commonplace. The style soon became more lively; they thought it pretty enough. It became severe and solemn, of a striking, elevated, and more difficult harmony. Some of the ladies began to think it quite tiresome, and to whisper a few criticisms to one another: soon half the party were talking. The master of the house was upon thorns, and Mozart himself at last perceived how little his audience were affected by the music. He did not abandon the principal idea with which he commenced, but he developed it with all the fire of which he was capable; still he was not attended to. Without leaving off playing, he began to remonstrate rather sharply with his audience, but as he fortunately expressed himself in Italian, scarcely anybody understood him. They became, however, more quiet. When his anger was a little abated, he could not himself forbear laughing at his impetuosity. He gave a more common turn to his ideas, and concluded with playing a well-known air, of which he gave ten or twelve charming variations. The whole room was delighted, and very few of the company were at all aware of what had passed. Mozart, however, soon took leave, inviting the master of the house, and a few connoisseurs, to spend the evening with him at his inn. He detained them to supper, and upon their intimating a wish to hear him play, he sat down to the instrument, where, to their great astonishment, he forgot himself till after midnight.

An old harpsichord tuner came to put some strings to his traveling pianoforte. "Well, my good old fellow," Mozart said to him, "what do I owe you? I leave tomorrow." The poor man, regarding him as a sort of deity, replied, stammering and confounded, "Imperial Majesty!—Mr., the *maître de chapelle* of his Imperial Majesty!—I cannot—It is true that I have waited upon you several times.—You shall give me a crown." "A crown!" replied Mozart, "a worthy fellow, like you, ought not to be put out of his way for a crown"; and he gave him some ducats. The honest man, as he withdrew, continued to repeat, with low bows, "Ah! Imperial Majesty!"

Of his operas, he esteemed most highly the *Idomeneo*, and *Don Juan*. He was not fond of talking of his own works; or if he mentioned them, it was in few words. Of *Don Juan* he said one day, "This opera was not composed for the public of Vienna, it is better suited to Prague; but, to say the truth, I wrote it only for myself, and my friends."

The time which he most willingly employed in composition, was the morning, from six or seven o'clock till ten, when he got up. After this he did no more for the rest of the day, unless he had to finish a piece that was wanted. He always worked very irregularly. When an idea struck him, he was not to be drawn from it. If he was taken from the pianoforte, he continued to compose in the midst of his friends, and passed whole nights with his pen in his hand. At other times, he had such a disinclination to work, that he could not complete a piece till the moment of its performance. It once happened, that he put off some music which he had engaged to furnish for a court concert, so long, that he had not time to write out the part which he was to perform himself. The Emperor Joseph, who was peeping everywhere, happening to cast his eyes on the sheet which Mozart seemed to be playing from, was surprised to see nothing but empty lines, and said to him, "Where's your part?" "Here," replied Mozart, putting his hand to his forehead.

The same circumstance nearly occurred with respect to the Overture of *Don Juan*. It is generally esteemed the best of his overtures; yet it was only composed the night previous to the first representation, after the general rehearsal had taken place. About eleven o'clock in the evening, when he retired to his apartment, he desired his wife to make him some punch, and to stay with him, in order to keep him awake. She accordingly began to tell him fairy tales, and odd stories, which made him laugh till the tears came. The punch, however, made him so drowsy, that he could go on only while his wife was talking, and dropped asleep as soon as she ceased. The efforts which he made to keep himself awake, the continual alternation of sleep and watching, so fatigued him, that his wife persuaded him to take some rest, promising to awake him in an hour's time. He slept so profoundly, that she suffered him to repose for two hours. At five o'clock in the morning she awoke him. He had appointed the music copiers to come at seven, and by the time they arrived, the overture was finished. They had scarcely time to write out the copies necessary for the orchestra, and the musicians were obliged to play it without a rehearsal. Some persons pretend that they can discover in this overture the passages where Mozart dropped asleep, and those where he suddenly awoke again.

Don Juan had no great success at Vienna, at first. A short time after the first representation, it was talked of in a large party, at which most of the connoisseurs of the capital, and amongst others Haydn, were present. Mozart was not there. Everybody agreed that it was a very meritorious performance, brilliant in imagination, and rich in genius; but everyone had also some fault to find with it. All had spoken, except the modest Haydn. His opinion was asked. "I am not," said he, with his accustomed caution, "a proper judge of the dispute: all that I know is, that Mozart is the greatest composer now existing." The subject was then changed.

Mozart, on his part, had also a great regard for Haydn. He has dedicated to him a set of quartets, which may be classed with the best productions of the kind. A professor of Vienna, who was not without merit, though far inferior to Haydn, took a malicious pleasure in searching the compositions of the latter, for all the little inaccuracies which might have crept into them. He often came to show Mozart symphonies or quartets of Haydn's, which he had put into score, and in which he had, by this means, discovered some inadvertencies of style. Mozart always endeavored to change the subject of conversation: at last, unable any longer to restrain himself, "Sir," said he to him, sharply, "if you and I were both melted down together, we should not furnish materials for one Haydn."

A painter, who was desirous of flattering Cimarosa, said to him once, that he considered him superior to Mozart. "I, Sir!" replied he, smartly; "what would you say to a person who should assure you that you were superior to Raphael?"

Mozart judged his own works with impartiality, and often with a severity, which he would not easily have allowed in another person. The Emperor Joseph II was fond of Mozart, and had appointed him his *maître de chapelle*; but this prince pretended to be a dilettante. His travels in Italy had given him a partiality for the music of that country, and the Italians who were at his court did not fail to keep up this preference, which, I must confess, appears to me to be well founded.

These men spoke of Mozart's first essays with more jealousy than fairness, and the Emperor, who scarcely ever judged for himself, was easily carried away by their decisions. One day, after hearing the rehearsal of a comic opera (*Die Entführung aus dem Serail*) which he had himself demanded of Mozart, he said to the composer, "My dear Mozart, that is too fine for my ears; there are too many notes there." "I ask Your Majesty's pardon," replied Mozart, dryly; "there are just as many notes as there should be." The Emperor said nothing, and appeared rather embarrassed by the reply; but when the opera was performed, he bestowed on it the greatest encomiums.

Mozart was himself less satisfied with this piece afterward, and made many corrections and retrenchments in it. He said, in playing on the pianoforte one of the airs which had been most applauded: "This is very well for the parlor, but it is too verbose for the theater. At the time I composed this opera, I took delight in what I was doing, and thought nothing too long."

Mozart was not at all selfish; on the contrary, liberality formed the principal feature of his character. He often gave without discrimination, and, still more frequently, expended his money without discretion.

During one of his visits to Berlin, the king, Friedrich Wilhelm, offered him an appointment of three thousand crowns a year, if he would remain at his court, and take upon him the direction of his orchestra. Mozart made no other reply than "Shall I leave my good Emperor?" Yet, at that time, Mozart had no fixed establishment at Vienna. One of his friends blaming him afterward for not having accepted the King of Prussia's proposals, he replied, "I am fond of Vienna, the Emperor treats me kindly, and I care little about money."

Some vexatious intrigues, which were excited against him at court, occasioned him, nevertheless, to request his dismissal; but a word from the Emperor, who was partial to the composer, and especially to his music, immediately changed his resolution. He had not art enough to take advantage of this favorable moment, to demand a fixed salary; but the Emperor himself, at length, thought of regulating his establishment. Unfortunately, he consulted on the subject a man who was not a friend to Mozart. He proposed to give him eight hundred florins, and this sum was never increased. He received it as private composer to the Emperor, but he never did anything in this capacity. He was once required, in consequence of one of the general government orders, frequent at Vienna, to deliver in a statement of the amount of his salary. He wrote, in a sealed note, as follows: "Too much for what I have done: too little for what I could have done."

The music sellers, the managers of the theaters, and others, daily took advantage of his well-known disinterestedness. He never received anything for the greater part of his compositions for the piano. He wrote them to oblige persons of his acquaintance, who expressed a wish to possess something in his own writing for their private use. In these cases he was obliged to conform to the degree of proficiency which those persons had attained; and this explains why many of his compositions for the harpsichord appear unworthy of him. Artaria, a music seller, at Vienna, and others of his brethren, found means to procure copies of these pieces, and published them without the permission of the author; or, at any rate, without making him any pecuniary acknowledgment.

One day, the manager of a theater, whose affairs were in a bad state, and who was almost reduced to despair, came to Mozart, and made known his situation to him, adding, "You are the only man in the world who can relieve me from my embarrassment." "I," replied Mozart, "how can that be?" "By composing for me an opera to suit the taste of the description of people who attend my theater. To a certain point you may consult that of the connoisseurs, and your own glory; but have a particular regard to that class of persons who are not judges of good music. I will take care that you shall have the poem shortly, and that the decorations shall be handsome; in a word, that everything shall be agreeable to the present mode." Mozart, touched by the poor fellow's entreaties, promised to undertake the business for him. "What remuneration do you require?" asked the manager. "Why, it seems that you have nothing to give me," said Mozart; "but that you may extricate yourself from your embarrassments, and that, at the same time, I may not altogether lose my labor, we will arrange the matter thus: You shall have the score, and give me what you please for it, on condition that you will not allow any copies to be taken. If the opera succeeds, I will dispose of it in another quarter." The manager, enchanted with this generosity, was profuse in his promises. Mozart immediately set about the music, and composed it agreeably to the instructions given him. The opera was performed; the house was always filled; it was talked of all over Germany, and was performed, a short time afterward, on five or six different theaters, none of which had obtained their copies from the distressed manager.

On other occasions, he met only with ingratitude from those to whom he had rendered service, but nothing could extinguish his compassion for the unfortunate. Whenever any distressed artists, who were strangers to Vienna, applied to him, in passing through the city, he offered them the use of his house and table, introduced them to the acquaintance of those persons whom he thought most likely to be of use to them, and seldom let them depart without writing for them concertos, of which he did not even keep a copy, in order that, being the only persons to play them, they might exhibit themselves to more advantage.

Mozart often gave concerts at his house on Sundays. A Polish count, who was introduced on one of these occasions, was delighted, as well as the rest of the company, with a piece of music for five instruments, which was performed for the first time. He expressed to Mozart how much he had been gratified by it, and requested that, when he was at leisure, he would compose for him a trio for the flute. Mozart promised to do so, on condition that it should be at his own time. The count, on his return home, sent the composer one hundred gold demisovereigns, with a very polite note in which he thanked him for the pleasure he had enjoyed. Mozart sent him the original score of the piece for five instruments, which had appeared to please him. The count left Vienna. A year afterward he called again upon Mozart, and inquired about his trio. "Sir," replied the composer, "I have never felt myself in a disposition to write anything that I should esteem worthy of your acceptance." "Probably," replied the count, "you will not feel more disposed to return me the hundred demi-sovereigns, which I paid you beforehand for the piece." Mozart, indignant, immediately returned him his sovereigns; but the count said nothing about the original score of the piece for five instruments; and it was soon afterward published by Artaria.

It has been remarked, that Mozart very readily acquired new habits. The health of his wife, whom he always passionately loved, was very delicate. During a long illness which she had, he always met those who came to see her, with his finger on his lips, as an intimation to them not to make a noise. His wife recovered, but, for a long time afterward, he always went to meet those who came to visit him with his finger on his lips, and speaking in a subdued tone of voice.

In the course of this illness, he occasionally took a ride on horseback, early in the morning, but, before he went, he was always careful to lay a paper near his wife, in the form of a physician's prescription. The following is a copy of one of these:

Good morning, my love, I hope you have slept well, and that nothing has disturbed you: be careful not to take cold, or to hurt yourself in stooping: do not vex yourself with the servants: avoid everything that would be unpleasant to you, till I return: take good care of yourself: I shall return at nine o'clock.

Constance Weber was an excellent companion for Mozart, and often gave him useful advice. She bore him two children, whom he tenderly loved. His income was considerable, but his immoderate love of pleasure, and the disorder of his affairs, prevented him from bequeathing anything to his family, except the celebrity of his name, and the attention of the public. After the death of this great composer, the inhabitants of Vienna testified to his children their gratitude for the pleasure which their father had so often afforded them.

During the last years of Mozart's life his health, which had always been delicate, declined rapidly. Like all persons of imagination, he was timidly apprehensive of future evils, and the idea that he had not long to live often distressed him. At these times he worked with such rapidity, and unremitting attention, that he sometimes forgot everything that did not relate to his art. Frequently in the height of his enthusiasm, his strength failed him, he fainted, and was obliged to be carried to his bed. Everyone saw that he was ruining his health by this immoderate application. His wife and his friends did all they could to divert him. Out of complaisance, he accompanied them in the walks and visits to which they took him, but his thoughts were always absent. He was only occasionally roused from this silent and habitual melancholy, by the presentiment of his approaching end, an idea which always awakened in him fresh terror.

His insanity was similar to that of Tasso, and to that which rendered Rousseau so happy in the valley of Charmettes, by leading him through the fear of approaching death, to the only true philosophy, the enjoyment of the present moment, and the forgetting of sorrow. Perhaps, without that high state of nervous sensibility which borders on insanity, there is no superior genius in the arts which require tenderness of feeling.

His wife, uneasy at these singular habits, invited to the house those persons whom he was most fond of seeing, and who pretended to surprise him, at times when, after many hours' application, he ought naturally to have thought of resting. Their visits pleased him, but he did not lay aside his pen; they talked, and endeavored to engage him in the conversation, but he took no interest in it; they addressed themselves particularly to him, he uttered a few inconsequential words, and went on with his writing.

HOW MOZART CONCEIVED OPERA

Romain Rolland

> The author of *Jean-Christophe* uses Mozart's letters as
> the starting point of an inquiry which is illuminating,
> even if many will disagree with it.

"His compositions constantly sing of love."

His gifts shine brightest in his dramatic works; and he
seemed to feel this, for his letters tell us of his preference for dramatic composition:

"Simply to hear anyone speak of an opera, or to be in the theater,
or to hear singing is enough to make me beside myself!" (October
11, 1777).

"I have a tremendous desire to write an opera" (*Idem.*).

"I am jealous of anyone who writes an opera. Tears come to my
eyes when I hear an operatic air. . . . My one idea is to write operas"
(February 2 and 7, 1778).

"Opera to me comes before everything else" (August 17, 1782).

Let us see how Mozart conceived an opera.

To begin with, he was purely and simply a musician. There is very
little trace of literary education or taste in him, such as we find in
Beethoven, who taught himself, and did well. One cannot say Mozart
was more of a musician than anything else, for he was really nothing
but a musician. He did not long trouble his head about the difficult
question of the association of poetry and music in drama. He quickly
decided that where music was there could be no rival.

"In an opera, it is absolutely imperative that poetry should be the
obedient daughter of music" (October 13, 1781).

Later he says: "Music reigns like a king, and the rest is of no account."

But that does not mean Mozart was not interested in his libretto

From *Musicians of Yesterday* by Romain Rolland, by permission of Routledge and
Kegan Paul Ltd.

and that music was such a pleasure to him that the poem was only a pretext for the music. Quite the contrary: Mozart was convinced that opera should truthfully express characters and feelings; but he thought it was the musician's duty to achieve this, and not the poet's. That was because he was more of a musician than a poet, because his genius made him jealous of sharing his work with another artist.

"I cannot express either my feelings or my thoughts in verse, for I am neither a poet nor a painter. But I can do this with sounds, for I am a musician" (November 8, 1777).

Poetry to Mozart simply furnished "a well-made plan," dramatic situations, "obedient" words, and words written expressly for music. The rest was the composer's affair, and he, according to Mozart, had at his disposal an utterance as exact as poetry and one that was quite as profound in its own way.

When Mozart wrote an opera his intentions were quite clear. He took the trouble to annotate several passages in *Idomeneo* and *Die Entführung aus dem Serail*; and his intelligent care for psychological analysis is clearly shown:

"As Osmin's anger steadily increases and the audience imagines that the air is nearly ended, the allegro assai with its different time and different style should make a good effect; for a man carried away by such violent rage knows no longer what he is about and is bereft of his right senses; so the music should also seem to be beside itself" (September 26, 1781).

Referring to the air, "*O wie ängstlich*," in the same opera, Mozart says: "The beating of the heart is announced beforehand by octaves on the violins. The trembling irresolution and anguish of heart is expressed by a crescendo, and whisperings and sighs are given out by muted first violins and a flute in unison" (September 26, 1781).

Where will such seeking for truth of expression stop? Will it ever stop? Will music be always like anguish and beating of the heart? Yes, so long as this emotion is harmonious.

Because he was altogether a musician, Mozart did not allow poetry to make demands upon his music; and he would even force a dramatic situation to adapt itself to his music when there was any sign that it would overstep the limits of what he considered good taste.

"Passions, whether violent or not, should never be expressed when they reach an unpleasant stage; and music, even in the most terrible situations, should never offend the ear, but should charm it and always remain music" (September 26, 1781).

Thus music is a painting of life, but of a refined sort of life. And melodies, though they are the reflection of the spirit, must charm the spirit without wounding the flesh or "offending the ear." So, according to Mozart, music is the harmonious expression of life.

This is not only true of Mozart's operas but of all his work. His music, whatever it may seem to do, is addressed not to the intellect but to the heart and always expresses feeling or passion.

What is most remarkable is that the feelings that Mozart depicts are often not his but those of people he observes. One could hardly believe this, but he says so himself in one of his letters:

"I wished to compose an andante in accordance with Mlle. Rose's character. And it is quite true to say that as Mlle. Cannabich is, so is the andante" (December 6, 1777).

Mozart's dramatic spirit is so strong that it appears even in works least suited to its expression—in works into which the musician has put most of himself and his dreams.

Let us put away the letters and float down the stream of Mozart's music. Here we shall find his soul, and with it his characteristic gentleness and understanding.

These two qualities seem to pervade his whole nature; they surround him and envelop him like a soft radiance. That is why he never succeeded in drawing, or attempted to draw, characters antipathetic to his own. We need only think of the tyrant in *Fidelio*, of the satanic characters in *Freischütz* and *Euryanthe*, and of the monstrous heroes in the *Ring*, to know that through Beethoven, Weber, and Wagner music is capable of expressing and inspiring hate and scorn. But if, as the Duke says in *Twelfth Night*, "music is the food of love," love is also its food. And Mozart's music is truly the food of love, and that is why he has so many friends. And how well he returns their love! How tenderness and affection flow from his heart! As a child he had an almost morbid need of affection. It is recorded that one day he suddenly said to an Austrian princess, "Madame, do you love me?" And the princess, to tease him, said no. The child's heart was wounded and he began to sob.

His heart remained that of a child, and beneath all his music we seem to hear a simple demand: "I love you; please love me."

His compositions constantly sing of love. Warmed by his own feeling, the conventional characters of lyric tragedy, in spite of insipid words and the sameness of love episodes, acquire a personal note and possess a lasting charm for all those who are themselves capable of love. There is nothing extravagant or romantic about Mozart's love; he merely expresses the sweetness or the sadness of affection. As Mozart himself did not suffer from passion, so his heroes are not troubled with broken hearts. The sadness of Anna, or even the jealousy of Elektra in *Idomeneo,* bear no resemblance to the spirit let loose by Beethoven and Wagner. The only passions that Mozart knew well were anger and pride. The greatest of all passions—"the entire Venus" —never appeared in him. It is this lack which gives his whole work a character of ineffable peace. Living as we do in a time when artists tend to show us love only by fleshly excesses or by hypocritical and hysterical "mysticism," Mozart's music charms us quite as much by its ignorance as by its knowledge.

There is, however, some sensuality in Mozart. Though less passionate than Gluck or Beethoven, he is more voluptuous. He is not a German idealist; he is from Salzburg, which is on the road from Venice to Vienna; and there would seem to be something Italian in his nature. His art at times recalls the languid expression of Perugino's beautiful archangels and celestial hermaphrodites, whose mouths are made for everything except prayer. Mozart's canvas is larger than Perugino's, and he finds stirring expressions for the world of religion in quite another way. It is perhaps only in Umbria that we may find comparisons for his both pure and sensual music. Think of those delightful dreamers about love—of Tamino with his freshness of heart and youthful love; of Zerlina; of Constance; of the Countess and her gentle melancholy in *Figaro*; of Susanna's sleepy voluptuousness; of the Quintetto with its tears and laughter; of the Terzetto ("*Soave sia il vento*") in *Così fan Tutte,* which is like "the sweet south, that breathes upon a bank of violets, stealing and giving odor." How much grace and *morbidezza* we have there!

But Mozart's heart is always—or nearly always—artless in its love; his poetry transfigures all it touches; and in the music of *Figaro* it would be difficult to recognize the showy but cold and corrupt characters of the French opera. Rossini's shallow liveliness is nearer Beaumarchais in sentiment. The creation of Cherubino was something almost new in its expression of the disquiet and enchantment of a heart under the mysterious influence of love. Mozart's healthy innocence skated over doubtful situations (such as that of Cherubino with the Countess) and saw nothing in them but a subject for merry talk. In reality there is a wide gap between Mozart's Figaros and Don

Juans and those of our French authors. With Molière the French mind had something bitter about it when it was not affected, hard, or foolish; and Beaumarchais is cold and bright. Mozart's spirit was quite different and left no aftertaste of bitterness; he was without malice, filled with love and life and activity, and ready for mischief and enjoyment of the world. His characters are delightful creatures who amid laughter and thoughtless jests strive to hide the amorous emotion of their hearts. They make one think of the playful letters Mozart wrote his wife:

Dear little wife, if I were to tell you all that I do with your dear picture you would laugh a good deal! For instance, when I take it from its cover I say, "God bless you, little Constance! . . . God bless you, you little rogue! . . . You rufflehead with the pointed nose!" Then when I put it back again I slide it in slowly, coaxing it all the time. I finish by saying very quickly, "Good night, little mouse, sleep well." I am afraid I am writing silly things—at least the world would think so. But this is the sixth day I have been parted from you, and it seems as if a year had gone. . . . Well, if other people could look into my heart, I should almost blush. . . . (April 13 and September 30, 1790)

A great deal of gaiety leads to foolery, and Mozart had a share of both. The double influence of Italian *opera buffa* and Viennese taste encouraged it in him. It is his least interesting side, and one would willingly pass it by if it were not part of him. It is only natural that the body should have its needs as well as the spirit; and when Mozart was overflowing with merriment some pranks were sure to be the result. He amused himself like a child; and one feels that characters like Leporello, Osmin, and Papageno gave him huge diversion.

Occasionally his buffoonery was almost sublime. Think of the character of Don Juan, and, indeed, of the rest of the opera in the hands of this writer of *opera buffa*. Farce here is mixed with the tragic action; it plays round the Commander's statue and Elvira's grief. The serenade scene is a farcical situation; but Mozart's spirit has turned it into a scene of excellent comedy. The whole character of Don Juan is drawn with extraordinary versatility. In truth, it is an exceptional composition, both in Mozart's own work and perhaps even in the musical art of the eighteenth century.

We must go to Wagner to find in musical drama characters that have so true a life and that are as complete and reasonable from one end of the opera to the other. If there is anything surprising in this, it is that Mozart was able to depict so surely the character of a skeptical and aristocratic libertine. But if one studies Don Juan a little closer, one sees in his brilliance, his selfishness, his teasing spirit, his pride, his sensuality, and his anger, the very traits that may be found in Mozart himself, in the obscure depths of his soul where his genius felt the possibilities of the good and bad influences of the whole world.

But what a strange thing! Each of the words we have used to characterize Don Juan has already been used in connection with Mozart's own personality and gifts. We have spoken of the sensuality of his music and his jesting spirit; and we have remarked his pride and his fits of anger, as well as his terrible—and legitimate—egoism.

Thus (strange paradox) Mozart's inner self was a potential Don Juan; and in his art he was able to realize in its entirety, by a different combination of the same elements, the kind of character that was furthest from his own. Even his winning affection is expressed by the fascination of Don Juan's character. And yet, in spite of appearances, this affectionate nature would probably have failed to depict the transports of a Romeo. And so a Don Juan was Mozart's most powerful creation and is an example of the paradoxical qualities of genius.

AN APPRECIATION OF *FIGARO* AND *COSÌ FAN TUTTE*

Alfred Einstein

> From the author's *Mozart, His Character, His Work*, a
> searching study of the composer, one well worth read-
> ing in its entirety.

"He was a great dramatist, and not just a great melodista."

All Mozart's musical forces were gathering for an outburst.
All he needed was the grand opportunity, and it came with Beaumarchais's *Le Mariage de Figaro*, which had reached the stage, not
without having triumphed over considerable obstacles, in 1784, and
had caused powerful reverberations throughout Europe. Let it not be
objected that Beaumarchais's *Le Barbier de Séville* had been available
since 1775, and had been set to music as an *opera buffa* by Paisiello
in St. Petersburg (with apologies for his boldness). *Le Barbier de
Séville* was a predestined *opera buffa*, and had indeed originally been
conceived by Beaumarchais as an *opéra comique*. The cheated old man
who wishes to marry his ward, the noble lover in disguise, the wily
servant, this time in the guise of a barber—these are typical figures
of the *commedia dell'arte*, and Rossini's genius, his diabolic buffoonery, was needed to rescue them for operatic immortality. What
might have distinguished *Le Barbier de Séville* from the usual *opera
buffa* would have been the conservation of the striking, witty,
sparkling original; but this original was essentially weakened and destroyed by Paisiello's literary hack, Giuseppe Petrosellini.

But *Le Mariage de Figaro* is quite another affair. It has been observed with truth that in Susanna there is a bit of Colombina left, in
Figaro of Arlecchino; that Don Bartolo and Marcellina are pure *buffo*
figures. But the Countess? The Count? Cherubino? The tiny roles of

Barbarina and her father, the gardener Antonio? Basilio the schemer? It took courage to see the *opera buffa* possibilities in this work and to realize them—courage that Mozart and Da Ponte can have gathered only from pieces like those of Bertati and Casti. They were fully conscious of what they were doing. Nothing was more common in opera librettos than perfunctory dedications to members of the nobility and crowned heads; nothing, on the other hand, was rarer than prefaces. But Da Ponte provided the original libretto (which has now become a rarity; I know of only two copies) with the following introductory remarks:

The duration prescribed for a stage performance by general usage, and the given number of roles to which one is confined by the same, as well as several other considerations of prudence, of costume, place, and public constituted the reasons for which I have not made a translation of that excellent comedy [the Beaumarchais original], but rather an imitation, or let us say an extract.

For these reasons I was compelled to reduce the sixteen original characters to eleven, two of which can be played by a single actor, and to omit in addition to one whole act, many highly effective scenes and many witty sayings, with which the original teems. For these I have had to substitute *canzonette*, arias, choruses, and other thoughts and words susceptible of being set to music—things that can be handled only with the help of poetry and never with prose. In spite, however, of all the zeal and care on the part of both the composer and myself to be brief, the opera will not be one of the shortest that has been performed on our stages. We hope that our excuse will be the variety of development of this drama, the length and scope of the same, the number of musical pieces necessary in order not to keep the performers idle, to avoid the boredom and monotony of the long recitatives, to paint faithfully and in full color the divers passions that are aroused, and to realize our special purpose, which was to offer a new type of spectacle, as it were, to a public of such refined taste and such assured understanding.

THE POET

An "imitation"—an "extract"! Da Ponte did not use the right word for his form of arrangement. We should call it a transfiguration of the Beaumarchais original. It is a simplification, which sacrifices none of the life of the original, and which transplants it into a new, purer, richer, and more ideal soil—that of music. I do not know whether it would be possible to drag Victor Hugo's *Le Roi S'amuse* out of its Romantic storeroom, now that Verdi's *Rigoletto* is in existence. But just as Shakespeare's *Othello* and *The Merry Wives of Windsor* maintain their own existence beside the two works of Verdi's old age, so Beaumarchais's *Figaro* holds its own beside Mozart's. It survives for its revolutionary tendency, for its wit and aptness of expression. The work by Mozart and Da Ponte is something different; a *Commedia per musica*, as the title reads (no longer *opera buffa*), a play in which social undertones are by no means lacking, but one that is gayer, more unconcerned, more human, and more inspired. It was in truth a "new type of spectacle," for the Viennese. The success of the work on May 1, 1786, does not seem to have been overwhelming, despite the brilliance of the cast, which included Storace (Susanna), Laschi (Contessa), Benucci (Figaro), and Mandini (Conte). It did not really take hold until it was produced in Prague. The demands it made upon its listeners were too unusual; in Florence, in 1788, the work was performed in two successive evenings, and at the first Italian performance, which took place in Monza, near Milan, in the autumn of 1787, the Archduke had the third and fourth acts newly composed by Angelo Tarchi, undoubtedly because he found them too long. Let us not be too shocked by this fact, for when the work was taken up again in the late summer of 1789, in Vienna, Mozart himself handled it very roughly, just as he later maltreated *Don Giovanni* when that work was produced in Vienna. In Mozart's operas the rule is always: the original version is the best.

We know from the memoirs of the Irish tenor Michael O'Kelly, who sang Basilio and Don Curzio in the first performance, which number in the opera was Mozart's own favorite: it was the Sextet in the third act, in which Don Bartolo and Marcellina reveal themselves as Figaro's father and mother, and are transformed from deadly enemies into guardian angels. Susanna, knowing nothing of all this, and bursting in upon the family embraces, misunderstands the situation until it is explained to her, when she joins in the bliss of the other three over the untying of the knot. In this bliss, only the Count and Don Curzio do not join. We have here a typical *buffo* scene—the finding of the long-lost child—as old as the comedies of Plautus and Terence, and repeated and varied a thousand times in a thousand comedies. Two of the participants, Bartolo and Marcellina, have been up to this point mere caricatures—particularly Bartolo, with his Profession Aria ("*La vendetta,*" No. 4), which is the crowning piece among all *buffo* arias. But at this point they both become human beings. Two lovers give voice to genuine happiness, two newly revealed parents express their genuine good will, and the Count, who has been led around by the nose, utters his genuine spite. The historical significance of *Le Nozze di Figaro* is that, thanks to Da Ponte's skill and Mozart's greatness, it no longer belongs to the category of the *opera buffa*, but rather, to use a favorite word of Wagner's, "redeems" the *opera buffa* and makes of it a comedy in music. No longer is anything of *buffo* style that is sung by any of the principal characters. The recitative and aria of the Count ("*Vedrò, mentr'io sospiro*," No. 17) is an outbreak of passion at the thought that a servant is to enjoy a piece of good fortune denied to him, the nobleman. What a moving figure is the Countess, in all her utterances! And Figaro, who in his first aria (the cavatina "*Se vuol ballare*") sounds the note of the entire opera, "cunning against force," and this with unprecedented brevity and directness, and the most amusing symbolism, brings the act to a glorious close with his military aria. Susanna—what an intelligent, lovable, little creature she is! Cherubino, of whom someone—I believe it was Kierkegaard—has rightly said that he is Don Giovanni as a boy, with all his feelings for the whole race of women in all its representatives compressed into two immortal arias! The unique greatness of Mozart becomes clear only when one imagines how an Italian would have composed these two arias, especially the second, an arietta, "*Voi che sapete*." An Italian composer always had the possibility of using folk tunes and for such purposes he would have found something Neapolitan or Venetian. But Mozart had to get along without such references; the source of all he used was in himself. It is significant that except for the fandango in the third act, Mozart renounced any Spanish flavor, any local color: he did not need it.

Our admiration mounts when we contemplate the ensembles. The Letter Duet of Susanna and the Countess, with its sublime "echo"; the little prestissimo of Susanna and Cherubino before the boy jumps out of the window; the Introduction, in which the two lovers are occupied with the preparation for their wedding and their married life, in ways that are even musically so sharply differentiated; the Duet of Susanna and the Count, in which Susanna, anticipating Freudian psychology, gives such irrelevant answers to the Count's importunate questions. But the numbers that constitute Mozart's greatest triumph are the larger ensembles and the two great finales; above all the first one, which in a thousand measures expands from a duet into a septet—a septet in which not alone two groups are juxtaposed (the Countess, Susanna, and Figaro on one side, and the Count, Marcellina, Bartolo, and Basilio on the other), but in which also every individual is subtly characterized. This piece exhibits a mastery of the counterpoint of characterization, and of the expression of feeling, such as has been attained by few and surpassed by none. Let the attempt be made in the Quintet of *Die Meistersinger* to separate Magdalena and David from the general G-flat major bliss at the end of the scene: it will not succeed. Mozart never made such mistakes, never sacrificed a character. And where the treatment of the voice is neutral, the flexible orchestra offers the finest commentary. This commentary sometimes passes beyond the framework of the scenic into the deeply personal, or even into the metaphysical. Before Susanna emerges from the closet, in the first Finale, Mozart slips in a measure —*molto andante*—of contemplation, a moment of mourning for the world and its people, of sadness at the nothingness of all things. Is this too much to say? I do not think so, even though of course such matters can only be felt, and never proved.

Da Ponte suggests the care he and Mozart took to achieve brief and pregnant expression. And they succeeded: *Figaro*, big as the score is, is not too long. Only two arias can be omitted—the ones for Marcellina and for Basilio at the beginning of the fourth act, which Mozart wrote for the sake of the two "secondaries." The second (*"In quegl' anni,"* No. 25) is a very curious one, of which up to now hardly any explanation has been forthcoming. Apart from this, the whole work, and each of its four (or rather two-times-two) acts, is a unity built up of arias, ensembles, recitatives, choruses, the splendid pompous march that ends the third act, and the Overture that introduces the "mad day" with a prestissimo. When the curtain falls on the fourth act with its *quid pro quo*—the act that has brought Susanna's *"Deh vieni non tardar,"* and the recognition scene of the two lovers—we are still by no means satisfied in regard to the future marital happiness of the poor Countess, but we know that in this work Mozart has added to the world's understanding of people and to its lightness of spirit. . . .

No work of Mozart's has experienced such opposition and occasioned so many attempts to "rescue" it as *Così fan Tutte*. The composer of *Fidelio*, who regarded the libretto of *Don Giovanni*, even, as scandalous, is said to have rejected it because of the frivolity of its subject matter. The composer of *Tannhäuser* and *Lohengrin* disapproved on other grounds. His thesis was that it was impossible to write as good music to a poor libretto as to a good one, since drama was the masculine element in opera and music the feminine:

The noble, straightforward simplicity of his [Mozart's] purely musical instinct, for instance his instinctive penetration into the arcana of his art, made it wellnigh impossible to him *there* to bring forth magical effects, as Composer, where the Poem was flat and meaningless. How little did this richest-gifted of all musicians understand our modern music-maker's trick of building gaudy towers of music upon a hollow, valueless foundation, and playing the rapt and the inspired where all the poetaster's botch is void and flimsy, the better to show that the Musician is the jack in office and can go to any length he pleases, even to making something out of nothing—the same as the good God! O how doubly dear and above all honor is Mozart to me, that it was not possible to him to invent music for *Tito* like that of *Don Giovanni*, for *Così fan tutte* like that of *Figaro*! How shamefully would it have desecrated Music! [1]

Here we have Wagner the theorist in all his glory as a counterfeiter of aesthetics and history. His testimony would have been somewhat more justified if he had applied it to the *Euryanthe* of his idol Karl Maria von Weber, and had compared this work with *Der Freischütz*. But Da Ponte's libretto for *Così fan Tutte* is, as far as craftsmanship goes, his best work—better than that for *Figaro* or *Don Giovanni*. Quite apart from the fact that it was his own independent creation, and accordingly gives the lie to those who consider Da Ponte only an arranger and literary freebooter, this libretto does not contain a single dead spot. The entire action develops gaily and logically, and at the end we have the aesthetic satisfaction that we get from a chess problem well solved, or a trick of magic. The trick is all the harder, and the solution all the more satisfying, because Da Ponte had only six characters to work with. Fiordiligi is the more "heroic" of the two ladies, while Dorabella is the more lighthearted; of the officers, Guglielmo, the baritone, is the more determined, while Ferrando, the tenor, has a softer and more lyric role. The threads of the action are all gathered in the hands of the old cynic, or worldly-wise man, as the eighteenth century called him, and the maid, Despina.

But the important thing is that Mozart's music for *Così fan Tutte* is not in any way poorer than that for *Figaro*. It is simply different. Mozart was at the peak of his creative ability, and he wrote the work *con amore*. On December 29, 1789, he invited his fellow Masons

[1] Translated by William Ashton Ellis, *Richard Wagner's Prose Works*, II, 36.

Puchberg and Joseph Haydn to a "little opera rehearsal" in his lodgings, and on January 20, 1790, to the "first instrumental rehearsal in the theater," which he would not have done if he had felt his work to be in any way inferior.

There are two ways of approaching Così fan Tutte, and perhaps even more, for every work of art has its inexhaustible secrets and resists every attempt to treat it categorically. One way is to forget the moralistic point of view of the nineteenth and twentieth centuries, and not to let oneself be shocked by the "trashy" plot. The other approach is the historical. Goldoni again gives us the key. He writes:

C'étoit un usage invétéré parmi les Comédiens Italiens, que les Soubrettes donnassent tous les ans, et à plusieurs reprises, des Pièces qu'on appelloit de transformations, comme l'Esprit follet, la Suivante Magicienne, et d'autres du même genre, dans lesquelles l'Actrice paroissant sous différentes formes, elle changeoit plusieurs fois de costume, jouoit plusieurs personnages, et parloit différens langages.[2]

Here we have the explanation for the figure of Despina, who in the finale of the first act appears as a doctor, effecting miraculous magnetic cures, and in the second act as a notary. Once we understand this figure, we understand the others as well. They are not at all mere marionettes, whose movements are accomplished merely by pulling wires. They do not have the same "reality" as Tosca and Scarpia, but, to remain within the field of comic opera, they do have the same as Eva and Beckmesser, Mistress Alice Ford and Sir John Falstaff— that is to say an operatic reality. Anyone who cannot put himself into the mood to accept this operatic reality should not go to the theater at all.

That Mozart's purpose was genuine "drama" is proved by evidence that survives. For Guglielmo, the baritone, he had composed the high-spirited burlesque aria, "Rivolgete a lui lo sguardo" (K. 584), in such extended form that it seemed to him to interrupt the flow of the first act. Accordingly, he replaced it with a shorter one ("Non siate ritrosi," No. 15) and entered the original aria in his thematic catalogue as: "an aria which was intended for Così fan Tutte; for Benucci." It may

---

[2] "It was an established custom amongst the Italian actors, for the waiting maids [soubrettes] to give several times every year pieces which were called transformations, as The Hobgoblin, The Female Magician, and others of the same description, in which the actress, appearing under different forms, was obliged to change her dress frequently, to act different characters and speak various languages." (Mémoires, 1, 43. Translated by John Black, Boston, 1877.)

confidently be said that this is the most remarkable *buffo* aria ever written. But in this thoroughly *buffo* opera Mozart was not concerned simply with buffoonery. There are, of course, typical *buffo* pieces in this score, among which are the arias of Despina, and the whole mad finale of the first act. But Mozart reserves the liberty to change his attitude continually. When the two lovers have taken their military farewell, Dorabella, the more impulsive of the two ladies, voices her state of mind in an aria (*"Smanie implacabili,"* No. 11) that would do credit to any fury robbed of her serpents. When the first attempt is made on the fidelity of the young ladies, Fiordiligi responds with an aria (*"Come scoglio,"* No. 14) that would be perfectly fitting in the most pathetic *opera seria*. It is pure parody. But not everything is parody. When things become serious, Mozart adopts quite another tone. In the first act, Ferrando sings an arietta in praise of the constancy of his beloved (*"Un'aura amorosa,"* No. 17, in A major), the lyric tenderness of which corresponds completely to the sensuous atmosphere of the whole act. But when he has evidence of Dorabella's unfaithfulness, he sings the arietta *"Tradito, schernito"* (No. 27, in C minor), in which the expression of his anguish is as genuine as it is brief. Consider the complete appropriateness of the tonalities, in relation to C major. When Fiordiligi makes the heroic decision to follow her beloved into the field she sings a rondo in E major (*"Per pietà, ben mio, perdona,"* No. 25), which voices a genuine struggle with herself, repentance, and joy at having come to a decision. It is no accident that Beethoven imitated this aria in Leonore's great aria, with the difference that instead of Mozart's two obbligato horns Beethoven naturally used three.

This opera is iridescent, like a glorious soap bubble, with the colors of buffoonery, parody, and both genuine and simulated emotion. To this, moreover, is added the color of pure beauty. We have already mentioned, as a moment of such pure beauty, the Quartet in A-flat in the second finale: three of the lovers sing in canon, while the fourth, Guglielmo, who cannot reconcile himself to defeat, grumbles a wrathful commentary. Another piece of this sort is the Farewell Quintet in the first act (*"Di scrivermi ogni giorno,"* No. 9). What was Mozart to do at this point? The two young ladies were weeping real tears, while the officers knew that there was no occasion to do so. Mozart raises the banner of pure beauty, without forgetting the old cynic in the background, "laughing himself to death." There is an evening glow over this whole score. Mozart is full of sympathy for his two victims, the representatives of frail femininity, unlike the old Verdi of *Falstaff*, who observes the gyrations of his characters as disinterestedly and ruthlessly as an Olympian. There is a touch of melancholy in the moral of the burlesque incident, and we can hear it already in the andante of the overture:

Anyone who has ears to hear will not fail to realize Mozart's personal sympathy with his creatures even in this most *buffa* of all his *opere buffe*. And consequently no one will take even this apparently most Italian of all his operas to be truly Italian—not because Mozart was a German, but because he was a great dramatist, and not just a great *melodista*. For Paisiello and Cimarosa were great melodists too.

A SINGER REMEMBERS MOZART

Michael O'Kelly

> Michael O'Kelly is a strange name to come across in eighteenth-century Vienna. This Irish tenor did live in Vienna and sang the part of the Notary, Don Curzio, in the first performance of *Figaro*. Later in life he wrote—or rather, had ghosted for him—a book of reminiscences. He had by that time retired to London, and after trying his hand as a composer, engaged in the wine trade. Sheridan called him "Composer of Wines and Importer of Music."

"As touchy as gunpowder."

I went one evening to a concert of the celebrated Kozeluch's, a great composer for the pianoforte, as well as a fine performer on that instrument. I saw there the composers Vanhall and Baron Diderstoff, and, what was to me one of the greatest gratifications of my musical life, was there introduced to that prodigy of genius—Mozart. He favored the company by performing fantasias and capriccios on the pianoforte. . . . After this splendid performance we sat down to supper. . . . After supper the young branches of our host had a dance, and Mozart joined them. Madame Mozart told me, that great as his genius was, he was an enthusiast in dancing, and often said that his taste lay in that art, rather than in music. . . .

He gave me a cordial invitation to his house, of which I availed myself, and passed a great part of my time there. He always received me with kindness and hospitality. He was remarkably fond of punch, of which beverage I have seen him take copious draughts. He was fond of billiards, and had an excellent billiard table in his house. Many and many a game have I played with him, but always came off second best. He gave Sunday concerts, at which I never was missing. . . .

From *Reminiscences of Michael O'Kelly*.

There were three operas now on the tapis, one by Regini, another by Salieri (*The Grotto of Trophonius*), and one by Mozart, by special command of the Emperor. . . . These three pieces were nearly ready for presentation at the same time, and each composer claimed the right of producing his opera for the first. . . . The characters of the three men were all very different. Mozart was as touchy as gunpowder, and swore he would put the score of his opera into the fire if it was not produced first; his claim was backed by a strong part: on the contrary, Regini was working like a mole in the dark to get precedence.

The third candidate was Maestro di Cappella to the court, a clever shrewd man, possessed of what Bacon called, crooked wisdom, and his claims were backed by three of the principal performers, who formed a cabal not easily put down. Every one of the opera company took part in the contest. I alone was a stickler for Mozart. . . .

The mighty contest was put an end to by His Majesty issuing a mandate for Mozart's *Nozze di Figaro*, to be instantly put into rehearsal; and none more than Michael O'Kelly (so he was called by Mozart) enjoyed the little great man's triumph over his rivals.

Of all the performers in this opera at that time, but one survives—myself. It was allowed that never was opera stronger cast. . . . All the original performers had the advantage of the instruction of the composer, who transfused into their minds his inspired meaning. I never shall forget his little animated countenance, when lighted up with the glowing rays of genius—it is as impossible to describe it, as it would be to paint sunbeams.

I called on him one evening, he said to me, "I have just finished a little duet (sung by Almaviva and Susanna—'Crudel perchè finora farmi languire così') for my opera, you shall hear it." He sat down to the piano and we sang it. . . .

I remember at the first rehearsal of the full band, Mozart was on the stage with his crimson pelisse and gold-laced cocked hat, giving the time of the music to the orchestra. Figaro's song, "Non più andrai, farfallone amoroso," Benucci (the Figaro) gave, with the greatest animation, and power of voice.

I was standing close to Mozart, who, "sotto voce," was repeating, "Bravo! Bravo! Benucci"; and when Benucci came to the fine passage, "Cherubino, alla vittoria, alla gloria militar" . . . the whole of the performers on the stage, and those in the orchestra, as if actuated by one feeling of delight, vociferated "Bravo! Bravo! Maestro. Viva, viva, *grande Mozart.*" Those in the orchestra I thought never would have ceased applauding, by beating the bows of their violins against the music desks. . . . The same meed of approbation was given to the finale at the end of the first act. . . . In the *sestetto*, in the second act (which was Mozart's favorite piece of the whole opera), I had a very conspicuous part, as the stuttering judge. All through the piece I was to stutter; but in the *sestetto*, Mozart requested I would not, for if I did, I should spoil the music. I told him, that although it might appear very presumptuous in a lad like me to differ with him on this point, I did, and was sure, the way in which I intended to introduce the stuttering, would not interfere with the other parts, but produce an effect; besides, it certainly was not in nature, that I should stutter all through the part, and when I came to the *sestetto* speak plain; and after that piece of music was over return to stuttering; and, I added (apologizing at the same time, for my apparent want of deference and respect in placing my opinion in opposition to that of the great Mozart) that unless I was allowed to perform the part as I wished, I would not perform it at all.

Mozart at last consented that I should have my own way, but doubted the success of the experiment. Crowded houses proved that nothing ever on the stage produced a more powerful effect; the audience (at the performance) were convulsed with laughter, in which Mozart himself joined. The Emperor repeatedly called out "Bravo!" and the piece was loudly applauded and encored. When the opera was over, Mozart came on the stage to me, and shaking me by both hands, said, "Bravo! young man, I feel obliged to you; and acknowledge you to have been in the right and myself in the wrong. . . ."

P.S. Perhaps Mozart was merely being amiable. His view, not O'Kelly's, was the right one. The stuttering of Don Curzio would interfere with the musical effect. At any rate, a stutterer does not stutter when he sings.—G.R.M.

AN IMAGINARY CONVERSATION
BETWEEN MOZART AND DA PONTE

Alexander Oulibicheff

A curious man, this Oulibicheff. Born in Dresden in
1795, he lived all of his life in Russia, where he died
in 1858. He was a nobleman and an amateur musician.
Loving Mozart's music above all other (he quite failed
to understand Beethoven), he published a three-volume
biography of Mozart which helped to reawaken interest
in the composer. The colloquy given here is highly fanciful; we may smile over it, yet allow it might have been
spoken.

"Let me see what there is in this devil story."

MOZART: My dear Abbé, I want a text for an opera, but do
not give me, I beg you, another French comedy. This time I have to
do neither with the court, nor with Vienna. I am to work for the
Prague public, who understand every syllable from me, and for the
orchestra in Prague, who play me at sight. The troupe is excellent, and
the singers can do everything I ask of them. It is precisely as if Mozart
were working for Mozart. It must do me honor. I should like to have
something out of the common run. Help me to it.

DA PONTE: You could not come more opportunely. I am just now
engaged upon a text. It is taken from an old comedy by Tirso de
Molina, and is called: *The Marble Guest, or the Scape-grace of Seville*. Molière and Goldoni have made comedies out of it; I have an
idea of working it up into an opera. It is the most remarkable tale of
diablerie. Nothing like it was ever offered to the dilettanti; only I
feared that no composer would be pleased with it.

MOZART: Let me see what there is in this devil story.

DA PONTE: In the first place there is an equestrian statue, who,
being invited to supper, gets off his horse, because it would not be

From *Dwight's Journal of Music*, May 8, 1852.

quite the thing to enter a saloon borne upon four feet. The statue refuses to eat anything; on the contrary, he holds forth to the master of the house, a precious scamp, in a very edifying discourse, and thereupon takes him down with himself to hell. That will be very fine, I assure you. A player with chalked face, a delft helmet, white glazed gloves, and a complete Roman suit of armor manufactured of old line (*Laughs.*) Moreover there will be lightning out of all the trapdoors, and devils of every hue. About one thing only I am in despair, you see. And that is the speech of the specter; for, although I flatter myself that I understand my trade as well as any one, I am not Shakespeare, that I can make ghosts speak.

Mozart: No matter what he says. Death will speak in my orchestra, and in a way to be understood. I know too well how *he* speaks. Excellent! The statue is a settled matter. What else is there?

Da Ponte: Next there is a beautiful lady; the statue is her father, who was killed in single combat by the reprobate, the hero of the piece. The Signorina weeps, is naturally quite inconsolable, and indeed the more so, since the traitor has nearly played her a very base trick, her, the daughter of a Commendatore, and what is more, the betrothed of the handsomest young man in Andalusia. She swears to be revenged. So far it all goes well for you, Maestro; but now comes the bad part. The young man, who expects to marry her, and who is charged with the duty of avenging her father, makes many promises, in fact he draws his sword; but before the knave, who is as resolute and brave as four, he loses his presence of mind, and the sword improves this opportunity to slip quietly back into the scabbard. Our lover is, I confess, a poor knight. You see him always following the footsteps of his beloved, like a prolongation of the train of her black robe. There was no means of representing him otherwise; so that the lamentations of the Signorina and her schemes of revenge bring nothing to pass.

Mozart: You would bring the impossible to pass! You would hasten the justice of heaven! You would wake up the dead from their graves! You ought to comprehend that it is the imperious cry, the superhuman cry for vengeance, which brings in the statue. Between these things there is an obvious connection. Abbé, I am in raptures with our prima donna; I would have chosen her among thousands. As for the bridegroom, he deserves not your reproaches. How can you desire the *poverino* to do battle with this incarnate devil, who offers a glass of wine to the ghost of the old man whom he has murdered? The daughter's husband would have gone after his father-in-law, and then, as in *Figaro*, we should have had no *tenore*. A fine advantage! *Caro amico*, you know not what such a man is; I understand your scapegrace; but patience! when you shall see him on the stage, facing the statue, his eyes flashing with desperation, irony and blasphemy upon his lips, while the hairs of the audience stand on end (I will look out for that!); when he shall say: *"Parla! che chiedi? che vuoi?"* ("Speak! what do you ask? what do you want?"); then you will recognize him. No, no, a reprobate of this stamp cannot be punished by the hand of a living mortal. It would make the devil jealous. Body and soul, the devil alone must have all; have compassion therefore on the young man. He promises, he would, he even tries: is not that all a prima donna could require of a loyal tenor in such a case! You see, the life of our lover is altogether an internal life; it is all spent in his love; it will be great and beautiful, my word for it. (*Looking over the manuscript.*) You make him swear by the eyes of his beloved, by the blood of the murdered old man. What a duet!

DA PONTE: Truly, Maestro, you are right. What a blockhead I was not to see how much wit I had; that seldom happens with my peers! But will you be as well contented with the rest, which I have yet to lay before you? This villain is a terrible devourer of women. In Spain alone he has already swallowed *one thousand and three*, and the devil of a man has traveled much. You will see that I could not bring all these ladies on the stage; but I needed at least one as the representative of this host of victims. I have taken her from Burgos, where our man stole her heart, and then, what know I how or where, deserted her. This *Didone abandonnata*, wife, widow, or young lady (for that is a point which I leave undecided), cannot digest her shame. She pursues him over hill and vale, and inquires of everyone she meets about the faithless fellow. At length she finds him deeply occupied with another. Instead of offering her excuses, the *briccone* laughs in her face and leaves her with his servant. The lady never loses courage. She is persuaded to wander through the streets by night with this very servant, disguised in the cap and gold-laced mantle of his master. She perseveres in loving the traitor, and after all hope is lost, seeks at least to convert him, though compelled to renounce his possession. Between ourselves, Maestro, I believe that she is mad. You see, we can make nothing else out of her.

MOZART: O the noble, the adorable person! Mad, say you? yes, for you poets, who regard nothing but the actions of persons and the words, which you put into their mouths at random. But to what different interpretations are not the words, nay even the actions liable! It is necessary to look into the heart, and, next to God, it is the musician only who can look in. Mad! At all events she is good enough to excite coarse merriment! Make her say what you will, but when my music like a mirror shall reflect the image of this high-minded and devoted soul, I trust my friends will see something very different from a mad woman in her. (*Looking through the manuscript.*) She comes to his last supper. That is altogether admirable; the unheeded voice of the guardian angel, letting itself be heard before the voice of judgment. (*After musing a while.*) Besides, this passionate and energetic person is the necessary link between the other persons, the two most prominent of whom, as I already perceive, are destined to a passive part. *Didone abandonnata* shall be the angel of the drama, and, so far as the music is concerned, the nucleus of the concerted pieces. She will afford us trios, quartets, perhaps even a sextet, should there be occasion. I have found a relish in the sextet, since we tried it in *Figaro*, although the lyric stuff was very poor. Is it not strange, my dear friend; the better you do your part, the less are you aware of it!

DA PONTE: I am satisfied, if you take it so. As to the sextet, there is an opportunity for one; we are not yet at the end of our list of persons; there is one who certainly will please you: a young rustic bride, who is open-hearted, full of feeling, a little coquettish, to be sure, and even somewhat imprudent, but only from necessity, as you shall see. A morsel worthy of you, my gallant Maestro!

MOZART: And of thee too, thou holy man of an Abbé. We know you.

DA PONTE: The scape-grace meets her with her wedding procession. He is a connoisseur, this scape-grace, we do him the justice to acknowledge that, and he has always a plenty of intrigues on hand. A moment suffices for him to lead the wedding guests aside as well as the bridegroom, who is a blockhead, a regular simpleton. The peasant bride is on the point of falling into the snare, like a lured bird, when someone grasps her arm and holds her back. This is our *Didone abandonnata*, who carries off the prize from the *briccone* in the very nick of time. This master in the art of seduction however is not put down; he tries to use force, which happily does not succeed. The bridegroom, blockhead as he is, is nevertheless enraged and means to have his rights; but it turns out, I do not know exactly why, that he, instead of administering blows, gets them himself, and well laid on.

He howls like one possessed. The little lady comes running in at his cry, and examines the bumps and bruises they have left upon the dear man with the butt of his own musket. A trifle! the little lady knows a specific, that will heal him in a moment. You must not forget, Maestro, that the night just commencing is that of her wedding day. I have done the best I could, *caro maestro*, and have written a sort of cavatina.

MOZART: Let us see the cavatina. (*Reads.*) "*Vedrai carino, &c.*" Hem! a very poorly disguised ——! Well, you could not have made it anything else; but my plan, do you understand it? is to describe in music the sweetest moment of life, the heart's supreme bliss and ecstasy! Another poet would have tried to express this in his way, and would have just spoiled it all for me; but you, whom I love as the apple of my eye, you, my devoted comrade, my faithful Pylades, you, the true poet of the composer, you take my hand, lay it upon a heart beating with rapture, and say to me: "*Sentilo battere*" ["Feel it beat"]. Now indeed, it is for me to feel and to make others feel. All the ecstasy of love shall express itself in this cavatina; glowing and chaste shall it be, in spite of the text. The text gives the language of a peasant girl; it becomes her; the music shall be its soul, the soul of Mozart, as he led his Constance to the nuptial bed. You see, I am already madly in love with our country maiden.

DA PONTE: (*Somewhat excited.*) I knew that she would please you.

MOZART: (*After reflecting anew.*) But, dear Abbé, to what genus does our common work belong? Plainly no *opera seria* will come of it. The great scape-grace and woman-devourer, the *Didone abandonnata*, about whom they make merry, the blockhead who is jeered and cudgeled, even the statue, who accepts an invitation to supper, all this seems to be far from suitable to the heroic kind. At the most, only the daughter of the Commendatore and her lover could come on in the *cothurnus*; and your renowned predecessor, Signor Metastasio, of glorious and enduring memory, would have rejected even these with contempt, because they are neither Greeks nor Romans, neither kings nor princesses. On the other hand, a piece, which ends with the death of the principal person, and whose closing decoration is a representation of Hell, is quite as far from being an *opera buffa*. What is it then?

DA PONTE: (*Almost angry.*) *Corpo di Bacco!* am I then a simpleton, that you can suppose I meant to make an *opera seria* of such materials? My purpose was, to write a *dramma giocoso*, and the comic element is nowhere wanting in the plot which I have the honor to explain to you. But you take the thing up in a way . . .

MOZART: Let us not get excited. Am I not *contentissimo* with all that you have given me? *Dramma giocoso* let it be then; what care I for the title of the work? after us perhaps somebody will find a better one for it. What is of the most importance to me is, that all sorts of contrasts are found united in it; everything in this opera must be brought out in strong colors. Foolery must not look paler than crime; nor love paler than anger and revenge. Else would the last form, that of death, crush all to atoms. There is something so fine in laughter! In *Figaro* I have only smiled; but here I want to laugh out heartily, to unburden myself in earnest; only about whom and with whom, is so far not quite clear to me. You know my views about your alleged crazy lady. The country bumpkin, to be sure, might entertain the public by his rôle, but this does not afford much material for the score. A blockhead in music is the same thing as in the world, *poco o niente.* Have you not perhaps still another person in reserve? You smile.

DA PONTE: I see, I must produce in self-defense the very thing which I kept back at first, in order to prepare a pleasant surprise for you. Yes, my dear, we have a *buffo ex officio,* and I agree to lose my place as poet to the imperial royal *troupe* in Vienna; yes, I will renounce my peculiarity as an Italian to become a *Tedesco* (a German) in the broadest sense of the word, if the *buffo* is not to your taste.

MOZART: I do not doubt it. You Italians are masters in buffoonery.

DA PONTE: You Italians! And who are *you,* then, sir composer of the *Marriage of Figaro?*

MOZART: I flatter myself, I am your equal in certain respects, though not in all.

DA PONTE: And do you presume to be more than an Italian in music?

MOZART: We will talk about that, when our present business is finished. Now the question is about the *buffo;* and if it is worth the pains, I will endeavor to make myself, so far as I am able, your compatriot.

DA PONTE: Paisiello would kiss my hand for his like. Judge yourself! Our buffoon is the servant, the secretary, the steward, the factotum of the *briccone.* Here it may be said: "Like master, like servant." He resembles his master about as much as a well-dressed ape might have resembled the devil, before the rebellious angel had cloven feet and tail. As to the *morale* of the creature, he is a coward, a lick-spittle, a great talker, and a jester, and for the rest the best man in the world. He frankly blames the conduct of his master; he mourns most heartily over the young birds, who let themselves be caught by his amorous oglings and caresses; and this pursuit, in which he is entirely disinterested, seems to him so diverting, that he cannot help seconding with all his powers the bird-catcher, whose dexterity has inspired him with a profound admiration. He curses every day the onerous drudgeries, the long fastings and the dangers, to which the adventures of the Don expose him; every day he takes his leave, and every day his sheer simplicity, a certain spirit of adventure, and more than all, his attachment to his master, whom he regards at the same time as a monstrous villain and as an admirable man, entangle him against his will in the most abominable transactions. You see him sticking his nose into every broil. If his own hide is in danger, the rogue slips through your fingers, like an eel, the very moment that you think you have him. Should he see the devil, he would first shut both eyes, then he would half-open one of them, because the devil is a sight not always to be seen. In short he is a compound of good nature and low drollery, of cowardice and lighthearted improvidence, of awkward apishness and instinctive cleverness, of natural and original stupidity, and of some borrowed understanding. Ha! what say you to him? Have I not given you a rich conception of our *buffo*?

MOZART: Yes, above price! sketched with a master's hand; the only character that you have perfectly comprehended! It only remains for me to put on the coloring; this time, if I fulfill your design, I am lucky.

DA PONTE: I forgot to tell you, that the pleasant rogue is the editor of a private journal, for which his master furnishes him the matter. Such a delectable journal, such an awful chronicle there never was before. In it you find entered, in the order of dates and places, the names, qualities, ages, and a complete inventory of all the beauties whom his patron has honored with his attentions. I presume that you would find also a historical sketch of each adventure. For the journal already forms an immense folio volume. Naturally enough, this servant is rather proud of his labors as editor. He reads it to everybody, who will or who will not listen. As to seizing the fit hour and audience, you will see that he has about as much tact as any of his colleagues, who drive the pen. The forsaken Dido awaits an explanation; now is the time or never, thinks the historian of the king of scape-graces. Surely, nothing can console her so well as a work, in which there is a chapter especially devoted to her; and instantly he prepares this edifying lecture for her. Is not this comic?

MOZART: Comic certainly, but scandalous, and almost horrible. I will put in an apology to the audience, that they may pardon you this joke. At bottom it is quite pardonable. Dido is an entirely victimized person in the dramatic point of view; one wrong more, one insult less, —she is used to that, poor lady. These are all glowing coals heaped upon the head of the *briccone!* We could not collect grievances enough against him, to bring the contents of the piece into harmony with the development and the finale. But, *a propos!* how many acts has the opera?

DA PONTE: Two acts, which will certainly outweigh four.

MOZART: What shall we have for the finale of the first? I should like a grand finale with choruses and scenic action.

DA PONTE: Verily that shall not be wanting. You shall have a splendid festival, to which the *briccone* invites all the passers-by. You shall have peasants, peasant girls, and masks, ball, music, and magnificent supper. Here is the knave of a master, planning the most abominable tricks, and the knave of a servant, paving the way; others are busied with plans of revenge; the crowd drink and dance, including the blockhead, whom they also persuade to dance, though his heart goes not to the violins. All is *pell-mell,* what we technically call a beautiful confusion. Suddenly in the midst of this gay whirl is heard a piercing shriek from an adjoining cabinet. What is the matter? They all look round, and find the young lady missing; the *briccone* too has disappeared. Ah! the traitor! ah! the archvillain! you understand. . . . They shriek, they swear, they storm, they beat the door with violence, it bursts open, and forth steps the *briccone,* sword in hand, dragging his servant by the hair. He the guilty one! O no! bold liar. He is surrounded, encircled, pressed upon, insulted, stunned, confounded; a hundred clubs are brandished over his head. The tenor makes the most of his lungs, the women support him with their screams, as the old geese do when the goslings fight; the musicians jump over their overturned desks and rush out; a storm, which happens to be raging out of doors, comes as if called to take part in the heathenish uproar. Shrieks and confusion, seem to know no bounds. Ah, *mein Herr!* are we fairly rid then of our scape-grace; the pitcher goes to water till it breaks. No, by no means! Our *briccone,* whose eyes glare like a tiger's, his drawn sword in his right hand, hurls back with his left whatever opposes his way; he cudgels the invited guests, receives no wound and disappears behind the scenes, with a loud, devilish laugh. The curtain falls; you clap your hands with approbation.

MOZART: (*Embracing the Abbé several times with enthusiasm.*) Friend! brother! benefactor! What demon or what god has poured all this into thy poor poet's brain? Know, that the world owes you a monument for this finale. Tell me no more; I know the thing now better than yourself. You are a great man. You task the powers of the musician terribly, but never did a more splendid opera subject come out of the head of an artist, and never will there come such another. Let me embrace you once more, my dearest friend, and thank you in the name of all the Faculty of composers, singers, instrumentalists and dilettanti, *nunc et in sæcula sæculorum!*

DA PONTE: (*Much flattered.*) O you are too good, dearest Maestro! Spare my modesty. In your opinion then I have produced a master-piece?

MOZART: (*Inspired.*) Without the slightest doubt. You, or the destiny of Mozart. It now remains for us to combine the concerted pieces; in relation to which you shall receive from me, as you did for *Figaro*, the most precise and circumstantial instructions. I will also give you the poetical thoughts of the arias, which shall characterize the persons as I conceive them. As to the action, there is nothing to be said.

DA PONTE: My rule, my metrical compass, my shears and file are at your service, and I will *say* all that your propose to *do*. You believe then, that our opera will rise to the stars?

MOZART: I know nothing about that, but I believe that sooner or later *Don Juan* will make some noise in the world.

MOZART AND SALIERI

Alexander Pushkin

> Antonio Salieri, Italian opera composer, was a rival of
> Mozart in the affection of the Viennese public. It was
> rumored that Salieri poisoned Mozart. Pushkin, whether
> he believed it or not, used the rumor as the basis of his
> small play. Rimski-Korsakov fashioned the play into an
> opera. The reference to Michelangelo Buonarotti at the
> end is an allusion to the story that the artist, in pursuit
> of utmost realism, actually murdered the model of the
> Christ in his *Crucifixion*.

Scene I

A room

SALIERI: Men say: there is no justice upon earth.
But neither is there justice in the Heavens!
That's clear to me as any simple scale.
For I was born with a great love for art:
When—still a child—I heard the organ peal
Its lofty measures through our ancient church,
I listened all attention—and sweet tears,
Sweet and involuntary tears would flow.
Though young, I spurned all frivolous pursuits:
All studies else than music were to me
Repugnant; and with stubborn arrogance
I turned from them to dedicate myself
To music only. Hard is the first step
And tiresome the first journey. I o'ercame
Early discomfitures; and craftsmanship
I set up as a pedestal for art;

Became the merest craftsman; to my fingers
I lent a docile, cold agility,
And sureness to my ear. I stifled sounds,
And then dissected music like a corpse,
Checked harmony by algebraic rules;
And only then, tested and proved in science,
I ventured to indulge creative fancy.
I started to create—but secretly—
Not daring yet even to dream of glory.
Not seldom, having spent in silent cell
Two or three days, forgetting sleep and food,
Tasting the joy and tears of inspiration,
I threw my labors in the fire and watched
My thoughts and songs—the children of my brain—
Flame up, then vanish in a wisp of smoke. . . .
What do I say? When the great Gluck appeared,
Revealing new, deep, captivating secrets—
Did I not then reject all I had learned,
All I had loved, and ardently believed,
And did I not walk bravely in his footsteps
Unmurmuring, like one who, gone astray,
Is bid by one he meets retrace his journey?
By vigorous and tense persistency,
At last, within the boundless realm of music
I reached a lofty place. At last fame deigned
To smile on me; and in the hearts of men
I found an echo to my own creation.
Then I was happy, and enjoyed in peace
My labors, my success, my fame—nor less
The labors and successes of my friends,
My fellow workers in the art divine.
No! Never did I know the sting of envy,
Oh, never!—neither when Piccini triumphed
In capturing the ears of skittish Paris,
Nor the first time there broke upon my sense
Iphigenia's opening harmonies.
Who dares to say that ever proud Salieri
Could stoop to envy, like a loathsome snake
Trampled upon by men, yet still alive
And impotently gnawing sand and dust?

No one! . . . But now—myself I say it—now
I do know envy! Yes, Salieri envies,
Deeply, in anguish envies.—O ye Heavens!
Where, where is justice, when the sacred gift,
When deathless genius comes not to reward
Perfervid love and utter self-denial,
And toils and strivings and beseeching prayers,
And puts her halo round a lack-wit's skull,
A frivolous idler's brow? . . . O Mozart, Mozart!

                                          (Enter MOZART.)

MOZART: Aha! You saw me enter! I was hoping
   To treat you to an unexpected jest.
SALIERI: You here! . . . How long have you been here?
MOZART: A moment.
   I started out to see you, bringing something
   To show to you; but just as I was passing
   The inn, I heard a fiddle. . . . Dear Salieri,
   In all your life you never yet have heard
   Such funny sounds! . . . A blind old fiddler there
   Was playing "*Voi che sapete.*" Heavens!
   I couldn't wait, I brought the fiddler with me
   To entertain you with his artistry.
   Come in!

                    (Enter a blind OLD MAN with a fiddle.)
           Now play us something out of Mozart!
     (The OLD MAN plays an air from Don Juan. MOZART
      bursts out laughing.)
SALIERI: And you can laugh?
MOZART: Why, yes, of course, Salieri!
   And do you not laugh too?
SALIERI: I do not, Mozart.
   I do not laugh when some poor, wretched dauber
   Besmears a masterpiece of Raphael's painting.
   I do not laugh when some grotesque buffoon
   Dishonors Dante with a parody.
   Begone, old man!
MOZART: Oh, wait! Here's something! Take it;
   Drink to my health.

                  (The OLD MAN goes out.)
          But, you, my dear Salieri,

Are not in a good mood today. I'll come
Another time.

SALIERI: What were you bringing me?

MOZART: Nothing—the merest trifle. One night lately,
As I was tossing on my sleepless bed,
Into my head came two or three ideas.
Today I wrote them down, and I should like
To hear your comments on them; but at present
You can't attend to me.

SALIERI: Ah, Mozart, Mozart!
When can I not attend to you? Sit down;
I am listening!

MOZART (*at the piano*):
                    Just imagine someone—well,
Let's say myself—a trifle younger, though—
In love—but not too deeply—just enamored—
I'm with some lady—or a friend—say you;
I'm cheerful . . . Suddenly a glimpse of death,
The dark descends—or something of the sort.
Now listen. (*He plays.*)

SALIERI: You were bringing *this* to me
And you could loiter at a common tavern,
To hear a blind old fiddler? God in Heaven!
Mozart, you are unworthy of yourself!

MOZART: Well, do you like it?

SALIERI: What profundity,
What boldness, and what art of composition!
You, Mozart, are a god and know it not!
I know it.

MOZART: Bah! Really? Perhaps I am—
However it may be, my godhood's famished.

SALIERI: Listen; this evening we shall dine together—
The Golden Lion inn is where we meet.

MOZART: That's very kind. But let me just run home,
To tell my wife not to expect me back
For dinner.   (*Goes out.*)

SALIERI: I'll await you; do not fail me.
No longer can I thwart my destiny.
For I am chosen to arrest his course.
If he lives on, then all of us will perish—

High priests and servants of the art of music—
Not I alone with my o'ershadowed glory.
And what will it avail if Mozart live
And scale still higher summits of perfection?
Will he thereby raise art itself? No, no,
'Twill fall again, when once he disappears.
He will not leave a single heir behind.
Then what can he avail us? Like a cherub
He brings to us some songs of paradise,
And wakens in us children of the dust
A wingless longing—then he flies away!
Well, let him fly away! We'll speed his going!

This poison—my Isora's parting gift—
For eighteen years I've carried on my person,
And often since that day has life appeared
Unbearable to me. And I have sat
At table with my unsuspecting foe;
Yet never to the whisper of temptation
Have yielded, not because I am a coward,
Nor yet because I do not feel an insult,
Nor from a love of life. I always tarried.
Whenever thirst for death would torture me—
"Why die?" I asked, and mused: "Perhaps—who knows?
Life yet may bring to me unlooked-for gifts;
The trance of genius yet may visit me
And the creative night and inspiration;
Perhaps a second Haydn may create
Great masterworks . . . and I'll rejoice in them. . . ."
While I was feasting with my hated guest,
"Perhaps," I thought, "a still more loathsome foe
I'll find; perhaps a still more loathsome insult
Will crash upon me from a lordly height—
Then, then your day will come, Isora's gift!"
And I was right! And I have found at last
My enemy; at last a second Haydn
Has drenched my soul with raptures all divine!
Now—is the hour! O sacred gift of love,
Today I'll pour thee into friendship's cup!

SCENE II

Private room at an inn; piano.

MOZART AND SALIERI (*At table.*)

SALIERI: What makes you look so glum today?
MOZART: Me? Nothing!
SALIERI: Mozart, I swear there's something on your mind!
    The dinner's good, the wine is excellent,
    Yet you sit silent, moping.
MOZART: I confess
    My *Requiem* is on my mind.
SALIERI: Aha!
    You're working at a *Requiem*? Since when?
MOZART: About three weeks. But one queer circumstance . . .
    Did I not tell you?
SALIERI: No.
MOZART: Then listen now:
    I came home late one night three weeks ago.
    They told me that a man had called to see me.
    Now, why I cannot tell, but all that night
    I thought: "Who can this be? What can he want
    Of me?" The following day a second time
    He called again and found me not at home.
    Next day, while I was playing on the floor
    With my young son, I heard them summon me.
    I left the room. A man, dressed all in black,
    With courtly bow, commissioned me to write
    A *Requiem*—and vanished. I sat down
    At once and starting writing. Since that hour
    My man in black has never called again;
    I'm glad of it; for I'd be loth to part
    With my creation, though the *Requiem* now
    Is finished quite. But meanwhile I . . .
SALIERI: Go on!
MOZART: I feel a bit ashamed confessing . . .
SALIERI: What?
MOZART: That day and night, my man in black gives ne'er
    A moment's peace to me. Behind me ever

He hovers like a shadow. At this moment,
It seems to me he's sitting at this table,
An uninvited guest.

SALIERI: What childish terrors!
Dispel these idle fancies. Beaumarchais
Was always saying: "Listen, friend Salieri,
Whenever gloomy thoughts beset your mind,
Why, then uncork a bottle of champagne,
Or read *Le Mariage de Figaro.*"

MOZART: Yes! Beaumarchais and you were friends, I know;
And wasn't it for him you wrote *Tarare?*
A glorious thing! There's one motif in that . . .
I keep repeating it when I am happy—
La-la, la-la . . . Ah, is it true, Salieri,
That Beaumarchais once poisoned someone?

SALIERI: No,
I doubt it. He was quite too comical
For such a task as that!

MOZART: He was a genius
Like you and me. But villainy and genius
Are two things that can never go together.

SALIERI: You think so?
(*Pours poison into* MOZART'S *glass.*)
Well, now drink.

MOZART: Your health, my friend,
I drink, and pledge that candid covenant
That links the names of Mozart and Salieri,
Two sons of harmony. (*Drinks.*)

SALIERI: Stop, stop, I say,
You've drunk it all! . . . and waited not for me?

MOZART: (*Throws his napkin on the table.*)
Well, now I've had my fill. (*Goes to the piano.*)
Salieri, listen,
I'll play my *Requiem.* (*Plays.*)
What! Are you weeping?

SALIERI: Yes, these are the first tears I've ever shed.
I feel both pain and pleasure, like a man
Who has performed a sad and painful duty,
Or like to one from whom the healing knife
Has cut a suffering limb. Friend Mozart, mark not

These tears. Continue playing, hasten thus
To fill my soul with paradisal strains.

MOZART: If only everyone could feel the power
Of harmony like you! But no, for then
The world could not exist; no man would stoop
To care about the needs of vulgar life—
For all would give themselves to art alone.
We are a chosen few, we happy idlers,
Born to contemn profane utility,
The priests of beauty—and of naught besides,
Aren't we, Salieri?—But I feel unwell.
Something oppresses me; I'll go and sleep.
Farewell!
SALIERI: Good-by. (*Alone.*)
                    You'll sleep a long sleep, Mozart.
But was he really right? Am I no genius?
So villainy and genius are two things
That never go together? That's not true;
Think but of Buonarotti. . . . Or was that
A tale of the dull, stupid crowd—and he
Who built the Vatican was *not* a murderer?

FIDELIO

John N. Burk

John N. Burk is the author of *The Life and Works of Beethoven* and annotator of the Boston Symphony programs.

"There will be no more performances."

When Beethoven, in his letter to Wegeler in 1801, spoke of his success in all musical forms except those of "opera and the church," he was revealing an ambition, which, at least so far as the opera was concerned, lay close to his heart. His eagerness when the opportunity came to him in 1804 overrode a certain lack of working experience, for his expertness in theater craft was necessarily drawn from nothing more substantial than the routine at Bonn, his studies of vocal writing with Salieri, his perusal of available scores by Cherubini, Méhul, or other contemporaries, and his direct observation in the theaters of Vienna, where he was often seen.

The crowded performances were a reminder of the glory which was showering upon talents far less than his own. Cherubini, much applauded in Paris, held his great respect. There was Paisiello in Naples; Paër, lately settled in Dresden. In Vienna Salieri, Volger, Seyfried, had enjoyed the production of many a stage piece, reaping esteem and reward. Beethoven hoped and strove mightily to do the same. The impresarios of Vienna remembered the success of his ballet *The Creations of Prometheus*. They were aware that his name would arouse anticipation and they were ready to gamble with it.

Since opera was the only form of music in Vienna which coincided with public entertainment, it alone could bring the ducats rolling in. Cherubini afforded an example of a long-famous composer discovered overnight in Vienna to be an effective writer of operas. In 1803, when the operas of Cherubini had been given in Italy and Paris for some twenty years, Schikaneder at the Theater-an-der-Wien and Baron Braun at the Burg Theater awoke suddenly to the fact that a golden opportunity was at hand. They fell over each other's heels importing his latest operas from Paris, and even came out simultaneously with the same piece, differently titled. Schikaneder offered to provide Beethoven with an opera libretto which he himself would write, and Beethoven received the idea favorably. He moved into the theater building where free lodgings were allowed him, according to custom, and is supposed to have made some sketches for an opera of which not even the subject is known. In the following season, Braun bought out the Theater-an-der-Wien. Schikaneder was excluded—so was Beethoven, from his opera project and probably from his lodgings as well. But fortune soon turned his way again. In November, 1804, the Baron put his former rival in charge of the theater—a tribute to the value of that arch-showman, and presently we find Beethoven back in his lodgings and at work upon another opera. The text was a German adaptation which Sonnleithner, Secretary of the Burg Theater, had made of a French piece then six years old—Bouilly's *Léonore*.

There began a struggle intense and prolonged. Beethoven alone with his libretto must subdue to his purpose an adversary far different from the pliant and responsible instruments which had always leapt to serve his greater thoughts. Now there were prosaic stretches of text, stage situations which must become a part of him and would not, the necessity of holding down his beloved orchestra as a background for vocal advantage. To adapt himself to the traditional Singspiel of the expired eighteenth century, infusing the stylized airs and ensembles with true and moving dramatic expressiveness, would have required a performer of miracles, a Mozart at the very least. Beethoven sometimes performed miracles, but he was not temperamentally constituted for this one. Mozart had the touch and go of the theater which could accept an inanity without hesitation and on the instant turn it into music of immortal beauty. Beethoven approached his subject slowly, laboriously, from within. In those parts where the characters and their dilemma took hold of him, the sheer power of his conviction overcame wooden conventions, and the story came to moving life. In none of his works was there a more remarkable manifestation of his will power.

The first libretto proposed to Beethoven (other than what he may have had from Schikaneder, the stage clown who wrote *The Magic Flute* text) was an extraordinarily happy choice. It was not a good piece of literature—no libretto of its day was that. But the subject had sprung from French Revolutionary ideals; it played upon the great, all-absorbing motive of liberation from tyranny, and was consequently the one subject that could have set Beethoven on fire. Bouilly, a French lawyer, and the librettist of Cherubini's *The Water Carrier*, had written the original book for Paris in 1798, as *Léonore, ou l'Amour Conjugal*, and Gaveaux had set it. Bouilly let it be known in his memoirs that the tale of the imprisonment of Florestan by a political enemy, and the efforts of his wife, Léonore, to liberate him by disguising herself as a jailer at the risk of her life, had a basis of fact in the days of the Terror. He had also intimated that he had set the scene in Spain for discretionary reasons. The book had been popular enough to make its way, in those days of free borrowing, into three languages. Paër had composed a score for an Italian version, *Leonora*, which opened the Dresden season in 1804, just at the time that Beethoven began to compose his German version. Sonnleithner had been called into service for this translation. The title was changed to *Fidelio*, so as to avoid confusion with Paër's opera; Beethoven naturally much preferred the real name to the assumed name of his heroine, and struggled in vain to keep the title. He showed his preference by naming two overtures "Leonore" when they were separately performed and published.

Beethoven could not rise above those scenes in Bouilly's text which were no more than a typical romantic effusion of the time. But the concept of cruel oppression overcome through a conjugal fidelity all-enduring and all-surpassing was to Beethoven more than the current coin of romantic tale-telling. It was a vitalizing impulse transcending pedestrian dialogue and stock situations. The pity of Florestan wasting away his life in a dungeon with no gleam of hope became something for every generation to feel, whatever its fashion in sentiment. The plight of his fellow prisoners, wan shadows of the men they once were—Beethoven lived and suffered in these with a compassion which too has outlasted all fashions. Leonore was to him woman's love at its noblest, deep and quiet, unfaltering and unquestioning.

Beethoven composed the scenes in order, as if to preserve in his own mind the continuity of unfoldment. The many pages of the sketchbooks, an astonishing tangle of notations decipherable only to himself, are proof of his devotion to his task, but proof no less of his labors to subjugate a resistant medium to his expressive intent. He made eighteen beginnings to the famous air *"In des Lebens Frühling-*

stagen" before he found what he was seeking: the full sense of Florestan's hopeless vision of the fair world which has been shut out to him. The jubilant final chorus "*O namenlose Freude*" was also arrived at by many stages.

Beethoven retired to Hetzendorf for the summer months of 1805 and between June and September made his last rounding out of the score. Returning to Vienna and his quarters in the Theater-an-der-Wien, he was able to hand to Sebastian Meier the complete music in performable shape. The opera was promptly put into rehearsal.

And now began the first episode in the unfortunate early career of *Fidelio*. When the initial performance was announced the attention of all Vienna was distracted by fearful speculations. The armies of France were moving steadily up the Rhine Valley, and across southern Germany. Austria lay before them, and Austria's capital would be Napoleon's certain objective. Ulm fell on October 20, and ten days later the news came that the boundary had been crossed. Bernadotte was in occupation of Salzburg. The progress down the Danube continued. Vienna, fair and proud, inviolate through her centuries, lay quite undefended. The nobility packed their jewels in their carriages and joined the trek of refugees which crowded the roads to Brünn or Pressburg. The best male singers were not available for *Fidelio*. Demmer, a tenor successful in light roles, had little idea of the character of Florestan. The villainous Don Pizarro fell to Sebastian Meier, who was a better stage manager than baritone. Anna Pauline Milder, the Leonore, had an ample voice; it was when she was only fourteen that Haydn had listened to her and exclaimed: "My dear child, you have a voice like a house!" Milder was to become famous in this part, but only later, with maturity and experience. She was now only twenty. The conscientious Seyfried rehearsed the opera, but the rehearsals were hasty and preoccupied. The tension and uncertainty which gripped Vienna made its way to the stage and orchestra.

On November 13, just a week before the scheduled first performance, the French battalions marched into Vienna. Napoleon had let it be known through his generals that he was the well-wisher of the Austrians, their protector against Russian barbarism. The Viennese were to be treated with courtesy; even the volunteer guards were to be left unmolested. The citizens did not know how to receive the invaders. The procession was a strange spectacle, and they gazed upon it in curious silence. The invaders were silent too. The emblazoned *grenadiers à cheval* were proud figures in their polished cuirasses, but the horses under them looked dejected. The infantry were mud-splashed and unshaven; here and there one carried a loaf of bread or a ham on the point of his bayonet. They seemed to come without end, day and night, some marching on toward Hungary or north-ward, some pitching camp in the suburbs, the officers taking occupa-tion of the princely mansions in the town. The reports of distant cannon could be heard; it was said that the French were engaged in a terrific battle with the Russians, that the Austrian army to the south was being annihilated by the Italians. But nothing was known. All communication was suppressed and, with it, all news. What could not be concealed was the presence of French wounded who were being brought in on stretchers from the Russian front. Austrian prisoners, too, were herded in. They could give no clear information except that the country was laid waste, the armies were living on it, and the people were starving.

The magistrates as much as ordered the townspeople to ignore what might be going on about them, and to forget their troubles in the pleasures of their parks. The Court theaters were commanded to be kept open. *Othello* was acted before an empty house on the night before the occupation. Operas of Cherubini or Zingarelli were to fol-low *Fidelio* at intervals.

There was no excitement over *Fidelio*, no anticipation. Almost all of Beethoven's friends were away, and those who remained had other things to worry about. The rehearsals were listless. In an overrun Vienna the rigid presence of men-at-arms seemed to make the private misfortunes of a legendary family in Spain dim and unimportant. Beethoven could gaze from his window in the Pasqualati house on the Mölker Bastei toward Hetzendorf and the Schönbrunn gardens where, in the heat of recent summer days, he had dreamed out his *Fidelio*. Now Schönbrunn was heavily guarded, for the Emperor Na-poleon sat in state at the Palace, receiving delegations. Napoleon knew nothing of an opera about to be produced, which had been composed a short while before in the paths beneath the Palace win-dow, where his sentries were now pacing. He did not know that the composer, a fiery little man who had once inscribed "Bonaparte" upon a symphony and then thought better of it, was gazing toward the violated Palace and speculating, quite correctly, that his own kind of power was more far-reaching in time and space, its impress upon mankind far more enduring. This proposition would have interested Napoleon not in the least. Music for him had a single function: to soothe and relax. He considered Cherubini taxing, more learned than tuneful. Finding him by chance in Vienna at the time, he patronized him for reasons of good appearance; it was fitting to surround himself with a retinue of culture. He much preferred Paisiello.

On November 20, 1805, *Fidelio* was first unfolded before a scattered assemblage who were mostly French officers, present because the Theater-an-der-Wien was open under orders and there was nothing else to do. Even if they had been able to follow the German text, these men of action would have preferred a more elegant and sprightly show to this one with its drab prison sets, and its woeful tale of virtue oppressed. On the second night, a young doctor from Edinburgh, Henry P. Reeve, attended *Fidelio* and described what he saw. "Beethoven presided at the pianoforte. He is a small, dark, young-looking man, and wears spectacles." Reeve found the plot, "a miserable mixture of low manners and romantic situations," "the music equal to any praise." This would look like musical acumen had not the Scottish doctor attended Zingarelli's *Romeo and Juliet* the following week, and found it likewise "above all praise." He finally reports that "a copy of complimentary verses was showered down from the upper balcony at the end of the piece." This vain attempt to stir acclaim for Beethoven is attributable to the faithful Stephan von Breuning. After three performances the public for *Fidelio* vanished altogether and the opera was dropped. Several critics managed to be there, despite conditions, and delivered their post mortems to the effect that Beethoven had written a dull opera without even the interest of his usual startling "singularities." None seemed to suspect that the opera might contain passages of imperishable beauty.

In December, the immediate emergency having passed, Baron Braun decided to give the opera another try; some of the initial expense might be saved, and there was the chance that, given a proper audience, it would after all prove worthy of its composer's reputation. It was generally agreed between the *régisseur* Meier and a group of Beethoven's friends that the first act moved too slowly. It must be cut. A night session was arranged at the Palace of Lichnowsky, at which the act was to be played and discussed with Beethoven. The imperious composer who never permitted questioning of his artistic judgment was strangely meek. He could not afford to be otherwise, for he knew not how to face the problems of dealing with the limitations and vanities of singers, the insistence of the stage director, the behavior of the crowds before the footlights, with their prejudices and their failure to respond at vital moments. All these people must be mollified if the whole venture were to be saved. Compromise on every side for the obdurate Beethoven! A composer like Gluck, who had the theater in his blood, could follow through his clear intentions to the bitter end. Beethoven knew how to be adamant; but now his unease and inexperience threw him upon the mercy and advice of others.

Treitschke and Meier of the Theater were at Lichnowsky's, and Clement, the leader of the violins. Von Collin, author of *Coriolan* and the playwright Lange would give literary advice. There was the tenor Röckel, a young man of twenty; there was Karl van Beethoven, interested in the salvation of a possible money-getter. Seyfried, as conductor at the theater and friend of Beethoven, must surely have been present.

Röckel has described the scene:

Meier had prepared me for the coming storm when Beethoven should be advised to leave out three whole numbers in the first act. . . . I had arrived in Vienna only a short while before, and there met Beethoven for the first time. As the whole opera was to be gone through, we went directly to work. Princess Lichnowsky played on the grand piano from the great score, and Clement, sitting in a corner of the room, accompanied with his violin the whole opera by heart, playing all the solos of the different instruments. The extraordinary memory of Clement having been universally known, nobody was astonished by it except myself. Meier and I made ourselves useful by singing as well as we could, he the lower, I the higher parts. Though the friends of Beethoven were fully prepared for the impending battle, they had never seen him in that excitement before, and without the prayers and entreaties of the Princess, an invalid, who was a second mother to Beethoven and acknowledged by himself as such, his united friends were not likely to have succeeded in an enterprise they had undertaken without confidence.

It must have been doubly hard for Beethoven to throw overboard music written with his heart's blood, some of it incomparably fine, and to yield to the combined pressure of his friends on such a subject. Once reconciled, he fell into a mood of reckless gaiety.

When after their efforts from seven until after one o'clock, the sacrifice of the three numbers was accomplished, and when we, exhausted, hungry and thirsty, went to revive ourselves with a splendid supper—then none was happier and gayer than Beethoven. His fury had been replaced by exhilaration. He saw me, opposite to him, intently occupied with a French dish and asked me what I was eating. I answered: "I don't know," and with his lion's voice he roared out: "He eats like a wolf without knowing what! Ha, ha, ha!"

Stephan von Breuning made the necessary condensations of the text, and Beethoven made the necessary excisions in the score. He reduced the acts from three to two. He was urged to rewrite the overture. The one then used, and now known as "No. 2," was too symphonic and involved, said the operatic experts. Undertaking a simplification, he became lost in his subject, and quite forgot the grave admonitions that not otherwise could his beloved *Fidelio* make him the successful operatic composer he longed to be. Without a text to cope with, alone with his beloved orchestra, he spoke in his true strength, producing a concert overture which, before the lowered curtain, told far more powerfully than the cumbrous stage could ever tell of loyalty, ringing conviction, joyous release. The new Overture ("No. 3") lost some of the quasi-theatrical directness and impact of the second, and became more symphonically involved. Instead of aiding the illusion to come, it was destined to crush the opening scene between Marzelline at her ironing board and Jaquino, her loutish lover, into silly puppetry. It was not until he made a fourth attempt at an overture and for a later revival wrote the one which still bears the name *Fidelio* that he found the suitable way lightly to bow in the pleasantly jogging, homely level of the opening scene.

The revised score for the second mounting of *Fidelio* was barely ready for rehearsal. There were signs of a favorable reception at the first performance (March 29), but things did not go well. Beethoven refused to conduct the second performance, for the orchestra, he complained, paid no attention to the dynamic indications. After two performances, the opera was once more withdrawn. Some remarkable critical statements accompanied the second going down of *Fidelio*— one of which referred to the glamorous liberating trumpet call as a "postilion horn solo," and another which waved aside the new overture as "abominable cacophony." Bruening attributed the second failure to cabals against the composer. It is easier to believe that Beethoven, unhappy and angry when he could not bring about an adequate performance with only one full rehearsal, became as usual a disrupting force.

Fidelio was mounted again in the following season; its audience perceptibly grew. But Beethoven now conceived the idea that he was being cheated of his full percentage. He went to the office of the Baron Braun and made his complaint. The Baron, knowing of Beethoven's reputed suspiciousness (Röckel tells this), protested mildly that his employees were trustworthy, and that if there were any shortage in the accounting he would lose more by it than Beethoven. Very likely the audiences would further increase. Until now they had been pretty well limited to the highest-priced seats—the stalls and first rows of the floor. It was to be hoped that the seats above would later be occupied.

"I don't write for the galleries!" exclaimed Beethoven.

"No?" replied the Baron. "My dear sir, even Mozart did not disdain to write for the galleries."

If the Baron wished to bring to an end his troubles with *Fidelio* and its vexatious composer, he could not have hit upon a surer way to do it.

"My score," Beethoven shouted. "Immediately. There will be no more performances. Give me my score!"

The Baron rang a bell and ordered that the score be returned at once to its author. So Beethoven, closing the door upon the career which had been his fondest ambition, found himself with his much-labored manuscript on his hands. Perhaps what had been most infuriating about the intendant's remark was its entire truth. Beethoven could tell himself proudly that he wrote for those of finer perceptions. So did Mozart, but that pupil of the school of necessity knew that to be a successful operatic composer, one must at the same time write for all and sundry. He had found the way, even before he had begun to grow up. Beethoven had not, so far as his opera was concerned, and nothing could have been more bitter to him than to hear it as a taunt from the lips of the man who controlled its destiny. *Fidelio* was quite without the combination of qualities by which the knowing composer contrives to win the mixed thousands in the dark spaces beyond the footlights—grateful displays of vocalism, incisive declamation, lush melody, spectacle, bright costumes, lively choruses. When Beethoven told Braun that he did not write for the galleries, he should rather have said that when an idea fully possessed him, he was incapable of courting the galleries with broadly externalized effects. His idea could grow and expand within him until it became irresistible, but not by resort to the obvious. The transfiguring power latent in *Fidelio* was so without ostentation that it could pass unnoticed. Only after the revival seven years later would it begin to win popular understanding.

Nevertheless, he labored with all that was in him to achieve adequate performance and general acceptance. It became his intermittent problem through about ten years of his life, from the end of 1803, when he made his first sketches, until 1814, when he made the second complete revision. They were the years of his greatest fertility. Into none of his music did he put more affectionate care. When his last illness was upon him, Beethoven extracted from his confusion of papers the manuscript score of *Fidelio* and presented it to Schindler with the words: "Of all my children, this is the one that cost me the worst birth pangs, the one that brought me the most sorrow; and for that reason it is the one most dear to me."

FIDELIO MISUNDERSTOOD

Donald Francis Tovey

Tovey showed us, in his famous program notes, how to
write about music with wit and clarity. That he should
have understood the misunderstood opera is to be expected.

"These old stagers might be very funny."

Someday *Fidelio* will become to English music lovers what
it is in Germany, the opera to which every right-thinking married
couple goes on the anniversary of their wedding. One step toward
this consummation is already nearly accomplished: it is now no
longer excruciatingly funny to be a right-thinking married couple, so
long as one does not interfere with couples whose mental co-ordinates
are Gaussian. The other step still remains to be taken. We are in
the throes of the discovery that opera is an interest of national importance; and therefore it behooves us to pay attention to the ortho-
doxies of the old-stager critics whose grandparents learnt from Wagner that *Fidelio*, besides having an impossibly bourgeois subject, is
not a good model for students in operatic technique. These old stagers might be very funny if they were not as mischievous as they are
pathetic. In 1902 I was surprised to learn, when I wrote the program
notes for the Meiningen Concerts, that it showed "paralysis of mind"
to speak of *Fidelio* as if it were a good opera. My surprise was caused
by no doubts as to the defects of *Fidelio*, which had been as obvious
to me as to any intelligent child of my age when I first heard it in
Berlin in 1888. And, lest I should miss them or be misled by them
then, they were explicitly pointed out to me by certain spiritual pas-
tors who worshiped every note of the music and almost every word
of the text. What surprised me was that, even in 1902, anybody
should still be so unused to the defects of *Fidelio* as to suppose that

From *Essays in Musical Analysis* by Donald Francis Tovey, by permission of Oxford
University Press.

they mattered. We know that *Paradise Lost* conspicuously fails in its purpose to "justify the ways of God to man." That failure is a defect, just as many features in the music and libretto of *Fidelio* are defects. But we also know that blank verse will not rhyme, that heroic couplets will not make Miltonic verse-paragraphs, and that the first irruption of spoken dialogue into music produces a disagreeable shock if you do not expect it. The old-stager school of critics does not always show that it can distinguish the working hypotheses of art forms from defects of execution.

Perhaps the listener, after being warned against the shock of the first irruption of spoken dialogue, may come to agree with Macfarren (who wrote an admirable and fearlessly critical analysis of *Fidelio* in the seventies) that the effect of the spoken words after the trumpet call is one of the greatest "thrills" ever achieved on the stage. The fact is that after Beethoven transformed the *Leonora* of 1804–6 into the *Fidelio* of 1814, all the remaining defects of the work were confined to the first part of the first act, which no amount of revision could make quite clear. The second act (originally the third) comprises the dungeon scene and the finale.

The dungeon scene is, in its now extant version, from first to last, "one of the greatest thrillers to be seen on any stage." That expression is as out of date as Pizarro's thirst for "crrimson blood and the hour of my rrevenge"—but 1814 is pretty near to the actual date of that expression. Thus, even the humble literary values of the libretto are those of an original and not of an imitation. And they are faithfully translated into the music of Beethoven. Someday I hope, with suitable though belated acknowledgment to the much-abused Macfarren, to produce a complete and historical analysis of *Fidelio*.[1] Meanwhile my account of the two great *Leonora* overtures must suffice, together with a few remaining *obiter dicta* on the present scene. The elements of operatic convention in it are clear enough to justify themselves, and they actually bulk much smaller in reality than in common report. Moreover, as we are dealing with first-rate melodramatic thrills, it is only fair to compare them with parallel phenomena in the cinema during the few years in which that modern art shall still give us opportunity to observe such phenomena.

For instance, it has been remarked, and justified as a good operatic convention, that Pizarro would in real life have a dozen chances of still killing Florestan while the music of the great quartet is pursuing

[1] Tovey never did, as far as I know. G.R.M.

its torrential course. I rather doubt this; few dramatic critics, and even fewer modern composers, know how short the apparently formal processes of classical music really are. The Wagnerite apostle Hueffer accused Mozart of "keeping Fate, in the person of the Count, with a drawn sword, at bay while Susanna and Cherubino sing an excellent duet" before Cherubino jumps out of the window. In actual stage timing Mozart gives Cherubino none too much time to make up his mind to risk a breakneck fall, and certainly only just enough time for the Count to come back with the crowbar he had fetched in order to force the Countess's locked door. However, supposing that Beethoven's quartet does stretch the action beyond realistic limits in order to achieve a musical purpose, that musical purpose fully occupies the listener's mind here and now, and only increases the dramatic tension, whereas in the cinema the only reason why the hero is tied to a barrel of gunpowder and left there to await the burning down of a six-inch candle is because common sense on the part of the assassins would make it impossible to announce that another episode of this hair-raising drama will be given next week.

SUFFERINGS AND GREATNESS OF RICHARD WAGNER

Thomas Mann

> This essay was written on the occasion of the fiftieth anniversary of Wagner's death and was delivered at the University of Munich on February 10, 1933, the year Hitler came into power. The world's viewpoint was different in those days which now seem very far away. Mann's viewpoint changed as an exile. Our attitude toward Wagner has changed. Nonetheless, I believe this to be the finest essay on Wagner extant. It is by a writer whose orientation toward music can be felt in all his works. The translation is by H. T. Lowe-Porter.

"The musical bond with night and death."

Il y a là mes blâmes, mes éloges et tout ce que j'ai dit.
MAURICE BARRÈS

Suffering and great as that nineteenth century whose complete expression he is, the mental image of Richard Wagner stands before my eyes. Scored through and through with all his century's unmistakable traits, surcharged with all its driving forces, so I see his image; and scarcely can I distinguish between my two loves: love of his work, as magnificently equivocal, suspect and compelling a phenomenon as any in the world of art, and love of the century during most of which he lived his restless, harassed, tormented, possessed, miscomprehended life, and in which, in a blaze of glory, he died. We of today, absorbed as we are in tasks which—for novelty and difficulty at least—never saw their like, we have no time and little wish to give its due to the epoch—we call it the bourgeois—now dropping away behind us. Our attitude toward the nineteenth century is that of sons toward a father: critical, as is only fair. We shrug our shoulders alike over its belief—which was a belief in ideas—and over its unbelief— that is to say, its melancholy relativism. Its attachment to liberal ideas of reason and progress seems to us laughable, its materialism all too crass, its monistic solution of the riddle of the universe full of shallow complacency. And yet its scientific self-sufficiency is atoned for, yes, outweighed, by the pessimism, the musical bond with night and death, which will very likely one day seem its strongest trait. Though another, not unconnected with it, is its willful love of mere largeness, its taste for the monumental and standard, the copious and grandiose —this again, strange to say, coupled with an infatuation for the very small and the circumstantial, for the minutiæ of psychological processes. Yes, greatness, of a turbid, suffering kind; disillusioned, yet bitterly, fanatically aware of truth; conscious too of the brief, incredulous bliss to be snatched from beauty as she flies—such greatness as this was the meaning and mark of the nineteenth century. Plastically represented, it would resemble a Michelangelo statue, an Atlas of the moral world, stretching and relaxing his muscles. Giant burdens were borne in that day—epic burdens, in the full sense of that strong word: one thinks not only of Balzac and Tolstoy, one thinks of Wagner as well. When the latter, in 1851, sent his friend Liszt a letter with the formal plan of the *Ring*, Liszt answered from Weimar: "Go on with it, and work on regardless! You ought to take for your motto the one the Chapter of the Cathedral of Seville gave to the architect who built it: 'Build us,' they said, 'such a temple that future generations will say the Chapter was mad to undertake anything so extraordinary.' And yet—there stands the Cathedral." That is genuine nineteenth-century.

The enchanted garden of French impressionistic painting, the English, French, and Russian novel, German science, German music—no, it was not such a bad age; in fact, it was a perfect forest of giants. And only now, looking back from a distance, are we able to see the family likeness among them at all, the stamp which, in all their manifold greatness, their age set upon them. Zola and Wagner, the *Rougon-Macquarts* and the *Ring of the Nibelungs*—fifty years ago who would have thought of putting them together? Yet they belong together. The kinship of spirit, aims, and methods is most striking. It is not only the love of size, the propensity to the grandiose and the lavish; not only, in the sphere of technique, the Homeric leitmotiv that they have in common. More than anything else it is a naturalism that amounts to the symbolic and the mythical. Who can fail to see in Zola's epic the tendency to symbol and myth that gives his characters their over-life-size air? That Second Empire Astarte, Nana, is she not symbol and myth? Where does she get her name? It sounds like the babbling of primitive man. Nana was a cognomen of the Babylonian Ishtar: did Zola know that? So much the more remarkable and significant if he did not.

Tolstoy, too, has the same naturalistic magnificence of scale, the same democratic amplitude. He too has the leitmotiv, the self-quotation, the standing phrases to describe his characters. He has often been criticized for his relentless carrying through, his refusal to indulge his reader, his deliberate and splendid longwindedness. And of Wagner Nietzsche says that he is surely the impolitest of all geniuses: he takes his hearer, as it were, and keeps on saying a thing until in desperation one believes it. Here they are alike; but more profoundly alike still in their common possession of social and ethical elements. True, Wagner saw in art a sacred arcanum, a means of salvation for a corrupted society, whereas Tolstoy, toward the end of his life, repudiated it altogether, as trivial and self-indulgent; but his disparity is not important. For as self-indulgence Wagner too repudiated art. He wanted it saved and purified for the sake of a corrupted society. He was all for catharsis and purification, he dreamed of an æsthetic consecration that should cleanse society of luxury, the greed of gold and all unloveliness; hence his social ethics were closely akin to those of the Russian epic writer. And there is a likeness in their destinies too; for critics have seen in the character of both a temperamental split, causing something like a moral collapse, whereas the truth is that both lives display throughout their course the strictest unity and consistency. It has seemed to people that Tolstoy, in his old age, fell into a kind of religious madness. They do not see that the Tolstoy of the last period lay implicit in characters like Pierre Besuchov in *War and Peace* and Levin in *Anna Karenina*. Similarly, Nietzsche would have it that Wagner toward the end was a broken man, prostrate at the foot of the Cross; he overlooks or wishes others to overlook the fact that the emotional atmosphere of *Tannhäuser* anticipates that of *Parsifal*, and that the latter is the final, splendidly logical summing up of a life-work at bottom romantic and Christian in its spirit. Wagner's last work is also his most theatrical—and it would be hard to find an artist career more consistent than his. An art essentially sensuous, based on symbolic formulas (for the leitmotiv is a formula—nay, it is a monstrance; it claims an almost religious authority) must be leading back to the church celebration; and indeed I do believe that the secret longing and ultimate ambition of all theater is to return to the bosom of the ritual out of which—in both the pagan and the Christian world —it sprang. The art of the theater is already baroque, it is Catholicism, it is the church; and an artist like Wagner, used to dealing with symbols and elevating monstrances, must have ended by feeling like a brother of priests, like a priest himself.

I have often thought about the likeness between Wagner and Ibsen, and found it hard to decide how much of it is due to their contemporaneity and how much to personal traits. For I could not but recognize, in the dialogue of Ibsen's bourgeois drama, means and effects, fascinations and wiles already known to me from the sound-world of the other artist; could not but be convinced of a kinship which in part of course lay in their common possession of greatness, but how very much too in their way of being great! How much they are alike in their tremendous self-sufficiency, in the three-dimensional rotundity and consummateness of the life-work of both; social-revolutionary in youth, in age paling into the ritual and mythical! *When We Dead Awaken*, the awesome whispered confession of the production-man bemoaning his late, too late declaration of love of life—and *Parsifal*, that oratorio of redemption: how prone I am to think of the two together, to feel them as one, these two farewell mystery plays, last words before the eternal silence! Both of them apocalyptic climaxes, majestic in their sclerotic languor, in the mechanical rigor of their technique, their general tone of reviewing life and casting up accounts, their self-quotation, their flavor of dissolution.

What we used to call *fin-de-siècle*, what was it but the miserable satyr-play of a smaller time, compared with the true and awe-inspiring end of the epoch whose swan-song was the last work of these two great wizards? For northern wizards were they both, crafty old weavers of spells, profoundly versed in all the arts of insinuation and fascination wielded by a devil's artistry as sensuous as consummate; great in the organization of effects, in the cult of detail, in all sorts of shifting meanings and symbolic senses, in the exploitation of fancy, the poetizing of the intellectual; and musicians they were to boot, as men of the north should be. Not only the one who consciously acquired his music because he thought it might be useful in his career of conquest; but also the other, though only privately, through the intellect and as a second string to the word.

But what makes them even to confusion alike is the way each subjected to an undreamed-of process of sublimation a form of art which, in both cases, stood at the time at rather a low ebb. In Wagner's case the form was opera, in Ibsen's the social drama. Goethe says: "Everything perfect of its kind must go beyond its kind, it must be something else, incomparable. In some notes the nightingale is still bird; then it surmounts its species, seeming to want to show to every other feathered fowl what singing really is." In just this sense Wagner and Ibsen made the opera and the social drama consummate; they made something else, incomparable, out of them. The other half of the comparison also rings true: sometimes, and sometimes even in *Parsifal*, Wagner is still opera; sometimes in Ibsen you can hear the creaking of the Dumas technique. But both are creative, in that sense of perfection and consummation; they have it in common that they took the accepted and made out of it something new, something undreamed-of.

What is it that raises the works of Wagner to a plane so high, intellectually speaking, above all older musical drama? Two forces contribute, forces and gifts of genius, which one thinks of in general as opposed; indeed, the present day takes pleasure in asserting their essential incompatibility. I mean psychology and the myth. Indeed, psychology does seem too much a matter of reason to admit of our seeing in it no obstacle at all on the path into the land of myth. And it passes as the antithesis of the mythical as of the musical—yet precisely this complex, of psychology, myth, and music, is what confronts us, an organic reality, in two great cases, Nietzsche and Wagner. A book might be written on Wagner the psychologist, on the psychology of his art as musician not less than as poet—insofar as the two are to be separated in him.

The technique of using the motif as an aid to memory had already been employed on occasion in the old opera; it was now gradually built up, by the profoundest virtuosity, into a system that made music more than ever the instrument of psychological allusion, association, emphasis. Wagner's treatment of the love-potion theme, originally the simple epic idea of a magic draught, is the creation of a great psychologist. For actually it might as well be pure water that the lovers drink, and it is only their belief that they have drunk death that frees their souls from the moral compulsion of their day. From the beginning Wagner's poetry goes beyond the bounds of suitability for his libretto—though not so much in the language as precisely in the psychology displayed. "The somber glow," sings the Dutchman in the fine duet with Senta in the second act:

> The somber glow I feel within me burning—
> Shall I, O wretch, confess it for love's yearning?
> Ah, no, it is salvation that I crave—
> Might such an angel come my soul to save!

The lines are singable; but never before had such a complex thought, such involved emotions, been sung or been written for singing. The devoted man loves this maid at first sight, but tells himself that his emotion has nothing to do with her; rather it has to do with his re-demption and release. Again, seeing her as the embodiment of his hopes for salvation, he neither can nor will distinguish between the two longings he feels. For his hope has taken on her shape and he can no longer wish it to have another. In plain words, he sees and loves redemption in this maiden—what interweaving of alternatives is here, what a glimpse into the painful abysses of emotion! This is analysis—and the word comes up in an even bolder and more modern sense when we think of the youthful Siegfried and observe the way Wagner, in his verse and against the significant background of the music, gives life to the springlike germination, the budding and shoot-ing up of that young life and love. It is a pregnant complex, gleaming up from the unconscious, of mother fixation, sexual desire, and fear —the fairy-story fear, I mean, that Siegfried wanted so to feel: a com-plex that displays Wagner the psychologist in remarkable intuitive agreement with another typical son of the nineteenth century, the psychoanalyst Sigmund Freud. When Siegfried dreams under the linden tree and the mother-idea flows into the erotic; when Mime teaches his pupil the nature of fear, while the orchestra down below darkly and afar off introduces the first motif: all that is Freud, that is analysis, nothing else—and we recall that Freud, whose profound in-vestigation into the roots and depths of mind has been, in its broad-est lines, anticipated by Nietzsche, shows an interest in the mythical, precultural, and primeval which is narrowly associated with the psy-chological.

"Love in fullest reality," says Wagner, "is only possible within sex; only as man and woman can human beings love most genuinely, all other love is derivative, having reference to this or artificially modeled upon it. It is false to think of this love (the sexual) as only one manifestation of love in general, other and perhaps higher manifestations being presumed beside it." This reduction of all love to the sexual has an unmistakably psychoanalytical character. It shows the same psychological naturalism as Schopenhauer's metaphysical formula of the "focus of the will" and Freud's cultural theories and his theory of sublimation. It is genuine nineteenth-century.

The erotic mother complex appears again in *Parsifal*, in the seduction scene in the second act—and here we come to Kundry, the boldest, most powerful creation among Wagner's figures—he himself probably felt how extraordinary she was. Not Kundry but the emotions proper to Good Friday were Wagner's original point of departure; but gradually his ideas more and more took shape about her, and the decisive conception of the dual personality, the thought of making the wild *Gralsbotin* (messenger of the Grail) one and the same being with the beguiling temptress, supplied the final inspiration—and betrays the secret depths of the fascination that drew him to so strange an enterprise.

"Since this occurred to me," he writes, "almost everything about the material has become clear." And again: "In particular I see more and more vividly and compellingly a strange creation, a wonderful world-demonic female (the *Gralsbotin*). If I manage to finish this piece of work it will be something highly original." Original—that is a touchingly subdued and modest word for the result he actually produced. Wagner's heroines are in general marked by a trait of lofty hysteria; they have something sleepwalking, ecstatic, and prophetic which imparts an odd, uncanny modernity to their romantic heroics. But Kundry herself, the Rose of Hell, is definitely a piece of mythical pathology; her tortured and distracted duality, now as *instrumentum diaboli*, now as salvation-seeking penitent, is portrayed with clinical ruthlessness and realism, with a naturalistic boldness of perception and depiction in the field of morbid psychology that has always seemed to me the uttermost limit of knowledge and mastery. And Kundry is not the only character in *Parsifal* with this extravagant type of mentality. The draft of this last work of Wagner says of Klingsor that he is the demon of the hidden sin, he is impotence raging against evil—and here we are transported into a Christian world that takes cognizance of recondite and infernal soul-states—in short, into the world of Dostoevsky.

Our second phenomenon is Wagner as mythologist, as discoverer of the myth for purposes of the opera, as savior of the opera through the myth. And truly he has not his like for soul-affinity with this world of thought and image, nor his equal in the power of invoking and reanimating the myth. When he forsook the historical opera for the myth he found himself; and listening to him one is fain to believe that music was made for nothing else, nor could have any other mission but to serve mythology. Whether as messenger from a purer sphere, sent to the aid of innocence and then, alas, since faith proves inconstant, withdrawing thither whence it came; or as lore, spoken and sung, of the world's beginning and end, a sort of cosmogonic fairy-tale philosophy—in all this the spirit of the myth, its essence and its key, are struck with a certainty, an elective intuition; its very language is spoken with a native-bornness that has not its like in all art. It is the language of "once upon a time" in the double sense of "as it always was" and "as it always shall be"; the density of the mythological atmosphere—as in the scene with the Norns at the beginning of the *Götterdämmerung*, where the three daughters of Erda indulge in a solemn-faced gossip about the state of the world, or in the appearances of Erda herself in the *Rheingold* and *Siegfried*—is unsurpassable. The overpowering accents of the music that bears away Siegfried's corpse no longer refer to the woodland youth who set forth in order to learn fear; they instruct our feeling in what is really passing there behind falling veils of mist. The sun-hero himself lies on his bier, struck down by blind darkness, and the word comes to the aid of our emotions: "the fury of a wild boar," it says, and "he is the accursed boar," says Gunther, pointing to Hagen, "who mangled the flesh of his noble youth." A perspective opens out into the first and furthest of our human picture-dreamings. Tammuz, Adonis whom the boar slew, Osiris, Dionysius, the dismembered ones, who are to return as the Crucified whose side a Roman spear must pierce that men may know him—all that was and ever is, the whole world of slain and martyred loveliness this mystic gaze encompasses; and so let no one say that he who created Siegfried was in Parsifal untrue to himself.

My passion for the Wagnerian enchantment began with me so soon as I knew of it, and began to make it my own and penetrate it with my understanding. All that I owe to him, of enjoyment and instruction, I can never forget: the hours of deep and single bliss in the midst of the theater crowds, hours of nervous and intellectual transport and rapture, of insights of great and moving import such as only this art vouchsafes. My zeal is never weary, I am never satiated, with watching, listening, admiring—not, I confess, without misgivings; but the doubts and objections do my zeal as little wrong as did Nietzsche's immortal critique, which has always seemed to me like a panegyric with the wrong label, like another kind of glorification. It was love-in-hate, it was self-flagellation. Wagner's art was the great passion of Nietzsche's life. He loved it as did Baudelaire, the poet of the *Fleurs du Mal*, of whom it is told that in the agony, the paralysis, and the clouded mind of his last days he smiled with pleasure when he heard Wagner's name: *"Il a souri d'allégresse."* Thus Nietzsche, in his paralytic night, used to listen to the sound of that name and say: "I loved him very much." He hated him very much too, on intellectual, cultural, ethical grounds—which shall not be gone into here and now. But it would be strange indeed if I stood alone in the feeling that Nietzsche's polemic against Wagner pricks on enthusiasm for the composer rather than lames it.

What I did take exception to, always—or rather, what left me cold —was Wagner's theory. It is hard for me to believe that anyone ever took it seriously. This combination of music, speech, painting, gesture, that gave itself out to be the only true art and the fulfillment of all artistic yearning—what had I to do with this? A theory of art that would make *Tasso* give way to *Siegfried*? I found it hard to swallow, this derivation of the single arts from the disintegration of an original theatrical unity, to which they should all happily find their way back. Art is entire and complete in each of its forms and manifestations; we do not need to add up the different kinds to make a whole. To think that is *bad* nineteenth-century, a bad, mechanistic mode of thought; and Wagner's triumphant performance does not justify his theory but only itself. It lives, and it will live, but art will outlive it in the arts, and move mankind through them, as it always has. We should be children and barbarians to suppose that the influence of art upon us is profounder or loftier by reason of the heaped-up volume of its assault upon our senses.

Wagner, as an impassioned man of the theater—one might call him a theatromaniac—inclined to such a belief, insofar as the first desideratum of art appeared to him to be the most immediate and complete communication to the senses of everything that was to be said. And strange enough it is to see, in the case of his principal work, *The Ring of the Nibelungs*, what was the effect of this ruthless demand of his upon the drama, which after all was the crux of all his striving, and of which, the fundamental law seemed to him to be precisely this utter, all-inclusive sense-appeal. We know the story of how this work was written. Wagner was working on his dramatic sketch of Siegfried's death; he himself tells us that he found it intolerable to have so much of the story lying before the beginning of the play, which had then to be woven in afterward as it proceeded. He felt an over-powering need to bring that previous history within the sphere of his sense-appeal, and so he began to write backward: first *Young Siegfried*, then the *Valkyrie*, then the *Rheingold*. He rested not until he had reduced the past to the present and brought it all upon the stage—in four evenings, everything from the primitive cell, the primeval beginnings, the first E-flat major of the bass bassoon at the commencement of the Overture to the *Rheingold*, with which then he solemnly and almost soundlessly set to. Something glorious was the result, and we can understand the enthusiasm of its creator in view of the success of a scheme so colossal, so rich in new and profound possibilities of effectiveness. But what was it, really, this result? Æsthetics has been known to repudiate the composite drama as an art form. Grillparzer, for instance, did so. He considered that the relation of one part to another resulted in imparting an epic character to the whole —whereby, indeed, it gained in sublimity. But precisely this is what conditions the effectiveness of the *Ring* and the nature of its greatness: Wagner's masterpiece owes its sublimity to the epic spirit, and the epic is the sphere from which its material is drawn. The *Ring* is a scenic epic; its source is the dislike of the antecedent doings that haunt the stage behind the scenes—a dislike not shared, as we know, by the classic nor by the French drama. Ibsen is much closer to the classic stage, with his analytical technique and his skill at developing the backgrounds. It is amusing to think that precisely Wagner's theory of dramatic sense-appeal was what so wonderfully betrayed him into the epic vein.

His relation to the single arts out of which he created his "composite art-work" is worth dwelling upon. It has something peculiarly dilettantish about it. In the still loyal fourth *Thoughts out of Season* (*Unzeitgemässe Betrachtungen*) upon Wagner's childhood and youth, Nietzsche says: "His youth is that of a many-sided dilettante, of whom nothing very much will come. He had no strict, inherited family tradition to make a frame for him. Painting, poetry, acting, music, came as naturally to him as an academic career; the superficial observer might think him a born dilettante." In fact, not only the superficial but the admiring and impassioned observer might well say, at risk of being misunderstood, that Wagner's art *is* dilettantism, monumentalized and lifted into the sphere of genius by his intelligence and his enormous will power. There is something dilettante in the very idea of a union of the arts; it could never have got beyond the dilettante had they not one and all been ruthlessly subordinated to his vast genius for expression. There is something suspect in his relation to the arts—something unæsthetic, however nonsensical that may sound. Italy, the plastic and graphic arts, leave him cold. He writes to Frau Wesendonck in Rome: "See everything for me too—I need to have somebody do it for me. . . . I have my own way of responding to these things, as I have discovered again and again, and finally quite conclusively when I was in Italy. For a while I am vividly impressed by some significant visual experience; but—it does not last. It seems that my eyes are not enough for me to use to take in the world."

Perfectly understandable. For he is an ear-man, a musician and poet; but still it is odd that he can write from Paris to the same correspondent: "Well, well, how the child is reveling in Raphael and painting! All very lovely, sweet, and soothing; only it never touches me. I am still the Vandal who, in a whole year spent in Paris, never got round to visit the Louvre. That tells the whole story." Not the whole; but after all something, and that something is significant. Painting is a great art—as great as the composite art-work. It existed before the composite art-work and it continues to do so—but it moves him not. He would have to be smaller than he is for one not to be wounded to the heart for the art of painting! For neither as past nor as living present has it anything to say to him. The greatness that grew up, as it were, beside him, the French impressionistic school— he hardly saw it; it had nothing to do with him. His relations with it were confined to the fact that Renoir painted his portrait; not a very flattering portrait—we are told that he did not much care for it. But his attitude toward poetry was clearly different. Throughout his life it gave him infinite riches—especially Shakespeare; though he speaks almost with pity of "literature-writers" in defense of the theory by which he glorifies his own powers. But no matter for that; he has made mighty contribution to poetry, she is much the richer for his work—always bearing in mind that it must not be read, that it is not really written verse but, as it were, exhalations from the music, needing to be complemented by gesture, music, and picture and existing as poetry only when all these work together. Purely as composition it is often bombastic, baroque, even childish; it has something majestically and sovereignly inept—side by side with such passages of absolute genius, power, compression, primeval beauty, as disarm all doubt; though they never quite make us forget that what we have here are images that stand not within the cultural structure of our great European literature and poetry, but apart from it, more in the nature of directions for a theatrical performance, which among other things needs a text. Among such gems of language interspersed among the boldly dilettante, I think in particular of the *Ring* and of *Lohengrin* —the latter, purely as writing, is perhaps the noblest, purest, and finest of Wagner's achievements.

His genius lies in a dramatic synthesis of the arts, which only as a whole, precisely as a synthesis, answers to our conception of a genuine and legitimate work of art. The component parts—even to the music, in itself, not considered as part of a whole—breathe something rank and lawless, that only disappears when they blend into the noble whole. Wagner's relation to his language is not that of our great poets and writers, it wants the austerity and fastidiousness displayed by those who find in words the best possession and the most trusted tool of art. That is proved by his occasional poems; the sugared and romantic adulations of Ludwig II of Bavaria, the banal and jolly jingles addressed to helpers and friends. One single careless little rhyme of Goethe is pure gold—and pure literature—compared with these versified platitudes and hearty masculine jests, at which our reverence for Wagner can only make us smile rather ruefully. Let us keep to Wagner's prose, to the manifestos and self-expositions on æsthetic and cultural matters. They are essays of astonishing mental virility and shrewdness, but they are not to be compared, as literary and intellectual achievements, with Schiller's works on the philosophy of art—for instance, that immortal essay on *Naïve and Sentimental Poetry*. They are hard to read, their style is both stiff and confused, again there is something about them that is overgrown, extraneous, dilettante: they do not belong to the sphere of great German and European prose; they are not the work of a born writer, but the casual product of some necessity. With Wagner every separate achievement was like that, always the product of necessity. Happy, devoted, complete, legitimate, and great he is, only in the mass.

Then was his musicianship too only the product of the demands made upon him by the whole overpowering product, only the result of strength of will? Nietzsche says somewhere that the so-called "gift" cannot be the essential thing about genius. "For instance," he cries, "what very little gift Richard Wagner had! Was ever a musician so poor as he still was in his twenty-eighth year?" And it is true that Wagner's musical beginnings were all timid, poor, and derivative, and lie much later in his life than is usually the case with great musicians. He himself says: "I still remember, round my thirtieth year, asking myself whether I possessed the capacity to develop an artistic individuality of high rank; I could still trace in my work a tendency to imitation, and looked forward only with great anxiety to my development as an independent original creator." That is a retrospect, he wrote it as a master, in 1862. But only three years earlier, when he was forty-six, in Lucerne, he had days when he simply could not get forward with the *Tristan*; he writes to Liszt:

How pathetic I seem to myself as a musician I cannot find words strong enough to tell you. At the bottom of my heart, I feel an absolute tyro. You should see me sitting here, thinking "It simply *must* go"; then I go to the piano and dig out some wretched trash, to give it up again, like a fool. Imagine my feelings, my inward conviction of my utter musical incapacity. And now you come, oozing it out of all your pores, streams and springs and waterfalls of it, and I have to listen to what you say of me! Not to believe that it is sheer irony is very hard. My dear chap, this is all very odd, and believe me, I am no great shakes.

That is pure depression, inapplicable in every word, and doubly absurd in the address to which it went. Liszt answers it as it should be answered. He reproaches him with "frantic injustice toward himself." Every artist knows this sudden shame, felt on confronting some masterly performance. For the practice of an art always, in every case, means a fresh and very careful adaptation of the personal and individual to the art in general; thus a man, even after he has received recognition for happy performances of his own, can suddenly compare them with the work of others and ask himself: "Is it possible to mention my own adaptation in the same breath with these things?" Even so, such a degree of depressive self-depreciation, such pangs of conscience in the presence of music, in a man who is in the middle of the third act of *Tristan*—there is something strange about it, something psychologically remarkable. Truly he had paid with a deal of poor-spirited self-abasement for the dictatorial self-sufficiency of his later days, when he published in the Bayreuth papers so much scorn and condemnation of the beautiful in Mendelssohn, Schumann, Brahms, to the greater glory of his own art! What was the source of these attacks of faint-heartedness? They could only come from the error he made at such moments: of isolating his musicianship and thus bringing it into comparison with the best, whereas it should only be regarded *sub specie* of his whole creative production—and vice versa; to this error is due all the embittered opposition that his music had to overcome. We, who owe to this wonder-world of sound, to this intellectual wizardry, so much bliss and ravishment, so much amazement at sight of this giant capacity, self-created—we find it hard to understand the opposition and the repulsion. The expressions that were used, descriptions like "cold," "algebraic," "formless," seem to us shockingly uncomprehending and lacking in insight; with a want of receptivity, a thick-skinned poverty of understanding that inclines us to think they could only have come from philistine spheres, forsaken alike of God and music. But no. Many of those who so judged, who were impelled so to judge, were no philistines, they were artistic spirits, musicians and lovers of music, who had her interest at heart and could with justice claim that they were able to distinguish between the musical and the unmusical. And they found that this music was no music. Their opinion has been completely counted out, it has suffered a mass defeat. But even if it was false, was it also inexcusable? Wagner's music is not music to the same extent that the dramatic basis (which unites with it to form a creative art) is not literature. It is psychology, symbolism, mythology, emphasis, everything—only not music in the pure and consummate sense intended by those bewildered critics. The texts round which it twines, filling out their dramatic content, are not literature—but the music is! Like a geyser it seems to shoot forth out of the myth's precultural depths—and not only seems, for it actually does it—and in very truth it is conceived, deliberately, calculatedly, with high intelligence, with an extreme of shrewdness, in a spirit as literary as the spirit of the texts is musical. Music, resolved into its primeval elements, must serve to force philosophic conclusions into high relief. The ever-craving chromatics of the *Liebestod* are a literary idea. The Rhine's immemorial flow, the seven primitive chords—like blocks to build up Valhalla—are no less so. I walked home one night with a famous conductor who had just finished conducting *Tristan*; he said to me: "That is not even music any more." He voiced the sense of our common emotion. But what we say today with acceptance, with admiration, could not but have sounded in the beginning like a furious denial. Such music as Siegfried's Rhine Journey, or the Funeral March, of unspeakable glory for our ears, for our spirits, they were never listened to, they were unheard-of in the worst sense of the phrase. This stringing together of symbolic musical quotations, till they lie like boulders in the stream of musical development—it was too much to ask that they be considered music as Bach, Beethoven, and Mozart are music. Too much to ask that the E-flat major triad at the beginning of the *Rheingold* be called music. It was not. It was an acoustic idea: the idea of the beginning of all things. It was the self-willed dilettante's exploitation of music to express a mythological idea. Psychoanalysis claims to know that love is composed and put together out of elements of sheer perversity; yet, and therefore, she remains love, the most divine phenomenon this world has to show. Well, now, the genius of Richard Wagner is put together out of streams of dilettantism.

But what streams! He is a musician who can persuade even the unmusical to be musical. That may be a drawback in the eyes of *illuminati* and aristocrats of the art. But when among the unmusical we find men and artists like Baudelaire—? For him, contact with the world of music was simply contact with Wagner. He wrote to Wagner that he had no understanding of music, and knew none except a few fine things by Weber and Beethoven. And now he felt an ecstasy that made him want to make music with words alone, to vie with Wagner in language—all of which had far-reaching consequences for French poetry. A pseudo music, a music for laymen, can do with converts and proselytes such as this; even the austerest music might be envious of them—and not of them alone. For there are things in this popular music so splendid, so full of genius, as to make such distinctions ridiculous. The swan motif in *Lohengrin* and *Parsifal*, the summer full-moon music at the end of the second act of the *Meistersinger* and the quintet in the third act; the A-flat major harmony in the second act of *Tristan*, and Tristan's visions of the lovers striding across the sea; the Good Friday music in *Parsifal* and the mighty transformation music in the third act; the glorious duet between Siegfried and Brünnhilde at the beginning of the *Götter-*

dämmerung, with the folk-song cadence; *"Willst Du mir Minne schenken"* and the ravishing *"Heil Dir Brünnhilde, prangender Stern"*; certain parts from the Venusberg revision of the *Tristan* time—these are inspirations that might make absolute music grow red with delight or pale with envy. I have selected them at random. There are many others that I might have cited to display Wagner's astonishing skill in modifying, modulating, and reinterpreting a motif already introduced: for instance, in the prelude to the third act of the *Meistersinger*, where Hans Sachs's Shoemaker's Song, already known to us from the humorous second act as a lusty workman's song, is lifted to unexpected heights of poetry. Or take the recasting—of rhythm and timbre—and the restatement that the so-called faith motif undergoes; we hear it first in the overture and many times throughout the *Parsifal*, beginning with Gurnemanz's great recitative. It is hard to refer to these things with only words at one's disposition to wake them. Why, as I think of Wagner's music, does some small detail, a mere flourish, wake in my ear, like the horn-figure, technically quite easy to describe, and yet quite indescribable, which in the lament for Siegfried's death harmonically foreshadows the love motif of his parents? At such moments one scarcely knows whether it is Wagner's own peculiar and personal art, or music itself, that one so loves, that so charms one. In a word, it is heavenly—though only music could make one take the gushing adjective in one's mouth without shame.

The general tone, psychologically speaking, of Wagner's music is heavy, pessimistic, laden with sluggish yearning, broken in rhythm; it seems to be wrestling up out of darkness and confusion to redemption in the beautiful; it is the music of a burdened soul, it has no dancing appeal to the muscles, it struggles, urges, and drives most laboredly, most unsouthernly—Lenbach's quick wit characterized it aptly when he said to Wagner one day: "Your music—dear me, it is a sort of luggage van to the kingdom of heaven." But it is not that alone. Its soul-heaviness must not make one forget that it can also produce the sprightly, the blithe, and the stately—as in the themes of the knights, the motifs of Lohengrin, Stolzing, and Parsifal, the natural mischievousness and loveliness of the terzetto of the Rhine maidens, the burlesque humor and learned arrogance of the Overture to the *Meistersinger*, the jolly folk-music of the dance in the second act. Wagner can do anything. In the art of characterization he is incomparable; to understand his music as a method of characterization is to admire it without stint. It is picturesque, it is even grotesque; it is all based upon the perspective required by the theater. But it has a richness of inventiveness even in small matters, a flexible capacity of entering into character, speech, and gesture such as was never seen in so marked a degree. In the single roles it is triumphant: take the figure of the Flying Dutchman, musically and poetically encompassed by doom and destruction, wrapped round by the wild raging of the lonely seas. Or Loki with his elemental incalculableness and malicious charm, or Siegfried's dwarf foster-father, knock-kneed and blinking; or Beckmesser's silly spite. It is the Dionysiac play-actor and his art—his arts, if you like—revealing themselves in his omnipotent ubiquitous power of depiction and transformation. He changes not only his human mask; he enters into nature and speaks in the tempest and the thunderbolt, in the rustling leaf and the sparkling wave, in the rainbow and the dancing flame. Alberic's tarn-cap is the comprehensive symbol of this genius for disguise, this imitative all-pervasiveness: that can enter as well into the spongy hopping and crawling of the lowly toad as into the carefree, cloud-swinging existence of the old Norse gods. It is this characteristic versatility that could encompass works of such absolute heterogeneity as the *Meistersinger*, sturdy and German as Luther himself, and *Tristan's* death-drunken, death-yearning world. It marks off each of the operas from the others, develops each out of one fundamental note that distinguishes it from all the rest; so that—within the entire product, which after all is a personal cosmos—each single work forms a closed and starry cosmos of its own. Among them are musical contacts and relations that indicate the organic nature of the whole. Accents of the *Meistersinger* are heard in *Parsifal*; in the *Flying Dutchman* we get anticipations of *Lohengrin*, and in its text hints of the religious raptures of *Parsifal*, as in the words: "*Ein heil'ger Balsam meinen Wunden*," "*Der Schwur, dem hohen Wort entfliesst*." And in the Christian *Lohengrin* there is a pagan residuum, personified by Ortrud, that suggests the *Ring*. But on the whole each work is stylistically set off against the rest, in a way that makes one see and almost feel the secret of style as the very kernel of art, well-nigh as art itself: the secret of the union of the personal with the objective. In every one of his works Wagner is quite himself, not a beat therein could be by anybody else, each bears his unmistakable formula and signature. And yet each is at the same time stylistically a world of its own, the product of an objective intuition that holds the balance with the personal will power and entirely resolves it in itself. Perhaps the greatest marvel in this respect is the work of the seventy-year-old man, the *Parsifal*: here the uttermost is achieved in exploring and expressing remote and awful the holy worlds—yes, *Tristan* notwithstanding, this is the uttermost point reached by Wagner, it witnesses to a power of blending style and emotion even beyond his usual capacity; to these sounds one surrenders with every new interest, unrest, and bewitchment.

"A bad business, this," writes Wagner from Lucerne in 1859, in the midst of his absorbing labors on the third act of *Tristan*, which have renewed his interest in the long-since envisaged and already sketched figure of Amfortas. "A bad business! Think of it, for God's sake: it has suddenly become frightfully plain to me that Amfortas is my Tristan of the third act, at his unthinkable culmination." This process of "culmination" is the involuntary law of the life and growth of Wagner's productions, and it is the result of self-indulgence. All his life long he was laboring to utter Amfortas, in accents broken by torment and sin. He was already there in Tannhäuser's "Ah, how the weight of sin oppresses me!" In *Tristan* they seemed to have reached their uttermost and shattering expression; but in *Parsifal*, as he recognizes himself, with horror, they must undergo another "unthinkable culmination." It is a matter of screwing up his language to the highest pitch and then unconsciously seeking ever stronger and intenser situations to go with them. The material, the single works, are stages and successive transformations of a unity possessed by the self-contained and consummate life-work—which "develops" but to a certain extent was present from the beginning. This is the explanation of the telescoping, the dovetailing of conceptions; from which it results, in an artist of this kind and caliber, that what he is working on is never merely the task in hand; for everything else is weighing upon him and burdening the productive moment. Something apparently (and only half apparently) planned, planned for a lifetime, comes out when we know that Wagner in 1862 wrote quite definitely to von Bülow from Bieberich that *Parsifal* would be his last work. This was a round twenty years before it was actually performed. The *Siegfried* will have been sandwiched in between *Tristan* and the *Meistersinger*, and the whole *Ring* worked up, in order to fill in the holes in the scheme. During the whole of *Tristan* he had to carry on at the *Ring*, and in *Tristan*, from the beginning, there are hints of *Parsifal*. The latter was present even during the sound and healthy, Luther-spirited *Meistersinger*; it had been waiting since 1845, the year of the first performance of *Tannhäuser*, in Dresden. In 1848 comes the prose draft which condenses the Nibelung myth into a drama: the putting on paper of *Siegfried's Death*, which was to end in the *Götterdäm-merung*. But meantime, between 1846 and 1847, the *Lohengrin* is composed, and the action of the *Meistersinger* drafted, as a satyr-play and humorous pendant to *Tannhäuser*. This fourth decade of the century, in the middle of which he will be thirty-two years old, rounds out the working plan of the whole of his life, which will be carried out in the following four decades up to 1881, all the plays being dovetailed in together by simultaneous working on them all. His work, strictly speaking, has no chronology. It originates, of course, in time; but it is there all at once, and has been there from the beginning. The last achievement, foreseen as such from the beginning, and completed with his sixty-ninth year, is then in so far release that it means the fulfillment, the end and the exitus, and nothing more comes after it; the old man's work on it, the work of an artist who has entirely lived out his powers, is nothing more than just work on it. The giant task is finished, is complete; the heart, which has held out the storms of seventy years, may, in a last spasm, cease to beat.

This creative burden, then, rested on shoulders which were far from being as broad as Saint Christopher's; on a constitution so weakly, to judge by appearances and by subjective evidence, that no one would have expected it to hold out to carry such a burden to its goal. This nature felt itself every minute on the verge of exhaustion; only by exception did it experience the sensations of well-being. Constipated, melancholy, sleepless, generally tormented, this man is at thirty in such a state that he will often sit down and weep for a quarter of an hour on end. He cannot believe that he will live to see the *Tannhäuser* finished. To undertake at thirty-six to bring the *Ring* to completion seems to him presumption; when he is forty, he "thinks daily of death"—he who will be writing *Parsifal* at almost sixty-nine.

His martyrdom is a nervous complaint, one of those organically intangible illnesses which victimize a man years on end and make his life a burden, without being actually dangerous. It is hard for the victim to believe that they are not; more than one place in Wagner's letters shows that he regards himself as devoted to death. "My nerves," he writes at thirty-nine to his sister, "are by now in complete decline; it is possible that some change in my outward situation will stave off death for some years yet; but cannot stop the process."

And in the same year: "I am nervously very ill, and after several efforts at a radical treatment of the disease have come to the conclusion that there is no hope of recovery. My work is all that keeps me up; but the nerves of my brain are already so ruined that I cannot work more than two hours in the day and then only if I lie down for two hours afterward and perhaps can fall asleep a little." Two hours daily. By such small stages, then, at least at times, this whole gigantic life-work is erected; struggling all the time against rapidly supervening exhaustion, complement to a tough elasticity which can in no long time restore the easily exhausted energies. And the moral name of this process is patience. "True patience displays great elasticity," Novalis notes; and Schopenhauer praises it as the genuine courage. It is this moral and physical combination of courage, patience, and elasticity that enables this man to carry out his mission; Wagner's history, as scarcely that of any other artist, gives us an insight into the peculiar vital structure of genius: this mixture of sensibility and strength, delicacy and endurance, which is compact of labor against odds and all-unexpected rewards, and out of which great works come. It is not surprising that in time it displays a sense of being kept on through the self-will of the task itself. It is hard not to believe in a metaphysical willfulness of the work that is struggling toward realization, whose tool and willing-unwilling victim the author is. "In fact I do very wretchedly indeed, but I do"—that is a despairing, self-mocking cry out of one of Wagner's letters. And he does not fail to set up a causal nexus between his sufferings and his art; he recognizes art and illness to be one and the same affliction—with the result that he tries to escape from them, naïvely, by the help of a water-cure. "A year ago," he writes, "I found myself in a hydropathic establishment, where I hoped and wanted to become an entirely healthy man by the healing of my senses. I was wishing for the kind of health that would make it possible for me to get rid of art, the martyrdom of my life; it was a last desperate struggle for happiness, for real, respectable joy in life, such as only consciously healthy people can have."

How touching is this confused and childish utterance! He looks to have cold water cure him of art; that is, from the constitution that makes him an artist. His relation to art, to his destiny, is complex almost beyond hope of unraveling, highly contradictory, involved— sometimes he fairly seems to be quivering in the meshes of a logical net. "So I am to do this too?" cries the forty-six-year-old man, after going at length and with animation into the symbolic and intellectual content of the *Parsifal* plan. "And music for it too! Thanks very much. Whoever wants to may do it, I'll fight it off as long as I can." The words have an accent of feminine coquetry; they are full of trembling eagerness for the work, awareness of the inward voice "Thou must," and the voluptuous pleasure of resistance. The dream of getting free, of living instead of creating, of being happy, continues to recur in the letters; the words "happiness," "disinterested happiness," "noble enjoyment of life," are everywhere expressed as the opposite to the artist existence; as also the conception of art as substitute for all direct forms of enjoyment. At thirty-nine he writes to Liszt: "I decline more and more surely from day to day. I lead *an indescribably worthless life.* Of real enjoyment of life I know nothing; for me enjoyment, *love* [he underlines the word] are imaginary, not experienced. My heart had to be absorbed in my brain, my life had to become artificial; now I can only live as 'artist,' all the human being is absorbed in that." We must admit that never before has art been characterized in stronger words, in more desperate frankness, as drug, intoxicant, *paradis artificiel.* And he has attacks of violent revolt against this artificial existence, as on his fortieth birthday, when he writes to Liszt: "I want to be baptized anew; will you be godfather? I'd like for us both to get clean away, out into the world! Come out with me into the wide world—even if we just went gaily to smash there, and sank into some abyss!" One thinks of Tannhäuser, clinging to Wolfram to drag him away to the Venusberg; for certainly the world and "life" are, as in a fever-dream of renunciation, conceived as the Venusberg, as a state of thoroughgoing bohemian *je m'en fichisme* and the self-destruction of mad dissipation—in short, as all that for which art offers him a "worthless" substitute.

On the other hand, or rather in strange alternation with this, art appears to him in a quite different light: as a means of release, as sedative, as a condition of pure contemplation and surrender of the will; for thus philosophy taught him to regard it, and with the docility and good will common to children and artists he was anxious to obey. Oh, he is idealist! Life has its meaning not in itself but in the higher things, the task, the creative activity, and thus "to be forever struggling to produce what is needed" as he is, "to be often for long periods of time unable to think of aught but how I must act in order to get outward peace for even a little while and get hold of what is necessary for existence, and to that end to have to depart so utterly out of my own character, to have to appear to people from whom I need things to be so entirely different from what I am—that is really maddening. . . . All these cares are so fit and natural to the man to whom life is an end in itself, who gets all the joy he finds in things out of the trouble he has to take to bring them about, and who can simply never understand why that is so absolutely disgusting to the likes of us, since it is the common lot of mankind! That anybody should look on life as not an end in itself, but as an indispensable means to a higher goal—who really does understand that at the bottom of his soul?" (Letter to Mathilde Wesendonck, Venice, 1858.) In truth, it is a shameful and degrading thing to be obliged to fight for life like that, to go on one's knees for it, when life itself is not at all what one wants, but one's higher goal lying above and outside life: art, creation, for whose sake one must fight for rest and peace, and which themselves appear in the light of rest and peace. And even when one has finally by dint of struggling achieved the conditions for work—which are not so easily satisfied—then only begins the actual and higher voluntary drudgery, the productive struggle involved in art. For what he fancied, in his deluded philosophizing while he struggled for the baser ends of existence, to be pure "idea" and redeeming wisdom, proves to be the real wheel of Ixion, the last and uttermost convulsion of the laboring will.

Purity and peace—a deep craving for these two lies in his breast, complementary to his thirst for life. And when the craving reacts against his attempt to seize upon immediate pleasure, then art—it is a fresh complication in his relations to her—appears to him in the light of a hindrance to his healing. What we have here is a variation of the Tolstoyan repudiation of art, the cruel denial of one's own natural endowment, for the sake of the "spirit." Ah, art! How right was Buddha when he called it the broadest path that leads away from salvation! There is a long and tempestuous letter written from Venice to Frau Wesendonck, in 1858, in which he sets this forth to his friend, in discussing his idea of a Buddhistic drama, *The Victors*. "Buddhistic drama"—there was precisely the difficulty. It is a contradiction in terms—as had become clear to him when he tried to utilize dramatically, and in particular musically, the idea of a being utterly free, lifted above all passions, such as the Buddha was. The pure and holy one, through knowledge tranquilized, is, artistically speaking, dead—that was quite clear. It was a piece of good luck that, according to the sources, Sha-kya Muni Buddha had a last problem to face, was involved in a final conflict: he had to come to the decision, despite his former principles, to receive the Dragon's Daughter into the company of the elect. And thus, thank God, he became a possible subject for artistic treatment. Wagner rejoices; but at the same moment the life-bound nature of all art, the knowledge of her temp-tress power, falls heavily upon his conscience. Has he not already caught himself in the act of preferring the play and not the spirit? Without art he might be a saint, with her he never will. If the highest knowledge and the deepest insight were vouchsafed him, it could only make him what he was, a poet, an artist; they would stand there before him, soulfully evident, an enchanting picture, and he would not be able to resist giving it created being. Worse yet, he would even take pleasure in the devilish antinomy! It is horrible—but fascinatingly interesting—one might make a romantic psychological opera out of it —and that, more or less, is what Wagner has done, in the letter to Frau Wesendonck, which is a sort of first draft. Goethe asserts: "One cannot withdraw from the world more securely than through art, one cannot knit oneself more securely to it than through her." That tranquil and grateful statement—see what becomes of it in the head of a romantic!

But whatever guise art adopts, and whether she is a betrayal of the joys alike of sense and of salvation, in any case the work goes on, thanks to that elastic power of recovery which he himself must admire in secret; the scores pile up, and that is the main thing. This man knows as little as do any of us the right way of living. He *is lived*, life squeezes from him what it wants—that is to say, his works—re-gardless of the mazes his thought wanders in. "My child, this *Tristan* is getting *frightful!* This last act! I am afraid the opera will be for-bidden—if the whole thing is not to become a burlesque through bad production. Only mediocre production can save me. Too good would make people crazy. I cannot imagine it otherwise. I have been driven as far as this! Alas! I was just in full train—adieu!" A note to Frau Wesendonck. A quite un-Buddhistic note, full of excited, half-terrified laughter at the madness and badness of what he is doing. This infirm and melancholic man—what a fund of good temper, what indestruc-tible resiliency he must have possessed! His disease, after all, consists in being a variation of the bourgeois variety of health. He gave out a vital magic that made Nietzsche call association with him the one great joyful experience of his life. And he had, before everything else, the inestimable power of throwing emotion on one side and giving free rein to the commonplace. Among his artists in Bayreuth, after a day of strenuous labor, he would announce the advent of rest and relaxation, crying out: "Now not another serious word!" He understood them perfectly, these little theatrical people whom he needed for the realization of his ideas; despite the great intellectual disparity, he was himself theater-blood through and through, a comrade of the Thespian car. His simple-minded friend Heckel from Mannheim, the first stockholder of Bayreuth, tells priceless things on this subject. "Very often," he writes, "the relations between Wagner and his artists were extremely jolly and free-and-easy. At the last rehearsal in the salon of the Hôtel Sommer he actually, out of sheer high spirits, stood on his head." Again one thinks of Tolstoy: I mean the time when the gray-bearded prophet and melancholic Christian felt such a superabundance of vitality that he actually jumped up on his father-in-law's shoulder. One is no less artist than are the tenors and soubrettes that call one master: a human creature inclined—at bottom—to being and making merry, an instigator to all kinds of festivities and diversions— in profound and most healthful contrast to the wise and knowledgeable and commanding intelligence, the perfectly serious human being, like Nietzsche. It is well to understand that the artist, even he inhabiting the most austere regions of art, is *not* an absolutely serious man; that effects and enjoyment are his stock-in-trade, and that tragedy and farce can spring from one and the same root. A turn of the lighting changes one into the other; the farce is a hidden tragedy, the tragedy— in the last analysis—a sublime practical joke. The seriousness of the artist—a subject to ponder. And perhaps to shudder at—if what we mean is the intellectual veracity of the artist being, for his artistic veracity, the famous "serious playing"—that purest, loftiest, and most moving manifestation of the human mind—does not come in here. But the other, what is to be said for it: and in particular for the seriousness of that seeker after truth, that thinker and believer Richard Wagner? The ascetic and Christian ideals of his later period, the sacramental philosophy of salvation won by abstinence from fleshly lusts of every kind; the convictions and opinions of which *Parsifal* is the expression; even *Parsifal* itself—all these incontestably deny, revoke, cancel the sensualism and the revolutionary spirit of Wagner's young days, which pervade the whole atmosphere and content of the *Siegfried*. It did not, it might not exist any longer. If the artist was intellectually sincere in these new, later, and probably definitive views, then the works of the earlier epochs, recognized as erroneous, sinful, and pernicious, must have been denounced and extirpated, burned by their creator's very hand, so as not to be any longer a stumbling block to humanity. But he does not think of it—actually the idea does not even occur to him. Who could destroy such beautiful compositions? So they continue to exist, side by side, and they continue to be played; for the artist has reverence for his biography. He yields himself to the varying psychological moods of life as it passes, and portrays them in works which to the eye of reason may contradict each other, but are individually all beautiful, and all worth keeping. To the artist, new experiences of "truth" are new incentives to the game, new possibilities of expression, no more. He believes in them, he takes them seriously, just so far as he needs to in order to give them the fullest and profoundest expression. In all that he is very serious, serious even to tears—but yet *not quite*—and by consequence, not at all. His artistic seriousness is of an absolute nature, it is "dead-earnest playing." But his intellectual seriousness is not absolute, it is only serious for the purposes of the game. Among comrades the artist is so ready to mock at his own seriousness that Wagner could actually send the *Parsifal* text to Nietzsche with the signature: "R. Wagner, Member of the Consistory." But Nietzsche was no comrade. Such good-natured winking could not appease the sour and deadly, the absolute seriousness of his feeling against the Popish Christianity of a production—of which, however, he does say that it is the highest sort of challenge to music. When Wagner, in a childish fury, threw a Brahms score down from the piano, the spectacle of such jealous desire for single domination made Nietzsche sad; he said: "At that moment Wagner was not great." If Wagner by way of relaxation talked nonsense and told Saxon jokes, Nietzsche blushed for him. I can understand Nietzsche's embarrassment at this alacrity in moving from one plane to another; but something in me—perhaps fellow feeling with Wagner as an artist— warns me not to understand it too well.

His acquaintance with the philosophy of Arthur Schopenhauer was the great event in Wagner's life. No earlier intellectual contact, such as that with Feuerbach, approaches it in personal and historical significance. It meant to him the deepest consolation, the highest self-confirmation; it meant release of mind and spirit, it was utterly and entirely the right thing. There is no doubt that it freed his music from bondage and gave it courage to be itself. Wagner had little faith in the reality of friendship. In his eyes, and according to his experience, the barriers of personality separating one soul from another make solitude inevitable, and full understanding an impossibility. Here he felt himself understood, and he understood completely. "My friend Schopenhauer"; "a gift from heaven to my loneliness." "But one friend I have," he writes, "whom I love ever to win anew. That is my old Schopenhauer, who seems so grumpy and is always so deeply loving." "When I have urged my feelings to their utmost, what a joy and refreshment to open that book and suddenly find myself again, to see myself so well understood and clearly expressed, only in quite a different language, which suffering quickly makes me understand . . . that is a wonderful and gratifying reciprocal effect, and ever new because ever stronger. . . . How beautiful, that the old man knows nothing of what he is to me, and *what I am to myself through him!*"

A piece of good luck like this, among artists, is only possible where they speak different languages; otherwise catastrophe and deadly rivalry ensue. But where the medium of one is thought, of the other form, all jealously engendered by the similarity or proximity of mental states is obviated. The *pereant qui ante nos nostra dixerunt* has no bearing, nor has Goethe's question: "Does one live, then, when others live?" On the contrary, the very fact of the other's existence means help at need, it means unexpected and blessed clarifying and strengthening of one's own being. Never probably in the history of the mind has there been so wonderful an example of the artist, the dark and driven human being, finding spiritual support, self-justification, and enlightenment in another's thought, as in this case of Wagner and Schopenhauer.

The World as Will and Idea: what memories of one's own young intoxications of the spirit, one's own joys of conception, compact of melancholy and gratitude, come up at the thought of the bond between Wagner's work and this great book! This comprehensive critique and guide, this poesy of knowledge, this metaphysics of impulse and spirit, will and idea as conceived by the artist, this marvelous thought-structure of ethical, pessimistical, and musical elements—what profound, epoch-making, human affinities it displays with the score of the *Tristan!* The old words come back in which the stripling described the Schopenhauer experience of his bourgeois hero: "He was filled with a great, surpassing satisfaction. It soothed him to see how a master mind could lay hold on this strong, cruel, mocking thing called life and enforce it and condemn it. His was the gratification of the sufferer who has always had a bad conscience about his sufferings and concealed them from the gaze of a harsh, unsympathetic world, until suddenly, from the hand of an authority, he receives, as it were, justification and licence for his suffering—justification before the world, this best of all possible worlds which the master mind scornfully demonstrates to be the worst of all possible ones." They come back, these old phrases of gratitude and homage that still express so well the tremulous rapture of the past—and of the present: that rousing out of brief and heavy sleep, that sudden and exquisitely startling awakening, to find in one's own heart the seed of a metaphysic which proves the ego to be illusion, death a release from that ego's insufficiency; the world a product of the will, and his own eternal possession, so long as he does not deny himself in knowledge, but finds his way from error to peace. That is the conclusion, the doctrine of wisdom and salvation subjoined to a philosophy of the will which has little to do with the wisdom of peace and rest, being a conception that could only have its source in a nature tormented by will and impulse; in which, indeed, the impulse to clarification, spiritualization, and knowledge was just as strong as the other sinister urgency; the conception of a universal Eros which expressly considers sex to be the focus of the will, and the æsthetic point of view, as that of pure and disinterested contemplation, the only and primary possibility of release from the torture of instinct. Out of the will, out of desire contrary to better knowledge, this philosophy, which is the will's intellectual denial, is born; and thus it was that Wagner, whose nature was profoundly akin to the philosopher's own, felt it and seized upon it with the greatest gratitude, as something essentially his own and answering to his needs. For his nature too was combined of urgent and tormenting desires for power and pleasure, together with longings for moral enlightenment and release; it was a conflict of passion and desire for peace. And thus a system of thought which is an extraordinary mixture of quietism and heroics, which calls "happiness" a chimera and gives out that the highest and best we can attain to is a life of heroic struggle, must have rejoiced a nature like Wagner's, must have seemed made to fit him and created for him.

The official works on Wagner assert in all seriousness that *Tristan* was not influenced by the Schopenhauerian philosophy. That seems to me a curious lack of insight. The archromantic worship of the night embodied in this sublimely morbid, consuming, enchanting work, deep-dyed in all the worst and highest mysteries of the romantic

essence, has about it nothing specifically Schopenhauerian. The sensuous, supersensuous intuitions in the *Tristan* come from a remoter
source: from the perfervid and hectic Novalis, who writes: "Union
joined not only for life but for death is a marriage that gives us a companion for the night. Love is sweetest in death; for the living death is
a bridal night, a sweet mysterious secret." And in the *Hymns to Night*
he complains: "Must morning always come? Does the domain of the
earthly never cease? Will it never be that love's sweet sacrifice shall
burn forever on the altar?" Tristan and Isolde call themselves the
"Night-consecrate"—the phrase actually occurs in Novalis: "Conse-
crated to the night." And still more striking from the point of view of
literary history, still more significant for the sources of *Tristan,* for its
emotional and intellectual bases, are its associations with a little book
of evil repute, I mean Friedrich von Schlegel's *Lucinde.* I quote a
passage from this work: "We are immortal as love. I can no longer say
my love or thy love, both being so utterly one, love as much given as
returned. It is marriage, eternal union and bond between our spirits,
not alone for what we call this world, but for a true, indivisible, name-
less, infinite world, for our whole, everlasting life and being." Here is
the mental image of the love- and death-potion: "Thus I too, if the
time seemed come, would drain a cup of laurel-water with thee, freely
and gladly, as the last glass of champagne we drank together, with the
words: 'Let us drink out the rest of our lives!'" And here is the
thought of the *Liebestod*: "I know you too would not outlive me, you
would follow to the grave your impatient spouse, from love and longing you would descend into the flaming abyss whither the Indian
woman is driven by a desperate law which by harsh and deliberate en-
forcement violates and destroys the most delicate sanctuaries of the
free will." And there is a reference to the "exaltation of voluptuous
ness," surely a very Wagnerian formula. Here indeed is an erotic,
mystical prose poem, in praise and adoration of sleep, the paradise of
rest, the holy silence of passivity, which in *Tristan* becomes the lulling
motif of the horns and the divided violins. And it was nothing less
than a literary discovery that I made, when as a young man I underlined the ecstatic passage between Julian and Lucinde: "Oh, eternal
yearning! For the fruitless desire and vain brilliance of the day die
down and expire, and a great night of love knows eternal repose,"
and wrote in the margin: "*Tristan.*" To this day I do not know whether
anyone has ever remarked this case of unconscious verbal memory and

imitation, as little as I know whether scholars are aware that Nietzsche took from *Lucinde* his title for the book he calls *Fröhliche Wissenschaft (Joyous Wisdom)*.

Its cult of the night, its execration of the day, are what stamps the *Tristan* as romantic, as fundamentally affiliated with all the romantic aspects of emotion and thought—and as such not needing the Schopenhaurian sponsorship. Night is the kingdom and home of all romanticism, her own discovery, always she has played it off against the empty vanities of the day, as the kingdom of sensibility against reason. I shall never forget the impression made upon me by Linderhof, the castle of the ailing and beauty-consumed King Ludwig; for I saw there the preponderance of the night expressed in the very proportions of the rooms. This little pleasure palace situated in the wonderful mountain solitudes has rather small and insignificant living rooms, and only one room of relative magnificence of size and decoration: the sleeping chamber. It is full of the heavy splendor of gilding and silk, its state bed lies under a canopy and is flanked by gold candelabra. Here is the true state apartment of the royal chalet, and it is dedicated to the night. This deliberate stress upon the night, the lovelier half of the day, is archromantic; and its romanticism is bound up with the whole mother- and moon-cult which since the dawn of human time and human sun-worship has stood opposed to the male and father-religion of the light. Wagner's *Tristan* belongs, generally speaking, to this world.

But when the Wagner authorities say that *Tristan* is a love-drama, as such contains the strongest affirmation of the will to live, and in consequence has nothing to do with Schopenhauer; when they insist that the night therein celebrated is the night of love *"wo Liebeswonne uns lacht,"* and that if this drama has a philosophy at all, then it is the exact opposite of the doctrine which would deny the will, and that precisely on that ground it is independent of the Schopenhaurian metaphysics—it seems to me that all this betrays a strange psychological insensitiveness. The denial of the will is the moral and intellectual content of Schopenhauer's philosophy, of secondary significance and not the crucial point. His philosophic system is fundamentally erotic in its nature, and insofar as it is that the *Tristan* is saturated with it. The quenching of the torch in the second act of the mystery play is emphasized in the orchestra by the death motif, the lovers' cry of transport: *"Selbst dann bin ich die Welt,"* with the longing motif out of the depths of the psychological and mythical accompanying music

—is that not Schopenhauer? Wagner is mythological poet not less in *Tristan* than in the *Ring*; even the love-drama deals with a myth of the origin of the world. "Often," so he writes from Paris in 1860 to Mathilde Wesendonck, "I look with yearning toward the land of Nirvana. But Nirvana soon becomes *Tristan* again. You know the story of the Buddhistic theory of the origin of the world? A breath troubles the clearness of the heavens"—he writes the four chromatic ascending notes with which his *opus metaphysicum* begins and ends, the G-sharp, A, A-sharp, B-natural—"it swells and condenses, and there before me is the whole vast solid mass of the world." It is the symbolic tone-thought which we know as the "*Sehnsuchts* motif," and which in the cosmogony of the *Tristan* signifies the beginning of all things, like the E-flat major of the Rhine motif in the *Ring*. It is Schopenhauer's "will," represented by what Schopenhauer called the "focus of the will," the yearning for love. And this mythical equating of sexual desire with the sweet and fatal world-creating principle that first troubled the clear heaven of the inane—that is so Schopenhauerian that the refusal of the experts to see it looks like obstinacy.

"How could we die," asks Tristan in the early, not yet versified draft; "what would there be of us to kill that would not be love? Are we not utterly and only love? Can our love ever end? Could I ever will to love, love no more? Were I now to die would love die too, since we *are* naught but love?" The quotation shows the unhesitating equation of love and will on the part of the poet. The latter stands simply for the love of life, which cannot end in death, though it is freed from the fetters of individuality. Most interesting it is too to see the love-mythus sustained as a conception of the drama and preserved from any historical or religious clouding or distortion. Phrases like "Whether bound for hell or heaven," surviving in the draft, are omitted from the production. We have here doubtless a conscious weakening of the historical element, but it is limited to the intellectual and philosophical and only happens in the interest of these. And it suits admirably with a most intensive technique of coloration, applied to the landscape settings, the cultural elements, the racial character-istics of the protagonists. It is stylistic specialization of incredible ability and certainty of touch. Nowhere does Wagner's skill at mimi-cry triumph more magically than in the style of the *Tristan*—this not as a matter of language merely, by phraseology in the spirit of the court epic; for with intuitive genius he is able to saturate his word-and tone-painting in an Anglo-Norman-French atmosphere, with a discernment that shows how completely the Wagner soul is at home in the prenational sphere of European life. The divorce from history, the free humanization, takes place only in the field of speculative thought, and then in the service of the erotic myth. For its sake heaven and hell are cut out. Christianity too, since it would amount to historical atmosphere. There is no God, no one knows Him or calls upon Him. There is nothing but erotic philosophy, atheistic metaphysics: the cosmogonic myth in which the *Sehnsuchts* motif evokes the world.

Wagner's good normal way of being ill, his rather morbid way of being heroic, are simply indications of the contradictions and crosscurrents in his nature, its duality and manifoldness, as manifested in such apparently contradictory elements as the psychological and mythological bents to which I have already referred. To call him romantic is still probably the most apt characterization of his nature; but the concept romantic is itself so complex and changeable that it seems to be less a category than the abandonment of categories.

Only in the romantic can popular appeal unite with the extreme of subtlety, with an overstimulated "heinous" indulgence (to use a favorite word of E. T. A. Hoffmann), in means and effects—and it alone can make possible that "double optic" of which Nietzsche speaks with reference to Wagner: that knows how to cater to the coarsest and the finest—unconsciously, of course, for it would be stupid to introduce the element of calculation—whose *Lohengrin* can enrapture spirits like the author of the *Fleurs du Mal* and at the same time serve to elevate the masses; that leads a Kundryish double life as a Sunday afternoon opera and as the idol of initiate and suffering and supersensitive souls. The romantic—in league, of course, with music, toward which it continually aspires, without which it can have no fulfillment—knows no exclusiveness, no "pathos of distance"; it says to nobody: "This is not for you"; one side of its nature stands with the least and lowest, and let nobody say that is the case with all great art. Great art may elsewhere too have succeeded in uniting the childlike and the elevated; but the combination of the extremely *raffiné* with fairy-story simplicity, the power to materialize—and popularize—the highly intellectual under the guise of an orgy of the senses; the ability to make the essentially grotesque put on the garment of consecration, the Last Supper, the bell, the elevation of the Host . . . to couple sex and religion in an opera of greatly daring sex appeal, and to set up that sort of holy-unholy artistic establishment in the middle of Europe as a kind of Lourdes theater and miraculous grotto for the voracious credulity of a decadent world—all that is nothing but romantic. In the classic and humanistic, the really high sphere of art, it is quite unthinkable. Take the list of characters in *Parsifal*: what a set! One advanced and offensive degenerate after another: a self-castrated magician; a desperate double personality, composed of a Circe and a repentant Magdalene, with cataleptic transition stages; a lovesick high priest, awaiting the redemption that is to come to him in the person of a chaste youth; the youth himself, "pure" fool and redeemer, quite a different figure from Brünnhilde's lively awakener and in his way also an extremely rare specimen—they remind one of the aggregation of scarecrows in A. von Arnim's famous coach: the enigmatic gypsy witch; the good-for-nothing, who is a corpse; the golem in female form; and the Field-Marshal Cornelius Nepos, who is a slip of mandrake grown beneath the gallows. The comparison sounds blasphemous; and yet the solemn personages in *Parsifal* have the same flavor of romantic extravaganza, they spring from the same school of taste as do von Arnim's disreputable crew, though the fact would be more obvious if the literary form were fiction instead of drama. As it is, the music, with its sanctifying, mythologizing power, shrouds it from view; it is music's power over the emotions that makes the ensemble appear not like a half-burlesque, half-uncanny impropriety of the romantic school, but as a miracle play of the highest religious significance.

Youth is typically susceptible to this elusive problem of art and the essence of the artist, it has a melancholy understanding of the ironic interplay of essence and effect; in this field I recall many an utterance of my own young days, characteristic of the Wagner passion that has gone through the fire of the Nietzschean critique, dictated by that "disgust of knowledge"—which is the foremost and peculiar lesson youth learns therefrom. Nietzsche said he would not touch the *Tristan* score with the tongs. "Who will dare," he cries, "to utter the word, the right word, for the *ardeurs* of the *Tristan* music?" I am more open to the rather comic old-maidishness of this question than I was when I was twenty-five years old. For what is there so venturesome about it? Sensuality, enormous sensuality, mounting into the mythical, spiritualized, depicted with the extreme of naturalism, sensuality unquenchable by any amount of gratification—that is the "word." And one asks whence comes the violent bitterness against sex that expresses

itself in such a psychological denunciation in the question of Nietzsche, the "free, very free spirit." Is not this Nietzsche the archmoral-
ist and clergyman's son? And what has become of his role as defender
of life against morality? He applies to the *Tristan* the mystic's formula:
voluptuous pleasure of hell (*"Wollust der Hölle"*). Good. And one
need only compare the mysticism of the *Tristan* with that of Goethe's
"blessed longing" and its "higher mating" to feel how little we are
in the Goethe sphere. But Nietzsche himself is after all no poorer instance than Wagner of the fact that the soul-state of the Western
world in the nineteenth century has deteriorated by comparison with
Goethe's epoch. And the sort of lashing to fury or drugging to calm
which are among Wagner's effects—the ocean too can show the same,
and nobody thinks of dragging its psychology to the light of day.
What is allowed to great nature should be allowed to great art; when
Baudelaire, in naïve artistic rapture, and quite without moral prejudice, speaks of the "ecstasy of bliss and understanding" which the *Lohengrin* overture put him in, and raves of the "opium intoxication,"
of the "desire that in high places circles," he shows much more courage and intellectual freedom than Nietzsche with his suspicious caution. Though, after all, the phrase in which Nietzsche characterizes
the Wagner craze as "a slight unconscious epidemic of sensuality"
still has its justification, and it is precisely the word "unconscious"
that, in view of Wagner's romantic popularity, may irritate such as
feel the need of clear thinking; may be a ground for "preferring not
to be there."

Wagner's power of concentrating the intellectual and the popular
in a single dramatic figure is nowhere better displayed than in the
hero of his revolutionary phase—in Siegfried. The "breathless delight"
with which the future director of the Bayreuth Theater one day witnessed a puppet show—he tells about it in his essay on Actors and
Singers—bore practical fruit in the setting of the *Ring*, which is an
ideal popular diversion with just the right kind of go-ahead hero. Who
can fail to recognize in him the little whip-cracker of the county fair?
But at the same time he is a northern sun-myth and god of light—
which does not prevent him from being something modern too, out
of the nineteenth century, the free man, the breaker of tablets and
renovator of a fallen society: Bakunin, in short, as Bernard Shaw, with
cheerful rationalism, quite simply calls him. Yes, he is a clown, a sun-
god, and an anarchistic social-revolutionary, all rolled into one; what

more can the theater demand? And this art of combination is simply an expression of Wagner's own mingled and manifold nature. He is not musician and not poet, but a third category, in which the other two are blended in a way unknown before; he is a theater Dionysius, who knows how to take unprecedented methods of expression and give them a poetic basis, to a certain extent to rationalize them. But insofar as he *is* poet, it is not in a modern, literary, and cultivated spirit, not out of his mind and consciously, but in a much deeper and devouter way. It is the folk-soul that speaks out of him and through him; he is only its tool and mouthpiece, only "God's ventriloquist," to repeat Nietzsche's good joke. At least, this is the correct and accepted theory of his artistic position, and it is supported by a kind of unwieldy awkwardness that his work betrays when considered as literature. And yet he can write: "We should not underestimate the power of reflection; the unconsciously produced work of art belongs to periods remote from ours, and the art product of the most highly cultivated period cannot be produced otherwise than in full consciousness." That is a blow between the eyes for the theory which would ascribe an entirely mythical origin to his works; and indeed, though these indubitably bear in part the marks of inspiration, of blind and blissful ecstasy, yet there is so much else, so much cleverness, wittiness, allusiveness, calculated effect; so much dwarfish diligence accompanies the labors of gods and giants, that it is impossible to believe in trance and mystery. The extraordinary understanding displayed in his abstract writings does not indeed act in the service of spirit, truth, abstract knowledge; but to the advantage of his work, which it labors to explain and justify, whose pathway it would smooth, both within and without. But it is none the less a fact. And there would remain the possibility that in the act of creation he was entirely shoved aside to make room for the promptings of the folk-soul. But my feeling of the improbability of this is strengthened by various more or less well-authenticated statements from those who knew him, to the effect that by his own account some of his best things were produced by dint of sheer hard thinking. "Ah, how I have tried and tried," he is reported as saying, "thought and thought, until at last I get hold of what I wanted!"

In short, his author- and creatorship has contact with both spheres: the one that lies "remote from ours" as well as the one where the brain long ago developed into the modern intellectual tool we know. And hence the indissoluble mingling of the dæmonic and the bourgeois which is the essence of him. Much the same is true of Schopen-hauer, who is accordingly Wagner's next of kin, both in time and in temperament. The unbourgeois extravagance of his nature, which he himself laid at the door of music ("It makes a purely exclamatory man of me," says he; "the exclamation point is the only satisfying punctu-ation to me so soon as I leave my notes"), this extravagance finds ex-pression in the exaggerated character of all his moods, particularly the depressive. It comes out in the strange destinies of his outer life—destiny being nothing more than the unfolding of character—his wry relations with the world, his hunted, outlawed, broken and battered existence; he puts it in the mouth of his *Wehwalt* Siegmund:

> Drew I to men or to women,
> Many I met, where I them found,
> If I for friend, for woman wooed,
> Ever still was I despisèd,
> Curses lay upon me.
> What right ever I wrought
> Still to them seemèd it wrong;
> What to me evil appear'd
> Others reckoned it right.
> Fell I on feud, whither I went;
> Where I me found, scorn met me.
> Long'd I for bliss, waked I but woe.

Every word comes from experience; not one but is coined out of his own life; in these fine lines there is no more than he wrote in prose to Mathilde Wesendonck: "Since the world, in all seriousness, does not want me"—or to her husband: "I am so hard to accommodate in this world, that a thousand misunderstandings are always likely to take place. This is my great trouble . . . the world and I knock our heads together and the thinnest skull gets cracked—no wonder I have my nervous headaches." The desperate humor of this is quite in character. Once, round his forty-eighth birthday, he speaks of the "crazy mood" he was in, in Weimar; it delighted everybody, but originated solely in the circumstance that he did not dare be serious, simply did not dare any more, for fear of going to pieces. "This is a fault of my tempera-ment, and it gets worse and worse. I fight against it, for sometimes it seems to me I shall weep myself away." What a luxury of debility! What *Kapellmeister Kreisler* eccentricity! All this passionate up and down, this frenzied and tragic emotionalism, reduced to its starkest elements, accursed, yet pining for rest and peace, he has concentrated in the figure of the Flying Dutchman; it lives and glows with the colors of his own anguish; the great intervals in which the score of this role swings to and fro are most calculated to create this impression of wild agitation.

No, this is no bourgeois—at least not in any sense of being adaptable or conformable to rule. And yet he has the atmosphere of the bourgeoisie, the atmosphere of his century, about him, as has Schopenhauer the capitalist philosopher: the moral pessimism, the mood of decline set to music—that is genuine nineteenth-century, and goes with its tendency to the monumental, its penchant for size—as though size were a property of morality. He has, I say, the atmosphere of the bourgeois, and not only in this general sense but in one much more personal. I will not insist that he was a revolutionary of the '48, a fighter for the middle class and thus a political citizen. For he was that only in his own peculiar way, as an artist and in the interest of his art, which was revolutionary and might hope for imagined advantages, better conditions, and more effectiveness from an upset of the existing order. But there are more intimate traits of character—despite its genius and its inspiration—which distinctly suggest the bourgeois attitude. As when he moved into that asylum on the green hill near Zürich and in the enjoyment of his sense of well-being wrote to Liszt: "Everything is arranged for permanence and convenience, and precisely as one would wish; everything is just in the right place. My study has the same fastidious air of comfort and elegance that is familiar to you; the desk stands by the big window. . . ." The fastidious order and also the bourgeois elegance he requires of his surroundings correspond to the element of shrewd and calculated industry which accompanies the dæmonic in his work, and supplies the bourgeois flavor of it. His later self-dramatization as *Deutscher Meister* with the black velvet cap had its good inward and natural justification; despite all volcanic manifestations it would be a mistake to overlook the Old German element, the loyal-eyed, industrious, and ingenious artisan, which is just as essential to it. He writes to Otto Wesendonck:

Let me tell you briefly the state of my work. When I began it I abandoned hope of being able to bring it to a conclusion in short order. . . . Partly because I was so full of cares and troubles of all sorts that I was often incapable of production. But partly also because I soon discovered my peculiar relation to my present work (which now I simply cannot do in a hurry, but can find pleasure therein only because I owe to good ideas that come to me even the smallest detail in it and work it out accordingly). I see this so clearly and unchangeably that I am obliged to give up any hasty or incomplete work which alone would enable me to finish in good time.

That is the "uprightness and good faith" which Schopenhauer inherited from his merchant forebears and which he claimed to have carried over into realms of the mind. It means solid, painstaking, accurate work, and it shows itself in the scores: they are clean, careful work, nothing slovenly about them—even that product of transport, the *Tristan*, is a model of clear, painstaking calligraphy.

But it cannot be denied that Wagner's taste for bourgeois elegance has its degenerate side; it betrays the tendency to put on a character that is quite remote from the sixteenth-century German *Meister* in the Dürer cap; it is bad nineteenth-century, it *is* bourgeois. The smack of the modern middle class (as distinct from the old civic spirit) is there, unmistakably in his human and artistic personality: all this luxury and extravagance, this silk and satin and *"Gründerzeit"* grandeur; it is of course a trait of his private life, but the roots of it go deep down. It is the time and the taste of the Makart bouquet with the peacock feathers which used to adorn the gilt and upholstered salons of the bourgeoisie; the fact is known that Wagner had the idea of engaging Makart to paint his scenery. He writes to Frau Ritter: "I've been having for some time now another craze for luxury (*ein Narr an Luxus*); whoever knew what it has to take the place of for me would consider me very modest indeed. Every morning I sit down and work in the midst of it; it is absolute necessity for me, for a day without work is torture." It would be hard to say which is more bourgeois, the love of luxury, or the torture felt at a day without work. But it is at this point that we discover the bourgeois striking back again into the disordered and unsavory realms of art, and taking on a character which, morbid as it is, has something dignified and even touching about it; something to which the word "bourgeois" is quite inapplicable. Here we enter a different field altogether, the fantastic domain of *stimulation*—Wagner treats of it, with restraint and circumlocution, in a letter to Liszt:

It is actually only with the most genuine despair that I take up my art again. If this must happen, if I must once more resign reality and plunge into that sea of fantasy, then at least my imagination must get help and support from somewhere. I cannot live like a dog, I cannot sleep on straw and drink bad brandy. I must be soothed and flattered in my soul if I am

to succeed at this grueling job of creating a world out of nothing. In order
to take up the plan of the *Ring* again and envisage its actual performance,
there had to be all sorts of contributing factors to give me the necessary
atmosphere of art and luxury. I *had* to be able to live better than I have
done in the past!

His *"Narr an Luxus"* is well known, the technique that had to come
to the help of his fancy: the wadded silk dressing gowns, the lace-
trimmed satin bed covers embroidered with garlands of roses, these
are the palpable expressions of an extravagance of taste which ran up
debts in thousands. Arrayed in them he sits down mornings to the
grueling job, by dint of them he achieves the "atmosphere of luxury
and art" necessary to the creation of primitive Nordic heroes and exalted natural symbolism, to the conception of his sun-blond youthful
hero striking sparks from the anvil as he forges his victorious sword—
all which goes to swell the breast of German youth with lofty feelings
of manly glory.

In reality the contradiction is without significance. Who thinks of
Schiller's rotten apples—the smell of which used to make Goethe
nearly faint—as an argument against the lofty sincerity of his works?
Wagner's working conditions happen to come higher than Schiller's—
and it would not be hard to think of costumes (for instance, dressing
up as a soldier or a monk) more suitable than satin dressing gowns
to the stern service of art. But in both cases we are dealing with an
artist pathology, harmless even though a bit weird; only philistines
would be misled by it. Yet after all there is some difference between
the two. In all Schiller's work there is no trace of the odor of decay
which stimulated his brain; but who would deny that there is a suggestion of satin dressing gowns in Wagner's art? True it is that
Schiller's purposeful idealism realizes itself much more purely and unequivocally in the influence his works exert than Wagner's ethical
attitude does in his. He was zealous for reform in a cultural sense, he
was against art as a luxury, against luxury in art; he wanted the purification and spiritualization of the operatic theater—which he conceived
of as synonymous with art. He referred with contempt to Rossini as
"Italia's voluptuous son, smiling away in luxury's most luxurious lap";
he spoke of the Italian opera as a "daughter of joy," of the French as
a "cold-smiling coquette." But his ethical attitude as artist, the hatred
and hostility these phrases suggest, does not find very happy expression in either the meaning or the method of his own art, which

brought the bourgeois society of all Europe to bow beneath its spell. What was it drove these thousands into the arms of his art—what but the blissfully sensuous, searing, sense-consuming, intoxicating, hypnotically caressing, heavily upholstered—in a word, the luxurious quality of his music? Eichendorff's song of the bold young bachelors, one of whom wastes his life in evil dissipations, characterizes temptation as "the wantoning waves," as "the billows' bright maw." Wonderful. None but a romantic could so suggestively characterize sin— and Wagner, in *Tannhäuser* and *Parsifal*, has done as much. And Wagner's orchestra, is it not just such a "bright maw" out of which, like Eichendorff's young Fant, one wakens "weary and old"?

If we must, in part, answer in the affirmative such questions as these, we are bound at the same time to recognize that we are dealing with what one calls a tragic antinomy, with one of the involved contradictions and incongruities in Wagner's nature. There are many of these, and a good part of them have to do with the relation between intention and effect in art; therefore it is highly important to emphasize here the complete and honorable purity and idealism of Wagner's position as artist, in order to obviate all possible misunderstandings on the score of the mass success his art achieved. All criticism, even Nietzsche's, tends to attribute the effectiveness of art to a conscious and deliberate intention of the artist, and to suggest calculation. Quite falsely and mistakenly: as though every artist does not do just what he *is*, what seems good and beautiful to *him*; as though there could be a kind of artist to whom his own effectiveness was a sham, instead of being, as it always is, an effect first of all upon him, the artist himself! Innocent may be the last adjective to apply to art; but the artist, he is innocent. An enormous success, such as that which Wagner's theater of music "aimed at," was never before vouchsafed to great art. It is fifty years since the master's death; and every evening this music envelops the globe. This art of the theater, this art of shaking the masses, owns such elements—imperialistic, world-subduing, despotic, powerfully *agaçante*, inflammable, demagogic elements—as to make one deduce a monstrous ambition, a Cæsar's will to power as the force that set them in motion. The truth looks different. "So much I tell you," Wagner writes from Paris to his beloved. "Only the conviction of my own purity gives me this power. I feel myself pure; I know in my deepest soul that I always worked for others, never for myself; and my constant sufferings are a proof to me." If that is not true, it is at least so sincere that skepticism is silenced. He knows naught of ambition. "Of greatness, fame, conquest of the masses," he assures Liszt, "I think nothing." Not even conquest of the masses? Perhaps, in the mild form of mastership and popularity, as ideal, wish-dream, as the romantic, democratic conception of art and artists, which the *Meistersinger* so sturdily and splendidly embodies. Yes, the popularity of Hans Sachs, against whom the "whole school" labors in vain seeing the people hold him dear—that is a wish-dream. In the *Meistersinger* there is a coquetting with the folk as final arbiter of art, which is the opposite of the aristocratic position and highly indicative of Wagner's democratic revolutionarism in art, his conception of it as a free appeal to the feeling of the people. What a contrast to the classic, courtly, and elegant notion of art obtaining in that time when Voltaire wrote: *"Quand la populace se mêle de raisonner, tout est perdu!"* And still, when this artist reads Plutarch, he feels, like Karl Moor, dislike of the "great men," and would not be like them for anything. "Hateful, violent, greedy little natures—because they have nothing in themselves and must always be sucking it in from outside. Away with your great men! I agree with Schopenhauer: not he who conquers, but he who overcomes the world, is worthy of admiration. God save me from these Napoleons!" Was he a world-conqueror, or a world-overcomer? And his *"Selbst dann bin ich die Welt,"* with its world-erotic theme and accent—of which of the two is that the formula?

In any case, the charge of ambition in the ordinary worldly sense is not tenable; because he worked at first without hope of immediate results, without any prospect of them under the actually existing circumstances and conditions. Worked in the void of fancy, as it were, for an imaginary ideal stage, the realization of which, for the time, was not to be thought of. Certainly there is no talk of shrewd calculation and ambitious exploitation of possibilities in the letter he writes to Otto Wesendonck: "For this I see: I am only wholly what I am when I create. The performance of my works belongs to a purer time —a time which I must first prepare for by my sufferings. My closest friends have only astonishment for my new labors: no one who has relations with our official art-life feels strength to hope. And they are right. Nothing shows me better how far ahead I am of everything round me." The loneliness of genius, its remoteness from actuality, has never been more arrestingly expressed than in these words. But we—we of the last decade of the nineteenth century and the first third of the twentieth, of the World War and the slow decline of capitalism; we in whose day Wagner's art bestrides the theaters of the civi-

lized worlds and triumphs everywhere in unabridged performances—we
are those "purer times" when he had to prepare through his sufferings.
Is the humanity of from 1880 to 1933 the one to prove the height
and goodness of an art by the giant success we have vouchsafed it?

Let us not ask. We see how his genius proves itself by the fact that
it seeks to come near the world, to adapt itself to the world—and
cannot. A comic operetta, a satyr-play to the *Tannhäuser*, a diversion
for him and his audience; the best of wills to create something light
and enjoyable—it turns out to be the *Meistersinger*. Well, then, something Italian, something tuneful, lyrical, and singable, with a small
cast, easy to produce, quite simple: and the result is—*Tristan*. One
cannot make oneself smaller than one is: one does what one is, and
art is truth—the truth about the artist.

Yes, the vast universal effectiveness of this art had, originally and
personally speaking, very pure and spiritual sources. This was first of
all due to its own lofty plane, where no deeper scorn is known than
that for effect, for "effect without cause." And next because all the imperial, demagogic, and mass-effective elements must be conceived in a
quite ultrapractical and ideal sense as having reference to all too revolutionary conditions yet to be achieved. In particular the innocence of
the artist comes in play, where the will to rouse enthusiasm expresses
itself, powerfully instrumented, in a national appeal, celebrating and
glorifying the German spirit, as happens quite directly in *Lohengrin*,
in King Henry's "German Sword," and in the *Meistersinger* on the
honest lips of good Hans Sachs. It is thoroughly inadmissible to ascribe
to Wagner's nationalistic attitudes and speeches the meaning they
would have today. That would be to falsify and misuse them, to be-
smirch their romantic purity.

The national idea, when Wagner introduced it as a familiar and
workable theme into his works—that is to say, before it was realized—
was in its heroic, historically legitimate epoch. It had its good, living
and genuine period; it was poetry and intellect, a future value. But
when the basses thunder out at the stalls the verse from the "German
Sword," or that kernel and finale of the *Meistersinger*:

> Though Holy Roman Empire sink to dust
> There still survives our sacred German art,

in order to arouse an ulterior patriotic emotion—that is demagogy. It
is precisely these lines—they already appeared at the end of the first

sketch, dated Marienbad, 1845—that attest the intellectuality of Wagner's nationalism and its remoteness from the political sphere; they betray a complete anarchistic indifference to the state, so long as the spiritually German, the *"Deutsche Kunst,"* survives. Even so he was not thinking of German art, but rather of his music-theater, which is far from being solely German, having taken unto itself not only Weber, Marschner, and Lortzing, but also Spontini and Grand Opera —but that is another matter. At bottom perhaps he thought, like that greatest unpatriot of them all, Goethe: "What do the Germans want? Have they not me?"

All his life long, Richard Wagner dreamed of an ideal public for his art, in the sense of a classless society, founded on love, freed from luxury and the curse of gold; thus as a politician he was much more of a Socialist, a believer in a cultural utopia, than he was a patriot in the sense of the all-powerful state. His heart was for the poor against the rich. His participation in the '48 cost him twelve years of torment and exile; later, repenting of his "reckless" optimism, in face of the *fait accompli* of Bismarck's empire, he minimized his share in it and identified it as best he could with the realization of his dream. He went the way of the German bourgeoisie: from the Revolution to disillusionment, to pessimism and a sheltered and contemplative resignation. And yet we find in his writings the opinion—in a certain sense the very un-German opinion: "Whoever tries to get away from the political befools himself!" So living and radical a spirit was of course aware of the unity of the problem for humanity, of the inseparability of mind and politics; he did not cling to the delusion of the German citizen, that one may be a man of culture yet not of politics—this madness to which Germany owes her misery. His attitude toward the Fatherland, from the founding of the empire to his settling down in Bayreuth, was always that of the solitary; misunderstood, repulsed, full of scorn and criticism. "Oh, how full of enthusiasm I am for the German league of the Germanic nation!" he writes from Lucerne in 1859. "God forbid that that reprobate of a Louis Napoleon should lay his hands on my dear German league: I should feel too upset if anything were to alter there!" In exile he was consumed with longing for Germany; but the return brought him nothing but bitter disappointment. "It is a miserable country," he cries, "and it is a just judgment that says the German is mean-spirited." But observe: these unfavorable comments refer solely to the German unreadiness to accept his work; their animus is quite childish and personal. Germany is good or bad according as it has faith in him or denies it to him. Even in 1875 he replies to a flattering remark that the German public has surrendered to him to a most unexampled extent, with the bitter comment: "Oh, yes, the Sultan and the Khedive have taken patrons' tickets."

It is an honor to his artist heart that at the same time he could envisage the fulfillment of his German desires in the foundation of the empire by Bismarck, the new empire for which Nietzsche could not find enough words of passionate execration; that he was ready and able to see in it the right soil for his cultural labors. The—little German—resurrection of the German Empire, a phenomenon of overpowering historical success, strengthened in Wagner, his friend Heckel says, a belief in the development of a German culture and art—in other words, the possibility that his artistic contribution, the sublimated opera, might be realized. It was this hope that gave rise to the *Kaisermarsch*; to the poem to the German army before Paris, which only shows that without music Wagner is no poet; to the incredibly bad taste of the *Capitulation*, a satire on Paris in her agony, in 1871, which is in every sense a betrayal of Wagner's higher self. But above all it gave rise to his manifesto "On the Production of the Festival Play: *The Ring of the Nibelungs*," to which he received one single reply—from friend Heckel, the piano dealer in Mannheim. The opposition to Wagner's plans and pretensions, the fear of siding with him, remained very great; but the foundation of the empire coincided with the foundation of the first Wagner Society and the issue of patrons' cards for the festival plays. The organization, full of compromises, as always, the realization, was beginning. Wagner was a good enough politician to link his affairs with the Bismarck empire; he saw in it an incomparably successful feat, and he attached his own fortunes to its chariot. The European hegemony of his art has become the cultural equivalent to the political hegemony of Bismarck. The great statesman to whose labors he thus married his own understood it not at all; he never troubled about it, he considered Wagner a crazy chap. But the old Kaiser—who understood no better—went to Bayreuth and said: "I never thought that you would bring it off!" The works of Wagner were installed as a national concern, as an official appanage of the empire; and they have remained more or less bound up with the red, white, and black—however little they have to do in their deeper essence and the quality of their Germanness with all or any empires based on power and war.

When we discuss the involutions and inconsistencies of Wagner's contradictory nature, we should not leave out of account the grandiose combination and interweaving of Germanness and cosmopolitanism: it is part of his being, characterizing it in the most absolutely unprecedented and thought-provoking way. There always has been, and there is today, a German art of high rank—I am thinking especially of the literary field—which belongs so entirely to the quiet and domestic Germany, is so peculiarly and intimately German, that it is able—albeit in a very high sense—to command influence and honor only within our borders, resigning entirely all claims upon a European audience. That is a destiny like another, it has nothing to do with values. Much more insignificant stuff, the universal commonplace of the day, easily crosses the frontiers and by its very nature is everywhere understood. But other works, equal in rank and value to the exclusively domestic product, may prove to be anointed with the drop of European and democratic unction that opens the world to them and assures them international currency.

Wagner's works are of this kind—though with him one cannot speak of a drop of oil, for they fairly drip with it! Their Germanness is deep, powerful, unquestionable. The birth of drama from music, as it is consummated, purely and enchantingly, at least once, at the height of Wagner's creative powers, in the *Tristan,* could only spring out of German life; and as German in the highest sense of the word we may also characterize its tremendous sense-appeal, its mythological and metaphysical tendencies; above all, its profoundly serious consciousness as art, the high and solemn conception of the art of the theater, with which it is filled and which it communicates. But in and with all that, it has a universal rightness and enjoyability above all German art of this high rank; and I shall remain within the frame of its creator's chosen circle of thought if I reason back from the practical manifestation to the informing will. *Richard Wagner as a Cultural Phenomenon,* a book by a non-German, the Swedish Wilhelm Peterson-Berger, is very shrewd and good on this point. The writer speaks of Wagner's nationalism, of his art as a national art, and remarks that German folk-music is the only field not comprehended in the Wagnerian synthesis. In the *Meistersinger,* and in *Siegfried,* he may, for purposes of characterization, strike the folk-key; but it is not the fundamental note or the point of departure of his tone-poesy, from which it gushes spontaneously, as is the case with Schubert, Schumann, and Brahms. It is necessary to distinguish between folk-art and national art: the first has a domestic, the second a foreign goal.

Wagner's music is more national than of the people. It has many traits indeed which *foreigners in particular* find German; but it has, according to this author, an unmistakably cosmopolitan cachet.

It seems to me that this analysis of Wagner's Germanness is very finely felt and expressed. Yes, Wagner is German, he is national, in the most exemplary, perhaps too exemplary, way. For besides being an eruptive revelation of the German nature, his work is likewise a dramatic depiction of the same; a depiction the intellectualism and the poster-like effectiveness of which is positively grotesque, positively burlesque; it seems calculated to move an eager and palpitating world-public to the cry: *"Ah, c'est bien allemand, par exemple!"* Well, then, this Germanness, true and mighty as it is, is very modern—it is broken down and disintegrating, it is decorative, analytical, intellectual; and hence its fascination, its inborn capacity for cosmopolitan, for world-wide effectiveness. Wagner's art is the most sensational self-portrayal and self-critique of the German nature that it is possible to conceive; it is calculated to make Germany interesting to a foreigner even of the meanest intelligence; and passionate preoccupation with it is at the same time passionate preoccupation with the German nature which it so decoratively criticizes and glorifies. In this its nationalism consists; but it is a nationalism so soaked in the currents of European art as to defy all effort to simplify or belittle it.

"You will serve the cause of one whom the future will hail as greatest among the great." Charles Baudelaire wrote this sentence in 1849 to a young German Wagner enthusiast and musical critic. The prophecy, astonishing in its assurance, springs from passionate love, from elective passion; and the critical acumen of Friedrich Nietzsche is displayed in the fact that he recognized this affinity without being aware of the expression of it. "Baudelaire," he says in the studies to the *Fall Wagner,* "was once the first prophet and advocate of Delacroix; perhaps today he may be the first Wagnerian in Paris." Only years later did he see the letter in which Wagner thanked the French poet for his homage—and he exulted. Yes, Baudelaire, the first admirer of Delacroix, that Wagner of the realm of painting, was actually the first Wagnerian in Paris and one of the earliest of true and passionate and artistically understanding Wagnerians. His article on *Tannhäuser,* written in 1851, was the decisive and pioneer utterance upon Wagner; it has remained historically the most important. The joy that Wagner's music gave him, the joy of finding oneself anew in the artistic conceptions of another, he had discovered in but one other case, his

literary acquaintance with Edgar Allan Poe. These two, Wagner and
Poe, are Baudelaire's gods—a singular juxtaposition to the German
ear! It puts Wagner's art all at once in a new light; it suggests associations with which our patriotic commentators have not familiarized
us. It opens up a whole world of color and fancy, lovesick for death
and beauty, the Western world of high and late romanticism; a pessimistic world, adept in strange intoxicants and refinements of the
senses, fanatically addicted to all sorts of æsthetical speculations and
combinations; in Hoffmannian, Kreislerian dreams of the correspondence and inner relation between colors, sounds, and odors, of the
mystical transformations of the mingled sense. . . . In this world we
are to see Richard Wagner: as the most glorious brother and comrade
of all these sufferers from life, given to pity, seeking for transport,
these art-mingling symbolists, worshipers of *"l'art suggestif,"* whose
need it is *"d'aller au delà, plus outre que l'humanité,"* to quote
Maurice Barrès, the latest convert of the cult, lover of Venice, the
Tristan city, the poet of blood, desire, and death, nationalist at the
end, and Wagnerian from beginning to end.

> *Sind es Wellen/sanfter Lüfte?*
> *Sind es Wogen/wonniger Düfte?*
> *Wie sie schwellen, /mich umrauschen,*
> *soll ich atmen, /soll ich lauschen?*
> *Soll ich schlürfen, /untertauchen,*
> *süss in Duften/mich verhauchen?*
> *In des Wonnenmeeres/wogenden Schwall,*
> *in der Duftwellen/tönenden Schall,*
> *in des Weltatmens/wehendem All—*
> *ertrinken—/versinken—*
> *unbewusst—/höchste Lust!*

That is the last and highest word of the world I mean, its crown
and triumph, stored and saturated with its spirit; and it was Wagner
and the early Nietzsche who conventionalized its European, mystic-
sensual art into something not too impossible for German culture,
and related it to the landmarks of tragedy—Euripides, Shakespeare,
Beethoven. Afterward Nietzsche regretted his act, being irritated by a
certain German lack of clarity in psychological matters; he overempha-
sized Wagner's European traits and poured scorn upon his German
mastership. Wrongly. For Wagner's Germanness was strong and
genuine. And that the romantic should reach its climax and achieve

its universal success in German and in the guise of the German *Meister* was determined for it beforehand, by its very nature.

A last word upon Wagner's relation to the past and to the future. For here too there reigns a duality, an interweaving of apparent contradictions, similar to the antithesis of Germanness and Europeanism which I have just analyzed. There are reactionary traits in Wagner, traces of reversion and cult of the dark past; we might interpret in this sense his love of the mystical and mythological; the Protestant nationalism in the *Meistersinger* as well as the Catholic spirit in *Parsifal*; his general fondness for the Middle Ages, for the life of knights and princes, for miracles and perfervid faith. And yet my feeling for the true nature of this artist phenomenon, conditioned through and through as it was by renewal, change, and liberation, strictly forbids me to take literally his language and manner of expression, instead of seeing it for what it is, an art-idiom of a very figurative sort, with which something quite different, something entirely revolutionary, keeps pace. This stormily progressive creative spirit, so charged with life despite all its soul-heaviness, its bond with death; this man who gloried in a world-destroyer born of free love; this bold musical pioneer, who in *Tristan* stands with one foot already upon atonal ground—today he would probably be called a cultural Bolshevist!— this man of the people, who all his life long and with all his heart repudiated power and money, violence and war; whose dream of a theater—whatever the times may have made of it—was one set up to a classless community; such a man no retrograde spirit can claim for its own; he belongs to that will which is directed toward the future.

But it is idle to conjure great men out of eternity into our now and here—to the end of asking them their views upon questions that were put differently in their day and thus are foreign to their spirit. How would Richard Wagner stand toward our problems, our needs and the tasks before us? That "would" has a hollow sound, the position is unthinkable. Views are of secondary importance, even in their own present; how much more so when that has become past! What is left is the man, and his work, the product of his efforts. Let us be content to reverence Wagner's work as a mighty and manifold phenomenon of German and Western culture, which will always act as the profoundest stimulus to art and knowledge.

THE MONSTER

Deems Taylor

This little tour de force seems to have become a minor
classic.

*"He would insult a man who disagreed with him about the
weather."*

He was an undersized little man, with a head too big for his
body—a sickly little man. His nerves were bad. He had skin trouble.
It was agony for him to wear anything next to his skin coarser than
silk. And he had delusions of grandeur.

He was a monster of conceit. Never for one minute did he look at
the world or at people, except in relation to himself. He was not only
the most important person in the world, to himself; in his own eyes
he was the only person who existed. He believed himself to be one of
the greatest dramatists in the world, one of the greatest thinkers, and
one of the greatest composers. To hear him talk, he was Shakespeare,
and Beethoven, and Plato, rolled into one. And you would have had
no difficulty in hearing him talk. He was one of the most exhausting
conversationalists that ever lived. An evening with him was an evening
spent in listening to a monologue. Sometimes he was brilliant; sometimes he was maddeningly tiresome. But whether he was being brilliant or dull, he had one sole topic of conversation: himself. What *he*
thought and what *he* did.

He had a mania for being in the right. The slightest hint of dis-
agreement, from anyone, on the most trivial point, was enough to set
him off on a harangue that might last for hours, in which he proved
himself right in so many ways, and with such exhausting volubility,
that in the end his hearer, stunned and deafened, would agree with
him, for the sake of peace.

It never occurred to him that he and his doing were not of the most intense and fascinating interest to anyone with whom he came in contact. He had theories about almost any subject under the sun, including vegetarianism, the drama, politics, and music; and in support of these theories he wrote pamphlets, letters, books . . . thousands upon thousands of words, hundreds and hundreds of pages. He not only wrote these things, and published them—usually at somebody else's expense—but he would sit and read them aloud, for hours, to his friends and his family.

He wrote operas; and no sooner did he have the synopsis of a story, but he would invite—or rather summon—a crowd of his friends to his house and read it aloud to them. Not for criticism. For applause. When the complete poem was written, the friends had to come again, and hear *that* read aloud. Then he would publish the poem, sometimes years before the music that went with it was written. He played the piano like a composer, in the worst sense of what that implies, and he would sit down at the piano before parties that included some of the finest pianists of his time, and play for them, by the hour, his own music, needless to say. He had a composer's voice. And he would invite eminent vocalists to his house, and sing them his operas, taking all the parts.

He had the emotional stability of a six-year-old child. When he felt out of sorts, he would rave and stamp, or sink into suicidal gloom and talk darkly of going to the East to end his days as a Buddhist monk. Then minutes later, when something pleased him, he would rush out of doors and run around the garden, or jump up and down on the sofa, or stand on his head. He could be grief-stricken over the death of a pet dog, and he could be callous and heartless to a degree that would have made a Roman emperor shudder.

He was almost innocent of any sense of responsibility. Not only did he seem incapable of supporting himself, but it never occurred to him that he was under any obligation to do so. He was convinced that the world owed him a living. In support of this belief, he borrowed money from everybody who was good for a loan—men, women, friends, or strangers. He wrote begging letters by the score, sometimes groveling without shame, at others loftily offering his intended benefactor the privilege of contributing to his support, and being mortally offended if the recipient declined the honor. I have found no record of his ever paying or repaying money to anyone who did not have a legal claim upon it.

What money he could lay his hands on he spent like an Indian rajah. The mere prospect of a performance of one of his operas was enough to set him to running up bills amounting to ten times the amount of his prospective royalties. On an income that would reduce a more scrupulous man to doing his own laundry, he would keep two servants. Without enough money in his pocket to pay his rent, he would have the walls and ceiling of his study lined with pink silk. No one will ever know—certainly he never knew—how much money he owed. We do know that his greatest benefactor gave him six thousand dollars to pay the most pressing of his debts in one city, and a year later had to give him sixteen thousand dollars to enable him to live in another city without being thrown into jail for debt.

He was equally unscrupulous in other ways. An endless procession of women marches through his life. His first wife spent twenty years enduring and forgiving his infidelities. His second wife had been the wife of his most devoted friend and admirer, from whom he stole her. And even while he was trying to persuade her to leave her first husband he was writing to a friend to inquire whether he could suggest some wealthy woman—*any* wealthy woman—whom he could marry for her money.

He was completely selfish in his other personal relationships. His liking for his friends was measured solely by the completeness of their devotion to him, or by their usefulness to him, whether financial or artistic. The minute they failed him—even by so much as refusing a dinner invitation—or began to lessen in usefulness, he cast them off without a second thought. At the end of his life he had exactly one friend left whom he had known even in middle age.

He had a genius for making enemies. He would insult a man who disagreed with him about the weather. He would pull endless wires in order to meet some man who admired his work, and was able and anxious to be of use to him—and would proceed to make a mortal enemy of him with some idiotic and wholly uncalled-for exhibition of arrogance and bad manners. A character in one of his operas was a caricature of one of the most powerful music critics of his day. Not content with burlesquing him, he invited the critic to his house and read him the libretto aloud in front of his friends.

The name of this monster was Richard Wagner. Everything that I have said about him you can find on record—in newspapers, in police reports, in the testimony of people who knew him, in his own letters, between the lines of his autobiography. And the curious thing about this record is that it doesn't matter in the least.

Because this undersized, sickly, disagreeable, fascinating little man was right all the time. The joke was on us. He *was* one of the world's great dramatists; he *was* a great thinker; he *was* one of the most stupendous musical geniuses that, up to now, the world has ever seen. The world did owe him a living. People couldn't know those things at the time, I suppose; and yet to us, who know his music, it does seem as though they should have known. What if he did talk about himself all the time? If he had talked about himself for twenty-four hours every day for the span of his life he would not have uttered half the number of words that other men have spoken and written about him since his death.

When you consider what he wrote—thirteen operas and music dramas, eleven of them still holding the stage, eight of them unquestionably worth ranking among the world's great musico-dramatic masterpieces—when you listen to what he wrote, the debts and heartaches that people had to endure from him don't seem much of a price. Eduard Hanslick, the critic whom he caricatured in *Die Meistersinger* and who hated him ever after, now lives only because he was caricatured in *Die Meistersinger*. The women whose hearts he broke are long since dead; and the man who could never love anyone but himself has made them deathless atonement, I think, with *Tristan und Isolde*. Think of the luxury with which for a time, at least, fate rewarded Napoleon, the man who ruined France and looted Europe; and then perhaps you will agree that a few thousand dollars' worth of debts were not too heavy a price to pay for the *Ring* trilogy.

What if he was faithless to his friends and to his wives? He had one mistress to whom he was faithful to the day of his death: Music. Not for a single moment did he ever compromise with what he believed, with what he dreamed. There is not a line of his music that could have been conceived by a little mind. Even when he is dull, or downright bad, he is dull in the grand manner. There is greatness about his worst mistakes. Listening to his music, one does not forgive him for what he may or may not have been. It is not a matter of forgiveness. It is a matter of being dumb with wonder that his poor brain and body didn't burst under the torment of the demon of creative energy that lived inside him, struggling, clawing, scratching to be released; tearing, shrieking at him to write the music that was in him. The miracle is that what he did in the little space of seventy years could have been done at all, even by a great genius. Is it any wonder that he had no time to be a man?

WAGNER EXPLAINS THE MUSIC OF THE FUTURE TO ROSSINI

Louis Biancolli

As translated and edited by the music critic in his book, *Great Conversations*.

"Ah! Monsieur Wagner—like a new Orpheus you have no fear of crossing the redoubtable threshold!"

It was with some misgivings that the French writer E. Michotte resolved in 1906 to publish a conversation between Richard Wagner and Gioachino Rossini which he had heard and taken down forty-six years before in Paris on a March afternoon in 1860. The problem for Michotte was not so much that of recalling as accurately as possible the detail and substance of the talk. The young journalist of a half-century before had provided for that handsomely. On his promise not to publish the talk, he had obtained the permission of both men to sit by and jot down the colloquy for his own personal record. Thus, the risks of a faulty memory were not his main difficulty. The problem was of another nature. To begin with, there was the stature and reputation of the speakers. To have Rossini speak was to invite pitiless scrutiny, for Rossini in 1860 had been the reigning wit of Paris. The sparkling quips of this Italian expatriate were the constant delight of Europe. Some of this flavorsome quality would have to come through Michotte's dialogue to give it an air of validity. And Wagner! Here was the storm center of a new school of opera, a man painstakingly, passionately seeking to be understood by way of an avalanche of words. Wagner speaking for himself would have to bear comparison with Wagner the voluminous self-apologist. Plainly, Michotte could make himself absurd by reproducing conversation which failed to live up to expectations.

What further complicated—and perhaps dramatized—Michotte's decision was that Wagner and Rossini had met only once. That meeting, moreover, had given rise to vast speculation as to the subjects discussed. Wagner had to some extent revealed its content in his own autobiographical writings and in a respectful magazine article that appeared in Augsburg some time after Rossini's death. Final confirmation of the meeting came with the publication of Wagner's *Mein Leben*, in 1911. To be sure, Michotte is not mentioned as the man who had brought them together. Yet even Wagner's most searching biographer, Ernest Newman, avers that Wagner's own two accounts of the interview "agree in essence with that of Michotte." In fact, the astute Mr. Newman has seen no reason for rejecting Michotte's record as a willful fabrication. "All in all," he concludes in the third volume of his *Life of Richard Wagner* (Knopf, 1941), "when full allowance has been made for Michotte's mistakes and embroideries, there seems little reason to doubt that he was present at the interview and that the talk was substantially as he represents it to have been."

If we are to take him at his word, Michotte was in an enviable position as regards both composers. He had met them both and admired them equally. While he never wearied of hymning the praises of Wagner's "music of the future," he was no less valiant in expounding the merits of Rossini in the vanguard circles of Paris. It would thus seem that history had chosen an ideal intermediary for the first and last encounter of the two most famous musical exiles of the Paris of 1860. Moreover, the contrast appealed strongly to the journalist Michotte. On the one hand, an Italian whose career as opera composer had long ended and who now dominated the Parisian scene as dean and *bon vivant*; on the other, a German whose strange new music was whipping up a storm of abuse, yet who was struggling with an unquenchable idealism to make himself heard as the bearer of new operatic tidings. For Rossini creative activity had come to an end. Secure in his fame and finances, he could look back on his succession of triumphs as he might on the work of another man. But Wagner was still fighting, one might say, for his life and his music. Recognition, such as it was, came from embattled little cliques and a few generous-minded celebrities like Franz Liszt. The conquest of the public was still in the future. And the shadow of elementary economic need was always at Wagner's heels. Yet he never doubted that his day was near. *Tristan und Isolde* was a finished product, the *Ring des Nibelungen* was by way of completion, and at the moment he was editing a French version of *Tannhäuser* for the Paris stage.

For Michotte a great obstacle in the way of arranging the meeting was the malicious newspaper campaign raging against Wagner. Many of the most vicious jokes were publicly attributed to Rossini. There was, for example, the anecdote of how Rossini once invited his friend, Carafa, a staunch Wagnerian, to dine with him. Rossini, whose cuisine was the talk of Paris, served his friend fish sauce without fish. When Carafa protested, Rossini impishly replied, "Sauce without fish is the right thing for any man who likes music without melody." Rossini wrote an angry protest to the newspaper which had attributed this *mauvaise blague* to him. Actually, the march from *Tannhäuser* was all that Rossini knew of Wagner's music. And that he happened to like. "For the rest," remarks Newman, "he had too much respect for an artist who was trying to enlarge the scope of his art to permit himself jests at his expense." Michotte's job was to assure Wagner that Rossini was utterly blameless, that he was above such petty tactics, and that he would be enchanted to receive his younger colleague. Wagner was persuaded. Unfortunately, after the meeting the campaign of vilification sharpened in the press. Rossini's name was again affixed to some waspish remarks, and Wagner, despite the intercession of Liszt, refused to see the Italian composer again. "The explanation of it all," ventures Newman, "probably is that in that hotbed of envy, hatred, malice and of uncharitableness he felt it useless to struggle against the powers of evil." Newman imputes the full blame to the work of "journalistic gangsters."

Suppose we follow Michotte on his little journey of preparation for that greatest of all days of his life. He begins by visiting Wagner in his modest quarters at No. 16 rue Newton, near the Barrière le l'Étoile. Outside, one can see the Bois de Boulogne, where Wagner is in the habit of taking a daily stroll with his little dog. The young Frenchman pays his respects to Minna Wagner, whom he finds very "simple and self-effacing," and then makes his arrangements with her husband. Wagner agrees to come to Michotte's chambers two days later in the morning, and from there the two will continue to Rossini's. Michotte resumes his travels and presently arrives at the fashionable site on the corner of the Chaussée-d'Antin and the Boulevard des Italiens. There Rossini occupies a sumptuous apartment on the first floor of an attractive house. It is here that literary and artistic Paris comes to pay tribute to the aging Italian master and savor his good food, good wine, and good talk. Michotte makes his proposal. "But, of course," Rossini assures him. "I shall receive Monsieur Wagner with the greatest pleasure. . . . You know my hours. Bring him whenever you wish." Rossini pauses thoughtfully; then: "I hope you have told him that I am completely innocent of these stupidities which have been fathered upon me." Two days later Wagner knocks on Michotte's door, and the two walk the short distance to Rossini's house. . . .

(MICHOTTE *and* WAGNER *climb the stairs to Rossini's apartment.*)

MICHOTTE: If Rossini is in the mood, you'll be charmed with his conversation. It will be a real pleasure. Don't be surprised if during your talk with him you see me taking some notes.

WAGNER: For the newspapers?

MICHOTTE: Not at all. Strictly for my own personal souvenirs. If the Maestro had the slightest suspicion I was going to give this to the press, he would scarcely open his mouth. In any case, he has complete faith in my discretion. He abominates any kind of publicity about his private life.

(MICHOTTE *and* WAGNER *are announced to* ROSSINI, *who is having breakfast. They wait a few minutes in the large drawing room.* WAGNER's *attention is drawn to a portrait of* ROSSINI, *life-size, showing him in a large green cloak and red skullcap.*)

WAGNER: That lively face, that ironic mouth—that's the composer of *The Barber*, all right. This portrait must date from the time Rossini was composing the opera.

MICHOTTE: Four years later. It was painted by Meyer in Naples in 1820.

WAGNER (*smiling*): He was a handsome lad, and in that country of Vesuvius where women kindle easily, he must have been quite devastating.

MICHOTTE: Who knows—if, like Don Juan, he had had a good bookkeeper like Leporello, he might have even exceeded the number "1003" entered in the notebook.

WAGNER: Now you're exaggerating! A "thousand" I'll concede, but three more besides, that's going too far!

(*The butler enters to announce that* ROSSINI *is ready to receive them.* MICHOTTE *and* WAGNER *enter the corner of the apartment that* ROSSINI *has reserved for himself. The room is to one side of the dining room. Four windows overlook the boulevard. There is a* bed in one corner, a Pleyel piano in another. A desk and secretary complete the furnishings. It is here that ROSSINI receives all manner of visitors, from the "lowest beggars to crowned heads," as MICHOTTE observes.)

ROSSINI (*the moment his visitors enter*): Ah! Monsieur Wagner— like a new Orpheus you have no fear of crossing the redoubtable threshold. (*Without giving* WAGNER *a chance to reply.*) I know that people have been blackening me to you. I am supposedly the author of all kinds of sarcastic gibes about you. I plead innocent. Besides, why should I behave that way? I am no Mozart or Beethoven. I certainly make no pretension of being a learned man. But I do pride myself on being polite and refraining from insulting a composer who I am told is striving to extend the boundaries of our art. These malicious people who take such a keen interest in my affairs should at least give me credit for common sense, if nothing more. As for having any contempt for your music—first, I should make myself acquainted with it. To become acquainted with it, I should hear it at the opera house. For it is only in the opera house—and not from a simple reading of the score—that it is possible to reach any fair conclusion about music that is intended for the theater. The one composition of yours that I know is the march from *Tannhäuser*. I heard it several times at Kissingen when I went there for a cure three years ago. It produced quite an effect, and I must confess quite frankly that for my part I found it very beautiful.

WAGNER (*with great deference*): Allow me to thank you, *Maître*, for your kind words. They touch me deeply. They prove how great and noble your character is—something I have never doubted. But please be assured that even if you had uttered some severe judgments about me, I would not have taken offense. I am quite aware that my music is often misunderstood. With the best will in the world, the judges can go wrong in appraising such a vast system of new ideas. That's why I am so anxious to see my operas performed as perfectly as possible. That would be the logical and complete demonstration of my theories.

ROSSINI: That's only fair, for actions speak louder than words.

WAGNER: To begin with, all my efforts are now concentrated on getting a performance of *Tannhäuser*. I had Carvalho listen to it recently. He was quite impressed and seemed prepared to risk producing it. But nothing has been decided yet. Unfortunately, a hostile campaign in the press is now threatening to become a very serious cabal against me. There is always the danger that Carvalho [1] may yield to this pressure.

Rossini (*aroused by the word "cabal"*): What composer hasn't been exposed to cabals, beginning with the great Gluck himself? Believe me, I was by no means spared myself. There was the night of the première of *The Barber*, to cite one instance. According to the practice of the time in Italy, whenever *opera buffa* was given, I sat at the clavicembalo accompanying the recitatives. I had to protect myself against the threats of an audience that had gone completely wild. I thought they were going to kill me. Even here in Paris—when I arrived for the first time in 1824 on an invitation from the director of the Italian Theater, I was greeted by the nickname of Monsieur Hullabaloo. The name stuck. And it certainly was not by pure coincidence that certain circles of the press and music turned their guns on me. They were joined in a common accord—*accord aussi parfait qui majeur*. [2] Nor was it any different in Vienna, when I came there to produce my opera *Zelmira* in 1822. Weber had already been writing some excoriating articles about me. After my opera was produced at the court Italian Theater, he hounded me relentlessly.

Wagner: Oh, I know how intolerant Weber could be! He was quite intractable from the moment the defense of German art became an issue. It was pardonable. I gather you quite naturally had nothing to do with him while you were in Vienna . . . ? A great genius and dying so prematurely! . . .

Rossini: A great genius, certainly—and a true one, because as a powerful creator, he imitated no one. . . . You're right. I had no dealings with him in Vienna. But let me tell you how I happened to see him later in Paris, a few days before he left for England. Shortly after he arrived he paid his respects to the composers then in the public eye—Cherubini, Herold, Boieldieu. He even called on me. Not having been forewarned of his visit, I must admit that I was prey to much the same emotion I had earlier felt in the presence of Beethoven. He was very pale and panting from climbing up my stairs. He was already a very sick man. The moment he saw me the poor fellow felt it necessary to tell me that he had been very harsh to me in his musical criticism. His embarrassment was only heightened by his struggle with the French language. I did not let him finish. "Look here," I said. "Let's not talk about that. Besides," I added, "I never

---

[1] *Tannhäuser* was finally produced in Paris on March 13, 1861.

[2] Untranslatable pun: "Accord [or harmony] as perfect as a major chord."

even saw your reviews. I don't know German. The only words of your devilish language that I as an Italian have been able to retain and pronounce after heroic application are *'Ich bin zufrieden.'* [3] I was quite proud of them," I said, "and in Vienna I made good use of them, with great impartiality, on any and all occasions, public and private, especially public. They procured me the good will of the Viennese, who pass for the most amiable of the Germanic peoples. And especially among the beautiful ladies of Vienna I earned a reputation for consummate urbanity—." *"Ich bin zufrieden!"* These words made Weber smile and put him immediately at his ease. "Moreover," I continued, "in discussing my operas at all, you really did me a greater honor than I deserved—I who am such a small thing beside the geniuses of your country. So I'm going to ask you to let me embrace you. And, believe me, if my friendship has any value in your eyes, I offer it to you completely and with all my heart." I embraced him warmly and I saw a tear appear in his eyes.

WAGNER: I believe he was already afflicted with tuberculosis then and he died of it shortly after.

ROSSINI: That's quite right. He struck me as in a pitiful condition at the time. He was very thin, his complexion was livid, and he had the dry cough of people suffering from lung ailments. Then, he limped. It was painful to see him. A few days later he came to see me again with a request for some recommendations for London, where he was going. I was depressed at the thought of his undertaking such a trip. I tried very hard to dissuade him, telling him he was committing a crime—suicide. It was useless. "I know," he replied. "I shall die there—but I've got to go. I must be there to produce *Oberon*. My contract calls for it. I've just got to go!" I had made some important ties in England during my stay there, and among the letters I gave Weber was one to King George, who happened to be very partial to artists and had been particularly affable with me. With a heavy heart I embraced this great genius once more, with a presentiment that I would never see him again. It was only too true. *Povero* Weber! . . . But we were talking about cabals. This is how I feel about them: There is only one way to fight them—passive silence. It's far more effective, believe me, than a furious rebuttal. Malice is legion. No one who wants to fight this sow ever manages to strike the last blow. I say, the devil take such sneak attacks! The more they rail at me, the more I reply with *roulades*. I rebuff their name-calling with *triolets*. I oppose

[3] "I'm satisfied."

my pizzicati to their buffooneries. And I swear to you that all the hubbub raised against my music by those who don't like it hasn't made me fire back at them one bass-drum broadside less in my cre- scendos, nor prevented me, when it suited my purpose, from horrify- ing them with one *felicità* the more in my finales. If you observe me wearing a wig, please rest assured that it wasn't this scum that caused me to lose a single hair of my head.

W<small>AGNER</small> (*trying not to laugh*): Oh, when it comes to that, Maes- tro, thanks to what you had in there (*touching his temple*), wasn't your passive silence really a powerful force backed by the public's acclaim? Actually one should pity the fools who dared hurl themselves against this power. . . . Incidentally, didn't you say a moment ago that you knew Beethoven?

R<small>OSSINI</small>: Quite so—in Vienna. It was in 1822, during the time I re- marked that my opera *Zelmira* was being produced there. I had al- ready heard some quartets of Beethoven in Milan—I don't have to tell you with what delight! I also knew some of his piano music. In Vienna I heard the "Eroica" Symphony for the first time. That music bowled me over. From that moment I had only one thought—to meet the great master, to see him, even just once. I consulted Salieri about this. I knew that he was in contact with Beethoven.

W<small>AGNER</small>: Salieri, the composer of *Danaides*?

R<small>OSSINI</small>: The same. He had made quite a name for himself in Vienna as a result of the success of many of his operas at the Italian Theater. He told me that he often saw Beethoven, but assured me that because of his violent and suspicious character, my request was not easy to satisfy. Parenthetically, this same Salieri had also been closely associated with Mozart. After Mozart's death, he was sus- pected and even seriously accused of having killed him with a slow poison out of professional jealousy.

W<small>AGNER</small>: In my time that rumor still persisted in Vienna.

R<small>OSSINI</small>: I had some fun one day when I told Salieri, in jest of course,—"It is lucky for Beethoven that his instinct for self-preserva- tion prevents his having you to dinner. You might dispatch him to the next world the way you did Mozart." "So I have the air of a poisoner?" replied Salieri. "Oh, no," I answered. "You have the air of an arrant blackguard!" I might add the poor devil seemed very little bothered by being taken for Mozart's murderer. What he could not endure was the remark of a Viennese journalist, a champion of German opera who had little love for Italian opera and Salieri in particular. Said the journalist: "Contrary to the *Danaides* story, Salieri had emptied his cask with very little effort, for there never was anything to speak of in it." This had quite a harrowing effect on Salieri. To return to Beethoven—Salieri, to satisfy my desire, did render me a service. He decided that the best way to approach him would be through the Italian poet Carpani, who was *persona grata* with Beethoven. Carpani agreed and persisted till Beethoven consented to receive me. Need I confess that in mounting the stairs to the modest lodgings of this great man I had some difficulty in controlling my emotions? When the door opened I found myself in a dirty, dingy hovel. The place was in a frightful mess. I especially remember the ceiling, which was right under the roof. It was all lined with huge cracks through which the rain must have poured in torrents. The portraits we know of Beethoven quite faithfully convey the features of his face. But what no painter could express was the indefinable sadness spread over his features. Beneath thick eyebrows his eyes glittered as from the depths of caverns. Though small, they seemed to pierce through you. His voice was sweet and perhaps a little veiled. When we entered, without paying any attention to us, he remained for some moments bent over some music proofs which he had just corrected. Then, raising his head, he said brusquely to me, in fairly good Italian, "Ah, Rossini—so it's you, the composer of *The Barber of Seville*! My congratulations! It's an excellent *opera buffa*. I read it with great pleasure. So long as Italian opera lives, *The Barber* will be performed. Don't ever try to do anything but *opera buffa*. It would be going against your destiny to attempt to succeed in any other genre." Here Carpani, who was with me, interrupted—in writing and in German, of course—since it was not possible to carry on a conversation with Beethoven in any other way. He said: "Maestro Rossini has already composed numerous serious operas—*Tancredi*, *Otello*, *Moïse*. I sent them to you not so long ago, advising you to look them over." "To be sure, I have run through them," replied Beethoven. "Look here, serious opera is not for the Italians. They don't have sufficient musical knowledge to handle true drama. And how could they acquire such knowledge in Italy? . . ."

WAGNER: That blow of the lion's claw would scarcely have assuaged Salieri's *Consternation* if he had been present. . . .

ROSSINI: It certainly would not! I related the whole thing to Salieri later. He bit his lips . . . without hurting himself too much, I suppose. For, as I said before, he was so contemptible that no doubt in the next world the King of Hell, to spare himself the embarrassment of roasting such a worm, must have ordered the job done elsewhere! . . . But let's come back to Beethoven. "Nobody can equal you in *opera buffa*," he continued. "Your language and your temperament have destined you for it. Look at Cimarosa. How far superior to the rest are the comic passages of his operas! The same thing is true of Pergolesi. I know you Italians make a great deal of his religious music. I admit that there's a very touching feeling in the 'Stabat.' But the form lacks variety. The effect is monotonous. On the other hand, his *Serva Padrona* . . ."

WAGNER (*interrupting*): Fortunately you did not follow Beethoven's advice, Maestro. . . .

ROSSINI: To tell you the truth, I did feel a greater aptitude for *opera buffa*. I was more eager to handle comic subjects than serious ones. But I scarcely had any choice in my librettos, which were imposed upon me by impresarios. How often it happened that I would receive the libretto piecemeal! Sometimes one act at the time. And I was supposed to write the music without knowing either what followed or how the story ended! Remember, I was obliged to support my mother, father, and grandmother. Roaming about from city to city like a nomad, I wrote three or four operas a year. And let me assure you that my income hardly permitted me to play the *grand seigneur*. I received a flat sum of twelve hundred francs for *The Barber*, plus a chestnut-colored suit with gold buttons, which the impresario gave me as a gift to make me look presentable while conducting the opera. It is very possible that suit was worth a hundred francs. Total, thirteen hundred francs. It took me only thirteen days to complete *The Barber*. That meant I was being paid a hundred francs a day. So you see (*smiling*) I was actually earning a big salary. It made me feel quite proud to think that my father when he was employed as trumpet player in Pesaro never earned more than two and a half francs a day.

WAGNER: Thirteen days! That certainly is a unique accomplishment! But I can't help marveling how under such conditions, forced to live that kind of Bohemian life, you were still able to write such music as *Otello* and *Moïse*, music which bears the mark not of improvisation but of carefully thought-out work and complete concentration of brain power. . . .

ROSSINI: Oh, I had facility . . . and plenty of instinct. Naturally my musical training had not been very profound. Lacking that—and where would I have acquired it in Italy?—the little I learned I found in German scores. A musical amateur in Bologna possessed a few—

The Creation was one, *The Marriage of Figaro, The Magic Flute.* He lent them to me, and since at fifteen I did not have the money to order them from Germany, I copied them avidly. Often I would only transcribe the vocal part, without looking at the orchestral accompaniment. On a loose sheet I would then write in my own accompaniment. This I would compare with Haydn's or Mozart's accompaniment. After which I would finish my copy by adding theirs. This system of study taught me more than all the courses at the Lyceum of Bologna. Ah, if I had only been able to study in your country, I feel I would have produced something better than I have.

WAGNER: Surely not better than the Darkness Scene in *Moïse,* the Conspiracy Scene in *William Tell,* and of a somewhat different order the *Quando Corpus Movietur*—to cite only a few examples. . . .

ROSSINI: What you cite there I admit frankly are some happy quarters of an hour in my career. But what are they beside the work of a Mozart or Haydn? I couldn't begin to tell you how much I admire the supple science and natural sureness in the writing of these masters. I have always envied them. But that must be mastered on school benches, and then it takes a Mozart to turn it to account. As for Bach —there's an overwhelming genius! If Beethoven is a miracle of humanity, Bach is a miracle of God! I have subscribed to the great edition of his complete works. Wait a moment, there's the latest volume printed, right there on my table! And I'm not exaggerating when I say that the day the next volume arrives will be a day of incomparable joy for me. How I would like, before leaving this world, to hear a complete performance of his *Passion According to St. Matthew*! Of course here in France there's no point in hoping for one.

WAGNER: It was Mendelssohn who first introduced the *Passion* to the Germans in a magnificent performance which he conducted himself in Berlin.

ROSSINI: Mendelssohn! What a lovable nature that man had! I remember with great pleasure the wonderful hours I spent with him at Frankfort in 1836. I had come to Frankfort to attend a marriage in the Rothschild family. It was Ferdinand Hiller who introduced me to Mendelssohn. What a pleasure it was to hear him play the piano! Among other things he played a few of his own delightful *Songs Without Words.* Then he played some Weber for me, and then I asked him to play Bach, a great deal of Bach! Hiller had told me that nobody played Bach better than Mendelssohn. . . . Mendelssohn was quite taken aback by my request. "How can you, an Italian, love

German music that much?" he asked me. "I love only German music," I replied, adding rather unceremoniously, "as for Italian music, I'm fed up with it!" He looked at me, bewildered. Which did not prevent him from playing several fugues and other pieces by the great Bach with admirable grace. Hiller later told me that after I left Mendelssohn recalled my sally to him and asked, "This Rossini, was he really serious? In any case, he certainly is a queer fish!"

WAGNER (*laughing heartily*): I can understand Mendelssohn's bewilderment, Maestro. . . . But may I ask you how your visit to Beethoven ended?

ROSSINI: Oh, it didn't last long. You can understand why, with one side of the conversation being conducted in writing. I made him understand how much I admired his genius and expressed my thanks for having been permitted to convey it in person. He replied with a profound sigh and one short phrase in Italian. "Oh! *un infelice!*"—"Oh —an unfortunate!" He paused a while and then asked me some questions about the opera houses of Italy, who the most celebrated singers were, whether Mozart's operas were frequently performed there, if I was satisfied with the Italian company of Vienna. Then, after wishing me a good performance and success for *Zelmira*, he rose and accompanied us to the door. Once more he said to me, "Above all, write more *Barbers of Seville*." While descending the ramshackle stairs, I was seized with such strong emotion in thinking how this great man was being neglected and abandoned that I could not restrain my tears. "Oh," said Carpani, "he prefers it that way. He's a peevish misanthrope and doesn't know how to keep a friend." That same evening, I attended a gala dinner at the house of Prince Metternich. Upset as I was by my visit to Beethoven and with that mournful *"un infelice"* still ringing in my ears, I could not help feeling confused by the flattering attention given me in this brilliant Viennese gathering. Without any ceremony, I shouted out what I thought of the way the court and aristocracy were behaving toward the greatest genius of our time, a genius about whom few seemed to trouble themselves and who was allowed to live in such distressful circumstances. They all replied the same way Carpani had. Nevertheless, I asked them if Beethoven's deafness shouldn't excite their pity, and if it was really charitable to use his idiosyncrasies as an excuse for not going to his aid. I added that such help would be very simple. A subscription could be raised among all the wealthy families of Vienna that without being very large would at least assure Beethoven enough income to keep him out of hardship. Not one person there agreed to my proposal. After dinner, the evening concluded with a reception which brought together the biggest names of Viennese society in Metternich's salon. There was even a concert. On the program was Beethoven's latest trio—it was always Beethoven, Beethoven everywhere, the way it used to be with Napoleon. The new masterpiece was listened to religiously and applauded with great enthusiasm. As I listened to it in such magnificent surroundings, I thought sadly how at that very moment, isolated in his dismal lodgings, that great man was perhaps working on still another masterpiece, another work of high inspiration destined, like the others, to regale with sublime beauty this same brilliant aristocracy from which he was excluded—an aristocracy enjoying his music but never troubling itself about the wretchedness of the man who had composed it. Despite my failure to procure an annuity for Beethoven, I did not lose heart. I tried next to raise the necessary funds to buy him a house. I managed to get some pledges for contributions. But when I added my own contributions to the others, the total proved too meager. So, it was necessary to give up this second project, too. The usual reaction was this: "You little know Beethoven. The day after he becomes the owner of a house, he will sell it. He can never stay for long in one place. He feels the need to change his apartment every six months and his housekeeper every six weeks. . . ." But enough about me and the others, who belong to the past and even the dead past. Let's discuss the present now, if you don't mind, Monsieur Wagner, and, even better, the future. For I notice that your name is invariably linked to that word in all the talk about you. Please don't suspect me of the slightest malicious intent. Now, first of all, tell me, are you definitely settled in Paris? And about your opera *Tannhäuser*. I feel certain you will succeed in having it performed. There has been so much noise about it that the Parisians are now dying of curiosity to hear it.

WAGNER: It's not quite finished yet. I'm working at it furiously with a collaborator who is not only very capable, but what is more important, very patient, too. For the difficulty is this—to make the musical expression perfectly understandable, it is necessary to identify, so to speak, each French word with the corresponding German word under the same notation. It's a frightful job and difficult of realization.

ROSSINI: But why don't you follow the example of Gluck, Spontini, and Meyerbeer and work from the start with a French libretto? Surely you now know the taste that prevails here and the special tempera-ment of the French for the things of the theater. It is inherent in the French spirit. I went through all this myself when I left Italy and gave up my Italian career to come to live and work in Paris.

WAGNER: In my case, Maestro, that would be out of the question. After *Tannhäuser*, I wrote *Lohengrin* and then *Tristan und Isolde*. From both the literary and musical standpoint, these three operas present a logical evolution in my concept of the absolute and defini-tive form of lyric drama. My style shows the inevitable effects of this gradation. And if it is true that I still see the possibility of writing other operas in the style of *Tristan*, I must confess myself absolutely incapable of returning to the style of *Tannhäuser*. So, if I decided to compose an opera for Paris on a French libretto, I could not and should not follow any other path than that which led me to write *Tristan*. The result would be that a work like *Tristan*, including such a dramatic disturbance of the usual forms of opera, would unquestion-ably be misunderstood and, things being what they are, the French would not accept it.

ROSSINI: Now tell me, Monsieur Wagner, what exactly was your point of departure in these reforms?

WAGNER: At the outset they were not developed as a system. I felt very strong doubts after my first attempt. I was not satisfied. Actually it was in the poetic rather than the musical conception that the idea of these reforms first took shape in my mind. In other words, my first efforts had a primarily literary purpose. Then, when I began seeking ways of enriching the meaning through deep musical expression, I found myself in a strange dilemma. I realized now how the freedom of my thought in an ideal domain was restricted when confronted with the formal demands of music drama. I mean those *arie di bra-vura*, those insipid duets fashioned on the same deadly model, and all those other *hors-d'œuvres* which interrupted the scenic action for no reason at all. And then those septets! For every respectable opera had to have its solemn septet in which all the main characters of the opera would abandon their roles and step up to the footlights together—all reconciled—and declaim their harmony (and my God, what harmony at times!) in one of those mawkish sermons.

ROSSINI (*interrupting*): Do you know what we used to call that in Italy: "the parade of the artichokes." Yes, I, too, realized how per-fectly ridiculous it was. It always made me think of a band of *fac-*

chini [4] stepping forward to sing for a few coins. But what could you do? It was the custom of the time, a concession made to the public— otherwise they would have thrown baked apples at us, and maybe not even baked.

WAGNER (*continuing, without giving much attention to* ROSSINI's *interruption*): And as for the orchestra . . . those routine accompaniments, wholly lacking in color, continually repeating the same formulas without regard to the diversity of character and situation. In a word, all that *musique de concert*, alien to the action, having no excuse for being there except convention—music which often mars even the very best operas. It all seemed to me so contrary to good sense and so incompatible with the high mission of a noble art worthy of the name.

ROSSINI: Among other things you just referred to the *aria di bravura*. *You* complain! It was my nightmare! Think of satisfying the *prima donna*, the *primo tenore* and the *primo basso* all at the same time! Some of the popinjays even went to the trouble of counting the number of measures in their aria and then coming to tell me that they would not sing because another member of the cast was given an aria that contained more measures than theirs. And when it wasn't the number of measures, it was trills and *grupetti* and so on.

WAGNER (*gaily*): That was taking one's measure with a vengeance! All the composer needed was a meter [5] to measure his music by!

ROSSINI: Yes, you might say an *ariameter!* Those people were quite ruthless, now that I think of it. It was they and only they that caused me to become bald at an early age—from making my head sweat so much. But let's go on with our discussion. . . . To be sure, there's no reply to the point you raise—provided the only thing to consider is the rational, rapid, and orderly development of the dramatic action. However, how are you going to maintain this independence of the literary conception, when you join it with musical form, which is all *convention?* You used the word yourself. If you're going to insist on absolute logic, it goes without saying that people don't sing when they talk. An angry man doesn't sing; a conspirator, a jealous man doesn't sing. (*Gaily.*) A single exception may be allowed, perhaps, for lovers, who may be regarded as making cooing sounds. To go still further—does anybody go to his death singing? That's opera for you— *convention* from one end to the other. And how about the orchestra-

[4] Street porters.
[5] Untranslatable pun here on *"mètre à musique"*—*"maître de musique."*

tion itself? While an orchestra is raging full blast, who can tell precisely whether what is being described is a storm, a riot, or a fire? Again and always—*convention!*

WAGNER: Granted, Maestro, that *convention* does operate on a vast scale—otherwise we would have to abolish lyric drama and even musical comedy. Still, it cannot be disputed that this *convention*, having been raised to the status of artistic form, should be so understood as to prevent its degenerating into excess and absurdity. It is that sort of abuse against which I have rebelled. But people have deliberately distorted my aims. Haven't they represented me as some arrogant upstart who makes disparaging remarks about Mozart?

ROSSINI (*with some humor*): Mozart—*l'angelo della musica.* But who would dare commit the sacrilege of laying a finger on Mozart?

WAGNER: I have been accused of repudiating practically the whole opera repertory, with some scant exceptions like Gluck and Weber. People persist, no doubt from having already committed themselves, in refusing to understand any of my writings. But why? I am far from denying the charm—as pure music—of many admirable pages of the truly great operas. But I am against having this music condemned to playing a servile role in some piece of light entertainment and I am opposed to its becoming the slave of routine or being used for strictly sensuous purposes without regard to the dramatic action. It is against such a role that I have revolted and wish to react. To my thinking, an opera, because of its complex nature, is a kind of organism in which is concentrated the perfect union of all the arts that form part of it— the art of poetry, the art of music, the art of decoration, and *plastique.* Doesn't it debase the mission of the composer to force upon him the role of mere instrumental illustrator of some libretto or other which prescribes in advance the number of arias, duets, ensembles, in a word, of *morceaux*—(which literally means things cut up into little bits)— that he has to translate into so many notes? Indeed, very much like a painter who adds colors to black engravings. To be sure, a great many composers have been inspired by a gripping dramatic scene and written immortal pages. But how many other pages of their score have suffered because of the vicious system I have just described? Thus, no real music drama can exist so long as these bad practices remain, so long as a complete mutual penetration is lacking between the music and the text, and so long as we fail to sense that *double conception* founded on a single thought from the very outset.

ROSSINI: That is to say, if I follow you, the composer should be his own librettist if he is to realize your ideal. That would seem to me, for many reasons, an almost unattainable condition.

WAGNER (*quite excited*): But why should it? What prevents a composer from studying literature, history, and mythology at the same time that he studies counterpoint? Such studies would lead him instinctively to fasten on those themes of poetry and tragedy best suited to his temperament. And even if he should lack the ability or experience to work out the dramatic intrigue himself, he certainly would know better where to find the playwright with whom he could collaborate in close sympathy. Besides, there are very few dramatic composers who have not revealed, at some time or other, a truly remarkable literary and poetic instinct. Often they have gone so far as to make drastic alterations in the text or sequence of scenes, to suit themselves. They instinctively grasped a scene better than their librettist. Not to look any further, let's take the example of the Conspiracy Scene in your own *William Tell*. You can't tell me that you followed, word for word, the text furnished you by your collaborators! I wouldn't believe it! Anybody examining it closely would soon discover effects of dynamics and declamation bearing the true imprint of what I might call "the musicality of spontaneous inspiration." I personally refuse to believe that they appeared that way in the sketch of the text which you had before you. A librettist, no matter what his ability, could not possibly know, especially in scenes full of ensemble complications, how to plan a distribution best suited to the composer in his efforts to achieve the musical fresco fashioned in his imagination.

ROSSINI: What you say is very true. As a matter of fact, that particular scene was considerably modified on my instructions, and not without difficulty. I composed *William Tell* at the country place of my friend Aquado. I spent a whole summer there, and I was cut off completely from my librettist. As it happened, it was Armand Marvast and Crémieux who came to my aid. Parenthetically, these two men became actual conspirators themselves, against the regime of Louis-Philippe. Marvast and Crémieux were also vacationing at Aquado's and both helped me make the necessary changes of text and versification to best "hatch the plot" against Gessler of my own conspirators.

WAGNER: Your experience bears out by implication what I have been trying to say. It would only require an extension of the same principle to prove that my ideas are by no means as inconsistent and impossible of realization as they might appear at first sight. I am convinced that through sheer inevitable logic and by a natural and perhaps slow evolution, there will be born not that "music of the future" which people persist in saying that I would pretend to achieve single-handed, but that "future of the music drama," in which the whole trend will play a part and from which a new and fecund orientation will arise in the minds of composers, singers and public.

ROSSINI: In short, a complete revolution! And do you really believe that the singers or the public, dazzled by all the old tricks of the game, would submit meekly to such a transformation of long-accepted practice? Singers who have been accustomed to showing off their virtuosity and who would now be asked to substitute for their brilliant exhibitions a sort of, yes, I can guess pretty well, declamatory chant? I doubt it very much.

WAGNER: I admit that a long period of education would be needed. But that could be done easily enough. As for the public, who does the educating? Does the public educate the composer, or the composer the public? Allow me to state one more thesis, of which I find you a brilliant example. Wasn't it really your thoroughly personal style that made Italy forget all your predecessors and won you an unprecedented popularity in an incredibly short time? And isn't it true that your influence became universal? With regard to the singers, who you say would offer great resistance, I feel they could only gain by submitting to a change which in the last analysis would ennoble them as artists. Once they perceive that lyric drama will no longer offer them a facile means of success through strong lungs or a charming voice, they will come to understand that the art of music has assigned them a higher mission. Forced to give up confining themselves within the strictly personal limits of their role, they will identify themselves with the philosophic and aesthetic spirit dominating the work. They will live, if I may so express it, in an atmosphere where, everything being a part of everything else, nothing can be secondary. Moreover, once they have learned to do without the short-lived success of a facile brilliance, once freed from the torture of holding their voices on insipid words and banal rhymes—the singers will readily see the chances of surrounding their names with a more lasting and artistic glory. Think how their psychological mastery of the role will be complete when they once have grasped its *raison d'être* in the dramatic scheme; when they have studied the ideas, customs, and character of the period in which the action unfolds, when they have added a faultless diction to a splendid declamation, noble and true in style.

ROSSINI: From the standpoint of pure art, those are certainly broad views and dazzling perspectives. But from the standpoint of strictly musical form, it is as I said before, a fatal trend toward declamatory chanting—"The funeral oration of the art of melody." Otherwise how could one possibly adjust the emotional pitch, so to speak, of each syllable of the text, to melodic form, which derives its special physiognomy from a precise rhythm and a symmetrical distribution of the units that constitute it?

WAGNER: I admit, Maestro, that a system pushed to such extremes would prove intolerable. But my aim, if you follow me, is not to discard melody, but on the contrary, to restore it in all its fullness. Isn't melody the final flowering of every musical entity? Without melody nothing can exist. However, let's be clear about this. My idea is to restore it beyond the narrow restrictions which force it into symmetrical periods, inflexible rhythms, prefixed harmonies and prescribed cadences. What I seek is a free melody, without shackles, and completely independent. A melody that can adapt itself not only to every special contour of character to the point where no role can be confused with any other, but one that can specify any definite fact or episode in the dramatic fabric. A melody, to be sure, of a certain precision, which by pliant application to the sense of the text can be restrained or extended according to the special effects sought by the composer.

ROSSINI (*interrupting*): A fighting melody!

WAGNER (*disregarding the interruption*): You yourself, Maestro, have given a sublime example of the kind of melody I have in mind. It is in the big scene of *William Tell*, where a sort of free song, accenting every word and sustained by the panting phrases of the cellos, reaches the highest summits of lyric expression.

ROSSINI: In other words I was writing the "music of the future" without knowing it!

WAGNER: What you wrote there, Maestro, was the music of all time, and that is the best there is.

ROSSINI: I must confess to you that the feeling that has most moved me in life has been my love for my mother and father, a love, I am happy to say, which they repaid with interest. It was there, I believe, that I found the note needed for the scene of the apple in *William Tell*. But one more question, Monsieur Wagner. How do you reconcile the simultaneous use of two or more voices with your system? To be perfectly logical you would have to prohibit them. . . .

WAGNER: Yes, it would, as a matter of cold logic, be necessary to model the musical dialogue on the spoken dialogue and restrict the characters to singing only in turn. On the other hand, it must be admitted that two different persons, at a given moment, may find themselves in the same emotional state, sharing a common feeling and thus joining their voices to identify themselves in a single thought. So with a large group of people. If they are animated by conflicting feelings, they may quite conceivably express them all at once, though each member of the group will do it his own way. Do you see now, Maestro, what infinite resources this system offers the composer of applying to each character and situation a specific melodic formula, which, while keeping its original character, lends itself freely to the broad currents and developments of the action? And take the ensembles. There each of the characters appears in his own individuality; yet all these different elements combine in a polyphony suited to the action. I repeat: such ensembles will no longer afford us those absurd spectacles in which people gripped by the most antagonistic passions are condemned at some given moment, without rhyme or reason, to unite their voices in a sort of *Largo d'apothéose*, where the patriarchal harmonies remind us that *"One cannot be happier than in the bosom of his family."* [6] As for the use of choruses—it's a psychological fact that large masses of people respond more energetically to a specific sensation than individuals. Sensations like terror, fury, pity. So it is logical to permit crowds to express these collective states in the language of opera without shocking common sense. Besides, the introduction of the chorus, assuming its logic in the situations of the plot, adds a powerful impact to the general dramatic effect. A hundred examples come to mind. Think of the strong impression of anguish aroused by the fiery chorus in *Idomeneo*—"*Corriamo, fuggiamo!*" Without forgetting, Maestro, that admirable fresco from your own *Moïse*—"*Le choeur est desolé, des ténèbres. . . !*"

ROSSINI (*slapping his forehead in mock amazement*): What, again? There is no longer any doubt about it—I, too, had a great propensity for "the music of the future!" You make my mouth water! If I were not so old, I would begin all over again, and then let the *Ancien Régime* beware!

WAGNER: Ah, Maestro, if you had only not thrown away your pen after *William Tell!* What a crime, and only thirty-seven! You don't

[6] *"On ne saurait être mieux qu'au sein de sa famille"*—a reference to the final chorus of Grétry's opera, *Lucille*.

realize yourself what you would have done with that brain of yours. You would have only begun. . . .

Rossini (*becoming serious again*): What do you expect? I had no children. If I had had, no doubt I would have gone on working. But to be perfectly honest, after having labored for fifteen years and composed in that so-called "lazy" period forty operas, I felt the need to rest and to go back to Bologna to live a tranquil life. Added to that, the Italian theaters, which already had left much to be desired during my career, had fallen into a state of complete decay. The art of singing had rapidly declined. It was all to be expected.

Wagner: How do you account for that in a country boasting such a superabundance of beautiful voices?

Rossini: I attribute it to the disappearance of the *castrati*. It is impossible to form any idea of the vocal charm and consummate virtuosity of these bravest of the brave. No doubt these gifts were a charitable compensation for their deficiencies in other matters. Moreover, the *castrati* became incomparable teachers. Instruction was usually entrusted to them in the schools attached to the churches and maintained at their expense. Some of these schools became famous. They were veritable academies of singing. Pupils flocked to them, and many of them frequently deserted the church choirs for a career in opera. But as a consequence of the new political regime installed by my rebellious compatriots, these schools were suppressed and replaced by "conservatories," where as far as the fine tradition of *bel canto* is concerned, they "conserve" nothing at all. As for the *castrati*, they vanished, and the practice of making new ones was abolished. There you have the cause of the irreparable decay of the art of singing. As a consequence, *opera buffa* was set adrift. And serious opera? The public, which in my time was already little disposed to rise to the level of great art, no longer showed any interest in this form of entertainment. The announcement of a serious opera on the billboards merely drew some plethoric spectators whose only desire was to breathe in some cool air away from the mob. So now you understand why I decided that the wisest thing for me to do was to shut up. I shut up, and so *finita la commedia*. (Rossini *rises and warmly squeezes* Wagner's *hands*.) *Mon cher* Monsieur Wagner, I don't know how to thank you for your visit and particularly for being kind enough to explain your ideas to me in such a clear and interesting way. I who don't compose any more, being instead at an age where one "decomposes" while waiting to be "redecomposed" once and for all, I am too old to turn my gaze toward the new horizons. But your ideas, whatever your detractors may say, are of a kind to make young men think. Of all the arts music is the one that, because of its ideal essence, is destined to undergo transformation. Such changes are limitless. Could one predict Beethoven, after Mozart? Weber, after Gluck? And certainly Beethoven and Weber aren't the end. Everyone should try, if not to go forward, at least to seek something new. Not like a certain Hercules, a great traveler I'm told, who, having arrived at a place from which he could no longer see clearly ahead, planted his column and then retraced his steps.

WAGNER: That might have been intended as a warning of private hunting grounds to prevent others from going any farther.

ROSSINI: *Chi lo sa?* Who knows? You're doubtless right, for history assures us that Hercules showed a gallant preference for lion-hunting. In any case, let's hope that no such erecter of columns will ever place any limits on our art. For my part, I belong to my time. It is up to you others, and especially you, with all your splendid vigor and vision, to make something new and succeed. I wish you that with all my heart.

(ROSSINI *accompanies* WAGNER *and* MICHOTTE *through the adjoining dining room. On the way he stops before an exquisitely inlaid mechanical organ made in Florence in the seventeenth century.*)

ROSSINI (*to* WAGNER): Wait a moment! This little organ is going to make you hear some old airs of my country. They may interest you.

(ROSSINI *releases a spring and immediately the instrument begins to play its whole repertory, with its archaic flageolet sounds. The pieces are all little folk tunes.*)

ROSSINI: What do you say to that? There's the past for you, the truly dead past! It is simple and naïve. Who was its unknown maker? Some fiddler or other, no doubt. It dates far back and it lives forever! Will as much of us survive a hundred years from now?

(WAGNER *and* MICHOTTE *take their leave of* ROSSINI.)

WAGNER (*while descending the stairs, to* MICHOTTE): I must admit I hardly expected to find in Rossini the simple, natural, and serious-minded man we just met. He seemed inclined to interest himself in every point that came up in our short conversation. Naturally, I couldn't expound in a few words all my ideas about the necessary development of lyric drama toward a new destiny. I confined myself to a few general remarks and some practical details to give him the general drift of my theories. You would have supposed that such a man would have found my statements extravagant, given the systematic spirit that prevailed in his time and of which he necessarily still carries some traces. Like Mozart, he possessed in the highest degree the gift of melodic invention. He had, too, a marvelous instinct for the theater and dramatic expression. What might he not have done if he had received a thorough musical education, and if, had he been less Italian and less skeptical, he had felt the religion of his art within him. There is no doubt that he would have reached the highest peaks. In a word, he is a genius gone astray from lack of good preparation and from not having found the milieu for which his high creative faculties had designed him. Still, I must say this much for him: of all the musicians I have met in Paris, Rossini is the only truly great one.

(WAGNER *and* MICHOTTE *separate,* MICHOTTE *hastening home to "put in order the notes I had taken during the conversation of these two celebrities.")*

WAGNER AND PAULINE VIARDOT-GARCIA

Anna Schoen-René

> A pupil of Pauline Viardot-Garcia, Anna Schoen-René enjoyed brief fame as a singer but was then forced by illness to abandon singing in favor of teaching. She was a member of the faculty of the Juilliard School of Music. Like most singers' reminiscences, hers may be taken with a grain of salt.

"The ugliest woman I have ever seen walk across the stage!"

In connection with my personal friendship with my great teacher Mme. Viardot-Garcia, it should be of interest to recall some memories which she told me concerning her friendship with Richard Wagner.

When Richard Wagner, during his exile from Germany, came to Paris to produce his *Tannhäuser*, Viardot was not a great admirer of his. She considered him a nervous person, always criticizing and berating other musicians. It was only after several disappointing experiences that she acknowledged his genius, and not altogether the petty person he had at first appeared to be. She told me that the failure of his opera in Paris was his own fault; that he antagonized everyone and dominated all the rehearsals, insulting the management and even the French government in his bitter moods. His most serious mistake had been in choosing French singers who did not understand his libretto or his music, and a mediocre German conductor whom he then humiliated by his harsh treatment. Altogether, she said (having attended the rehearsals), it was a very sad experience. Both she and her husband had begged him to abandon the performance. Even when a ballet was added to the Venusberg scene, to please the taste of the French audience, *Tannhäuser* was not a success in Paris.

Although he did not follow her advice in this matter, Wagner was a great admirer of Viardot. He called her "the greatest artist and musician of the century," and said that she was the only one who could sing any language in perfect style, and change her manner of singing to suit the requirement of the language.

In the days when there was a great deal of criticism of Wagner's compositions, and many were accusing him of ruining the voices which attempted his music, he told the following story about Viardot. (The story can be found in his autobiography, *Mien Leben,* but I tell it as Viardot recounted it to me.) The incident occurred at a rehearsal of *Norma* at the Grand Opera House in Paris, in which Viardot was singing and playing the leading role. Wagner was seated in one of the stage boxes. Viardot was not only singing with full voice, but was occasionally "marking." In addition, she was directing the stage performance. Filled with enthusiasm, Wagner rushed up to congratulate her at the conclusion of the rehearsal. Viardot noticed some music under his arm and asked him what it was. He handed her a score, saying, "This is my favorite composition, *Tristan and Isolde.* I am eager for you to be the first to sing it; but to begin with, let me hear your opinion of it." She took the score and seating herself at the piano on the stage, sang most of the first act, and Isolde's *Liebestod,* in the last act, with such pathos and beauty of voice that Wagner, tears in his eyes, kissed her hands and begged her to be the first Isolde. She refused.

Wagner, who spoke the unpleasant-sounding Saxonian dialect and had a harsh speaking voice as well as an atrocious singing voice, sat beside Viardot, alternating in the other parts. When she had finished, he looked at her in admiration and said, "No longer can anybody say that my compositions are hard on the voice. *No!* The singers are hard on my compositions!"

Although Viardot was enthusiastic about the opera and asked Wagner to come to her home the following day that her husband might hear it, she declined his offer to produce it on the stage. The next day she sang the entire score in the presence of the composer, her husband, Liszt, Anton Rubinstein, and Rossini.

On one occasion Wagner wrote and asked Viardot to send one of her pupils to Bayreuth to create the role of Kundry in *Parsifal* which Levi conducted. She recommended Marianne Brandt, the contralto with the golden voice, whose perfection only Schumann-Heink, in her best time, has been able to equal.

On Brandt's arrival in Bayreuth, Cosima Wagner met her at the station and took her directly to the rehearsal in the Festspielhaus. When Brandt walked on the stage, Wagner, who was conducting the rehearsal in the pit, threw up his hands in disgust. "She is impossible," he cried, "the ugliest woman I have ever seen walk across the stage!"

Marianne Brandt immediately turned and fled out of the hall and back to the station, to take the next return train to Munich. Following at her heels was Cosima Wagner, trying to apologize for her husband and to persuade Brandt that anything he said while conducting, however rude, should be forgiven, since he was in a nervous and irresponsible condition. Marianne Brandt would hear none of it, and Cosima followed her by train all the way to Nuremberg. Finally, as a last resort, she telegraphed Viardot, asking her to persuade the singer to return with her to Bayreuth for the sake of saving the performance, since Viardot had said she could recommend no other artist of the day to interpret the part. Brandt, devoted to her teacher, agreed on the condition that Wagner apologize to her. So the next day, at the rehearsal, Richard Wagner, the great master of the Bayreuth Festivals, did something which perhaps he never did before or afterward—he gave an apology before the entire orchestra and assembled cast. After he had heard Marianne Brandt sing, he went up to her and told her that she was the greatest singer, with the most beautiful, perfect voice, he had ever heard. As a result of this, a Kundry such as has never since been equaled was presented at Bayreuth at the first performance.

THE DEATH OF WAGNER

Ernest Newman

> At the sixteenth performance of *Parsifal* in Bayreuth, on August 29, 1882, Wagner, perceiving that the conductor Levi was indisposed, himself stepped into the pit and conducted the third act to the end. He departed for Venice two weeks later, much exhausted by the labors of the last year. He was in poor health and suffered frequent though not severe heart attacks. He died in Venice on February 13, 1883. The report of his death and of the world's reaction is taken from the fourth volume of Newman's biography.

"I shall have to take care of myself today."

On the sixth of February he went out, for the children's sake, to see the last night of the carnival. Perl caught sight of him there, threading his way among the masks with Daniela on his arm, and, familiar as he no doubt was with Keppler's accounts of his patient, he was astonished to see him looking so well: "His step was elastic, even youthful," he says, "his head was held high." But the strain and the excitement had evidently been too much for him. He developed a cold, and spent part of the next day in bed. Once more he recovered, and, depressed by the bad weather, he planned on the tenth an excursion with Siegfried to either Verona or Bologna, which, however, did not materialize. The next day he went for a walk, but returned in ten minutes with both hands pressed to his heart. He was ill at ease and fretful, but recovered toward the evening; and when Keppler called he found the pulse quite regular. Wagner read from Fouqué's *Undine*, discussed it, and dreamed of it in the night.

On the morning of the twelfth he worked at his essay on *Das Weibliche*, and at luncheon talked to Cosima at some length about his mother. In the afternoon he took a walk with Eva, and in the evening once more read to them from *Undine*: Joukowsky found him in good spirits and apparently well, and made a sketch of him reading. Wagner played with great earnestness the "Porazzi" theme and some bars of a scherzo he was planning to write, and, after the children had retired, the music of

> Tender and true
> 'tis but in the waters:
> false and base
> are those who revel above,

from the song of the Rhine Maidens as the curtain falls on the *Rhinegold*. "To think that I knew it so well even at that time!" he said to Cosima; and a little later, "They are very dear to me, these secondary beings of the depths, these creatures full of longing." With the record the next morning of these words of his, Cosima closed her diary forever.

On the thirteenth Joukowsky called as usual at a quarter to two for lunch: he found Cosima at the piano, in tears, playing Schubert's *"Lob der Thränen"*:

> *Nicht mit süssen Wasserflüssen zwang Prometheus unsern Leim;*
> *Nein, mit Thränen; drum im Sehren und im Schmerz sind wir daheim.*
> *Bitter schwellen diese Quellen für den erdumfang'nen Sinn,*
> *Doch sie drängen aus den Engen in das Meer der Liebe hin.*

Wagner was working in his own room: "I shall have to take care of myself today," he had remarked to his manservant, Georg Lang, that morning. At two o'clock he sent a message to the others that as he was not feeling well they were to begin lunch without him. Cosima went to see him, but he wished to be alone, as was his way when he was at grips with his implacable foe. She left the maid, Betty Bürkel, in the room next to Richard's. She heard him sighing and moaning from time to time: he was sitting bent over his desk, waiting for the anguish to pass. Suddenly his bell rang violently twice. Betty answered it, and then broke in upon the others with the news that the master had told her to bring "the doctor and my wife." Cosima at once went to him. A gondola had been ordered to take them all that afternoon to Wolkoff's house; Daniela sent off a note of excuse to him,[1] but

[1] This is the story as given by Glasenapp, quoting verbatim from Joukowsky's manuscript memoirs. According to Wolkoff himself, he waited until five o'clock, and then, not having received any message, he went to the Vendramin, where he met the painters

even yet no one seems to have suspected how serious Wagner's condition was. Meanwhile the maid had sent for Keppler. He arrived at three o'clock. The family and Joukowsky were sitting silent in the drawing room when Georg, sobbing and half-fainting, came in and said "The master is dead!" He was followed by Keppler, who bade them abandon hope.

In the other room the tragedy had quickly come to its long-appointed end. Cosima had found Wagner racked by a spasm of exceptional violence; apparently a blood vessel in the heart had been ruptured. Georg had loosened some of his clothing and eased him onto a seat, where Cosima sat down beside him and held him in her arms. While he was being moved, his watch, a gift from her, fell out of his pocket. "My watch!" he ejaculated. These were his last words. Cosima, still holding him close to her, believed he had fallen asleep; but Keppler, who had arrived a little while before, felt his pulse and found it had stopped. "We must not give up hope yet," he said: and laying Wagner on a couch he tried friction, Cosima clinging distractedly to the dead man's knees, unwilling to believe that what she had dreaded so long had really come to pass. The last glance he had turned upon her had been one of mute gratitude and love.

In the sudden desolation that had fallen on the house the faithful Joukowsky's thoughts were all for Cosima, who herself seemed at death's door, while Wagner, his last fight finished, lay on the couch in the profoundest peace his tortured spirit had ever known, his eyes closed, a gentle smile seeming to play upon the half-open mouth. All that night Cosima sat alone with the body, murmuring incoherent words of love into the deaf ears. She refused all care, all nourishment: she had lived in him and for him, and now she wanted to die with him. It was not until the late afternoon of the following day, twenty-five hours after he had died, that they succeeded in parting her from him.

The world was staggered by the news of Wagner's sudden death. Liszt, who was then in Budapest, at first believed it to be merely a

Passini and Ruben, who told him they had heard a rumor that Wagner was dead. This seems less credible than Joukowsky's account. See the *Memoirs of Alexander Wolkoff-Mouromtzoff* (A. N. Roussoff), *by Himself*, translated by Mrs. Huth Jackson, London, 1928, p. 215. It is one more illustration of the difficulty of arriving at the truth regarding the smallest matter of the past, even on the evidence of the people concerned in it.

journalistic false alarm. When he could no longer doubt he wrote to Cosima to ask if she would like him to go to her in Venice and accompany her back to Bayreuth. Through Daniela she declined his offer, for which he was not sorry. Like Cosima, he shrank from the publicity the funeral would involve, the stereotyped official condolences everywhere, the formal speeches, the musical performances and so forth. "Unless it is absolutely necessary for me to be there," he wrote to the Princess, "I prefer to keep away. . . . I will see Cosima in Bayreuth in six weeks' time, in calmer mood."

When Bürkel, to whom, as to a few others, Daniela had at once telegraphed, brought the news to the King, Ludwig mastered himself with difficulty: he could only say, "Frightful! Terrible! Let me be alone." After some hours of bitter self-communion he sent for Bürkel again and broke out distractedly, "Wagner's body belongs to me. Nothing must be done without my orders as regards the transport from Venice." A few days later, when Bürkel had returned from Bayreuth and told him of the universal grief, the King said with justifiable pride, "This artist whom the whole world now mourns, it was I who was the first to understand him; it was I who rescued him for the world." That was no more than the simple truth; it was to him, and after him to Cosima, that the world was indebted for the preservation of Wagner and the completion of his life's work. They two never doubted his mission, suffered for and with him, never forsook him, never shrank from any sacrifice for him.

When the wires flashed the news of the Meister's death Bülow was at Meiningen, only half-recovered from a severe illness. By a strange coincidence, Brahms had arrived in the town on the twelfth, and Bülow had pulled himself together sufficiently to greet him at the station, though he was confined to his bed the whole of the next day. It was not until the evening of the fourteenth that Frau von Bülow dared to break the news to him, and then only in the presence of his doctor. The next day she wrote to her mother:

The news of Wagner's death had so shattering an effect on my husband that the atmosphere here has been one since then of the profoundest melancholy. Even I had no notion of how passionate was the love he still felt in his innermost heart for Wagner, in spite of everything. Bülow's life is so closely interwoven with the name of Wagner that, in his own words, which he brought out with great difficulty, he felt as if his own soul had died with this fiery spirit, and only a fragment of his body still wanders upon earth.

Naturally, she added, the company of Alexander Ritter had been not only welcome but a positive necessity in some of his paroxysms of grief; while the presence of Brahms brought him only painful feelings of all kinds. Some days later, when he learned that Cosima's own life was in danger by her helpless abandonment to her grief and her abstinence from food, he sent her the historic telegram that was a masterpiece of kindliness and tact—"Sœur, il faut vivre."

Honest old Verdi, who never pretended, never compromised, never indulged himself in a single sentence of conventional complaisance, was cut to the heart by Wagner's death. "Sad sad sad!" he wrote to Giulio Ricordi on the fourteenth. "Frankly, when I read the news yesterday I was crushed. Let us say no more about it. A great individuality has gone, a name that will leave a powerful impress on the history of art." And reading his letter again before dispatching it, he, who rarely spoke in superlatives, crossed out the "potente," which he felt to be inadequate, and substituted for it "potentissima"—"a most powerful impress."

Adolf Gross and his wife had hurried to Venice as soon as they received Daniela's wire. Richter came from Vienna, a faithful Kurvenal groping to his place at the feet of the dead Tristan. While Frau Gross comforted Cosima as best she could, Adolf took on himself the heavy burden of keeping callers and inquisitive journalists from her, checking the impulses of the town authorities and others to intrude upon her grief with well-meant but unwanted official assurances of sympathy, and making arrangements for the departure. Wolkoff and others were anxious to have a death mask made by the sculptor Benvenuti, but Cosima would not hear of it: in the end Daniela, unknown to her mother, gave her consent, on condition that the mask should not go outside the family. Keppler embalmed the body, which was placed in a coffin ordered from Vienna: Cosima had cut off her beautiful hair, which had always been Wagner's delight, and laid it on the dead man's breast.

On the sixteenth the mournful cortège glided silently down the waters of the Grand Canal to the station, which Gross had prevailed upon the railway authorities, for Cosima's sake, to close for a while to the public. At two o'clock began the long slow journey to Bayreuth, Joukowsky, Gross and Richter accompanying the children, Cosima still blind and deaf to everything in the outer world that had suddenly become a desert to her, in a small coupé alone with all that now

remained of Richard Wagner. At Innsbrück they were joined by Levi
and Porges. At the Bavarian frontier town of Kufstein Bürkel was
awaiting them with a letter of condolence from the King, of which
Daniela took charge. They arrived in Munich at three o'clock in the
afternoon of the seventeenth; the station was filled with mourners
bearing torches and bringing flowers. The train remained there an
hour; and here, as elsewhere, it fell to Gross to keep, as far as was
possible, all sight and sound of the crowds from Cosima. It was not
until half an hour before midnight that they reached Bayreuth, where
a silent throng was awaiting the last homecoming of the Meister.
Cosima wished the body to be taken at once to Wahnfried, but this
could not be done: it remained all night in the station under a guard
of honor. At Wahnfried she missed her wedding rings, and Joukowsky
went back to the station to search for them. In the end they were
found on the floor of the room; they had slipped from her finger unnoticed by her, so wasted had she become after four days of virtual
starvation.

At four o'clock on the afternoon of Sunday, the eighteenth, the last
public tributes to Wagner were paid at the station. Muncker and
Feustel spoke out of the abundance of their hearts, a regimental band
played Siegfried's Trauermarsch, a male voice choir sang the unaccompanied chorus which Wagner had written for the homecoming of
Weber's remains to Dresden in 1844, and the King's aide-de-camp,
Count Pappenheim, laid a wreath on the coffin in his royal master's
name. Then the long procession set out for Wahnfried through the
packed, silent and half-lit streets, from every house of which flew a
black flag: the coffin was on an open hearse drawn by four horses.
At five o'clock it reached the house, where the public participation in
the mourning ended. Only two wreaths—those of the King—lay on
the coffin as it was carried through the outer gates. Snow was falling
as the cortège made its way to the place in the garden where Wagner
had prepared his own tomb years before. Twelve men bore the coffin
there—Muncker, Feustel, Gross, Wolzogen, Seidl, Joukowsky, Wil-
helmj, Porges, Levi, Richter, Standhartner and Niemann, while the
four children [2] grasped the corners of the pall. It was at the graveside
that the one jarring note was unwittingly struck. The address delivered by a local clergyman as he blessed the grave seems to have given
offense by its conventionally and too professionally religious tone:
"Denominational priests," said one writer afterward, "could not un-

[2] Blandine was not there.

derstand a spirit whose Christianity had no churchly tincture about it but was rooted solely in the personality of the Savior and His words."

One by one the friends went away in the deepening twilight, leaving only the children at the graveside, awaiting their mother. She came from Wahnfried leaning on Gross's arm; and in her presence the coffin was lowered into the vault. For a while she remained there, lost in her memories and her grief, till the children led her back to the house, the opening was walled up, and the great stone that Wagner had prepared long ago laid upon the mound. To that grave, forty-seven years later, the ashes of Cosima herself were brought.

AN APPRECIATION OF *DIE MEISTERSINGER*

Robert M. Rayner

> The challenge which Wagner's comedy offers to the analyst and the musical historian has been met by many an essay, an unconscionable wave of words. There exists an entire book devoted to this one music drama, a labor of love by the English writer, Robert M. Rayner. The excerpt here given deals chiefly with *Die Meistersinger* as a play, its characters, and its essential theme.

"It is designed to chastise with a smile."

The Bell-Clapper

In one of his letters to Liszt, Wagner likened creative power to a bell—the greater its caliber, the greater the external stimulus needed to set it vibrating. What was it that stirred his spirit into the prodigious output of nervous energy that gave us *Die Meistersinger*? Since 1845 he must often have called it momentarily up from the depths of his subconscious mind; but until that late autumn of 1861 he had always let it slip back again. Why did he now hold it fast and wake it to life and growth?

There cannot be a simple and definite answer to the question. Perhaps the ground was prepared by the need—brought home to him by the difficulties over the production of *Tristan* at Vienna—to write something that would be mountable in German theaters and acceptable to German audiences. Casting about for a subject, it was inevitable that he should bethink him of this sixteen-year-old project for a comic opera; and a day spent at Nuremberg just at this time recalled the "atmosphere" associated with it. He caught a vision of the old city, with its clattering open-fronted shops, its throngs of self-important burghers and merry apprentices and gaily dressed womenfolk.

From *Wagner and Die Meistersinger* by Robert M. Rayner, by permission of Mrs. Rowena Rayner.

The picture found expression almost involuntarily—so ready did visual concepts transmute themselves into sound in his mind—into the broad opening theme of the Overture. The wild mountain fastnesses of *The Ring* may have been suggested by the Alpine scenery amid which it was written, but "local color" would have been contrary to the whole spirit of that work; and although *Tristan und Isolde* is a Celtic legend, there is no trace of Celtic feeling in the music—it is timeless and placeless. In *Die Meistersinger,* on the other hand, Wagner transports us into sixteenth-century Germany. He could not have done so if he had not been there himself, first; and it was the sight of Nuremberg, a living museum of medieval German architecture, that carried him thither.

Moreover, it can hardly have been a mere coincidence that each time he took up the subject it was immediately after he had been immersed in *Tannhäuser.*[1] It seems as if on both occasions he had awakened out of the hothouse atmosphere of the Venusberg into the wholesome light of day, with its sunshine and breezes, the scent of wild flowers, and the song of a shepherd boy.

Then came the visit to Venice, the encouraging words of Mathilde, and the sight of a Titian canvas to quicken his sense of the glory of art. And as he brooded over the subject during those all-important days after his return to Vienna, he came to see in it far more than had been visible in 1845. Then it had appeared as a mere "satyr-play," with the Lover as the central character and Sachs as "the last embodiment of the folk-spirit in art"; but his experiences, both in Art and in Life, had since carried him up to a loftier outlook. He now saw that it could be made the vehicle for his artistic and philosophic *credo.* His career had been a long struggle to place Art in its true relationship with Life by means of the music drama—a relentless crusade against the pedantic routineers who dominated the operatic world. In that struggle he had scarcely deigned to parley with the foe; to it he had sacrificed his health, his ease, his wife, and his friends, and had mortified the desire for fame and success which was stronger in him than in most. Now he would create a work which would glorify all that gives to Art elevation and power and value for the human soul, and would ridicule all that degrades it, hampers it, and stultifies it.

All drama, comedic as well as tragic, must be based upon conflict.

[1] It will be recalled that for the Paris production of *Tannhäuser* in 1861 Wagner had rewritten a good deal of the music, and had composed a much more highly developed scene for the Venusberg.

Wagner had from the first conceived *Die Meistersinger* as a conflict between dried-up traditionalism personified by the Masters and the divine afflatus personified by Walther. More precisely, we might say that the protagonists are, on the one hand, the academic art in which beauty waits upon the judgment, and, on the other, the creative spirit which claims the right of expression unfettered by reflection and conscious "workmanship." The academic spirit is dramatized by staid and elderly bourgeois, opposed to a high-spirited young aristocrat; and the contrast is heightened by the circumstance that the academic musicians enforce an apprenticeship to art as if it were a handicraft; whereas the young enthusiast is a child of nature who admits that he has never applied himself to technical studies.

This conflict remained the backbone of the comedy in the revised version of 1861–62; but Wagner now saw that Art cannot live by enthusiasm alone—that the creative impulse needs to be guided, restrained, strengthened, by the technical skill that can only come from study of the precepts which experience has gained through centuries of "trial and error." Thus the true resolution of the conflict lay in the reconciliation of the two elements. There was nothing very novel about this conception, and it had long been latent in Wagner's mind. He had, indeed, given expression to it away back in 1846, in the lines which he had written in Bülow's album. But it was not until 1862 that the applicability of the apothegm to his long-planned *Meistersinger* drama came home to him with full effect. Then in a flash the project was lit up with a new significance and vitalized by a new urgency.

Jenseits Wagnerismus

So much for the spiritual conditions which made this the appropriate moment for him to take up the subject again; there were also technical reasons why he was now able to do so successfully. In the principles of musico-dramatic art which he had evolved during the past twelve years there was much that was universally true and applicable (at any rate, for *him*); but there was much, too, that was appropriate mainly to the works in which he was engaged at the time—first *The Ring* and later *Tristan*. The necessity of legendary subjects, the advantage of *Stabreim*, the avoidance of vocal tunes in set forms in favor of "endless melody" in the orchestra—all these principles had been fully exemplified in those works. By the time he came to *Die*

Meistersinger he had discovered that Wagnerism was not enough. He felt beyond the need to trouble himself about consistency in such matters. He was no longer under the domination of his own rules: they should henceforth be adapted or dispensed with, according to his will and pleasure. We catch in his letters a new consciousness of *mastery*, of supreme control over his medium. We feel that he is giving the rein to his creative instincts, unhampered by preconceived convictions as to whither they ought to lead him.

His emancipation began with the very adoption of the subject. For he had laid it down that music dramas ought to be without definite setting in place and time; whereas *Die Meistersinger* deals not with heroic or mythological personages, but with creatures of common clay like ourselves, living in historical times in a city still on the map. This had its effect on the character of the libretto, both as to prosody and as to diction. *Stabreim* might be the appropriate vehicle for the cosmic immensities of *The Ring*; the tensely ejaculatory style of *Tristan* might be suitable for an ecstatic tragedy of passion; but for a costume comedy the inevitable medium was easygoing rhymed tetrameters and trimeters, such as Goethe used for *Faust*. And a corollary of these rhymed meters was the construction of self-contained lyrical pieces such as he had deliberately eschewed in his recent works. This in turn gave direction to the music which was shaping itself in his mind— sometimes in vague outline, sometimes in thematic germs—all the time he was engaged on the book.

We must pause for a moment to consider this direction more closely.

Wagner was quite clear about his place in the history of music, and obligingly explained it to us at length in the course of his prose works. He was the lineal descendant of Beethoven; and this in two respects. Firstly, he intensified that "expressionism" which Beethoven had infused into the formal music of the eighteenth century; secondly, he brought into opera the practice of thematic development which that composer had carried farther than any of his predecessors in "pure" music. Beethoven, according to his view, had reached the limit of possibility in these respects within the restricted scope of instrumental music, and had tacitly admitted as much by breaking into song in the finale of his last symphony. This transference of symphonic processes to the theater was of course conditioned by the difference of purpose. Whereas symphonies are built on the framework of conventional designs [2]—"sonata form," minuet-and-trio, rondo, theme-with-variations, and so on—in opera the use of the themes is regulated by the course of the drama. They become the material of a musical "action" running parallel with the dramatic action, explaining and intensifying it.

Wagner's practice in the matter developed gradually, *pari passu* with his power of design and skill as a musician. In *The Dutchman* and *Tannhäuser* the themes thus used are few in number and mostly of considerable length (being conceived as vocal phrases based on long-winded sentences). Such themes are not susceptible of much manipulation, and their purpose is mainly "reminiscence"—a mere extension of what Beethoven had already done in *Fidelio* and Weber in *Der Freischütz*. In *Lohengrin* there is a notable advance; the themes tend to be shorter and more pithy, whole passages are built out of them, and they have greater influence in welding the work together organically. Then came the great gulf in the composer's career —his exile, his long abstention from composition, his theorizing in the prose works. When he again took up his music pen to compose *Rhinegold* he had by taking thought added many cubits to his technical stature. He now applied his newly formulated theories with the rigorous consistency of a fanatic. Most of his themes were now conceived instrumentally rather than vocally; and even when they were vocal, the short lines of the *Stabreim* tended to terseness. They are mostly condensed into emphatic figures which can be subjected to variations of orchestration and harmonization, combined with other themes concurrently or consecutively, built into sequences, or used as figures of accompaniment, according to the exigencies of the drama. The music becomes a continuous web of sound, woven out of threads spun from these cocoons; and "endless melody" is substituted for the self-complete "numbers" of earlier opera composers. In this Wagner was one of the pioneers of musical progress, which was toward the "articulation of minutiae"—the vitalizing of every part of the musical organism.

This elaboration of the orchestra's part provided a solution of one of the main problems of operatic composition—the treatment of narrative or conversational passages. The function of song is to express emotion; but a drama has to tell a story, and a story cannot be made intelligible without matter on an altogether lower plane of expression. Furthermore, audiences need a periodical relaxation of emotional ten-

---

[2] These designs are often pulled out of shape under the strains and stresses to which modern composers subject them, but they are seldom discarded altogether.

sion. How is the composer to treat these nonlyrical passages? In light opera the solution is simple—the parts that call for music have it, and the rest has none. But when this method is applied to works of a more elevated character, such as *The Magic Flute* and *Der Freischütz*, the effect is never quite satisfactory: the music having lifted us higher, the drop to speech level gives us a more uncomfortable jolt. And in a great tragedy like *Tristan* or *Otello* the bare thought of the music ceasing and the characters beginning to talk is hideous. Recitative— the nonlyrical vocalization of a string of notes designed more or less in imitation of the inflections of the voice in speech, accompanied either by chords on a clavier or by more or less formal interjections by the orchestra—was a step in advance; but there was still a disillusioning breach in the continuity of the fabric. Wagner contrived to keep the emotions of his audience in his grip all the time, by employing the orchestra to lend interest and significance to the periods of low emotional interest. His opponents objected that this "endless melody" in the orchestra involved "endless recitative" for the voices; and it is true that in *The Ring* his principle that music ought to be merely ancillary to the drama made him very chary about allowing his characters to break into melodious song. There are long stretches in that work wherein it is obvious that the orchestral fabric has been conceived first, as an expression of the ideas of the poem, while the actual words of the latter have been "musicalized" by a vocal line stuck on to the already existing harmonies. Long practice in this procedure gave him a skill in the sheer manipulation of musical notes that has rarely been equaled and never excelled (even by Bach); and this technical mastery was combined with a musical imagination that was tremendously vivid and active. In *Tristan* the white heat of his inspiration blurred the edges of his principles, and he became somewhat less self-conscious about them. It is a symphony in three vast movements. His dictum that the function of the orchestra is to explain and comment on the drama, like the chorus in the Greek tragedy, seems here at times to be reversed—the action on the stage seems to be doing little more than give the clue to the tremendous drama that is being bodied forth in the orchestra pit.

And when, some three or four years later, he set to work on *Die Meistersinger,* he had attained a poise which raised him above the crude extremes of Wagnerism altogether. This largely followed from the very nature of the subject. All the male characters in the drama are singers of songs by vocation; and the creation of a song is the pivot of

the action. Such a work could hardly be constructed on the characteristic Wagnerian pattern. His instinct for dramatic homogeneity made
Wagner give free play, for once in a way, to a sheerly musical impulse
toward vocal melody. The whole work is drenched in it—it is the
Apotheosis of Song. The orchestra still has its endless melody, and in
no other work is it more endlessly lovely; but again and again the
characters break forth into tune for tune's sake, with the orchestra subsiding into accompaniment. Many of these lyrical passages fall naturally into traditional "enclosed" song forms, some with distinct verses
and refrains, and orchestral ritornelli, and conventional 6/4 5/3 cadences on the dominant, and spreadings of one syllable over several
notes of the melody—formulae which Wagner had ridiculed unspar-
ingly in his prose works. Furthermore, many of these "numbers" have
all the *naïveté* of folk music—the two chorales, for instance, David's
Chaplet ditty and St. John song, the Night Watchman's call, and the
Dance of the Apprentices, and Sachs's *Schusterlied*, and the processional Guild songs, and Kothner's recital of the Tabulatur.

The process went even farther in the admission of concerted pieces.
Wagner had been loftily scornful over the absurdity of several characters singing together on the ground that people do not talk at the
same time in real life. But, as a matter of fact, they don't sing to each
other at all in real life, and Art is not to be regulated by considerations
of logical "naturalism." The intensification of words by music is the
very essence of opera, and the conversion of speech into song is a convention without which it could not exist. It is but a minor extension
of this convention for voices sometimes to be heard together, and
this combination of voices has an expressive power all its own, which
the composer can only discard at the cost of sorely impoverishing the
means at his disposal. Wagner's conscience was particularly sore about
the Quintet—he was at one time on the point of deleting it in deference to the principles which returned to plague him whenever he
awoke for a moment from his creative trance. Fortunately he allowed
his scruples to be soothed by Cosima—one of the traditional roles of
woman through the ages! And, having once made up his mind to
commit the crime, he put a bold face on matters and frankly presented
the piece for what it is—an interlude in which the action of the drama
is suspended while the characters line up along the footlights to indulge in music making, quite in the crusted tradition of grand opera.

The same searing of his conscience took place over the use of the
chorus. In *Oper und Drama* he had inveighed against such "swelling

of the harmonic volume of sound," with the remark that audiences are not interested in crowds but in persons. In *Rhinegold*, *Valkyrie*, and *Siegfried* there is no chorus at all, while in *Tristan* it is limited to a few bars of chanty-like unison by sailors. But in *Die Meistersinger* the "folk" is a generalized personage essential to the drama, inasmuch as one of Wagner's aims in the work was to cry up popular appraisement of works of art at the expense of the judgment of professed *cognoscenti*; and here again, having decided to throw his principles overboard, he did so with a will. Each of the three acts opens and closes with a chorus, or an ensemble of choral dimensions, save for the opening of Act III; and for overwhelming "mass effect" the last scene has not its like in all opera.

The Comedy

Die Meistersinger was Wagner's first and last attempt at comedy. Not that his preoccupation with serious issues necessarily precluded success therein, for, as Lando says, "Genuine humour requires a sound and capacious mind, which is always a grave one." But the making of comedies is a very special business, and Wagner had to adopt unaccustomed methods both as dramatist and as composer. The result is something quite unlike any other comic opera ever written or conceived.

Never was his ability to write his own "book" of greater advantage to him. When Weber planned to strike out new paths in German opera he could do no more than select one of several alternative subjects suggested by a professed "librettist," and leave all the rest to the latter—with the result that the *Euryanthe* into which he poured his heart and soul was stillborn. But Wagner could make his drama take a form exactly suited to his very peculiar musical capacities: instinctively he played up to his strength and minimized his weaknesses. Broad comicality, genial good humor, romantic love, mordant parody —all these aspects of comedy he felt to be within his scope, and for these he afforded an outlet; but sparkling wit, lighthearted persiflage, irresponsible gaiety—qualities which in various proportions characterize all other masterpieces in this genre, such as *Figaro*, *The Barber*, and *Falstaff*—were foreign to his musical nature, and he dispensed with the occasion for them in his "book."

What claims has it to high rank as a comedy? Wagner, we know, took himself very seriously as poet and dramatist; he would not have shunned comparison with the greatest exponents of the comic spirit,

Aristophanes, Shakespeare, Molière. That his libretto is not lacking
in literary merit may be judged from the fact that it, alone of his
works, has been performed as a spoken drama (by the students at a
German university), and that it has been edited, complete with notes
and vocabulary, in an American series of textbooks in German literature. It contains a good deal of very pleasant versification; and if to
an English reader this is sometimes reminiscent of old-fashioned
Christmas pantomime, it often rises to the level of poetry. Moreover,
the most humdrum passages are saved from banality by the racy idiomatic diction, with its touch of the archaic to preserve the historical
atmosphere.

Yet when all is said and done, no one reading it unacquainted with
the music could put it in the same class as *Le Misanthrope* or *The
Wasps*. Like all true comedy, it is designed to chastise with a smile
the weaknesses of human nature; but comedy is fundamentally a thing
of the mind rather than of the emotions, whereas *Die Meistersinger*
makes four-fifths of its effect through music which, deliberately and
as a matter of principle, appeals to the feelings rather than to the
mind. As a vehicle for that music, it is a masterly piece of work, dis-
playing great skill in adapting the meter to a variety of purposes—
Sachs's homely philosophizing, the merry leg-pulling of the apprentices, the argumentation of the Masters, the romantic visions of
Walther, Beckmesser's bathetic serenade.

The construction of the drama is in some respects as skillful as that
of *Tristan*. For one thing it adheres closely to the unities of time and
place, the action falling entirely within twenty-four hours and within
a square mile. And the exposition has none of the dreary narrative
that gives us such *mauvais quarts d'heure* with Wotan, and make
Gurnemanz the greatest bore on the operatic stage. To be sure, the
action halts now and again, especially in Act I, where David's explanation of Mastersinging and the Masters' discussions on the conditions
of the contest are somewhat too much of a good thing. But with these
exceptions it is a model of economical construction; and it is quite
in keeping with the general character of the work that Wagner should
here make use of an outmoded device, which he had eschewed in his
previous works—the soliloquy. It is, of course, another "irrational"
convention, for in real life people who bawl to themselves at the top
of their voices are not long left at large. But conventions are the material with which the dramatist has to work, and we must be thankful
that Wagner here saw his way to frankly accepting this one. The

meditations of Sachs are dynamic—they lead him to conclusions which are of prime importance for the action. It was far better to let him think them aloud than to bring on some unfortunate lay figure to be the passive recipient of his confidences. Another compliance with tradition is Sachs's Address after the Prize Song. It is a scarcely disguised allocution from the author to the audience, justified by the ancient custom which added epilogues to comedies.

Of all the exponents of the comic spirit, there is only one mind that had command of each of its elements—wit, intrigue, buffoonery, romance: Shakespeare. Aristophanes does not attempt the "songfully poetic" nor Molière the broadly farcical. We must not therefore count it heavily against Wagner that both his words and his music lack the witty glitter of Beaumarchais-cum-Rossini or Hofmannsthal-cum-Strauss. For he had the other components in abundant measure. The rich drollery of the Beckmesser scene in Act II is comparable with the best things in Aristophanes. It evokes the mirth that "lifts the brows as gunpowder lifts a fortress"; but for the most part the laughter that *Die Meistersinger* gives us springs from that illuminating inward delight that is a finer feast for the soul than any amount of cackling merriment. It has that health-giving virtue of the comic spirit which, as Meredith says, "enters you like fresh air into a study. You are cognisant of the true kind by the feeling that you take it in, savour it and have what flowers have to live on, natural air, for food. That which you give out—the joyful roar—is not the better part: let that go to good fellowship and the benefit of the lungs. Aristophanes promises that if folk will retain the ideas of the comic poet carefully, their garments shall smell odoriferous wisdom throughout the year." In this respect, at any rate, *Die Meistersinger* is worthy to rank with the greatest. Wagner was a terrible moralizer; but here his moral is so broad, so genial, of such universal application, that it irradiates the mind and warms the heart with a new faith in life. Lavender to keep our mental garments sweet and wholesome throughout the year—that was a happy thought of the old Greek's!

Dramatis Personae

In discussing the stimuli which impelled Wagner to set to work on the subject we noted a realization of the dramatic possibilities latent in the character of Hans Sachs. In the draft of 1845 he was merely one of the Masters, who, being more sympathetic toward the Lover than the rest, tricked the Marker into a course of action which led to the discomfiture of the latter and the success of the former. Wagner now saw that the part could be developed into something altogether larger and more significant; that the drama could thereby be lifted from the level of rather crude farce with an undercurrent of irony to that of genial comedy with an undercurrent of idealism, the "moral" of which could be enforced by an action, parallel with the external happenings of the play, in the mind and soul of the old cobbler. And that this conception continued to develop as he proceeded with the actual creation of the work there is evidence not only in his letters but in the actual music. For instance, in the Overture—the first part of the music to be got down on paper—there is no allusion to Sachs at all. Wagner hardly began to envisage that personality in terms of music until some months later, when he sketched the Introduction to Act III.

In 1851, in the course of an account of the abandoned project in *A Communication to My Friends,* he wrote:

I conceived Hans Sachs as the last manifestation of the art-producing folk-spirit, and contrasted him in this capacity with the philistine master-singing burghers, to whose droll, tabulatur-poetic pedantry I gave personal expression in the figure of the "Marker."

Just that and no more. But when he took the subject up again ten years afterward there began in his mind a shifting of the center of gravity in the drama similar to that which took place during the creation of *The Ring.* There the great tragic figure of the mighty but frustrated Wotan loomed ever larger until it thrust back the blithe exuberant youth who had been the focus of interest in the original *Siegfried's Death.* Sachs did not become exactly a tragic figure, but he is "instinct with knowledge and experience of the tragic," and he has a serious outlook on life which is the outcome of long brooding on human vicissitudes. It was this conception of Sachs as a philosopher which ripened as the work grew under Wagner's hands, until it found musical expression in the "*Wahn*" motive which dominates the third act. The old cobbler's outlook, conveyed in the monologue at the beginning of that act, may be epitomized as follows: Mere objective fact does not explain human nature, nor satisfy the needs of the human soul. The highest function of Art is to redeem man's peace of soul by means of that power of Illusion (*Wahn*) which works its wonders wherever our ordinary way of looking at things avails us no farther.

This was the point to which Wagner's own spiritual experiences had brought him by the end of 1861, and his idealization of Sachs was really a Wagnerization. Nevertheless, the essential traits of the historical cobbler-poet were still recognizable in the Sachs of *Die Meistersinger*. That humorous shrewdness of expression, that genial warmth of heart, that sturdy common sense, that faith in hard work and pride in his handicraft—all these qualities are as characteristic of our own Sachs as of his prototype in real life. So, too, are the love and respect that he won from his fellow citizens. Doubtless some of his ideas would have been beyond the scope of a citizen of sixteenth-century Nuremberg—for one thing, he seems to have studied Schopenhauer. But we know that the historical Sachs had an open-mindedness and a freshness of outlook which made him among the first to welcome the Reformation in its early stages, combined with a spiritual steadiness that made him withdraw from active support of the movement when it developed into fanaticism. The Sachs of the opera has the same qualities, only they are displayed in connection with Art instead of Religion. His rejection of traditional formalism in favor of directly observed truth is essentially the Lutheran attitude of mind. He does not condemn the laws of the Guild: on the contrary, he upholds them against Walther and persuades him to adopt them. But he learns from him, and impresses upon his colleagues, the need for adapting their laws to the spirit of inspiration. He personifies the reasoning faculty which must be part of the make-up of the true artist.

The notion has long been current that the central theme of *Die Meistersinger* is Sachs's love for Eva, and his noble surrender of his hopes of winning her in the competition in order that she may be won by her lover. But for this view there is no warrant either in the work itself or in anything that Wagner ever said or wrote about it. He was more self-conscious about such matters than any other great composer that ever lived, and was very fond of explaining the significance of his dramas; therefore the absence of any such interpretation is strong presumption that it never occurred to him. True, in his well-known "program" to the Introduction to Act III he says that the opening phrase expresses "the bitter plaint of a resigned man who shows a cheerful and energetic countenance to the world," and that when this musical phrase accompanies the Cobbler's Song in Act II it suggests to Eva's comprehension the hidden grief that underlies that song. But this does not imply that the "plaint" is connected with love for

Eva, or that she so interprets it; all that he suggests is that it brings home to her the constitutional pessimism that underlies Sachs's bluff cheerfulness.

It is interesting to trace the history of this misinterpretation of the drama. It seems to have first been formulated in Houston Stewart Chamberlain's *Das Drama Richard Wagners* (1892); and the fact that the author was a member of the inner Sanhedrin of the Wagner cult gave it a sort of official stamp which it did not deserve. Let us see exactly what he says.

In *Die Meistersinger* we are witnesses of the last great victory which Sachs wins over himself: a renunciation brave, conscientious and proud; and the simple workman appears to us as great as any of the glorious heroes. . . . It is not in striking actions that Hans Sachs's greatness of soul is revealed, but in the insignificant facts of daily life. And that interior struggle, the renunciation of the hand of Eva, of the last happiness which life could offer him—it is not one of those struggles in which the soul is torn by the assault of the outward man. No; a man such as Sachs could not for an instant have harboured the idea of tearing a young girl from her lover, or even of disputing with him for her. The struggle which he sustains is altogether an inward one—against his own grief. That is the tragic conflict, those are the depths of the human heart to which the drama conducts us; and as later in *Parsifal*, the struggle ends not in the fall of the hero, but in his victory. His soul attains the supreme serenity of a mild and gentle resignation. Such is the drama of *Die Meistersinger*.

It is this last sentence which led later commentators astray. Undoubtedly Sachs has the tenderest affection for Eva; probably it would have given him great happiness to have made her the child-wife of his declining years.[3] Possibly he had some vague idea of entering the competition with a song of his own, though we see no sign of his having prepared one. Whatever his intentions might otherwise have been, he abandons them with a ready if rueful smile when he sees how matters stand with the young people, and promptly devotes his attention to contriving a happy issue for them. All this lends a special interest to his personality and endears him to us; but it is quite subordinate to the main action of the drama. Yet nearly every later writer has adopted Chamberlain's view. In Alfred Ernst's well-known book *L'Art de Richard Wagner* the only mention of *Die Meistersinger* is a study of the

[3] It may be recalled that the historical Sachs actually married a young girl a year after the death of his first wife in 1550, and that the marriage proved a very happy one.

character of Hans Sachs which places him among Wagner's "renunciatory heroes"—Erik, Wolfram, and King Mark. He goes on:

It is desirable to see clearly in what Sachs's renunciation consists. He loves Eva in a somewhat fatherly fashion, no doubt, since he formerly carried her as a baby in his arms; but the difference in age is not so great as certain commentators have supposed. Sachs is not an old man like Mark; he is in the maturity of life, and in the full force of his genius. Eva, from fear of falling to Beckmesser, faces the possibility of becoming the wife of Sachs, if she cannot belong to Walther.[4]

This involuntary dream of love, of happiness with Eva, is what he sacrifices, and the sacrifice is painful. His feeling for her is sweet to his heart; and although he has never dared to formulate it, he has tasted its unavowed delights, and he has to renounce this sentiment, to break this charm.

Much of this is finely perceived. Where we join issue with the author is over the statement that this is the central interest of the drama.

The hold which the idea gained over students of Wagner is amusingly shown by the case of another eminent French critic, Edmond Schuré. In the first edition of his *Drame Musicale* he made no mention of it, but declared that "the foundation of the drama is the struggle of genius with the counters of notes and syllables." But soon after Chamberlain's book had appeared, De Brinn Gabast in his *Les Maîtres Chanteurs* (1894) furiously combated Schuré. "No!" he vociferates, "a thousand times no! That struggle exists in the drama but it is not the foundation of it. The center of it is the soul of Hans Sachs and its real problem is the renunciation of Eva." Schuré gave ground before this onslaught, and added a Note to his second edition which appeared a year later.

In his very penetrating book *Das Drama Richard Wagners* Mr. Houston Chamberlain has very justly brought out the silent heroism of Hans Sachs, the greatness of his renunciation, and how completely he stands alone in the greatness of his soul. For no one understands the depths of his heart, neither the rigid Masters nor Walther himself. It is only Eva, with her feminine power of divination, who gives a furtive glance into those depths. For a moment the maiden's heart is penetrated by the loneliness and hidden torment of the Master. But she, too, soon forgets, for happiness is blind and ungrateful; suffering alone is clairvoyant and sympathetic

[4] Surely a very forced interpretation of Eva's coy suggestion.

towards suffering. Sachs carries through his sacrifice with genial good-nature; he does not permit his grief to raise its voice within himself; he stifles it with a smile.

Since then, critics and commentators have accepted this interpretation almost without exception. Let us see if there is any justification for it in the opera poem.

In Act I Sachs refers to Eva twice in the course of the Masters' discussions. He urges that she ought not to be forced to marry the winner of the competition against her will; and, a little later, in reply to Beckmesser's insinuation that he himself has an eye on the prize, he jocularly remarks: "The singer who is to have any chance of receiving the prize from Eva will have to be a younger man than you or I!" [5] Do either of these utterances suggest any feelings for Eva beyond an elderly man's affection for his neighbor's daughter whom he has known from babyhood? At this moment he knows nothing of the love affair of the young people—which, indeed, is only a few hours old; and Walther has not even dreamed the dream which is destined to win the prize on the morrow. Sachs is admittedly the most famous and talented member of the Guild—that is why Beckmesser is jealous of him. Thus he would have every chance of winning Eva in the only way that she is attainable; yet he goes out of his way to urge that she shall be left free to reject the winner. But it is quite clear that he has no intention of entering the competition; otherwise his above-quoted reply to Beckmesser would be a mean piece of deceit quite foreign to his character. Clearly then, if he has ever harbored a thought of wooing Eva he has already put it behind him, and this "renunciation" cannot be the "true action" about to be unfolded.

When at the beginning of the next act he returns home, his heart is full—but not of the fact that Eva's fate is to be decided on the morrow; he never gives her a thought. It is Walther's song that is still ringing in his head. In his first monologue, as he sits at his bench, it is upon the purely artistic question connected herewith that he ponders. And when Eva comes across from her father's house opposite, and sits beside him, there is no hint of bitterness in his affectionate greeting. She half-playfully asks him why he does not enter the competition, for which as a widower he is eligible; but it is a painful misapprehension to suppose, like M. Ernst, that she regards the cobbler

[5] *Aus jüng'rem Wachs*
　Als ich und Ihr, muss der Freier sein
　Soll Ev'chen ihm den Preis verleih'n.

as a *pis-aller* if her aristocratic lover fails to make good. A girl who within a few hours of exchanging rapturous vows with the lover of her dreams could carefully make sure of having somebody else to fall back upon would be a horrid young person. No; her half-conscious aim is to get him to tell her what has passed at the Singing School; perhaps, too, she hopes to win her old friend's sympathy and support for her lover and herself in their difficulties. And Sachs himself: does his response suggest that he takes her words seriously, or that his heart is lacerated by her coquetry? Not in the least. He playfully repudiates all thought of winning her, and goes on to tease her by pretending to agree with his colleagues' condemnation of Walther's song. By so doing he provokes her into an outburst which reveals to him how the land lies, but he displays not the least personal feeling at the discovery that she has given her heart to another. On the contrary, he forthwith sets about smoothing out the path of true love by a comic frustration of Beckmesser's Serenade, and by guiding the lovers into a path which will lead to their permanent happiness.

At the beginning of Act III David points out to the cobbler how capital it would be if he would carry off the prize, and thus provide the house with a new mistress; but Sachs merely dismisses him with a playful proverb and resumes his meditation—"his talk with David not having disturbed the current of his thoughts," as the stage directions expressly state. And the famous Monologue that follows does not touch upon Eva and her fate—it arises out of the riot of the previous night, and its subject is the illusions that dominate human nature. Later on, when the happy ending is in sight and Eva throws herself upon his neck in an outburst of gratitude to the man who has brought it to pass, declaring that if she were heart-whole it is Sachs himself whom she would have chosen—how does he reply? With the remark that he is not such a fool as to court the troubles that befell King Mark in the legend of *Tristan and Isolde*! Doubtless he only puts it like that in order to set the young people at ease; but the response is not that of a man deeply in love. In the Quintet that follows, Sachs does at last give expression to his vague dream. He would have liked to sing for the maiden in the contest, but has realized that this cannot be; and now Walther's song has convinced him of the claims of youth to win "the Poet's Prize." These last words are significant—they indicate once more that Art takes precedence of all else in Sachs's mind. And when in the final scene Pogner wrings his hand, he is expressing gratitude, not for a "renunciation" of Eva (there is no indication that the goldsmith ever thought of Sachs as a prospective son-in-law), but for the overthrow of Beckmesser, whose success, in view of Eva's repugnance, would have placed him in a very embarrassing position.

The Wagnerians would doubtless reply that, the action being within Sachs's soul, it is expressed in the orchestral commentary rather than in the words of the drama. Lichtenberger, for instance, says in his *Le Drame Wagnérien*:

> What decided Wagner to take up the subject again, was the possibility of superimposing on the social and literary satire a human drama which is played within the bosom of Hans Sachs. This drama is so intimate and so hidden that it is hardly to be perceived in the text of the poem; it is only revealed so to speak by the music.

But it is not. In Act I there is not a bar that could possibly have any such significance. In Act II the music that accompanies the bewitching scene between Sachs and Eva is woven out of three themes which depict the personality of Eva and her anxiety as to her lover's fate. The music gives no hint of the reactions of Sachs, even when she suggests that he might himself be a candidate for her hand. We meet themes that depict "Sachs as Cobbler" and "Sachs as Friend" and "Sachs as Philosopher," but none that depicts "Sachs as Lover." That profoundly serious "Philosophy" motive, of which so much is made in Act III, has clearly nothing to do with Eva, for it is first developed during the *"Wahn"* Monologue, in which Sachs never thinks of her.

No. Sachs has a warm affection for Eva, he is deeply concerned for her happiness, he has sometimes repressed a sigh that he is too old for her; but "the Renunciation of Love" is not the main trait of his character or the underlying theme of the drama. His main preoccupation is with the problems of creative art. He stands for the deliberate and conscious element in it. Brought up in the traditions of Mastersinging, he comes through the action of the drama to a realization that these traditions are sterile unless fecundated by the inspiration of genius, while genius needs the guidance which can alone be given by technical study based on the practice of the "Old Masters." And alongside this broadening of his artistic outlook there is another spiritual development of wider and more general bearing—a perception of the vanity of human passions, and of Art's high mission to interpret Man's "illusions." It would be out of keeping with Sachs's sturdy common sense,

his essential bigness of spirit, to think of him as the victim of sentimental infatuation for a young girl.

The Masters incarnate the conventional limitations of art against
which Wagner was in rebellion all his life; but he has not portrayed
them in any hostile spirit. He saw, and he makes us see, the wholesome simplicity of their bourgeois life within the narrow horizon set
by their old walls and their hoary traditions. They are (with one exception) worthy and honorable men, who feel themselves the accred-
ited guardians of all that is best in Art. Lacking creative power they
think the more of the rules that should guide creation—these at any
rate they can elaborate and master; and they are shocked at any artistic phenomenon which threatens to make them think out these
canons afresh. They are just a little ridiculous in their pompous satisfaction with themselves and with their precious Guild; but we all
know people just like that, whom wc love none the less for their crusty
conservatism.

In Veit Pogner, the senior member, we see the idealism which was
the most engaging aspect of Mastersinging. Perhaps there is a touch
of vanity in his famous offer. He intends thereby to raise the reputation of the Nuremberg Guild for high devotion to their craft; but he
also will show the world that he, a simple burgher, can rival the high-
born personages who sometimes offered rich prizes at such compe-
titions. It is outside our modern range of ideas for a father thus to
pledge his daughter's future happiness. This aspect of the story fails
to convince—it is a stage device which we have to accept as we do
Lear's partition of his kingdom, or the disguises in *Twelfth Night*,
with the reflection that this acceptance is part of our contribution to
the making of the play. And Wagner has done a good deal to reconcile us to it. He lets us see that the old man's pride in his scheme
is shaken when he finds that it may lead to Eva losing Walther, whom
he would gladly have as a son-in-law. He knows nothing of the love-at-
first-sight between the pair when he makes his announcement; he
finds it out when he overhears Eva's whispered question to Magdalena, early in Act II. Even before that, during his evening walk with
his daughter on his arm, he has sensed the disquiet in her secret
thoughts; and when they reach home he at first thinks of calling on
Sachs, to ask for his advice and help, but reflects that he has gone too
far to turn back. And when in Act III the cobbler has saved the situation by his tact and knowledge of human nature, the old jeweler's
relief and gratitude overflow.

Then there is Fritz Kothner the Baker, who acts as convener and Master of the Ceremonies. He exemplifies the Masters' orotund self-importance at its richest and fruitiest. With what unction does he intone the sacred tables of the Mastersinging Law; how magisterially he inquires into the antecedents of the candidate for admission; how deprecatingly he shakes his head when the Knight announces a secular subject for his song instead of the sacred theme which would surely have been more seemly!

The third outstanding personality among the Masters is, of course, the sublime Sixtus Beckmesser, Town Clerk and Marker to the Worshipful Guild. Mechanical self-satisfied routine, crass egotism, malicious jealousy—these failings are to be found, in greater or less degree, in every such society, and poor Sixtus has to be the scapegoat to carry them all into the wilderness. A keen but narrow mind, coupled with rigid adherence to rules and regulations, has stood him in good stead among colleagues in whom formality and routine are in high favor: in the City Council he has been made Town Clerk, and in the Guild he has been chosen Marker. These influential appointments have mightily swelled his vanity, and now Pogner's announcement seems to open a way to fortune through his unrivaled knowledge of song craft. He seeks to assure himself in advance of the old man's support. He tries to win the favorable notice of Eva by serenading her. He espies possible rivals in Sachs and Walther, and sticks at nothing in his anxiety to eliminate them. Finally he blunders into sharp practice that leads to his own undoing.

Yet although he is ridiculous, he is never obnoxious. It is a remarkable thing that Wagner, almost an egomaniac, often so acrimonious and spiteful to foes and even to lukewarm friends, could display such godlike universality of sympathy in the creation of this character. We know that he identified Beckmesser with Hanslick, whom he hated to the point of publicly affronting him, yet the Marker is limned with hardly a touch of that malice which might have been expected in the circumstances. We laugh at Beckmesser but we never despise him, and in the end we come almost to love him. When at the end he rushes off, frustrated and furious, we hope that he will get over his chagrin and live down this public humiliation; and that, chastened perhaps by this bitter experience, he will find his way to happiness in the lonely old age that lies before him.

Walther von Stolzing embodies the creative impulse, the divine fire of genius. In some sense he is an avatar of Walther von der Vogelweide, whose poetic spirit he has imbibed "by quiet hearth in winter-time." Like that old *Minnesinger*, he comes of a knightly family whose fortunes have fallen into decay; like him he has grown up in intimate communion with nature amid the rural solitudes that surround his ancestral home; and just as the earlier Sir Walther betook him to Vienna to mend his fortunes, so this later one has come to Nuremberg with the same purpose.

He gives himself no airs in his dealings with the *bons bourgeois* with whom he comes into contact there, but he is distinguished from them as much by his bearing—frank, impetuous, high-spirited—as by his poetic gifts. Song wells forth from his heart, passionate and un-premeditated. We feel for him the affectionate admiration that we might have felt for Shelley, could we have known him. But the combination of gentle blood with artistic temperament makes him singularly unbalanced in the practical affairs of life. He is a creature of impulse—sometimes lofty, always engaging, but often indiscreet. It is impulse that makes him fall in love with Eva at first sight, and seek her out in church. It is impulse that kindles in him the sudden resolution to win admission to the Guild—at a session which is to open in five minutes' time. It is impulse that spurs him to plan an elopement the moment that the course of true love does not run smooth. It is impulse that makes him, when vexed and thwarted, ready to fall on Beckmesser, on Sachs, on the old Night Watchman whose blast sounds like a challenge in his distraught ear. It is impulse that causes him to reject the emblem of Masterhood, even from the hands of his future father-in-law. Yet we feel that this is a quality becoming to youth and genius, the outcome of freedom and idealism; and in the radiant glow of happiness with which the opera ends, one vital element is the fact that Walther's faith in his muse has been triumphantly justified.

It is an endearing trait in him that with all his proud impetuosity, he submits instinctively to the good will and good sense of Hans Sachs. Thrice at critical moments he allows himself to be guided by it: first, when the strong arm of the cobbler pulls him out of the hurly-burly through which he had thought of fighting his way with Eva; then when he accepts his advice in reshaping his song; lastly, when he reconsiders his refusal to become a Master.

But our greatest assurance for the future well-being of Walther springs from the personality of his bride. For Eva, the simple burgher maiden, has just those qualities of saving common sense which the poetic young noble lacks. Her disposition is complementary to his in much the same way as Juliet's is to Romeo's. Just as the new experience of love gives decision and circumspection to the child Juliet, while it throws Romeo off his balance and impels him to one hasty indiscretion after another, so it gives to Eva a clear-sighted practicality which saves the situation for her and her impetuous Walther. But for the fact that she, unlike poor Juliet, was able to lay a restraining hand on her lover's arm, things might have gone as badly in Nuremberg as in Verona.

Wagner does not seem to be able to conceive of love as coming otherwise than in a flash. The continuous growth of affection depicted in Wordsworth's "She was a phantom of delight," rooting deeper and deeper in the soul with the passing of the years, seems outside his range of experience and imagination. With him love is always the sacred beam from Paradise that smites with the irresistible suddenness of lightning. It is thus with Senta and the Dutchman, with Elsa and Lohengrin, with Isolde and Tristan, with Sieglinde and Siegmund, with Brünnhilde and Siegfried. This is not to say that his womenfolk have not distinct personalities. Eva only resembles her high-born sisters, the daughters of gods or kings, in the way that the sudden realization of love sweeps away every other consideration from her mind. She belongs far more to this earth than any of the others. She is no sanctified dreamer like Elsa or Elisabeth, nor has she the heroic proportions of Isolde and the supernatural personages of *The Ring*. She is a rosy-cheeked child of Nature. Her lively sense of humor and arch tenderness remind us sometimes of Rosalind, her refreshing *naïveté* and native intelligence recall Gretchen and Clärchen. Yet her qualities are all her own, for they are depicted less in her words than in the music that irradiates them. And along with the artless charm of the hedge rose she has thorns that can prick, as Sachs finds when his teasing provokes her to a little spurt of very burgher-like temper.

Such is Ev'chen Pogner—of all Wagner's womenfolk the most human, the most lovable, the most harmonious.

In David we see the limitations of Wagner's sense of the comic. The young fellow has many engaging traits: his high spirits, his self-importance among the other apprentices, his love and admiration for his master, the genuine talent which he shows in his own little trial song, his devotion to the Guild of which we are sure that he will one day be a very worthy Master. But his love affair with Magdalena, who as Eva's nurse (*Amme*) can scarcely be less than twice his age, is neither convincing nor altogether pleasing. There is a parodistic touch about it which seems hardly concordant with the beautiful humanity that pervades the work as a whole. True, callow youths do become enamored of women of riper age; but they generally grow out of it before there is any harm done, whereas here we see the lad definitely tied up to his aging sweetheart. As to Magdalena herself, she hardly comes to life. She is a revival of that old-fashioned dramatic device, the *confidante*, and it was a tradition of comic opera that this character should be paired off with the *tenore buffo*. Still, we have all known people who seem equally colorless, and yet make an indispensable contribution to the good and the beautiful in life, as Magdalena does in the Quintet.

THE SONG OF THE LARK

Willa Cather

Music, particularly operatic music, meant a great deal
to Willa Cather. References to opera and opera singers
are numerous in her works. Her early novel, *The Song
of the Lark* (1914–15), is a study of a singer, perhaps
suggested to her by personal experiences with singers of
the period whom Cather counted among her friends.
In later years she revised the novel, and for this new
edition she wrote a preface which limns the author's
conception of the artist: "The life of nearly every artist
who succeeds in the true sense (succeeds in delivering
himself completely to his art) is more or less like
Wilde's story, 'The Portrait of Dorian Grey.' As Thea
Kronborg is more and more released into the dramatic
and musical possibilities of her profession, as her artistic life grows fuller and richer, it becomes more interesting to her than her own life. As the gallery of her
musical impersonations grows in number and beauty,
as that perplexing thing called 'style' (which is the
singer's very self) becomes more direct and simple and
noble, the Thea Kronborg who is behind the imperishable daughters of music becomes somewhat dry and
preoccupied. Her human life is made up of exacting
engagements and dull business detail, of shifts to evade
an idle, gaping world which is determined that no artist
shall ever do his best. Her artistic life is the only one
in which she is happy, or free, or even very real. It is
the reverse of Wilde's story; the harassed, susceptible
human creature comes and goes, subject to colds,
brokers, dressmaker, managers. But the free creature,
who retains her youth and beauty and warm imagination, is kept shut up in the closet, along with the scores
and wigs."

From *The Song of the Lark* by Willa Cather, by permission of Houghton Mifflin
Company.

Two excerpts from the novel are given here. The first describes the impression Thea's singing makes on her lifelong friend, Dr. Howard Archie. The second, taken from the close of the novel, describes Thea's triumph when she appears as Sieglinde.

One bright morning late in February, 1909, Doctor Archie was breakfasting comfortably at the Waldorf. He had got into Jersey City on an early train, and a red, windy sunrise over the North River had given him a good appetite. He consulted the morning paper while he drank his coffee and saw that *Lohengrin* was to be sung at the opera that evening. In the list of the artists who would appear was the name "Kronborg." Such abruptness rather startled him. "Kronborg": it was impressive and yet, somehow, disrespectful; somewhat rude and brazen, on the back page of the morning paper. After breakfast he went to the hotel ticket-office and asked the girl if she could give him something for *Lohengrin*, "near the front." His manner was a trifle awkward and he wondered whether the girl noticed it. Even if she did, of course, she could scarcely suspect. Before the ticket stand he saw a bunch of blue posters announcing the opera casts for the week. There was *Lohengrin*, and under it he saw:

Elsa von Brabant . . . Thea Kronborg.

That looked better. The girl gave him a ticket for a seat which she said was excellent. He paid for it and went out to the cabstand. He mentioned to the driver a number on Riverside Drive and got into a taxi. It would not, of course, be the right thing to call upon Thea when she was going to sing in the evening. He knew that much, thank goodness! Fred Ottenburg had hinted to him that, more than almost anything else, that would put one in wrong.

When he reached the number to which he directed his letters, he dismissed the cab and got out for a walk. The house in which Thea lived was as impersonal as the Waldorf, and quite as large. It was above 116th Street, where the Drive narrowed, and in front of it the shelving bank dropped to the North River. As Archie strolled about the paths which traversed this slope, below the street level, the fourteen stories of the apartment hotel rose above him like a perpendicular cliff. He had no idea on which floor Thea lived, but he reflected, as his eye ran over the many windows, that the outlook would be fine from any floor. The forbidding hugeness of the house made him feel as if he had expected to meet Thea in a crowd and had missed her. He did not really believe that she was hidden away behind any of those glittering windows, or that he was to hear her this evening. His walk was curiously uninspiring and unsuggestive. Presently remembering that Ottenburg had encouraged him to study his lesson, he went down to the opera house and bought a libretto. He had even brought his old *Adler's German and English* in his trunk, and after luncheon he settled down in his gilded suite at the Waldorf with a big cigar and the text of *Lohengrin.*

The opera was announced for seven-forty-five, but at half-past seven Archie took his seat in the right front of the orchestra circle. He had never been inside the Metropolitan Opera House before, and the height of the audience room, the rich color, and the sweep of the balconies were not without their effect upon him. He watched the house fill with a growing feeling of expectation. When the steel curtain rose and the men of the orchestra took their places, he felt distinctly nervous. The burst of applause which greeted the conductor keyed him still higher. He found that he had taken off his gloves and twisted them to a string. When the lights went down and the violins began the prelude, the place looked larger than ever; a great pit, shadowy and solemn. The whole atmosphere, he reflected, was somehow more serious than he had anticipated.

After the curtains were drawn back upon the scene beside the Scheldt, he got readily into the swing of the story. He was so much interested in the bass who sang King Henry that he had almost forgotten for what he was waiting so nervously, when the Herald began in stentorian tones to summon Elsa von Brabant. Then he began to realize that he was rather frightened. There was a flutter of white at the back of the stage, and women began to come in: two, four, six, eight, but not the right one. It flashed across him that this was something like buck fever, the paralyzing moment that comes upon a man when his first elk looks at him through the bushes, under its great antlers; the moment when a man's mind is so full of shooting that he forgets the gun in his hand until the buck is gone.

All at once, she was there. Yes, unquestionably it was she. Her eyes were downcast, but the head, the cheeks, the chin—there could be no mistake; she advanced slowly, as if she were walking in her sleep. Someone spoke to her; she only inclined her head. He spoke again, and she bowed her head still lower. Archie had forgotten his libretto, and he had not counted upon these long pauses. He had expected her to appear and sing and reassure him. They seemed to be waiting for her. Did she ever forget? Why in thunder didn't she— She made a sound, a faint one. The people on the stage whispered together and seemed confounded. His nervousness was absurd. She must have done this often before; she knew her bearings. She made another sound, but he could make nothing of it. Then the King sang to her, and Archie began to remember where they were in the story. She came to the front of the stage, lifted her eyes for the first time, clasped her hands and began, *"Einsam in trüben Tagen."*

Yes, it was exactly like buck fever. Her face was there, toward the house now, before his eyes, and he positively could not see it. She was singing, at last, and he positively could not hear her. He was conscious of nothing but an uncomfortable dread and a sense of crushing disappointment. He had, after all, missed her. Whatever was there, she was not there—for him.

The King interrupted her. She began again, *"In lichter Waffen Scheine."* Archie did not know when his buck fever passed, but presently he found that he was sitting quietly in a darkened house, not listening to, but dreaming upon, a river of silver sound. He felt apart from the others, drifting alone on the melody, as if he had been alone with it for a long while and had known it all before. His power of attention was not great just then, but in so far as it went he seemed to be looking through an exalted calmness at a beautiful woman from far away, from another sort of life and feeling and understanding than his own, who had in her face something he had known long ago, much brightened and beautiful. As a lad he used to believe that the faces of people who died were like that in the next world; the same faces, but shining with the light of a new understanding.

What he felt was admiration and estrangement. The homely reunion, that he had somehow expected, now seemed foolish. Instead of feeling proud that he knew her better than all these people about him, he felt chagrined at his own ingenuousness. For he did not know her better. This woman he had never known; she had somehow devoured his little friend, as the wolf ate up Red Ridinghood. Beautiful, radiant, tender as she was, she chilled his old affection; that sort of feeling was no longer appropriate. She seemed much, much farther away from him than she had seemed all those years when she was in Germany. The ocean he could cross, but there was something here he could not cross. There was a moment, when she returned to the King and smiled that rare, sunrise smile of her childhood, when he thought she was coming back to him. After the Herald's second call for her champion, when she knelt in her impassioned prayer, there was again something familiar, a kind of wild wonder that she had had the power to call up long ago.

After the tenor came on, the doctor ceased trying to make the woman before him fit into any of his cherished recollections. He took her, in so far as he could, for what she was then and there. When the knight raised the kneeling girl and put his mailed hand on her hair, when she lifted to him a face full of worship and passionate humility, Archie gave up his last reservation. He knew no more about her than did the hundreds around him, who sat in the shadow and looked on, as he looked, some with more understanding, some with less. He knew as much about Ortrud or Lohengrin as he knew about Elsa—more, because she went farther than they, she sustained the legendary beauty of her conception more consistently. Even he could see that. Attitudes, movements, her face, her white arms and fingers, everything was suffused with a rosy tenderness, a warm humility, a gracious and yet—to him—wholly estranging beauty.

During the balcony singing in the second act the doctor's thoughts were as far away from Moonstone as the singer's doubtless were. He had begun, indeed, to feel the exhilaration of getting free from personalities, of being released from his own past as well as from Thea Kronborg's. During the duet with Ortrud, and the splendors of the wedding processional, this new feeling grew and grew. At the end of the act there were many curtain calls and Elsa acknowledged them, brilliant, gracious, spirited, and with her far-breaking smile; but on the whole she was harder and more self-contained before the curtain than she was in the scene behind it. Archie did his part in the applause that greeted her, but it was the new and wonderful he applauded, not the old and dear. His personal, proprietary pride in her was frozen out.

Doctor Archie saw nothing of Thea during the following week. After several fruitless efforts, he succeeded in getting a word with her over the telephone, but she sounded so distracted and driven that he was glad to say good night and hang up the instrument. There were, she told him, rehearsals not only for *Walküre*, but also for *Götterdämmerung*, in which ʳhe was to sing Waltraute two weeks later.

On Thursday afternoon Thea got home late, after an exhausting rehearsal. She was in no happy frame of mind. Madame Necker, who had been very gracious to her that night when she went on to complete Gloeckler's performance of Sieglinde, had, since Thea was cast to sing the part instead of Gloeckler in the production of the *Ring*, been chilly and disapproving, distinctly hostile. Thea had always felt that she and Necker stood for the same sort of endeavor, and that Necker recognized it and had a cordial feeling for her. In Germany she had several times sung Brangaene to Necker's Isolde, and the older artist had let her know that she thought she sang it well. It was a bitter disappointment to find that the approval of so honest an artist as Necker could not stand the test of any significant recognition by the management.

Thea had her dinner sent up to her apartment, and it was a very poor one. She tasted the soup and then indignantly put on her wraps to go out and hunt a dinner. As she was going to the elevator, she had to admit that she was behaving foolishly. She took off her hat and coat and ordered another dinner. When it arrived, it was no better than the first. There was even a burnt match under the milk toast. She had a sore throat, which made swallowing painful and boded ill for the morrow. Although she had been speaking in whispers all day to save her throat, she now perversely summoned the housekeeper and demanded an account of some laundry that had been lost. The housekeeper was indifferent and impertinent, and Thea got angry and scolded violently. She knew it was very bad for her to get into a rage just before bedtime, and after the housekeeper left she realized that for ten dollars' worth of underclothing she had been unfitting herself for a performance which might eventually mean many thousands. The best thing now would be to stop reproaching herself for her lack of sense, but she was too tired to control her thoughts.

While she was undressing—Thérèse was brushing out her Sieglinde wig in the trunk-room—she went on chiding herself bitterly. "And how am I ever going to get to sleep in this state?" she kept asking herself. "If I don't sleep, I'll be perfectly worthless tomorrow. I'll go down there tomorrow and make a fool of myself. If I'd let that laundry alone with whatever nigger has stolen it— *Why* did I undertake to reform the management of this hotel tonight? After tomorrow I could pack up and leave the place. There's the Philamon—I liked the rooms there better, anyhow—and the Umberto—" She began going over the advantages and disadvantages of different apartment hotels. Suddenly she checked herself. "What *am* I doing this for? I can't move into another hotel tonight. I'll keep this up till morning. I shan't sleep a wink."

Should she take a hot bath, or shouldn't she? Sometimes it relaxed her, and sometimes it roused her and fairly put her beside herself. Between the conviction that she must sleep and the fear that she couldn't, she hung paralyzed. When she looked at her bed, she shrank from it in every nerve. She was much more afraid of it than she had ever been of the stage of any opera house. It yawned before her like the sunken road at Waterloo.

She rushed into her bathroom and locked the door. She would risk the bath, and defer the encounter with the bed a little longer. She lay in the bath half an hour. The warmth of the water penetrated to her bones, induced pleasant reflections and a feeling of well-being. It was very nice to have Doctor Archie in New York, after all, and to see him get so much satisfaction out of the little companionship she was able to give him. She liked people who got on, and who became more interesting as they grew older. There was Fred; he was much more interesting now than he had been at thirty. He was intelligent about music, and he must be very intelligent in his business, or he would not be at the head of the Brewers' Trust. She respected that kind of intelligence and success. Any success was good. She herself had made a good start, at any rate, and now, if she could get to sleep— Yes, they were all more interesting than they used to be. Look at Harsanyi, who had been so long retarded; what a place he had made for himself in Vienna! If she could get to sleep, she would show him something tomorrow that he would understand.

She got quickly into bed and moved about freely between the sheets. Yes, she was warm all over. A cold, dry breeze was coming in from the river, thank goodness! She tried to think about her little rock house and the Arizona sun and the blue sky. But that led to memories which were still too disturbing. She turned on her side, closed her eyes, and tried an old device.

She entered her father's front door, hung her hat and coat on the rack, and stopped in the parlor to warm her hands at the stove. Then she went out through the dining room, where the boys were getting their lessons at the long table; through the sitting room, where Thor was asleep in his cot bed, his dress and stockings hanging on a chair. In the kitchen she stopped for her lantern and her hot brick. She hurried up the back stairs and through the windy loft to her own glacial room. The illusion was marred only by the consciousness that she ought to brush her teeth before she went to bed, and that she never used to do it. Why—? The water was frozen solid in the pitcher, so she got over that. Once between the red blankets there was a short, fierce battle with the cold; then, warmer—warmer. She could hear her father shaking down the hard-coal burner for the night, and the wind rushing and banging down the village street. The boughs of the cotton-wood, hard as bone, rattled against her gable. The bed grew softer and warmer. Everybody was warm and well downstairs. The sprawling old house had gathered them all in, like a hen, and had settled down over its brood. They were all warm in her father's house. Softer and softer. She was asleep. She slept ten hours without turning over. From sleep like that, one awakes in shining armor.

On Friday afternoon there was an inspiring audience; not an empty chair in the house. Ottenburg and Doctor Archie had seats in the orchestra circle, got from a ticket broker. Landry had not been able to get a seat, so he roamed about in the back of the house, where he usually stood when he dropped in after his own turn in vaudeville was over. He was there so often and at such irregular hours that the ushers thought he was a singer's husband, or had something to do with the electrical plant.

Harsanyi and his wife were in a box, near the stage, in the second circle. Mrs. Harsanyi's hair was noticeably gray, but her face was fuller and handsomer than in those early years of struggle, and she was beautifully dressed. Harsanyi himself had changed very little. He had put on his best afternoon coat in honor of his pupil, and wore a pearl in his black ascot. His hair was longer and more bushy than he used to wear it, and there was now one gray lock on the right side. He had always been an elegant figure, even when he went about in shabby clothes and was crushed with work. Before the curtain rose, he was restless and nervous, and kept looking at his watch and wishing he had got a few more letters off before he left his hotel. He had not been in New York since the advent of the taxicab, and had allowed himself too much time. His wife knew that he was afraid of being disappointed this afternoon. He did not often go to the opera, because the stupid things that singers did vexed him, and it always put him in a rage if the conductor held the beat or in any way accommodated the score to the singer.

When the lights went out and the violins began to quaver their long D against the rude figure of the basses, Mrs. Harsanyi saw her husband's fingers fluttering on his knee in a rapid tattoo. At the moment when Sieglinde entered from the side door, she leaned toward him and whispered in his ear, "Oh, the lovely creature!" But he made no response, either by voice or gesture. Throughout the first scene he sat sunk in his chair, his head forward and his one yellow eye rolling restlessly and shining like a tiger's in the dark. His eye followed Sieglinde about the stage like a satellite, and when she sat at the table listening to Siegmund's long narrative, it never left her. When she prepared the sleeping draught and disappeared after Hunding, Harsanyi bowed his head still lower and put his hand over his eye to rest it. The tenor—a young man who sang with great vigor—went on:

> *Wälse! Wälse!*
> *Wo ist dein Schwert?*

Harsanyi smiled, but he did not look forth again until Sieglinde reappeared. She went through the story of her shameful bridal feast and into the Walhalla music, which she always sang so nobly, and the entrance of the one-eyed stranger:

> *Mir allein*
> *Weckte das Auge*

Mrs. Harsanyi glanced at her husband, wondering whether the singer on the stage could not feel his commanding glance. On came the crescendo:

> *Was je ich verlor,*
> *Was je ich beweint,*
> *Wär' mir gewonnen.*

> (All that I have lost,
> All that I have mourned,
> Would I then have won.)

Harsanyi touched his wife's arm softly.

Seated in the moonlight, the Volsung pair began their loving inspection of each other's beauties, and the music born of murmuring sound passed into her face, as the old poet said—and into her body as well. Into one lovely attitude after another the music swept her, love impelled her. And the voice gave out all that was best in it. Like the

spring indeed, it blossomed into memories and prophecies, it recounted and it foretold, as she sang the story of her friendless life, and
of how the thing which was truly herself, "bright as the day, rose to
the surface" when in the hostile world she for the first time beheld
her Friend. Fervently she rose into the hardier feeling of action and
daring, the pride in hero-strength and hero-blood, until in a splendid
burst, tall and shining like a Victory, she christened him:

Siegmund—
So nenn' ich dich!

Her impatience for the sword swelled with her anticipation of his
act, and throwing her arms above her head, she fairly tore a sword
out of the empty air for him, before Nothung had left the tree. *In
höchster Trunkenheit*, indeed, she burst out with the flaming cry of
their kinship: "If you are Siegmund, I am Sieglinde!" Laughing, singing, exulting—with their passion and their sword—the Volsungs ran
out into the spring night.

As the curtain fell, Harsanyi turned to his wife. "At last," he sighed,
"somebody with *enough*! Enough voice and talent and beauty, enough
physical power. And such a noble, noble style!"

"I can scarcely believe it, Andor. I can see her now, that clumsy girl,
hunched up over your piano. I can see her shoulders. She always
seemed to labor so with her back. And I shall never forget that night
when you found her voice."

The audience kept up its clamor until, after many reappearances
with the tenor, Kronborg came before the curtain alone. The house
met her with a greeting that was almost savage in its fierceness. The
singer's eyes, sweeping the house, rested for a moment on Harsanyi,
and she waved her long sleeve toward his box.

"She *ought* to be pleased that you are here," said Mrs. Harsanyi.
"I wonder if she knows how much she owes to you."

"She owes me nothing," replied her husband quickly. "She paid her
way. She always gave something back, even then."

"I remember you said once that she would do nothing common,"
said Mrs. Harsanyi thoughtfully.

"Just so. She might fail, die, get lost in the pack. But if she achieved,
it would be nothing common. There are people whom one can trust
for that. There is one way in which they will never fail." Harsanyi retired into his own reflections.

After the second act, Fred Ottenburg brought Archie to the Harsanyis' box and introduced him as an old friend of Miss Kronborg. The head of a musical publishing house joined them, bringing with him a journalist and the president of a German singing society. The conversation was chiefly about the new Sieglinde. Mrs. Harsanyi was gracious and enthusiastic, her husband nervous and uncommunicative. He smiled mechanically, and politely answered questions addressed to him. "Yes, quite so." "Oh, certainly." Everyone, of course, said very usual things with great conviction. Mrs. Harsanyi was used to hearing and uttering the commonplaces which such occasions demanded. When her husband withdrew into the shadow, she covered his retreat by her sympathy and cordiality.

The chorus director said something about "dramatic temperament." The journalist insisted that it was "explosive force," "projecting power."

Ottenburg turned to Harsanyi.

"What is it, Mr. Harsanyi? You know all about her. What's her secret?"

Harsanyi rumpled his hair irritably and shrugged his shoulders. "Her secret? It is every artist's secret"—he waved his hand—"passion. That is all. It is an open secret, and perfectly safe. Like heroism, it is inimitable in cheap materials."

The lights went out. Fred and Archie left the box as the second act came on.

Artistic growth is, more than it is anything else, a refining of the sense of truthfulness. The stupid believe that to be truthful is easy; only the artist, the great artist, knows how difficult it is. That afternoon nothing new came to Thea Kronborg, no enlightenment, no inspiration. She merely came into full possession of things she had been refining and perfecting for so long. Her inhibitions chanced to be fewer than usual, and, within herself, she entered into the inheritance that she herself had laid up, into the fullness of the faith she had kept before she knew its name or its meaning.

Often when she sang, the best she had was unavailable; she could not break through to it, and every sort of distraction and mischance came between it and her. But this afternoon the closed roads opened, the gates dropped. What she had so often tried to reach lay under her hand. She had only to touch an idea to make it live.

While she was on the stage she was conscious that every movement was the right movement, that her body was absolutely the instrument of her idea. Not for nothing had she kept it so severely, kept it filled with such energy and fire. All that deep-rooted vitality flowered in her voice, her face, in her very fingertips. She felt like a tree bursting into bloom. And her voice was as flexible as her body; equal to any demand, capable of every *nuance*. With the sense of its perfect companionship, its entire trustworthiness, she had been able to throw herself into the dramatic exigencies of the part, everything in her at its best and everything working together.

RICHARD STRAUSS DISCUSSES *DER ROSENKAVALIER* AND *SALOME*

In his *Observations and Reminiscences,* Strauss made
certain demands on his interpreters. It is not too surprising to learn that these demands are not often fulfilled. The translation is by G. R. Marek.

Der Rosenkavalier

Two important demands on the interpreters: Just as Clytem-
nestra ought to be played not as a superannuated and desiccated witch
but as a beautiful, proud woman of fifty years, whose disintegration is
due to mental rather than physical causes, so should the Marschallin
be a pretty young woman, no older than thirty-two years. True enough,
in a bad humor she calls herself an "old woman" in comparison to the
seventeen-year-old Octavian, but surely she is not David's Magdalena,
who by the way is likewise portrayed too old. Octavian is neither the
first nor the last lover of the beautiful Marschallin, and she must not
act the closing of the first act too sentimentally, as tragic farewell to her
life, but must retain some measure of Viennese grace and lightness,
with one mournful and one joyous eye. As to the conductor—don't drag
the tempo, beginning with F Major 2/4!
  The most misunderstood figure has been our friend Ochs. Most of
the bassos put on the stage a horrible and vulgar monster with grue-
some make-up and proletarian manners, such a figure as would rightly
antagonize civilized audiences (French and Italian). That is altogether wrong. Ochs is a country Don Juan. He is handsome, approximately thirty-five years old, and an aristocrat even if half a peasant. He
knows how to behave in the Marschallin's salon with sufficient decency
so that the servants do not throw him out after five minutes. Inside
he is a vulgarian; outside presentable enough for Faninal not to refuse him on first looking him over. Most important, it is necessary to
play the first scene of Ochs in the boudoir with the greatest delicacy
and discretion, if it is not to be as repulsive as the love affair of an

old general's wife with a sergeant. In short, Viennese comedy—not Berlin farce!

Salome

In Berlin, in Max Reinhardt's Little Theater, I saw Wilde's *Salome* with Gertrud Eysoldt. After the performance, I met Heinrich Gruenfeld, who said to me, "This would make the right operatic subject for you!" I was able to reply, "I'm already at work composing it." Before this, the Viennese poet, Anton Linder, had sent me the drama and had offered to fashion it into an "opera text" for me. I agreed, and he sent me a few skillfully versified scenes; I was unable to decide, however, how to begin the composition. Then one day he proposed: "Why don't you compose without further ado, 'How beautiful is the Princess Salome tonight'?" From that moment on it was not difficult to cleanse the drama of all its literary characteristics so that in the end it became very good "libretto." Now, after the dance and the whole final scene have been steeped in music, it is no great trick to declare that the drama "cried out for music." Certainly—but somebody had to perceive that first!

I had long found fault with all operas on Oriental or Jewish subjects, believing that they lack the true color of the East, the aura of burning sun. The necessity of supplying such color forced me to invent an exotic harmonic scheme, iridescent with strange cadences, like taffeta. . . .

Once the brave Schuch [1] had shown the courage to accept *Salome*, the difficulties began. They began with the first piano reading rehearsal, at which all soloists had gathered with the intention of handing back their parts to the conductor. All, that is, except the Czechoslovakian Burian who, as the last to be consulted, responded, "I already know the part by heart." Bravo! Now the others began to feel ashamed, and the work of the rehearsal began in earnest. At the first stage rehearsal the dramatic soprano, Wittich, went on strike. She had been entrusted with the part because she was equal to its demands: as the sixteen-year-old princess with the voice of Isolde, she could be heard above the full orchestra. Now she protested. "It is not fair to write anything like this," and then, summoning all the dignity of the wife of a Saxon mayor, "I won't do it: I'm a decent woman." She drove the stage director Wirk to desperation, accusing him of

[1] The conductor.

"perversity and cruelty." And yet Wittich, whose figure was not ideal for the role, had some right on her side, although hardly in the way she meant it. What I have seen other singers do in later performances in the way of shimmying and snakelike movements, teetering with Jokanaan's head, does surpass all measures of decency and taste. Anybody who has been to the Orient and has observed the restrained behavior of Oriental women can understand that Salome, being a chaste virgin and an Oriental princess, can only be acted with most simple and elegant gestures. If not, the result of her tragic fate is likely to create disgust and horror rather than pity. (Parenthetically, I want to mention that the high B-flat of the bass cello at the murder of the Baptist is not supposed to represent cries of pain but the repressed sigh of the impatiently waiting Salome. This ominous moment so frightened Graf Seebach [2] at the dress rehearsal, since he feared that it would cause the audience to snicker, that he convinced me to soften the point by adding a prolonged B-flat of the English horn.) Generally speaking, the acting of all the performers must be restrained, must be as simple as possible, in contrast to the wild, excited music. Herodias, often played as a neurasthenic who keeps running up and down, should remember that he is in fact a parvenu from the East and that with all his erotic excesses he is trying to impress his Roman guests with his dignity and his position, imitating the great Caesars of Rome. Tumult on the stage as well as in the pit is—too much! The orchestra alone suffices. My father, to whom a few months before his death I played excerpts on the piano, grumbled in despair, "God! What nervous music! It sounds like nothing but ants crawling up and down your trousers." Perhaps he wasn't altogether wrong. Cosima Wagner, for whom I played part of the score at her insistent request (I myself counseled her against hearing it), remarked after the final scene, "This is pure insanity. You are good only for the exotic, my son Siegfried for the popular."

Salome's success in Dresden was to be expected, since in that town new operas were usually accorded initial welcome. However, all the head-shaking prophets in the Bellevue Hotel were agreed that the opera, though it might be given in a few of the largest theaters, would certainly disappear in short order. After three weeks Salome was, I believe, accepted by ten theaters. In Breslau, played by an orchestra of seventy, it had a sensational success. Now began the inanities of the press, the opposition of the clergy and of the Puritans in New York,

[2] The impresario of the Dresden opera.

where the work had to be canceled after the première at the insistence of a certain Mr. Morgan. The Kaiser permitted the performance only after Hülsen [3] conceived the idea of having the morning star shine in the sky, to signify the coming of the three kings. Wilhelm II said, "I am very sorry that Strauss composed this *Salome*. I am quite fond of him in other respects, but with this thing he will do himself no end of harm." From this harm I was able to construct my villa in Garmisch!

[3] The impresario in Berlin.

THE DUSK OF RICHARD STRAUSS

Wallace Brockway and Herbert Weinstock

> Although written in 1941, nothing in the years inter-
> vening till Strauss's death has made necessary a revision
> of the estimate.

"The false dawn of modern music."

During the two decades following the death of Wagner, the
most important music composed in Germany was a series of big
orchestral works by Richard Strauss. They began with *Aus Italien* in
1887, and ended with the *Sinfonia Domestica* in 1903. Every one of
them, without exception, was a *succès de scandale*, though not all of
them won the public they had shocked. They established the right of
a young man who had begun as a classicizing, textbook composer to
assume the leadership of the *Zukunftsmusiker*, those Musicians of the
Future parented by Liszt and Wagner. Also, by their overt theatrical-
ism and programmatic drama, even the first of them hinted that it
would not be long before their composer began writing opera. Were
not his tone poems themselves substantially operas without stage action and words—Wagnerian music drama grafted onto the symphonic
poem of Liszt? Strauss's choice was wise: in his reaction from academic classicism, it was less risk to carry the symphonic poem a step
farther than to try, at the high noon of Wagner's apotheosis, the same
with opera. But in 1893, Wagner was ten years dead, and Strauss, on
the basis of *Don Juan* and *Tod und Verklärung*, was himself a *Meister*.
And so, he wrote *Guntram*, his first opera. A really popular opera did
not come from him for a dozen years: when *Salome* was produced in
1905, Strauss had completed all his tone poems.

In the tone poems, Strauss had perfected a manner of his own—an
unmistakable way of arranging ideas of any provenance whatever.
But when it came to composing *Guntram*, this most assured of eclec-

tics turned his back on this manner, and borrowed everything—type of subject matter and musical style—from Wagner. Like Wagner, too, he even wrote the libretto, which was based upon those ideas of redemption through love which had haunted Wagner's mind through his long series of stage works. The very names of the principal characters—Guntram, Freihild, and Friedhold—might have come from the *Ring*. The music, even to the turn of melody and closely imitative way of using leitmotivs, led straight back to Bayreuth. *Guntram* can be interpreted in two ways: it was either public proclamation that Strauss believed himself equipped to vie with Wagner, using the *Meister's* own tools, or it was a confession that Strauss had not yet devised his own style for the opera house. Most critics voted *Guntram* tiresome when it was staged on May 12, 1894, at Weimar, but Ernest Newman, in his minority report, later (1908) wrote: "Altogether *Guntram* is a great work, the many merits of which will perhaps some day restore it to the stage from which it is now most unjustly banished." Strauss himself got two things from the Weimar production: first, a realization that the public, having begun to tire somewhat of Wagner, would not stomach imitation Wagner, and second, a wife, Pauline de Ahna, who had sung Freihild.

In his second try for operatic acclaim, Strauss took a seven-mile leap by securing a libretto that was as shocking to some as his tone poems had been. Shock was a *sine qua non* of Strauss's technique—he simply had to have it to work successfully either in the concert hall or in the opera house. The libretto of his second opera, *Feuersnot* (besides containing attacks on Strauss's critics), is not only shocking, it is obscene, being a mixture of Rabelais and the German idea of the comic —not a bland mixture. For this farce, Strauss amended his Wagnerism in two directions. He allowed simple tunes, naïve, folksy, banal, to contaminate the Wagnerian stream, and from his tone poems he brought over a connoisseur's understanding, and use, of harmonic *Schrecklichkeit*. This tempered use of unresolved discords, unprepared modulations, and warring contrapuntal streams meant that Strauss was all but ready to project into opera his own carefully manufactured dual personality. *Feuersnot* found him arrived, but without all his baggage unpacked. It had the meager success that its trial-flight character deserved: outside Germany, it is hardly known at all. Its single American production at Philadelphia, on December 1, 1927, is notable chiefly because Nelson Eddy played the minor role of Hämmerlein.

In *Salome,* Strauss let himself go, arriving in one bound at an operatic position as advanced as that which he had attained, years earlier, in his purely instrumental work. Rather as a *coup,* he had managed to secure Oscar Wilde's notorious play, which in the Germany of that day was considered only less lofty than Shakespeare or Goethe. Except for a few brief excisions, Strauss accepted the play, in Hedwig Lachmann's faithful German version, just as it was—a self-contained work of art, and a work of art so jeweled, so static, so immalleable, that it did not require music, and would not have mixed well with it.

Strauss did not attempt to mix the two: he wrote a tone poem with human voices as added instruments in the orchestra, the whole designed to be accompanied by a stage spectacle of an aggressively sense-stimulating nature. For the suggestive, heavily perfumed, and rigidly mannered text, he wrote music that exaggerated each of its qualities. The music tells more than it has to say, is downright aphrodisiac, and ends in tetanic catalepsy. Throughout, the music so overshadows the stage action as to reduce it to mime, and even the greatest of dramatic singers cannot utterly overcome the posed, almost hieratic quality of the drama. Strauss's *Salome* is more decadent than Wilde's play simply because it takes itself more seriously. Or, perhaps, only seems to—with Strauss one is never sure, though now that its magnificent tissue has begun to wear thin and reveal the cotton body to which the brocade is stitched, it is tempting to write *Salome* off as the cold-blooded fabrication of a supercraftsman. And even in the tissue, which used to look so golden and cunningly patterned, it now seems that there are patches of the carelessly commonplace. But what remains of *Salome* is enough, when a powerful singing actress is found for the title role, to provide a good evening in the opera house. . . .

Salome dazzled the world with its piled-up brilliance, its quenchless energy, its battery of shattering effects. It was a magnificent envelope containing little, and musically it was bound to fade. It was a symptom of the bustling imperial Germany of the early twentieth century, with its boasts, its strutting muscularity, its sumptuary excesses, and its glee in the superficials of progress. *Salome* was another course in the continuous champagne banquet of expanding Germany, and it was, though not in the old sense, a national opera. Those who were able to see through the dazzle, being neither too shocked nor too carried away, saw through to the synthetic core and said that Strauss lacked conviction. They said that *Salome* had no inwardness, and it was even whispered that Strauss's creative peak was passed. In 1908, Ernest Newman ended his monograph on Strauss, one of the first in English, on an ominous note: "His new opera, which is to be produced early next year, will probably show whether he is going to realize our best hopes or our worst fears."

The next opera was *Elektra*. For many, it confirmed their worst fears. It was louder, more cacophonous, more unrelievedly psychopathic. *Salome* had emitted a mingled odor of perfume and decay; *Elektra* omitted the perfume, and the decay had become decomposition. Here was stench in terms of music. Hugo von Hofmannsthal, they said, had distorted Sophocles and made him hideous, and Strauss had further uglified the result. It was the end, they said, and Strauss, besides being degenerate, was certainly insane. There could be no doubt that so foul a betrayal of art would soon shrivel up and disappear.

But *Elektra* has done nothing of the sort: recent performances have tended to confirm the opinion, at first expressed cautiously, and then with ever-growing conviction, that *Elektra* is a tragic masterpiece of the very first order. It has not faded: it is as shattering, as moving, as profound in terror, as on the night of its première. What we can now hear that many of its first baffled listeners could not, because of their consuming interest in its more obvious, less significant aspects, is the abiding conviction that holds *Elektra* together. The noise, the cacophony, even the reek of twisted neuroses and unleashed passion—all have integral functions. In short, *Elektra* is not a deliberate shocker—it merely, since it deals with the naked psyche, has no reticences. Within the limits imposed by the climatic character of the situations, the characters achieve a wholeness that is the best proof of Strauss's searching care in projecting personalities. So intense was that care that the tender lyricism of certain scenes escapes that banality which is all too often Strauss's only counterpoise to the horrible and the grotesque.

Elektra is formally and technically more satisfactory than *Salome*. Little in the libretto or the music is extraneous to the establishment of the atmosphere of tragedy and, in the largest sense, the display of Elektra's struggle with fate. To these great issues Strauss's sure-fire theatrical devices—his pictorialism, his automatic program-making, his underlining of each situation—are tributary. In *Elektra*, he kept his unstaunchable cleverness in its place. The extreme chromaticism and discord, which sometimes seem willful in *Salome*, are always relevant in *Elektra*, in which they are much more abundantly used. *Elektra*, too, is more singable than *Salome*. The voice parts, instead of doubling instruments in the orchestra, are throughout the note of color that sustains the balance of the palette. In *Salome*, the tone-poem base and the stage action practically dispossess the voice; in *Elektra*, Strauss, become a master of vocal declamation, establishes the parity of the vocal line without sacrificing the equilibrium of the whole structure. He did not damp down the orchestra, the result being that the singers have to work hard. But they work to effect. . . .

Schumann-Heink's feeling that Strauss would, in some measure, recant was justified by his next stage work, which was quite different from anything he had done before. "This time I shall write a Mozart opera," he said—and *Der Rosenkavalier* was the result. Hofmannsthal supplied the libretto, this time a farce satire laid in the Vienna of the mid-eighteenth century, and written in a broad Viennese dialect that shocked its first Vienna hearers, though they used the same idiom themselves. Hofmannsthal's book is a masterly mélange of the ridiculous, the coarse, and the pathetic, to all of which Strauss gave due consideration when he set it. This time, he disappointed the expectations of those in his audience who had come to regard him as a provider of clinical studies, pathological thrillers. *Der Rosenkavalier* is shocking, but it is not psychotic: the affair between the mature Marschallin and the seventeen-year-old Octavian is only mildly perverse, while Baron Ochs is merely a lecherous country squire. Of course, the version given in Germany is far more outspoken than that used at the Metropolitan, where, for example, the Marschallin is discovered on a sofa in Act I, and not in bed, and where some lines have been excised. But the libretto is no more suggestive than that of *Le Nozze di Figaro* or *Così fan Tutte*, while compared to *Salome* or *Elektra*, *Der Rosenkavalier* is healthy, bawdy fun—with just a tinge of Hofmannsthal's overripeness. . . .

Der Rosenkavalier has become a popular fixture at the Metropolitan—sixty-two performances by the end of the 1940–41 season—and several other great opera houses. It is probably the most popular opera composed since *Madama Butterfly*, and the chief reason is its uncommon allure. Not only is *Der Rosenkavalier* the most digestible of Strauss's three major operas, but one of the most digestible of modern stage works making use of an advanced harmonic technique. It is his most lush and entrancing work, like a single lyric outpouring. It is somewhat odd that Strauss, in his "Mozart" opera, cast his spells in the form of Viennese waltzes, but the answer to those who would have preferred him to use gavottes and minuets is that his anachronism comes off, for Strauss orchestrates a waltz as brilliantly as did Ravel. (Imagine a gavotte scored for full Straussian orchestra!)

It would have been better if Strauss had never brought up Mozart, for then *Der Rosenkavalier* could have been judged on its own merits, which are great.[1] The man who could create the sheer delight of the senses that is the scene of the presentation of the silver rose need not call falsely on the name of Mozart. But Strauss as much lacks proportion about himself as about the volume and complexity of his orchestration—*Der Rosenkavalier*, for all its charm, is overfreighted, too noisy, too elaborate. A smaller orchestra would have helped. As scored, the emotions of the characters are larger than life, and the orchestral riot that breaks forth when the Marschallin's lover leaves her, for the first time, without a kiss, is but one sample of a grave disproportion. These are major lapses in taste, but they do not prevent *Der Rosenkavalier* from brimming over with beauty. Nor is that all. It is peopled with convincing characters, two of whom—the Marschallin and Baron Ochs—are unforgettable full-lengths.

Der Rosenkavalier was a work of Strauss's high prime—he was not yet forty-seven when it had its première. Since then, he has written eight operas, two ballets, many songs, a symphony, a piano concerto for the left hand alone, a hymn for the opening of the Olympic Games, and a considerable miscellany of other music, his most recent effusion being an apparently Axis-inspired *Festmusik* to mark the twenty-six hundredth anniversary of the accession to the throne of Japan of the Emperor Jimmu. All of the operas have had titanically publicized premières, all have solved separate technical problems, and all have pages that do not shame the creator of *Salome, Elektra,* and *Der Rosenkavalier.* But, alas! only pages. Strauss seems to have fallen victim to something closely akin to premature senility. None of his

[1] By coupling his name with Mozart's, Strauss invited attack from his ill-wishers, among whom is Cecil Gray, who for years has pursued the G.O.M. of German music with unmitigated scorn. Writing in *A Survey of Contemporary Music,* he lashed out: "The divinely innocent and virginal Mozartean muse cannot be wooed and won like an Elektra or a Salome; all we find in *Der Rosenkavalier* is a worn-out, dissipated *demimondaine,* with powdered face, rouged lips, false hair, and a hideous leer. Strauss' muse has lost her chastity. Does he himself actually believe that *Der Rosenkavalier* is like *Figaro?* Are we to regard this declaration as a pathetic self-deception, or as the last crowning perversity? It would be difficult to say, and it is perhaps more charitable to infer the former."

later stage works has the cohesiveness, the vigor, or the over-all imagination that unified each of his three great operas. Technical victories are won, often of dazzling brilliance, but ever with material awkwardly, or not at all, related to his surroundings, or with material either appallingly banal or shoddily imitative of his own past inspirations.

In these later works, too, Strauss's indulgences in other people's styles break all restraint, and are substituted shockingly for his own lack of style. Cecil Gray was not too harsh when he complained: "The impurity of style and juxtaposition of dissimilar idioms which was always one of his outstanding faults is carried to a disconcerting extreme in *Ariadne auf Naxos* and *Die Frau ohne Schatten*. In the first, Mozart dances a minuet with Mascagni, and Handel with Offenbach; in the second, Wagner is reconciled to Brahms, and Mendelssohn to Meyerbeer. Needless to say, this admixture of styles is not effected with any deliberate satirical intention, but from sheer lack of taste and cynical indifference."

Of these later operas, the one that aroused the most hope was *Ariadne auf Naxos*, principally because it followed on the heels of *Der Rosenkavalier*. It was the main feature of a Strauss festival at Stuttgart, and the composer himself conducted its première, on October 25, 1912, with Jeritza as Ariadne, Jadlowker as Bacchus, and Sigrid Onegin in a minor role. It turned out to be a divertissement tacked on to a performance of Molière's *Le Bourgeois Gentilhomme* (itself with Strauss's vivacious incidental music—modern treatment of Lully). Its idea is good: a farce handling of the old *opera seria*, the tragic action being interrupted by five traditional masks from the *commedia dell'arte*, one of whom (Zerbinetta) sings a complex burlesque coloratura aria that is supposed to give the final *coup de grâce* to the traditional "mad scene." In this most trivial of his operas, Strauss overreached himself by emphasizing too much the total inconsequentiality of the proceedings. He used an orchestra of only thirty-seven players, which helped along its unquestioned intimacy, but made it hopeless for a large house even after he had given it a prologue and detached it from *Le Bourgeois Gentilhomme*. For this reason, the Metropolitan has never attempted it, though it has been given both in Philadelphia (November 1, 1928) and at the Juilliard School, New York (1934). At the Philadelphia performance, Helen Jepson, as Echo, made her operatic debut.

Die Frau ohne Schatten came in 1919. This elaborate moral allegory—an attempt to give *Die Zauberflöte* a sequel—was followed, in 1925, by *Intermezzo*, to Strauss's own book. Based on a little incident in his own life, *Intermezzo* is interesting only because of Strauss's attempt to provide set numbers suitable for true *bel canto* singing, the connecting tissue being a free, light type of declamation that has some of the naturalness of ordinary speech. Three years later, Strauss composed the last of his operas that have been heard at the Metropolitan—the ponderous, complicated, and apathetic *Die aegyptische Helena*, whose dreariness is a libel on the vivacious Helen of Troy. On that November 8, 1928, five months after the world première at Dresden, the sumptuous Urban settings, the choice of the beauteous and popular Jeritza for the name role, and the scholarly conducting of Bodanzky could not hide the fact that neither Hofmannsthal nor Strauss was any longer anything more than mediocre. It disappeared after one season.

The following year, Hofmannsthal died, leaving Strauss the libretto of a Viennese musical comedy, *Arabella*. In it, Strauss is remembering, but not always vividly, *Der Rosenkavalier*, and its several lyrically charming pages are not enough to carry a three-act opera. *Die schweigsame Frau* (1935), an extraordinarily raucous affair based on Ben Jonson's *Epicœne, or The Silent Woman*, had a Stefan Zweig libretto, and it was this collaboration with a Jew that temporarily made Strauss *persona non grata* with the Führer, who, moreover, resented his past collaboration with another "non-Aryan," Hofmannsthal. *Der Friedenstag* (1938), a political morality play along lines acceptable to the Nazi regime (even though it celebrates peace), restored the old gentleman to favor, and when *Dafne* was produced later the same year, high Nazi officials were in the audience, and Strauss had to respond to twenty curtain calls. The final kiss of peace came in 1939, when Hitler journeyed to Vienna expressly to hear *Der Friedenstag* and congratulate Strauss on his seventy-fifth birthday.

It is a long, sad story—these last thirty years. It is the story of one of the foremost masters of every kind of musical technique sinking to complete spiritual incompetence. . . . He occupies much the same position in the history of German opera that Puccini occupies in Italian: just as the latter came after Verdi, and developed certain new ideas in the musical atmosphere without himself becoming an evolutive force, so Strauss followed Liszt and Wagner, carrying their methods to extremes, and leaving them there without any tentacles waving to the future. What Paul Rosenfeld said of Strauss in general almost a quarter of a century ago applies peculiarly to his operas: "To us, who once thought to see in him the man of the new time, he seems only the brave, sonorous trumpet-call that heralded a king who never put in his appearance, the glare that in the East lights the sky for an instant and seems to promise a new day, but extinguishes again. He is indeed the false dawn of modern music."

WOZZECK

Olin Downes

Downes was an early champion of the work.

"Perhaps the most remarkable opera of the modern age."

Alban Berg's *Wozzeck* is perhaps the most remarkable opera of the modern age. One says "perhaps," because he would be a bold man indeed who would say what the world of fifty years hence will think of it. Is this weird, sordid, tragical and compassionate creation a last word in musical decadence and ultrasophistication, or is it a score prophetic of a tonal art subtler, emotionally more sensitive, psychologically more profound, than any other composer has predicated?

It is simple to say that this is a "period piece," the consequence of the despair and decadence of the exhausted Europe of the 1920's, following the First World War; that it represents a mood and an outlook of the past, applicable neither to the present nor the future of our civilization; that therefore it will in due course be outmoded and discarded by future generations. But this does not fit with present indications. *Wozzeck* saw the light in 1925, when it was looked upon as an anarchical offshoot of the Schönberg school of atonality—a first-class aberration, as the Doctor calls Wozzeck's hallucinations in the opera—of a composer of dubious powers. But the opera slowly gained headway, first in Middle Europe and neighboring countries. Then its radius began to widen. At this writing, it is twenty-seven years old. In the past five years alone it has advanced remarkably in the public's interest. It was an attractive feature of the international music festivals of Salzburg in 1951, Florence and Paris of 1952. England heard it for the first time in the previous year. . . . It was quiet for a long time in the United States, after two pioneer performances under Leopold Stokowski in New York and Philadelphia in 1931. It became a feature of the spring repertory of the New York City Opera Company in April of 1952. The Western world is more interested in this work in the mid-century than ever before. There is a further fact of great importance: in the year 1952 *Wozzeck* remains, at least so far as musico-dramatic technic is concerned, the most advanced opera of the modern era.

When *Wozzeck* first appeared, it gave the impression of an isolated experiment, an oddity of a certain school and trend of musical thought. It had, certainly, novel features. Its most unusual characteristic was Berg's use of eighteenth-century musical forms, such as the toccata, the fugue, the suite, the passacaglia, as part of its substructure; forms which would seem to stiffen and formalize the progress of the action, but which do nothing of the sort as Berg utilizes them. Then there was his use of the *Gesangsprache*—the song-speech, which is but a slight variant, if any, of Schönberg's *Sprechgesang*—speech-song. The singers employ a vocal production which is between singing and speaking, and which clings closely in rhythm and inflection, but *not* in pitch, to the music. As for the system of "atonality"—nontonality —Schönberg had fully established that before Berg had come prominently into public view. It is the system which dispenses entirely with the principles of harmonic relations and the gravitation of chords to tonal center which have been in force from the time of J. S. Bach to the present day. Some claim that this is merely twelve intervals of the chromatic scale, arranged in a tonal anarchy, resulting in music, if it can be called music, without form, and void. The atonalists have a remedy for that situation, in their invention of the device of the "tone-row." This is a series of tones made arbitrarily, we might say geometrically, from the fixed order, and serving as a structural basis for the composition; much as the old plain chant, used as a *"cantus firmus,"* was employed by the medieval masters to provide a center of departure for the counterpoint of the voices. Much could be said regarding the validity or nonvalidity of this theory, which has gained many adherents sinch Schönberg formulated it. The discussion is not essential here. In all music, particularly in the domain of opera, we are not concerned with the composer's technical methods, but with what he says. And the future will judge Berg by this criterion alone. And the present discovers that he has much to say.

But behind these external novelties of procedure, it is clear that *Wozzeck* has ancestors. Wagner is there, as he is in the whole development of Schönberg and his school. Debussy, also, is there, and the Strauss of *Salome* and *Elektra* and also Puccini, strangely as he may figure in this company. But these are assimilations, not imitations, and only represent the immense amount of discovery and invention accumulated by great masters of opera music for Berg's employment in his own way. Looked at from this angle, *Wozzeck* is one of the most eclectic scores that have been composed, and one that clings to no single system or method of composition to communicate its contents. Common chords are there, as well as other chords that had not been before on land or sea; and all are potent in original ways. Like it or not, the opera comes over the footlights. It is first-class theater. One may ask whether he is hearing music. It is all organized and integrated, masterfully, toward a dramatic end. The form is perfectly balanced and unified, and worked out in most exquisite and intricate style. The artist is passionately sincere, as well as master of his means. He is a neurasthenic: there is no question about it. He is both realist and psychologist. Fortunately—it is the redemption of his work, if there is redemption for it—he is two things, not one. He is a most sensitive artist, and a humanitarian to the bottom of his soul. This double aspect of his nature is luminous in the score. The story is sordid and tragical to a degree. It is told in terms prevailingly of bitterness and sardonic portrayal, yet also with tenderness and pity. By the side of passages about as dissonant as the human ear, fairly well inured to the ugliness of much contemporaneous art can tolerate, are other passages of a sudden shining beauty, even exultation, which move us deeply with the thought of the mercy of Him who is not unmindful of the fall of the sparrow. Of such constituent elements, as it appears to the writer, is this opera of Berg's made. It is significant that he, the disciple of Schönberg, had his doubts of the theory of atonality.

Another striking circumstance in the history of this opera, based on the drama by Georg Büchner (1813–37), is the manner in which the subject of social injustice is treated by Büchner, who died in exile by reason of his democratic political beliefs, and the recurrence of this theme in Berg's consciousness a century later. An actual event in Germany led to Büchner's play, or at least the sketches for it that were found among his papers after he died. This event was the murder in Leipzig, in 1821, by one Johann Christian Woyzeck, an ex-soldier and apoplectically inclined barber, age 41, of his mistress, a widow of 46, with whom he consorted for two years, but who, at the same time, appears to have had an unfortunate penchant for soldiers. Resentful of her treatment of him, and in a jealous rage at her accessibility to others, Woyzeck one day bought a knife and killed her.

What made the case unusual in view of its tawdry criminal character was the lawyer's defense of a killer who made no attempt to escape his sentence, appearing to seek the supreme penalty rather than evade it. The trial centered upon the question of whether this man was a deliberate criminal or a maniac. It was shown that he had had hallucinations and a persecution complex, and believed that he was pursued with inimical purpose by Freemasons. For a period of eighteen months, noted psychiatrists and legal lights were engaged to thrash out the question. The presiding judge, Hofrat Clarus, remained convinced of Woyzeck's moral guilt. Finally Woyzeck was executed in the Leipzig marketplace, August 27, 1824. But the case did not end there. It was argued publicly and at great length for fourteen years, until in 1838 Hans Meyer published complete documents of the case and supported the Hofrat's decision. A. H. J. Knight, in his book, *Georg Büchner*, points out the significance of the long discussion of the affair, which he attributes in large part to the general intellectual attitude of the 1820's—E. T. A. Hoffmann's period, incidentally—toward the visionary mind, "the point being that the decade in question was divided, more than any previous decade, between a materialistic and a romantic explanation of the processes of the human mind and nature in general." This attitude of mind was doubtless Büchner's, whose father was a doctor and a free-thinker, and through whose office Büchner had complete access to the documents of the Woyzeck case.

Georg Büchner, an anatomist, a poet and dramatist who died in his twenty-fourth year, and who promised, had he lived, to become one of the greatest men in German literature, never completed or published the play which inspired Berg's opera the century after. His only publications were a drama, *Dantons Tod*, of which an opera has lately been made,[1] a treatise upon "The Nervous System of the Barbel" [2] which won him his doctorate at the University of Zürich, and a political pamphlet, *Der Hessische Landbote*, which got him into trouble. *Woyzeck*, which was the original name of the drama—was found among his papers after he died, as a series of sketched scenes, on partly unnumbered pages, some of them hardly legible, and some represent-

---

[1] *Dantons Tod*, Gottfried von Einem, 1947.

[2] Large European fresh-water fish with fleshy filaments hanging from mouth; Büchner was a student of Comparative Anatomy.

ing alternate versions of the same episodes. The confusion and im- preciseness of this material were such that Ludwig Büchner,[3] when he published a volume of his brother Georg's posthumous writings in 1850, did not dare include *Woyzeck* among them. But in 1875 the novelist, Karl Emil Franzos (1848–1904), secured access to this manu- script and published it with his own editing in 1879. It was the Fran- zos version, presented for the first time that season on the stage, which Berg saw in 1914, and used for his opera. It was not till 1922 that Fritz Bergemann completed his edition of Büchner's *Collected Works and Letters*, which exhibited in a glaring light certain of Franzos' errors. The extent of these may be gauged by the fact that Franzos had even misspelled the title of the drama, which was *Woy- zeck* and not *Wozzeck*. However, *Wozzeck* has remained ever since the title of the opera and various translations of the play. Franzos' own editorial interpolation, in the scene of Wozzeck's self-destruction in the pool of the last act, also remains. "He drowns" is the stage direction of Franzos, not Büchner. But the point need hardly con- cern us. The episode serves well Berg's purpose—Berg, who said wisely that the composer must be his own stage manager.

And in certain respects the brief, sketchy nature of the scenes of *Wozzeck*, as they fell into Berg's hands, also served his purpose in a way ideal for the composer. . . . Novels have been cut, tightened, altered in sequence to make drama, and dramas have in turn been shortened and condensed to make practicable scenarios for treatment by the composer. Here the material of the various episodes was al- ready present in a highly condensed form, which concentrated action and emotion in a few sentences, and left the composer room to ex- pand these moments freely with his music. Berg, however, used the surgeon's knife with great skill. The twenty-six scenes he cut to fifteen, five each for the three acts, and he connected his scenes, as Debussy does in *Pelléas et Mélisande*, by orchestral interludes between the fall- ing and rising of each curtain. He had commenced work upon the libretto in 1914, when he was called to military duty, for which he was later found unfit. He finished the book in 1917. He finished the composition of the music in 1920, and completed the orchestration in April of 1921. Four years later came the première of the opera.

[3] Physician and noted philosopher.

OPERA HOUSES AND AUDIENCES

WHAT MAY BE SEEN AT THE OPERA

Henry Sutherland Edwards

> Edwards was a nineteenth-century English historian.
> Opera was his special love. He wrote a two-volume
> study, *The Prima Donna*, a *History of the Opera*, and
> a *Life of Rossini*. Like Cyrano, he could say the things
> he said in this poem lightly enough himself—but would
> "allow none else to utter them."

I've seen Semiramis, the queen;
   I've seen the Mysteries of Isis;
A lady full of health I've seen
   Die in her dressing-gown, of phthisis.

I've seen a wretched lover sigh,
   "*Fra poco*" he a corpse would be,
Transfix himself, and then—not die,
   But coolly sing an air in D.

I've seen a father lose his child,
   Nor seek the robbers' flight to stay;
But, in a voice extremely mild,
   Kneel down upon the stage and pray.

I've seen "Otello" stab his wife;
   The "Count di Luna" fight his brother;
"Lucrezia" take her own son's life;
   And "John of Leyden" cut his mother.

I've seen a churchyard yield its dead,
   And lifeless nuns in life rejoice;
I've seen a statue bow its head,
   And listened to its trombone voice.

I've seen a herald sound alarms,
　Without evincing any fright:
Have seen an army cry "To arms"
　For half an hour, and never fight.

I've seen a naiad drinking beer;
　I've seen a goddess fined a crown;
And pirate bands, who knew no fear,
　By the stage-manager put down;

Seen angels in an awful rage,
　And slaves receive more court than queens,
And huntresses upon the stage
　Themselves pursued behind the scenes.

I've seen a maid despond in A,
　Fly the perfidious one in B,
Come back to see her wedding day,
　And perish in a minor key.

I've seen the realm of bliss eternal
　(The songs accompanied by harps);
I've seen the land of pains infernal,
　With demons shouting in six sharps!

HANS CASTORP LISTENS TO THE GRAMOPHONE

from *The Magic Mountain*

Thomas Mann

> In the snowy fastness, Hans Castorp, the febrile hero
> of the novel—"life's delicate child"—discovers music.
> He alone among the guests of the sanitorium takes
> charge of the "mysterious object" standing in the salon.

Evening, after the social quarter-hour, when the guests were
gone, was his best time. He remained in the salon, or returned stealth-
ily thither, and played the gramophone until deep in the night. He
found there was less danger than he had feared of disturbing the
nightly rest of the house; for the carrying power of this ghostly music
proved relatively small. The vibrations, so surprisingly powerful in
the near neighborhood of the box, soon exhausted themselves, grew
weak and eerie with distance, like all magic. Hans Castorp was alone
among four walls with his wonder-box; with the florid performance of
this truncated little coffin of violin-wood, this small dull-black temple, before the open double doors of which he sat with his hands
folded in his lap, his head on one side, his mouth open, and let the
harmonies flow over him.

These singers male and female whom he heard, he could not see;
their corporeal part abode in America, in Milan, Vienna, St. Petersburg. But let them dwell where they might, he had their better part,
their voices, and might rejoice in the refining and abstracting process
which did away with the disadvantages of closer personal contact, yet
left them enough appeal to the sense, to permit of some command
over their individualities, especially in the case of German artists. He
could distinguish the dialect, the pronunciation, the local origin of

these; the character of the voice betrayed something of the soul-stature of individuals, and the level of their intelligence could be guessed by the extent to which they had neglected or taken advantage of their opportunities. Hans Castorp writhed when they failed. He bit his lips in chagrin when the reproduction was technically faulty; he was on pins and needles when the first note of an often-used record gave a shrill or scratching sound—which happened more particularly with the difficult female voice. Still, when these things happened, he bore with them, for love makes us forbearing. Sometimes he bent over the whirring, pulsating mechanism as over a spray of lilac, rapt in a cloud of sweet sound; or stood before the open case, tasting the triumphant joy of the conductor who with raised hand brings the trumpets into place precisely at the right moment. And he had favorites in his treasure-house, certain vocal and instrumental numbers which he never tired of hearing.

One group of records contained the closing scenes of a certain brilliant opera, overflowing with melodic genius, by a great countryman of Herr Settembrini, the doyen of dramatic music in the south, who had written it to the order of an Oriental prince, in the second half of the last century, to celebrate the completion of a great technical achievement which should bind the peoples of the earth together. Hans Castorp had learned something of the plot, knew the main lines of the tragic fate of Rhadames, Amneris, and Aïda; and when he heard it from his casket could understand well enough what they said. The incomparable tenor, the princely alto with the wonderful sob in its register, and the silver soprano—he understood perhaps not every word they said, but enough, with his knowledge of the situation, and his sympathy in general for such situations, to feel a familiar fellow-feeling that increased every time he listened to this set of records, until it amounted to infatuation.

First came the scene of the explanation between Rhadames and Amneris: the king's daughter has the captive brought before her, whom she loves, whom she would gladly save for her own, but that he has just thrown away for the sake of a barbarian slave—fatherland and honor and all. Though he insists that in the depth of his soul honor remains untarnished. But this inner unimpairment avails him little, under the weight of all that indisputable guilt and crime, for he has become forfeit to the spiritual arm, which is inexorable toward human weakness, and will certainly make short work of him if he does not, at the last moment, abjure the slave, and throw himself into the royal arms of the alto with the sob in her register—who, so far as her voice went, richly deserved him. Amneris wrestles fervidly with the mellifluous but tragically blind and infatuated tenor, who sings nothing at all but "In vain" and "I cannot," when she addresses him with despairing pleas to renounce the slave, for that his own life is in the balance. "I cannot" . . . "Once more, renounce her" . . . "In vain thou pleadest"—and deathly obstinacy and anguished love blend together in a duet of extraordinary power and beauty, but absolutely no hope whatever. Then comes the terrifying repetition of the priestly formulas of condemnation, to the accompaniment of Amneris's despair; they sound hollowly from below, and them the unhappy Rhadames does not reply to at all.

"Rhadames, Rhadames," sings the high priest peremptorily, and points out the treason he has committed.

"Justify thyself," all the priests, in chorus, demand.

The high priest calls attention to his silence, and they all hollowly declare him guilty of treason.

"Rhadames, Rhadames," sings the high priest again. "The camp thou hast left before the battle."

And again: "Justify thyself." "Lo, he is silent," the highly prejudiced presiding officer announces once more; and all the priests again unanimously declare him guilty of treason.

"Rhadames, Rhadames," for the third time comes the inexorable voice. "To Fatherland, to honor and thy King, thy oath thou hast broken"—"Justify thyself," resounded again. And finally, for the third time, "Traitor," the priestly chorus proclaims, after noting that Rhadames has again remained absolutely silent. So then there is nothing for it: the chorus announces the evildoer for judgment, proclaims that his doom is sealed, that he must die the death of a deserter and be buried alive beneath the temple of the offended deity.

The outraged feelings of Amneris at this priestly severity had to be imagined, for here the record broke off. Hans Castorp changed the plate, with as few movements as possible, his eyes cast down. When he seated himself again, it was to listen to the last scene of the melodrama, the closing duet of Rhadames and Aïda, sung in the underground vaults, while above their heads in the temple the cruel and bigoted priests perform the service of their cult, spreading forth their arms, giving out a dull, murmurous sound. *"Tu—in questa tomba?"* comes the inexpressibly moving, sweet and at the same time heroic voice of Rhadames, in mingled horror and rapture. Yes, she has found her way to him, the beloved one for whose sake he has forfeited life and honor, she has awaited him here, to die with him; and the exchange of song between the two, broken at times by the muffled sound of the ceremonies above them, or blending and harmonizing with it, pierced the soul of our solitary night-watcher to its very depth, as much by reason of the circumstances as by the melodic expression of them. They sang of heaven, these two; but truly the songs were heavenly themselves, and heavenly sweet the singing of them. That melodic line resistlessly traveled by the voices, solo and *unisono*, of Rhadames and Aïda; that simple, rapturous ascent, playing from tonic to dominant, as it mounts from the fundamental to the sustained note a half-tone before the octave, then turning back again to the fifth—it seemed to the listener the most rarefied, the most ecstatic he had ever heard. But he would have been less ravished by the sounds, had not the situation which gave them birth prepared his spirit to yield to the sweetness of the music. It was *so* beautiful, that Aïda should have found her way to the condemned Rhadames, to share his fate forever! The condemned one protested, quite properly, against the sacrifice of the precious life; but in his tender, despairing *"No, no troppo sei bella"* was the intoxication of final union with her whom he had thought never to see again. It needed no effort of imagination to enable Hans Castorp to feel with Rhadames all this intoxication, all this gratitude. And what, finally, he felt, understood, and enjoyed, sitting there with folded hands, looking into the black slats of the jalousies whence it all issued, was the triumphant idealism of the music, of art, of the human spirit; the high and irrefragable power they had of shrouding with a veil of beauty the vulgar horror of actual fact. What was it, considered with the eye of reason, that was happening here? Two human beings, buried alive, their lungs full of pit gas, would here together—or, more horrible still, one after the other—succumb to the pangs of hunger, and thereafter the process of putrefaction would do its unspeakable work, until two skeletons remained, each totally indifferent and insensible to the other's presence or absence. This was the real, objective fact—but a side, and a state of affairs quite distinct, of which idealism and emotion would have none, which was triumphantly put in the shade by the music and the beauty of the theme. The situation as it stood did not exist for either operatic Rhadames or operatic Aïda. Their voices rose *unisono* to the blissful sustained note leading into the octave, as they assured each other that now heaven was opening, and the light of its eternity streaming forth before their yearning eyes. The consoling power of this æsthetic palliation did the listener good, and went far to account for the special love he bore this number of his program.

He was wont to rest from these terrors and ecstasies in another number, brief, yet with a concentrated power of enchantment; peaceful, compared with the other, an idyll, yet *raffiné*, shaped and turned with all the subtlety and economy of the most modern art. It was an orchestral piece, of French origin, purely instrumental, a symphonic prelude, achieved with an instrumentation relatively small for our time, yet with all the apparatus of modern technique and shrewdly calculated to set the spirit a-dreaming.

Here is the dream Hans Castorp dreamed: he lay on his back in a sunny, flower-starred meadow, with his head on a little knoll, one leg drawn up, the other flung over—and those were goat's legs crossed there before him. His fingers touched the stops of a little wooden pipe, which he played for the pure joy of it, his solitude on the meadow being complete. He held it to his lips, a reed pipe or little clarinet, and coaxed from it soothing head-tones, one after the other, just as they came, and yet in a pleasing sequence. The carefree piping rose toward the deep-blue sky, and beneath the sky stretched the branching, wind-tossed boughs of single ash trees and birches whose leaves twinkled in the sun. But his feckless, daydreaming, half-melodious pipe was far from being the only voice in the solitude. The hum of insects in the sun-warmed air above the long grass, the sunshine itself, the soft wind, the swaying treetops, the twinkling leaves—all these gentle vibrations of the midsummery peace set itself to his simple piping, to give it a changeful, ever surprisingly choice harmonic meaning. Sometimes the symphonic accompaniment would fade far off and be forgot. Then goat-legged Hans would blow stoutly away, and by the naïve monotony of his piping lure back Nature's subtly colorful, harmonious enchantment; until at length, after repeated intermission, she sweetly acceded. More and higher instruments came in rapidly, one after another, until all the previously lacking richness and volume were reached and sustained in a single fugitive moment that yet held all eternity in its consummate bliss. The young faun was joyous on his summer meadow. No "Justify thyself," was here; no challenge, no priestly court martial upon one who strayed away and was forgotten of honor. Forgetfulness held sway, a blessed hush, the innocence of those places where time is not; "slackness" with the best conscience in the world, the very apotheosis of rebuff to the Western world and that world's insensate ardor for the "deed." The soothing effect of all which upon our night-walking music-maker gave this record a special value in his eyes.

There was a third. Or rather there were many, a consecutive group of three or four, a single tenor aria taking up almost half the space of a whole black rubber plate. Again it was French music—an opera Hans Castorp knew well, having seen and heard it repeatedly. Once, at a certain critical juncture now far in the past, he had made its action serve him for an allegory. The record took up the play at the second act, in the Spanish tavern, in crude Moorish architecture, a shawl-draped, roomy cellar like the floor of a barn. One heard Carmen's voice, a little brusque, yet warm, and very infectious in its folk-quality, saying she would dance before the sergeant; one heard the rattle of castanets. But in the same moment, from a distance, the blare of trumpets swelled out, bugles giving a military signal, at which sound the little sergeant starts up. "One moment, stop!" he cries, and pricks up his ears like a horse. Why? What was it then, Carmen asked; and he: "Dost thou not hear?" astonished that the signal did not enter into her soul as into his. "Carmen, 'tis the retreat!" It is the trumpets from the garrison, giving the summons. "The hour draws nigh for our return," says he, in operatic language. But the gypsy girl cannot understand, nor does she wish to. So much the better, she says, half stupidly, half pertly; she needs no castanets, for here is music dropped from the sky. Music to dance by, tra-la, tra-la! He is beside himself. His own disappointment retreats before his need to make clear to her how matters stand, and how no love affair in the world can prevent obedience to this summons. How is it she cannot understand anything so fixed, so fundamental? "I must away, the signal summons me, to quarters!" he cries, in despair over a lack of understanding that doubly burdens his heavy heart. And now, hear Carmen! She is furious. Outraged to the depths of her soul, her voice is sheer betrayed and injured love—or she makes it sound so. "To quarters? The signal?" And her heart? Her faithful, loving heart, just then, in its weakness, yes, she admitted, in its weakness, about to while away an hour with him in dance and song? "Tan-ta-ra!" And in a fury of scorn she sets her curled hand to her lips and imitates the horns: "Taran-tara!" And that was enough to make the fool leap up, on fire to be off! Good, then, let him be off, away with him! Here are helmet, saber, and hanger—away, away, away with him, let him be off, let him be off, off to the barracks! He pleads for mercy. But she goes on, scorching him with her scorn, mocking him, taking his place and showing in pantomime how at the sound of the horn he lost what little sense he had. Tan-tara! The signal! O heaven! he will come too late! Let him go, let him be off, for the summons sounds, and he, like a fool, makes to go, at the very moment when she would dance for him. From this time, so she will account his love!

He is in torments. She cannot understand. The woman, the gypsy girl, cannot, will not understand. Will not—for in her rage and scorn speaks something more and larger than the moment and the personal: a hatred, a primeval hostility against that principle, which in the accents of these Spanish bugles—or French horns—called in the love-lorn little soldier. Over that it was her deepest, her inborn, her more than personal ambition to triumph. And she possesses a very simple means: she says that if he goes he does not love her—precisely that which José cannot bear to hear. He beseeches her to let him speak. She will not. Then he compels her—it is a deucedly serious moment, dull notes of fatality rise from the orchestra, a gloomy, ominous motif, which, as Hans Castorp knew, recurred throughout the opera, up to its fatal climax, and formed also the first phrase of the soldier's aria, on the next plate, which had now to be inserted. "See here thy flow'r treasured well"—how exquisitely José sang that! Hans Castorp played this single record over and over, and listened with the deepest participation. As far as its contents went, it did not fetch the action much further; but its imploring emotion was moving in the highest degree. The young soldier sang of the flower Carmen had tossed him at the beginning of their acquaintance, which had been everything to him, in the arrest he had suffered for love of her. He confesses: "Sometimes I cursed the hour I met thee, and tried all vainly to forget thee" —only next moment to rue his blasphemy, and pray on his knees to see her once more. And as he prayed—striking the same high note as just before on the "To see thee, Carmen," but now the orchestration lends all the resources of its enchantment to paint the anguish, the longing, the desperate tenderness, sweet despair, in the little soldier's heart—— Ah, there she stood before his eyes, in all her fatal charm; and clearly, unmistakably, he felt that he was undone, forever lost— on the word undone came a sobbing whole-tone grace-note to the first syllable—lost and forever undone. "Then would an ecstasy steal o'er me," he despairingly asseverated in a recurrent melody repeated wailingly by the orchestra, rising two tones from the tonic and thence returning ardently to the fifth: "Carmen, my own," he repeats, with

infinite tenderness but rather tasteless redundancy, going all the way
up the scale to the sixth, in order to add: "My life, my soul belongs
to thee"—after which he let his voice fall ten whole tones and in deepest emotion gave out the "Carmen, I love thee!" shuddering forth
the words in anguish from a note sustained above changing harmonies, until the "thee" with the syllable before it was resolved in the
full accord.

"Yes, ah, yes," said Hans Castorp, with mournful satisfaction, and
put on the finale: where they are all congratulating young José because the meeting with the officer has cut off his retreat, and now it
only remains open to him to desert, as Carmen, to his horror, had
before now demanded he should.

> Away to the mountains, away, away,
> Share in our life, careless and gay,

they sang in chorus—one could understand the words quite well:

> Freely to roam, the world our home,
> Gaily to pass o'er land and sea
> And enjoy, all else excelling,
> Sweet liberty!

"Yes, yes," he said, as before; and passed on to a fourth record,
something very dear and good.

It is not our fault that it was French again, nor are we responsible
for its once more striking the military note. It was an intermezzo, a
solo number, the Prayer from Gounod's *Faust*. The singer, a character warmly sympathetic to our young man's heart, was called in the
opera Valentine; but Hans Castorp named him by another and
dearly familiar, sadness-evoking name; whose one-time bearer he had
come largely to identify with the operatic character whom the wonder-
box was making vocal—though the latter to be sure had a much more
beautiful voice, a warm and powerful baritone. His song was in three
parts: the first consisting of two closely related "corner" strophes,
religious in character, almost in the style of the Protestant chorale, and
a middle strophe, bold and *chevalieresque*, warlike, lighthearted, yet
God-fearing too, and essentially French and military. The invisible
character sang:

> Now the parting hour has come
> I must leave my lovèd home

and turned under these circumstances to God, imploring Him to take under His special care and protection his beloved sister. He was going to the wars: the rhythm changed, grew brisk and lively, dull care and sorrow might go hang! He, the invisible singer, longed to be in the field, to stand in the thickest of the fray, where danger was hottest, and fling himself upon the foe—gallant, God-fearing, altogether French. But if, he sang, God should call him to Himself, then would He look down protectingly on "thee"—meaning the singer's sister, as Hans Castorp was perfectly aware, yet the word thrilled him to the depths, and his emotion prolonged itself as the hero sang, to a mighty choral accompaniment:

> O Lord of heaven, hear my prayer!
> Guard Marguerite within Thy shelt'ring care!

ITALIAN OPERA IN NEW YORK

Lorenzo da Ponte

> Mozart's librettist ended his life in America, being un-
> successful at one thing after another. He tried the
> grocery business, the wine and liquor trade, dealing in
> tobacco, and giving instructions in the Italian language
> at Columbia College, where he was befriended by the
> Reverend Clement Moore, author of "A Visit from St.
> Nicholas." His memoirs were published in New York.

"*My* Don Giovanni."

Although I was glad to see the cultivation of Italian letters
was daily increasing both in New York and in other towns of the
United States, I believed there was another means of diffusing them
and bringing them more into esteem, but to tell the truth, I did not
dare to hope for it. So what was my joy when several people assured
me that the famous Garcia[1] with his wonderful daughter [2] and other
Italian singers, was coming from London to America—to New York, to
be exact—to start Italian opera, the object of my greatest desire. Indeed he came, and the effect was amazing. It is impossible to imagine
the enthusiasm roused among the cultured part of the nation by our
music, when performed by artists of the first rank and great merit.
Rossini's universally admired and famed *Barbiere di Siviglia* was the
opera which was as the root from which sprang the great musical tree
of New York. A young American of great ability and a lover of music,
was speaking of it to his friends as if ex cathedra in my presence one
day shortly before our singers arrived. As his opinions seemed to me
to be mistaken, I said jokingly to him, "Be silent, Solomon, you don't
yet know anything about music."

[1] Manuel Vicente Garcia (1775–1832), the Spanish singer and composer.
[2] Marie-Felicité, better known as Madame Malibran.

From *Memoirs of Lorenzo da Ponte*, by permission of Routledge & Kegan Paul Ltd.

He began to get angry with me, but I begged him to calm himself, and promised him I would soon convince him.

Some time after, Garcia arrived. Rossini's *Barbiere di Siviglia* was announced for the opening of the theater,[3] and I took the young man and some of my other pupils to the fifth rehearsal. The wonderful music enraptured them and others who were present in an ecstasy of delight. Perceiving by the perfect silence, the look of faces and eyes, and the continued clapping, what a marvelous effect the music produced, I went up to the incredulous one when the rehearsal was over, and asked him what he thought of it. "Signor Da Ponte," he said generously, "you are right. I own with real pleasure that I did not know an iota about music."

The first performance produced a similar effect on everyone who had any ear at all or had no particular interest to speak ill of it,[4] either in order to assign the first place in music to other countries or exalt to the skies the "crowning" of some seductive warbler. In spite of their talk, the excitement over our music was so continuous, that there were very few evenings when the theater was not filled by a very large and select audience, and those rare occasions were due, I think, to a lack of patience on the part of the Spanish director.

What interest I took in the continuation and success of the undertaking may readily be imagined without my telling. I well foresaw the advantages to our literature, and how our language would be spread abroad through the attractions of the Italian opera, which is regarded by all the cultured nations in the world as the noblest and most delightful of spectacles which human genius has invented, and to the perfecting of which the noblest arts assist.

But however fine and esteemed Rossini's operas might be, it seemed to me that it would be an excellent thing to be more sparing of their performance and to alternate them with those of some other composer, both for the fame of Rossini and for the cash box of the producers. A good chicken is certainly a delicious dish, but when it was repeated many times in a banquet given by the Marchioness of Monferrato to the King of France, he asked her if nothing but chicken grew in that part of the world.

I spoke to Garcia about it. My idea pleased him, and on hearing that I proposed my *Don Giovanni* set to music by the immortal Mozart, he uttered a cry of joy and said, "If we have got a cast suf-

[3] The Park Theatre, Park Row.

[4] One gloomy journalist honored the Italian music with the epithet "monstrous."

ficient to give *Don Giovanni*, we'll give it at once. It is the finest opera in the world."

I was overjoyed at his reply, partly because I hoped it would be very successful, and partly from a great wish, which was natural enough, to see a drama of mine performed in America. When we looked into matters, it was found that there was no one in the company capable of singing the part of Don Ottavio. I undertook to find someone, and I found the man. As the impresario did not want to incur fresh expense, my friends and pupils and I between us paid for him, and *Don Giovanni* was staged. My hopes had not deceived me. Everything pleased, everything was praised and admired, words, music, actors and execution. Garcia's lovely, animated and charming daughter distinguished herself and shone in the part of Zerlinetta as her unrivaled father did in that of Don Giovanni.

Public opinion was in truth divided on the transcendent merits of these two prodigies of the musical world. Some preferred Rossini, others the German, and I really could not say whether *The Barber of Seville* or *Don Giovanni* had more partisans. It must be observed, however, that Mozart, either because he is no longer living, or because he is not Italian, not only has no enemies but is raised to the skies by the impartial and discerning; while Rossini has a very numerous set of enemies, some jealous of his fame, and others enemies from malice or the mean instinct to criticize and condemn anything wonderful that Italy may produce. . . .

An American gentleman, a great lover of music and well acquainted with our language (like the one who had lived many years in Italy and visited all the chief towns), was sitting near me at the theater during the performance of a successful drama. Toward the middle of the first act, turning to me with a smile, he said, "Signor Da Ponte, when this aria is finished, I shall settle down and go to sleep. When such and such a piece begins, please wake me up if I'm still asleep. I am pretty sure I shall sleep, for this wretched drama is the best soporific in the world, as are unfortunately nearly all those that come from Italy." I did not know what to answer him, and in a few moments I heard him snoring. I woke him up at the piece he had mentioned, after which he fell asleep again, or pretended to, and so for the rest of the opera, and then we separated.

Two or three days after, my *Don Giovanni* was to be played. In the morning I went to the theater and found his name written in the usual list of reserved seats, and as there was room for me in the same box, I at once put my name down for it. He was already in his seat when I arrived, so I sat at his side. Toward the end of the first act I wished to speak to him, but he almost angrily made me a sign to be silent, and when, after the finale, the curtain fell, he said, "Now speak. Oh, it is Signor Da Ponte! What did you want to say to me?"

"I wanted to ask you when you were going to settle down and go to sleep," I replied.

"Not before tomorrow," he answered. "You don't go to sleep at a performance of an opera like this, and you don't sleep after it all night."

A STORMY PERFORMANCE OF NORMA

Max Maretzek

> Maretzek was one of that popular breed of operatic impresarios of the nineteenth century, who by turns took over one opera house after another, competed with P. T. Barnum, and made and lost a good deal of money, mostly lost it. A *bon vivant* and picturesque figure, he too felt compelled to give the world his memoirs (1885) and he dedicated them to Berlioz. Whether the performance of *Norma* actually took place as he describes it is anybody's guess.

"Never was there a greater amount of merriment."

It was on a stormy evening in December, that the operatic Napoleon entered the dressing room of *our* king of modern tenors. He found him painting his face. In the first place, the two monarchs glanced at each other. Their glances were such as a lion and a tiger might exchange, in measuring each other's strength. The Napoleon of the Opera exulted, like a successful Machiavel, over his last demonstrable success, that of having vanquished the queenly Truffi. On the other hand, the prince of tenors was literally burning with indignation, and panting to avenge his blonde ally.

After a moment of awful silence, the Napoleon of the Opera said, with that laconic brevity which distinguishes him—"Friday, *Norma*.—You, Pollio!"

These four words were pronounced very slowly, and with an expression which would have caused a tremor in any other than the king of tenors.

Passing quietly a damp towel over the rouge upon his cheeks and the lamp black upon his eyebrows, he calmly responded—"Never."

"Never?"

"Neve-e-e-e-e-r!"

"Why?"

From *Crotchets and Quavers*.

"Arnoldi has taken the part. It is, and must remain his property."

"He took it, simply because you were sick."

"Only at your request. I was sick, simply to oblige you."

"But the public wishes specifically to hear you with Madame Laborde."

"Have the kindness then, to inform the public that the principal tenor of this operatic troupe only sings with the queen of prima donnas."

"That, sir, shall certainly be done."

Having registered this declaration, the Napoleon of the Opera rushed out of Benedetti's dressing room, and dashed upon the stage. He appeared before the astonished audience as unexpectedly as the ghost of Banquo rises through the trap at Macbeth's banquet, and, *apropos des bottes*, announces to the public who had assembled in the Astor Place Opera House, to hear and quietly enjoy *Lucretia Borgia*, that Benedetti had positively refused to sing in *Norma* on the Friday following.

Before anyone could understand what this extraordinary announcement might mean, he has vanished from the stage, and again stands before Benedetti.

Waving his hand, he grandiloquently exclaims, "I have now given you your deserts."

"Then I will now give you yours, you puppy and liar," replies the incensed royalty.

So saying, he draws his sword, and attempts with the flattened side of it (the edge was as blunt as stage swords invariably are) to castigate the manager.

A fierce struggle ensued. Unhappily, my dear Berlioz, (remember that I say this as one of the unlucky race of managers), the prince of tenors soon found the Napoleon of the Opera entirely in his power. Turning him round, he administered a kick to his enemy. It took effect in that part of his body where the completed dorsal bone terminates, and the leg has not yet begun. With its force, he was sent three or four paces beyond the limits of Benedetti's dressing room.

His equilibrium had been so forcibly disturbed, that he plunges out of it, and falls upon the boards. He is totally unable to resume the offensive with so powerful an opponent, and Benedetti remains the victor.

A committee of the subscribers who had heard the statement of the manager, then repaired to Benedetti to inquire into its truth; and what think you was his response?

With true Italian subtlety, he informed them that he had never dreamed even for one moment, of refusing to sing the part of Pollio. "Oh! dear, no!" he only required that some sort of apology should be made to Signor Arnoldi, "who was a very admirable singer." I leave you to imagine the spirit in which this last observation was made by Benedetti. You, who know, even better than I do, the hatred with which an Italian vocalist looks upon all who in any way supplant him or her, even for a moment, will be at no loss in divining this.

Satisfied with the expression of willingness to sing, upon the part of Benedetti, the committee retired, and left Mr. Fry to enjoy the fruits of the declared enmity which he had so wantonly provoked.

The public, however, are invariably the supreme judges in all matters of this description, and they were by no means so readily appeased. They had not heard the tenor's Italian and soapily improvised explanation. Simply did they understand, that the manager as well as the vocalist were both in the wrong. The manager, very decidedly so, by his perverse interruption of the quiet and orderly performance of the *Lucretia,* for the purpose of making an accusation of insubordination against one of his principal singers. This was when, be it remembered, he had yet eight and forty hours before him. In this period of time, he might very certainly, had he so chosen, have exhausted the various diplomatic means of persuasion which were at his disposal, before adopting the harsh and compulsory measure of appealing to the public. The error of the tenor was at the least as obvious. He had no right, upon his first impulse, to refuse positively singing at the side of an excellent and most estimable artist, whom, with a purblind insolence only to be found in Italian vocalists, he believed not equal to his own degree of merit.

Accordingly, upon the Friday evening in question, three distinct parties were to be found in the Astor Place Opera House.

These were the personal friends of the manager, those who supported the refractory tenor, and the public.

The first of these came simply and purely for the purpose of hissing Benedetti and sustaining Mr. Fry in his attempt to control him. This was, it must be confessed, my good friend, a very praiseworthy example of private friendship. The second of the three parties were the friends of the culprit. These appeared on this night with the purpose of doing precisely the contrary. This, you must grant, was at the least, to the full as praiseworthy. But the public also chose to be present en masse. A part of them undoubtedly came with the simple view of enjoying the row which was expected by all, a virtuous pleasure which is in general keenly appreciated by them. The remainder had, however, paid their money solely to have the satisfaction of giving a lesson to each of the belligerents.

Plans for the evening's campaign had been arranged beforehand by either of the two first parties.

Benedetti, who would be exposed to the primary outbreak of the popular indignation, artfully fomented by the friends of the management, was prepared with a lengthy speech. In it, he would touch upon every possible point of accusation against him. He would explain, modify, denounce, entreat, bully, and apologize—appealing to the well-known generosity and kindliness of the public, while he announced his thorough good will, and asserted his at the least as thorough good faith toward the management. In fact, it was a very commonplace, everyday sort of theatrical speech, with which he had primed himself—a sort of oration which the public, friend of mine, ought long since to have known by heart, but by which it is still content to be deceived on almost every occasion.

Thus read the program issued from the camp of the manager.

Benedetti was by all means to be hissed off the stage. Then, when the confusion had reached its highest point, Mr. Fry was to appear before the audience. After a flattering reception, he was to address the audience, and request, as a personal favor, their pardon for Benedetti. Was it not at once obvious, that all who were present would say, "What a noble-hearted, fine and generous fellow we now have for a manager!" After this, he would give utterance to a few modest remarks, composed expressly for this occasion, and then retire, followed by a sedulously prolonged and deafening cheering.

Now, let us see what really chanced upon this evening.

The house was crammed from the top to the bottom. Every seat was taken. The avenues in the parquet were thronged by those who had been attracted by the scandal. It was another proof, my dear Berlioz, that Art is by no means the principal thing to be cultivated by a management that would rejoice in attracting large audiences.

When the introduction was over,[1] Benedetti appeared. He was im-

---

[1] The opera on this occasion was of course the *Norma*.

mediately greeted by a storm of hisses, which were as quickly broken in upon by thunderous acclamation. This at length stilled, and he began to sing. That man, however, who would have heard a note after he had touched the first *bar*, must have had good ears. Screams, whistles, clapping of hands, hisses, trampling of feet, roaring, menacing outcries and gesticulations of every kind filled the theater. You might have imagined that the inmates of some half a hundred madhouses had broken loose, and crowded it upon this occasion. To catch a note from the orchestra, was as impossible as to listen to the singing. After a brief time, chaos having roared itself hoarse, began to shape itself into some intelligible form, and a few cries of "Order! order!" were occasionally heard.

"What order?" retorted the friends of the manager. "Off the stage with the rascal!"

"No! no! Go on, and give us a tune," roared the public.

"Order! order!"

"Off the stage with him! He wouldn't sing when we wanted him. He shan't sing, now."

"Apologize to Fry."

"Fry be d—d! Apologize to Madame Laborde."

"Never mind Laborde! Apologize to the public."

"The Public doesn't want an apology."

"Give us a song."

"Yes! yes! 'Yankee Doodle'!" shouted a portion of the public.

"We don't want 'Yankee Doodle.' 'Carry him back to Old Virginey.'"

"Order! Order!"

For some time, Benedetti stood all this very quietly. Occasionally, he would open his mouth with the attempt to sing. It was perfectly hopeless, and his lips would close again almost as quickly as they had separated. At length, he advanced a few steps, and performed a curious specimen of pantomime, supposed to be expressive of his desire to speak. As you and myself both know, the public is at all times a curious animal. Its curiosity at present, therefore, restored order. But this order menaced Mr. Fry's program of proceedings with the destruction of its utility. He and those of his friends who were with him, behind the scenes, trembled, lest by these means their own tactical arrangements might be turned by their astute enemy against themselves.

"Ladies and gentlemen!" said Benedetti, "I came here to sing—"

"So you did!"

"Why the deuce don't you, then?"

"Give us 'Yankee Doodle'!" roared out a voice from the gallery.

Benedetti gazed on the audience with an air of unabashed majesty, as he mildly inquired—"Shall I sing or withdraw?"

"Sing!"

"Withdraw!"

"Yes!"

"No!"

"Yes! Yes!"

"No! no!" were the cries and screams that broke from every part of the theater, while in the same roar from the gallery—"Give us 'Yankee Doodle'!" was again heard.

"No! No!"

"Yes! Yes! Yes!"

Now, whether this "Yes! yes!" applied to singing or withdrawing, or the vocalization of "Yankee Doodle," it would be impossible to say, and Benedetti stood for a moment completely nonplused.

To correct his misappreciation of their desires, he therefore repeated the question; and, drawing himself up in a graceful and expressive position, was preparing to proceed with the rest of his previously prepared speech, when the acuteness of one of Madame Laborde's friends frustrated his intention. This was Monsieur Nourrit, an old stager and old stage manager, who, seeing the turn matters were about to take, pulled the wire and gave the signal for dropping the curtain. Down it at once came, before the internally irate and externally most pacific tenor, cutting short any further colloquy between himself and the public.

With a brief compliment to Nourrit for his strategic skill, Mr. Fry settled his new pair of spectacles securely upon the bridge of his nose, and rushed out to the footlights.

But what was his astonishment to find that the flattering reception indicated in his program was by no means accorded him! There must have been some unaccountable error committed by those to whom his arrangements had been entrusted. He gazed wildly around the house, but hisses, catcalls, and objurgations couched in the most derogatory terms, were all that could be afforded him. In his horror, he would not even have endured it as long as Benedetti had done, but for the suggestions of some of the members of his orchestra. These, with a keen relish for his most unmistakable nervousness, encouraged him not to leave the battle ground. At length, agitated and trembling, he was permitted to stammer out his speech, hissed by the friends of the tenor, applauded by his own, and laughed at by the public, after which the performance was allowed to go on.

Never, possibly, had Benedetti or Laborde sung better, and very certainly, never was there a greater amount of merriment elicited from its hearers by any farce, than was then called forth by the lyrical tragedy of *Norma*.

THE ORIGINAL PURPOSE OF THE METROPOLITAN OPERA

Irving Kolodin

> Music and record critic, Mr. Kolodin has served as an
> official but wholly unprejudiced biographer to our lead-
> ing opera house.

"It is a relic of another day's thinking."

Opera has been given continuously at the Metropolitan
Opera House, 1423 Broadway, New York City, for nearly seventy-five
years—since its first season of 1883. In that time no work by a native
American—indeed, no work created on the North American Continent—has had any lasting success in its repertory. In this as well as in
other ways it has taken on a coloration peculiarly American.

As opposed to those countries (now including England) where
opera is given largely in the vernacular, opera at the Metropolitan is
given largely in the language of its original text. As opposed to those
countries (now, also, including England) where opera is state or
municipally supported, opera at the Metropolitan continues to struggle
along with only negative assistance from governmental groups. Mostly
this assistance has taken the form of tax relief. Though the budget of
the city of New York is larger than that of many European countries,
it gives not one penny of aid to this world-celebrated institution.

The international tinge of the Metropolitan and its lack of subsidy
thus denominate it "American," though it gave opera for seven seasons in German only, reached its greatest glory under the direction
of two Italians, and has most recently been directed by a Canadian
and an English subject of Austrian birth. One American, Herbert
Witherspoon, interrupted this sequence; but he died before his work
was fairly begun.

The Metropolitan is oddly American, too, in outliving the circumstances that brought it into being—indeed, the whole mental atmosphere that determined its location, size, and structure. Like the national Capitol in Washington (once a central point of a concentrated federation), it is a relic of another day's thinking, no longer suitable for the purpose it serves, and vastly more costly to maintain for that reason. It has eaten up its original cost many times over in deficits that persist for lack of plan or direction in meeting the changes, social and economic, of half a century.

Few of us today could imagine a society in which a mere whim could determine the existence of such a structure as the Metropolitan. Lilli Lehmann has recorded the circumstances in her memoirs, *My Path through Life* (New York: G. P. Putnam's Sons; 1914): "As, on a particular evening, one of the millionairesses did not receive the box in which she intended to shine because another woman had anticipated her, the husband of the former took prompt action and caused the Metropolitan Opera House to rise."

The box denied was, of course, in the Academy of Music, on Fourteenth Street, the fashionable home of opera in New York from 1849. The person denied was a Vanderbilt, most probably Mrs. William H. Her husband had but recently inherited a fortune from the family founder, Commodore Vanderbilt. Virtually all the boxes in the Academy were held by older elements of New York society, sufficiently venerable to be known as the Knickerbocker gentry. Their money dated from the Revolution; those whose money dated only from the War Between the States were considered tainted, no matter how much of it they had.

William H. Vanderbilt came into most of the family fortune (ninety-four million dollars) when his father died, in 1877. The heir lived only until 1885, by which time he had doubled the stake entrusted to him. In a time of such untaxed accumulation of wealth, the hundreds of thousands of dollars required to create the most lavish theater were barely consequential.

Vanderbilt could doubtless have done it by himself and held the theater as a physical chattel, as his heirs did as a social chattel through the long life of his daughter-in-law Grace Orme Wilson Vanderbilt (still living, in her eighties, in 1952, and the last recognized *grande dame* of New York society). But he was willing enough to share the burden with other eager millionaires excluded from the Academy of Music's box list.

The critical period may be dated from April 4, 1880, when it was noted in the *New York Times* that George H. Warren, a lawyer and broker affiliated with Vanderbilt, had conferred with a group of Academy stockholders: August H. Belmont and Messrs. Lorillard, Van Hoffman, and Dinsmore. All the Academy people could offer was a plan to add twenty-six boxes to the existing thirty. Obviously the old box-holders would remain the inner brotherhood. The offer was rejected.

Within the week (on April 7) Warren announced to the press that $800,000 had been subscribed to create a new opera house. He identified the leading participants in the plan as: "The two Roosevelts, Iselins, Goelets, the Astors, the three Vanderbilts, the Morgans, myself, and others." Had the building been erected on the first site chosen, the Metropolitan for all of these years would have stood on Vanderbilt Avenue, adjacent to Grand Central Terminal (between Forty-third and Forty-fourth streets); but the deeds to some plots forbade erection of a theater where the Biltmore Hotel now stands.

In mid-March, 1881, the present site on Broadway between Thirty-ninth and Fortieth streets was secured at an investment of $600,000. At the same time the capitalization was increased to $1,050,000. The rumor that this was a Vanderbilt project was dealt with in the *New York Times* of March 9, 1881: "Of the 10,500 shares, W. H. owns 300, W. K. 300, and Cornelius 150." This gave the one faction five boxes, however, not to mention those possessed by in-laws and business dependents.

Delays in taking possession of the site and ousting stubborn leaseholders made completion of the project by the target date of October, 1882, impossible. Even after construction had begun, with a foundation costing $125,000, increased costs of building materials caused gossip that the whole venture would be abandoned, or an apartment building substituted. At a meeting called to decide the issue in 1882, only fifty-one of the seventy stockholders appeared. Thirty-seven (a narrow majority of the whole) voted to go ahead on a capitalization now of $1,700,000. The final expenditure was $1,732,478.71.

Perhaps because of the added expenditure, it was decided to fill in the corners of the structure (originally indented for a modest kind of eye appeal) with rent-yielding apartments. As it was not unknown for a single ball, wedding reception, or other social function of the day to cost the host $200,000, the factor of cost alone could not have been considered crucial in this decision. Rather, it was that same concept of "good business" which impelled the elder Vanderbilt to haggle over the charge for a load of manure when he was a traction tycoon, and a struggling truck farmer (his son William H.) was the customer.

There are those who would cite the Metropolitan's exterior as no uglier, really, than that of the Bayreuth Festspielhous. Aesthetically the margin between them is narrow. But if severity is a characteristic of Wagner's exterior design, utility is a criterion of its interior planning. No such balance can be found in the American structure of 1883. At that, its instigators cannot be held wholly blamable. They can hardly have imagined that it would survive into an era of telephone, wireless, television, and jet planes. That it would survive such then still unbuilt marvels as the Singer Building, the New Theater—thirty years younger—and the Ritz Hotel (a construction of 1914) would have been regarded as palpable nonsense.

Whatever the majority sentiment, at least one member of the board of directors had a grasp of the business realities inherent in operating an opera house. Following one meeting to increase capitalization, James A. Roosevelt (fourth cousin of Franklin Delano) told a *Times* reporter on March 14, 1882: "We never expected that it would pay. No opera house in the world has ever paid as an investment, and none ever will."

If payment was lacking, other compensations were not. The house was first used on May 24, 1883, when the stockholders met to apportion the boxes. In a gambling spirit, location went by chance. From one hat, young Miss Warren drew a name; from another, Miss Townsend drew a number. As there were three less stockholders than the seventy boxes in the two tiers, Nos. 9, 24, and 35 remained unassigned. At the same meeting, an assessment of $5,000 was placed on each stockholder to underwrite completion of the business properties. And, to relieve the "pressure" on the dauntless millionaires, the Bowery Savings Bank granted a mortgage of $600,000.

Having gone so far as to provide New York with its most magnificent gaslit structure, the innovators intended to go no further. Operation of the theater was obviously the province of a professional who would entertain the public as Colonel Mapleson entertained it at the Academy of Music, and possibly make a profit as well. At that, the proposition was an inviting one, for the stockholders posted a guarantee of $60,000, against possible losses in a season of sixty-one performances. "All" the operator had to do was dress the stage and engage an orchestra, stars, and supers.

The contract was finally awarded to Henry E. Abbey, well known as a theatrical entrepreneur and manager of concert artists. His adviser on operatic matters was Maurice Grau, well versed in producing operettas and musical comedies. What Grau learned was of considerable value when he came into prominence a decade later; but it was an expensive education for Abbey. Henry H. Krehbiel (in *Chapters of Opera*) quotes an Abbey associate (Schoeffel) as saying that the loss of the single season was $600,000. Doubtlesss this included the fifty-four road performances.

In any case, the expense of outfitting nearly a score of operas would have placed a staggering burden on any single season's income. As well as paying such stars as Nilsson and Campanini one thousand dollars a performance, Abbey's lavish hand provided a wardrobe in which "every costume, every shoe and stocking was provided . . . by Worth of Paris." The witness to this extravagance was Lilli Lehmann, who came to New York two seasons later. Such matters could not fail to impress the unpretentious Lilli, whose frugality, when a reigning prima donna, extended to riding the horsecar to and from the theater rather than engaging a hack.

The directors met the obligation of their guarantee to Abbey, and also granted him the use of the theater for a benefit. This remarkable show added $16,000 to his personal fortune, but solvency was far away. He offered to run the theater for a second season without compensation of any kind if the stockholders would absorb his losses of the first, but the offer was laughed aside.

Had Ernest Gye, impresario of Covent Garden, London, not been married to the soprano Emma Albani, the history of the next decade could have been quite different. Gye had been in the running for the lease before Abbey was selected, and negotiations were resumed with him on the assumption that he might still be interested. His wife, he replied, would have to be considered in any plans he might make, which brought an end to the conversations. The stockholders were loyal to Nilsson, and no company of the time could accommodate more than a prima donna.

In the end the stockholders had neither Nilsson nor Gye. Faced with the penalty of keeping the theater dark (and meeting tax charges anyway) while the Academy of Music crowd enjoyed a triumph, they accepted from Leopold Damrosch an offer that transformed the Metropolitan, for a period of seven years, into a German opera house. A moving spirit in the musical life of New York since his arrival from Germany ten years before, Damrosch proposed his own services

as conductor and director for a season's salary of $10,000. The or-
chestra would be his own Symphony Society; choristers from the Oratorio Society (which he also conducted) could be utilized; and he
would recruit his principals from central Europe, thus avoiding the
expensive stars of the Italian and French theaters. An appeal to the
quarter-million persons of German extraction in New York would be
made by attention to the long-neglected Wagner repertory.

Damrosch was authorized to proceed in early August. Despite the
handicap of this late date, his knowledge of the situation on both
sides of the Atlantic supported his program. He gathered a company
able to perform *Rigoletto*, *William Tell*, and *La Juive* (in German),
as well as the promised Wagner. At a four-dollar top (Abbey had asked
seven), the public response was keen. By January, 1885, business was
running so far ahead of the previous year that Damrosch was encouraged to plan a second season. His salary was reduced to $8,000, but
he would share in the profits.

Damrosch did not live to see his scheme prosper, however. The
overwhelming work load of opera performances, plus his concert routine, made him an easy victim to pneumonia, and he died on February
11. The fight for the vacated post was both ugly and unpleasant, with
a prominent member of the company, Anton Schott, making noisy
claim to recognition. He later claimed credit for directing attention
to Anton Seidl, who was engaged as music director to succeed Damrosch; he did not otherwise add luster to the meager record of tenors
for sagacity.

As executive, the stockholders appointed Edmund G. Stanton, already serving as secretary to the board of directors. Young Walter
Damrosch was sent abroad to negotiate with Seidl, and to give glamor
to the roster by adding Max Alvary, Emil Fischer, and Lilli Lehmann
to the company.

The reduction in loss from $40,000 in the first Damrosch year to
$25,000 in the first year under Seidl was gratifying. The ecstatic ap-
proval of the largely German-dominated press was welcome. When
Mapleson gave up the fight at the Academy of Music in 1886, the
Metropolitan's stockholders could relax in contentment. Even his as-
persions against the "new yellow brewery on Broadway" could be
shrugged aside; likewise his historic farewell: "I cannot fight Wall
Street." Seidl was given a three-year contract, and the Germanization
of the theater proceeded.

As too frequently in the pattern of Metropolitan operation expedience and convenience took precedence over any other considerations of how a representative opera house should be conducted. If Abbey was willing to risk his fortune, Italian opera sufficed. If Damrosch and Seidl could save money by giving German opera, German opera sufficed. Many of the difficulties that beset the Metropolitan in those early years were inherent in the ill-assorted coterie that had produced the money in the first place. They accepted a yearly assessment as part of the expense of social position, but with more than a few mental reservations about other responsibilities.

So it was German opera for the next little while. When the time came for another decision in the spring of 1889, the advance sale for the next season stood at $80,000. This impressive figure could not be denied, and a vote to continue opera in German was upheld, 43 to 3. As may be noted, twenty-five stockholders did not even bother to vote.

So long as there was no alternative to German opera at minimum losses, impatience, indeed boredom with its "heavy" intellectual pressures, were endured. When the novelty of the Wagner repertory wore off, and damaging experiments with such minor composers as Nessler, Brüll, Smareglia, even the Duke of Saxe-Coburg, aroused objection in the press, a change became inevitable. The box-holders were all for getting out of the responsibility of opera-producing as soon as possible.

The alternative that presented itself could have been much worse. Abbey had recovered from his first season's losses and was again making money with such singers as Patti, Albani, Nordica, and Del Puente. Grau, now in his early forties, did most of the planning and direction of the company. When the company presented a season of old favorites in the Metropolitan in the spring of 1890, the tunes and their singers cast their usual spell. When the existing commitments to the German group were fulfilled, the lease was given to Abbey and Grau, to begin with the fall of 1891.

This decision was by no means unanimous, nor was it welcomed by that part of the press which represented the interests of the German-descended public. Without opera in German, they reasoned, there would be no German opera, a matter of distress to those wedded to contemporary ideas of Italian opera being "old-fashioned," and Wagner representing "the music of the future." In addition, many of the box-holders who had joined up in the first flush of social enthusiasm for the new meeting-place were finding the continuing responsibilities irksome.

As sometimes happens (if the participants are fortunate enough), a cumbersome situation was resolved by *force majeure*. For the Metropolitan stockholders it was the fire of August 27, 1892, which consumed, along with wood and walls, the softer elements of the membership. Only those who cared enough about opera not to count its cost or those who had so much money that the cost did not matter took up the burden of refinancing and reconstruction. By far the largest number of the newly formed Metropolitan Opera and Real Estate Company were in the second category, and they soon evolved a formula whereby important money losses were held to a minimum for three decades.

Through the terms of the lease with each producing group (until the sale of the property in 1940), the stockholders waived a rental charge, taking instead the use of the boxes for all subscription performances. Thus the opera-producing faction had no fixed rental to meet. On the other hand, those who occupied the most desirable seats in the theater—the only ones to which special prestige was attached—were relieved of any obligation or responsibility for the quality of work done. The contradiction inherent in this division of function has complicated much of the recent history of opera at the Metropolitan.

BACKSTAGE AT THE MET
from *Time* Magazine

"An extraordinary exercise in skill, timing, and logistics."

Most Americans, forever fascinated by the backstage know-how of the movies, TV, the theater or the circus, know little about how an opera is staged. It is actually an extraordinary exercise in skill, timing and logistics, far more involved than play production. Many opera plots include supernatural happenings and require complicated equipment; what is more, everything from magic fireworks to the basso's whiskers must move according to the music. Technically, one of the most demanding operas is Gounod's *Faust*, which opened the Metropolitan Opera in 1883. Last week *Faust* had its 317th Met performance, a matinee.

The Met is an old and barely adequate house. What it lacks in convenience it must make up with backstage savvy, proudly displayed by a crew of 152 electricians, carpenters ("grips"), prop men, *et al*. Best place from which to watch them at work is 44 feet above the stage, in the gloom of a narrow fly gallery. There, about lunchtime, Electrician Charlie Suhren started setting the lights for the first scene. As soon as his job was done, Charlie retired to a remote eyrie high in the cathedral vault of the stage, where he played solitaire until it was time to reset the lights for the next scene.

12 Noon. Almost all the cast and chorus are in the house, scattered through four floors of dressing rooms, getting into costumes, making up, vocalizing.

12:30. Carpenters and stagehands check in. Others have already hung all the drops (painted linen) in proper order, ready to be lifted or lowered. The newcomers go to work on the first-scene set, Faust's study.

12:45. Executive Production Manager David Pardoll adjusts a carnation in his lapel, leaves his tiny first-floor office and goes to his regular post in the wings.

12:50. The setting for Faust's gloomy study is in place. Books are piled on the desk and a large armchair has been carefully placed so that it screens an open trapdoor from the view of the audience.

12:52. A short, stooped man carrying a vocal score sits down quietly beside Pardoll. His name is Antonio Dell'Orefice, and he is one of the Met's seven "maestros"—unobtrusive musician of clerklike appearance whose job it is to follow the score and cue curtains, entrance, exits.

12:55. Master Mechanic Louis Edson looks over the stage set and okays it. General Manager Rudolf Bing marches purposefully across the stage but speaks to no one. Faust (Tenor Thomas Hayward) steps out of the elevator from his third-floor dressing room, looking uncomfortable in his heavy overcoat and old-man's false forehead and wig. Chief Electrician Rudolph Kutner checks with his assistant, stationed at a control panel in the hooded apron box next to the prompter's box.

12:57. Faust checks his props, takes his seat by the fireplace, opens a book on his lap. Backstage voices are hushed. In the darkness behind the study, the set for Scene 2 is all ready to be pulled into place: three sideshow stalls, a circular bandstand, the entrance to the Bacchus Inn. The chorus files in and Chorus Master Walter Taussig mounts a stepladder that is steadied by a stagehand. When he reaches eye level with a small hole in the canvas sidewall of Faust's study—through which he will be able to watch the conductor—Taussig opens his score, focuses a battery light on it and waits.

12:58.30. Pardoll sends Conductor Kurt Adler into the pit.

12:59. Pardoll signals for the house lights to be turned down. A stagehand grips the rope triggering the hydraulic mechanism that controls the curtain. Other stagehands are standing immobile in the wings. It is very quiet and cool. The opera is poised for flight.

1:00. Pardoll says: "Ready, everyone." The stooped maestro in the wings slides back a small panel and looks out at Conductor Adler. Adler starts the prelude. Four minutes later the maestro murmurs, "Ready!", then gestures abruptly. The stagehand bends his back to the curtain rope, and the heavy, golden brocade parts, rises majestically.

1:05. Faust sings of his despair. When he sees the coming of daylight, he closes the shutters. The pale sunbeams (supplied by a spot high up on Suhren's fly gallery) disappear. He threatens to kill himself, but—as Chorus Master Taussig on his stepladder gives the beat— women's voices offstage urge Faust to live.

1:08. In the basement, directly below Faust's vocal soul-struggles, Mephistopheles (Basso Nicola Moscona) paces nervously, dressed in evening clothes, red-lined Inverness cape, with top hat and cane. Three grips stand ready at the trapdoor platform. Another maestro, with a score on his lap, sits near by. Mephistopheles clears his throat, begins la-la-la softly. The maestro, straining to hear the orchestra, says "Ready!" and Mephisto steps onto the platform.

1:13. Faust sings, "A moi, Satan, à moi!" and throws his book into the fireplace. An electrician switches on a fan, which sends flame-colored paper streamers upward into sight of the audience. The basement maestro makes an abrupt pronouncement: "Up with him!" The stagehands lift the platform and Mephisto into the air. The audience first sees him sitting on the arm of the chair that screens the trapdoor, nonchalantly swinging his foot and cane. Meanwhile, behind the rear study wall, Marguerite (Soprano Nadine Conner) is climbing a narrow set of stairs to a platform, aided by a stagehand.

1:19. Mephisto flourishes his cane. Behind the scenery, backstage spots begin to glow, lighting Singer Conner; as a result, Faust and the audience see the vision of Marguerite through a scrimmed hole in the middle of Faust's bookcase. Faust, enraptured, signs away his soul to the Devil, drinks the potion to restore his youth. While Mephisto struts about flashing his cape to distract the audience, Faust rips off his old-man disguise and springs forward as a young man.

1:22. Curtain comes swiftly down and stagehands swarm on to strike the study set. Flats are restacked swiftly for transfer to trucks waiting back of the stage on Seventh Avenue, ready to take them to the warehouse (there is not enough room at the Met to store all the scenery). Choristers and dancers pour out from the wings to take their places in the Kermesse set for Scene 2. Gay carnival lanterns, already lighted, are strung across the stage. More than 170 people are moving about in seeming confusion.

1:24.30. Pardoll says, "Places, everyone." In the instant before curtain time the cast comes to Faustian life: a hand is raised in the beginning of a greeting, a head thrown back and a wine beaker tipped to the mouth; a pair of dancers in the wings are "on the mark" for a madcap dash across the stage; a girl on a ladder reaches up for a lantern.

1:25. Pardoll looks out at Conductor Adler, flips a switch and a small blue light goes on in the orchestra pit. Music. The curtain rises on "students, burghers, soldiers, maidens and matrons" three minutes after it fell on Faust's study.

The performance moves on through the carnival scene, the garden scene (a rubberized pool, rocks and lilies), the church, the public square (a tricky set with two flights of stairs). As the sets are changed, everyone backstage talks in normal tones, knowing that the thick silk-and-linen curtain deadens the noise. Pardoll urges everyone to keep an eye out for loose tacks. Even so, Met dancers are resigned to at least one pierced foot per season.

3:57. The last scene is under way. Marguerite, languishing in prison, calls on the angels to save her. The chorus, already in street clothes, is massed in the wings.

4:07. Marguerite dies far out on the apron, and Mephisto pronounces her damned forever. Offstage, the angel chorus contradicts him. Marguerite is saved. She rises, turns, a scrim comes down slowly and the prison walls vanish upward. Master Mechanic Edson cautions: "Ready, boys." Half a dozen stagehands stare at a glowing red bulb, and when the light flicks off, they pull their ropes like bell ringers. Pearl-gray drops rise as the pearly gates open before Marguerite. The sighs and stirrings of the audience can be heard through Gounod's music.

4:09. The great gold curtain comes down with a sound like a chorus of schoolgirls whispering secrets.

4:10. Pardoll shepherds the principals through their curtain calls. Meanwhile, all the colored lights die, the harsh work lights come on and the last drop is flown. The great stage is once more an ugly warehouse. The maestros put away their scores and go out to eat. Charlie Suhren puts away his cards and climbs up to the fly gallery to change the colors on his spotlights. Production Manager Pardoll deposits his carnation in a glass of water.

Before the last star has changed to street clothes, the first scene is being set for the night's performance (*Aïda*).

OPERA WAR

Vincent Sheean

> This is the story of the exciting days (1906) when New
> York had two great opera companies and the Metro-
> politan faced real competition, all to the benefit of
> New York's operagoers. The war was declared by Oscar
> Hammerstein I, German-American cigar maker, play-
> wright, and theatrical entrepreneur. He introduced to
> New York *Pelléas and Mélisande, Louise, Salome,* and
> *Elektra,* among others. After four years of intense com-
> petition, he sold out to the Metropolitan, and agreed
> that he would not produce opera in the United States
> for a period of ten years. The present excerpt from
> Vincent Sheean's biography follows the course of the
> enterprise to the open declaration of hostilities. Ham-
> merstein was eventually defeated, more by his own reck-
> lessness than by the lances of competition.

"The war was on and the warrior was happy."

The Manhattan Opera House was actually completed, as all
the newspapers of the day inform us, about one hour before the curtain rose on its first performance. Apparently the paint was, as usual
with Hammerstein, still wet in many places. There was never enough
time for Hammerstein: he seems to have made his dates purposely
difficult to meet, perhaps with the notion that if he did not, there
would be some doubt of getting the job done at all.

Originally he entertained the idea that he could give opera at
fairly reasonable prices—opera for the masses. He discovered very early
that this would not be possible if he used internationally known
singers, all of whom demanded large fees, and if the chorus and orchestra were to be kept up to standard. The fiendish expense of opera
production was by no means unknown to Hammerstein, but he had

never until now embarked on the really big enterprise of a full international company. He learned, to his sorrow, how expensive rehearsals can be and how necessary they are, and it is immensely to his credit that he gave his principal conductor, Cleofonte Campanini, all the rehearsal time he demanded during the first three seasons.

Leaving the actual building of the house more and more to Arthur, the Old Man set himself throughout 1905 to the task of organizing his company. He wanted, of course, some internationally famous singers to counterbalance the Metropolitan's Caruso and Sembrich.

The most famous singer in the world was undoubtedly Nellie Melba, and Hammerstein determined to get her at almost any cost. Aside from Caruso, the reigning tenor of the Italian opera houses was Alessandro Bonci, who had never yet been heard in the United States. Maurice Renaud was an idol at the Paris Opéra; he was a baritone of the grand style, a Don Giovanni beyond compare at the time. The Metropolitan had held a contract with him and had allowed it to lapse, paying him damages, and thus he too had not yet been heard in New York. Charles Dalmorès, then young and very handsome, was at the beginning of his renown as a dramatic tenor in French and Italian operas. The sumptuous basso of Vittorio Arimondi, the *buffo* skills of Charles Gilibert, and the imposing contralto of Eleanora de Cisneros were all available. De Cisneros (born Eleanor Broadfoot) had been heard briefly at the Metropolitan in small parts; her subsequent career had been in Europe. Mary Garden was the queen of the Opéra Comique in Paris, and although Hammerstein was unable to get her to America for his first season, there is no doubt that he had her in mind from the beginning. He went to Europe to sign contracts with these and other singers.

It is impossible not to tell the Melba story, although it is equally impossible to guarantee its veracity. It appears that Mme. Melba had no wish to come to the United States at all, and no particular desire to associate herself with a new opera company in any case. Mr. Hammerstein went to see her at the Grand Hôtel in Paris, where she was living during engagements at the Opéra. He could not prevail upon her. Melba was immensely successful and rich; large fees did not dazzle her any more; she was in demand in every opera house in the world, from St. Petersburg to Buenos Aires. Her silvery tones were still at their loveliest, and there was a cloud of legend about her. Her romance with Philippe d'Orléans, pretender to the throne of France, may have been partly responsible for her reluctance to revisit America, as it was also responsible for much of her contemporary legend.

For whatever reasons, Hammerstein failed utterly. The legend is that in his last interview, in her sitting room at the hotel, he accepted her decision with a bow and then, taking a wad of thousand-franc banknotes from his coat pocket, he opened it out fanwise and threw it into the air. The banknotes fell all over the room. Mme. Melba stared at him in utter amazement. He bowed again and left. As he walked down the corridor he was pursued by the sound of Melba's helpless laughter, apparently a highly robust noise. She signed the contract the next day.

The most decisive of Hammerstein's acts in the formation of his company was the engagement of Cleofonte Campanini as principal conductor. This remarkable animator and inspirer of great operatic performances was the younger brother of the heroic tenor Italo Campanini and was married to Eva Tetrazzini, elder sister of Luisa. Hammerstein had made an effort to get the services of Arturo Toscanini, then chief conductor at La Scala in Milan, but without success. Toscanini at that time was much too wedded to the Scala to think of America; and when he finally came over, it was to join the Metropolitan as part of an arrangement including Giulio Gatti-Casazza as general manager.

Campanini, older than Toscanini, had worked in his youth at the Metropolitan, but in his maturity had not yet appeared in the United States. He was an indefatigable worker who could rehearse all day every day and conduct practically every night. His command of all the forces—orchestra, chorus, and principals—was of an electrical kind which New York had not so far experienced. For a new opera company containing many artists who had never sung together it was all-important to have a conductor of this quality, and Hammerstein recognized it so amply that he gave Campanini practically unlimited authority over every detail of performance. As the Metropolitan had nothing of similar caliber—Arturo Vigna, its chief Italian conductor, was a listless time-beater—Hammerstein began with a formidable advantage. Campanini's prestige in the opera houses of Europe was also useful, as many singers who were otherwise timorous about the new enterprise were reassured by his presence.

Another element in Hammerstein's company for which he was personally responsible was his chorus. He recruited it from the young people of the New York voice studios, for the most part, adding experienced choristers from Italy just as the season was about to begin. His chorus had youth, looks, voices, and ambition. It is seldom that one reads such praise as the New York music critics lavished upon this chorus, so often the least regarded part of opera production.

In this particular season the choristers were making news at the Metropolitan in a wage dispute with Conried; they went on strike and the Metropolitan was without a chorus for a few days. Hammerstein wanted no difficulties of that sort, and when his American chorus asked for half-pay for the three weeks of preseasonal rehearsal, he gave it to them at once.

In the staff assembled through 1905 to deal with the administration of the new opera company there were some notable figures. William J. Guard, the press agent of the Manhattan, made a place for himself in New York life then and for many years afterward when he went to the Metropolitan. "Billy" Guard he was called, and he was both amiable and astute; Hammerstein often had occasion to be grateful for his high professional skill. There was no need to persuade the papers to write about Hammerstein—he was now and had been for years eminently newsworthy—but there were often times when manipulation of the news became necessary. The subscription department and box office in general were in the hands of Lyle Andrews, another Hammerstein stalwart.

Arthur Hammerstein, having built the theater, was now pressed into service by his father as a sort of general aide-de-camp ("my four years of opera torture," he called it) and learned how to face the innumerable difficulties of the impresario. Jacques Coini, a stage director of great talent, was imported from Brussels to see the staging of the operas, and Hammerstein's old friend Mme. Freisinger, who had worked with him on earlier productions, undertook to supply all the costumes. When Hammerstein went to her he was without ready cash—the building of the theater had taken all he possessed —so the good lady invested twenty thousand dollars of her own money in the materials she needed to dress the repertoire.

Hammerstein's plans aroused intense curiosity in the press and public. This was not only because of his picturesque personality, but because the actual enterprise was so daring, so hazardous, so improbable. One man alone, without financial backing other than the profits of his vaudeville theater, was undertaking to rival the entrenched and highly organized Metropolitan Opera.

Hammerstein was owner, builder, and architect of his own theater, producer, director, everything rolled into one. There was something intensely appealing about his valor, his high spirits, his unquenchable optimism. He seemed to know and care so little about the powers of New York society and finance, the great Astor-Morgan combination upon which he was making war. As we read the press of 1906 we come across constant expressions of the admiration and wonder with which the writers—W. J. Henderson, Richard Aldrich, and the rest—watched his course. They all knew, probably a good deal more accurately than he did, what he was up against, what forces would almost inevitably combine to crush him. The favorable attitude of the press was a result of this admiration, and Hammerstein made use of it abundantly. Almost every day he would give forth some kind of statement, divulging his projects piecemeal so that each separate item got its full value in the newspapers.

In some of these statements he was playing the press as a fisherman plays a big fish. All through 1905–6 there were statements of one sort or another about the De Reszke brothers. Mr. Hammerstein was "negotiating" with them; Mr. Hammerstein "hoped" to get Jean de Reszke out of retirement; Mr. Hammerstein was going to bring Édouard de Reszke back in any case. The fact seems to be that there never was any question of Jean de Reszke returning to the stage or to America. Hammerstein did have an option on the services of Édouard de Reszke, but sacrificed it when he heard the basso sing a concert in Paris; the voice was no longer equal to the needs of opera. Whatever the truth of the matter, the name of the De Reszke brothers was always good for a newspaper story, and Hammerstein used it for that purpose. The same was true of Melba and, to a lesser degree, of Bonci.

Hammerstein joined battle almost at once over *La Bohème*, and for Melba's sake. Her Mimi was famous, the great success of all her later career, and Hammerstein "positively announced" it a number of times although the publishing house of Ricordi in Milan retorted that the Metropolitan had exclusive rights to it.

The right and wrong of the matter cannot be determined exactly. Certainly Hammerstein thought he had a verbal agreement with George Maxwell, Ricordi's New York representative, covering all the Puccini operas. He was also convinced that it was not the Ricordi firm but the Metropolitan and Conried who tried to do him out of these works. He had originally announced *Madama Butterfly*, then new, and afterward *La Bohème: Bohème* was at one time scheduled as his opening-night opera. Ricordi went to court and Hammerstein had to forgo his *Bohème* for a while.

In this, as in numerous other difficulties he encountered in 1905–6, he was always inclined to see the hairy hand of Heinrich Conried. There were persistent stories that singers had been warned against appearing in Hammerstein's company; that some artists had been told they would never be paid; that a sort of whispering campaign was going on, emanating from Conried, to discredit Hammerstein and discourage any prospective member of his company.

It may all have been true and it may partly have been imagined; Hammerstein was always more than ready to believe ill of Conried. However, with Campanini at his side and Melba definitely contracted for ten performances, Hammerstein could overcome the whispering campaign easily enough. His major difficulties came not from slander or ill-will but from the sheer physical necessities of preparing an opera season from scratch, with not a dress or a stage set or a trombone ready to hand.

The hours of work Hammerstein put in during this period of preparation were prodigious. He is said to have been active as many as twenty hours out of the twenty-four, and there was hardly a detail of the preparation which did not require and receive his close personal attention. He had deliberately chosen to challenge the Metropolitan, and even invited conflicts in repertoire, singers, and dates. He went so far as to set his opening for the same night as the Metropolitan's, and postponed it only because he was not ready.

He might have sidestepped some of the conflict if he had wished to do so. For example, he need not have given his performances on the same nights as the Metropolitan: Tuesdays and Thursdays, when no operas were performed at the Metropolitan, would presumably have released a large public to Hammerstein if he had produced on those days. But he chose to run in direct opposition to the older opera house, giving his performances at the same time as theirs: Mondays, Wednesdays, Fridays, and two on Saturdays. His announced reason for not utilizing Tuesdays and Thursdays was that these nights were required for rehearsal. It is not easy to understand why he could not have rehearsed on Mondays and performed on Tuesdays, and his statements on the subject are not convincing. To my way of thinking, he really *wanted* the direct conflict with the other opera house. It appealed to his combative spirits; it was a large part of his fun.

Similarly, he might have avoided a good many other elements of rivalry. Aïda, for example, is an opera peculiarly suited to the Metropolitan's architecture, acoustics, and style. It might quite reasonably have been left to the Metropolitan while Hammerstein devoted his energies to something else. But no: he could not leave it alone, but must challenge the direct comparison by producing his own Aïda. The sharper the conflict, the better he liked it. So he would pit Ponci against Caruso, Melba against Sembrich, in an all-out "opera war" in which somebody was bound to get rather badly hurt.

After the arrival of Mary Garden, it is true, Hammerstein's repertoire did begin to differentiate itself more markedly from that of the Metropolitan. Hammerstein brought whole productions for her from Paris. This, however, was in the second season. In his first season and during the year of preparation for it, Hammerstein had not really found his bearings, operatically speaking, and his sovereign desire to fight with the Metropolitan seems to have been the determinant of all his choices.

As he explained it himself, his task at the beginning was to build a sort of standard repertoire which would thereafter remain as the base of the operation. While he was still in the early stages of this process, working with singers who were often strangers to one another, he had to give a great deal of rehearsal time to the bread-and-butter operas, the ever familiar Aïda, Faust, Carmen, and Rigoletto. Hammerstein's fame does not rest on those productions—except possibly Carmen—but, like all opera managers, he thought he could not run a season without them. It is no doubt true that the bread-and-butter works are necessary and basic if there is but one opera house in a city, but when there are two running at the same time, it is hardly imperative for them to duplicate their efforts. Or so it would seem to the onlooker, and in retrospect: at the time, and to Oscar Hammerstein, it was different. He wanted a full-fledged "international opera" season in flat opposition to the Metropolitan, and this was the way he went about it.

The characteristic of Hammerstein in opera as in all his other theater enterprises was, to begin with, haste. He was always in a hurry, always jumping ahead of himself. Most men undertaking to create a new opera company would have taken two or three years, at least, to do what Hammerstein did in one. The simple physical labor involved in a production of Aïda, for example, is immense: costumes, scenery, chorus, ballet, orchestra. In Hammerstein's case, nothing was ready-made; everything had to be created. Nowadays at the Metropolitan there are two hundred and fifty persons on stage during the triumphal scene of *Aïda*. Hammerstein did not run to quite such display, but he aimed at it.

Where everything and everybody is new and time is short, there must be a general feeling of shakiness through the whole period of preparation. It is not surprising, therefore, that substitutions had to be made from time to time, and that postponements took place; the fact of the matter is that Hammerstein started his first season without knowing how it was going to end.

An opera season ought to be, and usually is, planned with the utmost exactitude a full year in advance. The girl who is going to sing a small part in *Carmen* on a given date in April a year from now is assigned to the part already; there are many shake-ups and breakdowns in the course of a season, but on paper, at least, it is plotted to the inch. Nothing has ever been devised to take care of such contingencies as sudden illnesses except having two or three singers for each part, and even then there may be last-minute difficulties of the most hair-raising nature. A New York winter is sometimes hard on delicate throats, and nobody—not even a conductor—is free from physical hazards.

Hammerstein's immense daring at the outset, in forming a company that had virtually no available substitutes for leading parts, was rewarded by exceptional luck. He got through the first season with hardly any of the mishaps his improvisation had invited. True, Maurice Renaud had a period of hoarseness after his first arrival in New York, but otherwise it seemed that all the Hammerstein singers were immune to the misfortunes of weather and bronchial disturbance. During the very same period, numerous substitutions and changes were forced on the Metropolitan by the illnesses of singers—including both Caruso and Sembrich, healthy performers if ever there were such. It seems to have been Hammerstein's luck at its high tide—which, like his luck at its low tide, was phenomenal.

For, with all his strenuous work, his employment of skilled agents in Europe, his own tour there, and his twenty-hour-a-day schedule, he ended his preparation with a company dangerously close to minimum level. He had exactly one dramatic soprano, Mme. Russ, for all the heavy parts in Italian opera; he had, until the advent of Melba later on, just one coloratura, Mlle. Regina Pinkert; and throughout the season he had only one leading dramatic contralto, Mme. de Cisneros. His lyric tenor was Bonci, with no replacement. His Italian dramatic tenor was Amedeo Bassi, with no replacement. His French tenor was Dalmorès, with no replacement. He was a little better off in baritones (Renaud for a short time, Ancona for the season, Sammarco later, Seveilhac throughout), but his only basso for leading parts was Vittorio Arimondi in both Italian and French.

Even adding the mezzo-soprano Bressler-Gianoli for a long series of performances as *Carmen,* the limitations of such a company are manifest. It would tax anybody's ingenuity even to contrive a repertoire to fit this array of artists, and quite obviously Hammerstein would be obliged sometimes to ask them to sing in successive performances (as he did) or even twice in one day (as he did). The loyalty of the company to the impresario was shown by the fact that these heavy demands were all met, sometimes to the vocal discomfort of the singer.

We may be sure that Hammerstein knew what risks he was running, and took them deliberately because of his limited treasury. He had been piling up money for the Manhattan Opera House and its company as fast as he could, but the theater itself was costing a fortune and every principal singer was to receive a substantial fee. Mme. Melba's contract demanded that she be paid before the curtain rose on any of her performances—paid in cash. This was not so unusual as it might be today. Sarah Bernhardt operated on the same principle for years, as did others who could enforce it.

Hammerstein's desire for well-rehearsed performances with fresh direction, costumes, and sets, his employment of the perfectionist Campanini, his anxiety to see that the theater itself was adequate and appropriately decorated, were all heavy drains upon the available resources. He had not the slightest chance of getting through his season at all unless he could bring in enough money at the box office to pay for the running expenses after the start was made. Even with all the earnings from the Victoria Theatre his finances were precarious throughout, and he knew in advance that they would be. . . .

While Oscar went to Europe and concentrated on the formation of his company, the theater was steadily going up under Arthur's direction. As it neared completion there were long articles about it in the press, describing the "modern French" style (it was Louis XIV) and its red, buff, and gold decorations. Arthur was at his wit's end to get the house finished in time, particularly as his father had actually announced the opening night to coincide with that of the Metropolitan on November 26, 1906. This date could not be kept, and the opening night of the Manhattan was then announced for Monday, December 3, 1906, one week later. Even so, as we have seen, the theater was not pronounced finished until about one hour before curtain time, and not all the paint was yet dry.

This means that the rehearsals took place while the workmen were still busy in the house. Campanini rehearsed the orchestra diligently at times when it would have been difficult for anybody else to hear them, such was the pounding of hammers; he started his rehearsals at a time when the stage could not be used at all. When the stage in whole or in part could be used, full rehearseals with orchestra, chorus, and principals were held while the workmen and decorators were still operating. The pandemonium must have been extreme. All nerves were on edge, all tempers frayed. At this period—and, it is said, on the very day of the opening—while Oscar Hammerstein was in an aisle watching the rehearsal, a reporter from one of the New York papers came to him and asked him to hear a certain American baritone.

"He's going to be the greatest of all American baritones some day," the reporter said.

"I can wait," said Hammerstein.

The Metropolitan Opera approached the season of 1906–7 under certain handicaps. Conried was ill. Caruso had been arrested in the monkey house of the Central Park Zoo, one week before the opening of the season, on the charge of annoying a lady. On the other hand, the opening-night opera, *Roméo et Juliette*, offered the debut in the United States of Miss Geraldine Farrar, an American girl of twenty-four who had already won great popularity in Berlin as well as the admiration of the German Crown Prince.

At the next performance Caruso made his first appearance of the season in *La Bohème*, with Mme. Sembrich and Scotti. There is much evidence that he was extremely nervous and afraid of his audience until, at the end of Rodolfo's narrative, there was tumultuous applause. From then on the episode of the monkey house at the Zoo was forgotten, so far as the opera and its public were concerned.

Farrar's debut was a success, on the whole; Caruso was an idol, as always; and Sembrich had "never sung better." Vigna, the Italian conductor, was chided a bit, but nowhere near so sharply as he was to be later after New York had heard Campanini. There were interesting new productions announced—the first *Madama Butterfly* and the first *Salome*. There was a visit from Puccini in prospect; there was a German repertoire with casts that Hammerstein could not touch.

And yet he had one advantage over the established company. New York was more than a little tired of the Metropolitan. This was not true of New York society, which owned the boxes (the "Diamond Horseshoe") and went to the opera without regard to what was presented or how. It was, however, true of most of the critics, whose tone in reviewing Metropolitan productions was often captious in the extreme. It was true of a large public besides, as Hammerstein proved.

There was, therefore, some basis for his confidence. He may have overestimated his own strength, but it was in his nature to do so, and luck was on his side. There were wonders quite beyond Hammerstein's control, such as the vocal supremacy of Nellie Melba at the age of forty-six. It is certain that Hammerstein engaged Melba for her fame; how was he to know that she would sing for him better than she had ever sung before? These and other elements of good fortune were to attend him. Among such elements the Metropolitan's general debility in organization, its lack of true ensemble, its inferior conductors, and its old-fashioned style in production were to be counted. Moreover, nobody could have foreseen that one of Conried's greatest cards in the game, his production of Richard Strauss's *Salome*, would have to be withdrawn because of moral objections after a single performance.

Pitching the established Metropolitan against the new and untried Manhattan, we may see that for the latter (in spite of great excellences that will be noted later) it was essentially a gamble that came off, a leap in the dark which landed well. In 1906 and early 1907 Conried was in the habit of referring to "the so-called opera house in Thirty-fourth Street." By the season's end he was engaged in a scramble to get singers away from Hammerstein and to keep his own. The alteration in the Metropolitan's own tone tells the story.

The press campaign for some months before the opening of the Manhattan was incessant, and grew to a high pitch before the first curtain went up. Hammerstein himself gave interviews and statements in a steady flow, also contributing articles to the press from time to time. In one of these, two days before his opening, he said substantially what he said on the first night: "To the public of New York, to those who love the arts and to those who love effort and achievement of any sort, I dedicate the Manhattan Opera House" (*Evening Telegram*, December 1, 1906).

The special talents of William J. Guard were also at work. There were a great many stories about singers, and some of them bear the mark of the skilled press agent. "Hammerstein's Lost Tenor" was one headline: it referred to Amadeo Bassi, "last heard of in Buenos Aires." The arrival of Bonci and a score of other singers produced more of the same. They got to New York on November 18, and there were stories of various kinds: one that Mme. Giacomini, a minor mezzo-soprano, was suing her landlord at an Italian boardinghouse for her opera costumes. (The dire suggestion of conspiracy to hurt Hammerstein?)

One of the oddest of these inventions was to the effect that Caruso had challenged Bonci to a duel. No amount of denial could keep this from the front pages for at least a day. Another story claimed that Eleanora de Cisneros narrowly escaped injury to herself and her wardrobe in a collision of ships en route to America.

From time to time in the final week—and actually on the final day —Hammerstein was interviewed in the midst of carpenters and painters while rehearsals were progressing. There were recurrent stories about *La Bohème*, which Hammerstein steadily asserted he was going to produce in spite of any opposition, and which he eventually did produce. The tone of all this press agitation was favorable in the sense that it gave full weight to Hammerstein's difficulties while feeding a public curiosity which had grown steadily through the months.

Then, at last, the house and its company were ready—ready in a sense; ready enough to keep the date Hammerstein had fixed for himself and for the public. In the language of a headline in the New York *American* (Decembr 3, 1906): "Last Workmen to Leave New Manhattan as Arrival of Audience Begins." This was, as it happens, simply true.

The actual opening of Hammerstein's opera house aroused the interest of the whole United States. The opera was *I Puritani*, almost forgotten in America; but if it had been *Puss-in-Boots*, it would have made no difference to the public. The throngs that made their way to Eighth Avenue and Thirty-fourth Street—an outlandish region to many of them—were eager, above all, to see the theater, to see Oscar, and to see the rest of the audience. The fame of Bonci had indeed preceded him, and there were no doubt many who came for him, but by and large it was an audience of curiosity.

Every seat in the huge auditorium (there were 3,100) was sold, and the standing room behind the last rows was packed to suffocation. There were also crowds outside who could not get in. Although this huge audience had started to gather in good time, neither the traffic police nor Hammerstein's house staff was fully prepared to deal with such a crush. It proved impossible to get the "automobiles and wagonettes" through Thirty-fourth Street in any reasonable order and time.

The long, slow procession stretched all the way from Fifth Avenue, moving an inch at a time. There was but one entrance for the public to the Manhattan Opera House (there are three at the Metropolitan), and this fact added to the confusion. It was, on the whole, a good-humored crowd, and no actual quarrels or casualties were reported, but the whole press the next day gave an account of the mob scene and advised Hammerstein to take steps in future to deal with it. No such scene, as a matter of fact, ever occurred again, although the house was often filled to capacity; not only did Hammerstein learn how to deal with it, but the public that turned out simply to stare, not to enter the theater at all, was never again like this.

Hammerstein, at the peak of his form, watched the crowds and the crowds watched him. He was in all parts of the house; he was with the conductor, the stage director, the singers, the box office; he was resplendent in silk hat and cigar, lit or unlit, as millions of Americans were now accustomed to view him.

It became necessary, as he saw quite early in the evening, to hold the curtain. There was unparalleled confusion in the seating of the ticket-holders even after they had obtained entrance to the theater. The ushers were not sufficiently familiar with the house, and the general hysteria of the opening night did nothing to help them. The muddles were innumerable and the house had nowhere near settled down or even found itself at eight o'clock, although the crowd had already formed at half-past seven. One of the difficulties was the dense formation of standing-room ticket-holders all around the periphery of the bowl, through whom it was almost impossible to penetrate.

Hammerstein therefore held the curtain for half an hour. By that time some semblance of order had come into the house, although the audience was still struggling in during the first act and there were still crowds outside, unable to obtain admission. The first outburst of enthusiasm came when Cleofonte Campanini came to the conductor's podium and raised his baton. New York did not know him, but enough curiosity about him had been aroused already to ensure a reception.

Receptions, "ovations," and the like were the order of the evening, as so often on first nights. There was one of a slightly erroneous nature when Mario Ancona, the baritone, made his entrance. This big, fat baritone, the owner of a superb natural voice, bore no resemblance to the tiny, elegant tenor Bonci. And yet somewhere in the gallery cries of "Viva Bonci!" arose and had to be hushed by the more knowing members of the audience.

The fact was that in that huge audience hardly anybody had heard *I Puritani* before, and the plot, if it can be called a plot, was unknown. It had been produced in New York decades earlier; Patti had sung it there in her day, and so had Sembrich, who had made her world debut as Elvira in Athens; but by now it was new again. The difficulty in producing the opera did not reside in the music for the coloratura soprano, but in the tenor's part, which, having been written for Rubini, had a range beyond the capacity of all but the rarest voices. This was, of course, why Hammerstein chose it, or acquiesced in it, as a debut for Bonci: he was probably the only tenor of the century who could have sung it at all without transposing a great deal of the music.

I Puritani was an opera that Caruso had dropped from his repertoire early in his career; he did not have the required kind of voice. Bonci did. Thus, it showed up not only Bonci's advantages, but Caruso's disadvantages, if such they were.

The comparison of Bonci to Caruso would have been, in any case, a primary component of Hammerstein's season: it filled many, many columns of newsprint during the next few months. From this distance in time it seems a little foolish to have concocted a rivalry between voices that were fundamentally so different. Bonci had a perfectly produced high tenor voice of the utmost beauty and used it with the utmost elegance of style. His breathing was phenomenal and his taste beyond criticism. As the *New York Times* remarked some months later, "There never was an Italian singer with a finer style than Bonci."

Caruso's voice was, even then, much more robust, and he committed errors of taste and judgment in practically every performance. He had, however, a luscious tone that penetrated to every part of the house, his middle and lower voice surpassed that of almost any other tenor, and—when he did not force them—his high notes, up to C, were as clear as a golden trumpet. His appeal to the widest public had already been confirmed, and it remained sure to the very end. It is possible that the constant comparison of his errors with Bonci's perfection may have irritated him, but he had all possible revenges: the public never lost its predilection for him, his phonograph records were extraordinary and have survived, his fortune was great, and he will be remembered. Bonci, except by specialists, is already forgotten.

At the Manhattan's first night the purely operatic interest of the audience, aside from its curiosity about the theater itself and Oscar Hammerstein, was nevertheless centered upon Bonci and the inescapable comparison. He was received with great applause at his entrance. Many in the audience may have heard him in Europe, but the reception was due most of all to the general excitement of a first night, an "opera war," and a "duel of tenors." As the evening went on and he had greater opportunities to display his extraordinary vocalism, the applause rose to great heights. Reading between the lines, one may be permitted to guess that he was not quite so perfect in this performance as in some later in the season, but nothing could disturb the violin-like purity of his delivery, especially in the upper part of the voice. The reviews on the following day paid full tribute to all his qualities, although most of them pointed out that the sensuous (or "luscious" or "resplendent") beauty of Caruso's tone was not his.

On the same night Caruso and Sembrich were singing *Marta* at the Metropolitan, a revival, and in spite of the mob scene at the Manhattan the older house was also full. New York's appetite for opera had risen—perhaps with its population, perhaps with the influx of European immigrants in recent years—to the point where it seemed possible for two opera companies to exist.

The rest of the cast of *I Puritani* was not so warmly reviewed as Bonci. The Elvira was Mlle. Regina Pinkert, now making her first appearance in the United States. She was only twenty-four, had made her debut at La Scala in Milan at seventeen, and was singing in the opera company at Kiev, in the Ukraine, when Hammerstein's agents found and engaged her. She apparently had a good command of flowery, light music, although she was not a sensational coloratura by any means. The men besides Bonci were Mario Ancona, whose opulent baritone had been heard at the Metropolitan ten years before, and Vittorio Arimondi, a commanding basso.

The reviewers were struck, from the very first, by Campanini's conducting. He had been working under difficulties, as we have seen, and yet he animated and controlled the entire performance in a way New York had not known in works of this kind. There were rough spots—which under such conditions could not have been avoided—but the impression made by Campanini was deep from the very beginning. It grew steadily deeper all through this and succeeding seasons until it forced the Metropolitan to bring Toscanini to America as the only possible counterattack.

Another element of Hammerstein's strength which has already been mentioned was his youthful and good-looking chorus, every member of which had been picked and trained to sing accurately and as if they belonged to the drama. The New York *World* spoke of their "volume, resonance, quality, precision of tone, accuracy of intonation and boldness of attack." Other accounts complimented their appearance. In this and succeeding performances the chorus seems to have been a constant surprise to the critics. No doubt the Metropolitan's chorus, at fifteen dollars a week and no pay for preseason rehearsals, had deteriorated so badly that a fresh collection of young people with good voices was startling to hear and to behold.

And Hammerstein—! After the second act, Bonci, now fully recovered from his severe first-act stage fright, drew Oscar onto the stage to take bows with the singers. As the newspapers later remarked, Hammerstein seemed more nervous even than Bonci. He tried to depart by a door that had not been made to open—the kind of contretemps which delights an audience.

Again at the final curtain he was brought out for bow after bow. At last, in response to the audience's clamor, he stepped forward to make his little speech. This time, apparently, he was not nervous in the least. If he had not planned to make this speech, at this moment when he looked out at his admiring first-night audience he seems to have known precisely what he wished to tell them. He proposed to make it perfectly clear that he, and he alone, had created this institution.

"Ladies and gentlemen," he began, when the audience had quieted to hear him, "I am very much gratified. There is a sensation of pride and of fear."

There was a burst of appreciative laughter, the first of several. He went on, in part:

"I can only say that this is an effort toward the furtherance of industry and music. I am compelled to add that I am the only one who has created this institution. I have had no assistance, financially or morally. The burden has all been upon me and the responsibility is all mine. I have no board of directors, nobody to tell me what I should and should not do. (*Laughter*)

"I have concluded in my years of decline—for you can see that I am already out of my boyhood days—that if I can aid with that which I have earned honestly—can aid the cause of music—it would be something I could look back upon with what you call pride. I have never expected to make a dollar out of this enterprise.

"Many people endow libraries (*Voice from the gallery: 'One on Carnegie!'*) and hospitals: but I have yet to see one who has endowed opera. When the curtain falls tonight it is the beginning of a series of trials—nothing else.

"The ensemble which surrounds this institution is so large and is composed of so many celebrities of music that every opera for the next three or four weeks is experimental, and depends for success or failure on this audience and this city (*Applause and cheers*)."

In Proscenium Box 13, listening to this, were Mr. and Mrs. Otto Kahn of the Metropolitan's board of directors. With their party was Mr. Eliot Gregory, also a director of the Metropolitan. Other members of the Metropolitan forces were scattered through the audience, including a number of singers. How they reacted to Hammerstein's pointed thrusts is not known, but Hammerstein's attitude toward society patrons of opera was abundantly clear even without the implications of his little curtain speech. It was apparent in the very design of his theater.

Hammerstein must have decided, even before he built his opera house, even while he was worrying over the blueprints for the theater, that he would ignore the support or nonsupport of high society. He had boxes—forty of them—but they were arranged, like the rest of the theater, for their relationship to the stage and not to one another. The *New York Times* of the day after says, in a special "social" story apart from the news story and the review of the opera:

While the world of fashion went to the Metropolitan and applauded Sembrich and the famous quartet in *Marta*, the musical people found their way to the Manhattan Opera House to hear Bonci, the famous tenor, and the other new singers. It is evident that Mr. Hammerstein is not catering for the Metropolitan element.

The auditorium is designed for seeing and hearing, but not for the display of jewels and gowns. Still, the first-night audience at the Manhattan was quite representative, and there were many notable and prominent people present, although at the Metropolitan not one of the parterre boxes was empty, and the audience there was as brilliant as on the opening night a week ago.

So far there was no defection from the time-honored list of the Metropolitan subscribers.

There then follows a very long list of "exceptions"—persons belonging to New York society who had undertaken the hazardous journey to Eighth Avenue and Thirty-fourth Street to hear opera. The society reporter further states:

On matters sartorial the first night audience followed a go-as-you-please style of dressing. Not only were the standees clad, as are many of the same class of genuine music-lovers at the Metropolitan, in white cotton blouses and plaid walking-skirts topped by serviceable but non-ornamental headgear, but they wore these in many of the orchestra as well as gallery seats, removing, of course, the view-obstructing chapeaux, while next to them sat women in the most gorgeous of highly colored or white dinner and evening dresses, wearing lofty aigrettes and quantities of pearls, diamonds and other precious gems. The display of jewels was indeed a very handsome one.

This candid chronicler remarks that the house was so built that the occupants of the first tier of boxes, the equivalent of the Metropolitan's "Diamond Horseshoe," could not be seen except from the other boxes and the front of the orchestra. The rest of the house had a "splendid view of the stage" but not of the inmates of these boxes. "It seemed the aim of the management last evening to make as little of the social feature of the opening as possible." One of the signs of this aim was that "the intermissions were short."

All this may seem trivial detail, but nobody acquainted with the problems of opera in the United States could deny that the support of fashionable society is of great financial importance. Oscar Hammerstein had at this time no acquaintance with, and no use for, persons in high society. He undoubtedly thought that their influence had laid a dead hand on the Metropolitan, turning it into something more like a horse show or a garden party than an institution for the performance of operatic music. It is not conceivable that he could have built his house in this precise way, with a noticeable disregard for the boxholders' desire to display their jewels, if he had not considered the entire situation and taken his decision. . . . Probably he associated all of New York society with the Metropolitan; and as he had quite consciously chosen to give battle to the Metropolitan in every possible domain, his disregard for society was a part of the whole, or an inevitable concomitant.

His greatness and his courage were shown in this as much as in the larger purpose. If he intended to revivify opera in New York, to shake it loose from dead tradition and routine, as he clearly did intend, then to emancipate it from the bondage of high society was a definite part of the enterprise.

He was to gain and suffer from this. There were times in the next few weeks when he had to face half-empty orchestra seats and boxes. The galleries were filled from the beginning, but no great opera house can continue—unless it is heavily subsidized—on the patronage of those who pay least for their tickets. Yet his courage in trying brought him considerable reward in the esteem of the public and the critics—so much so that we find the press actually scolding the public on some occasions for ingratitude in not supporting Hammerstein more fully.

And with this growth of esteem for his endeavor, as was inevitable, his opera house did actually become fashionable. Not, of course, with the Morgan-Vanderbilt-Astor clans who, among them, owned most of the Metropolitan boxes as well as the house itself and had a great vested interest in loyalty to the old establishment; but with the numerous younger members of New York society who began to realize his aim and to appreciate it.

When Melba arrived, this process became obvious: at her performances society was out in force. Later on, with Mary Garden, a new element of fashionable support was added—that of the seekers after novelty, the intellectual snobs, those who wished to know and discuss the latest in all things. Certain of her admirers among the critics (Huneker, Van Vechten, and others) created for Garden a kind of cult which drew heavily from the ranks of New York society. Thus Hammerstein, without courting it and even, as we have seen, by ignoring it, did obtain a great deal of support after a while from the ranks of the rich and grand, and particularly from their youth. Perhaps he always knew that this, too, would come.

At all events, when he had finished his remarks before the curtain on the opening night, there could be no doubt in anyone's mind that Hammerstein meant to maintain his opera house without a Diamond Horseshoe, or go down trying.

Having said what he had to say, Oscar left the stage. For a long time the audience continued to call for him, but he did not come out again.

For Hammerstein this was a very solemn moment, nothing less than the coronation of a lifetime. Probably it should not surprise us that after audience and performers were gone, the lights out, and the theater locked up for the night, he rode alone in a streetcar to Forty-second Street, ate an oyster stew at Childs, and went to his two rooms on the Victoria's balcony and to bed. That he celebrated his triumph thus, we are told by those who should know—those who can remember or have heard the story from those who could remember the great night.

It is quite consonant with all the rest of his character that he should have stuck to his streetcar, his Childs restaurant, and his lonely chambers on this night of nights. His reflections, we may suppose, were of grim but undeniable satisfaction. He had "done it"—one of the headlines of the next day (New York *Journal*) quotes him as crying out: "I did it!" when the curtain fell on *I Puritani*. He had done it against every imaginable form of opposition, in which he counted the devious and unrelenting hostility of Heinrich Conried; he had done it against the wishes of his own sons, who were nevertheless aiding him to the limit; he had done it, most of all, by himself. . . .

In this very week—his first—a crisis of magnitude arose over the hoarseness of Maurice Renaud. Renaud did not want to make his American debut when he was not in good voice. He had been one of the most difficult of all singers for Hammerstein to obtain, and his contract, covering every contingency possible or impossible, covered forty-eight legal pages. Hammerstein's immediate task, on the very day after the triumphal opening, was to persuade Renaud to make his American debut on the next night (Wednesday) in *Rigoletto* even if a rest became necessary afterward. In this, too, he succeeded.

And on that very day—the papers having been signed and filed the day before—New York learned that Hammerstein had no intention of giving up *La Bohème*. In the United States Circuit Court, where G. Ricordi of Milan had brought suit to restrain him from producing *La Bohème*, on the ground that Conried owned the exclusive rights to it by contract, Hammerstein declared that his own oral contract of the preceding March was valid and could be proved. He thus served notice that he fully intended to proceed with his plans—and, perhaps, thumbed his nose once more at Conried.

Hammerstein's words about "the beginning of a series of trials" were all too literally true. For about three weeks he had them in sufficient number to keep even his indefatigable spirit fully occupied.

For his second performance his chief worry was Renaud and his obstinate throat condition. Renaud was, next to Bonci, the principal European celebrity to be introduced to New York in the early part of the season. Fees in those days were always exaggerated in the press, and Renaud's was usually given as $1,600. Judging by the final Hammerstein-Kahn contract, in which his fee is given as $1,000, I should think that his fee in 1906–7 was about $750 for each performance, possibly $800.

Renaud's contract had been drawn up with a multitude of precautions to protect the singer. There were stipulations of all sorts, such as that his valet was to have an outside cabin on the steamer coming and going, and that a carriage was to be provided for him for all rehearsals. Hammerstein himself revealed these facts in an interview printed the following week. He had treated Renaud with every consideration, and the result was that when the baritone felt his voice to be in improper condition for his first performance, he asked Hammerstein to deduct his fee. Hammerstein did not do so.

We do not know how Hammerstein "coaxed" (his own word) this famous singer to sing before he thought himself quite ready. We only know that he did so. Renaud made his American debut as Rigoletto on Wednesday, December 5, 1906, with a resounding success. Hammerstein did two special things for him. First, he caused an announcement to be made from the stage, between the first and second acts, to the effect that M. Renaud was suffering from hoarseness and asked that this fact be considered. Second, Renaud was allowed to rest indefinitely after this performance until he felt himself perfectly well and confident.

We all know the nervousness of singers, even the greatest of them, about their throats. Caruso's letters to his wife are full of anxiety over his throat. In this case, however, Renaud could have omitted the announcement of his illness and nobody would have been the wiser. Every critic in New York reviewed him glowingly, and most of them said that they never would have known he was hoarse if he had not announced it. He was a "singing actor," as the later phrase had it, rather than a simple exponent of vocalism: his artistry was greater than his natural voice. He seems to have been an artist of such consummate skill, power, and conviction that he could not be resisted.

Nevertheless, the loss of Renaud from subsequent casts for the next twelve days was uncomfortable for Hammerstein. He was obliged to substitute Mario Ancona, whom (as we shall see later) he never really liked, and who was in any case an old story to New York, having been for years at the Metropolitan. Ancona had a rich voice, but as an artist he was, by all accounts, never in Renaud's class. And besides all that, Hammerstein had banked heavily on Renaud to give luster to his casts, and in those early weeks they needed it. Renaud was not able to appear again until December 17.

This first performance of *Rigoletto* afforded, aside from Renaud's debut, a better opportunity to judge Bonci's powers. The diminutive tenor did not sing many of the same roles as Caruso; the Duke in *Rigoletto* was one. On this occasion, with no stage fright and the assurance that he had been well received—buoyed up, as well, by Renaud's presence, as all first-rate artists are by each other—he greatly deepened the impression he had made on the first night. Some critics had found his exquisite singing in *I Puritani* "lacking in warmth": they did not find it so in *Rigoletto*. When he sang *"La donna è mobile,"* it was impossible to restrain the audience, and Campanini, who as a rule was inflexibly opposed to encores, had to give in and repeat the air.

Mlle. Pinkert's reviews were mixed and none of them exceptionally good. When Hammerstein looked back over this first season of his, it must have afforded him some ironic amusement to reflect that the Polish soprano, only twenty-four years old, gave some critics the impression of having lost "the bloom of youth" from her voice—a thing that was never said of Nellie Melba, almost twice her age.

There were several interesting details of a nonmusical character about the night of Hammerstein's second opera. For one thing, Geraldine Farrar was present in a box with Mr. and Mrs. Walter Damrosch. For another, Mme. Sembrich and her husband, Professor Stengel, occupied a stage box opposite them. We have no evidence that Conried disliked having his singers (and board of directors!) present at the opposing house, but he cannot have been too greatly pleased.

Another operatic event took place on the same night. Mlle. Lina Cavalieri, once of the Folies-Bergère, made her debut at the Metropolitan in the title role of *Fedora*, with Caruso and Scotti. The new opera was not well received and the new soprano was praised more for her looks than for her singing, but she was to play quite a part in Hammerstein's activities later on. Cavalieri was then and remained for many years a woman of the most exceptional loveliness, yet her operatic career seems to have been a deviation rather than a fulfillment: she began in the Folies-Bergère and finished her public career as the director of a beauty shop in Paris. The havoc that she was to create among younger members of the ruling families at the Metropolitan, the Astors and the Vanderbilts, was yet to come; it was a part of the long and complicated "opera war."

As his third performance Hammerstein had chosen *Faust*, for the debut of Charles Dalmorès.

This celebrated French tenor was at the time thirty-four years old, tall and handsome, the possessor of a powerful voice of fine quality, and qualified both as musician and actor. He had been trained in the conservatories of Nancy, Lyon, and Paris, but originally he was a player of the violoncello and the French horn. Indeed, he was at first refused for the Paris Conservatoire on the ground that he was "too good a musician to waste his time in becoming a mediocre singer." After his debut in 1899 in Rouen he sang at La Monnaie in Brussels and had been for the two preceding seasons at Covent Garden in London. His renown was yet to come: in fact, it was in his long series of performances with Mary Garden that he became really famous. At this time he was not known in New York, even by reputation, except to a few. He had been one of the first singers Hammerstein had engaged on his trip to Europe some months before—thus indicating, along with Renaud, the direction in which Hammerstein's mind was turning.

The soprano for this performance was Pauline Donalda, a Canadian girl of twenty-three who had also been singing with success at Covent Garden. She had a particularly appealing presence, it seems, and a fresh young voice; she was better received than any other of Hammerstein's sopranos until the arrival of Melba.

The *Faust* performance was not well attended. It was what the papers called a "light house," particularly in the orchestra and boxes, although from there on to the ceiling the tickets were all sold. Dalmorès and Donalda were equally unknown; Renaud had been obliged to cancel his appearance; Arimondi as Mephistopheles was not a drawing card. Hammerstein must have reflected on that night that his "series of trials" was on its way.

And yet the reviews of the performance as a whole were good, and the *Times* remarked that those who were present had a very good time indeed. Again the chorus came in for praise: "What a chorus!" the *Times* critic, Richard Aldrich, exclaimed, and devoted an entire paragraph to the subject. In every performance through its early period the chorus, the orchestra, and Campanini drew the admiration of the critics, whatever they said of the principals. The chorus, orchestra, and conductor at the Metropolitan were seldom mentioned.

Campanini was a tired man at the end of that week. He conducted not only the first three evening performances, all-important for the initial effect of the new venture, but also the repetition of *I Puritani* at Saturday's matinee (December 8). To open his Saturday-night series at popular prices Hammerstein had nothing ready except a repetition of *Faust*, with Jean Altschewsky instead of Dalmorès. Arimondi had to sing Mephistopheles, Donalda Marguerite, and Seveilhac Valentine, on two successive nights. The conductor at the "pop" performance was Leandro Campanari, one of Campanini's two assistants. To sing difficult operatic parts on two nights running is a strain on any voice, but Hammerstein was forced to demand it; he had no alternative.

On that Friday night of the first week, when he was offering *Faust* to a "light house," an almost equally "light house" gathered at the Metropolitan for the première of *La Damnation de Faust*, with Farrar, Rousselière, and Plançon.

Hammerstein ended his first week in expansive and even exultant mood. Reading the quotations from his various interviews, one gets the impression that he was probably startled to find that he had gone through the week without disaster. He laughed at the idea that an occasional poor house might discourage him. You cannot expect a mob every night, was the gist of his argument: wait until you see my *Carmen* and my *Aïda*!

During his second week, still handicapped by the absence of Renaud, and with only the Renaud operas rehearsed and prepared, Hammerstein must have gone through a great deal more anxiety than he would allow to be seen. The operas of the week were *Rigoletto, Don Giovanni, Carmen, Don Giovanni* at the Saturday matinee, and for the popular-priced Saturday night another *Carmen*. This was running periously near the edge of breakdown. He could not make Ancona sing in every performance, and the French baritone Seveilhac was not of the first quality; yet these were the only baritones he had to sing the Renaud parts, and he had no other operas ready. He has himself related how he amazed Mme. Bressler-Gianoli, the Swiss mezzo-soprano, by asking her to sing on two successive nights; she had "never heard of such a thing." But in this poverty-stricken week she did.

He got through this one, too, thanks to Bonci and to that same Swiss mezzo. Bonci sang three times—Monday, Wednesday, and Saturday matinee—with uniform success. His Don Ottavio in *Don Giovanni*, always one of his very finest achievements, was praised to the skies. It was not so with his companions. Donalda (Zerlina) was always reviewed kindly, even sweetly—she must have been a very pretty girl—but not in the tone used of great singers. Mme. Giannina Russ, who made her debut as Donna Anna on the Wednesday night, was adjudged rough and unsuited to Mozart's music. Ancona was acceptable in this, as in everything else, because of his voice, but he was in no sense a true substitute for Renaud. Charles Gilibert, the French buffo, did very well with Leporello, and Campanini was increasingly praised, but the entire press by this time had made up its mind that Hammerstein's casts were weak on the side of the women.

This statement was to be repeated constantly throughout December until it must have set Hammerstein's teeth on edge. Every day he must have prayed for Melba, but he could not have been sure of anything about her, contract or no contract, until she had actually sailed from Europe on December 22. Nothing could prevent her from having an illness, real or imaginary, and a doctor's certificate is accepted in all opera houses, even up to curtain time, as a legal basis for abrogation of contract.

There was one amazing stroke of luck—if it was luck—in this second week. The Swiss mezzo-soprano Bressler-Gianoli made a stunning success in *Carmen*, one of the greatest ever known in New York. Her conception of the role was totally different from Calvé's and yet it cohered as a really powerful and integrated character, a dramatic and musical creation. Her voice was rather dark and she sang all the music as written, with none of the transpositions or substituted notes common among sopranos who try that part. She made no effort to look different from the other cigarette girls—indeed, the *Times* remarked that of the entire factory she was the shabbiest—but she seems to have been some sort of tornado on the stage, a force of nature. She had actually sung Carmen some years before in New York, with an organization called the New Orleans French Opera, which quickly disbanded. This had been more or less forgotten; few thought of it when

Hammerstein brought her back. The impact of her performance now, with Dalmorès as Don José and Campanini conducting at the peak of his natural ferocity, seems to have been something New York had never experienced before.

The success of this *Carmen* was a godsend to Hammerstein. He may have expected it (he said he did), but as an experienced show-man he also knew that it is impossible to be certain of your public until it has spoken. Bressler-Gianoli's Carmen drew larger houses at every repetition until it became that joy of managers, a certain and inevitable sell-out every time it was announced. The usual Micaela in this long run of *Carmen* was Donalda; at first the Toreador was Ancona, but Renaud after his recovery took it for some performances, Seveilhac for others. . . .

Melba's arrival at the end of December gave the whole Manhattan company new life. It was surrounded by considerable excitement in the press and among her innumerable friends and admirers—an ex-citement that needed no stimulation from the press agent. Melba by this time was a dominant figure in opera everywhere, and the curiosity over her return to America was great. On her last visit, in 1904, she had been in the midst of a long illness; after only one per-formance at the Metropolitan (in *La Bohème*) she had been obliged to cancel all other engagements. Hammerstein must have thought: *Thank God she's here! Now I wonder what she'll do on the stage!*

She was, as a personality, one of the most arguable of all prima donnas. The Melba stories, both in her favor and against her, are al-most without number. There can be little doubt that her enormous popularity throughout the world had to some extent gone to her head; she was human, after all, and such fortune comes to very few creatures in this life. If she liked a certain kind of toast, as she did, it was promptly named after her (and has since been commercialized everywhere); if she liked a certain combination of peach and ice cream, the same thing happened; there were flowers and perfumes and all sorts of objects which bore her name or were associated with her. Her particular kind of fame, so pervasive and unlocalized, transcended opera and even the theater itself, becoming a part of the general consciousness. She was, as they say, a household word, and more literally than could be said of almost anybody else in her time.

Whether she was really as imperious, demanding, grandiose, and unreasonable as some of the stories would indicate can hardly be ascertained now. There are stories to prove that she was, certainly, but there are just as many to prove that she was not. She was extremely kind when her heart was moved, and the available evidence is that Hammerstein had in some way moved her heart. She had no other reason for revisiting New York: she could have made just as much or more money in any of the great opera houses of Europe, and her American fame was already well established. We are led to the conclusion that she liked and admired what he was doing (his "pluck," as she called it) and actually wanted to help him. She would not do so, of course, without a whacking big fee, for she was an excellent businesswoman; but, after all, fees had presented no problem to Melba for some years past.

She certainly had some prima-donna habits, such as taking bows alone. There is a story to the effect that the first time John McCormack sang with her at Covent Garden and started out to take a bow, she said to him: "In this house nobody takes bows with Melba." As she practically owned Covent Garden, this is probably true. We also know that conductors were intimidated by her, but this, after all, was at least in part their fault. It is related that in this first season at the Manhattan Campanini stopped her in the middle of a rehearsal to correct a tempo and do the passage over again. She stared at him in unaffected amazement. It probably had not happened to her in years. But without protest she went back and did it over in his way.

With all her business acumen, she was certainly both kind and generous. Numbers of young singers were aided by her, and she was a great giver of presents. In this Manhattan season she sold her autographs, which were in great demand, and sent all the proceeds to a home for blind children on Long Island. In Australia, where she was a sort of uncrowned queen—audiences in theaters rose when she entered as a member of the public—her beneficence is well remembered.

Still, she was a prima donna, the greatest of her time, and the Manhattan company was put on its toes by her mere presence. It is good for such a company to be put on its toes: the evidence is that all performances, not only the ones in which she appeared, improved after her arrival.

Melba sang for the first time on Wednesday, January 2, in *La Traviata*, with Bassi and Ancona, Campanini conducting. The house was packed to the walls and many who tried could not get in at all. Hammerstein was saved indeed: for not only did she shed the glamour of her presence on the huge crowd, but she sang as she had not sung in years, if ever.

It was, by all authoritative accounts, a voice unlike any other except, perhaps, that of Adelina Patti some decades earlier. It was pure and "silvery" (that word is constantly used) with a perfectly equalized range from the B-flat below middle C to the F above high C. The breath control, phrasing, and modulations were all beyond criticism. The only debate at the time (and one sees it even in the sedate pages of *Grove's Dictionary of Music and Musicians*) was as to how much of this was art and how much nature. It is indeed a tribute to Melba that nobody could really tell where nature ended and art began. She had had only one year of "master" training, with Mathilde Marchesi in Paris, teacher also of Calvé and Eames. After that she had made a series of phenomenal debuts: at La Monnaie in Brussels (October 12, 1887) as Gilda; at Covent Garden, London (1887), as Lucia; at the Opéra in Paris (1889) as Ophélie.

Now she was approaching her forty-sixth birthday, at the very least. Richard Aldrich in the *Times*, after remarking upon her illness on her last trip to America, found her still in possession of all those marvelous qualities of pure vocalism which had so often been admired here in other years. "Her voice has its old-time lusciousness and purity, its exquisite smoothness and fullness; it is poured out with all spontaneity and freedom. Mme. Melba's singing of the music of Violetta was a delight from beginning to end."

It was Melba's evening, of course, but the critics were also delighted by some other aspects of the production. For one thing, Hammerstein had decided to do it in the décor and costumes of 1848, which is what the drama demands (can one imagine the dramatic situation of *La Dame aux Camélias* in any other period?). Nowadays this would occasion no remark, but audiences in New York and elsewhere had been accustomed for years to seeing the work dressed in a seventeenth-century style that, although thoroughly false, was supposed to take the curse off the old prejudice against opera "in modern dress." By this time 1848 was no longer "modern," but the habit of anachronism had persisted until Hammerstein did away with it.

Campanini's conducting, no doubt because of Melba, had some extra electricity that night; the chorus was superb in its two scenes; Ancona was well received, as usual; only Bassi, the tenor, was not equal to the rest of the company. Aldrich remarks upon his "mouse-like and querulous style," and the other critics were equally unappreciative of his efforts. Hammerstein, however, had taken the choice that almost any impresario would have taken on this occasion. He did not want to do anything that could take away from the effulgence of Melba as the center of the evening. This is the obvious reasoning, aside from money considerations, that would lead him to put his secondary tenor and baritone with her instead of Bonci and Renaud. It could also very well be that these singers, particularly Bonci, did not care much about being mere adjuncts to Melba's debut. Such is the way of opera houses.

The success of Melba in this season surpassed anything she had ever done in America before. Every time she sang, the house was filled to its uttermost limits. She had been engaged for ten perform-ances and she remained for fifteen; she was supposed to sing once a week and in several weeks she sang twice. There seems to have been no end to her kindness, her benevolence, her indulgence, in this par-ticular year. Considering how sharp she could be, and had been, with other managers, it is only possible to conclude that she liked Ham-merstein as much as she said she did. Moreover, no human being, not even a Melba, can be quite insensible to the atmosphere in which she was doing her work, an atmosphere that called out the very best she had to give and made her glow with special satisfaction.

This atmosphere requires a little explanation. She was not only "saving Hammerstein from disaster," as the standard reference books have it, but she was, in Hammerstein's house, the *prima donna asso-luta*. There was literally no other woman in the company who came within planetary distance of her accomplishment, popularity, and fame. According to my reading of Mme. Melba's character, this in itself was a situation that supplied great satisfactions. In almost any other company there would have been a few other luminaries, but in the Manhattan, for this one season, Melba was alone. This, plus the feeling that she was really needed, really wanted, and that the public was responding as never before, put her into the angelic mood in which she not only sang better, but felt better and behaved better than at any time in years. She said it herself, and I think she knew.

All of her succeeding performances were greeted rapturously by the largest audiences that the house could accommodate, and with actually mounting enthusiasm by the critics. For her second perform-ance, the week after her first, Hammerstein gave her Bonci and Re-naud with Campanini for a performance of *Rigoletto*. It was ex-pensive and delicate casting. Usually Melba's name alone was carried in capital letters in the advertisements, but for this evening (Friday, January 11, 1907) all three were so displayed: MELBA, BONCI, RENAUD.

Rigoletto, a masterpiece easy to victimize by routine treatment, was brought to life by a superlative performance under Campanini's sovereign control. Every one of the principals sang and acted better than before. Melba was supreme; Bonci "added a volume of luscious tone which surprised even his warmest admirers"; Renaud "sang and acted with a power that carried all before him" (*New York Times*). The presence of three such artists in one cast usually has the effect of keying each of them to a higher pitch of achievement, as it did in this case—and as it did with Campanini himself. The *Times* declared that this was "the best production of *Rigoletto* seen in New York for many years."

Pleasant reading for Caruso, Sembrich, and Conried!

On that very evening, as it happened, Conried was introducing one of his novelties at the Metropolitan: a revival of Meyerbeer's *Africaine*, in Italian as *L'Africana*, with Fremstad and Caruso. It was very coldly reviewed by the critics and had to be dropped. Even Caruso could not save it. The music was too high for Fremstad and the rest of the cast was indifferent, but the worst element, according to the press, was the crude and patchy conducting of Arturo Vigna. This unfortunate man had done quite well at the Metropolitan up to now, but he could not stand the constant comparison with Campanini. As a result, Conried was already attempting to make advances to Toscanini in Milan (as is shown in Gatti-Casazza's memoirs). The Metropolitan, which had been so haughty toward "the so-called opera house in Thirty-fourth Street," was beginning to feel the breeze.

Melba, we may be sure, knew more about this than any of us could know today. She saw the Metropolitan growing agitated, she read its bad reviews, she saw the immense crowds she attracted to the Manhattan, and, although we have no positive knowledge of any real grudge she had against the Metropolitan, she must at least have felt gratified at the effects of her own power—gratified or amazed.

For the astonishing fact is that from now on all the performances at the Manhattan began to get good reviews and most of them to attract large houses—not only the "Melba nights"—and the Metropolitan, except for the première of *Butterfly* (February 11), had some notable mishaps. For example: on Friday, January 18, Hammerstein produced *Les Huguenots* (in Italian) with the same singers who had, most of them, failed to arouse much admiration earlier in the season, and it drew a huge house and excellent criticisms in the press. The same "distaff side" that had been found wanting before—Mme. Russ and Mlle. Pinkert—was now praised, quite possibly because they had actually improved, and another lady, Mme. de Cisneros, had a decided success. And this was the very night when Conried was giving the première of Puccini's *Manon Lescaut* in the presence of the composer, with Cavalieri, Caruso, and Scotti singing. Where, the onlooker demanded, did so many operagoers come from? Had New York gone "opera mad"?

By mid-January of Hammerstein's first season, as we have seen, the complacency of the Metropolitan was no longer unruffled. For the time, however, the war between the opera houses was openly fought only by the challenger. The older house sat in apparent calm, although, if Hammerstein's accusations were not only the product of his angry imagining, subtle maneuvers were going on beneath the surface in an effort to suppress the upstart. The first battle of the war was apparently to be over whether or not Hammerstein was to succeed in putting *La Bohème* on the Manhattan's stage for Mme. Melba.

The Puccini Question is murky now and was murky then. What was the secret of the cabal that attempted to keep Hammerstein from producing *La Bohème?* Was it, as Hammerstein firmly believed, a nefarious plot on Conried's part, an inimical maneuver on the part of the Metropolitan? It may well have been. It cannot be proved now. Certainly *La Bohème* had already been produced all over the world, and by all sorts of companies, without a whimper out of the firm of Ricordi, which owned the rights. All they asked was $150 a night for royalties. It had been played by traveling opera companies in New York and more or less everywhere else in the United States. Hammerstein had an oral agreement with George Maxwell, the Ricordi representative in New York, dating from March, 1906, which would have permitted him to produce *La Bohème* and all the other Puccini works.

Now, suddenly, Ricordi had sought an injunction to keep Hammerstein from producing *La Bohème* on the ground that the Metropolitan owned the exclusive rights to that and all other Puccini operas in New York.

Hammerstein needed *La Bohème*—not only to give some slight flavor of modernity to his otherwise antique repertoire, but also because Mme. Melba wanted it. In fact, Melba was just as determined to sing it as Hammerstein was to produce it. She had sung it everywhere else and she wanted to sing it at the Manhattan. Moreover, as her last appearance at the Metropolitan had been in *La Bohème* and had been badly marred by her illness, she undoubtedly wanted to show what she could do with it now. Any singer would have felt the same.

The Metropolitan, or at least Conried, took a hand in the matter directly by inviting Puccini to America for the première at this house of his latest work, *Madama Butterfly*, which was to take place February 11, with Farrar, Homer, Caruso, and Scotti in the cast. The composer arrived in New York on the liner *Kaiserin Augusta*, delayed by fog, on Friday, January 18, the night of the première of his *Manon Lescaut* at the Metropolitan. He got there just in time to hear and see the performance, which he professed to admire—although, from his parting remarks six weeks later, I doubt that he did. From that time onward he was treated as Metropolitan Opera property. He threw himself zealously into the preparation of *Madama Butterfly*, probably as a simple measure of self-defense against the ineptitudes of the conductor Arturo Vigna, but no doubt also for a substantial fee from Conried. And from the beginning to the end of his stay in America he was asked—in fact, almost every day—what he thought of the question of Hammerstein's production of *La Bohème*. From beginning to end he said he knew nothing whatever about it; it was a matter between Ricordi and Hammerstein.

Puccini was an honest man, as any reader of his letters must know. He would not have shied off so obstinately from this question if there had been any clear right and wrong involved—or, let us say, if he had not felt that there was something wrong somewhere. If, to put it crudely, Conried had bribed Ricordi to adopt the attitude that was adopted, I feel sure that Puccini had nothing to do with the business.

And the whole curious crisscross of interests, animosities, and fears which runs through this entire "opera war" was thereafter exhibited for weeks. Puccini did not want to offend either Ricordi or the Metropolitan; he equally did not wish to offend Hammerstein directly. How could he know which opera company would come out ahead? Cleofonte Campanini, threatened with a boycott from some of the Ricordi-controlled opera houses of Italy, could not or would not conduct *La Bohème* publicly, although he was willing to prepare it. Nobody was especially eager to offend Mme. Melba, whose powers in several opera houses of the world were at that time very great, possibly as great as those of Ricordi. Her popularity in America was such that it may have influenced even the courts; certainly it influenced the press. From the tone adopted by the press at the outset of this dispute, and confirmed steadily thereafter, Hammerstein must have had wide sympathy in his effort to put on *La Bohème*. As the press said more than once, he was only trying to do what many lesser companies had done before him, and the claim to exclusive rights by the Metropolitan, although probably valid, was a new arrangement, a new contract, hastily run up in the endeavor to do harm to Hammerstein.

Puccini had a "wonderful time" in America, and went sight-seeing to Niagara as soon as his duties with *Madama Butterfly* were over. He worked hard on *Butterfly*, which then, as afterward, he considered his best opera. He obtained a good result, for the press in general held it to be the best production the Metropolitan had offered in Italian for a long time. He worked with orchestra, chorus, principals, and stage director, although he was unwilling to conduct this or any other opera. Arturo Vigna was the conductor, but, owing to Puccini's work, he turned in a far better performance than usual.

And the Puccini "wave" at the Metropolitan reached a great height that year, unquestionably because of the composer's visit and the effort to impress and please him. Four of his operas were in the repertoire and received twenty-one performances, more than those of any other composer. It would be a strange coincidence if this courtship of Puccini were not somehow connected with Conried's claim to exclusive rights for his works. In short, it looks as if Hammerstein may have been right in his suspicions, and that the Metropolitan management did in fact go to great lengths in the matter.

Ricordi's ace card was possession of the orchestral score of *La Bohème*, which had never been printed. The Milan firm took extraordinary precautions to see that no one of the existing manuscripts of the score (all of which were numbered and placed in various parts of the world) could possibly fall into Hammerstein's hands. The impresario made diligent search, through agents in the United States and elsewhere, and after much difficulty he came into possession of a mutilated orchestral score that had been used by a touring company from England some years before. Campanini knew the score so well, having memorized it and conducted it often, that he was able to supply the missing parts.

Thus Hammerstein proceeded with his plans and produced *La Bo-*

hème on Friday, March 1, with Melba, Trentini, Bonci, Sammarco, Arimondi, and Gilibert. Fernando Tanara actually conducted the performance while Campanini sat in a box, but Campanini had rehearsed and prepared it in every detail.

The situation in court was that Ricordi's case for an injunction was pending and Hammerstein's answer had been given (as we have seen) on the eve of the Manhattan opening. As soon as Melba had had her three performances as Mimi and sailed away to Europe, Hammerstein voluntarily withdrew his opposition to the case and the court then granted the injunction. By this time it meant nothing; Hammerstein and Melba had had what they wanted, and by the next year almost anything might happen.

Melba's brief repertoire made all the difference to Hammerstein. He could present her in operas that were already in production: *Lucia* (January 28) with Bonci, and *Faust* (February 8) with Dalmorès, along with repetitions of *La Traviata* and *Rigoletto*. These four constituted her list until the *Bohème* production, and it would be difficult to imagine reviews more favorable than those she received at each performance; yet in the *Bohème*, according to the *New York Times*, she "sang the music more beautifully than she has done anything else this season in New York."

That *Bohème*, Melba's and Hammerstein's victory, was full of surprises. For example, Emma Trentini, a lively soprano who reminded many persons of Fritzi Scheff, had a genuine personal success as Musetta. She had been in the company all season, singing small parts without any remarkable effect, and had even sung Micaela in some of the numerous performances of *Carmen*. But Musetta was really her part, and she scored heavily, foreshadowing the time when she, like Scheff, would progress from opera to operetta. Bonci displayed a "full voice" in *La Bohème* as never before, and the new baritone Mario Sammarco made a great effect, as he did in everything. . . .

There were some disappointments, of course, but the complexion of everything in Hammerstein's project looked very rosy through February and March. Bonci's *Fra Diavolo*, which the critics thought "delightful," was sparsely attended by the public. Bressler-Gianoli had to go away at the end of the fifteenth week, after having performed *Carmen* at least once and sometimes twice a week; her run of *Carmen* was one of the longest known in a single season. Dalmorès had a cold for a while and sang over it.

But, despite incidents of this sort, everything, including finance, looked better than Hammerstein had had any right to expect some months earlier. For one thing, he had obtained a loan of $400,000 from Frank Woolworth, founder of the Woolworth stores, with the Manhattan Opera House as security. This was to make sure of his coming season, although he already believed that the present season would end with some profit, however small.

Hammerstein negotiated this loan personally. He did not know Mr. Woolworth, but, hearing that he was interested in music and had often been at the Manhattan, he went to see him without preparation. He returned with a subscription to a box for every performance, and the loan of $400,000 in addition. We begin to understand what people meant when they called him "persuasive."

Melba's farewell for the season took place on Monday, March 25, in *La Bohème*. When the opera was over and bows had been taken, she appeared again to sing the Mad Scene from *Lucia*—a sort of extra caper more common in those days than now. After this, the stage was cleared and a caterer took over; it was Hammerstein's supper party for all the principals of the company and their wives or husbands. At that supper party (where they had *suprême de volaille Hammerstein* and ended with *pêche Melba*) Oscar must have felt expansive and more than a little incredulous. There he sat, surrounded by some of the finest singers and musicians in existence, with every likelihood of ending his season solvent, and with a substantial sum of money in the bank, thanks to Mr. Woolworth, toward next season's outlay. Needless to say, he had composed a piece for the occasion, a sort of potpourri called "Memories of the Manhattan Opera Season," which the orchestra dutifully played. He was the same magnificent Oscar, but this time his splendor was real. Moreover, he had Melba on his right and Calvé on his left.

Yes, Calvé.

Melba's departure would have left Hammerstein in precisely the same position as at the beginning of the season if he had not enlisted the services of another famous soprano. His "distaff side" had been a weakness, as he had good reason to remember; never again did he attempt to get through a season or any part of a season without prima-donna sopranos who could appeal to a large audience. He had learned that lesson so well that in future he tended in the other direction and supplied himself with such a wealth of prima donnas that it was difficult to carry out all their contracts. In this very month of

March and even more in April, the papers were filled with stories of Hammerstein's contracts, signed or possible, with celebrated singers.

But now, with four more weeks to go and no Melba, he had been able to corral Emma Calvé to take over in her own repertoire of *Carmen, Cavalliera,* and *La Navarraise.* More than a decade before, he had wanted Calvé to sing for him in variety at the Olympia. Now he was achieving that ambition, too, but in a way that delighted him more.

We are not informed about the behavior of Mmes. Melba and Calvé to each other on the occasion of that historic supper party. It must have been choice and rare, whether it was in the realm of cordiality or that of pinpricks. Both ladies were famous for their rudeness to rivals or other personages of equal rank in opera. A much younger singer, Mary Garden, endured some sizzling language from both of them when she had become, to their annoyance, an international prima donna. On one occasion when Garden and Melba sang at Windsor Castle after a state dinner for the King of Greece, Melba said to the court chamberlain, Lord Farquhar: "What a dreadful concert this would have been if I hadn't come!" Once Garden had supper at the Savoy in London with Calvé and others after a performance at Covent Garden. She was wearing a special perfume created for her. Mme. Calvé sniffed the air and declared that she would have to change tables. "I shall not be able to eat, or I shall be sick," she said. These were the amenities of which we hear a good deal from those days. (Both incidents took place only a year or two after Hammerstein's Melba-Calvé supper.)

At all events, Melba departed and Calvé arrived. Melba's last performance was at the beginning of Hammerstein's seventeenth week; Calvé's first was two days later, Wednesday, March 27, in *Carmen.* . . .

Melba's instrumental style, which kept the abundant beauty of tone under control at all times, did not wear out either her throat or her temperament. She was never "carried away" by her own performances, and in her repertoire it was perhaps not desirable that she should be. As a result, Calvé left the operatic stage in 1910, when she was fifty (more or less), and Melba did not say farewell to Covent Garden until 1926.

It may be worth noticing that Calvé's beauty had, in spite of some gain in weight, endured better than her voice, whereas with Melba it was the opposite. The *Times* remarked of Melba's Marguerite that same season: "The years have told on Mme. Melba's presence as they have not been able to tell upon her voice."

What Hammerstein had, therefore, in his two world-famous sopranos was one who had conserved her vocal resources and one who had not: Melba was at her very peak and Calvé was beginning to go, although even as she declined she remained one of the most interesting performers in the world.

Melba's farewell statement may be quoted in its brief entirety. It was issued the day before she sailed:

I have never enjoyed any season in America so much as the one now closing. All through I have been in splendid health and spirits and I shall never forget the kindness with which I have been received. I am proud to have been associated with Mr. Hammerstein in his launching of New York's new opera house. What courage Mr. Hammerstein has shown and what wonders he has done! I think there must be something in the conditions of American life to encourage him, for I know of no opera manager in any city of the world who, single-handed and under circumstances of such difficulty and competition, would have risked his fortune in opera.

His pluck appealed to me from the first, and I leave as I came, his loyal friend and admirer.

When the curtain fell after the last "popular-priced Saturday night" (another *Aïda*, of which there had been many), Oscar Hammerstein was no doubt happy and full of wonder that he had actually won so great a battle. He did not, however, have much time to think it over. While the certified public accountants surveyed the books to see what really had happened, the "opera war" was in full tilt. It had started up in February, through the Puccini episode and others, and from now on it gained momentum all the time, with hardly even a lull in the summer. When Hammerstein and Conried went to Europe, their doings and utterances were reported from there, too. It was, without a doubt, an era of some madness, for which Hammerstein was largely responsible, but the public joined in with zest and the press could not have omitted the daily communiqués if they had wished to do so. . . .

Both managers began to make raids on each other, and a sort of double warfare ensued in which one part was above ground and reported in the press, the other subterranean and in some cases not known until years later. So far as the open warfare was concerned, Hammerstein was the more belligerent. In fact, his love of issuing statements, giving interviews, making plans public, would probably have flourished regardless of the stimulus it gave him to annoy Conried.

But in secret there were many activities that only came to light later. Thus, Conried made a determined effort to get Campanini for the Metropolitan and offered him a good deal more money than Hammerstein was paying. Campanini refused from the first and did not even tell Hammerstein: he had retained from his youthful experience a detestation of the Metropolitan and its methods, and in addition he was king at the Manhattan. Could anybody be king at the Metropolitan when every artistic effort was subject to the caprices (or the ignorance) of the Morgan-Astor-Vanderbilt directorate? . . .

Bonci was another matter. Conried got him. It was very annoying to the Metropolitan to have its leading tenor constantly compared to Hammerstein's leading tenor, and the solution Conried found—costly though it was—seemed reasonable enough from some points of view: take Bonci, add him to Caruso, and the supply of Italian tenors is thereby exhausted. It was not, of course, true: there were other Italian tenors of the first rank, and Hammerstein had no trouble finding them.

Caruso's fee had been, in this 1906–7 season just past, $1,440 for each of sixty-two performances. For the next season Conried was obliged to pay him $2,000 for each of sixty-eight performances. The jump in fee was due, of course, to Hammerstein. Just as Conried worked on Bonci, so Hammerstein worked on Caruso. . . .

Nearly every day, from the end of February onward, the newspapers carried some announcement, rumor, or speculation about the doings of the rival managers. Hammerstein (from the time he got the $400,-000) erupted into statements about new works, conductors, and singers. Some things came to pass and some did not. He was going to produce Wagner with Hans Richter conducting: Cosima Wagner's hatred of the Metropolitan had made her exert her influence, said the press. Ernestine Schumann-Heink, later on, announced that she was "proud" to leave the Metropolitan for Hammerstein. Conried was going to bring Chaliapin from Europe and Hammerstein was going to bring Mary Garden (both of these were rumors long before they were facts).

Hammerstein's season ended April 19, Conried's a week earlier. Each had given twenty weeks of opera and each promised the same for next season. Hammerstein really did not have Mary Garden's signature to a contract when he began to use her name in March, 1907, for she refused to sign with an agent; she said: "If Mr. Hammerstein wants to talk to me, he should come to Paris and do it." He did, however, have messages of such encouragement (from the French music publisher Durand to the American music publisher G. Schirmer) that he regarded this acquisition as certain. He did have a signed contract with Schumann-Heink, and it was announced on March 18 that he had signed the day before with the agent for Lillian Nordica. Mme. Nordica had left the Metropolitan at the end of the preceding season (in a huff, it seems), but had refused to sign with Hammerstein because she felt unsure of his experiment. Now, on tour in the Far West, she telegraphed that she, too, was "proud" to join him.

Mme. Nordica's Metropolitan fee had been $1,250 for each of twenty performances, one of the highest received by any woman singer in the house (Eames's alone was a little higher). We do not know precisely what Hammerstein had to pay her, and there was, especially at this time, a tremendous lot of misrepresentation going on about the size of the fees in the "opera war," but it is safe to guess that Hammerstein must have paid $1,500 at least, perhaps $1,750.

He had already announced Melba and Calvé; now he had Nordica and Schumann-Heink as well, with a strong likelihood of Mary Garden. Instead of being "weak on the distaff side," he was going to be overloaded with prima donnas.

At the end of his season he had the task of dismissing a number of singers: that is, of refusing to renew his options on their services. To Ancona, whom he never really liked, he laid down severe conditions for possible renewal: he must lose thirty pounds, acquire a waistline, etc., etc. Hammerstein is supposed to have poked his forefinger at Ancona's protruding belly. "That is not fat," said the singer, "that is my chest." With Mlle. Pinkert, the Polish coloratura, it was worse: she screamed, fainted, had assorted hysterics in Italian, and refused to accept her salary in dollars, although she had been doing so all year. (She wanted it in gold francs.)

The Bonci affair filled columns and columns of newsprint during the closing weeks of Hammerstein's season. The gist of it was that Conried simply bribed him away by paying $1,500 for each performance instead of $1,000, as Hammerstein's option provided for the tenor's second season. Bonci's contract was incredibly complicated and had so many peculiar clauses in it—about sums to be deposited in a bank in Florence; about Hammerstein as "an Italian citizen" (through his agent) and other legal fictions—that the clear option Oscar held for the next two years was shadowed. It was the kind of contract in which Clause S is carefully framed to cancel out Clause C, and Clause M to erase Clause F. Oscar went to court about it almost automatically—he loved going to court—but, aside from the pleasure of annoying Conried, he really did not care much about Bonci.

As he explained to the reporters when the story about Bonci's defection first appeared, there were other tenors. He showed them a contract signed just two weeks before with Giovanni Zenatello, the brilliant young Italian tenor who had been making great successes in Europe. This man, Hammerstein said, could sing anything, robust modern works as well as old lyric ones, and Bonci could sing only his own repertoire, all very old.

Bonci took refuge in his agents: he "knew nothing about the contracts." Conried confirmed the signature. The tenor was summoned to court on April 1 (all this time he was singing once or twice a week for Hammerstein) and endured some little embarrassment. In the end, he went to the Metropolitan and Hammerstein did not mourn, although, as he pointed out in a published letter, Bonci might have stayed in Europe a long time if he, Hammerstein, had not brought him to New York.

The certified public accountants showed that the first season of the Manhattan Opera had achieved a profit of $11,000. This is amazing in itself and Hammerstein had not expected even so much. However, Arthur Hammerstein is on record as believing that there was a profit of about $100,000, and Oscar Hammerstein himself said that his box office took in about $750,000 during the season. The whole system of bookkeeping and of money transfers was so peculiar, with that famous truck loading up currency at the Victoria Theatre and dumping it out at the Manhattan, that it would have been difficult for any expert to be sure. The main point is that he made some money, after lavish and often unexpected expenditures.

In the same season the Metropolitan lost $84,039.[1] Some of its productions had been destroyed in the San Francisco fire and had to be replaced, but of course *all* of Hammerstein's were new in every particular, so this explanation does not explain. The simplest reasoning leads us to conclude that both opera companies were under severe financial strain because of the competition, but that the Manhattan made a little money and the Metropolitan lost a respectable amount.

[1] Kolodin: *The Story of the Metropolitan Opera,* p. 228.

It was the first time in a good many years that the Metropolitan had ended the season with a loss.

The war was on and the warrior was happy. Hammerstein's ebullience at the end of the season was the delight of the press. He talked not only of an opera house in Philadelphia—this was quite serious, and the *Times* reported that he had made a number of exploratory visits there—but also of Boston and Chicago, as well as of a number of other less likely cities from time to time. He talked of so many different kinds of new repertoire that it would have required a dozen opera houses to stage them all. The press took these improvisations with a grain of salt, but only one grain, and that a tentative one. It all sounded crazy, but who could tell? It had been equally crazy to think of a full opera season in opposition to the Metropolitan, and lo! Lo indeed! In the tone in which these grandiose imaginings were reported it is possible to detect skepticism, but skepticism tempered by the salutary reflection that the man who had already performed one impossibility might equally well perform others.

HOW LA SCALA WORKS

Martin Mayer

> In 1946 the bombed-out opera house in Milan was re-
> opened by a concert conducted by Toscanini. Since
> then La Scala has regained some of its ancient glory,
> though the quality of many of its performances is de-
> batable. This report shows what happens when an opera
> house is operating with government subsidy, a condi-
> tion very different from that our musical enterprises
> have to face. It is only fair to add that all at La Scala
> is not quite so rosy as it would appear from this report.

"We think of nothing here but music."

Late last March,[1] as the opera season was ripening to full
bloom, the Teatro alla Scala of Milan presented the world première
of two one-act operas. The first aroused no excitement, but the second
achieved an uproarious fiasco. One outraged customer threw his shoes
at the singers to demonstrate his feelings. To appreciate his action
you must conjure up the sight, rare in the United States, of an entirely formal audience; and then imagine a dignified gentleman leaving the opera house, in tuxedo, boiled shirt, black tie—and stocking
feet. I wish I had seen him.

From the point of view of the directors of La Scala, however, the
evening was on balance a success. Musicians and critics from all over
the Western world had come again to La Scala to participate in an
event that might become part of the history of music. The executive
staff had exercised the muscles of judgment, the artistic staff had
flexed the mysterious fibers of creation. Whether these particular
operas were worth the work was a question that would be answered
decades later. But La Scala's management could see no question at all
about the general principle of presenting new operas. In Milan on

[1] 1953.

this evening a museum had become a workshop, a library had sprung to life.

The constant search for new operas to perform is one of five pillars on which rests La Scala's eminence as the world's greatest opera house. The other four, too, are strange to American ears: complete control over musical matters by the conducting staff; forty cheap evenings a year, to keep Milan's working population in touch with the operatic world; a devotion to music's past, the previously unpopular operas of dead composers; and finally money to burn.

By comparison, the Metropolitan Opera House of New York stands on a bed of mud, an unlucky house entirely out of the main stream of New York. It has no money, its staff spends half the year trying to extract cash from rich Patrons of Art and poor listeners to the weekly radio broadcasts. The Met never revives an unfashionable old opera, and hasn't presented a world première since 1943.[2] Whenever the Met cuts prices—for a students' matinee, or a "popular" Saturday night—it puts on stage an inferior cast led by a conductor from the second or third string. And musical matters are in nobody's control, because nobody has the time.

This is not to slam the loyal, talented people of the Met. Considering its poverty of resources, a remarkable job is done every night. Far too little honor is given to the singers, and far too much blame to the management. Over the years the Met has built up a tradition of brilliant improvisation, sound performances manufactured from bits of string, rat's tails, and seashells. The present company at the Met executes that tradition about as well as any company ever has. Given the riches of La Scala, they could—but no, they could only sit down and cry.

Behind the theater there used to be a house; American bombers took care of that in 1943. The management of La Scala and the city and citizens of Milan looked at the rubble for almost a decade and wondered what to do with it. Meanwhile, La Scala needed a rehearsal hall for the orchestra and a place to make records; the big theater was too busy for the one and acoustically troublesome for the other. The decision was made to build a rehearsal and recording studio, and the project turned over to Dottore Ingegnere Marcello Fravelani-Rossi, a gentle, scholarly man with a brush mustache and graying hair, who is La Scala's technical director. He suggested that a rehearsal and recording studio would also be an ideal place for

[2] One is planned in the season of 1957–58.

chamber-music concerts. And then the management, in Fravelani-Rossi's words, "remembered an old idea of Arturo Toscanini's that there should be a *Piccola Scala*, a small opera house where ultramodern works and works from the seventeenth and eighteenth centuries could be successfully given for a small, serious audience."

Orfeo, for instance, is a great work, but it makes no effect whatever in a large house. The operas of Alessandro Scarlatti, of Handel, of Haydn, of Mozart himself, even of Rossini—are all harmed by presentation in the huge barn of an opera house. They were written to be played by small orchestras and heard by small audiences. And now La Scala, alone of the world's great opera houses, will have the means to present them as they were written.

The right-sized house, of course, is only a start. Singers trained to Verdi and Wagner are usually ineffective in anything earlier than Mozart: There is something wrong in the very coloration of the voice, which is a matter more profound than style. But La Scala has a school, the only full-time, fully professional opera school in the world, which trains young singers specifically to the pre-Romantic repertory. Six or seven promising voices, all owned by graduates of conservatories, are taken into the school every year; and after three years of intensive training (during which they receive a regular weekly salary) they become the *Cadetti della Scala*.

Opera in the United States might best be described as an unexceptionable entertainment. It never causes excitement, it never creates shock. It exists separate from the body of intellectual achievement; its audiences are never sure enough of their opinions or fond enough of their importance to make much fuss about anything. Our tradition of operagoing is a conservative one; Americans who go to operas generally wish to hear what they heard ten or twenty years ago.

In Italy, however, opera has held its senior place among the theatrical arts. No first night at a play has the theatrical importance of the excitement of a first night at La Scala—and La Scala has twenty *prime* a season. Every opera has its own first night, and each first night is an occasion requiring formal dress.

For these twenty *prime* nearly half of La Scala's thirty-two hundred seats sell for sixteen dollars each (eleven dollars by subscription to all). Two of the twenty might be world premières—"We baptize operas," says Dr. Luigi Oldani, La Scala's secretary-general—another a contemporary work never before played in Italy; another a rarely played opera from the seventeenth century; another an old opera that has been out of the repertory for at least fifty years. Of the remaining fifteen at least ten would be newly reset and newly staged and studied afresh by a new cast. To miss a first night at La Scala is to risk the loss of an original, important experience. The excitement is built in.

These first nights are often international affairs, because La Scala is always importing talent. Among the new designers for 1954 were Pablo Picasso and Ludwig Sievert; among the stage directors were Heinz Tietjen and Otto Erhardt, Roberto Rosselini (who botched up Honegger's *Jeanne d'Arc au Bûcher*), the Met's Herbert Graf, and Pierre Bertin of the Comédie Française. Eight living composers, including Gian-Carlo Menotti, were represented in the repertory, and among the works by the dead were Béla Bartók's *Duke Bluebeard's Castle*, Richard Strauss's *Elektra*, and Ferruccio Busoni's *Arlecchino*. The hit of the season was Luigi Cherubini's long-neglected *Medea*, with Leonard Bernstein conducting and the great Maria Callas (an American citizen) in the title part. Bernstein was not the only imported conductor—Dimitri Mitropoulos, Artur Rodzinski, and Herbert van Karajan each conducted works that were particular personal pets.

Though the *prime* are expensive, the joys of these performances are by no means reserved for the wealthy. After the first night, prices drop by half; the third night is cheaper still; the fourth night goes for a five-dollar top. That takes care of the subscription audience, eighty nights a year; for the other forty to forty-five performances of each season, the house is scaled at sixteen cents to $1.60 and at nine to eighty-five cents.

These are La Scala's *Serate per i Lavoratori*, quite literally "workers' evenings," and tickets to them can be bought only at the offices of Milan's labor unions. The same cast that sang on the first night sings at the workers' evenings, the same conductor conducts; though there is always a drop in the voltage of excitement after the *prima* there is no lowering of musical quality. I went to one of these workers' evenings to hear Renata Tebaldi's beautiful *Tosca*, and the audience was as impressive as the performance—serious, knowledgeable, correctly enthusiastic. Radio Italiana has contributed heavily to this knowledge with its 150 full-length opera broadcasts a year; but the main source of wisdom was clearly La Scala itself.

Italy remembers Toscanini not only as the thorough workman who was sure of what he wanted and had remarkable ways of getting just that, but above all as the heroic anti-Fascist who gave up his life's love, the top job at La Scala, and his life's dream, the top job at Bayreuth, because he would not work for the friends of Mussolini or Hitler. Fascism is very real and recent in the musical world of Italy, where Mussolini's boys still hold a number of the best jobs; the name Toscanini sounds a clear bell through the haze.

How much of the vitality and scholarship of contemporary La Scala traces back to Toscanini's days as director is something nobody can know, because everything good is attributed to him. But La Scala's most precious tradition is unquestionably Toscanini's legacy. All the great singers sing at La Scala, but it is a conductor's house. The conductor gets top billing in the advertisements and first praise or blame for a performance, and in all musical matters his authority is supreme.

Last year, the Met opened with Gounod's *Faust*, under the leadership of Pierre Monteux. Monteux shortly found better things to do —but *Faust* was a hit, so the Met turned it over to other conductors and played it throughout the season. La Scala's smash was Cherubini's *Medea*.

"We could have given ten, twelve, fifteen performances," Dr. Oldani says. "Unfortunately, Maestro Bernstein had other engagements. So the opera was withdrawn." Every conductor trains a cast to his own conception of a work, and no conductor can get the best efforts of any cast that another man has trained. At the Paris Opéra and at the Met, conductors are simply assigned to a job, and the management keeps the most successful operas going whoever comes, whoever goes. At La Scala the conductors (in consultation with Oldani and Sovrintendente Ghirlinghelli) made their own assignments: They would never even consider directing an opera another man had prepared. Its conductors don't like cast changes, either. Since singers (and guest conductors) are customarily engaged by the month, an opera is usually removed from the season's repertory within a month of its first performance.

Opera is the most complicated known form of entertainment, and pulling an opera into one piece takes immense amounts of time. Time is expensive where musicians are concerned; musicians are paid by the hour, whether for rehearsal or for performance. The Vienna Staatsoper therefore works its orchestra to the extent of nine performances a week, and the Met averages more than six. La Scala, because its conductors demand rehearsal time, makes do with less than five. This forbearance gives La Scala about 150 full orchestral rehearsals for every season, or an average of seven for each opera. La Scala's 150 rehearsals for twenty operas contrasts with the Met's seventy for twenty-five operas, and Vienna's twelve to fifteen for fifty operas. The quality of performance at the three houses is roughly in this ratio, too.

It is hard to describe the quality of a La Scala performance. Not everything is to be praised. The sets are usually unimaginative and often ugly—surprisingly so, considering the money spent on them and the great names hired as designers. The brilliant design tradition that is presently making over the face of Italy has not touched La Scala's sets. They function well and never interfere with the action, but their drab colors and clumsy proportions damage illusion. The Met, though sometimes ludicrous, and Paris, though often vulgar, give an opera more help with their stage sets. Elsewhere, La Scala demands better.

The orchestra, the best paid in Italy (its members average about $35 a week), is always magnificent, faultless in sound, impeccable in rhythmic execution. The separate wind band that tootles from onstage is extraterrestrial. The singers are the best Milan's money can buy: wonderful sopranos and basses, good altos, weak tenors (there is a world-wide shortage of tenors), and poor baritones (the best baritones are Americans and sing only occasionally at La Scala). The stage direction—let's forget the unfortunate Rosselini—is of the highest professional quality. Two-hundred-man armies in full regalia, wind bands of thirty or forty musicians, whole monasteries of monks move across La Scala's vast stage in perfect order, each man knowing where to go and what to do. Individual acting is always, of course, an individual matter; on the whole, thanks again to the great amount of rehearsal time and the fact that nobody is expected to sing more than seven times a month at most, the level of acting at La Scala is higher than at other opera houses. . . .

But these are facts rather than feelings, and it is the feel of an opera that counts. At La Scala the feeling is one of complete unity, a professional polish evenly applied to every aspect of the production, a work of art asserting itself from the stage. Part of this impression comes from the even flow of the stage direction, part from Giuseppe Piermarini's perfect eighteenth-century design for an opera house. From the outside La Scala is a square brown box with a squat porch stuck on the front. Inside, the house is elegant, gilded, and imposing (though not nearly so imposing as the Met), and the acoustics are miraculous. The sound is precisely the same at the front of the house and at the rear, at the side of the balcony and the center of the orchestra. Here all the classical works of voice projection really work and the orchestra can play as loud as the conductor wishes and the voices can still be heard. Whether Piermarini was lucky or was history's greatest master of acoustical science nobody knows. But La Scala, rebuilding a bombed-out house in 1946–47, was frankly afraid to tamper with the proportions of the architect's 1778 design.

Most important, of course, is the concentration of control in the hands of the conductors. At La Scala more than anywhere else, an operatic performance represents the execution by several hundred people of a single man's conception. The talent for tyranny is always a conductor's greatest asset, and La Scala's conductors, though no Toscaninis, are eternally masters of the iron hand. They say, probably accurately, that La Scala's orchestra is too brilliant, wild, and reckless to respond to kinder treatment. Every conductor listens to suggestions from his artists, and a man would be a fool to brush off Renata Tebaldi's instinctively perfect musical phrasing, or Maria Callas's overwhelming sense of musical characterization. But La Scala's conductors tend to compromise only when they can make the artist's suggestion an integral part of their own idea. The artist whose proposal is rejected does as instructed; responsibility and power are entirely with the conductors.

At the Met, Paris, and Vienna, performances are generally won or lost by the brilliance of the singers; and management at all three houses says, reluctantly, that the audience "comes to hear *bel canto.*" At La Scala the singers alone cannot produce what the audience expects. It has eight conductors for twenty operas as against four for fifty at Vienna, three for twenty at Paris. In addition to the four non-Italians, La Scala's conducting staff consists of *Primo Direttore* Victor de Sabata, Carlo Giulini, Gianandrea Gavazzeni, and Antonino Votto. De Sabata,[3] a kindly, frail man with violent nervous energy, is world-famous; Giulini, apparently the most generous with singers, and Gavazzeni, apparently the most scholarly, I know only from report and isolated hearing. But I watched Votto work in three very dissimilar operas—Verdi's *Don Carlos,* Puccini's *Tosca,* and Wolf-Ferrari's *I Quattro Rusteghi*—and I consider him one of the greatest of operatic conductors.

He is utterly passionless when conducting. Singers don't like him,

[3] Now retired.—Editor.

they say he has no heart. His beat is very firm, his gestures short but sharp, commanding complete obedience; in the second-act finale of *Don Carlos* he kept between thumb and baton the orchestra, a wind band of twenty-eight onstage, a chorus of eighty, eight temperamental singers, and two hundred supernumeraries. Under his direction every piece of the opera was placed exactly into its appointed niche, all friction was removed from the works, and the thing was made to run with crushing momentum, though not without delicacy and even humor. Votto is a disciple of Toscanini, and this is the Toscanini method, by which the Old Man revolutionized operatic conducting in the 1910's and 1920's. Modified in the 1950's to allow an opera more contemplative grace, it still provides that unity and force which make La Scala productions more exciting and more convincing than those of any other opera house. It is Toscanini's bequest to his best-beloved liege.

Teatro alla Scala means "Theater at the Stairs," and there once was a flight of steps there a long time ago. Milan, like New York, has leveled its ancestral hills. The stairs were gone before Giuseppe Piermarini's time, but the site had been that of a church, Santa Maria alla Scala, and the reference was kept. La Scala is a kind of shrine to the Milanese, a temple to their cultural importance. In the lobby of the theater stands statues not only to Rossini, Bellini, Donizetti, and Verdi, but to Stendhal, "who loved to call himself a Milanese."

La Scala's work is not exclusively operatic. The opera season runs from early December to early June, followed by a brief symphony season before the July vacation. August is devoted to making records and lucrative contracts. September sees the orchestra playing for the local and imported ballet troupes, October another symphony season, devoted mostly to classical German and contemporary Italian music. The final weeks of November are given over to intensive rehearsals for the opera season, and then the cycle begins all over again.

All told, La Scala puts on close to two hundred public performances a year, and sells them out at substantial prices. Because the place is a shrine, not even the most conservative Milanese would dream of canceling his subscription because of a distaste for the mass of modern music. And because it is a shrine the Italian government (through the tax on Totocalcio, the national football pool) and the city of Milan (through its ordinary budget) put up between them a subsidy equal to La Scala's entire revenue from selling tickets. "We think of nothing here but music," says Dr. Oldani.

THE BATTLE OF THE CLAQUE

Joseph Wechsberg

Annoying as it can be, the paid claque is an ancient theatrical institution. It may date back to Nero, who hired five thousand soldiers to applaud his singing. The professional claque as we know it was formed in Paris around 1820. *Clacqueurs* were specialists: one was known as a Laugher, another as a Weeper, a *Bisseur*, etc. It has been argued that the claque performs a useful function in that it teaches an audience when and where to applaud. I doubt it.

"I am a true democrat . . . but in the fourth gallery I firmly believe in the authoritative system."

The claque at the Vienna Staatsoper was an exclusive group of forty innocent opera lovers with uncompromising ideas about good music and good singing. Joseph Schostal, the claque chef, a dignified man with black sideburns, high-toned principles, and great authority, who gave us free standing room admissions in the fourth gallery in return for applause, never failed to remind us of the claque's "classical tradition." I became a full-fledged member of the illustrious body in the twenties, when I studied music at the Vienna Conservatory. Every once in a while, Schostal called a meeting at his permanent headquarters, the back room of the Peterskeller, a traditionless beer cellar across from the Staatsoper, and over foam crowns of *Gösserbräu* reminisced about the history of the claque.

The founder of the noble institution was the great Schoentag, who commanded a social position in Kaiser Franz Josef's Vienna before the turn of the century. Schoentag went out riding in the Prater in the luxurious equipage of Ernest Marie Van Dyck, the great Belgian *Wagnertenor*—"best Parsifal they ever had in Bayreuth," Schos-

From *Sweet and Sour* by Joseph Wechsberg, by permission of Houghton Mifflin Company.

tal said; "studied the part under Mottl"—and played whist with Hans
Richter, director of the Hofoper, as it was called in those feudal days.
Once the Kronprinz Rudolf honored the claque chef by inviting him
to supper at the Hotel Sacher and letting him pay the bill. The Kronprinz was a great patron of the claque before he became the Hero of
the Mayerling Saga. Some lesser members of the imperial household
exercised their cordial relations with the claque to promote subtly
the artistic futures of the blue-eyed, slim-ankled coryphees of the
ballet.

Schoentag's successor was a man by the name of Wessely, who, like
almost all prominent Viennese, hailed from the fertile plains of
Moravia. Wessely lived the life of a *grand seigneur,* was called "my
dear friend" by Lilli Lehmann, had a son in a Kaiserliches Husaren-
Regiment, and owned a house in Hietzing, a swank suburban district.
He died of a broken heart when Hofoperndirektor Gustav Mahler,
in a temperamental whim, abolished the claque.

"Then came the horrible, the claqueless interregnum," Schostal
said. "It was a wild, chaotic time, with several hand-clapping outlaws
operating inside the Opera. Then there was Freudenberger."

We knew the sad tale of old Freudenberger. We saw him in the
fourth gallery every time *Fidelio* was given. He would slip in through
a side door, carrying a half-torn, battered score of Beethoven's opera.
He shuffled along the wall, trying not to look at people, his lips silently moving—the ghostly appearance of a white-bearded patriarch. As
claque chef, he had been a close friend of the Austrian playwright and
novelist Hermann Bahr and his wife, the great dramatic soprano Anna
von Mildenburg. Later Freudenberger's artistic judgment became
somewhat dimmed by the demon alcohol. The claque operates 'way
up in the fourth gallery, and after too many siedels of Schwechater
beer, Freudenberger was unable to climb up the two-hundred-odd
stairs leading to the "Fourth." He would spend the evening in a
Beisel, the local equivalent of a beer joint, leaving the conduct of
applause to his incapable underlings. Soon plain anarchy reigned in
the fourth gallery, and the artists who had paid cash to Freudenberger and didn't get the proper applause were in a rebellious frame
of mind.

"This proves what lack of leadership will do," Schostal would
say. "I am a true democrat in my political convictions, but in the
fourth gallery I firmly believe in the authoritative system."

In the twilight era of Freudenberger, Schostal, then a youthful music student, all but slept at the Opera. He was there every evening and during the daytime hung around the stage doors—there were separate entrances for singers (male), singers (female), orchestra members, chorus, ballet, stagehands, executives—and when one of his idols went by, he would take off his hat and meekly exclaim, *"Hoch!"* One night before a performance of *Samson et Dalila,* the prima ballerina, Jammerich, a temperamental lady, refused to go out on the stage unless the Freudenberger gang was silenced and "that nice young man Schostal" was called in to organize the applause for her. "I want him to come here right away," she said to the horrified Hofoper executives. *"I zih mi net aus*—I won't undress." And to prove that she really meant business, she didn't undress.

A runner was dispatched to the fourth gallery and in no time Schostal, dumfounded and trembling, found himself sitting in the prima ballerina's private dressing room. The dancer explained that she wanted special applause after the ballet in the first act, "something that makes their rear ends jerk up from their seats."

"I agreed to give all I had and the prima ballerina smiled and began to get out of her many petticoats," Schostal said. "I remember well. First a purple taffeta one with ruffles, then a light-purple one made of fine silk, with Brussels laces, then a pinkish one of tulle, sort of shirred, and then a beautiful petticoat of ethereal white batiste." When he got to this point of his story, Schostal took out a handkerchief and mopped his brow in nostalgic excitement. "She was a great dancer," he said, with a deep sigh, and there was finality in his voice.

Schostal was an idealist and a businessman who managed to make a fortune out of his love of good opera. He refused to take money from singers whom he didn't consider worthy of the Staatsoper, and got infuriated when some Viennese newspapers, envious of the claque's influence on matters operatic, called us *eine amerikanische Gangstergruppe.* Schostal had his own scientific theory of applause. "The driving power of the initial applause must overcome the inherent inertia of the audience," he said. Many singers considered him their artistic father confessor and several times Franz Schalk, director of the Staatsoper, invited him to sit in on auditions of young artists, which Schostal rightly considered the high point of his career. Once Hans Liebstoeckl, the editor of the *Extrablatt,* offered him the job of music critic, but Schostal refused. It didn't seem ethical to mix applause with criticism. Liebstoeckl said, "The claque chef of the Barcelona Opera is also the town's leading music critic," but Schostal said, "No, sorry."

Schostal was anxious to keep up the high artistic standard of applause and devoted much effort to the training of new men. At the end of the 1925 season several claque members whose homes were in the "province" were called back from Vienna by their enraged families because the boys spent more time at the Staatsoper than in school. Schostal then decided to hold regular auditions for new candidates. They took place at the janitor's box under the Kärntnerstrasse arcades, in an area with walls and floors of large marble squares, where the acoustics came nearest to applause conditions in the fourth gallery.

Schostal originally intended to hold his auditions in the "Fourth," but the management of the Staatsoper failed to see his point. He would sit down on the large bench which was customarily reserved for Leo Slezak, Erik Schmedes, Richard Schubert, and other aging tenors, and the candidate, after a thorough examination in operatic airs, recitatives, leitmotivs, detailed knowledge of popular scores, and "general music understanding," was ordered to produce some *Probeapplaus*— test applause. If a man wanted to make the grade, he had to produce what Schostal called *den dunklen Klang*—the deep, dark sound. High-pitched hand-clapping was considered girlish and strictly taboo.

Few men came up with the hollow-sounding, sepulchral applause that had the professional touch. Schostal would glance at Herr Nusterer, the janitor, a tall, mustachioed man in an admiral's uniform, who looked on the gloomy side of things and had only two sorts of comment. A candidate would be either "bad" or "very bad." If Schostal liked the candidate and Nusterer's comment was "bad," Schostal would accept the new man for a trial period. After the audition, Schostal and Nusterer would send to the Peterskeller for a *Frühschoppen* beer.

Schostal had a strange respect for Nusterer, who had been *Portier* at the Opera for over twenty-six years and had never been at a single performance. Once he had gone into the auditorium during the third act of *Walküre*, looking for Herr Dr. Richard Strauss, but the spectacle of eight full-bosomed ladies jumping all over the stage and screaming, "Hojotojo!! Heiaha-ha!!" had been too much of a shock. Nusterer lived in Mauer, a suburb mainly populated by grimly underpaid federal employees, and he hated Wagner because the interminable performances of *Meistersinger, Tristan,* and *Götterdämmerung* usually made him miss the "last blue" trolley car, which left the Operngasse at five minutes past eleven.

"If a man for twenty-six years has worked at the Opera and never heard a performance, he must be either an archmoron or have character," Schostal said. "Nusterer is no moron, so I have decided that he's got character. That's why I ask his opinion about our new candidates. Nusterer is the Voice of the People."

Nusterer's great ambition was to converse in the English language. The Staatsoper and the Burgtheater in Vienna were the only two theaters on earth which had no daytime box offices. The box offices were opened only half an hour before the beginning of the evening performance. There were a few agiotage peddlers, hiding behind the marble pillars and in the niches near the entrance, who had tickets concealed in their pockets as though they were dirty postcards, but they charged innocent passers-by twice the official price. The only place where tickets were sold at regular prices between 9:00 A.M and 3:00 P.M. was the Bundestheaterdirektion at the Bräunerstrasse, a ten-minute walk from the Opera.

Anglo-Saxon visitors staying at the Bristol, the Imperial, or other Ringstrasse hotels, who came to the Staatsoper for tickets, always got lost in search of the box office before they wound up at Nusterer's lodge. It was always a great moment for the *Portier* when he could tell those *Valuta-Aristokraten* from England and America how to get to the Bräunerstrasse. He had learned English all by himself from a then popular book entitled *Learning English—A Pleasure*.

"Döss iss simpel," Nusterer would say. "Jöst nomadize over the Operngasse and takens the firsht street for your lefft. Net right, net *gradaus*, böt lefft. Jöst promenade and follow your nose. Pörsue the Augustinerstrassen öntil the Josefsplatz. Dös iss a tulli platz, the Josefsplatz. Firsht for your right and firsht house for your lefft—and da sa ma." Seeing a blank expression on the faces of his customers, Nusterer continued, "Nachurell', today iss *ausverkauft*, bought out. Maybe tomorrow bought out. Böt keep smiling. Dös iss simpel. Go buy tickets to Theater-an-der-Wien. *Gräfin Mariza*, they give. Or the Ronacher girls. Graceföl and déshabillée—böt iss all right for *die gnädige Frau*."

Nusterer entertained cordial relations with the claque chef. Schostal paid for the *Frühschoppen* and in return was given by Nusterer advance information on who would be on police duty at the evening performance. The *Portier* had his own channels to the Polizeipräsidium. Every night there were four *Kriminalinspektoren,* plain-clothes men, on duty inside the house, two in the parterre standing room, one in the fourth and one in the third gallery. We never understood why they had a man posted in the third gallery. No *claqueur* would be seen dead or alive in the "Third," where the acoustics were deplorable; third-gallery tickets were sold only to innocent travelers from the hillbilly districts of Styria, Sudetenland, the Hungarian bush, and the American Far West.

There were signs inside the Opera reading "*Alle störenden Bei- so wie Missfallsbezeugungen sind verboten*—All Disturbing Manifestations of Ap- and Disap-proval Are Prohibited," and the four *Inspektoren* on duty were always after offenders, most of whom naturally belonged to the claque. All policemen liked Staatsoper duty because they were paid an extra seven schilling per evening and besides received a *Dienstsitz,* a duty seat. They never used the seats for themselves but brought their *Pupperln* along. The girl friends sat down and the cops remained in the standing room. One *Inspektor,* an elderly man with four children, whom I'll call Weber, brought as many as three different *Pupperln* in one week. I remember a Botticelli blonde who came always to Mozart and early Verdi operas, and a luscious redhead who preferred the more lascivious side of the repertoire— *Thaïs, Salome, Elektra, Schéhérazade,* and the Venusberg scene from *Tannhäuser.*

The Botticelli blonde was on the *Dienstsitz* one evening when Emanuel List sang the Cardinal in Halévy's *La Juive,* a part that in Vienna was associated with the great Richard Mayr. Mayr was one of the claque's best clients, but List was an excellent man, and Schostal's private ambition was always to give able people a break. He loved the challenge of a difficult assignment. Knowing what he was up against, Schostal alerted the *Hohlposcher*—Hollow Sound Men—a powerful task force of six master *claqueurs* who were alerted only on critical evenings. I remember three of them, Gold, Ritter, and Hofbauer, strong and fearless men. When they started to applaud, it was as though a regiment of heavy tanks were rumbling over a cobblestoned street at high speed.

List sang the air of the Cardinal in great style and Schostal from his command post under the first lamp on the extreme left gave his "cue," a faint nod of his bald head. The Hollow Sound Men, strategically posted behind the marble pillars, broke into a deafening drumfire that shook the house and roused the audience into a "spontaneous" ovation. The din was so formidable that people sitting near-by put their fingers into their ears. An elderly, bald misanthrope with the face of an unhappy baboon turned around and shook his fists against us. The Hollow Sound Men ignored him coolly. They started another heavy barrage after the duet of the Cardinal and Leonora, which was even more earsplitting. All of a sudden the bald man jumped up and shouted, *"Polizei! Polizei!"* and ran out of the gallery. The *Hohlposcher* didn't even bother to pull his leg as he ran out past them, and Schostal said, "Guess he wants to make the last train for Steinhof." Steinhof was Austria's largest insane asylum.

After the second act, Kriminalinspektor Weber and his blonde *Pupperl* came up to our command post. Weber gave the girl ten groschen and told her to get him a glass of water, and when she had gone, he turned toward Schostal. "I'm afraid you're in serious trouble, *Herr Doktor*," he said. Schostal's influence was known among the Force, and many coppers called the claque chef *Herr Professor* or *Herr Doktor*. "A fellow just asked me to arrest you. He says he'll get the District Attorney to prosecute you for serious bodily injury."

We were stunned. According to paragraph 152 of the Austrian penal code, *schwere körperliche Beschädigung* meant busting in a man's skull or breaking his shinbones, putting him out of action "for at least twenty days," and none of us had as much as touched the madman. Weber said, "You see, he's got some trouble with his ears, and when you started that salvo, he got ill. *Himmelherrgott*, that was a blast! My Grerterl almost fell down from my seat. He made me write down a protocol. You will have to see Hofrat Ritzberger to-morrow morning."

The *Hofrat*, chef of the police Strafsektion and a great friend of the claque chef, was already well informed about the misadventure, when Schostal came to see him. He got up from his chair and they shook hands. The *Hofrat* said, "Well, well, well—what now?"

"A man with ear trouble has no business coming up in the fourth gallery," Schostal said. "The next time he will file a claim against the Staatsoper, the *Bundestheaterverwaltung*, and the entire Republic of Austria, because the bass tubas in the second act of *Walküre* made him sick. You remember the bass tubas when Hunding gets killed by Wotan, *Herr Hofrat*?"

Ritzberger offered Schostal a *trabuco* cigar and explained that legally there was a difference between the *Walküre* bass tubas and the salvo of our Hollow Sound Men. "A man who buys a ticket legally must anticipate the bass tubas because they are a fixture of the Opera, like curtains and lights. The claque isn't—yet. However, I'll add a postscript to the protocol when I send it over to the District Attorney. I hope he won't press any charges which would get you before a jury." Three bad weeks went by, during which the claque showed notable restraint and a certain lack of enthusiasm. Then Hofrat Ritzberger called up Schostal and told him that the D.A. had not bothered about the case. That night, at a performance of *The Flying Dutchman* with Friedrich Schorr, the claque was again in great form.

The Hollow Sound Men caused more trouble at a memorable evening of *La Fanciulla del West*, with Maria Jeritza as Minnie and Alfred Jerger as Sheriff Jack Rance—both clients of the claque. In the second act Minnie plays her famous poker game with the Sheriff, cheats, and wins after using cards that she had hidden under the upper part of her stocking. It was a great scene and Jeritza made the best of it, and there was always a terrific ovation for her. The girls of the Jeritza Club, an amateurish fan organization of thin-voiced subsub-debs under the leadership of one Herr Silberstein of the *Bodenkreditanstalt*, shouted like mad.

In the general bedlam, Mr. Jerger, the able baritone, was completely forgotten. Finally he couldn't stand it any more. One evening he got in touch with Messrs. Gold and Hofbauer of the *Hohlposcher* and asked them, for the sake of artistic justice, to put in a few cries of "Hoch Jerger!" The Hollow Sound Men dutifully reported Jerger's request to Schostal, during the roll call under the arcades, when Schostal gave out standing room admission, shortly before the performance. There was always a lot of noise and excitement during the roll call and Schostal didn't give the matter much attention, but told the task force to go ahead on their own.

Too late the claque chef realized what he had let himself in for. At the end of the second act, the Hollow Sound Men raced down the stairs from the gallery, broke through the *Parkett* auditorium and ran up to the orchestra pit, where they started *unisono* to shout, "Hoch Jerger!" There was a magic about their booming basso profundo voices and the well-domesticated Viennese audience took up the hint immediately. Within a few seconds even old Jeritza admirers found themselves shouting, "Hoch Jerger!" many, as they later shamefacedly explained, against their better judgment. Things got so bad that Silberstein of the Jeritza Club approached the Hollow Sound Men and meekly asked them to let his girls have "just one curtain call for Jeritza alone." By that time a general reaction had set in; everybody was tired and hoarse, and the Jeritza ovation fell flat.

Up in the fourth gallery Schostal watched this major disaster with trembling hands. Madame Jeritza was one of the claque's outstanding clients and there was no saying what she might do. "*Mea culpa!*" the claque chef murmured. "I'll have to take a walk to Canossa." The Hollow Sound Men were sorry for what they had done, and wanted to go with the chef to apologize to Madame Jeritza. Schostal was deeply moved. "I appreciate your loyalty, men," he said. "But it was my fault and I have to face her alone."

He told us later what happened when he accompanied Madame Jeritza from the Staatsoper to her home at Stallburggasse 4. "She was furious and I can't blame her. 'Have you heard those hooligans?' she said. 'I got so mad I couldn't even look out for them. Who were they —morons from the province who thought this was the Sunday afternoon football game on the Hohe Warte?' " Schostal breathed heavily. "I told her that I was beside myself—that it won't happen again. And it won't," he added, a Boris Godunov-like expression in his fierce eyes.

The Hollow Sound Men displayed conspicuous bravery beyond and above the call of duty in what the annals of the Viennese police call the Battle of the Claque. This took place in 1925, one night after the première of Richard Strauss's *Intermezzo*. It was a conflict among Vienna's cab drivers that precipitated the Battle. There were two groups of taxicabs in Vienna, the fifty-groschen taxis, dilapidated vehicles of proletarian domestic origin—Steyr, Wanderer, Tatra—and the eighty-groschen de luxe conveyances—early vintage Studebakers, Panhard-Levassors, Fords, Lancias, and other elegantly superannuated foreign-make limousines. The fifty-groschlers and the eighty-groschlers both parked at the Operngasse, but the more aristocratic eighty-groschen cabbies seldom spoke to the fifty-groschen hoi polloi, and there was quite a feeling of class consciousness.

Schostal, who attended to the *Wagenvertrieb* around the Staatsoper, insisted that all prominent singers ride in the more dignified eighty-groschen cars. After the evening performance, when the singers at the stage door were waiting for cabs, he would never let a humble fifty-groschen man approach any of his clients.

"They've got broken windows, bad springs, and no heat," he would say. "You can't take a chance with them."

Finally the fifty-groschlers couldn't stand it any longer. A deputation approached the claque chef at his Peterskeller headquarters. "We don't care about the carfare," the spokesman, a red-bearded ex-wrestler from Hernals, Vienna's Third Avenue, said. "We'll be happy to drive them home gratis but we want to go home and be able to tell our wives that we, too, are driving the Lehmann and the Jeritza. We are getting sick and tired of being heckled by our wives and children. 'All day around the Opera and never one of them *Kammer-sänger* in your cab,' they say." The ex-wrestler paused for a last man-to-man appeal. "If you were married, *Herr Doktor,* you would know what a wife can do to you."

Schostal finished his beer and wiped his mouth. "I am very sorry," he said finally. "But I cannot possibly permit Frau Kammersängerin Lehmann to ride in a Steyr that may never reach her destination. She should forever ride in a Rolls-Royce, filled with Persian rugs and crystal mirrors," he added poetically. The red-bearded spokesman muttered dark threats, and the deputation left in a rage.

A few nights later, after the sensational première of *Intermezzo,* Schostal saw to it that Madame Lehmann, who won a triumph as Christine, was taken back home in the most luxurious eighty-groschen car, a black Buick limousine that was called *"der nobliche Booeek"* around the Staatsoper. Then all members of the claque adjourned to the Peterskeller to discuss the Strauss première over *Rindsgulasch* and beer. All of a sudden the door was torn open and a mob of blood-thirsty fifty-groschlers broke into the room. They were led by the red-bearded ex-wrestler, who seized a beer seidel—not his own, at that —and threw it against Schostal. If the claque chef hadn't shielded his face with the brand-new score of *Intermezzo,* he would have been badly hit. The expensive score got wet all over with stale beer. It was this sight that infuriated us members of the claque more than the raging cabbies. Beer glasses and plates with goulash were thrown through the air, but the cab drivers outnumbered us five to one and they advanced steadily. Schostal jumped on a beer barrel, from where he directed the battle, proving that real leadership shows itself in moments of dire stress.

"We have to hold them until our eighty-groschen reinforcements arrive," he shouted. The Hollow Sound Men fought like lions. Gold took off his braces and whirled them around in a mad circle, hitting 'em right and left, while Hofbauer tore legs off a heavy table and bravely attacked the ex-wrestler. Meanwhile Immerglück, a gray-haired, fifty-year-old boy, crawled down under the tables on hands and

knees, the way the Nibelungen do in the first act of *Siegfried*, and managed to get out on the Operngasse, where he hollered for the eighty-
groschen men to come to our support. Unfortunately most of the de
luxe cabbies were out on rides, taking the singers home. One by one
they returned, and there were also a few *Nächtler*, night chauffeurs,
who took our side and heroically dived into the scramble, but there
is no doubt that only the arrival of twenty-odd policemen saved the
claque from complete annihilation.

We all, fifty-groschlers, eighty-groschlers, night chauffeurs, claque
members, and three beer-drinking members of the Philharmoniker,
who had come to our support out of nowhere, were taken to the nearest police *Wachtstube*. The Hollow Sound Men looked badly beaten
up, Gold's pants were falling down because he couldn't find his braces,
and Schostal was holding the pitiful remains of the expensive *Intermezzo* score under his elbow. Another pitched battle flared up in the
police wagon when a fifty-groschler spat at the man who had brought
Madame Lehmann home in his "Booeek," but the police officer on
duty in the *Wachtstube* handled the matter efficiently. Schostal, well
known on the police premises as a champion of Law and Order, was
released at once. The members of the claque, the three Philharmoniker, the eighty-groschlers, and the night chauffeurs remained at
the station for another hour, and were sent home with a few words of
mild reprimand. The fifty-groschen rowdies were held behind bars all
night long and fined twenty schilling each for rioting and disturbing
the peace.

THE OPERA BOX: THE SORROWS OF A NEW YORK HOSTESS

Alice Duer Miller

What happens when you are trying to give your opera tickets away? Related by the American writer in *Harper's Bazar*, March, 1908, but still applicable.

"How selfish the idle rich are!"

Many people who are at a loss to understand the point of view of those who are willing year after year to undertake all the infinite trouble which most entertaining involves, could imagine a great deal of pleasure could be derived from an opera box. Those who own one tell a different story.

In the first place, the opera comes so often. We should not think of pledging ourselves to give a dinner party once, twice, or three times a week during the entire season; yet on a small scale that is what the owner of a box is forced to do. The ideal number is five—two women and three men. You ask some good-looking girl, who will sit up straight and wear pretty clothes and contribute her beauty to the appearance of the house; then there is yourself and your husband. No one else is needed except two "nice men." But unfortunately, the visible supply of nice men is limited, and most of them who are known to go about are engaged weeks ahead, and some of those who are not cannot abide music; and you may easily spend three days in writing notes, and two more at the telephone, without finding any man to accompany you, except your husband—a state of things which would not please the "good-looking girl" at all. If a dinner party begins to go wrong you can let it go—have a cold, and recall your invitations, but you cannot leave your box empty. There it is, a terribly expensive opportunity for giving pleasure to someone.

Perhaps it is a horror of wasting it, perhaps it is mere respect for the appearance of the house, but box-owners are very careful to fill

From *Harper's Bazaar*, March, 1908.

their boxes; and when they find that on a given evening a superior attraction is going to call them away they sit down and write some little note like this:

My dear Mrs. Gadding:

It would be such a pleasure to me if you could use my box for the 27th. I am enclosing the tickets in the hope that you will accept them.

Very sincerely yours,

Rita Starr

But Mrs. Gadding is also among the seventy-five particularly carefully chosen souls who are going to the Vespers' costume dinner, and she does not much like Rita's assumption that she is not. She sends the box back, not too quickly, with a line to say that she has a previous engagement. She might be weak enough to add where that engagement was, were it not that she realizes Rita will see her there in due time.

So Rita casts about in her mind, and suddenly remembers her husband's Aunt Gertrude, who is so fond of music, and whom they have not asked to the opera for more than a year.

Dearest Aunt Gertrude: [she writes, trying to curb her hurried pen so that it shall trace characters legible to the old] will you do Bob and me the great honor of occupying our box on the 27th? We thought it would be nicer for you to make up your own party, and so we are sending you all the six tickets.

I have been wanting to come and see you every day for the past month, but you know how busy I am.

Your affectionate niece,

Rita

She rings and despatches it with a feeling of duty well done. But she has reckoned without her aunt. Within two hours she gets the tickets back by the hand of her aunt's elderly manservant.

My dear Rita:

Many thanks for your kindness in thinking of me. I am, as you know, very fond of music, and some night when you and Bob wish me to go to the opera I shall be very glad to do so; but I think I shall wait until then. I know I am old-fashioned, but I could as little enjoy entertaining my friends in your box during your absence as I could giving a dinner party at your expense.

Your loving

Aunt G.

Rita, who is essentially a child of her times, cannot understand such scruples, and remarks to Bob that "some people do contrive to make it very hard to be civil to them."

And here it is the twenty-first, and she has not much time, so she scribbles a line on her visiting card to her best friend:

DEAR NELLIE: Couldn't you take the box for the 27th, just to oblige yours, R.?

Again those hateful tickets return.

Thanks, dear. This is the eleventh box I have had offered me for the 27th. Have already accepted two.

Rita begins to feel resentful, as if her friends were willfully leaving her in the lurch. She consults a small book she keeps to help her out in these crises. No use in asking the Van Aspics, or the Hooks; they will surely be going to the Vespers, and yet, no harm to try. Then there is Bob's partner and his fat wife. Perhaps if she sent the box to them she would not have to invite them to dinner this year. See what a comfort that would be! And then there are those cousins of Bob's, who live somewhere in West Eighty-ninth Street, and all entertained a sentiment for Bob before his marriage. She hastily scratches down a list while she dresses, and as she goes through the hall on her way to the theater, she tells her butler to telephone these ladies in the order named, and offer the box for the twenty-seventh.

When she comes home at midnight, he meets her, and tells her triumphantly that Mrs. Van Aspic accepts the box with pleasure for the twenty-second, and that he has despatched the tickets.

"For the twenty-second! Oh, Cleverbridge," cries poor Rita, "I said the twenty-seventh! The twenty-second is tomorrow, and you know I have people dining here to go to the opera with *me*."

Cleverbridge looks aggrieved. He will go to his grave believing that she said the twenty-second, but he bows and says: "I'm sorry to have misunderstood you, madam."

It takes Rita all the next day to disentangle this complication and get back her tickets for her own guests. The Van Aspics had already begun to make up their party, and are not at all appeased by being offered the box for the twenty-seventh. Of course they are going to the Vespers. Rita knew it perfectly well. They have a faint notion that she just changed her mind about the twenty-second, and took her box away on purpose.

In the end Rita summons her husband, and suggests that he should call up his cousin Louisa and ask her if she could go on the twenty-seventh. Bob, who always feels a little guilty that Louisa is not very often asked to his house, although at one time he almost lived at her mother's, agrees with alacrity, and presently comes upstairs with the soothed expression of a man who has been in conversation with one who appreciates him.

"She'll take it," he said. "Seems awfully pleased."

"I hope you said, Bob, that if she could not use it any of the other thirteen sisters would do as well."

"There are only four, Rita, and I did not say so. I thought it seemed nicer to make it something personal to Louisa."

But Rita has lost interest. At last the box is off her mind. Or is it?

Five days pass. It is the twenty-seventh. She is actually dressing for the Vespers—a process which begins at six, although dinner is not set until eight-thirty, and everyone knows no one will come before nine—when Bob knocks at the door. He enters quite sorrowfully, his head whitened, a sheet around his neck to protect his fine clothes from the powder, and a note in his hand—a note thick with six tickets.

Rita gives a faint scream when she sees it.

"Don't tell me it's back again," she cries, turning up her chin to the costumer, who is engaged in placing a patch upon it.

"Yes," says Bob. "It seems she feels symptoms of approaching grippe, and—"

"I told you to say the sisters would do, Bob."

"She mentions that she did feel tempted to give it to Annie, but on second thoughts knew it would be more polite to return it to me."

"Oh, Bob, your relations have too fine feelings for me," says Rita, smiling. "Some people's politeness gives more trouble than rudeness. Now the only thing to do is to telephone the garage and send the tickets back by the automobile, and tell Louisa to give them to Annie or the ashman. I don't want to see them again."

Perhaps Bob does not succeed in softening this message sufficiently, for when they return from the costume dinner, which was followed by a vaudeville, which was followed by a supper, they see on the hall table an envelope enclosing the tickets, without any note.

So the Starrs' box stood empty through one of the most perfect performances of the year; and the directors saw it, and thought that their stockholders had no real love of music; and Rita's friends in the parquet saw it, and thought she might at least have offered it to them; and her critics in the galleries saw it, and thought how selfish the idle rich are: too sated to enjoy things themselves, too lazy to give them to others.

HOW TO ACT IN OPERA

Alfred V. Frankenstein

> More years ago than he himself cares to remember, Alfred Frankenstein, who as music and art critic of the San Francisco *Chronicle* dispenses blame and praise for the operatic activities of that civilized city, proposed a new school for operatic acting. Since these words were put on paper, the quality of operatic acting seems to have improved; there is perhaps less need today for such a school. Or hasn't it? And is there?

"Basic Attitude No. 1 is the Bucket Balance.*"*

For many years, man and boy, professional and amateur, it has been my pleasure to observe many of the world's greatest operatic stars on the stages of Berlin, Rome, Florence, Paris, New York, Chicago and San Francisco. As a result of this polyglot experience I have perfected what is now in process of being patented under the name of the *All-American Five-Point System of Operatic Acting.* Just as there are five positions basic to the art of the classic ballet, so operatic acting is reduced in this system to five basic attitudes, which, by variation, permutation, combination, synthesis, conjunction and conglomeration create an entire language of gesture suitable for use in any and all situations in any and all operas.

Basic Attitude No. 1 is the *Bucket Balance.* This is a position derived from the peculiar thing that happens automatically to one's left arm when carrying a heavy pail of water in the right hand. Its plain, or stiff-armed form has an important variant, the *Cursive Bucket Balance,* done with a more supple motion from the elbow. Both these gestures are universally useful. They can be employed to indicate jealousy, ecstasy, choler, or (as is usually the case) nothing at all.

A second highly important variant of the *Bucket Balance* is the *In-*

By permission of Alfred V. Frankenstein.

visible Churn. When indulged in at arm's length this movement is much favored by chorus people to signify animated conversation. When done with a short jab and crooked elbow, the clenched fist close to the chest, it indicates villainy. This latter form, however, might be called one of the several variations of:

Basic Attitude No. 2, the *Heart Attack.* This action, one hand placed firmly over the upper ribs, is too well known to require description, as is its first transformation, the *Double-Breasted Heart Attack.* In this same category comes the *Asthma Clutch,* similar to the *Heart Attack,* but with the fingers at the base of the throat. Also under this general heading one must place the *Lemon Squeeze,* wherein the hands are joined in a tight clasp about four inches in front of the breast bone.

Basic Attitude No. 3 is *Worse Than Death.* The head is lowered, the hand grasps the back hair, and the bent arm forms a kind of frame for the head. This can be done either seated or standing. It often alternates with:

Basic Attitude No. 4, the *Guy Rope Stance.* The hands are extended stiffly downward, at an angle of about forty-five degrees from the body, the chest is thrown out, and the feet are often parted in a kind of frozen stride. The whole picture is designed, as far as possible, after the appearance of a governor on a motor. Required of wronged husbands when the bad news breaks, but useful in other situations as well.

Fifth and last of the Basic Attitudes is the *Fevered Brow.* The back (never the palm) of one hand is placed on the forehead, the head itself is frequently tilted either backward or forward, and the other arm is always extended in a *Bucket Balance.* The *Fevered Brow* is usually completed with a determined, side-swiping motion of the hand away from the head indicating that the incredible revelation that produced the gesture in the first place is too dreadful to be believed. It then frequently goes into the *Guy Rope Stance.*

These are the movements and positions basic to every operatic work of every school and nationality, and therefore are universally applicable. There is also a rich field of gesture and action peculiar to specific works and specific roles which I also propose to teach. I shall, for instance, give careful instruction to *Carmen* chorus ladies on the approved method of singeing their eyebrows while smoking cigarettes that stick straight up in the air. Embryo Valkyries graduating from our academy will be thoroughly proficient in the *Bloodhound Snoop,*

Seven O'Clock in the Morning (an exercise for the development of the right biceps done with a spear instead of a dumbbell) and other calisthenics of Wagnerian interpretation. No one training for any part in *Aïda* can afford to dispense with *Heil Hitler* and the *Egyptian Double-Breasted Heart Attack*. The approved methods of hunting for hidden objects in places where they very obviously have not been hidden will occupy an important place in the curriculum. All manner of shudders, staggers, flops and falls will be appropriately codified. And the subject of placing daggers under the armpit will call for a course all its own.

NATASHA GOES TO THE OPERA
from *War and Peace*

Leo Tolstoy

> One of the most delightful of the humorous scenes in
> *War and Peace*. How adroitly Tolstoy transports Na-
> tasha from the absurd to the receptive mood, an experi-
> ence which the author himself must have undergone a
> number of times! The specific opera of the scene has
> not been identified; it probably was not meant to be.

The floor of the stage consisted of smooth boards, at the sides
was some painted cardboard representing trees, and at the back was a
cloth stretched over boards. In the center of the stage sat some girls
in red bodices and white skirts. One very fat girl in a white silk dress
sat apart on a low bench, to the back of which a piece of green cardboard was glued. They all sang something. When they had finished
their song the girl in white went up to the prompter's box and a man
with tight silk trousers over his stout legs, and holding a plume and a
dagger, went up to her and began singing, waving his arms about.

First the man in the tight trousers sang alone, then she sang, then
they both paused while the orchestra played and the man fingered
the hand of the girl in white, obviously awaiting the beat to start singing with her. They sang together and everyone in the theater began
clapping and shouting, while the man and the woman on the stage—
who represented lovers—began smiling, spreading out their arms and
bowing.

After her life in the country, and in her present serious mood, all
this seemed grotesque and amazing to Natasha. She could not follow
the opera nor even listen to the music, she saw only the painted cardboard and the queerly dressed men and women who moved, spoke and
sang, so strangely in that brilliant light. She knew what it was all
meant to represent, but it was so pretentiously false and unnatural that
she first felt ashamed for the actors and then amused at them. She
looked at the faces of the audience, seeking in them the same sense of

ridicule and perplexity she herself experienced, but they all seemed attentive to what was happening on the stage, and expressed delight which to Natasha seemed feigned. "I suppose it has to be like this!" she thought. She kept looking round in turn at the rows of pomaded heads in the stalls and then at the seminude women in the boxes, especially at Hélène in the next box, who—apparently quite unclothed —sat with a quiet tranquil smile, not taking her eyes off the stage. And feeling the bright light that flooded the whole place and the warm air heated by the crowd, Natasha little by little began to pass into a state of intoxication she had not experienced for a long while. She did not realize who and where she was, nor what was going on before her. As she looked and thought, the strangest fancies unexpectedly and disconnectedly passed through her mind: the idea occurred to her of jumping onto the edge of the box and singing the air the actress was singing, then she wished to touch with her fan an old gentleman sitting not far from her, then to lean over to Hélène and tickle her.

At a moment when all was quiet before the commencement of a song, a door leading to the stalls on the side nearest the Rostovs' box creaked, and the steps of a belated arrival were heard. "There's Kuragin!" whispered Shinshin. Countess Bezukhova turned smiling to the newcomer, and Natasha, following the direction of that look, saw an exceptionally handsome adjutant approaching their box with a self-assured yet courteous bearing. This was Anatole Kuragin whom she had seen and noticed long ago at the ball in Petersburg. He was now in an adjutant's uniform with one epaulette and a shoulder-knot. He moved with a restrained swagger which would have been ridiculous had he not been so good-looking and had his handsome face not worn such an expression of good-humored complacency and gaiety. Though the performance was proceeding, he walked deliberately down the carpeted gangway, his sword and spurs slightly jingling and his handsome perfumed head held high. Having looked at Natasha he approached his sister, laid his well-gloved hand on the edge of her box, nodded to her, and leaning forward asked a question, with a motion toward Natasha.

"*Mais charmante!*" said he, evidently referring to Natasha, who did not exactly hear his words but understood them from the movement of his lips. Then he took his place in the first row of the stalls and sat down beside Dolokhov, nudging with his elbow in a friendly and offhand way that Dolokhov whom others treated so fawningly. He winked at him gaily, smiled, and rested his foot against the orchestra screen.

"How like the brother is to the sister," remarked the count. "And how handsome they both are!"

Shinshin, lowering his voice, began to tell the count of some intrigue of Kuragin's in Moscow, and Natasha tried to overhear it just because he had said she was *"charmante."*

The first act was over. In the stalls everyone began moving about, going out and coming in.

Boris came to the Rostovs' box, received their congratulations very simply, and raising his eyebrows with an absent-minded smile conveyed to Natasha and Sonya his fiancée's invitation to her wedding, and went away. Natasha with a gay coquettish smile talked to him, and congratulated on his approaching wedding that same Boris with whom she had formerly been in love. In the state of intoxication she was in everything seemed simple and natural.

The scantily clad Hélène smiled at everyone in the same way, and Natasha gave Boris a similar smile.

Hélène's box was filled and surrounded from the stalls, by the most distinguished and intellectual men, who seemed to vie with one another in their wish to let everyone see that they knew her.

During the whole of that entr'acte Kuragin stood with Dolokhov in front of the orchestra partition looking at the Rostovs' box. Natasha knew he was talking about her and this afforded her pleasure. She even turned so that he should see her profile in what she thought was its most becoming aspect. Before the beginning of the second act Pierre appeared in the stalls. The Rostovs had not seen him since their arrival. His face looked sad, and he had grown still stouter since Natasha last saw him. He passed up to the front rows not noticing anyone. Anatole went up to him and began speaking to him, looking at and indicating the Rostovs' box. On seeing Natasha Pierre grew animated and hastily passing between the rows, came toward their box. When he got there he leaned on his elbows and smiling, talked to her for a long time. While conversing with Pierre, Natasha heard a man's voice in Countess Bezukhova's box and something told her it was Kuragin. She turned and their eyes met. Almost smiling, he gazed straight into her eyes with such an enraptured caressing look that it seemed strange to be so near him, to look at him like that, to be so sure he admired her, and not to be acquainted with him.

In the second act there was scenery representing tombstones, and there was a round hole in the canvas to represent the moon, shades were raised over the footlights, and from horns and contrabass came deep notes while many people appeared from right and left wearing black cloaks and holding things like daggers in their hands. They began waving their arms. Then some other people ran in and began dragging away the maiden who had been in white and was now in light blue. They did not drag her away at once, but sang with her for a long time and then at last dragged her off, and behind the scenes something metallic was struck three times and everyone knelt down and sang a prayer. All these things were repeatedly interrupted by the enthusiastic shouts of the audience.

During this act every time Natasha looked toward the stalls she saw Anatole Kuragin with an arm thrown across the back of his chair, staring at her. She was pleased to see that he was captivated by her and it did not occur to her that there was anything wrong in it.

When the second act was over Countess Bezukhova rose, turned to the Rostovs' box—her whole bosom completely exposed—beckoned the old count with a gloved finger, and paying no attention to those who had entered her box began talking to him with an amiable smile.

"Do make me acquainted with your charming daughters," she said. "The whole town is singing their praises and I don't even know them."

Natasha rose and curtsied to the splendid countess. She was so pleased by praise from this brilliant beauty that she blushed with pleasure.

"I want to become a Moscovite too, now," said Hélène. "How is it you're not ashamed to bury such pearls in the country?"

Countess Bezukhova quite deserved her reputation of being a fascinating woman. She could say what she did not think—especially what was flattering—quite simply and naturally.

"Dear count, you must let me look after your daughters! Though I am not staying here long this time—nor are you—I will try to amuse them. I have already heard much of you in Petersburg and wanted to get to know you," said she to Natasha with her stereotyped and lovely smile. "I had heard about you from my page, Drubetskoy. Have you heard he is getting married? And also from my husband's friend Bolkonski, Prince Andrew Bolkonski," she went on with special emphasis, implying that she knew of his relation to Natasha. To get better acquainted she asked that one of the young ladies should come into her box for the rest of the performance, and Natasha moved over to it.

The scene of the third act represented a palace in which many candles were burning and pictures of knights with short beards hung on the walls. In the middle stood what were probably a king and a queen. The king waved his right arm and, evidently nervous, sang something badly and sat down on a crimson throne. The maiden who had been first in white and then in light blue now wore only a smock, and stood beside the throne with her hair down. She sang something mournfully, addressing the queen, but the king waved his arm severely, and men and women with bare legs came in from both sides and began dancing all together. Then the violins played very shrilly and merrily and one of the women with thick bare legs and thin arms, separating from the others, went behind the wings, adjusted her bodice, returned to the middle of the stage, and began jumping and striking one foot rapidly against the other. In the stalls everyone clapped and shouted "Bravo!" Then one of the men went into a corner of the stage. The cymbals and horns in the orchestra struck up more loudly, and this man with bare legs jumped very high and waved his feet about very rapidly. (He was Duport, who received sixty thousand rubles a year for this art.) Everybody in the stalls, boxes and galleries began clapping and shouting, with all their might, and the man stopped and began smiling and bowing to all sides. Then other men and women danced with bare legs. Then the king again shouted to the sound of music, and they all began singing. But suddenly a storm came on, chromatic scales and diminished sevenths were heard in the orchestra, everyone ran off, again dragging one of their number away, and the curtain dropped. Once more there was a terrible noise and clatter among the audience, and with rapturous faces everyone began shouting: "Duport! Duport! Duport!" Natasha no longer thought this strange. She looked about with pleasure, smiling joyfully.

"Isn't Duport delightful?" Hélène asked her.

"Oh, yes," replied Natasha.

HOW TO ACT WHEN HEARING OPERA
from *La Vie Parisienne*

> About the time the Metropolitan Opera opened in
> New York, the French journal *La Vie Parisienne* pub-
> lished a guide to all music and particularly to the opera.
> This guide was to serve experts "who do not under-
> stand anything about anything."

"Begin with 'ideal' and go on to 'divine.'"

MUSICAL ABC or *What One Should Feel and Say in Listening to the Great Masters*

AUBER: Praiseworthy personality. Enthusiasm unnecessary. It is sufficient if you speak with respect of this composer.
How To Act During the Performance: It is permitted to converse
or to be distracted, to use one's lorgnette, to cough or to blow one's
nose. It is even permitted to hum the melodies which the singers
up there are singing.

BEETHOVEN: Mighty genius. Bow down in deepest homage. No contradiction!!! That's the way it is.
How To Act During the Performance: Deepest concentration.
Everyone has to see that you are paying the closest attention. Solemn silence. Your deep emotion is betrayed only by a hardly
noticeable shaking of your head.

BERLIOZ: Misunderstood during his lifetime. Since his death our ears
have got used to worse things. Declare that he is extremely strong
and awfully interesting. Strange. Strange. Strange.
How To Act During the Performance: Your glance should be
wild and half-demented. Your hands clenched, your throat dry. And
put as much cotton in your ears as you can stuff into them.

GOUNOD: Not one dissenter. The whole world is enraptured. Sway
with the world in your enthusiasm. He wrote three things: *Faust,*

Faust, and *Faust.* All the exclamations you can think of. Begin with "ideal" and go on to "divine."

How To Act During the Performance: Crouch and clutch yourself. Tremble, shiver and give forth all signs of sensuous delight. Then murmur in an ecstatic voice inarticulate sounds like "mmmm-oooh."

MOZART: One either loves him to the point of insanity or one finds him insipid. It is a question of taste and temperament. Also of education. Therefore you will do well to feel your way around and get the other man's opinion before you voice your own.

How To Act During the Performance: Listen without any sign of excitement. From time to time make a noise with your closed mouth which may remind one of the bleating of a peacefully grazing sheep. This shows that these peaceful melodies are related to the pleasures of a shepherd.

MEYERBEER: Practically the whole world is agreed on admiring him. Few adversaries. Therefore you may praise safely.

How To Act During the Performance: Make a sad face as if you were making your will and repeatedly say "Terrific" in a decided, solemn tone. Nothing more, but roll the "r's" properly. Don't say too much. "Terrific" covers the subject.

MASSENET: His position is not as yet clarified. A few adore him, others do not acknowledge him.

How To Act During the Performance: Cup first your right ear, then your left, not to lose anything. Your body should be in a relaxed attitude. Lean your head on your hand and give your eyes a longing expression. The safe procedure is to find everything charming. You don't have to believe it, of course.

OFFENBACH: There are some who want to burn his scores. That is exaggerated. You simply say that he has talent.

How To Act During the Performance: Do not be dignified. Rock to and fro. Put on an embarrassed air, then put your left thumb in your vest and hook your right thumb in your trouser pocket. Then say, "Crazy," and smile with a tolerant smile.

ROSSINI: Don't spare the praise. The Swan of Pesaro. The creator of *William Tell.*

How To Act During the Performance: Applaud every bar and scream *"Bravo! Bravi! Brava!"*

VERDI: You can say that you prefer to hear all the works he wrote before *Aïda* performed on the barrel-organ. But that is enough criticism. Beginning with *Aïda,* declaim, "I am filled with admiration." If you follow this suggestion, you will be taken for an accomplished connoisseur.

How To Act During the Performance: Throw your arms in the air and scream at *Aïda* performances. As to the rest, phooey! bah! pooh!!!

WAGNER: As a Frenchman you detest him in direct proportion to the degree of your patriotism. As a listener, it depends on how much you can stand. Say: "I confess that it remains incomprehensible to me. Certainly that is my fault. My ears hurt me. My God! I think I am becoming deaf!"

How To Act During the Performance: Leave.

FOR AND AGAINST TRANSLATION

Perhaps the liveliest operatic controversy in English-speaking countries centers on the question whether or not opera should be given in the vernacular. The controversy is hardly new. It was important enough in the eighteenth century to prompt a discussion in *The Spectator*. After two hundred years, at the time this anthology is being compiled, no conclusion has been reached.

THE SPECTATOR LOOKS AT OPERA

Joseph Addison

Equitis quoque jam migravit ab aure voluptas
Omnis ad incertos oculos et gaudia vana.

But now our nobles too are fops and vain,
Neglect the sense, but love the painted scene.

HORACE

It is my design in this paper to deliver down to posterity a faithful account of the Italian Opera, and of the gradual progress which it has made upon the English stage: For there is no question but our great-grandchildren will be very curious to know the reason why their forefathers used to sit together like an audience of foreigners in their own country, and to hear whole plays acted before them in a tongue which they did not understand.

Arsinoe was the first opera that gave us a taste of Italian music. The great success this opera met with, produced some attempts of forming pieces upon Italian plans, which should give a more natural and reasonable entertainment than what can be met with in the elaborate trifles of that nation. This alarmed the poetasters and fiddlers of the town, who were used to deal in a more ordinary kind of ware; and therefore laid down an established rule, which is received as such to this day, "That nothing is capable of being well set to music, that is not nonsense."

This maxim was no sooner received, but we immediately fell to translating the Italian operas; and as there was no great danger of hurting the sense of those extraordinary pieces, our authors would often make words of their own which were entirely foreign to the meaning of the passages they pretended to translate; their chief care being to make the numbers of the English verse answer to those of the Italian, that both of them might go to the same tune. Thus the famous song in *Camilla*, "Barbarous woman, yes, I know your meaning,"

From *The Spectator*, No. 18.

which expresses the resentments of an angry lover, was translated into that English lamentation—"Frail are a lover's hopes," etc. And it was pleasant enough to see the most refined persons of the British nation dying away and languishing to notes that were filled with a spirit of rage and indignation. It happened also very frequently, where the sense was rightly translated, the necessary transportation of words which were drawn out of the phrase of one tongue into that of another, made the music appear very absurd in one tongue that was very natural in the other. I remember an Italian verse that ran thus word for word, "And turned my rage into pity"; which the English for rhyme sake translated, "And into pity turned my rage." By this means the soft notes that were adapted to pity in the Italian, fell upon the word *rage* in the English; and the angry sounds that were to rage in the original, were made to express pity in the translation. It oftentimes happened likewise, that the finest notes in the air fell upon the most insignificant words in the sentence. I have known the word *and* pursued through the whole gamut, have been entertained with many a melodious *the*, and have heard the most beautiful graces, quavers and divisions bestowed upon *then, for,* and *from*; to the eternal honor of our English particles.

The next step to our refinement, was the introducing of Italian actors into our opera; who sung their parts in their own language, at the same time that our countrymen performed theirs in our native tongue. The king or hero of the play generally spoke in Italian, and his slaves answered him in English: the lover frequently made his court, and gained the heart of his princess, in a language which she did not understand. One would have thought it very difficult to have carried on dialogues after this manner, without an interpreter between the persons that conversed together; but this was the state of the English stage for about three years.

At length the audience grew tired of understanding half the opera, and therefore to ease themselves entirely of the fatigue of thinking, have so ordered it at present that the whole opera is performed in an unknown tongue. We no longer understand the language of our own stage; insomuch that I have often been afraid, when I have seen our Italian performers chattering in the vehemence of action, that they have been calling us names, and abusing us among themselves; but I hope, since we do put such an entire confidence in them, they will not talk against us before our faces, though they may do it with the same safety as if it were behind our backs. In the meantime I cannot forbear thinking how naturally an historian, who writes two or three hundred years hence, and does not know the taste of his wise forefathers, will make the following reflection, "In the beginning of the eighteenth century, the Italian tongue was so well understood in England, that operas were acted on the public stage in that language."

One scarce knows how to be serious in the confutation of an absurdity that shows itself at the first sight. It does not want any great measure of sense to see the ridicule of this monstrous practice; but what makes it the more astonishing, it is not the taste of the rabble, but of persons of the greatest politeness, which has established it.

If the Italians have a genius for music above the English, the English have a genius for other performances of a much higher nature, and capable of giving the mind a much nobler entertainment. Would one think it was possible (at a time when the author lived that was able to write the *Phædra and Hippolitus*) for a people to be so stupidly fond of the Italian opera, as scarce to give a third day's hearing to that admirable tragedy? Music is certainly a very agreeable entertainment, but if it would take the entire possession of our ears, if it would make us incapable of hearing sense, if it would exclude arts that have a much greater tendency to the refinement of human nature: I must confess I would allow it no better quarter than Plato has done, who banishes it out of his commonwealth.

At present, our notions of music are so very uncertain, that we do not know what it is we like, only, in general, we are transported with anything that is not English: so if it be of a foreign growth, let it be Italian, French, or High Dutch, it is the same thing. In short, our English music is quite rooted out, and nothing yet planted in its stead.

WHAT'S WRONG WITH OPERA IN NEW YORK?

Oscar George Sonneck

> The man who was chiefly responsible for making the Music Division of the Library of Congress in Washington one of the best music libraries in the world pleads pro translation.

Nobody in his right senses will question the excellence of opera performances in New York or in the three cities so slavishly imitating New York. The performances by no means always bear out the boasts that opera has reached a state of perfection in New York not to be found elsewhere in the world, but the average is high enough for the most fastidious taste. It is not the quality, nor the quantity of opera in New York with which I find fault, but the fundamental aspect of your—from an art-economic viewpoint—so dangerously top-heavy institution. Opera in New York impresses me like an enormously expensive hothouse full of enormously expensive exotic plants of luxuriant growth. In my humble opinion, the Metropolitan Opera House Company shares this distinction with Covent Garden, its twin, that it is a huge incubator of an *antiquated system of opera*.[1] Antiquated, because all other nations have found out long ago that a healthy operatic life depends on opera in the vernacular. Does anybody suppose for a moment that Italian opera would have become ingrown into the Italian nation's daily life, if for centuries opera had stubbornly been performed in Italy in English instead of in Italian? Does anyone believe for a moment that Wagner, and what Wagner means to the German mind, would have been possible, if the Germans had not thrown off the foreign yoke long ago? Is anybody naïve enough to fancy that French opera would be so fascinatingly French, if the

[1] Please note that I did not say "antiquated opera house or antiquated operas," or other nonsense of that kind. I am criticizing the *system* of presentation of opera as antiquated.

clear-cut maxim pronounced by Perrin and Cambert, the founders of French opera, in 1659, in the preface to their very first joint creation, that operas to be properly appreciated should be performed in the language of the audience, had not been heeded by Lully and his successors down to Debussy?

But I do not intend to shake the yellow banner of "Votes for Opera in English" at you. I have been an advocate of opera in English for so many years that I no longer allow myself to be dragged into argument on the subject. I now answer all questions of *why*, wearily with the counterquestion of *why not?* In your newspapers and elsewhere the arguments for and against opera in the vernacular—which, by the way, had a very respectable artistic and even financial record in our country before it was temporarily side-tracked by the present system —have been thrashed out so often and so thoroughly that it would serve no useful purpose to add here to the number of dead and wounded. Only this I wish to say, that in my opinion every argument, except one, usually advanced against opera in the vernacular, which in our country, of course, means opera in English, deals with difficulties, but difficulties are never reasons for or against the adoption of reforms. This one exception is the argument that a performance of an opera in its original language comes nearest to aesthetic perfection.

In theory, yes, in practice, not necessarily so; but, quite aside from the ludicrous inconsistencies of the champions of this argument, it is the argument of the selfish aesthetic gourmet, not the argument of the man who has the best interests of opera at heart, as viewed from the standpoint of national need. An opera may or may not lose something of its aesthetic significance by translation, but this eventual loss is more than offset by the gain that opera in the vernacular, from the standpoint of the auditor desirous of understanding and not only hearing and seeing opera, stops being a *pantomime with vocalises* and becomes, what it was intended for by its creators, a musical drama. Whenever this libretto bugaboo is paraded before me, I cannot help thinking of Germany. There Goethe, Schiller and Shakespeare form the triumvirate of the dramatic repertoire. Not Shakespeare in English, but Shakespeare in translations that are works of art; and the love of educated Germans for Shakespeare, their appreciation of his genius, their familiarity with his works, is something wonderful to behold. This being the case, I ask the simple question: Did Shakespeare suffer or gain by his conquest of Germany through the medium of artistic translations?

The more radical opponents of opera in the vernacular sometimes deny that the texts of operas sung in English would really be so much better understood than the texts if sung in the original language. They point to some rather notable failures in this respect, when opera in English with very commendable good will was tried on our audiences. The argument has been answered in several ways, but one telling answer or explanation, it seems to me, has been neglected. It is this, that a language sung and a language spoken, sound very different. Language sung is a jargon, the understanding of which depends on an acquired taste and on practice. Supposing a Frenchman who has never been to opera hears for the first time his language sung from the stage by artists famed for their clear diction and enunciation. I guarantee that he will not understand five per cent of the words this first time, and that without the fault of the singers. But with continued practice of his ear, he will gather in a higher and higher percentage, until it may reach forty or fifty. In other words, the success of opera in the vernacular depends as much on the practice of the audience to listen to its own language in the disguise of musical speech, as on the practice of the singers to sing therein and the practice of the composer to compose therein. At any rate, it seems to me that a system of opera which *might* enable the practiced listener to understand forty per cent of the words—which means a proportionate better understanding of the subtle relations between text and music—is decidedly more sensible than a system of opera which offers him only five chances in a hundred.

In this connection I should like to draw attention to a correlated fact, usually overlooked in the discussion of the problem. The artificiality of our present system has not been so apparent here as it would be in cities abroad, because the population of New York is so cosmopolitan. Especially the German language has no terrors for a considerable percentage of your operagoers, for the very simple reason that they are German-Americans and understand German. But the German emigrants to the United States now amount to only about fifteen thousand persons a year; moreover, it is a well-known fact that the second and surely the third native generation of German-Americans loses its command of the German language completely. The more the consequences of such facts spread to our art-economics, the more apparent even to New Yorkers, the artificiality of their operatic system will become.

That opera in English will be a panacea for all the evils in our operatic life, or that opera in English *per se* will produce great American opera composers, is not my contention, but this much I predict without hesitation: Unless the system is again reversed *preponderantly* —I do not say exclusively—in favor of opera in the vernacular, we shall not have a healthy operatic life in this country. Nor do I fear for the ultimate outcome. The readjustment will be difficult and will require extraordinary executive ability and bulldog tenacity, but it will come sooner or later. Then, not the type of art-speculator who dabbles in more or less shrewd experiments with public taste, will stand out in our operatic history as the moving force, but those men who have been for years the practical pioneers in this movement for opera in the vernacular and whose faith in the common sense of our people will yet be vindicated. Their itinerant companies often leave much to be desired from the purely artistic standpoint, but nevertheless they are doing more for a proper dissemination of opera as an intelligible form of art in *America at large* than the Metropolitan Opera House Company and all its imitators put together. And should luck so favor the English-speaking nations as to give us in the near future opera composers of the victorious sweep of a Gounod or Puccini, not to mention giants like Wagner and Verdi, the doom of the present system will be sealed irresistibly and rapidly. To harp on the deserved or undeserved failure of a few American operas by composers without previous individual or collective experience as opera composers as proof that English-speaking people cannot produce real opera composers, is eminently silly. If English-speaking people could produce a musico-dramatic genius like Henry Purcell once, nothing prevents them from doing so again. It is a question of nature's caprice, of talent, and of opportunity, combined, not a question of national temperament, just as our national temperament does not hinder us from turning out in almost unlimited numbers opera singers who have conquered first the Old World and then the New, and who can hold their own against the best of foreign artists.

THE CASE FOR TRANSLATED OPERA

Deems Taylor

Another argument, eloquent I think, for translation.

The curtain rises on a performance of *Rigoletto*. The opening chorus is all that our average, intelligent American businessman had hoped for—gay, lively music, with certainly nothing complicated or abstruse about it. He can't make out the words, but that would be too much to expect of any opening chorus. Then two men enter. One of them is the leading tenor, as our disciple discovers from the outburst of applause that greets his appearance. The other is a tenor, too, but not so good. The two hold a brief conversation in song, not one word of which the American understands. He is a little disappointed when he realizes that they are singing Italian, for we had forgotten to tell him that the performance was to be given in a foreign language. However, a soprano enters, rather young and good-looking, and the tenor sings her a pretty song. Matters might be worse. The music is certainly tuneful and well sung, and perhaps our American can get a general idea of the story by watching the actors.

But the plot is a trifle puzzling. A hunchback enters—a baritone, and, judging by the applause, another big shot—to whom the other members of the cast seem to have taken a dislike. An old man is dragged in, singing bass, and makes a long and indignant speech to the leading tenor, who seems annoyed. The hunchback refuses to take the old man seriously, whereupon the old man turns and gives him a piece of his mind, ending with what looks like a good old-fashioned curse. This frightens the wits out of the hunchback, who cowers in terror as the old man is led away by the gendarmes.

During the intermission, our American has plenty to think about. The leading tenor, he decides, is somebody important—a king, probably—and not far wrong, at that; he was a king, until the censor made

Verdi change him into a duke. The hunchback must be his court jester, and the old man is presumably a political prisoner, though why he should be so sore at the hunchback remains a mystery. Ah, well. Things will probably clear up in the next scene.

But they don't clear up. The scene shows a garden on one side and a street on the other, with a wall running down the center of the stage. The hunchback enters and sings a solo. Then a basso appears and sings another solo, the only distinguishable word of which is something that sounds like "sparra—foo—cheel, sparra—foo—cheel" over and over. Then the basso leaves, and the hunchback, after another solo, unlocks a gate in the wall—he might have saved time by stepping over it—and enters the garden, whereupon a beautiful girl appears—at least she is dressed in white and wears a blond wig—and throws herself into his arms. They have quite a chat. An older woman appears and joins in, after which the hunchback and the girl sing a duet.

By this time, the unfortunate American is hopelessly befuddled. Abandoning all hope of disentangling the plot, he decides to concentrate upon the beautiful voices and the orchestra. But a whole evening of unrelieved, meaningless singing and playing is too much. It is a rare power of concentration that can stand the strain of a vocal concert lasting nearly three hours. About halfway through the third act, our American, having received a vicious jab in the side from a scowling neighbor, comes to with a start, to realize that he has been fast asleep, and probably snoring.

Americans are a hardy race, and so, little daunted, our hero tries again another night. This time, the opera being *Die Walküre*, he takes precautions. His knowledge of German, picked up during the war, is confined largely to *"Kamerad," "wie viel,"* and *"danke schön,"* which, he dimly suspects, will not get him very far with Wagner. So he buys an English translation of the libretto, which he studies earnestly, reading and rereading it until he feels that he has a firm grip on the plot.

So he goes to *Die Walküre*. The introduction to the first act is exciting, and the first scene, with the exhausted fugitive staggering into the hut to take refuge from the storm, he finds doubly impressive because he knows what it is about. But as the action progresses, he finds himself more and more out of touch with what is going on upon the stage. These people stand about, without moving, for hours. Just talking. And he keeps getting ahead of them. He is sitting up, waiting for Siegmund to pull the sword out of the tree, just as that hero is warming up to an account of his life's history for Hunding's benefit. The orchestra is magnificent, and the voices are fine; but there are no set musical numbers, and as he remembers only the general idea of each scene, and has no idea what the actors are saying, he finds it hard to keep his attention from wandering.

During the intermission he overhears an enthusiastic lady telling another, "I love to just sit and close my eyes and listen to the voices and the orchestra." So he tries that, with the result that, not being a student of music, but only an average theatergoer, he ignominiously falls asleep, just as he did at *Rigoletto*. Some time later he awakes with a start, to find Brünnhilde standing exactly where she was when his nap began. This is the end. He is a brave man, but he knows when he is licked. Declaring that opera is too highbrow for him, he goes back to his theater and talkies, leaving Art to shift for herself.

There is just one important reason why the American opera audience is so small. It is the fact that opera, as produced in this country, is sung in virtually every language except that of the inhabitants of this country. There is one other country in which this is done—England. And England and America are the two highly civilized countries in the world where opera has never taken root. A hundred and fifty years ago, the question of language was not so acute. Opera then was the only spectacular, and almost the only musical entertainment to which the public had access. There were no elaborately staged musical shows; no spectacular motion pictures; no public song recitals or symphony concerts. To the average man, opera was a little bit of all these. But the picture has changed. So far as concerns spectacle, ballet, orchestral music, even singing, opera finds itself today outstripped by its newer competitors. It must hold its place as a musical form of dramatic entertainment—the *dramma per musica* of its Renaissance inventors—if it is to survive at all.

Europe has, of course, long recognized this fact. Mention the famous air, *"La fleur que tu m'avais jetée,"* to a German, and he will not know what you are talking about. But if you call it *"Hier, an dem Herzen treu geborgen,"* he knows at once that you are referring to the Flower Song from *Carmen*. He has never heard Bizet's masterpiece sung in any language but his own. Standing outside the Paris Opéra Comique one day, I saw posters announcing a forthcoming performance of what I assumed to be a new opera—*Paillasse*. Not until, reading further, I came to the cast of characters and saw the familiar Nedda, Canio, Tonio, Silvio, did I realize that it was only our old friend,

Pagliacci, which, as this was a French opera house, was being sung in French. My friend Edward Johnson, general director of the Metropolitan Opera Association, knows the roles of Tristan, Parsifal, and Lohengrin in Italian, because he has sung them in Italy. He does not know them in the original German, because he has never sung in Germany, and he does not know them in English, because he was never asked to sing them in English.

To realize why opera has never really taken root here, why its audience is one-twentieth of what it should be, and why so few American composers have written grand operas, try to imagine the state of the American theater today if it had faced the conditions under which its sister art has had to struggle. Suppose that, fifty years ago, a group of public-spirited New Yorkers had built a magnificent theater and installed therein a company of first-rank actors, prepared to give the finest plays written. For fifty years, then, this company has been presenting the works of Molière, Racine, Rostand, Hauptmann, Sudermann, Schiller, Goldoni, Ibsen, Shakespeare, and other playwrights. None of these plays, however, has been done in English. The French plays have been played in French, the German ones in German, Ibsen in Norwegian, Dostoevsky and Tchekoff in French or Italian—never English—translations. The company, which at first was entirely European, is now about one-third American. Most of these American actors have received their training in Europe, and know their roles only in foreign tongues; for even Shakespeare, in this imaginary theater, is played in Italian.

Under such conditions, just how large a theatrical audience would the United States have developed? What would the average citizen make of a performance of *Faust* in German, or *The Cherry Orchard* in Italian? How many theaters would have sprung up in response to popular demand, how many American playwrights would we have developed, how many American actors would be playing today? How large a following do you suppose Walter Hampden would have built up for his *Cyrano* if he had played it in French? How big a hit would *Liliom* and *The Swan* have been if they had been offered in the original Hungarian? What would Katharine Cornell's position be today if she had received all her training abroad and played only in German and Italian?

This comparison is not, of course, wholly fair. There is no music to fill in the gaps of a spoken play. In opera, on the other hand, there is undeniably much pleasure to be had from listening to the music, even if the action is unintelligible. But the fact remains that however great that pleasure may be for the listener who is unusually sensitive to music, it is not enough to attract and hold the listener who is not definitely musical. If you don't believe me, look at the state of opera in this country today.

Most of the greatest composers of opera—Gluck, Weber, Wagner, Verdi, Strauss, and Puccini, for instance—have been as much concerned with the dramatic qualities of their librettos as with the aesthetic qualities of their music. Music is only half the opera. If it is all, as some people insist, why scenery and costumes? Why the pretense of a story? Why expect any acting of the singers? Why not save time and expense, hire a concert hall, play and sing the music without words, and let it go at that?

Opera is theater. And the essence of the theater is that the spectator sees a story unfolded in his presence, is in on the ground floor, so to speak, when things happen. And it is one of the paradoxes of the drama that the words are essential, and yet not important. They are not important in that, as you watch a play, you are conscious not so much of the individual words of a scene as of the ideas of which those words are an expression. They are essential in that, if the lines are incomprehensible, you have no chance to get at the ideas.

But in opera, they tell me, this problem can be solved by studying the libretto beforehand, so as to familiarize oneself with the story. In the first place, that's a bore. When I go to a play, I don't have to bone up on it beforehand, as if I were getting ready for a mid-term examination. Why must I do research work in order to understand an opera? In the second place, no amount of homework can take the place of understanding every line as it is delivered. Unless I go to the trouble—which nobody would—of actually memorizing the entire libretto, both in the original language and in English, I bring to the performance only a general idea of the purport of each scene. When the curtain goes up on the first act of *La Bohème* I remember that the studio is cold, and that Rudolfo and his companions finally decide to burn his play in order to keep warm. So I sit, firmly clutching that idea, while four singers get through ten minutes of chatter that is only incidentally interesting from a musical point of view, but which I would probably find amusing if I knew what they were talking about.

Tony, your barber, understands the words of the operas that he attends in your country's greatest opera house. When he goes to *Pagliacci* and hears "*Vesti la giubba*," he not only listens to a tenor singing a famous aria but he follows a dramatic situation, hears an actor playing a touching scene. No wonder he is several times as enthusiastic about opera as you are. If the Metropolitan, most of whose repertoire is sung in either Italian or German, managed to pay its way for more than a score of years, that phenomenon may not be unconnected with the fact that New York's Italian-speaking population outnumbers that of Milan, while her German-speaking residents would populate Leipzig.

The Metropolitan is still probably the greatest single opera house in the world, giving every year performances of about fifty different Italian, French, and German operas that average better than similar performances in Italy, France, and Germany. A few years ago I traveled four thousand miles to hear, among other things, some festival performances of opera in Salzburg and Munich; and Salzburg's *Der Rosenkavalier* was just about as good as the Metropolitan's, while Munich's *Die Meistersinger* was not only just about up to the Metropolitan's average but presented singers whom I had already heard at the Metropolitan. New York's famous opera house is an international museum of opera, just as New York's other Metropolitan is an international museum of painting and sculpture. At the Metropolitan—the opera house, that is—you can hear all of Europe's great operas, produced in a manner that frequently surpasses the European standard, with most of Europe's great singers.

Nevertheless, unless opera can be sold to America, unless it can find a new, large, popular audience, it may shortly pass out of existence. That audience must be trained, since it does not now exist; and the only way to train it is to make it take opera and like it. And the only way to do that is to produce opera, somewhere, strictly for an American audience, and wholly from the American point of view.

Somebody—perhaps it was Plato (quotations are not my strong point)—said that "to know what to ask is to know half the answer." Which encourages me to the belief that I know fifty per cent of the solution of this opera problem. At least I know what I should like to see, without regard to whether it is possible or could ever be made so. I should like to see some American opera companies, run by Americans—schools of opera appreciation, so to speak, to which the Metropolitan would be a postgraduate course. What would they be like, and how would they differ from what now exists?

First of all, such a company would be housed in a modern theater. By "modern," I mean designed for a contemporary audience of citizens of a republic, rather than for an imaginary audience of kings, nobles, and rabble. Our existing opera houses, even the newest of them, pay more or less respectful tribute to the famous houses of Europe; and the more famous a European house is, the less likely is it to have anything that we need. Covent Garden, in London, dates from the fifties; the Paris Opéra was begun in 1861; and La Scala, in Milan, goes back to the seventies—1778, to be exact.

Suppose we admit that these houses have served their purpose, and forget them, putting our hypothetical opera company in a theater equipped with a revolving stage, projection booths before and behind the curtain, plenty of storage space, plenty of rehearsal rooms, the last word in lighting systems, and so on. The auditorium will be shallow, to bring everyone as close as possible to the stage, will seat not more than three thousand people—the Festival Opera House at Bayreuth seats only twenty-four hundred—and the best places in the house will not be given over to the boxes—or rather they will be; for I would put the boxes downstairs in the rear of the house, where the occupants can see and hear perfectly without being seen.

The general manager of such a company would be a theatrical producer of culture and taste. He would be interested in opera, and know something about it, and interested in music, although his most important qualification would be his showmanship. Two years before his house opened he would carefully go through the hundred-odd operas that compose the existing repertoire, picking out, not those that he thought he ought to produce, or those that impresarios always produce, or those that the music critics would like to see produced, but those that he believed would have some dramatic and musical interest for an average better-class American theater audience.

This would give him a working repertoire of about thirty-five operas. One or two of your especial favorites would undoubtedly be omitted, but be patient; remember, this is a popular opera house. Having selected his repertoire, he would proceed to have it translated into English. And here I must digress to explain what I mean by "English."

Mention opera in English to the average operagoer, and he thinks you mean the curious doggerel into which librettos are generally translated for English-speaking readers and auditors. It has its merits, but it is hardly a language in which I should ever care to hear an opera sung. It is the result, partly of the practice among foreign publishers of paying as high as one hundred dollars for an "English" translation, and partly of their habit, when commissioning a translator, of hiring someone who knows the language of the original, but does not know any English. He may know it in the sense that he speaks it, but he cannot write it clearly, beautifully, or always intelligibly. Judging from the way he fits the words to the notes, he knows nothing whatsoever about music.

What I mean by a translation of a libretto is an English version written by someone who is a master of the English language, who is sensitive to music and knows a little about it, and who is able to reconcile the rhythms and accents of music to those of English poetry—an English version, in short, that has the same literary and poetic distinction as the original, and fits the music just as well. Most people would say that such a thing is impossible, and most people would be wrong. It has never been tried. To my knowledge, no first-rank American writer of English has ever been asked to prepare a singing translation of a foreign-language libretto—chiefly, I suppose, because he would be expensive. He would probably have to be paid as much as the prima donna gets for three or four performances of the opera. Offhand, I can think of half a dozen Americans who could do the job to perfection—Brian Hooker, Maxwell Anderson, Stephen Benét, Archibald MacLeish, John Erskine, and Edna St. Vincent Millay.

While his English librettos were being prepared, our producer could be recruiting his company and his chorus. It would obviously be impossible to develop a group of American singers into such a company of international stars as the Metropolitan can offer, inside of a year; but one could make a creditable start. It is not a question of voice. We have produced many magnificent voices in this country, and could produce many more if there were any demand for them. But voice is no longer enough for an opera singer. He must be an actor, and a good one, and, for an American audience, he ought to be able to look something like the character he is impersonating. Perhaps the best way to train our opera company of beginners would be to select candidates with good voices, interesting personalities, and a knowledge of singing style—they could be found—and then make them do what Lawrence Tibbett did—put in a hard course of training in theatrical stock companies. Six months would be enough to weed out those who were hopeless as actors, and another six months would develop the survivors into good raw material for the stage director.

I envy the stage director. He could work, for once, free from the dead hand of operatic tradition. To understand how tradition works, and why it is necessary to bear in mind that every opera company in the world is a repertoire company, presenting anything between fifteen and fifty operas in a given season. Naturally, with such a large number of works to perform, no company has any great amount of rehearsal time to give to anything but new productions. In consequence, and also because singers travel from one company to another, the stage business, the properties, and the plan of the scenery for any opera tend to become standardized.

When an opera is first produced, the positions of the singers on the stage, even their important gestures, are carefully worked out and rehearsed. If it survives, and is produced in another opera house, these positions and gestures are more or less faithfully copied. So with its third production, and its fourth, and so on. In time, after ten years or so, it may be receiving simultaneous performances in a score of opera houses, scattered throughout the Western world, all substantially alike.

The practice has obvious advantages. When the manager of an opera company decides to produce some hitherto unperformed opera, half his singers have probably sung it elsewhere, and are thoroughly familiar with the staging. His scene designer, having the original plans before him, is saved the trouble of having to work out fresh solutions of construction problems. Singers become easily interchangeable—like automobile parts. The Metropolitan, let us say, engages a tenor by cable from Buenos Aires. Two weeks later he arrives in New York. It would be quite possible for him to dock at five in the afternoon, go direct to the opera house, dress, and step upon the stage at eight o'clock for the evening's performance of *La Bohème*, without ever having seen another member of the company, knowing exactly what they are going to do and where they will be upon the stage at any given moment.

But, inevitably, a traditional performance tends to become stereotyped and mechanical. Some perfectly accidental and meaningless gesture, some mannerism of the singer who first performs a role, may be solemnly perpetuated through two or three generations, with never a question as to its suitability or significance.

They tell a story of a young tenor who was studying the title role of Verdi's *Otello*. At a certain moment in one scene, the coach informed

him, while the chorus was singing and he was not, he must turn, go
upstage, mingle with the crowd, and then come back in time to sing
his concluding measures. Dramatically speaking, there was no sense
to this procedure, and the tenor objected. But the coach was adamant.
"That is the tradition of the part," was his only explanation.

"But why?" the tenor persisted.

The coach didn't know and didn't care.

"Who created this role?"

"Tamagno."

The name of the world-famous tenor was enough to crush any be-
ginner's objections, but still the young singer was not satisfied. A
year later, when he was in Italy, he hunted up Tamagno and asked
for an interview.

"Maestro," he began deferentially, "I have come to ask you about a
certain piece of business in *Otello*"—and proceeded to outline the
troublesome scene.

The old man looked puzzled. "Did I do that?"

He thought hard for a moment, then took down a copy of the vocal
score and studied it. Suddenly his face brightened.

"I have it!" he cried triumphantly. "It is very simple. You will
notice that in the final passage Otello has to sing a high B-flat. So,
while the chorus is singing, I go upstage to spit!"

If this were all that tradition did to opera, we might make the best
of it. But it does worse, in that it tends to keep methods of acting
and stage handling completely static. Generally speaking, the opera
lags, mechanically and histrionically, half a century or more behind
the spoken theater. Rossini's *The Barber of Seville* was first produced
in 1816. I would lay odds of eight to five that if a member of the
original first-night audience could be resuscitated and taken to a performance of *The Barber* in almost any opera house in the world today,
he would notice nothing new or strange about it. *Rigoletto* is performed today with much the same kind of acting and *mise en scène*,
and about the same scenery, that it received in its world première in
1851. When Wagner's *Ring* cycle was first performed complete, at Bayreuth in 1876, it represented the last word in modern scene designing,
acting, lighting, and stage direction. The lighting has been a little
modernized since then, but any attempt to bring the acting, or even
the scenery, a little more abreast of contemporary stage ideas, is
greeted with roars of disapproval of such violation of the sacred tra-

ditions established by the master. Yet do you suppose that Wagner, who was nothing if not a progressive, would stage the *Ring* today exactly as he did over sixty years ago?

I still remember the historic night at the Metropolitan when Maria Jeritza dared to sing *"Vissi d'arte"* lying on her stomach. We critics wrote reams about this epoch-making event in operatic history. Yet, in the modern dress version of *Hamlet,* I once saw Basil Sydney deliver all of Hamlet's soliloquy lying flat on his stomach, and the critics didn't even bother to mention it. In the contemporary theater it is taken for granted that actors and directors will try to find new ways to do old things. In the opera, what was good enough for our great-grand-fathers is good enough for us.

Our imaginary opera company being, as I say, a local affair, and being composed of singers who need not fit into European productions that have remained unchanged since the sixties, would be free to put on its repertory according to the best standards of American scene designing, stage direction, and acting, and without regard to any tradition that could not pass an intelligence test. Bosom-heaving would, I imagine, be reduced to a minimum, and arm-waving would be largely confined to the traffic cops outside the opera house.

It would be an interesting opening night. The performance would be pretty crude in spots, I imagine. The singers would hardly be in the same class with the great singing actors of operatic history. At least, though, the audience would be able to understand two-thirds of what they were saying; which is two-thirds more than the average American audience now understands. Think of being able to follow the action of an opera as if it were a play, with the added emotional excitement of the music! The orchestra would be first-class, and the conductor as well. The latter would be, if a good one were available, an American; otherwise, not—the occasion being a theatrical and not a patriotic one. The lights and the sets and the stage direction would be, as they generally are in the American theater, unconventional and interesting. Despite the company's lack of experience, there would be something about the whole performance—something new and electric and dramatic—that would hold its hearers spellbound.

They would come again, I think. Not to perform a duty, or absorb culture, or be seen by somebody socially eligible, but to spend an evening in the theater—the theater that is music. I think they would come often enough, and in sufficient numbers, to make the company able to pay its way; and, in other cities, other companies. People would get to know the operas, not merely as concerts but as dramas; and some they would reject, and some they would take to their hearts. When they came to New York they would drop in at the Metropolitan as a matter of course, exactly as they would drop in at any other great theater. America would have, in short, an operatic audience; one that was on an equal footing, in its interest and understanding, with French, German, Italian, and other audiences, including the Scandinavian.

YES, BUT MOSTLY NO

Olin Downes

We are of those who approve as a utility measure, when and
where advisable, the singing of opera in the language of the country
where that opera is performed. Where there are new and uninformed
audiences, listeners to whom opera itself is an unfamiliar experience,
it is a first necessity to know what the singing is all about, what the
dramatic motivations are which the composer is revealing by means of
his music.

The shorter the cut to that understanding between the dramatic
composer and his audience the better for the effect of his work. Opera
is drama transmuted by music. The first approach to an opera is
not that of an analysis of the score, the docketing of the themes as a
sort of Baedeker survey of the tonal landscape, or learned explanations of the manner in which melodies and motives are interwoven and
express the situation on the stage. The first and the last essential is
for the listener to understand not only what the characters are doing,
but what they are thinking and feeling as the situations develop. Repeated listening and a consciousness of the dramatic tensions involved
are the keys to the assimilation and "understanding" of the music.

It might seem that nothing compares to this primary importance of
understanding the words of an opera. But there are other requisites for
its most artistic and dramatic representation. The music is born of
the language in which it was conceived and created, and from which
it is tonally and psychologically inseparable. This is no companionate
union, in which words and music, similarly rhymed and metered, go
amicably hand in hand toward an expressive goal. It is a unity of
speech and song which is indivisible, and for which no substitution
of other elements than those which constitute the original identity is
possible. Approximation of the original substances, rough equivalents

By permission of the *New York Times*.

these can be. This is all that the best and most sensitive translation can achieve. But the genius of a language is the genius of the music which it inspires. Music takes wing from the word and is a transmutation of it.

You can no more find an English substitute for the Italian words which carry the melody of *"Cielo e mar"* in *La Gioconda*, or, let us say, for that ugly, powerful word, *"Spitze,"* in *Götterdämmerung*, than you could find the French or German idiom that would match the poignant outpouring, "Nobody knows de trouble Ah've seen," or the cantillation of the words "Deep River," if you spent infinity trying. Word and tone are one and inseparable.

Who will sing "heaven and sea," or "ocean and sky" to Ponchielli's aria, and think that by the substitution of words other than the native Italian that he can evoke in the consciousness of the listener, in just four syllables and as many notes, the sense of the music of the summer night and the moonlit sea?

What composer in any language, except Wagner with the German of his own devising, could use with such suggestion the jagged unlovely syllables as those of the oath on the spearhead that dooms Siegfried to his end by that weapon in the hands of Hagen? *"Spitze,"* in the mouth of the raging Brünnhilde, and the metallic trumpet echoing her cry of revenge in the orchestra, is irreplaceable. It is the vicious point of the spear, thrust home. No word in any approximate English translation could have such an inescapable connotation. The word "spear" is smooth and symmetrical, swift too, but it has no such cutting edge or thrust of hate in it and it could never provoke such a savage Wagner, speaking musically and textually, as the tongue of his fathers can give.

AGAINST TRANSLATION

Herbert F. Peyser

> I vote with Peyser. Exceptions: television, opera work-
> shops, intimate performances. But for the Metropoli-
> tan or the San Francisco Opera House or Covent
> Garden . . .?

Twenty years ago I was heartily in favor of translating all
operas into the language of the people to whom they were sung. Today I am just as heartily opposed to it. I attribute this change of front
largely to the circumstance that, living for the past five years in Germany and Austria, I have listened in and out of season to practically
nothing but translated opera. I can recommend no better corrective
than such an experience to those theorists and visionaries who believe
that the performance of all operas in English versions is the secret of
domesticating the lyric drama in America.

Before considering the matter more closely let me make it clear
that the singability of the English language is not a point at issue. In
America the whole problem of translated opera has been confused
and obscured for years by the clamor of those who lose sight of the
real questions in dispute and who imagine that any disbelief in the
efficacy of translated opera amounts to a repudiation in principle of
the English tongue for the purposes of song. This, of course, is merely
a waste of time and a darkening of counsel. It ought to be as preposterous to argue that English is singable as to rush to arms in defense of the multiplication table. Every language in the world is singable if it is used according to the physical canons of the human voice.
The folk song is the all-sufficient proof of that.

The stock arguments retailed in America on behalf of translated
opera are by this time fairly familiar. It is claimed that as long as
operas are presented in foreign languages the greater number of listeners cannot understand what is being sung and that the action of the
piece they are witnessing must consequently remain more or less unin-

By permission of *Musical America*.

telligible to them. Hence their enjoyment of what they see and hear
in the opera house is necessarily restricted and it follows that the popular relish of opera cannot be more than skin-deep. Therefore opera can
never become an integral part of the average citizen's life, a native experience in his daily round like the movie palace or the baseball field.
Now, if he can hear his operas in his own language this barrier will fall
and in proper season opera will become as familiar and as prizable
a feature of his life as it is of the Italian's, the Frenchman's, the German's. Opposition to translated opera (so it runs on) has partly been
engineered by snobs who like to flaunt their knowledge of foreign
tongues; partly by persons distressed at the ordinary low standard of
English operatic translations, partly by alien artists too lazy or un-
talented to acquire an acceptable English pronunciation, partly by
other persons with axes to grind. The assumption is that greater care
in the translation of librettos and a more universal employment of
singers whose mother tongue is English will speed the ultimate establishment of opera in the language of the people. With this conclusively achieved we shall be squarely in the path to the opera written
in America for Americans by Americans.

The trouble with most of these pleas, assumptions and half-truths
is that they misconceive the real nature of the problem. Before the
day comes when Americans will hear all their operas in English as
Germans hear all theirs in German and Frenchmen all theirs in
French, some bigger obstacles than slipshod translations, recalcitrant
artists, haughty impresarios and incorrigible snobs will have to be
swept out of the way. It should not be necessary to remind the reader
that efforts to popularize the operas of the standard repertory in English texts have been neither few nor negligible. In America some of
them have been of considerable artistic merit. In London and the
English provinces grand opera in the vernacular has flourished after a
fashion for decades. Yet neither in England nor in America have such
enterprises ever acquired more than a limited and a small-scale
significance. At the Metropolitan after the war several Wagner operas
were sung in English translations which, if not without their faults,
had at least been discreetly groomed. They were performed, moreover,
by the same artists usually cast for the Wagner parts, a number of
them native Americans. Why did these English versions survive only
a short time, why was haste made to revert to the original texts the
moment German was once more adjudged house-broken? Was snobbery the reason? Has snobbery in the long run ever killed a cause that

was really popular or pumped life into one that commanded no support beyond that furnished by the snobs themselves?

The reason why opera translated into the popular tongue has never gained an extensive or a lasting foothold in England and America lies neither in the defects of translations, the antagonism of cliques, the opposition of foreign singers, the untutored diction of native ones or some fancied musical insufficiency of the English language. It lies first and foremost in the Anglo-Saxon psychology and in the reaction of this psychology to opera as such. That the average English translation of an opera is usually poorer than the average foreign one happens not so much because the English translators are, man for man, less skilled than their colleagues in other lands as because the public for which they work is psychologically what it is.

Neither the American nor the Englishman has ever accepted as the Continental European has done the fundamental convention of opera. That the characters of a stage piece should sing of their actions and emotions instead of speaking them, that their song should sometimes assume highly artificial forms, that their movements and demeanor should be regulated by the impositions of the music rather than by the more obvious logic of nature—these things have always exercised a more or less estranging effect upon even cultivated Americans or Englishmen, let alone on the musically illiterate. They irritate such a person at times and very easily stir him to ridicule at others. They feed his sense of humor more than they do that of any of the other nations that share a common musical birthright. The more the words this individual hears fall below a certain level of dignity and the closer their sound and sense approach the commonplace and the colloquial, the more disturbing, incongruous or downright funny it strikes him that they are sung rather than spoken. Unless the intention is deliberately comic, to sing a sentiment or a statement is, in the Anglo-Saxon view, to enhance, ennoble or idealize it. But to "ennoble" a colloquialism or a platitude by communicating it in poetic or in musical terms is almost willy-nilly to achieve satire. This state of things is, in fact, one of the chief sources of the humor of Gilbert and Sullivan. It explains why time out of mind an American will smile in the opera house when he hears in his own language a phrase to which the European will listen with unruffled composure and even with gravity. And to the maker of English operatic translations (and the author of English librettos generally) it lays down a law which he can flout only at his peril.

The foreign librettist is not in the same boat. One work after another of the great masters of opera proves it. Again and again you
will encounter in these works passages which, translated into English
for all they are worth, will cause an English-speaking audience to
react to them in greater or lesser degree as a European audience would
never dream of doing. Why is it that an Italian public at *Traviata*
finds absolutely nothing incongruous or disturbing when Violetta
in a snippet of recitative bids her maid "*Apri la finestra*"? Why is it
that when she does the same thing with the words "*Offne das Fen-
ster*" a German audience is equally unperturbed? Yet why is that if
the Lady of the Camellias were to sing in Butte, Des Moines, Brooklyn or Oklahoma City "Open the window" some might laugh and
some might wince? Theorize, split hairs and argue as fiercely and as
long as you will, this is just what is likely to happen. Why is it that
when he comes to the words of David in *Meistersinger*, "*Möchtet ihr
nicht auch die Wurst versuchen*," Frederick Jameson renders them:
"Here, too, a sausage, would you but try it"? Why is it that the
Corders, tackling in the same opera Magdalena's "*Jetzt Evchen,
komm! Wir müssen fort*" produced "Now, Eva, come! We ought to
trot"? Simply because these men were conscious, however darkly, of
pitfalls and obligations. Jameson chose to sacrifice the homely colloquialism of the German original, thereby perhaps escaping the de-
risive or embarrassed laugh that would have greeted something like
"And wouldn't you like to try the sausage?" What he gives us in its
place, however, is stiff and starched librettese and not for a moment
what a lad like David would have said. The Corders tried honestly
enough to preserve Wagner's colloquial flavor but the result is good
intention gone mad. I might go on till the crack of doom citing heart-
breaking instances of this and other kinds. (Mozart is full of them,
Puccini is full of them, *Hänsel und Gretel* is full of them, even *Fidelio*
is full of them—and if you want to gain a real idea of the problems
involved in translating a popular opera for Anglo-Saxon audiences
just take a stab or two at *Carmen*!) But my point is that the man
who attempts such a translation for such a purpose has got to keep this
racial peculiarity ceaselessly before his mind's eye. The job is almost
as hard and as poignant as sitting clothed in a strait jacket on the
horns of a dilemma.

I know it has been claimed in times past (and perhaps it is in
America even today) that some of that small talk which amuses or
distracts us when we hear it sung in our tongue sounds just as bad

to the Europeans who hear it either in the original or in the language of their own countries. Yet the short and the long of it is that they don't and the fact obstinately refuses to be argued away. Those who are old enough to remember Victor Herbert's *Madeleine* at the Metropolitan may recall how they giggled or squirmed when they heard it announced that the heroine was to have for her dinner "soup and fresh asparagus." Has anyone ever seen a French audience squirm when in the first act of *Louise* there is some talk as to whether *"la soupe est prête"*?

However, I have other grounds for believing that the game of translated opera is not worth the candle. For one thing, I believe that the argument to the effect that as soon as all operatic works are performed in the language of the people who listen to them these people will understand the action and the tragedy or humor of the texts that is otherwise lost on them—I believe this argument to a very large extent fallacious. In the first place, it presupposes conditions that very rarely exist. It assumes a standard of enunciation on the part of the average singer that is seldom justified by experience. It takes for granted that operatic conductors will exercise over their orchestras a greater dynamic control than they ordinarily do. It banks on the composer in a manner often highly unwarranted. It largely presupposes that his orchestration is so contrived that it will hardly ever mar the intelligibility of the words, that his treatment of the voice parts is such that the text reaches the listening ear unhampered by an uncongenial *tessitura* or pulled out of its natural word shapes and inflections by those elongations, syllabic extensions and other irregularities with which music has a way of tyrannizing over language, of distorting and of voraciously consuming it. The idea that in order to understand the text of an opera in something like its completeness from a stage performance alone one needs principally to understand the language of the libretto is an illusion that will not hold water when put to the practical test under average conditions. I make this claim on the strength of having listened for more than thirty years both in America and in Europe to operas in languages I understand as well as I do English. And I think I am scarcely alone in my belief. If all one required to get the dramatic hang of an opera were a pair of normal ears and a familiarity with the language, libretto salesboys the world over would soon find Othello's occupation gone.

In the second place, there is, to my thinking, a flaw in the argument that, as soon as an American audience hears all its operas in English, it will grasp the plot of the piece that was heretofore obscure to it, understand without further hindrance what is being sung and, so understanding, take grand opera forever and aye to its hitherto reluctant bosom. Such a point of view leaves out of account that neither in America nor anywhere else is it the habit of audiences to strain their ears and concentrate on the text. If this text is understood, so much the better, if not, so much the worse. Has anyone ever heard of a singer with a good voice discharged from an opera company because his diction was not clear? Does anyone imagine that an opera containing beautiful music and other elements of success would be refused or discarded solely because some fault of the composer's prejudiced the intelligibility of the words? The thing in opera that matters first and last—whether the opera be by Handel, Mozart, Rossini, Verdi, Wagner, Debussy, Křenek, Deems Taylor or Alessandro Scarlatti—is the music. The more the hearer concentrates, line by line, on the book, the less he absorbs and enjoys, measure for measure, of the score.

It is only when the text can be caught without special effort, only when it can be understood without perceptibility detracting from the attention claimed by the music that the normal operagoer troubles himself about what the singer is saying. This is as true when the listener understands the language of the opera as when it is Greek to him. He may wonder from time to time what was said in this aria or in that scene. But so long as his interest is primarily engaged by the composer the librettist is a minor quantity, be his name Salvatore Cammerano, Hugo von Hofmannsthal or Richard Wagner. Give an audience a synopsis of the plot and it will ask very little more. (Such synopses, by the way, are printed in the programs of most large European opera houses. Why?) This is as true in Vienna, Paris, Dresden, Schweinfurt, Dijon, Brünn and Parma as in Cleveland, Louisville, Houston and New York. The details of the action or the utterances may go hang—and usually do. The world over, it is a lucky ear that without special exertion catches as much as fifty per cent of the remarks addressed to it from beyond the operatic footlights. And most ears decline to practice special exertions.

Another vital issue is involved in the question of translated opera— an issue to which the American propagandists for the experiment have given insufficient thought or which they have neglected altogether. I have reference to the matter of style—of a correct, an authentic interpretation as distinguished from a falsified one. Out of innumerable performances I have witnessed in different European countries

I can recollect scarcely one which did not in larger or smaller degree misrepresent an operatic work of foreign origin the moment it set out to render it in another tongue. It will not do to brush the question aside with the claim that a German production of, let us say, *Carmen*, must inevitably suffer from the inability of the German race to grasp the French spirit; that Italians will deprive *Meistersinger* or *Siegfried* of their true character because Italians cannot encompass the distinctive elements of the German nature; or that the *slancio* which Italians give out of the fullness of their souls to *Cavalleria* or to *Rigoletto* is absent from a French presentation of these works for the reason that it forms no part of the Gallic temperament. All these things are the truth, but not the whole truth.

A deeper, more specific reason why something goes basically wrong when music written by one people is sung in the language of another springs from the fact that the pace, the rhythm, the contour, the physiognomy of a nation's music are primarily determined by the character and the movement of that nation's language. It is the German tongue which has molded the vocal writing of Schubert and Brahms and shaped the declamation of Wagner, just as *"Chi vuol la Zingarella," "Largo al Factotum," "Celeste Aïda,"* and *"Mi chiamano Mimi"* could only have grown out of the Italian language and *"Salut demeure," "Nous irons à Paris,"* or *"C'est l'extase langoureuse"* from the French. And when you mate the music of one race with the language of another your success in creating the illusion of agreement between the two will only be in proportion to the kinship of the original tongue and the one substituted for it. To the extent that the language into which you translate the original differs from it in what I might term its density, its intonation, its mobility, its overtones—to that extent you will be nearer to or farther from a stylistically correct performance when you sing your opera in it.

I have never heard a "correct" performance of *Carmen* in Germany. This is not because the German translation is especially inept, not even because most German women are scarcely Carmens by nature. It is principally because the German language and Bizet's music are mutually antagonistic. The former forbids the latter to move at its proper pace. It hangs clogs on it. It compels the singer to move more slowly than the French artist does. The conductor has no choice but to follow suit—now slightly, now considerably, but, in the aggregate, with differences perceptible enough to alter the specific gravity of the opera and subtly to transform the whole spirit of the work. Consider for a moment the German rendering of Carmen's *"L'Amour est un oiseau rebelle"*—*"Ja die Liebe hat bunte Flügel."* The paraphrase as such is not so bad. But try to sing it to the first phrase of the Habeñera and note what happens. Mark, for one thing, what the consonants do.

If you think I have selected a biased and inconclusive example, let me draw your attention to the Teutonic edition of *"Vissi d'arte, vissi d'amore"*—*"Nur der Schönheit weiht' ich mein Leben."* Poetically this is rather a clever job and it fits the music supply enough. But sing it to yourself and carefully digest the change that has come over the familiar melody.

A language determines not only a racial style of song but also the tone formation and production of the singers belonging to that race. The throaty voice, the *"Knödel Stimme"* of the German tenor is as much a by-product of the German language as the *"voce bianca"* of the Italian is of the *"lingua Toscana."* And so even a German tenor singing Turiddu in Italian or an Italian soprano singing Elsa in German is likelier than otherwise to prove a misfit. Why was Léon Rothier when he used to sing Pogner in the Metropolitan *Meistersinger* invariably a square peg in a round hole? He was an intelligent artist and he labored industriously with his German which was often no worse in its way than the French of, let us say, Giuseppe Danise. The main reason he never carried conviction in the part was due to the essentially French intonation and tone quality he was incapable of disguising.

From half a dozen different standpoints the translation of an opera from its original language into another implies a falsification in its style of performance, a corruption of its spirit (yes, even if the work is called *Boris* or *The Bartered Bride* or *Halka* and even if I do not know ten words of Russian, Czech or Polish!). The correctness and the authenticity of most of the representations it has sponsored for half a century have been the justifiable boast of the Metropolitan and the envy of the most enlightened music lovers abroad. Is this lordly advantage on the point of being surrendered (for foreign operas translated into even the best of English are going to be falsified as surely as ever was Bizet or Verdi in Germany or Wagner and Weber in Paris) on the specious plea of bringing opera closer to a people whose real desire for it I gravely doubt? I, for one, am too good an American to hope so.

SINGERS AND CONDUCTING

HOW A TENOR REVOLVES AROUND THE PUBLIC

Hector Berlioz

> One of Berlioz's *Evenings with the Orchestra*. This version has been newly translated by Jacques Barzun. You may choose your own tenor for the protagonist.

"You belong to the theater, not the theater to you."

A very dull modern German opera is being given.

General conversation. "My God!" exclaims Kleiner the Younger as he comes into the orchestra; "how can a man stand so many vexations? As if it weren't enough to have to listen to this wretched work, without having it sung by that infernal tenor? What a voice! What a style! What musicianship! What pretensions!"

"Shut up, you misanthrope!" retorts Dervinck, the first oboe; "you'll wind up as brutish as your brother; you have the same tastes, the same ideas. Don't you know that a tenor is a being apart, who holds the power of life and death over the works he sings, over the composers, and consequently over poor devils of players like you and me? He is not a denizen of this world, he is a world in himself. More, he is deified by the dilettanti, and he takes himself so completely for a god that he is forever talking of his 'creations.' Just take a look at this book someone sent me from Paris, and you will see how this celestial body revolves around the public. You who are everlastingly delving into Humboldt's *Cosmos* will readily grasp the phenomenon."

"Read it out to us, Kleinerchen," say the majority of musicians; "if you read properly, you shall have a Bavarian cream."

"You mean it?"

"We certainly do."

"All right, then."

BEFORE DAWN

The as yet unknown tenor is in the hands of an able teacher, who is full of knowledge, patience, feeling, and taste, and who begins by making of him a perfect sight reader and a good harmonist, gives him a broad, pure method, initiates him into the beauties of master-pieces—in a word, trains him in the grand style of singing.

Hardly has the tenor caught a glimpse of the emotional power with which he is endowed before he aspires to the throne. In spite of his teacher he wants to make his debut and rule supreme. But his voice is not yet formed. A second-class theater opens its doors to him; he makes his debut and is hissed. Incensed by this outrage, the tenor obtains permission to break his contract and, his heart full of contempt for his fellow countrymen, hies himself to Italy.

At first he runs into mighty obstacles in the way of a new start, but he ends by overcoming them; he is pretty well received. His voice changes, it becomes full, strong, incisive, fitted to express the violent passions as well as the softest sentiments; its timbre gradually acquires purity, freshness, and a delightful simplicity. These qualities finally make up a talent whose effect is irresistible. He is a success. The Italian managers, who are good businessmen, sell, buy back, and resell the poor tenor, whose paltry salary remains the same even though he brings riches to two or three theaters a year. He is exploited and squeezed dry in a thousand ways, so much and so often that in the end his thoughts revert to his native land. He forgives her and even goes so far as to admit that she was right to be severe at his debut. He knows that the director of the Paris Opéra has his eye on him. He accepts an offer and crosses the Alps again.

SUNRISE

The tenor makes a fresh debut, this time at the Opéra, and before a public predisposed in his favor by his Italian triumphs. Exclamations of pleasure and surprise greet his first melody: from then on, his success is assured. Yet this is but the prelude to the emotions he is to stir before the evening is over. The audience has admired the fusion of feeling and of discipline with an organ of enchanting sweetness; there remain to be heard the dramatic accents, the bursts of passion. A number comes during which the daring artist, stressing each syllable, gives out some high chest notes with a resonant fullness, an expression of heart-rending grief, and a beauty of tone that so far nothing had led one to expect. A petrified silence reigns in the house, people hold their breath, amazement and admiration are blended in a mood akin to fear. There is in fact reason for fear until that extraordinary phrase comes to an end; but when it has done so triumphantly, the wild enthusiasm of the listeners is beyond imagining.

We reach the third act. An orphan returns to his father's thatched cottage; his heart, seared by a hopeless love, and his senses, affected by the blood and slaughter he has just witnessed at the wars, collapse under the shock of the most appalling contrast conceivable: his father is dead; the cottage is empty; all is still and silent; it is peace, it is the grave. Both the bosom on which it would be so sweet to shed tears of filial piety and the heart beside which his own could alone beat with less pain are separated from him by the infinite—*she* will never be his. . . . The situation is poignant and worthily treated by the composer. Here the singer reaches a height no one would have thought him capable of. He is sublime. And from two thousand panting lungs break forth cheers such as an artist hears only twice or thrice in his lifetime, cheers that repay him sufficiently for his long and arduous labors.

It is all bouquets, laurel wreaths, recalls. Two days later the press, overflowing with enthusiasm, broadcasts the name of the radiant tenor to all parts of the world where civilization has penetrated.

It is at this point that, if I were a moralist, I might toy with the idea of addressing a homily to the triumphant hero, somewhat in the style of Don Quixote's speech to Sancho when that worthy squire was about to take possession of the government of Barataria:

"You have reached the summit," I would say. "In a few weeks you will be famous; frantic applause will be yours and likewise endless engagements. Authors will pay court to you; managers will no longer keep you waiting in their anterooms, and if you ever write to them, they will answer you. Women whom you do not even know will speak of you as their protégé or very intimate friend. People will dedicate to you their books in prose or verse. Instead of the five francs you give your janitor at Christmas, you will have to give him a hundred. You will be exempted from service in the National Guard. You will get leave from the Opéra from time to time, so that the provincial towns can fight over your presence and performances. Flowers and sonnets will be heaped around your feet. You will sing at the *soirées* given by the Prefect, and the Mayor's wife will send you apricots. You are on the verge of Olympus at last; for as the Italians call their women singers *dive* (goddesses), it naturally follows that the great men singers are gods. Well, you have now been promoted deity; try to remain a good fellow none the less—and don't look down on people who offer you good advice.

"Remember that the voice is a fragile instrument, which may be spoiled or broken in a minute, often without any discoverable cause; and that such an accident is enough to hurl the greatest of the gods from his high throne and reduce him to mortal rank, and sometimes even lower than that.

"Don't be too hard on the poor composers.

"When from the depths of your elegant carriage you see in the street Meyerbeer, Spontini, Halévy, or Auber going on foot, do not greet them with a slight nod of patronizing friendship. They would laugh at it in pity, and passers-by would look upon it with indignation as supreme impertinence on your part. Do not forget that a number of their works will be admired and full of vitality when the memory of your high C from the chest is sunk in oblivion.

"Should you visit Italy once more, do not become infatuated with some feeble spinner of cavatinas and, on your return, palm him off as a classic, telling us with an impartial air that Beethoven 'was also talented.' For no god can escape ridicule.

"When you accept a new role, do not allow yourself to make any changes in it except by the author's leave. Bear in mind that a single note added, curtailed, or transposed may make a melody commonplace or distort its expression. You have in any case no right to do this at any time. To modify the music one sings, or the book one is translating, without saying a word about it to the man who wrote it only after much thought, is to commit a shocking breach of trust. People who borrow without giving notice are called thieves; unfaithful interpreters are libelers and assassins.

"If by any chance there should arise a rival whose voice has more bite and power than your own, do not, in the midst of a duet, start matching lungs with him. Take it for granted that you must not fight the iron pot, even and especially if you are a piece of Ming china.

"When on tour, beware also of saying to the provincials, by way of reference to the Paris Opéra and its chorus and orchestra: '*My* theater, *my* chorus, *my* orchestra.' Provincials do not enjoy being taken for fools any more than Parisians do. They know full well that you belong to the theater, not the theater to you, and they would find your fatuous conceit the acme of the grotesque.

"And now, friend Sancho, receive my blessing; go and govern Barataria. It is a rather low-lying island, but the most fertile, perhaps, to be found on earth. Your people are but slightly civilized. Therefore encourage public education, so that in a couple of years' time they will no longer suspect of witchcraft those who can read. Do not take too seriously the flattery of those you invite to your table; don't keep repeating your damnable slogans; don't get upset when you have an important speech to deliver; and never break your word. May those who entrust their interests to you feel sure that you will not betray them; and in whatever you do, may you never be accused of being sharp (or flat) anywhere in the world."

THE TENOR AT HIS ZENITH

His salary is one hundred thousand francs, with a month's leave annually. After the first role that brought him dazzling success, the tenor attempts a few others with varied results. He then accepts some which he gives up after three or four performances if he does not excel in them as he did before. In so doing he may spoil the career of a composer, annihilate a masterpiece, ruin a publisher, and do enormous harm to the theater. Considerations of this kind are to him nonexistent. Art for him is nothing but gold coin and laurel wreaths, and the most likely means to obtain both quickly are the only ones he cares to use.

He has noticed that certain melodic formulas, certain vocalizations, certain ornaments, certain fortissimi, certain concluding platitudes or vulgar rhythms have the property of immediately drawing applause of a sort. This seems to him reason enough to rely on these devices; indeed, to insist on the composer's supplying them in his roles, regardless of expression, originality, or elevation of style; meanwhile showing hostility toward loftier and more individual productions. He knows the effect of the old methods he is in the habit of using. He is ignorant of the effect of the new methods submitted to his attention, and though an interpreter, he does not regard himself as one who can afford to remain disinterested. When in doubt, he abstains as far as he can.

The timidity of a few composers who have given in to his unreasonable demands has already made him dream of introducing into our theaters the musical practices of Italy. There is no use telling him that *Maestro* means "Master," and that the name has been rightly conferred on the composer; that it is *his* conception that must strike the audience free and unimpaired through the medium of the singer. It is the master who gives out light and casts shadows; it is he who is king and answerable for his acts; he proposes and disposes; his ministers must have no other object, seek no other glory, than that of rightly grasping his plans and, by putting themselves exactly at his point of view, ensuring their realization.

(Here the reader's entire audience shouts "Bravo!" and so far forgets itself as to applaud. The tenor on the stage, who just then was yelling out of tune more than usual, takes the applause for himself and throws a gratified glance at the orchestra.)

The reader continues:

The tenor will not heed. He wants to vociferate in drum-major style. Ten years on the stage south of the Alps have made him an addict to hackneyed themes with pauses during which he can hear himself applauded, or can mop his brow, fix his hair, cough and swallow a lozenge. Or again he insists on senseless vocalizes, interspersed with threatening, angry, or tender accents, and laced with low notes, shrill cries, buzzings of hummingbirds, screechings of guinea-fowl, runs, arpeggios, and trills. Whatever the meaning of the words, the character of the part or the situation, he feels free to accelerate or slacken the tempo, to add scales up and down and ornaments of every species, not to mention *ah's* and *oh's* that make the phrase absurd. He dwells on short syllables, gallops through long ones, disregards elisions, introduces aspirate *h's* where none exist, and takes breath in the middle of a word. He no longer has standards; anything goes—provided it helps the emission of one of his favorite notes. Who would notice one absurdity more or less in such good company? The orchestra either keeps its counsel or else humors him. The tenor lords it over everyone and tramples on everything. He struts about the theater with the air of a conqueror; his crest gaily glints above his proud head; he is king, hero, demigod, god.

Only, it is hard to make out whether he is weeping or laughing, whether he is in love or in anger. There is no melody left, no expression, no common sense, no drama, no music; there is simply an emission of vocal sounds, and this alone matters; this is the great thing. He goes to the theater to hunt down the public as others go to the forest to hunt the stag. Forward boldly! Let us give tongue! Tally-ho! Tally-ho! Let art be our quarry!

Soon the example of this vocal fortune makes the management of the theater impossible. It awakens and fosters mad hopes and ambitions among all the singing mediocrities. "The leading tenor gets one hundred thousand francs; why," asks the second tenor, "shouldn't I get eighty thousand?"—"And I fifty?" puts in the third.

To feed these gaping vanities, to fill up these chasms, the manager vainly cuts down the expenses of the company, reduces and cripples orchestra and chorus by giving the artists who make them up porters' wages. Vain are his efforts, useless his sacrifices—until the day when he tries to find out exactly how he stands, attempts to compare the hugeness of the tenor's salary with the work done, and discovers with a shock the following curious result:

The first tenor, with a salary of a hundred thousand francs, sings approximately seven times a month; he therefore takes part in eighty-four performances a year, and receives a little over eleven hundred francs an evening. Taking a role comprising eleven hundred notes or syllables, this represents one franc a syllable. Thus in *William Tell*:

My (*1 fr.*) presence (*2 frs.*) may well seem to you an outrage (*8 frs.*).
Mathilda (*3 frs.*), my indiscreet steps (*5 frs.*).
Have dared to find their way as far as this, your dwelling (*13 frs.*).

Total, thirty-two francs: your words are golden, my lord.

Given a prima donna receiving a mere pittance of forty thousand francs, Mathilda's answer of course comes cheaper (commercial parlance), each of her syllables averaging a mere eight sous, but even that is not so bad:

It's easy to forgive (*2 frs., 8 sous*) the wrongs (*16 sous*) one has a part in (*2 frs.*).
Arnold (*16 sous*), I (*8 sous*) expected you (*32 sous*).

Total, eight francs.

So the manager pays, goes on paying, pays again and again, till the day comes when he can pay no more and is compelled to close his theater. As his brother managers are in a no more flourishing condition, some of the immortals have to resign themselves to teaching sol-fa (those who can) or singing to a guitar in the public squares, with four candle-ends and a green carpet.

THE SUN SETS—STORMY SKIES

The tenor is on his way out. His voice can neither go up nor come down. He has to decapitate every phrase and sing only what lies in his middle register. He wreaks havoc upon the old scores and clamps an unbearable monotony upon the new as a prerequisite to their being heard at all. His admirers are disconsolate.

Composers, poets, or painters who have lost their sense of beauty and truth, those whom vulgarity no longer shocks, who lack the strength even to follow up their own fugitive ideas, and whose only pleasure is to set traps under the feet of their active and flourishing rivals—such men are already dead and buried. And yet they believe themselves to be still alive; a happy illusion sustains them, they mistake exhaustion for fatigue, impotence for moderation. But compare with this the loss of an organ! Who could deceive himself about a loss of that magnitude? Especially when the loss is that of a voice that was marvelous in range and strength, in the beauty of its inflections, the nuances of its timbre, its dramatic expression, its perfect purity?

I have sometimes been moved to deepest pity for these unfortunate singers, and filled with a great indulgence for the whims, vanities, exactions, immoderate ambitions, exorbitant pretensions, and infinite absurdities of some of them. They live but a day, and die once for all. Hardly do the names of a few famous ones survive, and even these owe their rescue from oblivion to the fame of the composers whose interpreters they were, all too often unfaithful interpreters at that. We know of Caffarelli because he sang at Naples in Gluck's *Tito*. The memory of Mmes. Saint-Huberty and Branchu has been kept in France because they created the roles of Dido, of the Vestal, of Iphigenia in Tauris,[1] and so on. Who among us would ever have heard of the diva Faustina were it not for Marcello, who was her teacher, and for Hasse, who married her? Let us therefore forgive these mortal gods for making their Olympus as brilliant as they can, for subjecting the heroes of art to such long and rugged trials, and for being inappeasable except by the sacrifice of ideas.

It is cruel for them to see the star of their fame and fortune sinking moment by moment below the horizon. What an anguishing celebration is that of their farewell appearance! How broken in heart must the great artist be when he last treads the boards and haunts the recesses of the theater of which he was for so long the tutelary

[1] In the operas, respectively, of Piccini, Spontini, and Gluck.

spirit, the king, the absolute sovereign! Dressing in his room, he soliloquizes: "I shall never be here again; this helmet with its brilliant crest will adorn me no more; never again will this private receptacle open its lid to receive the perfumed notes of fair enthusiasts!"

A knock: it is the callboy to announce the beginning of the piece. "Poor lad, no more trouble for you from my bad temper; no more abuse or cuffs to fear! Never again will you come to me and say: 'The overture has begun, sir. The curtain is up, sir! The first scene is over, sir! Your turn to go on, sir! They are waiting for you, sir!' Alas, no! It is I who now say to you: 'Santiquet, take off my name, which is still on the door; Santiquet, carry these flowers to Fanny; go at once, she won't care for them tomorrow; Santiquet, drink this glass of Madeira and take away the bottle; you shan't have to drive off the boys of the chorus in order to guard it; Santiquet, just make a parcel of these old wreaths, cart away my little piano, put out the lamp, lock the door; all is over.' "

Under the load of these sad thoughts the virtuoso enters the wings. He meets the second tenor, his closest enemy, his understudy, who outwardly weeps heartily, but inwardly laughs luscious tears.

"And so, my dear old chap," says the demigod in a doleful voice, "you're leaving us? But what a triumph is in store for you this evening! It is a great moment!"

"Yes, for you," replies the leading singer gloomily; and turning his back on him: "Delphine," he says to a pretty little dancer whom he has allowed to worship him, "give me my box of sweets."

"Oh, my box is empty," retorts the wanton creature, spinning on one foot, "I gave them all to Victor."

No matter. He must choke down grief, despair, fury; he must smile and sing. The tenor is on the stage; he is playing for the last time the work which he made a success, the part he *created*. He casts a final glance at the scenery which has reflected his glory, which has so often resounded with his tender accents, his passionate flights. He looks at the lake on whose shore he has waited for Mathilda, at the Grütli, from which he has shouted *Liberty!*—at the pale sun that for so many years he has seen rise at nine o'clock at night.[2]

He would like to cry, to sob his heart out; but he gets his cue, his voice must not tremble, the muscles of his face must express no other emotion than that of the part. The public is there—thousands of

---

[2] These details refer to Rossini's *William Tell*, whose Paris première Berlioz witnessed in 1829.

hands are prepared to applaud you, my poor old god: should they remain still, you would discover that the private sorrow you have just
suffered and stifled is as nothing compared to the lacerating torture of
the public's indifference on an occasion such as this. Once your slave,
the public is today your master, your emperor. Now then, make your
bow, there's the applause. . . . *Moriturus salutat.*

And so he sings, and by a superhuman effort recovers his youthful
verve and voice; he arouses transports of enthusiasm beyond any yet
seen; the stage is strewn with flowers like a hardly closed grave. His
heart throbbing with a thousand conflicting emotions, he walks slowly
off. The public wants to see him once more, and loudly calls for him.
What a sweet and cruel anguish there is for him in that final ovation!
It is easy to forgive him for prolonging it a little. It is his last joy, his
glory, his love, his genius, his life, shuddering as they die together.

Come, then, poor dear great artist, blazing meteor whose course
is run, come forward and hear the ultimate voice of our affectionate
admiration, as well as of our gratitude for the many pleasured moments you have given us; come and relish them, be happy and proud;
you will always remember this hour, though we shall forget it tomorrow.

He comes forward gasping for breath, his heart swollen with tears.
Loud cheers greet his appearance; the people clap their hands, call
him by the grandest, dearest names; Caesar crowns him. But the curtain comes down at last, like the cold weighted knife of the guillo-
tine; a chasm yawns between the conqueror and his triumphal chariot,
a chasm not to be bridged, a chasm hewed by the years. All is over!
The god is no more!

Dark night . . .

Eternal night . . .

PATTI: AN APPRECIATION

Eduard Hanslick

Patti charmed the famous Viennese critic and inspired him to some of his best writing, a portrait of what a singer can or ought to be. Was he prejudiced? See George Bernard Shaw below.

"Such delicate shading . . . I have never heard before."

When extraordinary natural gifts are combined with consummate artistry, the person thus endowed is capable of offering an utterly individual pleasure almost independent of the composition at hand, of being both artist and poet in a work whose author was neither. If we go today to hear operas such as *Linda, Sonnambula, I Puritani*, etc., we do it not to hear the works themselves—all dull— but to hear Patti. It is her talent and her voice which breathe new life into these empty and ineffectual melodies.

The aural image of such intoxicating vocal accomplishments fades all too swiftly; unlike a score, they cannot be recalled at home by reading. Thus, it is well to establish the characteristics of great singers while the memory of them is still fresh. In my personal contacts with Adelina Patti I had occasion to record numerous observations which will, I believe, be of interest to a wide circle of music lovers and add illustratively to her story. From the parquet alone one cannot determine just how much is attributable to natural gifts and how much to the labor of learning and the profit of instruction. That can be determined only in the singer's studio. And in Adelina Patti I have learned to know a musical organization perfect beyond all others—I may, indeed, say: a musical genius.

Nature endowed her with three assets in uncommon degree: refinement of hearing, quickness to grasp and to learn, and a secure memory. The infallible purity of her intonation is common knowledge. But a recent example may serve to demonstrate the extent to which the impression of the correct interval has become an integral part of that ever-compliant instrument, the throat, quite independently of any auxiliary devices. The occasion was the Patti benefit performance of Gounod's *Faust*. Following the Jewel Song, there was prolonged applause and then a riotous ovation. Wreaths flew from the boxes. Gigantic bouquets and even whole baskets of flowers were brought up from the orchestra, all acknowledged by innumerable bows. Finally, just as the spectacle seemed to be subsiding, there came even more fervent shouts demanding a repetition of the aria. Without giving any signal to the orchestra, Patti attacked the trill on the B-natural. The orchestra entered in the next measure—and all was precisely in tune. The noisy, tiring interruption, lasting some quarter of an hour, had not disturbed her certainty in the free attack on the correct pitch. It is understandable that she finds the false intonation of others painful. She is unusually considerate in her judgment of her colleagues, and the only expression of disapproval I ever heard from her concerned out-of-tune singing—which is, unfortunately, not uncommon at the Vienna Court Opera.

Patti's memory borders on the miraculous. She learns a new part completely by singing it two or three times *sotto voce*, and what she has once learned and sung publicly she never forgets. Of the operas she has sung often, she had neither the vocal nor the piano score with her in Vienna. Of all of the operas she sang during her last visit, she reread only *Semiramide* prior to the performance, and this only because she had sung it rarely and, in the last two years, not at all. In the final performance of *Don Pasquale*, I visited her in her dressing room after the first act. In the course of the conversation she asked to see a piano score of the opera. She opened it to the second act, sang two measures *sotto voce*, and laid the book aside, continuing with the conversation. "What was it?" I asked. "Nothing," she answered. "I know the opera by heart all right, although I sang it last a year ago. But I sang *Linda* day before yesterday, and I just remembered that a certain part in *Linda* starts exactly like a part in the second finale of *Don Pasquale*. I just wanted to make sure that I would not fall into the wrong theme."

This is the only case I know of where she experienced a moment of uncertainty. It seems to speak as much for her memory as for her musical presence of mind. She once sang me a mazurka of Strauss's which I had played for her some ten years before and which she had not heard again. Her voice, schooled from earliest childhood and treated with an instinctive security—as we treat the most ordinary gesture—hardly requires systematic exercise. She practices solfeggio for half an hour every day, normally *mezza voce*. She does not run through her roles. She never practices facial expressions before the mirror. "That leads only to mugging," she says.

Patti first came to Vienna at the age of twenty early in 1863, appearing with her opera troupe at the Carltheater. She stayed until May. I was not especially anxious to make her personal acquaintance, since she was said to be unfriendly, but in the end I complied with the repeated requests of her brother-in-law, Strakosch, and went with him one morning to visit her. I can still see her before me, a small, pale, slender figure in a red wool Garibaldi blouse, seated in an armchair at the window, caressing her dog, Cora. I was soon on good footing with both, with the dog because I coaxed and with Adelina because I didn't. With her father, her brother-in-law, and her faithful companion, Louisa, she had rented a small private apartment where she lived simply and quietly during this first year in Vienna. She had no fondness for parties, visits, or flirtations, and this coincided with the tastes of Strakosch, who took good care of her. Apart from myself, there were few visitors. The manager and conductor of the Italian opera called now and then, as did the family of the banker Julius Fischof, in-laws of Strakosch.

Adelina was a child of nature, half timid and half wild, what the French call *sauvage*, good-humored and violent, inclined to sudden, quickly passing fits of temper, directed usually against Strakosch, who tried to appease her. She had not yet learned to restrain herself, to be amiable with people for whom she did not care—an art which she later learned to perfection. Even today, as a French *grande dame*, she has not lost her kindness of heart, but the American child of nature of 1863 was more stimulating and appealing. When I happened in at mealtimes, which were frequently changed, I had to join them without demur. Hardly another "diva" can have eaten more simply or in a more bourgeois manner. After meals, I would play waltzes by Strauss and Lanner, which she loved to hear. Sometimes she would impulsively push tables and chairs aside, Strakosch (an excellent waltz player) would take over at the piano, and we would dance as a single, enraptured couple around the room. It was highly comical when Strakosch, worried about her voice, would plead with us to stop. "For heaven's sake, Lina," he would cry, "you must sing tonight."

"Leave that to me," she would answer, laughing, and the waltz would go on.

I also had occasion to become acquainted with her marked talent for languages. One day I said something in German to Strakosch which I did not want her to understand. In mock anger she suddenly began speaking in broken German. She had understood everything, although she had lived in Vienna only four weeks and had never heard or read a German word before. At home she spoke English, which she described as her mother tongue, but she also commanded a full knowledge of Italian and French.

The young Patti was preoccupied in those days solely with music and the theater. Such energetic singleness of purpose bears secure fruits, but it also has its disadvantages. I have never found in Adelina the slightest concern for higher questions of humanity, for science, politics, religion, or even for literature. A book was always the rarest item in her apartment. We professors, however, cannot restrain the desire to make such charming beings also a bit literary, and thus I urged her, in this first year, to read something. She agreed to try a nice English novel. I brought her Dickens' *Great Expectations*, which I deemed suitable because of its fortunate mixture of comic and tragic elements. The book starts with a tale about an old woman who, deserted by her bridegroom on her wedding day, goes insane from the shock. She dresses in her faded bridal dress, sits before her half-petrified wedding cake, and waits for her lover.

When I asked Adelina, a few days later, how she had liked the novel, she answered excitedly that she had started it but did not intend to continue. "It's nothing but lies which nobody will make me believe. That an old woman wouldn't give up her old bridal dress and her old wedding cake can't be true and isn't possible. I am no longer a child to whom one can give such things to read." The simplicity of her attitude was charming, but it restrained me from further literary attempts. It may be that her horizon has broadened in this respect with the passage of years. I don't know.

Patti's repertoire at that time consisted exclusively of naïve or half-serious roles. Even now, when her voice and her dramatic talents have developed and become intensified, she seems most perfect to me in parts like Zerlina in *Don Giovanni*, Norina in *Don Pasquale*, or Rosina in *The Barber of Seville*. These parts blend most naturally with her artistic individuality and her appearance—considerations whose sovereign importance is not always sufficiently appreciated by the critics.

At that time (1863), she sang these naïve parts, if not better, at least with more pleasure and youthful exuberance than today, when her full sympathy belongs exclusively to expressly dramatic parts. Life, too, has made her more serious. She had a strong affection even then for dramatic roles, but she was wisely told to wait for the future. She did not like to hear the naïve parts described as her particular domain. She once replied, tossing her head, "I am no *buffa.*" Once, after a performance of *Don Giovanni*, she said, ignoring my praise of her Zerlina: "I should prefer to sing Donna Anna, and I shall sing her yet!"

Her first role in Vienna was *Sonnambula.* In order to reproduce conscientiously this first impression, I should like to quote a part of my review of that performance:

If Patti's singing, acting, and personality are regarded as a whole, one must confess to having hardly ever met a more charming individual on the stage. I have heard greater artists as singers, and more brilliant voices. I recall more sophisticated actresses, and more beautiful women. But Patti's charm consists in making one forget them. What she offers is so completely hers, so harmonious and lovable, that one allows oneself to be captivated and accepts capitulation with pleasure. When this slip of a girl steps lightly on the stage, inclines her childish face, radiant with artless pleasure, and regards the audience, intelligently and good-naturedly, with her big, shining doelike eyes, she has already conquered. When she begins to sing and act, both eye and ear are happy to say yes to the rash judgment of the heart. What a youthful fresh voice, ranging evenly and effortlessly from C to the F above the staff! A silver-clear, genuine soprano, it is wonderfully pure and distinct, particularly in the higher tones. The middle register has a suspicion of sharpness, but the impression is rather of brisk morning freshness. The lower register still lacks force. The voice is not extraordinarily soft and warm, and its strength is impressive only in relation to the singer's slight frame. It seems hardly capable of big climaxes or great dramatic effects, but it is advisedly never extended to the limit of what it can master completely. Her bravura is considerable, more brilliant in leaps and staccati than in legato. Over all, however, is immeasurable charm.

The author of this certainly very measured praise was attacked as an enthusiast by the anti-Patti faction of the Viennese press. Several papers then would have liked to represent her as a flash-in-the-pan, of whom nobody would speak a few years later. Time has furnished conclusive proof to the contrary.

Patti's Lucia came in for particularly adverse criticism in that first year. I, too, was not as enthusiastic about this role as I was about her Rosina or Norina. One had only to see her to be persuaded that she was better suited for naïve parts than for tragic or heroic ones. But what is there of the tragic or heroic in this Lucia of Donizetti? She was a charming, weak, rather spoiled creature, who promises everything to her lover in the first act, can refuse nothing to her brother in the second, and has no recourse other than insanity in the third. Patti does not play her in "grand style," but there is no place for "grand style" in this opera. What has been criticized as lack of greatness rests more or less in her slight physique. The slender figure cannot possibly stride imposingly; the arms cannot make full sweeping gestures or present plastic studies for a Niobe. In a word, Patti is prevented by her appearance from lifting Lucia from the atmosphere of Donizetti into something higher and more imposing. Of the singers I have heard, none has sung the role with greater mastery.

Most perfect and most charming, however, were the cheerful parts, especially Zerlina. Mozart himself, in his fondest dreams, can hardly have seen a more natural and charming embodiment of this creature of his fantasy, with whom, according to Oulibicheff, he seems to have fallen in love himself. Patti's Zerlina creates the illusion of a beautiful natural phenomenon, perfect, artless, inexplicable, and incapable of reproduction, even through the ultimate devices of art. Nature is the superior and decisive device which she possesses for this role, and it is just about the only one she applies. The whole accomplishment is replete with the inborn serenity of a perfectly attuned personality, with a grace at once natural and individual. The majority of Zerlinas lapse either into false sentimentality or open flirtatiousness. Patti's Zerlina borders neither on the one nor on the other. When she encounters Don Giovanni she is a cheerful young girl, somewhat thoughtless and vain, but harmless and inexperienced. And it is with the curiosity of surprised childish vanity, not with the repulsive sophistication of coquetry, that she listens to his blandishments. In her precious *"Andiam!"* there is neither an assumption of passion nor a suggestion of eager acquiescence. There is nothing, indeed, but the unthinking impulsiveness of a flattered peasant girl who, as soon as she realizes the danger, finds her way back with the instinct of innocence. Thus, Patti, more through instinct than reflection, not only overcomes the dubious in Zerlina but even evokes the beautiful image as if there were nothing dubious about it. I need hardly add that she sings

the part not only according to the spirit but also according to the letter of the score.

Similar accomplishments, coupled with brilliant virtuosity, animate
her Rosina and Norina. Her Sonnambula and Lucia may be wanting
in warmth and depth of feeling, but it is impossible to imagine a
Rosina or Norina more graceful, more brilliant, or more natural. The
song is clear, strong, and fresh as a lark's trill; the acting inspired with
delightful wit and the most graceful realism. Rosina offers perhaps the
best material for an appreciation of her miraculous technique. She
is the only contemporary singer who has a thorough command of the
traditions of the Rossini style. She furnished new proof of this in
Semiramide, the last new part she sang in Vienna. Granted that even
she can restore to this faded work only an illusion of life, I still enjoyed the rare opportunity of hearing it from the only singer presently
capable of singing it with complete mastery. The dean of European
music critics, W. von Lenz in Petersburg, has named her the "Paganini of vocal virtuosity." He was prompted not only by her comparable virtuosity but also by a comparable sense of disembodiment of
tone. "No other violinist," he wrote of Paganini, "achieved such
physical identity with the instrument. Once he began, he seemed, so
to speak, to continue. When I first heard Patti, I was struck at once
with the fact that she launches a tone in a manner characteristic only
of great instrumentalists. She attacks the first note with a security and
an exactness of intonation which the majority of singers achieve only
in the course of a cantilena."

I first saw Patti again in the spring of 1867, in Paris. She was
doing nothing new. The repertoire of the Opéra Italien was the most
commonplace in the world, but the public crowded the theater whenever she sang, regardless of the role. New, however, was her social
progress. She had an elegant apartment on the Avenue de l'Impératrice.
There were visitors galore and even brilliant parties, where I met a
number of celebrities. I made the acquaintance, among others, of the
gifted illustrator Gustave Doré and of that famous sportsman the
Marquis de Caux, both of whom were infatuated with her. She
treated them both with the same friendliness and impartiality—and
without a thought of serious involvement. The consistent endeavors
of the Marquis were, however, eventually successful. They were married in London, in 1869.

Those who observed Adelina in the company of the Marquis—before, as well as after, their marriage—were aware that she did not marry for love. She had no knowledge of love in the sense of *la grande passion*. Thus, she was able to believe that she could marry a man without this unknown element, a man in whom she saw an accomplished gentleman and whom she knew to be her enthusiastic admirer. Aristocratic society was open to her as a queen in her own right even before she became a marquise, but the title and the exalted connections of her suitor may have flattered her childlike mind.

She returned to Vienna in the spring of 1872, after an absence of nine years, to fulfill an engagement at the Theater-an-der-Wien. Since then she has returned every year, singing three years ago in the newly built house of the Comic Opera, and last year and the year before in the Court Opera. Each year, despite the frequency of her appearances, she has been a charming novelty, and we critics have been subjected to ever greater embarrassment in our efforts to write something new about a phenomenon so perfect. To the operas which she had sung here before were added: *Il Trovatore* and *Rigoletto* of Verdi; *Dinorah* and *The Huguenots* of Meyerbeer; *Romeo and Juliet* and *Faust* of Gounod; *Linda di Chamounix* of Donizetti; *I Puritani* of Bellini; *Martha* of Flotow; and *Semiramide* of Rossini.

The reunion was artistically most pleasing. The homage she had received in Europe had not turned her head. She never considered herself an infallible "diva." She strove conscientiously for perfection. Her natural charm has remained unspoiled, but, at the same time, her art has ripened to a marvelous fruit. If, in 1863, we had to warn enthusiasts against regarding as a phenomenon of the art of perfect singing what was, indeed, a phenomenon in its totality, we must now recognize in her the greatest of singing artists. The irresistible charm which so surrounded her first appearance, and her pure joy in singing and acting, have not been lost with her youth. Graced by God with talent, she is, at the same time, one of the happiest of His creatures, simply by virtue of her inexhaustible joy in her vocation. This doesn't always go hand in hand with success. Her sister Carlotta longs for the day when she need no longer sing.[1] For Adelina, singing and acting are vital requirements. Such passionate artistic natures quickly establish a magnetic relationship with the public. She has grown not only musically but also dramatically. Her understanding seems to have deepened, her acting to have gained in refinement, her ever-attractive

---

[1] (1840–99) a celebrated coloratura.

pantomime to have become exemplary. Such expressive, delicately detailed acting as her farewell to Alfredo in the second act of *La Traviata* was still beyond her grasp in 1863. Her voice, too, has gained strikingly; one enjoyed especially the greater fullness and beauty of the low notes. They sounded immature nine years ago; now they remind one of the dark tones of a Cremonese viola.

Of her new parts the most effective was that of Leonora in *Il Trovatore*. Especially admirable was her singing of the two big arias. The slow movements she sings broadly and expressively. The dubious triviality of the allegros she overcomes by two devices. First, she gives free rein to a brilliant virtuosity which completely overshadows the composer. One must have experienced the silver-clear impact of this infallible voice, which toys with the most astounding difficulties and attacks the most distant pitches, the highest notes, with a security rare even among instrumentalists. And she knows how to soften the coarseness of these allegros, to ennoble them by musical phrasing, by facial expression and gesture. The effect of a look or a gesture is not everything, but it may contribute a lot. Not every singer can make such characteristics her own, just as not every singer can have that sharply profiled, marble-pale face with the two black flames which glow with every upward surge in the music.

Her *La Traviata* is equally good. It is even more convincing and attractive, because the part and the whole opera are superior to *Il Trovatore* in naturalness, feeling, and musical charm. *La Traviata* represents considerable progress from the stylistic violence of *Il Trovatore*, and its origin in an effective, cleverly made play is a dramatic advantage. The character and the plot of *La Traviata* develop before our eyes. They are understandable and compel our participation more or less, while the persons and situations in *Il Trovatore* arrive on the stage as if shot from a pistol. The events leading up to the tragedy in *Il Trovatore* are, moreover, so unintelligible that few manage to grasp which of the two young men was kidnaped and burned and which wasn't. Patti's Violetta has one fault—a fault which I would rather praise than condemn. She is no Traviata, no *Dame aux Camélias*. The piquant *haut-goût* of the demimonde, which Désirée Artôt,[2] the sophisticated French singer, bestowed on this figure with so much elegance, is completely wanting. When Patti enters in the first scene, bubbling with childlike gaiety, the camellias in her corsage seem trans-

[2] (1835–1907) a pupil of Pauline Viardot-Garcia, one-time fiancée of Tchaikovsky.

formed into lilies. Her rendering of the first aria resembles a shower of flowers, and in the last act she finds the most touching accents. Such delicate shading from piano to expirating pianissimo, as in the death scene, such remarkable transitions from *mezza voce* to fortissimo, as in her duet with Alfredo, I have never heard before.

A DIFFERENT VIEW

George Bernard Shaw

It is still possible for a prima donna to bounce on the stage and throw her voice at the heads of the audience with an insolent insistence on her position as a public favorite, and hardly the ghost of a reference to the character she is supposed to impersonate. An ambitious young artist may easily be misled by illustrious examples of stage misconduct. To tell an average young opera singer that she is a Patti or a Nilsson is to pay her the highest compliment she desires. Yet Madame Patti's offenses against artistic propriety are mighty ones and millions. She seldom even pretends to play any other part than that of Adelina, the spoiled child with the adorable voice; and I believe she would be rather hurt than otherwise if you for a moment lost sight of Patti in your preoccupation with Zerlina, or Aïda, or Caterina.

THE OTHER SHOE
from *The Mapleson Memoirs*

Col. J. H. Mapleson

Col. Mapleson, a flamboyant English impresario of the nineteenth century, wrote—as impresarios were wont to do—a book of memoirs, *The Mapleson Memoirs*. He too knew Patti and knew her well.

"Ultimately the other shoe was got on."

From Philadelphia we went to Boston, where, unfortunately, the booking was not at all great, it not being our usual time for visiting that city. Moreover, I had to go to the Globe Theatre. On the second night of our engagement we performed *La Traviata*. That afternoon, about two o'clock, Patti's agent called upon me to receive the five thousand dollars for her services that evening. I was at low water just then, and inquiring at the booking office found that I was two hundred pounds short. All I could offer Signor Franchi was the trifle of eight hundred pounds as a payment on account.

The agent declined the money, and formally announced to me that my contract with Mme. Patti was at an end. I accepted the inevitable, consoling myself with the reflection that, besides other good artists in my company, I had now eight hundred pounds to go on with.

Two hours afterward Signor Franchi reappeared.

"I cannot understand," he said, "how it is you get on so well with *prime donne*, and especially with Mme. Patti. You are a marvelous man, and a fortunate one, too, I may add. Mme. Patti does not wish to break her engagement with you, as she certainly would have done with anyone else under the circumstances. Give me the eight hundred pounds and she will make every preparation for going onto the stage. She empowers me to tell you that she will be at the theater in good time for the beginning of the opera, and that she will be ready dressed

From *The Mapleson Memoirs*.

in the costume of Violetta, with the exception only of the shoes. You can let her have the balance when the doors open and the money comes in from the outside public; and directly she receives it she will put her shoes on and at the proper moment make her appearance on the stage." I thereupon handed him the eight hundred pounds I had already in hand as the result of subscriptions in advance. "I congratulate you on your good luck," said Signor Franchi as he departed with the money in his pocket.

After the opening of the doors I had another visit from Signor Franchi. By this time an extra sum of £160 had come in. I handed it to my benevolent friend, and begged him to carry it without delay to the obliging prima donna, who, having received £960, might, I thought, be induced to complete her toilette pending the arrival of the forty pounds balance.

Nor was I altogether wrong in my hopeful anticipations. With a beaming face Signor Franchi came back and communicated to me the joyful intelligence that Mme. Patti had got one shoe on. "Send her the forty pounds," he added, "and she will put on the other."

Ultimately the other shoe was got on; but not, of course, until the last forty pounds had been paid. Then Mme. Patti, her face radiant with benignant smiles, went onto the stage; and the opera already begun was continued brilliantly until the end.

A MEMORY OF SALZBURG AND FIDELIO

Vincent Sheean

A reminiscence of a past but not forgotten era in Salzburg.

"You have it or you do not have it."

Lotte Lehmann, who afterward became my especially cherished friend, was the reigning queen of the Vienna Opera at that time.[1] Vienna loved her for appearances in many operas she never sang in countries farther west—*Manon* and *Bohème*, for example, *Eugen Onegin* and several Italian works—as well as for the pieces by Strauss, Beethoven, Wagner and others which she sang in London and America. She had beauty, voice, style, intelligence, everything a singer may need in that arduous career, but along with it she had some very particular gift of emotional communication which it would be as difficult to define as to acquire. You have it or you do not have it; it comes, apparently, from on high, and in my own life I have never seen or heard anybody else on the stage with whom it was a sovereign and compelling quality as it was with Lehmann. Later on, after she stopped singing in opera, this capacity to communicate feeling in every shade came to another fruition and she had a whole new career as a Lieder singer—the best of whom I have knowledge, in the entire German literature from Beethoven to Wolf and Strauss. In 1935 she was hardly beginning as a *Liedersängerin*, and her one recital in Salzburg, with Bruno Walter at the piano, was only an adumbration of what she could and did achieve afterward. (This is in retrospect: at the time we were all enraptured!)

Lehmann's fame in the West, already great, was based chiefly upon

[1] The 1930's.—Editor.

her incomparable Sieglinde—far and away the best of the time—and beautiful impersonations of Elisabeth, Elsa and Eva; upon *Ariadne auf Naxos*; upon an occasional Italian foray such as her Desdemona in Lor.don; and, most of all, upon the Marschallin in *Der Rosenkavalier*, which had been all her own for about ten years. Some of her triumphs in Strauss works—*Die Frau ohne Schatten* and *Arabella*, for instance—never reached England and America except as echoes from Central Europe, and the kind of season customary in London, New York and Chicago gave no opportunity for her to sing her whole Vienna repertoire or even much of it. Four or five parts were all that most of us had heard from this unique artist, but they were enough to establish our regard for her in a very high and special place with a firm foundation.

Toscanini chose *Fidelio*, with Lehmann as Leonore, for his first performance at Salzburg. Her Leonore in Vienna nine years before, under Franz Schalk, had been acclaimed by all of Central Europe during the Beethoven celebrations of 1926, but fame alone, or public recognition, never swayed Toscanini in his choice of a leading artist for any great work. On the contrary; he frequently delighted in excavating artists hitherto unknown and showing what they could do. Sometimes he even seemed to have a prejudice against singers who were too famous or too established, I thought in after years, and insisted upon his unknowns even when they were not the best he could have had. In the case of Lehmann he was swayed not by her fame as Leonore but by his own ardent admiration, which on one occasion, I was told, led him to declare at the end of a difficult passage in rehearsal: "You are the greatest artist in the world."

Well, she was. The sheer ecstasy which she and Toscanini between them got into certain passages of *Fidelio* could not otherwise have come into being. I mean, for example, the part of the *Hoffnungsarie* beginning *"Ich folg' dem innern Triebe,"* or the duet *"Namenlose Freude."* For my own part, I held my breath in those passages every time (I have no idea what Lehmann did) and to this day I am unable to say what the secret was. With other singers (Flagstad, for example, who sang it with Walter later on in New York) nothing of the kind occurred although the notes were the same and were taken just as fast. In fact, it is my conviction that in the complete *Fidelio* recording which Toscanini made some years later he took those passages even faster than he did in Salzburg, but the ecstasy is not there. Ecstasy is not a matter of speed. Nor can any time beat account for the magical tranquillity of that first-act quartet as Toscanini, Lehmann and the others did it in Salzburg (*"Es ist so wunderbar"*). There was an element in this *Fidelio* at Salzburg which defies technical definition. It was not perfect—not as, for example, *Falstaff* was perfect or nearly so—because in this *Fidelio* there were singers who were not physically able to reach the exalted mood in which Lehmann and Toscanini performed. The incandescence of the conductor and the soprano produced the very curious effect of making one pass over these imperfections almost without noticing them—noticing them, that is, afterward or remembering them with a certain childish wonder, but paying them no real heed during the performance.

Fidelio is certainly not a work for ordinary repertoire—it requires much too much; it leaves its best participants purged to extinction; when it is really recreated as it was in Salzburg, it leaves even its audience much in need of food, drink and sleep. But just the same it does not deserve the reputation it has had for a century or more of being "unsingable" or "undramatic" or "unoperatic." The main line of the drama is absorbing and the music sets it forth with the passion and skill and sincerity of a master. The central soprano part has long been reserved, in Germany anyhow, for those mammoth voices which otherwise sing only Brünnhilde and Isolde. The general idea is that unless a woman has a voice suitable for a fire engine she cannot sing the part of the faithful wife. I am sure Beethoven had no such notion, and Lehmann supplied the proof—if it were needed—that a richly human voice, warm and full, has far more to offer in this music than any *hochdramatische* goddess. Most Leonores look like the Soviet women competitors in the Olympic Games, with sound to match. Lehmann was not a sylph in 1935, but her appearance in that ungrateful costume was more convincing than any other I remember, and every note of her voice conveyed the meaning of the part. Her speaking voice, for instance, had a slow tenderness (sounds like *"kühl"* and *"schwül"*) which extended the beauty of the music even to that part of the drama which is now, I think unwisely, so often omitted. Those who remembered Lehmann's Leonore in all its moods and tenses, its whole range, must know very well that this music is not "unsingable" and the character not at all beyond the acting range of an authentic talent.

True, the tenor part does seem more or less unsingable, but only because we have never heard it sung properly. Someday a tenor will come along who has the resources and the skill to do it. In the meantime, when we can get a Leonore like Lehmann we find the tenor's shortcomings obliterated in the general blaze of great music greatly performed.

Blaze is the word that comes to mind most often in thinking of this collaboration between Lehmann and Toscanini. They seemed to take fire from each other; the resulting conflagration warmed all of us for as long as memory can last, but I never shall know what caused it.

AS I SEE LEONORE

Lotte Lehmann

> Demonstrating that a singing actress works not by voice alone.

"I have never been able to sing this without being stirred to the depths of my being."

I have known unforgettable experiences with each conductor with whom I have sung *Fidelio*. Schalk, who first induced me to sing this beautiful role, imbued the opera with all the nobility of his being. Singing it with him I felt liberated from this earth. I am grateful that it was he who through many intensive rehearsals first revealed Beethoven to me. The Beethoven Centenary, in which I sang Leonore for the first time, in a new production of *Fidelio*, was a great event for the people of Vienna. There was scarcely a person who didn't take a vital interest in the celebration. Music was the very breath of life to the Austrians. They grew up with it and were so intimate with the treasures of their musical heritage that everyone seemed to regard Beethoven and Mozart as his own personal property. Those days of the centenary festivities, when even the bakers' boys delivering their rolls whistled Beethoven airs through the streets, painted Vienna in all its loveliest hues—a Vienna which perhaps may someday rise again from the rubble and ashes of destruction.

Bruno Walter gave his whole soul to this noblest of all operas. It was as if the whole gamut of human emotion from the depths of tragedy to the heights of joy pulsed from his heart.

And Toscanini? He made *Fidelio* flame through his own fire. There was thunder and lightning in his conducting—his glowing temperament, like a flow of lava, tore everything with it in its surging flood. I shall never forget the wave of intoxicated enthusiasm which broke from the Salzburg audience after the third Leonore Overture. There

From *My Many Lives* by Lotte Lehmann, by permission of Boosey and Hawkes, Inc.

was something almost frightening in its storm—but the Maestro let it break over him with his characteristic look of helplessness. It was as if he were saying: "You should honor not me but Beethoven."

I was always exhausted after the terrific strain of the prison scene and at first paid no attention to the music, but just sat waiting in the wings, grateful for a moment of rest after such drama. But the fire which flamed from the conductor's stand out to the remotest corners of the house always tore me out of my exhaustion. Even behind scenes we all joined in shouting enthusiastic "bravos."

To sing the Leonore is a wonderful but at the same time exceptionally strenuous task. At least, for me it was almost beyond the limit of my power. I never had a highly dramatic voice—it was for this reason that my longing to sing Isolde remained only a dream—and the part of Leonore made me feel that it demanded the utmost which I was capable of giving. But what a task it was! What joy to impersonate such a human role! I found in it the most exalted moments of my opera career and was shaken by it to the depths of my being.

Our performance of *Fidelio* at the Vienna Opera was ideal and our guest performance at the Grand Opera in Paris a triumph. Alfred Roller, the great stage designer, had created in his characteristic style a magnificent and somber setting. The broad gallery around the prison courtyard in the second scene of the first act was especially impressive. During the conversation between Pizarro and Rocco I could move around this gallery, and so convey the impression that I understood something of the fiendish plot which Pizarro was unveiling to the trembling Rocco but that the complete significance of the scheme was not entirely clear to me. A friend of mine once made a lovely remark about this stealthy listening from the upper gallery: "It is as if the soul of Leonore holds watch over the sinister threads which are being spun below as in a spider's web—as if above them her soul draws a protecting circle against these evil intentions and ill will."

Fidelio in Salzburg, Vienna, Paris, London, Stockholm, Hamburg, Berlin—was always the same tremendous experience. I could never become "accustomed" to singing Leonore—for me she was always new, always deeply exciting and utterly moving.

The part of Leonore imposes greater dramatic problems than any other role: she must be convincing as a man, while she is actually the most feminine of women. It must be clear that it is only through her great love that Leonore is capable of enduring the torment of her disguise.

One must picture Leonore as she was before tragedy threatened to destroy her life: she was the beloved wife of a man of high position in the political world. She was adored and honored. Then, through the clever intrigue of Pizarro, her husband was lured into a trap: he disappeared—she did not know where they had taken him. She has only known that he must be suffering in some prison and that his bitterest opponent in the political field, Pizarro, must be involved in his disappearance. But Leonore has not been contented to weep and complain in helplessness as would have been the average woman of her time. Where others would have given up in despair she *acted*. An evil plot has robbed her of her husband, a clever plot must bring him back to her—that is her decision. . . . She suspects which prison it is in which he is languishing. She knows the ways of Pizarro, she knows that he would only have taken him to the place from which there would be the least possibility of escape. She knows of a dark dungeon which would seem the most secure—no one could escape from it. Victims of political enmity—political "criminals"—have been thrown into this prison. How many innocent beings have suffered in this grave of the living! To reach it is Leonore's goal. But how? A woman could never accomplish this, and even if she did succeed in doing so without being recognized she knows that she would never be admitted. So she must disguise herself as a man. Secretly she learns to walk as a man, to make movements which until now have been completely foreign to her nature. She must be convincing if she wants to succeed. And she must succeed for she must free her husband. She practices carrying herself like a man until her bearing becomes convincing and natural.

She has the good fortune to be engaged as the helper of the prison master, Rocco. She has forged her way closer to her goal. But she has not found her husband among the prisoners to whom she must bring food. So, in her disguise, she serves here without really knowing whether her husband Florestan suffers within these dark walls. And now a distressing complication has arisen: Marzelline, Rocco's young daughter, has fallen head over heels in love with this handsome youth who seems so different from the young men whom she knows. Different from Jaquino, Rocco's helper, whose love until now had been quite welcome but now seems only a nuisance—for how could he compare with Fidelio's beauty?

Leonore—or rather "Fidelio," for this is the name under which she lives here in disguise—sees that Marzelline is a spoiled daughter and that her father, Rocco, would gladly do anything to make her happy. If Leonore should seem to reject Marzelline's none too subtle indications of love, Rocco might in the end tell Fidelio that he must leave in order to save his daughter from a broken heart. That must be avoided! She must win Rocco's confidence, his *complete* confidence. . . . So she accepts Marzelline's advances and plays the lover. It hurts her to deceive these harmless and simple people who have been so kind to her. In moments of depression she hates herself for being able to do this. But the rescue of Florestan is everything to her. It is worth while to play an apparently unworthy role in order to achieve this goal.

The portrayer of Leonore must have a deep understanding of this whole situation and must know what she is feeling the moment she enters the stage. She is returning from a mission which has been a torture to her: she has had to fetch new chains from the blacksmith and knows that they may perhaps be placed about her husband—to make certain that he will never escape. She has suffered from this torturing thought and has also suffered physically from the weight of the chains, for never before has she carried so heavy a burden.

So she enters the door almost upon the point of collapse spiritually and physically.

She is pale—there are deep shadows beneath her eyes. She leans for a moment against the frame of the door as if to gather strength. . . . But her eyes search the faces of Rocco and Marzelline anxiously and questioningly: whenever she has been away she is fearful lest something might have betrayed her secret—she is always on guard, always anxious. But no—they both look at her with the same confidence as before.

I have always enjoyed speaking the dialogue very much and regret that it is now cut for the most part. I have never felt that the transition from the spoken word to the music seemed an interruption. On the contrary, the spoken words seemed to make the drama, which in this particular opera is especially vital and powerful, even more natural and human. In speaking it is very difficult to find the right balance: it is so easy to make everything too pathetic—and I myself have never had the feeling of completely solving this problem. For example, when (after the heavenly quartet) Leonore asks Rocco if she may accompany him down to the lowest dungeon, and he tells of the approaching death of one of the political prisoners, there is the danger that Leonore may react so violently that it will seem unnatural. If Leonore should reveal her anxiety through the horror which it is almost impossible for her to suppress, wouldn't Rocco notice it and immediately become distrustful? Leonore almost betrays herself when she cries out: "Two years, did you say?" This victim who is about to die had been in this prison for two years—and it was two years ago that her husband was taken from her. Now she realizes that she is on the point of reaching her goal: it must be Florestan of whom the old man is speaking. She is overcome with emotion and with a superhuman effort tries to retain her composure. To make all this seem natural and sufficiently discreet is the task of a great tragedienne—a task which I certainly never quite fulfilled.

I once talked with Max Reinhardt about the problem of the dialogue and found that he had quite a different conception. He said that he would have the whole dialogue stylized, almost without any expression, more as a kind of melodious speech which flows out of the music back into the music. Very interesting, very original! It is a pity that he never produced *Fidelio*. It would certainly have been a very rich and revealing experience to portray Leonore in the light of his interpretation. Perhaps he would have opened for me an entirely new approach.

It is and has always been my highest goal to make every opera *as humanly convincing as possible*. Gestures, even if they must be stylized when borne by the music, must nevertheless always arise from genuine human feeling.

There are endless opportunities for subtle differentiations in acting Leonore: this very feminine woman must behave consciously as a man when she knows that she is under observation, but when she is alone she is feminine and soft. For example, the whole first part of the great aria (after the violently dramatic recitative at the beginning) should be sung with almost no movement—as if lost in prayer. Here she should be completely under the spell of her desperate struggle that she becomes Leonore and not at all Fidelio. In the second part she is overwhelmed by the immensity of her task and is so completely under the spell of her desperate struggle, that she becomes "Fidelio" from head to toe, even though she is alone. But she speaks of victory and success—and victory and success are dependent upon her own cleverness, her own skill in carrying out the plan which she has conceived: the excusable deception of these innocent people for the sake of her husband. . . . With the fanfare of trumpets she again becomes the man who in her absorption had given place to the loving woman.

In the following duet with Rocco, her strength almost leaves her. She will go with Rocco down to the dungeon—she will see the man whose death Pizarro has decreed. She will probably find that he is her husband. . . . But she must go down, for she must dig his grave that this murderous crime may be concealed from an avenging world. This task seems so superhuman that the mere thought of it almost crushes her; she loses herself in tears—tears which she, the man, must not shed in the presence of Rocco. . . . When, in his desire to spare the youth, he declares that it is better for him to go alone she regains control of herself. With a violence which forces Rocco to yield she again offers to help him. For the moment the danger is surmounted. Rocco agrees.

The meeting with Pizarro brings new danger to Leonore. She sees before her the man who seeks to destroy her husband—she knows now that he is planning in cold blood to murder the being dearest to her. . . . Yet she must control herself, she must not yet draw the hidden pistol to point it at his evil heart. She must wait for the right moment.

It is important for the impersonator of Leonore to convey the terrible conflict of her emotions without unnaturally and overobviously forcing herself into the foreground. Any striking gesture would attract the attention of Pizarro—and could she risk that? On the other hand it is absolutely essential that her inner trembling be perceptible. When at the end of the first act Leonore goes away with Rocco they pass in front of Pizarro who is standing in the center of the stage. Leonore must not look up at him with a challenging glance or a conspicuous gesture as I have seen her do. The quieter, the more rigid and withdrawn she seems as she passes him, the more credible is it. She must move as if she were an automaton, as if she were obeying an inner command. The command is: "Pull yourself together, don't be excited, don't do anything which will make you conspicuous. . . ." She passes him slowly, with bowed head, her steps falter almost unnoticeably—but she moves on rigidly as if driven by an inner compulsion. And Pizarro, somewhat disturbed, follows the silent youth with his eyes as he disappears through the door on his way to the most tragic of all the dungeons.

In the first scene of the last act Leonore's task is made easier by the fact that Rocco is deeply affected by the sight of the poor prisoner who has been condemned to die at the hand of a murderer. He pays no attention to his helper whose emotion he readily understands, thinking it is only the expression of a sympathy which any one must feel in seeing such a pathetic half-starved being before him.

Leonore, now realizing that it is her husband who languishes here in chains, has momentarily but one wish: to make things bearable for him at least for the moment—to help him, to get him water, bread—anything which might revive him. When Florestan, grateful for the small piece of bread, touches her hand she again almost becomes the victim of her emotions: turning away from him she fervently presses to her lips the hand which his has grazed. Florestan had only caught a fleeting glimpse of her face, and with a sudden shock has asked: "Who is that?" A vague resemblance has gripped his heart, an improbable resemblance to his wife which he realized half unconsciously. But Rocco's explanation that it is his son-in-law has shattered every hope in Florestan, hope which he hadn't for a moment felt with any certainty.

Left alone with her husband—before the entrance of Pizarro—Leonore does not dare reveal herself to him. If he should give way to his emotion he might ruin everything—and so even though alone with him she has the painful task of continuing to play "Fidelio." She can only try to give him courage, to give him faith in providence which even at the last moment may still save him.

Like an animal ready to attack she creeps nearer when Pizarro discloses his cruel intention of murdering Florestan. She must jump between them at the very last moment, just at the instant when Pizarro, confident that everything has been prepared and that he is in no danger, is inattentive.

Of course the fact that she doesn't simply shoot him right away is one of the improbable things which have a way of happening in operas. . . . But how fortunate it is that because of this improbability the trio, mounting to a raging presto, introduces more exciting drama than could possibly have developed if the act had been logical and quick! For the dramatic signal of the trumpet, pronouncing freedom can, due to this delay, arise from the storm of the drama, flooding it with the radiance of salvation. The signal breaks like a ray of white light into the raging darkness. The quartet: "O you are saved, God be praised, God be praised" is almost unbearable in its divine beauty.

I have never been able to sing this without being stirred to the depths of my being—and my collapse after all had left and I was alone with Florestan was scarcely "acted". . . .

Until the last moment Leonore continues to be watchful; her pistol is constantly directed at Pizarro and it is only during the prayer of gratitude, "O you are saved," that the threatening weapon is lowered

—for this is such pure song, so filled with the joy of deliverance and liberation that the pointed pistol would disturb the visual effect, and it is better to be a little illogical and forget that Pizarro might take advantage of this moment to put an end to his hated enemy, even though his plot has been defeated. The pistol drops from Leonore's hand at the moment when Pizarro goes up the stairs. He had hurled his murderous knife at her in an effort to kill the woman whose bold deed has ruined his life. But Leonore is quicker than he and has warded off the weapon with a quick movement—and now at last all danger has been surmounted. Without a sound she sinks to the ground unconscious.

At this point it is of the utmost importance that Florestan should not speak too soon. This prolonged moment of exhaustion should not be interrupted. And his voice must tremble, almost without tone —only not as is so often the case with pathos—the more simply, the more in a whisper he speaks, the better. Leonore's "Nothing, my Florestan, nothing . . ." is also a toneless stammering—and with these words she pulls herself out of her momentary loss of consciousness and staggers into his arms. The following duet is, if I may express myself so daringly, a reeling dance of ecstasy, a clinging together, separating, coming together again, feasting their eyes upon one another, being blissfully united—there is nothing to be found in any opera more exalted, more beautiful or more gripping. This duet is vocally very taxing and exposed, but through its inner surge one is borne over its dangers as if by the hands of angels—and I have scarcely ever had the feeling that this exultant hymn makes too great a demand upon one's resources.

When Leonore appears with Florestan in the last scene she must seem completely changed: to be sure she is still in the costume of a man—but she no longer assumes the behavior of a man. She is absolutely feminine, soft, submissive. Leaning against Florestan, supporting and leading him, she has eyes only for him and scarcely takes any notice of her surroundings. She has achieved her goal: she has saved him, her task is accomplished, now she is ready to step into the background, to be nothing more than the wife of her beloved husband. Even when Pizarro, in the last throes of his despair, tries to involve Rocco in his somber plot through his senseless accusation that he would have committed the murder with the help of Rocco, she only reacts with a languid defense. What he has done is clear and convincing. Rocco has only been an innocent victim of this cruel intrigue. The accusation is so senseless that it seems hardly worth while to say anything in his defense. Fernando, the minister who has appeared as their liberator, understands the situation completely and pays no attention to Pizarro's accusation. He orders him to be led away, and with his presence disaster disappears from the life of Florestan.

When Leonore is presented to Fernando as Florestan's wife she bows before him with the graciousness of a great lady. She is now again a woman of high position who is accustomed to receiving homage. So her bow of greeting should be one of equality, not humility.

The wonderful moment has come in which Florestan is to be freed of his chains. Bowing deeply before her, Fernando asks Leonore to remove them. Through her act she has brought about his release, and now she should be the one to remove his shackles.

This moment is so unspeakably beautiful that even in recalling it I feel tears coming into my eyes. From the breathless: "O God, O what a moment!" this prayer of gratitude soars with ethereal beauty; Leonore's voice rising above the chorus floats upward to God in inner transfiguration.

The opera ends with a great hymn of joy. Here one should not "act" too much. Here everything is music, ecstasy.

MARIA MALIBRAN

Richard G. White

> The story of a unique and unfortunate artist, taken
> from a history of operatic performances in New York.
> Richard Grant White (1821–85) was an American
> music critic and editor of an edition of Shakespeare.
> His son was Stanford White, the architect.

*"Malibran worked all her wonders . . . in the little space of
ten years."*

The first Italian opera heard in America was Rossini's masterpiece *Il Barbiere di Seviglia,* which was produced at the Park Theatre
in 1825 by the famous Garcia company. Angrisani appeared as Basilio,
Garcia as Almaviva, and Signorina Garcia as Rosina. Angrisani was
one of the best Italian-singing basses of his day. Garcia had then
hardly a rival among tenors; and his daughter, Signorina Garcia, soon
became, as Madame Malibran, to Italian opera what Rachel was afterward to French tragedy; and she began her wonderful career in New
York, where her talent was first recognized and was first appreciated
at its real value, and where she soon became the idol of the public,
tasting here first that intoxicating adulation which she was afterward
to drink without measure.

Manuel Garcia was a Spanish Hebrew who had risen to operatic
distinction in Paris as a tenor, both *di forza* and *di grazia,* and who,
in such parts as Otello, Almaviva, and even Don Giovanni, was without an acknowledged equal. His daughter, Maria Felicita, after some
years of pupilage under her father, and some little operatic experience
in Italy as his supplement and support, went with him to London
when she was sixteen years old, and was engaged at the Italian opera
there, in 1824, as a chorus singer! Only a year afterward, when the
prima donna—the great prima donna of the day—fell suddenly ill,

From *Opera in New York.*

Garcia, who never lost anything for lack of confidence, boldly offered the services of his girlish daughter in place of those of—Pasta! They were accepted, and, on the twenty-fifth of June, 1825, she appeared before a London audience as Rosina, and so pleased her audience that she was engaged for the rest of the season, six weeks, at a salary of five hundred pounds. She afterward sang at the Manchester, York, and Liverpool festivals; but, notwithstanding some splendid manifestations of her talent, by one of which she provoked the jealous wrath of Velluti, the eminent *musico*, or male soprano, of his day (the last of his sexless sort who attained distinction), she had not yet reached a recognized position, and, indeed, her fortunes were so low that she was on the point of accepting an offer of marriage from a humble orchestral musician.

Fortunately, just at this time her visionary and eccentric father projected a scheme of Italian opera in America, and put it at once into execution. The rapidity of his movements are not less remarkable than his daring. On the twenty-ninth of November of the very year in which in June, she had made at London her first appearance in *Il Barbiere*, she appeared in the same opera at the Park Theatre, in New York. When we remember that, after the close of the London operatic season, about the first of August, the Garcias had made a concert tour through England, and that at that time the ocean was crossed only in sailing vessels by a few people who had prayers put up in churches for their safety, and when we consider, too, the painful and protracted negotiations which are now necessary to secure the presence of a company of second-rate artists, the sudden appearance of the Garcia company in New York approaches the marvelous.

The success of the strange art and of the stranger artists, especially that of Signorina Garcia, was, like the performances, something quite unknown before in America. Nor was it the ephemeral consequence of novelty and surprise. The performances went on twice a week until the end of August, 1826, nearly a year. To *Il Barbiere* were added *La Cenerentola*, *Otello*, *Semiramide*, and *Don Giovanni*—each of them a new experience, an unimagined delight, to the audience—each of them a new occasion of triumph to the young prima donna, "the Signorina" as she was fondly called by the musical people of the day.

Maria Garcia was the most accomplished vocalist, the most dramatic singer, in all respects the most gifted musical artist, of modern days; and she had such beauty of person and charm of manner that she became the most supreme of prima donnas—a sort of women who from their first appearance have been accustomed to see the world at their feet. She was the idol of society in New York, and was hardly less admired and beloved by the general public. Such a creature had not been seen before for half a century, and was not to be seen again for quite as long. Her voice was a contralto, but it was a contralto which enabled her to sing with equal ease the music of *Semiramide* and of *Arsace*. She had at ordinary command three full octaves, and in private she could surpass even this wonderful compass. As an actress she was made by nature equally mistress of the grand, the pathetic, and the gay. Her face was, perhaps, not in all points regularly beautiful; but it was full of beauties each eminent in its kind, and had an ever-enduring, always-varying charm. Her dark, bright eyes fascinated all on whom their brilliant glances fell, and by her smile, which revealed brilliant and beautifully shaped teeth, not only all men, but even all women, seem to have been carried captive. Her figure was so exquisitely beautiful in all points that it was somewhat extravagantly said that she might be studied for an improvement upon the Venus de' Medici. The poise of her daintily shaped head upon her shoulders was an appeal to admiration, and her graceful carriage would have been dignified had she been a little taller. To the power of varied expression in her face there seems to have been no limit; but that most natural to it, and most commonly seen upon it, was a fascinating radiation of happiness from her own soul to all within her influence. Nor did her manner and her look belie her nature. According to all evidence, she was as good as she was beautiful and fascinating—"as good as an angel." There is no record of any other such supremacy, personal, vocal, and dramatic, except in the great Gabrielle, who turned the head and won the heart of all Europe three-quarters of a century before her; and Gabrielle was far below her morally, and in all that makes woman most admirable and lovable.

It is greatly noteworthy that the career of such a woman as this should have been really begun and shaped in New York, the New York of 1825. But so it was. In New York she received the first recognition of her talents; in New York she first felt the glow of triumph, and was conscious of the possession of sustained power. In New York, too, she passed from maidenhood to wifehood, and acquired the name by which, notwithstanding a second marriage, she was afterward always known and will be known while the world reads the history of music. She had not been long upon the stage of the Park Theatre when M. François Eugène Malibran, a French merchant of New York, proposed marriage to her. He was fifty years of age, she seventeen; but she was willing; and after a brief opposition on the part of her father she became Madame Malibran in March, 1826—only four months after her appearance here, and in the midst of her operatic and social success. Garcia's opposition to this marriage was purely selfish, as its sad event proved. His concern was not for his daughter's happiness, but for her salary—the gain which he expected to reap as her father and business manager from her brilliant future, to which he was looking. As to her, she may have sought an escape from his selfishness, tyranny, and brutality—for he was selfish, tyrannical, and brutal beyond measure and past sufferance; but she also, as the experience of the world has shown, may have been fond of this man who was old enough to be her father. It is necessary to look for no other motive on his part than that of passionate love for a girl so beautiful, so gifted, so charming, and so good. But, sad to relate, it does seem as if he had a base and selfish motive in his proposal, and that, with a Frenchman's eye to the profit of marriage, he sought a wife whose income, so long as she had health, could not but be very large. For she had been a wife but a few months when her husband, who had overcome her father's opposition by promising him a present of a hundred thousand francs for the loss of his daughter's services, was bankrupt and (as the old laws on such matters were then in force in New York) a prisoner for debt. It is hardly probable that a merchant of his sort was ignorant of the calamity that was impending over him; and his subsequent conduct confirms this natural conclusion. The young wife gave up for the benefit of his creditors all claims which she had upon his property—an act which added greatly to her popularity. Her father abandoned her in his disappointment and rage, and, going to Mexico with his family, left her alone and penniless, with an imprisoned and disgraced husband, among strangers. She, not losing courage, renewed the study of English, and of English song, which she had begun in England (for, with the departure of her father, performance of Italian opera was of course at an end); and before long she appeared at the Bowery Theatre, then newly built and called "The New York." Her first appearance there was in *The Devil's Bridge*; her next in *Love in a Village*. Success again crowned her efforts; her performances were very profitable to the manager; and from every night's receipts a certain sum was regularly sent to M. Malibran. She also sang in the choir of Grace Church, then at the corner of Broadway and Rector Street. It is rather startling to think of the greatest prima donna, not only of her day but of modern times—the most fascinating woman upon the stage in the first half of the nineteenth century, as singing the soprano parts of psalm tunes and chants in a little church in a small town then less known to the people of London and Paris and Vienna than Jeddo is now.

Malibran, however, soon wearied of this life; and breaking loose from her selfishly dependent husband, she went to Paris, where she arrived in 1827. Thus in a short time she had crossed the Atlantic twice —then no trifling matter, of course—had achieved the success of a great prima donna, had become a wife, had seen her husband ruined and imprisoned, had been deserted by her father and her family, and, left alone in a strange country, had mastered a new domain of her art and a new language, had won a new popularity, and had filled the humble position of a choir singer—and she was a girl not yet eighteen years old. Thenceforward her life belongs to the history of music in Europe; but her career and her success as an artist, and her joys and sorrows as a woman, began in New York. She awoke an enthusiasm and an admiration, mingled with high regard, which surpassed all the attainments in this respect of her predecessors, so far as we can learn, and of all her successors, as we know. Before her first were wreaths of flowers and coronals cast upon the stage. It was at Paris when she performed *Tancredi* at the Théâtre Favart, for the benefit of Sontag, her rival; but when this first homage from Flora to Euterpe fell before her feet, we may be sure that it brought up to her never-forgetting and tenderly grateful soul the memory of the New York experience that first gave her assurance that she was a great dramatic singer.

The incidents of Malibran's later life are so well known to all who take an interest in musical affairs, that any particular recounting of them would be superfluous here, even irrespective of the limits and the purpose of these articles. There is one story of her, however, which does not appear in her memoirs, and I believe has never been in print. When she was singing at Covent Garden Theatre, in London, the tenor was Templeton, a Scotchman with a beautiful voice and fair vocalization, but dull, without style or expression, and a mere split-stick upon the stage. All at once, Malibran declared she would not sing with Templeton. The manager, supposing that she objected to him as an artist, and knowing her kindness and good nature, asked her the reason of her decision. After a little hesitation she replied, "Last evening Mr. Templeton was going to kiss me." The manager, who knew Mr. Templeton as well as he knew Malibran, sent for the tenor immediately, and in the presence of the haughtily shrinking prima donna, told him of her accusation. "Modum Molly Brawn," was the stolid Scotchman's reply—"Modum Molly Brawn, I wadna kuss ye on ony accoont." "Molly Brawn," who was then pestered by a gilded throng made up of half the male butterflies in London, appreciated the situation instantly, broke into a peal of laughter, and matters were restored to their former condition.

Malibran worked all her wonders and achieved all her triumphs in the little space of ten years. Within three years from the time when she soared into happiness upon the applause of the Park Theatre, she had conquered the whole musical world of Europe, where she queened it gently for a short, glorious reign of six years. Her only rival was Henrietta Sontag. They had their partisans; they were both great singers; both were beautiful; they were jealous; they were publicly compared; their several successes were made thorns in each other's sides. Malibran fully acknowledged the talent of her rival. She would sometimes weep and say, "Why does she sing so divinely?" At last the two were reconciled. It was at a concert at the house of the Countess Merlin. There was a little scheme among the musical amateurs to bring them together; and in the course of the evening it was proposed to them to sing the great duo from *Tancredi*. There was in both a brief shrinking—natural and inevitable—from the struggle; but soon they consented, and approached the pianoforte, excited not only by their own emotions, but by the murmurs and applause of the whole company. The performance more than fulfilled all the high expectations it had awakened, and caused so profound a sensation of delight and admiration that, at the end of the duet, they looked a moment in each other's eyes, then silently clasped hands and kissed—a sight to see. Thereafter they were friendly rivals; but Malibran, because of her superior dramatic power and greater versatility (a trait of her genius which was most remarkable), attained an unquestioned superiority, which she maintained while she lived. When she was at the fullness of her power, and at the highest pinnacle of her art, she was thrown from her horse, and received injuries from which she never recovered, and she died in 1836, at the youthful age of twenty-nine—being, in the shortness of her life and the suddenness of her rise to undisputed eminence, as singular among prima donnas as she was in the splendor of her vocal and mental gifts, and in the charm of her person and the beauty of her character.

CARUSO

Francis Robinson

The Assistant Manager of the Metropolitan Opera is
the author of a pictorial biography of the tenor. This
essay was written for a collection of Caruso's records.

"Still a living presence at the Metropolitan."

Enrico Caruso belongs to the ages. Death could not still his
voice nor dim the luster of his name. The most ready proof of this is
his records which seem to defy the law of diminishing returns. He recorded over a period of eighteen years. Almost twice that time has
elapsed since his death, in which the royalties paid to his estate are
correspondingly almost double his earnings from the phonograph during his lifetime. There has been no decline. These are mere figures. Immortality is something even more substantial than the columns of a
balance sheet.

A generation has passed and the man whose name spelled grand
opera to millions of people is still a living presence at the Metropolitan. Visitors from all over the world come to the Broadway lobby
of the opera house to see the mammoth, laurel-crowned head, so
like a Caesar and so unlike Caruso. On the red walls of Sherry's hangs
a portrait of him in *La Juive,* the last opera he ever sang, looking
more like a road company Shylock than the noble Eléazar we know he
was. The bas-relief on the parterre floor was unveiled the year after
his death and Mrs. Caruso herself presented the silver bust in the
family circle foyer. But neither bronze nor oil on canvas nor silver
can contain him. Caruso, heart and voice, was gold. "Always the word
golden comes to the lips," Huneker wrote of him. "Golden, with a
thrilling human fiber."

His open-handedness was not the price of the loyalty and affection
heaped on him, but true generosity born of consideration for the
needs and feelings of others. Nobody ever heard him speak ill of a

By permission of Radio Corporation of America.

colleague and no member of the company had anything but praise for him. He had no rival.

Too much has been written of Caruso's gifts and not enough about his achievements. The lovable, happy-go-lucky boy gave way to the worker and fighter and artist. In his singing class he was known as "a glass voice" because he broke so easily. At Salerno (the manager locked him in the theater on Sundays when there were two performances and hoisted him his dinner of cream cheese and sardine sandwiches by hook and line) he cracked on a high note at his debut. To the everlasting credit of the Salerno public a troublesome top note in such a voice did not matter too much. But he continued to crack. Every time he came to the B-flat in the Flower Song from *Carmen* it split wide open. A man may not add a cubit to his stature but Caruso by sheer determination built a top to his voice.

Just as diligently he set about to extend his repertoire. At the Metropolitan he sang thirty-seven different roles in as many operas. He permanently influenced the over-all repertoire, establishing the popularity of *Aïda*, which holds the record for number of performances there, and *I Pagliacci*. In the fifteen years before he arrived, *Aïda* had forty-six performances at the Metropolitan. In the sixteen years Caruso did Rhadames it had 101, of which he sang sixty-four. *Pagliacci* he sang seventy-six times.

Caruso's formal education would not have added up to a year but he got along in seven languages and managed to sing acceptably in three other than his own. His English was enlivened by the racial tendency to make two syllables where only one had been before and by his *r*'s which rolled around the concert platform like hoops. Of his bouts with French, Geraldine Farrar recalls he swore he could detect no difference between the sound of "*des yeux*" ("of the eyes") and "*des cieux*" ("of the skies"). "Yet," says Miss Farrar, "he *did* learn the difference" and came to sing French, especially *Faust*, extremely well.

His figure was not meant for tragedy but this he overcame by the conviction of his performances. At the beginning of his career, when he was thin as an anchovy, his acting was pronounced "awful." Ten years later the press was still flaying him for such "incomprehensible blunders" as wearing white gloves into Marguerite's dungeon, and worse, keeping them on. One commentator found the offending gloves as correct for the Duke as they had been wrong for Faust. P. G. Hurst writes in *The Golden Age Recorded*: "His entrance in *Rigoletto* fastidiously adjusting his gloves; his play with a pack of cards in *La donna è mobile*; his handshakes to the courtiers—all were distinguished by a neatness of action and movement quite beyond the compass of a bad actor." Call this detail, behavior and deportment, if you like; nevertheless, it was adding up to the unforgettable portraits he drew of Samson and Eléazar and John of Leyden.

Finally, there was his responsibility to the public and to the management, a sense of obligation which was fanatical and literally hastened his end. Nobody expects a man bleeding at the mouth to sing but that was Caruso. He never spared himself. His record of cancellations was almost zero. Once he was announced to sing, he sang—in eighteen seasons at the Metropolitan 607 times.

There are also gaps in the Caruso literature on his importance as the pioneer in recording. When the phonograph was in its infancy the big artists must have felt somewhat like the actors who later slipped sheepishly, and often anonymously, down to Fourteenth Street or over to Astoria to emote before the primitive movie cameras. Emilio de Gogorza recorded under at least three different aliases. Caruso put an end to all that. He gave respectability to recording; and where he led the others followed. It was the beginning of an industry.

He was twenty-nine and already famous when he was approached in Milan by F. W. Gaisberg of the Gramophone and Typewriter Company. He made the following proposition which was relayed to London: ten arias, to be done in a single afternoon, at a fee of one hundred pounds—about fifty dollars a record. London cabled back: "FEE EXORBITANT, FORBID YOU TO RECORD." At this point Gaisberg becomes the hero of the story. Mainly because he was too embarrassed to go back to Caruso with such an answer, he took matters in his own hands and ordered the recording session to proceed. Caruso sauntered in, tossed off his ten arias in two hours—without blemish, Gaisberg says—and was on his way.

Enrico was the eighteenth of twenty-one children and the first with "the strength to live" past infancy. His mother knew what to give and what to withhold from a sensitive boy. It was she who found the money for his first lessons. If Marcellino Caruso had had his way his son might never have got past the factory clerkship he was holding down at sixteen. In his time off Enrico sang at one of the public bathing places which line the Bay of Naples.

There are no records from the opera of his debut, a little number called *L'Amico Francesco*, and forgotten, like its composer, except for

Caruso's having touched it. The music world sat up and took notice when he created the lead in *Fedora* in Milan but that was the Teatro Lirico and not La Scala. Contracts came pouring in from everywhere including Russia and South America. His Scala debut, in the words of Mr. Gatti, was "not lucky." He was not well and sang only to save the performance. But in *L'Elisir d'Amore* he had "a success that remained a sensation in the annals of the Teatro alla Scalla." His home town was another story. The *sicofanti* of San Carlo rejected him in *L'Elisir*. Caruso vowed, "I will never again come to Naples to sing; it will be only to eat a plate of spaghetti." New York adored him as Nemorino and ironically it was in this, his only comedy part, that he began to spit blood on the stage of the Brooklyn Academy of Music that December night in 1920.

Rigoletto was the work in which he made his London, Paris and New York debuts. At La Scala he was a member of the Quartet at a solemn commemoration conducted by Toscanini the week after Verdi's death. "He sang like an angel," is Gatti's simple testimony. It was for Caruso that Gatti gave *La Forza del Destino* its first production at the Metropolitan. According to Mrs. Caruso he considered *"Solenne in quest' ora"* with his old friend Scotti the best of his recorded duets.

The first and last acts of *La Bohème* provided the best opportunities for the horseplay Caruso indulged in during his rollicking early days. Anything might happen in that garret and often did. One evening at Covent Garden Marcello, going out to get medicine for the dying Mimi, found the sleeves of his coat sewed up. Another time Colline's stovepipe hat had been thoughtfully filled with water. This very freedom on the stage once saved a bad situation in Philadelphia. Just before the Coat Song Andrès de Segurola, panic-stricken, whispered, "I've lost my voice!" Caruso replied calmly, "Stand still and move your lips." With his back to the audience Caruso sang the bass aria. He recorded the number privately, had six copies struck, then ordered the master destroyed. "I don't want to spoil the bass business," he said.

One of his bitter disappointments was that Puccini did not give him the première of *Tosca*. Nevertheless, Caruso was the perfect Puccini singer and became a close friend of the composer. He and Scotti created Pinkerton and Sharpless in *Madama Butterfly* both in London and at the Metropolitan. When Puccini heard him in New York in *Manon Lescaut* he exclaimed, "He is singing like a god."

Mrs. Caruso is our authority that he regarded the excerpt from *La Juive* his best recorded aria. To her, his most lifelike record is "*Sei morta nella mia vita.*" "It's as if Rico were in the next room," she says. The romanza from the Good-night Quartet is frequently referred to in the adorable letters to his young wife. From Mexico City he reports, "I sung that song with all my soul and everybody were emotionated." Later from Havana, "I win another battle with my second performance of 'Martha.' I took the public by the—what you call the lower part of the mouth, 'il mento,' [chin] and shake terribly until he came down at my feet."

The aria from *Martha* was the last thing he ever sang and his final triumph. Caruso had allowed a forlorn student to trail him to Sorrento that agonizing last summer. The boy was committing mayhem on "*M'appari.*" "Let me show you," Caruso said, and began to sing. "His voice," Mrs. Caruso remembers, "was like a shower of stars." Delirious with joy he shouted, "I have not lost my voice! I can sing!"

A few weeks later in fearful heat and pain the end came—Naples, Hotel Vesuvio, 9:05 A.M., August 2, 1921. Back at their villa near Florence Mrs. Caruso decided to face the final ordeal. "I knew that one day I would have to hear his voice again on a record." One afternoon she sent the servants from the house and went into the music room alone. She chose "*Luna d'estate,*" one of his gayest songs. The needle had traced only a few turns of the record when Gloria, then not two years old, came stumbling through the doorway. "Daddy, Daddy," she called.

Always the tantalizing question arises, "What if he had lived?" He was only forty-eight and at the height of his powers. Had he not been struck down he might easily have gone on another ten years at the top. And what if he had survived the illness? The verdict of one of the physicians is he would have kept his voice but never again would he have had the breath to fill that great chest.

Caruso had his wife and baby to live for. More than once in his letters he spoke of wanting to retire. But the most idolized singer of all time not singing? One remembers the entry Yeats made in his diary a few days after the death, at thirty-seven, of J. M. Synge:

We pity the living and not such dead as he. He has gone upward out of his ailing body into the heroical fountains. We are parched by time.

TWO LETTERS

by Enrico Caruso

The spelling is Enrico's.

"I mounted myself and taked my public."

MEXICO CITY

Oct. 26, 1919. 8:30 P.M.

MY ONLY SWEETEST DORO:

Here I am after the performance of *Aïda* which was really triumph. There were some univeness but we finished the performance very well. I will describe you how everything goes.

Today was a beautiful day with the sunshine terribly hot. We beginning the performance and at moment to go on the stage this was illuminated plenety by the sun. I had like a shower of rays in my eyes terribly hot. Like Swedish bath. Then I was forced to close my eyes and impossible to look the condocter. The basso, worse than a bad corist, beginning to sing, with a voice like an old dog, doing "WHAU WHAU!!" Both things made me nervous and I beginning to sing "Celeste Aïda" with my eyes closed and a bag of sunshine on my face. Impossible to sing well and my aria was sang without feeling and for a chance I dont make a terrible *crak* before the end. I finisched well and had a good applause. But the public understand that I was not satysfide and I think himself was the same because the ovation was not enthuiastic. The second scene was same thing and there was not enthusiasm even that I sang very well. Somebody told me that the cause was the basso.

The scene of the triumph passed. Then came the scene of the Nilo [Nile]. I mounted myself and taked my public. There were many calls and people were crazy. I dont know the exact words to express what the public doit. Heats, umbrellas, hendekacifs, canes all in the aria, and a shouts that arrived in heaven. I think many people will have no voice for many days.

I must give my soul to take the public.
I will leave you for tomorrow.
You will excuse me, yes? Thanks.
All my love with all my soul.

Yours
RICO

HOTEL SEVILLA HAVANA CUBA
Monday May 31 1920 1:30 A.M.

MY DEAREST DORO SWEETHEART:

. . . I went to the theatre and show your cable to Bracale. He was nearly fainting down. He told me that he will come to New York with me and implore you to accept the proposition because, he said, we cannot throw out from the window two hundred thousand dollars. I try my best to calm him, and I think now he is calm and put his soul in peace.

Then I went in my dressing-room to prepare myself for "Pagliacci." I was so nervous that you cannot imagine. But what a "Pagliacci" I sung! Surprised myself and everybody was crazy! I never see people crying like in such performance.

EVELYN INNES

George Moore

> George Moore's novel is a psychological study of a
> woman who achieves her ambition and fulfills her
> dream only to turn away from them in disappointment
> and seek recluse in the life of a nun. Sir Owen Aster is
> attracted by Evelyn's beauty and voice and offers her
> the means to pursue her career. Evelyn becomes a
> famous opera singer, one of her great roles being Mar-
> guerite in *Faust*. But her real ambition is to sing
> Wagner.
> Later she becomes enamored of Ulick Dean, a critic
> and himself a composer. The conflict caused by her at-
> traction toward both men forms the main body of the
> novel. The present excerpt from *Evelyn Innes* is Moore's
> imaginative interpretation of the process by which a
> singing actress "creates" a role.

The score [1] slipped from her hands and her thoughts ran in
reminiscence of a similar scene which she had endured in Venice
nearly four years ago. She had not seen Owen for two months, and
was expecting him every hour. The old walls of the palace, the black
and watchful pictures, the watery odors and echoes from the canal
had frightened and exhausted her. The persecution of passion in her
brain and the fever of passion afloat in her blood waxed, and the
minutes became each a separate torture. There was only one lamp.
She had watched it, fearing every moment lest it should go out. . . .
She had cast a frightened glance round the room, and it was the
specter of life that her exalted imagination saw, and her natural eyes
a strange ascension of the moon. The moon rose out of a sullen sky,
and its reflection trailed down the lagoon. Hardly any stars were
visible, and everything was extraordinarily still. The houses leaned
heavily forward and Evelyn feared she might go mad, and it was

[1] Of *Tristan*.

through this phantom world of lagoon and autumn mist that a gondola glided. This time her heart told her with a loud cry that he had come, and she had stood in the shadowy room waiting for him, her brain on fire. The emotion of that night came to her at will and lying in her warm bed she considered the meeting of Tristan and Isolde in the garden, and the duet on the bank of sultry flowers. Like Tristan and Isolde, she and Owen had struggled to find expression for their emotion, but, not having music, it had lain cramped up in their hearts, and their kisses were vain to express it. She found it in these swift irregularities of rhythm, replying to every change of motion, and every change of key cried back some pang of the heart.

This scene in the second act was certainly one of the most difficult—at least to her—and the one in which she most despaired of excelling. It suddenly occurred to her that she might study it with Ulick Dean. She had met him at rehearsal, and had been much interested in him. He had sent her six melodies—strange, old-world rhythms, recalling in a way the Gregorian she used to read in childhood in the missals, yet modulated as unintermittently as Wagner; the same chromatic scale and yet a haunting of the antique rhythm in the melody. Ulick knew her father; he had said, "Mr. Innes is my greatest friend." He loved her father, she could see that, but she had not dared to question him. Talking to Owen was like the sunshine—the earth and only the earth was visible—whereas talking to Ulick was like the twilight through which the stars were shining. Dreams were to him the true realities; externals he accepted as other people accepted dreams —with diffidence. Evelyn laughed, much amused by herself and Ulick, and she laughed as she thought of his fixed and averted look as he related the tales of bards and warriors. Every now and then his dark eyes would light up with gleams of sunny humor; he probably believed that the legends contained certain eternal truths, and these he was shaping into operas. He was the most interesting young man she had met this long while.

He had been about to tell her why he had recanted his Wagnerian faith when they had been interrupted by Owen. . . . She could conceive nothing more interesting than the recantation by a man of genius of the ideas that had first inspired him. His opera had been accepted, and would be produced if she undertook the principal part. Why should she not? They could both help each other. Truly, he was the person with whom she could study Isolde, and she imagined the flood of new light he would throw upon it. Her head drowsed on the pillow, and she dreamed the wonderful things he would tell her. But as she drowsed she thought of the article he had written about her Marguerite, and it was the desire to read it again that awoke her. Stretching out her hand, she took it from the table at her bedside and began reading. He liked the dull green dress she wore in the first act; and the long braids of golden hair which he admired were her own. He had mentioned them and the dark velvet cape, which he could not remember whether she wore or carried. As a matter of fact, she carried it on her arm. His forgetfulness on this point seemed to her charming, and she smiled with pleasure. He said that she made good use of the cape in the next act, and she was glad that he had perceived that.

Like every other Marguerite, her prayerbook was in her hand when she first met Faust; but she dropped it as she saw him, and while she shyly and sweetly sang that she was neither a lady nor a beauty, she stooped and with some embarrassment picked up the book. She passed on, and did not stop to utter a mechanical cry when she saw Mephistopheles, and then run away. She hesitated a moment; Mephistopheles was not in sight, but Faust was just behind her, and over the face of Marguerite flashed the thought, "What a charming—what a lovely young man! I think I'll stop a little longer, and possibly he'll say something more. But no—after all—perhaps I'd better not," and, with a little sigh of regret, she turned and went, at first quietly and then more quickly, as though fearful of being tempted to change her mind.

In the garden scene, she sang the first bars of the music absent-mindedly, dusting and folding her little cape, stopping when it was only half folded to stand forgetful a moment, her eyes far off, gazing back into the preceding act. Awaking with a little start, she went to her spinning wheel, and, with her back to the audience, arranged the spindle and the flax. Then stopping in her work and standing in thought, she half-hummed, half-sang the song "Le Roi de Thulé." Not till she had nearly finished did she sit down and spin, and then only for a moment, as though too restless and disturbed for work that afternoon.

Evelyn was glad that Ulick had remarked that the jewels were not "the ropes of pearls we are accustomed to, but strange, medieval jewels, long, heavy earrings and girdles and broad bracelets." Owen had given her these. She remembered how she had put them on, just as Ulick said, with the joy of a child and the musical glee of a bird. "She laughed out the Jewel Song," he said, "with real laughter, returning lightly across the stage"; and he said that they had "wondered what was this lovely music which they had never heard before!" And when she placed the jewels back, she did so lingeringly, regretfully, slowly, one by one, even forgetting the earrings, perhaps purposely, till just before she entered the house.

"In the duet with Faust," he said, "we were drawn by that lovely voice as in a silken net, and life had for us but one meaning—the rapture of love."

"Has it got any other meaning?" Evelyn paused a moment to think. She was afraid that it had long ceased to have any other meaning for her. But love did not seem to play a large part in Ulick's life. Yet that last sentence—to write like that he must feel like that. She wondered, and then continued reading his article.

She was glad that he had noticed that when she fainted at the sight of Mephistopheles, she slowly revived as the curtain was falling and pointed to the place where he had been, seeing him again in her overwrought brain. This she did think was a good idea, and, as he said, "seemed to accomplish something."

He thought her idea for her entrance in the following act exceedingly well imagined, for, instead of coming on neatly dressed and smiling like the other Marguerites, she came down the steps of the church with her dress and hair disordered, in the arms of two women, walking with difficulty, only half recovered from her fainting fit. "It is by ideas like this," he said, "that the singer carried forward the story, and made it seem like a real scene that was happening before our eyes. And after her brother had cursed Marguerite, when he falls back dead, Miss Innes retreats, getting away from the body, half mad, half afraid. She did not rush immediately to him, as has been the operatic custom, kneel down, and, with one arm leaning heavily on Valentine's stomach, look up in the flies. Miss Innes, after backing far away from him, slowly returned, as if impelled to do so against her will, and, standing over the body, looked at it with curiosity, repulsion, terror; and then she burst into a whispered laugh, which communicated a feeling of real horror to the audience.

"In the last act, madness was tangled in her hair, and in her wide-open eyes were read the workings of her insane brain, and her every movement expressed the pathos of madness; her lovely voice told its sad tale without losing any of its sweetness and beauty. The pathos of the little souvenir phrases was almost unbearable, and the tragic power of the finish was extraordinary in a voice of such rare distinction and fluid utterance. Her singing and acting went hand in hand, twin sisters, equal and indivisible, and when the great moment in the trio came, she stepped forward and with an inspired intensity lifted her quivering hands above her head in a sort of mad ecstasy, and sang out the note clear and true, yet throbbing with emotion."

The paper slid from Evelyn's hand. She could see from Ulick's description of her acting that she had acted very well; if she had not, he could not have written like that. But her acting only seemed extraordinary when she read about it. It was all so natural to her. She simply went on the stage, and once she was on the stage she could not do otherwise. She could not tell why she did things. Her acting was so much a part of herself that she could not think of it as an art at all; it was merely a medium through which she was able to relive past phases of her life, or to exhibit her present life in a more intense and concentrated form. The dropping of the book was quite true; she had dropped a piece of music when she first saw Owen, and the omission of the scream was natural to her. She felt sure that she would not have seen Mephistopheles just then; she would have been too busy thinking of the young man. But she thought that she might take a little credit for her entrance in the third act. Somehow her predecessors had not seen that it was absurd to come smiling and tripping out of church, where she had seen Mephistopheles. She read the lines describing her power to depict madness. But even in the mad scenes she was not conscious of having invented anything. She had had sensations of madness—she supposed everyone had—and she threw herself into those sensations, intensifying them, giving them more prominence on the stage than they had had in her own personal life.

TOSCANINI CONDUCTS OPERA

Lawrence Gilman and Olin Downes

Those of us who were fortunate enough to hear Toscanini conduct opera—works as totally dissimilar as *Parsifal* and *Aïda*—experienced the proof of the assertion that it is the conductor who is the vitalizing factor in operatic performance.

"What he accomplished . . . is not easy to speak of with composure."—GILMAN

"The head of ice and the heart of fire."—DOWNES

Toscanini's *Parsifal* by Lawrence Gilman

New York *Herald Tribune*, Sunday, October 4, 1931

As one reflects upon the European festival season which has now become history, the conviction grows that its cardinal event was the setting forth of *Parsifal* at Bayreuth under Toscanini. Indeed, it would perhaps be more accurate to say that scarcely any musical disclosure of the last half-dozen years in Europe can be placed beside this as a contribution to aesthetic enlightenment. . . .

Wagner's *Parsifal,* that mystical reverie in which the most passionate and despotic artist of the nineteenth century speaks to us gravely and weightily of quiet things—of mercy and tenderness, and the beauty of compassion, and the wisdom of the pure in heart—this curious and anachronistic work, so disaffecting to the impatient and the inconsiderate, is in need of periodic attestation by those who can bring to the task not only faith, but persuasiveness and authority of an exceptional kind.

From the New York *Herald Tribune*, October 4, 1931. By permission of the New York *Herald Tribune*.

That Mr. Toscanini is an advocate of this order needs no special emphasis, so far as his achievements in the interpretation of music in general are concerned; but he had yet to manifest, for the non-Italian world, his ability to discourse with the highest eloquence of *Parsifal* in its musico-dramatic entirety—though his manner of dealing with certain concert excerpts at Philharmonic performances in New York had not been lost upon the observant.

I heard the last of the five performances of *Parsifal* which Toscanini conducted at Bayreuth. I do not know what the measure of his achievement may have been in his exposition of the score in the earlier performances; but what he accomplished in that which closed the Festival is not easy to speak of with composure. . . .

A few creative artists . . . persistently shut their eyes to the truth which Gilbert Murray set down in the preface to his translation of the *Agamemnon*: that "all art moves in its course from Religion to Entertainment." Mr. Toscanini is among these irreconcilables. For him, no art that is great art, whether or not it be "religious" in the narrower and limiting sense of the word, has even moved from the temple. Yet the explicitness with which *Parsifal* illustrates Wagner's conception of the essential function of the theater seems to have made inevitable its confrontation by Toscanini. He is doubtless its predestined custodian. His raptness in his chosen task; his attitude of consecration; his utter self-effacement; the image he summons of the priest preparing his sacrificial rite: these things marked him out for *Parsifal* and *Parsifal* for him; and the event fulfilled the prophecy.

I had been prepared to find this Toscaninian *Parsifal* more subtly cadenced, more rarefied in mood, more exquisite in texture and nuance than any I had known; and I was not disappointed. There were subtleties within subtleties, an infinite sensitiveness in the tracing of line and the application of harmonic and instrumental color, a saturation of the musical idea in beauty of a transilluminated purity—as, to recall a few among innumerable instances, the subduing enunciation of the altered theme of Faith as it threads the singer's words in the latter part of Gurnemanz's narrative; and the slow unfolding of the A-flat passage for the strings which accompanies Kundry's visit to the spring with her pitcher, and her announcement of Parsifal's approach. At such moments the music seemed to disengage some superearthly essence, some disembodied loveliness of sound and signification that hovered above the unseen instruments in the covered pit, unevoked by earthly lips or fingers.

But I was scarcely prepared to find this Latin *Parsifal* ampler in breadth and weightier in drive and impact than Muck's superb Teutonic one.

Toscanini's tempi were slow, but with a slowness that was never languid nor devitalized. The music's pace seemed inevitable, and it was often overwhelming in effect as in the episode of Parsifal's adoration of the sacred spear, that prodigious *"Sehr langsam"* for the muted and unison strings and wind (I had never before, by the way, heard the brief seventh-chord for the bassoons and double basses that points the long-held C-sharp of the other strings given the significant value that it had under Toscanini).

But this version was salient not merely because of its surpassing eloquence in the realization of those moods of hieratical solemnity and elevation which are characteristic of *Parsifal*; nor was it remarkable only for its summoning into the listener's perceptual field of those hovering presences and Pentecostal lights which irradiate certain pages of the score. The reading had not only breadth and depth and weight, intensity of accent and loftiness of mood, and that mystical poignancy which is of the music's essence, but it was sharply and startlingly dramatic. The tautness and incisiveness and vitality of the rhythms in such passages as the first entrance of Kundry and the stormy introduction to the second act were scarcely less remarkable than the probing intensity with which Toscanini charged certain of those terrible measures in which the music seems to bear the cumulative burden of humanity's immemorial woe, transfixing the spirit with its lancing pity and its grief—when one feels as if it had remembered Hamlet's plea, and drew its breath in pain.

At every point and in every realized mood the effect was heightening, intensifying, affirmative, renewing one's conviction of the wondrousness of the marvelous score. And this was its essential virtue. As so often before, this unaccompanied artist exercised his signal gift for bringing us into quickened contact with a masterwork which some had begun to take too much for granted. It was no longer an accustomed and familiar thing: again we heard the *Parsifal* of Wagner with new and unfilmed ears, recharged, magical, a thing of wonders and revelations.

Creative *Aïda* by Olin Downes
New York Times, April 3, 1949

Passing his eighty-second birthday, Mr. Toscanini has afforded the audience of the nation, and we hope of even wider areas, a consummative example of interpretation in his broadcast performance in two parts of Verdi's *Aïda*, completed yesterday afternoon in Radio City. Thanks enough can hardly be given the National Broadcasting Company which made such a performance available to every listener with a radio or television set at his disposal, wherever he might happen to be.

It is not this writer's belief that any radio transmission can catch completely the innermost nuance or pulsation of such a performance, which is to be experienced completely only perhaps by those within actual earshot. Something is denatured in the transmission, to say nothing of the fact that it is still necessary, as we understand it—knowing nothing whatever of the technical process—to limit the sonorous range from very soft to very loud in any broadcasting. These limitations, though they lessen every year, do inhere in radio transmission.

On the other hand, such is the power in the province of the art which we ourselves are incapable of regarding as anything but the supreme art of them all—the art of music—that the thought and emotion back of the notes responsible for their projection come through unmistakably. The listener must sense strongly the creative impulsion of such a Toscanini interpretation. Whatever the acoustical boundaries, if the listener is at all sensitive himself he is likely to "get it." He may not get the complete impression that he does if he sits in Studio 8H, but he will be caught in the evocative power of such a re-creation of music.

And "re-creation" it is! We have the impression that Mr. Toscanini does not like this word, and we shall not be violating an inviolable confidence if we recall at this moment a sort of unspoken protest of some years ago which came to us from this selfless artist. We had used the word "re-creation," as we recall it, commenting upon one of his performances. A few hours later came an envelope containing a letter of Verdi on this subject.

It is such a simple but eloquent comment on that master's part that a paragraph from it may not be amiss here. We avail ourselves here of the excellent translation of this letter by Edward Downes in the volume of letters selected by Franz Werfel and Paul Stefan and published by L. B. Fischer of New York. Verdi wrote Giulio Ricordi:

As to conductors' inspiration . . . to "creative activity in every performance" . . . That is a principle which forever inevitably leads to the baroque and untrue. It is precisely the path that led music to the baroque and untrue at the end of the last century and in the first years of this, when singers made bold to "create" (as the French still say) their parts, and in consequence made a complete hash and contradiction of sense out of them. No: I want only one single creator and I shall be quite satisfied if they perform simply and exactly what he has written. I often read in the papers about effects that the composer never could have thought of; but for my part I have never found such a thing. I understand everything you say about Mariani; we are all agreed upon his merit. But it is not a question of a single performance, were he ever so eminent, it is a question of art itself. I deny that either singers or conductors can "create" or work creatively —this, as I have always said, is a conception that leads to the abyss.

Granted the truth of that principle, it nevertheless, in the ultimate of a master's interpretation, becomes untrue! The writer believes that when he said a week ago of the first two acts of Aïda that those who had not heard Toscanini conduct it had not heard Aïda, he wrote the fact. And this does not mean at all that the performance reached unheard-of heights because of Toscanini's fabulous clarity and precision or dramatic temperament or orchestral command.

It is something that goes farther and is more consummative than all that; something that fuses together in one flaming unity all the elements of an art, adding those of the spirit to those of the mind and senses; something that releases the jewel of the artistic creation from the matrix of its conception in the composer's consciousness; that sets the music in a free and supreme place of its very own, where it has no connection with or obligation to the source, even, of its existence.

That is the creative force which we are trying to define which is present in the greatest interpretations of Mr. Toscanini. Needless to say, he does not always achieve such a height. No artist could. The consummative may occur often enough in their work just to torment the greatest artists. But no oftener!

A friend said to Toscanini recently, after his performance of the

Beethoven "Pastoral" symphony: "The spirit of Beethoven is in you."
Toscanini replied a little sadly: "Only sometimes."

The wholly exceptional level of anything that he attempts is the
result of his genius and his artistic conscience. But when the goal is
reached, as certainly it has been in the *Aïda* performances and in
certain of the rehearsals, the achievement is not only evocative, it is
creative in the truest sense of the word.

It cannot be otherwise with an interpreter of the highest rank. It
could not be, however greatly such an interpreter might desire to
keep the performance on a purely objective level. Something has
gone into the business which frees the music of every bond—even of
the man who composed it, to say nothing of the interpreter.

But this is not done merely by a process of purification. By a sovereign act of intellectuality and imperious creative power the music
has been put beyond the reach, one would almost say, of any outside
power, on its throne. By a very act of supreme humanity, it has been
set free of any human agency. The umbilical cord has been severed
because of the creative release so selflessly and decisively achieved.
And this triumph makes the listener aware, as he may not have
been before, of the extent of music's miracle.

The beauty of this supremely artistic process is the logic, the
method, and construction which have brought it to accomplishment.
A Toscanini performance is not accomplished by devices of magic. It
begins with the most practical and energetic working out of every detail in the score. The details of *Aïda* happen to be numerous, if only
in point of the great ensembles and the richness of detail in the instrumentation. Each of these details has in turn to be perfected and
adjusted to the grand line of the reading—always the conductor's
task.

Then comes the interpretive study and the vitalizing of every
word of the text that the characters sing, as well as the transfiguration
of the word by the tone, and the fitting together of the whole. In
the synthesis of the performance one thrills to feel the brain of Toscanini, which is so powerful and aristocratic in its texture, summarizing the whole concept, and passionately vitalizing each element of it.

All this precedes the moment when the head of ice and the heart
of fire become one precipitating force which fashions this music,
with the power of the demon in it: the presence of something sublime, even terrifying, evoked from the invisible world by the spirit of
man.

TOSCANINI'S FIRST APPEARANCE AT THE METROPOLITAN

Giulio Gatti-Casazza

> From Gatti's memoirs, compiled with the aid of Howard Taubman.

"It was proved that Toscanini was right."

Toscanini's first rehearsal with the orchestra [1] before the season began was *Götterdämmerung*.

He made a short speech and began the rehearsal with no score before him. To tell the truth, he has been unwilling to introduce himself in this fashion, but I had insisted so much that he, although far from convinced, ended by complying with my request.

The orchestra was very attentive and really admirable. But after a few measures, Toscanini stopped. Addressing the first cellist, he said, "That note should have been B-flat."

"No," replied the musician, "that's not what I have here, nor have I ever had it. In all the years that I have been playing, I have always played the note as A-natural."

"Well," said Toscanini, "you have always committed an error," and, seeing by the face of the musician that he was not convinced, Toscanini added, "It seems to me that I have not convinced you. Would you like to have me get the full orchestra score for verification?"

The cellist answered, "Yes, I'd like to see the full orchestra score."

The score was brought; it was proved that Toscanini was right and the musician wrong. A sensation! The orchestra was conquered. At the end of the rehearsal the men gave Toscanini a tremendous salute. He had won the battle decisively.

[1] 1908.

From *Memories of Opera* by Giulio Gatti-Casazza. By permission of Charles Scribner's Sons.

THE CRISIS OF OPERA

THE CRISIS OF MODERN OPERA

Henry Pleasants

> No musical publication of recent years has caused such
> vehement critical disapproval and such name-calling as
> *The Agony of Modern Music* by Henry Pleasants. We
> need not follow the author in his comprehensive con-
> demnation of the serious music of our day. But we may
> ponder what he says about opera—and hope for the
> better.

*"Parlando operas that disdain the agreeable sensuous com-
munication of song."*

The harmonic epoch of European music was born in the
opera house.

Although its evolution has been dominated by the trend from an
originally vocal art to an ultimately instrumental art, opera has remained one of its great representative forms. All the evolutionary
factors in European music have been present in the evolution of
opera, and many of them originated in opera.

It would be impossible, of course, to write a complete history of
European music with reference to opera alone, but any satisfactory
history of opera will cover all the evolutionary factors essential to a
critical understanding of European music. A critical coverage of
Monteverdi, Alessandro Scarlatti, Handel, Gluck, Mozart, Cimarosa,
Beethoven, Rossini, Meyerbeer, Weber, Donizetti, Bellini, Verdi,
Gounod, Massenet, Wagner, Mascagni, Puccini, Strauss, Debussy,
and Berg would provide all that is needed to describe the arc of the
rise and fall of European music.

The decisive factors throughout the story are harmony and the
orchestra. That it is impossible to list the singer among these factors
gives to the story the flavor of perversity that so distinguishes the his-

tory of European music. This history offers, in its boldest outlines, the spectacle of an instrumental art born of a vocal art, which made a singer of the orchestra, and collapsed when the vocal objective was forgotten.

The singer himself has remained without influence. At each step along the way he has had to yield to the overriding demands of the orchestra. He has had his moments, to be sure. There were times in both the eighteenth and nineteenth centuries when the singer ruled the roost, and composers did his bidding. But the trend of musical evolution was against him. History records these as bad periods. They were terminated by reform movements born of the conviction that there was more to music than mere singers could provide.

This "more" was always found in harmony and in the orchestra. The implications of harmony seemed more substantial than the blandishments of a tune, however meltingly or forcefully delivered, and the instrument of harmony was the orchestra. Thus it is that the three-century history of opera shows the singer in a long battle with the orchestra, a battle punctuated by dramatic fluctuations, but with the outcome never in doubt.

The tragedy is that the nature of the conflict and its implications were not understood, even by the contestants. The reform composers, notably Gluck, Wagner, and Verdi, never fully realized that in favoring the orchestra they were imposing upon it vocal responsibilities. And the singers who acquiesced in the surrender of their primacy, themselves fascinated by the orchestra and the challenge of orchestra participation, failed to realize that what they were losing was their life's blood of vocal melody.

Nor were the implications of the conflict apparent to the public. They are not understood to this day. The operagoing public, to be sure, still favors *The Barber of Seville, Lucia, Norma, Il Trovatore, Tannhäuser,* and *La Bohème,* all singers' operas. But few are disposed to challenge the historical judgment of *Otello* or *Falstaff* as Verdi's masterpieces, or of *Tristan und Isolde* as Wagner's. One simply deplores the unenlightened condition of public taste. The public accepts the disparagement—and continues to pay allegiance to its favorites.

Thus it is that the low estate of contemporary opera, while recognized, is not understood as a consequence of evolutionary forces still enthusiastically applauded. History goes no further than noting that, up to the time of *Der Rosenkavalier,* opera was a living art and that since then it has not been. There is little disposition to seek in Wagner, Verdi, and Strauss the root of the evil.

Characteristic of modern opera generally are the assignment of the musical expressive function of the orchestra and the reduction of the singer to the role of a recitative-articulating actor. The idiom of the orchestra, in turn, is what is familiar to all of us as modern music. In this respect the iniquities of modern opera are identical with the iniquities of modern music in general, with the single exception that opera is better suited than other forms to deriving some benefit from the descriptive faculties that came to the fore in the decadence of the art.

The contemporary idiom of the singer is the parlando recitative, inherited from the last great manifestations of Italian opera, and the declamatory style inherited from Wagner. Gone are the arias, duets, trios, quartets, quintets, sextets, septets, and grand choruses that so delighted the audiences of Mozart, Beethoven, Weber, Rossini, Donizetti, Bellini, Verdi, Puccini—and even of Wagner and Strauss.

All successful operas have succeeded because they have given musical pleasure and excitement, because the audience's attention has been held and its spirit moved by beautiful singing, stirring drama, a great spectacle or—as is the case with the most successful operas—by the three in combination. No opera has succeeded that did not give singers something to sing. At its best, opera is the extension of the theater in song, the expressive faculties of vocal melody being exploited to broaden and intensify the emotional communication.

Opera owes its existence as an art of the theater to the dramatic implications of harmony. This is why opera, like the symphony and the symphonic poem, exists only in European music. Harmony is articulate, however, only in song, whether the singing be entrusted to voices or to instruments. In opera the singing was originally entrusted to singers, since the purpose was the representation of drama, and the technique the articulation of drama by singing actors. But as the orchestra emerged as the ideal instrument of harmonic music, the singer had to adjust himself to a concept of music that recognized the orchestra as the dominant executive agent.

Modern opera is the result of interpreting this as a trend directed, not only against the singer, but also against song. Overlooked is the fact that in *Tristan und Isolde* and *Otello* the orchestra sings. Wagner and Verdi sensed instinctively that there can be no music without song. When they inhibited the singing of their singers by grafting the vocal line to the text, they saw to it that the melodic loss was made good in the orchestra. Their successors simply noted the absence of set vocal pieces and concluded that Wagner and Verdi had evolved something better than song.

Thus it is that for fifty years composers have given us recitative and parlando operas that disdain the agreeable sensuous communication of song, vocal or instrumental, without substituting for it the precise articulation of the spoken word. They have given us operas which, uncommunicative musically, are dependent for communication upon the text. The singer is restricted to declamation in order that the text may be understood. And then he is drowned out by a clamorous orchestra in order that the composer may still claim to have written an opera.

The contemporary composer makes a point of integrating music and drama, and achieves neither one nor the other—nor anything else. If one listens to the music, the experience is unrewarding, since, as the composer will be the first to proclaim, it is unintelligible without reference to the drama. But if one listens to the drama, nothing comes of it but frustration, since the text is normally lost in the orchestral din.

The villain of the piece, of course, is Wagner. Modern opera, like all modern music, is reactionary, and no other composer is so stigmatized by the reaction as Wagner. The length of his operas, his system of leitmotivs, the size and richness of his orchestra, the fullness of his harmonies, the ecstasies of his progressions, the philosophical pretensions of his libretti—all are rejected. But these have to do with manner rather than with method. Wagner's method—the integration of music and drama, with music subordinate to the text—has survived. The irony of this is that no composer has ever so flagrantly and successfully violated his own proclaimed method. Wagner's music has survived, not because of his method, but in spite of it.

The simple fact is that people go to the Wagnerian music dramas to hear the music—in the orchestra and on the stage. They go to hear The Ride of the Valkyries, the *Waldweben*, Wotan's Farewell, the Magic Fire Music, *Winterstürme*, "*Du bist der Lenz*," Siegfried's Funeral March and Rhine Journey, Brünnhilde's Immolation, "*O sink hernieder Nacht der Liebe*," the *Liebestod*, and so on—all musical episodes of lyric, epic, and sometimes even dramatic grandeur.

Hardly anyone understands the words. Hardly anyone cares, except possibly the singers, for whom they serve as memory props and a guide to expressive vocal coloration. The audience is required to sit a long time between these musical pleasures. It puts up with a good deal of awful boredom during those barren stretches where Wagner really practiced what he preached. A good many people consider it worth the trouble, and some are even impressionable enough to persuade themselves that they enjoy the ugly, empty wastes of Wagnerian recitative.

The purely musical basis of Wagner's popularity is something contemporary composers of opera have never perceived. They have held to his method and discarded his manner, not recognizing that what was valid and vital in Wagner was precisely his manner, including particularly the excesses and extravagances the contemporary composer so heartily despises.

Wagner was a musician, a composer in spite of himself. He achieved success and immortality in the theater just as Bellini and Meyerbeer and Verdi did—by writing hit tunes. He was music's greatest unwitting hypocrite. He was determined to bridle the singer. But instinctively he realized the telling effect of a well-prepared, forcefully delivered high C as the climax of a long melodic line. And Wagnerian opera today is dominated by the tenor and the prima donna just as any other opera is; indeed, even more so, since so few singers can meet their requirements.

Wagner compounded the paradox by adding a new virtuoso—the conductor. In his music, for the first time, orchestra and singer are on an equal footing. When the singer does not sing, the orchestra does. Often they sing together. For the orchestra's song the conductor is responsible. Since Wagner's time, with the primacy of the orchestra established, the conductor has been to opera what the *castrato* was to the opera of the seventeenth and eighteenth centuries.

It would probably have been impossible to continue much farther in the Wagnerian direction—that is, in the direction pointed by Wagner's musical manner. There had to be a limit to loudness and richness and bigness. Wagner did not reach it. But he came close, and Strauss had no difficulty in finishing the job with *Salome*, *Elektra*, and *Der Rosenkavalier*.

The contemporary composer's error has been, not in failing to take up where Wagner and Strauss left off, but in failing to understand what Wagner had been. They were influenced by his theories and his method, and ignored the obvious musical reasons for his success. They neglected to note that the essential musical nature of opera had not been changed, least of all by Wagner, and that in the opera house, as in the concert hall, vocal melody, or an instrumental substitute for it, is the alpha and omega of music.

This is an axiom Verdi never overlooked, even in theory. It has made him, for the contemporary composer, a more complicated point of departure.

Despite the great successes scored by singers in Wagner's music dramas, the impact of Wagner's personality, the novelty of his idiom, and the evangelistic fervor of its propagation blinded even the sophisticated to the essentially melodic source of his popularity. Hanslick, for instance, for all his insight, kept attacking the Wagnerian method as if it were the method that really counted.

Verdi's course from *Nabucco* to *Falstaff* was more gradual, and was accomplished without the fanfare of theoretical revelation and the dogma of a reform platform. But Verdi could not entirely escape the trend of the time. He never lost sight of the singer, but he did, toward the end, begin to lose sight of song. Hanslick felt this when he heard *Otello* in Milan in 1887, shortly after the première, and commented:

Song remains the decisive element, but it follows closely the course of thought, feeling, and word. Independent, self-sufficient, symmetrically constructed melodies appear less frequently than does that cross between recitative and cantilena which now dominates modern opera. . . . If the right choice of color for every mood and the emphatic notation of every turn of speech were the single objective of opera, then we could unhesitatingly declare *Otello* to be an improvement over *Aïda* and Verdi's finest work.

This devotion to the poem does not, however, release the opera composer from other obligations. He must above all else be a musician, and on this basis we expect music not only in accord with the text but also attractive to us simply as music—individual, original, and self-sufficient. . . . We demand of the opera composer beauty and novelty of musical ideas, particularly melodic ideas. And from this point of view *Otello* strikes me as less adequate than *Aïda*, *La Traviata* or *Un ballo in maschera*.

To the succeeding generation it did not appear, as it did in the case of Wagner, that Verdi had reached a limit. They reckoned that his was a direction offering reasonable prospects of further profitable vistas. This proved to be the case, if in a limited degree. The job of running out the vein, performed for German opera by Strauss and for French opera by Debussy and Charpentier, was done for the Italians by Leoncavallo, Mascagni, Giordano, and Puccini. But again the composers committed a critical error, or, to put it more precisely, an error in criticism.

Their mistake was in thinking of the succession of Verdi's operas in general terms of continuous progress, from bad to good to better to best, the last applying to *Otello* and *Falstaff*. In terms of technical mastery and dramatic sophistication this was certainly the case. But it was not the case in terms of music. The composer, the student of music, the sophisticated listener, may think of *Otello* as being superior to *Aïda*, and of *Falstaff* as being superior to *Otello*. But as pure music *Aïda* is superior to both of them.

The composers turned to *Otello* and *Falstaff* to find out what it was that Verdi was driving at. They found something very much akin to the Wagnerian concept of integrated music drama, free of Wagner's Germanic trappings. What they failed to understand was that even Verdi could be wrong, or at least go too far. Verdi's destination was *Aïda*. He had developed a considerable momentum in getting there, and in *Otello* and *Falstaff* he overshot the objective. He did not come to grief. He had too much stability for that. But his successors foundered in rapid succession.

It is easy to understand, at this distance, the temptation *Otello* and *Falstaff* represented. They offered more concentrated, more pointed, more modern excitement and pleasure. The pace is faster, the action more direct and, in the case of *Otello*, more violent and shocking. The form is less conventional. The set piece has almost vanished. There are some in *Otello*, although less numerous and less conspicuous than in *Aïda*. There are very few in *Falstaff*. In other words, they represented, when superficially examined, and from the point of view of the time, a liberation from the operatic conventions, a step toward real music drama, a closer approximation than Wagner was able to achieve of a complete jelling of the various arts involved in opera.

Such an appreciation was correct enough, but the conclusions drawn from it were as mistaken as those drawn from the similar appreciation of Wagner, and hardly less disastrous, although easier to forgive. Verdi was the more honest progressive of the two, or at least the more consistent, and his results were more convincing. Wagner's visions were a bit ridiculous. Verdi's never were. He had as good a sense of the theater as Wagner, and a more conscious under-standing of the essentially musical nature of opera. Thus it was easy to believe that *Otello* and *Falstaff* owed their success and the high esteem in which they were held to what was new in them rather than to what was old.

This was true as far as the critics and the initiated public were concerned. But it was not the new that kept the operas in the reper-toire. It was what still survived of the earlier Verdi. Critics may praise as they will the declamatory style of *Otello*. But what keeps it in the repertoire is the opening chorus, the Drinking Song, the first act duet, the Credo, the Iago-Otello duet at the close of the second act, the great choral scene and Otello's monologue at the end of the third act, and Desdemona's arias in the fourth. There are fewer such melodic excursions in *Falstaff*, which is why *Falstaff* is less often in the repertoire than *Otello*.

Contemporary composers would have done better had they not dismissed the fact that *Aïda* is still more popular than either *Otello* or *Falstaff* and always will be. Their error was in listening to the critics rather than to the box office. About this even Verdi, for whom the box office was never an institution to be taken lightly, may have been deceived. By the time *Otello* was produced he had achieved a position in the hearts of his countrymen and others where failure would have been next to impossible. But the fact was that Verdi, along with the main stream of music, had moved away from his popular base. He, too, had been seduced by the lure of a music that would be more than song.

This is the tragedy of European music in miniature. In aspiring to more than song its composers denied those very lyric faculties of music which prompt people to express themselves musically and which make the musical expression of others intelligible. Preoccu-pied with harmony and instrumentation, they forgot that the musi-cian's primary purpose in life is to sing.

European music collapsed, but not just because its distinctive technical resources were exhausted. It collapsed because composers thought of composition in terms of technique. They knew a lot about composition, but they no longer knew anything about music. They had forgotten, if they ever knew, what music is. Nowhere is this more convincingly demonstrated than in the history of opera.

The normal means of communication is speech. All speech is col-ored by variations of pitch and rhythm employed spontaneously to supplement the precision or imprecision of words with a sense of the feelings associated with them. Thus all speech is in some degree musical, and all speakers composers, in however rudimentary a way. Verbal communication is never entirely dissociated from musical communication. Musical expression begins when a baby first uses its vocal cords.

Poetry is a musical extension of speech. It is distinguished from speech by a rhythmical organization whose purpose is to encourage, support, and animate a vocal tone more consciously and more consistently sustained than is customary or practical in speech.

The advantage of the sustained tone of poetry over the unsustained tone of speech is its plasticity. The melodic variation can be enriched and accentuated, and the opportunities for expressive coloration are infinitely increased, if only because the tone is of longer duration and gives the speaker more time for its lyrical exploitation. Poetry is, in short, a step toward song. Although an understanding of the words is still essential to a satisfactory communication, the melodic component is on at least a level with the verbal.

If one wishes to go beyond the poet's capacities for sensuous or melodic communication, song is the next step. Here the voice is fully sustained, and the melodic component of the communication dominant, if not exclusive. The words rather cease to count. The communication is sensuous rather than ideational, general rather than precise. The words are hardly more than a guide to the singer. They are not essential to the audience. This is why songs in all languages are effective everywhere, regardless of the language in which they are sung, provided only that they are good songs and well sung.

Song has the advantage over prose and poetry of an incomparably greater range of expressive coloration and emphasis, since the tone can be regulated in pitch, augmented or diminished in volume, and accelerated or retarded in movement in a purely musical way. Because of sustained plastic, malleable tone, music can work in expressive spheres where prose, bound to the word, and poetry, released from absolute verbal precision but still constrained by a text, cannot go. This is why the poet writes verse instead of prose, and it is why the musician should work with song rather than with verse.

The historical course of music since Beethoven's time has been in the opposite direction. Musicians have acted as though music's ideational imprecision were a fault, and as though its salvation lay in finding in it the narrative and descriptive faculties which are the natural attributes of speech, poetry, painting, and sculpture. This was because the picturesque and dramatic implications of harmony and orchestra led them to assume that music's ultimate objectives were dramatic and picturesque.

There have been similarly misguided ambitions in the sister arts. Prose writers have abandoned syntax and rhetoric in order to achieve something akin to poetry. Poets have abandoned the precision of word and meter in order to achieve something akin to music. Painters have abandoned description in order to achieve something akin to architecture. The over-all picture is plainly pathological—a disheartening spectacle in which creative artists, secretly aware that they cannot match or surpass their predecessors, crib from their neighbors in order, at least, to be original.

In opera this general tendency has found expression in a denial of purely musical values in favor of textual or descriptive values. Instead of making opera the extension of the theater in song, composers since Wagner's and Verdi's time have tended to make it a theatrical extension of music. They have behaved as if song were something to be ashamed of—and have produced a songless music of which they should be ashamed.

Parlando recitative or dry declamation has replaced the aria and the concerted piece. Choral commentary has replaced the exuberant song of massed voices. Ballet has disappeared, by which opera has been deprived, not only of song, but of dance. Even the orchestra, opera's last great singer, has become an humble provider of commas, periods, exclamation points, descriptive color, inflated dynamic contrasts, and mood-painting. The faculties of free, emotional, sensuous expression in song, which are music's purest and most utterly native property, have been denied, as if composers were all ascetics, and song a cardinal sin.

Asceticism is one of the abiding ills of modern music. Asceticism and music do not go together. Music is a spontaneous, uninhibited expression of feeling. Without feeling there can be no music. Asceticism is opposed to the expression of feeling and the indulgence of the senses. This is why ascetic faiths and philosophies have no music and why, in certain austere faiths, music is associated with evil.

It is in the opera house that the ascetic character of modern music is most keenly felt. A symphony without song may deceive by its thematic workmanship and the skill and ingenuity of its orchestration.

In the opera house, with attention diverted from the orchestra to the stage, the absence of song is insupportable. For there is less music in the declamation of modern opera than in the spoken lines of the modern theater.

The kind of declamation or parlando recitative now fashionable in modern opera defeats rather than assists the musical objective. By restricting the voice to arbitrary pitches in a manner incompatible with the melodic-structural character of song, the composer puts the singer in an emotional strait jacket. The vocal line to which he is constrained offers less opportunity for melodic expression than the flattest sort of speech.

Nothing has been written in the opera since the end of World War I that could compare as music with any Shakespearean speech, even as delivered by a third-rate actor. Thus it is that modern opera reveals the full calamity of serious music. An art that originated as the creative extension of the rudimentary music of speech has ended, in the more radical of its present forms, by being less musical than the gurgle of a newborn babe.

There is little, as usual, that the composer can do about it, even if he recognizes the fact. If he tries to write musically he ends, like Krěnek twenty years ago, in a no-man's land between serious and popular music, or like Menotti today, somewhere between the present and Puccini. Or he finds, as did Weill, that he can compete successfully with the really popular composers, and does so. In either case he ceases to be taken seriously as a serious composer. If he continues in directions still taken seriously he may make a reputation, but he will hardly make money. Certainly he will not make music.

Music still lives in the theater. It probably always will. But it lives in the theater today, in America, at least, in the music of Gershwin, Kern, Rodgers, Porter, Schwartz, and Berlin. Their shows have never been fully recognized as opera. But it is not what a thing is called that counts. It is what it is. If opera is the extension of the theater in song, then these shows are operas, regardless of the spoken dialogue and regardless of who does the orchestration.

By the same definition most modern opera is not.

L'ENVOI

Donald Jay Grout

From Professor Grout's A *Short History of Opera.*

Throughout its career opera has been both praised and censured in the strongest terms. It was lauded by its creators as "the delight of princes," "the noblest spectacle ever devised by man." On the contrary, Saint-Evremond, a French critic of the late seventeenth century, defined an opera as "a bizarre affair made up of poetry and music, in which the poet and the musician, each equally obstructed by the other, give themselves no end of trouble to produce a wretched work." Opera has been criticized on moral as well as on aesthetic grounds; the respectable Mr. Haweis in 1872 regarded it "musically, philosophically, and ethically, as an almost unmixed evil." Despite both enemies and friends, however, it has continued to flourish, and there is no reason to expect that it will not, in some shape or other, be with us for a long time to come.

From A *Short History of Opera* by D. J. Grout, by permission of Columbia University Press.